S0-EIA-838

Guide to
BRITISH PROSE FICTION EXPLICATION

Nineteenth and Twentieth Centuries

A
Reference
Publication
in
Literature

Nancy C. Martinez
Editor

Guide to
BRITISH PROSE FICTION EXPLICATION

Nineteenth and Twentieth Centuries

LYNNDIANNE BEENE

G. K. HALL & CO.
An Imprint of Simon & Schuster Macmillan
New York

Prentice Hall International
London Mexico City New Delhi Singapore Sydney Toronto

G. K. Hall & Co.
An Imprint of Simon & Schuster Macmillan
1633 Broadway
New York, New York 10019

Library of Congress Catalog Card Number: 96-27135

Printed in the United States of America

Printing number
1 2 3 4 5 6 7 8 9 10

Library of Congress Cataloging-in-Publication Data
Beene, Lynn.
Guide to British prose fiction explication : nineteenth and twentieth centuries / LynnDianne Beene.
p. cm. — (Guides to prose explication series) (A reference publication in literature)
Includes bibliographical references (p.).
ISBN 0-8161-1987-2 (alk. paper)
1. English fiction—19th century—Explication. 2. English fiction—20th century—Explication. I. Title. II. Series. III. Series: A reference publication in literature.
PR861.B38 1996
823.009—dc20 96-27135
CIP

This paper meets the requirements of ANSI/NISO A39.48.1992 (Permanence of Paper).

For all those who teach and learn—and teach to learn.

There are some people who read too much: the bibliobibuli. I know some who are constantly drunk on books, as other men are drunk on whiskey or religion. They wander through this most diverting and stimulating of worlds in a haze, seeing nothing and hearing nothing.

–H. L. Mencken

Contents

The Author

LynnDianne Beene is currently a Professor of English Language and Literature at the University of New Mexico, Albuquerque. She has published works on such topics as technical communications, contemporary British popular fiction, and rhetorical and grammatical applications to fiction and nonfiction. She is the author of *Solving Problems in Technical Writing* with Peter L. White and *John Le Carré*, a book-length examination of the espionage novelist. She is at present working on a survey of grammar models and a study of novelist D. M. Thomas.

Preface

Truly, bibliographers have uncommon genes. Those who labor to all hours in various libraries, who haunt the InterLibrary Loan departments, who live easily with numbers and abbreviations, and who learn to reach for a tissue to check a dust-induced sneeze while still verifying entries and adjusting the continuous-feed paper to the printer perplex their coworkers and companions. With notecards, massive printouts, reference texts unopened since their purchase, they walk around with looks of nonplussed satisfaction. Hot on the trail of a seemingly obscure detail, they take on the look of Robert Altick's scholar adventurers. When they meet for coffee—stronger beverages would, presumably, dull their enterprising spirits—bibliographers laugh over relics held as gems where others would merely wonder why.

Such is the intensity one must bring to a project such as this volume, a continuation of the explication series begun with Joseph M. Kuntz's *Poetry Explication* (Joseph M. Kuntz and George W. Arms, *Poetry Explications: A Checklist of Interpretation Since 1925 of British and American Poems Past and Present* New York. Swallow, 1950). It is a piece of a whole, a major publishing project nurtured by G. K. Hall under the wise (and understanding) general editorship of Nancy Martinez. This volume surveys selected British prose fiction works from the nineteenth and twentieth centuries. The survey includes some writers that readers will miss and omits others that will, to some critics' discerning viewpoint, be missed. Irish writers such as James Joyce and Joyce Cary, like Scottish-born

Walter Scott, are obvious; however, New Zealand native Katherine Mansfield, Canadian Margaret Atwood, or India-born Lawrence Durrell may cause some to stop, particularly when readers consider that other writers from these countries and other former British colonies are absent. Pragmaticism, the availability of resources, and the authors' sense of identification shaped the decisions to include or exclude a writer. Authors who identify with the British Isles more than with the countries of their birth were obvious choices. Thus, though Thackeray was born in Calcutta, his novels come close to establishing the norm for the Victorian novel as do those of the Bengal-born Orwell for the present century. They were included where other writers, such as Doris Lessing, were not.

Moreover, the work charts fiction from roughly the beginning of the nineteenth century to nearly the present day. For instance, some readers may ask why Fanny Burney is not recorded but Jane Austen is. Unlike Austen, who died early in the century, Burney lived well into the nineteenth century but her fiction thematically and stylistically belongs to the previous century. Although her fiction continues the comic traditions of eighteenth-century works and ignores the turbulence of her world, many of Austen's greatest novels were written and published in the nineteenth century (e.g., *Pride and Prejudice*, 1812; *Emma* perhaps three years later). Further, her success in many ways stimulated women to write prose fiction later in the century. For these reasons, and because her novels are among the most readable, Austen found her way into the survey.

The general guidelines established in the original *Poetry Explication* defined the concept of explication and directed the choice of critical works. As with the initial volume, this bibliography surveys various articles that do more than make an individual text's meaning clear. Some entries do provide detailed readings of complete works. More often, however, entries detail some aspect of a text: they analyze some allusion, character, event, image, or source; they evaluate a linguistic, compositional, or expressive aspect of a work or of a complete novel; they synthesize evaluations of parts to the whole or the whole to the parts; or they seek to explain an element of a work, a complete work, or a series of works by alluding to contemporary theorists' insights. Readers will not find articles that gauge a work's production, revision, authorship, or reception unless such commentaries contribute substantially to a close reading of the work. For many earlier novelists, reviewers' notes placed their novels in a cultural context that explains why, for example, some characters react as they do. For current writers about whom critical perceptions are evolving, explications appear in reviews of their current work, making these reviews a far more valuable source for prose fiction than similar reviews would be for poetry.

Thus, the critical works registered here vary from contemporary professional reviews to semiotic interpretations, from New Critical approaches to new historicist readings, from linguistic subtleties to cross-cultural estimations. Overall, the bibliography is organized according to the format of others in this series:

1. Prose fiction writers are listed alphabetically by last name, with the writer's most commonly recognized name as the indicator. Hence John le Carré is listed under his pseudonym, rather than his given name, David John Moore Cornwell.

2. Novels and short stories are listed alphabetically by title (excluding initial articles).

3. Explications are listed alphabetically by the author's surname following each prose fiction work. Full publication data are included within the citation for all essays and for most books. Reprints are cited following the major entry.

4. Names of journals and periodicals are abbreviated according to the standard Modern Language Association abbreviations and are listed immediately after this Preface.

No bibliographer, however muted or mutated that individual's genes may be, compiles such a work without drawing on the resources of others and, at times, straining those resources to their ultimate. Several graduate students contributed their time and bibliographic curiosity to this work. In particular, Michele Marsee, William Foreman, Megan O'Neill, and Elizabeth Moorehead worked when it would have been much easier for them to rest. Krystan V. Douglas, friend and compatriot in mischief, provided the right words at the right time without being asked. Juliette Cunico had all the encouragement with her, much of which she shared with me and much of which I hope to return to her as she needs it. Countless Zimmerman Library staff members smiled patiently as I ferreted out aging books, begged to take precious reference works home "for just one night," and indulged my newfound ability to flood Interlibrary Loan with computer-generated requests. Friends from Randy and Dedre, Floyd and Terry, Bel, Mary Sue, Karen, Suzanne, Kristy, Bill, Patsy, Jan, and more other individuals than I can herein name suffered through my countless reports on the work's progress. Most of all, however, a thanks to the Friz, who watches, wonders, holds, and loves.

LynnDianne Beene

Abbreviations

A&E	Anglistik & Englischunterricht
ABAJ	The American Bar Association Journal
ABACJ	The ABAC Journal
ABR	The American Benedictine Review
Accent	
ACF	Annali di Ca' Foscari: Rivista della Facoltà di Lingue e Letterature Straniere dell'Università di Venezia
ACM	The Aligarh Critical Miscellany
Acme	Annali della Facoltà di Lettere e Filosofia dell'Università degli Studi di Milano
ADAM	International Review
AI	American Imago
AIM	The Annals of Internal Medicine
AJES	The Aligarh Journal of English Studies
AJFS	The Australian Journal of French Studies

ABBREVIATIONS

AJP	The American Journal of Psychoanalysis
Albion	
AlS	Alei-Siah
ALS	Australian Literary Studies
America	
AmH	American Humor
AmO	American Opinion
AmPQ	The American Philosophical Quarterly
ASch	The American Scholar
Analog	Analog Science Fiction-Science Fact
AnaU	Analele Universitatii, Bucuresti, Limbi Germanice
AngF	Angel's Flight
Angles	Angles on English Speaking World
Anglia	Zeitscrift für Englische Philologie
Annees	
ANQ: A Quarterly Journal of Short Articles, Notes, and Reviews	
AntigR	The Antigonish Review
Antithesis	
AR	The Antioch Review
ArAA	Arbeiten aus Anglistik und Amerikanistik
Arbor	
Arcadia: Archiv für das Studium der Neueren Sprachen und Literaturen	
Archiv: Archiv für das Studium der Neueren Sprachen und Literaturen	
ArEB	The Arizona English Bulletin
Ariel: A Review of International Literature	
ArmD	The Armchair Detective: A Quarterly Journal Devoted to the Appreciation of Mystery, Detective, and Suspense Fiction
The Arnoldian: A Review of Mid-Victorian Culture	
ArQ	The Arizona Quarterly: A Journal of American Literature, Culture, and Theory

Artes

ASUI Analele Ştiinţifice ale Universitâţii "Al.I. Cuza" din Iaşi (Serie nouâ), e. Lingvisticâ

ASNSP Annali della Scuola Normale Superiore di Pisa: Classe di Lettere e Filosofia

Athenaeum Studi Periodici di Letteratura e Storia dell'Antichità

Atlantis: A Women's Studies Journal/Revue d'Études sur la Femme (*formerly* Atlantis: A Women's Studies Journal/Journal d'Études sur la Femme)

AtM Atlantic Monthly

AWR Anglo-Welsh Review

AUMLA: Journal of the Australian Universities Language and Literature Association: A Journal of Literary Criticism and Linguistics

AusQ Australian Quarterly

BACLA Bulletin de l'ACLA/Bulletin of the ACLA (*superseded* by Revue de l'ACLA/Journal of the CAAL)

BarRev The Barat Review

Basilian The Basilian Teacher

BCDE Bulletin of the [Calcutta] Department of English

Belfagor: Rassenga di Varia Umanita

Bestia

BET The [Boston] Evening Transcript

BI Books at Iowa

Biography: An Interdisciplinary Journal

BIS Browning Institute Studies: An Annual of Victorian Literary and Cultural History

BJA The British Journal of Aesthetics

BJRL The Bulletin of the John Rylands University Library

BkA Books Abroad

Blackfriars

The Black Scholar

BLM	Bonniers Litterära Magasin
BM	The Booklover's Magazine
BNYCSLS	The Bulletin of the New York C. S. Lewis Society
BNYPL	The Bulletin of the New York Public Library
BO	Black Orpheus: Journal of African and Afro-American Literature
BOMB	
Booster	
boundaryII	boundary 2: An International Journal of Literature and Culture
BRH	Bulletin of Research in the Humanities
Britain Today	
BRLV	Bruxelles Revue des Langues Vivantes
BrN	Brontë Newsletter
Broom	
BSSA	Bulletin de la Société de Stylistique Anglaise
BSEAA	Bulletin de la Société d'Études Anglo-Américaines des XVII et XVIII Siecles
BSJ	The Baker Street Journal
BST	Brontë Society Transactions
BSUF	The Ball State University Forum
Bulletin: Municiple University of Wichita	
BuR	The Bucknell Review: A Scholarly Journal of Letters, Arts and Sciences
BUSE	Boston University Studies in English
BWVACET	The Bulletin of the West Virginia Association of College English Teachers
BYUS	Brigham Young University Studies
CA&E	College of Arts and Essays
C&L	Christianity and Literature
CahiersI	Cahiers du Centre d'Études Irlandaises

CahiersN	Les Cahiers de la Nouvelle
CahiersRLI	Les Cahiers du Centre d'Études et de Recherches sur les Littéraires de l'Imaginaire
CalUB	Calcutta University Bulletin
Caliban	
CalR	The Calcutta Review
CamJ	The Cambridge Journal
CamR	The Cambridge Review
CanH	The Canadian Holmes
CanL	Canadian Literature
CarM	The Carnegie Magazine
CarQ	The Carolina Quarterly
CatW	Catholic World
CaudaP	Cauda Pavonis: Studies in Hermeticism
CCent	The Christian Century
CCrit	Comparative Criticism: A Yearbook
CCTEP	Conference of College Teachers of English Studies
CdP	Cuadernos de Poética
CE	College English
CEA	The CEA Critic: An Official Journal of the College English Association
CE&S	Commonwealth Essays and Studies
CentR	The Centennial Review
Century	
CHA	Cuadernos Hispanoaméricanos: Revista Mensual de Cultura Hispanics
Chatelaine	
ChildL	Children's Literature: Annual of the Modern Language Association Division on Children's Literature and Children's Literature Association

ChiR	Chicago Review
ChLN	The Children's Libraries Newsletter
ChT	Christianity Today
CIEFLB	The Central Institute of English and Foreign Languages Bulletin
CimR	The Cimarron Review
Cithara	Essays in the Judaeo-Christian Tradition
CJ&B	Criminal Justice and Behavior
CJH	The Canadian Journal of History/Annales Canadiennes d'Histoire
CJIS	The Canadian Journal of Irish Studies
CL	Comparative Literature
CLAJ	The College Language Association Journal
CLAQ	Children's Literature Association Quarterly
CLE	Children's Literature in Education
	Clearing House
CR	The Clergy Review
CLIO	CLIO: A Journal of Literature, History, and the Philosophy of History
ClNP	Clinical Neuropharmacology
CLQ	The Colby Library Quarterly
CLS	Comparative Literature Studies
	Clues: A Journal of Detection
CMat	Critical Matrix: Princeton Journal of Women, Gender, and Cultural (*formerly* Critical Matrix: Princeton Working Papers in Women's Studies)
CMF	Casopis pro Modernii Filologii
CML	Classical and Modern Literature: A Quarterly
CNews	The Carlyle Newsletter
CNIE	Commonwealth Novel in English
CollL	College Literature

Colóquio	Colóquio/Letras
Comhar	
Commentary	
Commonweal	
Communiqué (Petersburg)	
Continentes	Dos Continentes
CoRev	The Commonwealth Review
ConL	Contemporary Literature
ConnR	The Connecticut Review
Conradiana: The Journal of Joseph Conrad Studies	
Conradian	The Conradian
ContempR	Contemporary Review
Costerus	
CQ	The Cambridge Quarterly
CQR	The Church Quarterly Review
CR	The Critical Review
CRCL	The Canadian Review of Comparative Literature/Revue Canadienne de Littérature Comparée
Cresset	
CRev	The Chesterton Review: The Journal of the Chesterton Society
Criterion	
CritI	Critical Inquiry
Critic	
Criticism	A Quarterly Journal for Literature and the Arts
Crit	Critique: Studies in Contemporary Fiction
Critique	Revue Générale des Publications Françaises et Etrangères
CritQ	Critical Quarterly
Crosscurrents	
Crotocos	

ABBREVIATIONS

CRUX	A Journal on the Teaching of English
CSMF	Critique: Studies in Modern Fiction
CSM	The Christian Science Monitor
Cycnos	
CuyahogaR	The Cuyahoga Review
CVE	Cahiers Victoriens et Edouardiens: Revue du Centre d'Études et de Rescherches Victoriennes et Edouardiennes de l'Université Paul Valéry, Montpellier
CWLM	Chung-wai Literary Monthly: Studies in Chinese and Foreign Literatures
Daedalus	Journal of the American Academy of Arts and Sciences
DD	Dutch Dickensian
Descant	
DHL	D. H. Lawrence: The Journal of the D. H. Lawrence Society
DHLR	The D. H. Lawrence Review
Diacritics: A Review of Contemporary Criticism	
Dial	
Dialoog	
Dickensian	The Dickensian
Dieu Vivant	
DilR	Diliman Review
Dionysos	The Literature and Addiction TriQuarterly (*formerly* Dionysos: The Literature and Intoxication TriQuarterly)
Discourse	Journal for Theoretical Studies in Media and Culture
DL	Deus Loci: The Lawrence Durrell Quarterly
DLSUDia	DLSU Dialogue
DLSUGraJ	The DLSU Graduate Journal
DR	Dalhousie Review
DQR	The Dutch Quarterly Review of Anglo-American Letters
DQu	The Dickens Quarterly

DSA	The Dickens Studies Annual: Essays on Victorian Fiction
DSGW	Deutsche Shakespeare-Gesellschaft West: Jahrbuch
DS	Dickens Studies
DSN	The Dickens Studies Newsletter
DTel	The Daily Telegraph
DubR	The Dublin Review
DUJ	Durham University Journal
DVLG	Deutsche Vierteljahrsschrift für Literaturwissenschaft und Geistesgeschichte
DWB	Dietsche Warande en Belfort: Tijdschrift voor Letterkunde en Geestesleven
E&S	Essays and Studies
ÉA	Études Anglaises
EAA	Estudos Anglo-Americanos
EA&A	Études Anglaises et Américaines
EAS	Essays in Arts and Sciences
ÉBC	Études Britanniques Contemporaines
ECent	The Eighteenth Century: Theory and Interpretation
ECF	Eighteenth-Century Fiction
ECLife	Eighteenth-Century Life
EConr	L'Epoque Conradienne
ÉdT	Études de Lettres
ECW	Essays on Canadian Writing
Edda	Nordisk Tidsskrift for Litteraturforskning/Scandinavian Journal of Literary Research
Egoist	
ÉI	Études Irlandaises: Revue Francaise d'Histoire, Civilisation et Littérature de l'Irelande
EIC	Essays in Criticism: A Quarterly Journal of Literary Criticism
EigoS	Eigo Seinen

Éire	Éire-Ireland: A Journal of Irish Studies
EJ	English Journal
EK	Eibungaku Kenkyu
EL&L	English Language and Literature
ÉLawr	Études Lawrenciennes
ÉLC	Études Sur la Littérature Contemporaine
ELH	(*formerly* English Literary History)
ELN	English Language Notes
ELT	English Literature in Transition (1880–1920)
ELWIU	Essays in Literature
EN	Enemy News: Journal of the Wyndham Lewis Society
Encounter	
Enclitic	
Encyclia: The Journal of the Utah Academy of Sciences, Arts, and Letters	
English: The Journal of the English Association	
EngM	English Miscellany
EngR	The English Record
EngStColl	English Studies for College
EP	Études Philosophiques
Epos	Revista de Filologìa
ES	English Studies: A Journal of English Language and Literature
ESA	English Studies in Africa
ESC	English Studies in Canada
Esprit	
ESRS	Emporia State Research Studies
Essays by Divers Hands	
ETC: A Review of General Semantics	
Études	
Europe	Revue Littéraire Mensuelle

EWNS Evelyn Waugh Newsletter and Studies (*supersedes* Evelyn Waugh Newsletter)

Expl The Explicator

ExTimes [Edinburgh] Expository Times

Extrapolation: A Journal of Science Fiction and Fantasy

F&R Faith and Reason

Fabula: Zeitschrift für Erzählforschung/Journal of Folktale Studies/Revue d'Études sur le Conte Popular

Fantasiae

FDig Family Digest

FemR The Feminist Review

FemS Feminist Studies

Fforum Folklore Forum

FJS Fu Jen Studies: Literature & Linguistics

Florilegium: Carleton University Annual Papers on Late Antiquity and the Middle Ages

FN Filologiceskie Nauki

FLitS Foreign Literary Studies (China)

FMLS Forum for Modern Language Studies

Folio Essays on Foreign Languages and Literatures

Folklore

Fortnightly

Forum

Foundation: The Review of Science Fiction

Frontiers Frontiers: A Journal of Women's Studies

GaR The Georgia Review

GEF The George Eliot Fellowship Review (*superseded* by George Eliot Review)

GEGHLN The George Eliot-George Henry Lewes Newsletter

Genders

Genre	
GettR	The Gettysburg Review
GissingJ	The Gissing Journal (*formerly* The Gissing Newsletter)
GKW	G.K.'s Weekly
GL&L	German Life and Letters
GlyphT	Glyph Textual Studies
Golsuorsi	
Gothic	
GrandS	Grand Street
Granta	
Greyfriar: Siena Studies in Literature	
GRM	Germanisch-Romanische Monatsschrift
GSJ	Gaskell Society Journal
Guilde du Livre	
GypS	Gypsy Scholar
Harpers Magazine	
The Hatcher Review	
HBM	The Horn Book Magazine
HEI	History of European Ideas
Hermathena: A Trinity College Dublin	
Hibernia	
HibJ	Hibbert Journal
HirUS	Hiroshima University Studies
Hispanófila	
HKBCACJ	The Hong Kong Baptist College Academic Journal
HLQ	The Huntington Library Quarterly: A Journal for the History and Interpretation of English and American Civilization
HM	The Harvard Magazine
HN	The Hemingway Review

Hochland	
HofM	The History of Medicine
Horen	Die Horen: Zeitschrift für Literatur, Kunst und Kritik
HR	Hispanic Review
HSE	Hungarian Studies in English
HSELL	Hiroshima Studies in English Language and Literature
HSL	The University of Hartford Studies in Literature: A Journal of Interdisciplinary Criticism
HSt	Hamlet Studies: An International Journal of Research on 'The Tragedie of Hamlet, Prince of Denmarke'
HT	History Today
HudR	The Hudson Review
HUSLA	Hebrew University Studies in Literature and the Arts
Humanist	The Humanist
HumAR	Humanities Association Review/La Revue de l'Association des Humanités
Humor	International Journal of Humor Research
HumS	Humanities in Society
HUSL	Hebrew University Studies in Literature and the Arts
HusR	The Husson Review
IAN	Izvestiia Akademii Nauk Turkmenskoi SSR, Seriia Obshchestvennykh Nauk
IAT	Izvestiia Akademii
IbSE	Ibadan Studies in English
IdD	Ilha do Desterro: A Journal of Language and Literature
IFR	The International Fiction Review
IJESt	The Indian Journal of English Studies
IJWS	The International Journal of Women's Studies
ILit	Indian Literature
IllQ	The Illinois Quarterly

Il Lattore di Provincia

The Illustrated [London] News

ILR	The Indian Literary Review: A Tri-Quarterly of Indian Literature
IncL	The Incorporated Linguist

Inklings: Jahrbuch für Literatur und Ästhetik

InozF	Inozemma Filolihiia
Insula	Revista de Letras y Ciencias Humanas

Interpretation: A Journal of Political Philosophy

Interpretations: A Journal of Ideas, Analysis, and Criticism

IowaR	The Iowa Review
IPEN	The Indian P.E.N.
IRA	The Irish Renaissance Annual

Irish Press

ISh	The Independent Shavian
ISP	Igirisu Shosetsu Panfuletto

Italica

IUR	Irish University Review: A Journal of Irish Studies

Jabberwocky: The Journal of the Lewis Carroll Society

JAF	Journal of American Folklore
J&KUR	Jammu and Kasmir University Review
JASt	Journal of Asian Studies
JBeckS	Journal of Beckett Studies
JBritS	Journal of British Studies
JCL	Journal of Commonwealth Literature
JDECU	Journal of the Department of English (Calcutta University)

JDSG: Jahrbuch der Deutschen Schillergesellschaft

JDF	Jahrbuch Deutsch als Fremdsprache
JDSG	Jahrbuch der Deutschen Schillergesellschaft
JEGP	Journal of English and Germanic Philology

JELL	Journal of English Language and Literature
JEP	Journal of Evolutionary Psychology
JES	Journal of European Studies
JETT	Journal of English Teaching Techniques
JHI	The Journal of the History of Ideas
JHSex	Journal of the History of Sexuality
JIL	Journal of Irish Literature
JiS	Jezik in Slovstvo
JJB	James Joyce Broadsheet
JJLS	James Joyce Literary Supplement
JJQ	James Joyce Quarterly
JJR	James Joyce Review
JKSUA	The Journal of King Saud University, Arts
JLM	Journal of Modern Literature
JLSTL	Journal of Literary Studies/Tydskrif Vir Literaturwetenskap
JMMLA	Journal of the Midwest Modern Language Association
JNT	Journal of Narrative Technique
JPC	Journal of Popular Culture
JRead	The Journal of Reading
JPRS	Journal of Pre-Raphaelite and Aesthetic Studies
JRR	Jean Rhys Review
JSA	Joyce Studies Annual
JSL	Journal of the School of Languages
JSSE	Journal of the Short Story in English
JUkGS	Journal of Ukrainian Studies
Junction	
JWSLit	The Journal of Women's Studies in Literature
Kaleidoscope	
Káñina	Revista de Artes y Letras de la Universidad de Costa Rica

KanQ	Kansas Quarterly
KFR	Kentucky Folklore Record
KJ	The Kipling Journal
KN	Kwartalnik Neofilologiczny
KPAB	Kentucky Philological Association Bulletin
KR	The Kenyon Review
KRev	The Kentucky Review
KS	Kenkyu Shuroku
KSJ	Keats-Shelley Journal: Keats, Shelley, Byron, Hunt, and Their Circles
KSR	Keats-Shelley Review
KuKl	Kultur og Klasse
KulturaP	Kultura: Szkice, Opowiadania, Sprawozdania
KultuurL	Kultuur Leven
Kunapipi	
LA	Living Age
L&B	Literature and Belief
L&C	Language and Culture
Lang&C	Language & Communication: An Interdisciplinary Journal
L&FAR	Liberal and Fine Arts Review
L&H	Literature and History
L&K	Literatur und Kritik
L&L	Life and Letters
L&L&LM	Life and Letters and The London Mercury
L&LC	Literary and Linguistic Computing: Journal of the Association for Literary and Linguistic Computing
L&M	Literature and Medicine
L&P	Literature and Psychology
L&U	The Lion and the Unicorn: A Critical Journal of Children's Literature

Labrys	
Lang&C	Language and Culture
Lang&H	Le Langage et l'Homme: Recherches Pluridisciplinaires sur le Langage
Lang&Lit	Language & Literature
LanM	Les Langues Modernes
LangQ	Language Quarterly
Lang&S	Language and Style: An International Journal
LCrit	The Literary Criterion
LdProv	Il Lettore di Provinci
LE&W	Literature East & West
LeF	Le Figaro
LeS	Lingua é Stile: Trimestrales di Filosofia del Linguaggio Linguistica e Analisi Letteraria (*formerly* Lingua é Stile: Trimestrale di Linguistics e Critica Letteraria)
LFQ	Literature/Film Quarterly
LHY	Literary Half-Yearly
Library Review	
Licorne	La Licorne
LingLit	Linguistics in Literature
LiNQ	Literature in North Queensland
Listener	
LIT	Lit: Literature Interpretation Theory
Lit&L	Literatur und Leben
Ling&Lit	Linguistics and Literature
LitE	The Literary Endeavour: A Quarterly Journal Devoted to English Studies
LitO	Literature of the Oppressed
LitR	The Literary Review: An International Journal of Contemporary Writing
Litt	Littératures

LittPrag	Littéraria Pragnesia: Studies in Literature and Culture (*supersedes* Philologica Pragensia)
LitW	Literary World
LJGG	Literaturwissenschaftliches Jahrbuch im Auftrage der Görres-Gesellschaft
LJHum	Lamar Journal of the Humanities
LM	Langues Modernes
LMag	London Magazine
LO	Literaturnoe Obozrenie: Organ Soiuza Pisatelei SSSR
LockHB	Lock Haven Bulletin
LOS	Literary Onomastics Studies
LPrag	Litteraria Pragensia
LQR	Law Quarterly Review
LRB	London Review of Books
LuK	Literatur und Kritik
LugR	Lugano Review
LWU	Literatur in Wissenschaft und Unterricht
M&DA	Mystery and Detection Annual
Maatstaf	
Magazine	
MAL	Modern Austrian Literature
Mallorn: The Journal of the Tolkien Society	
MalR	Malahat Review
MARev	Mid-American Review
MathT	Mathematics Teacher
MCRel	Mythes, Croyances et Religions dans le Monde Anglo-Saxon
Meanjin	
Mercury	[London] Mercury
Merkur	Deutsche Zeitschrift für europäisches Denken
MFAN	Mystery FANcier

MFS	Modern Fiction Studies
MGSL	Minas Gerais, Suplemento Literario
MidHLS	Mid-Hudson Language Studies
Minas Tirith Evening Star: Journal of the American Tolkien Society	
Mirror	
Misc	Miscellanea
MissQ	Mississippi Quarterly: The Journal of Southern Culture
MissR	Missouri Review
MJLF	Midwest Journal of Language and Folklore
MLN	(*formerly* Modern Language Notes)
MLNew	The Malcolm Lowry Review
MLQ	Modern Language Quarterly: A Journal of Literary History (*formerly* Modern Language Quarterly)
MLR	Modern Language Review
MLS	Modern Language Studies
ModA	Modern Age: A Quarterly Review
ModBL	Modern British Literature
Der Moderne Englische Roman	
ModST	Modernist Studies: Literature and Culture 1920–1940
Month	
MOR	Mount Olive Review
Moreana	Bulletin Thomas More
Mosaic	A Journal for the Interdisciplinary Study of Literature
MP	Modern Philology: A Journal Devoted to Research in Medieval and Modern Literature
MQ	Midwest Quarterly: A Journal of Contemporary Thought
MQR	Michigan Quarterly Review
MR	Massachusetts Review: A Quarterly of Literature, the Arts and Public Affairs
MSE	Massachusetts Studies in English

MSpr	Moderna Språk
MTJ	Mark Twain Journal
MVA	Mitteilungen des Verbandes deutsher Anglisten
Mythlore	Mythlore: A Journal of J. R. R. Tolkien, C. S. Lewis, Charles Williams, and the Genres of Myth and Fantasy Studies
N&Q	Notes & Queries
Nabokovian	The Nabokovian
Names	The Journal of the American Name Society
NAMM	North American Mentor Magazine
NAR	North American Review
Nation	
Nation&A	Nation and Athenaeum
NatlR	The National Review
NCF	Nineteenth-Century Literature (*formerly* Nineteenth-Century Fiction)
NConL	Notes on Contemporary Literature
NCS	Nineteenth-Century Studies
NDEJ	Notre Dame English Journal
NDH	Neue Deutsche Hefte Studiekamraten
NDQ	North Dakota Quarterly
Neohelicon: Acta Comparationis Litterarum Universarum	
Neophil	Neophilologus
NEQ	New England Quarterly: A Historical Review of New England Life and Letters
NewB	New Blackfriars
NewC	The New Criterion
NewComp	New Comparison: A Journal of Comparative and General Literary Studies
New Letters: A Magazine of Fine Writing	
NewR	The New Republic

New Review	
NewS	New Statesman
NewS&L	The New Statesman and Leader
NewS&N	New Statesman and Nation
NewS&S	New Statesman & Society
Newsweek	
NewWR	New Welsh Review
NewY	The New Yorker
NewYSJM	The New York State Journal of Medicine
NewW	The New Worlds
NG/FH	Die Neue Gesellschaft/Frankfurter Hefte
NLH	The New Literary History: A Journal of Theory and Interpretation
NM	Neuphilologische Mitteilungen: Bulletin de la Société Néophilologique/Bulletin of the Modern Language Society
NMIL	Notes on Modern Irish Literature
NHCL	The New Hampshire College Journal
NNER	The Northern New England Review
Novel	A Forum on Fiction
NOR	The New Orleans Review
NPP	Northhamptonshire Past and Present
NR	The Nassau Review: The Journal of Nassau Community College Devoted to Arts, Letters, and Sciences
NRDM	Nouvelle Revue des Deux Mondes
NRF	Nouvelle Revue Française
NRFH	Nueva Revista de Filología Hispánica
NRP	Nueva Revista del Pacífico
NS	Die Neuren Sprachen
NsM	Neusprachliche Mitteilungen aus Wissenschaft und Praxis
NSR	Die Neue Schweizer Rundschau

NTg	De Nieuwe Taalgids: Tijdschrift voor Neerlandici
NULR	The Natal University Law Review
NVSAWC	The Newsletter of the Victorian Studies Association of Western Canada
NWi	The North Wind: Journal of the George MacDonald Society
NYLF	The New York Literary Forum
NYRB	The New York Review of Books
NYRS	The New York Review of Science
NYTBR	The New York Times Book Review
Oberon	Magazine for the Study of English and American Literature
Observer	The Observer
Okike: An African Journal of New Writing	
OJES	Osmania Journal of English Studies
OL	Orbis Litterarum: International Review of Literary Studies
OLR	The Oxford Literary Review
OnomasticaC	Onomastica Canadiana
OnsE	Ons Erfdeel: Algemeen-Nederlands Tweemaandlijks Cultureel Tijdschrift
The Opera News	
The Opera Quarterly	
Orcrist	
OrientW	Orient West
Overland	
P&L	Philosophy and Literature
PAPA	Publications of the Arkansas Philological Association
Paragraph	Paragraph: A Journal of Modern Critical Theory
The Paris Review	
ParR	Par Rapport
Pasajes	

Paunch

PCCTET Proceedings of the Conference of College Teachers of English of Texas

PConL Perspectives on Contemporary Literature

PCP Pacific Coast Philology

PCrit Paris Critique

PCulR Psychocultural Review

PeakeS Peake Studies

Permskii Universitet

Perspective

Persuasions Journal of the Jane Austen Society of North America

PH La Palabra y el Hombre: Revista de la Universidad Veracruzana

Plein-Chant

Philogia Pragensia

Philosophy The Journal of the British Institute of Philosophical Studies

PhS Philosophical Studies: An International Journal for Philosophy in the Analytic Tradition

PLL Papers on Language and Literature

Plum Lines Supplement

Plural

PMLA Publications of the Modern Language Association

PNR The PN Review

Poetica Zeitschrift für Sprach- und Literaturwiseenschaft

Poétique Revue de Théorie et d'Analyse Littéraires

PolR The Polish Review

POMPA Publications of the Mississippi Philological Association

PostS Post Script: Essays in Film and the Humanities

PoT Poetics Today

PowN Powys Notes

PPR	Philosophy and Phenomenological Research
PQ	Philological Quarterly
PR	Partisan Review
PRAN	Proust Research Association Newsletter
PraSE	Prague Studies in English
PreRR	The Pre-Raphaelite Review
Pretexts	Pretexts: Studies in Writing and Culture
PRev	The Powys Review
Problemi	Problemi: Periodico Quadrimestrale di Cultura (Yugoslavia)
Proteus	A Journal of Ideas
ProverbiumY	Proverbium: Yearbook of Internationl Proverb Scholarship
PSc	Prairie Schooner
PSt	Prose Studies: History, Theory, Criticism
PsyAR	The Psychoanalytic Review
PsycholRep	Psychological Reports
PsyHR	The Psychohistory Review
PULC	The Princeton University Library Chronicle
Punch	
PURBA	The Panjab University Research Bulletin (Arts)
PVR	The Platte Valley Review
QL	La Quinzaine Littéraire
QLL	Quaderni di Lingue e Letterature
QQ	The Queen's Quarterly
Quaderni di Filologia Germanica della Factolta di Lettere e Filosofia dell'Universita di Bologna	
Quadrant	
Quest	New Quest
Quimera: Rivista de Literatura	
R&C	Race & Class

R&L	Religion and Literature
RAEI	Revista Alicantina de Estudios Ingleses
Rag: Abiko Literary Quarterly	
RAL	Research in African Literatures
Rally	
RANAM	Recherches Anglaises et Americaines
Raritan	The Raritan: A Quarterly Review
Razgledi: Spisanie za Literatura Umetnost i Kultura	
RCEI	Revista Canaria de Estudios Ingleses
RCF	The Review of Contemporary Fiction
RChL	Revista Chilena de Literatura
REALB	Real: The Yearbook of Research in English and American Literature
RecL	Recovering Literature: A Journal of Contextualist Criticism
Red Letters: A Journal of Cultural Politics	
Renascence	Essays on Value in Literature
Representations	
RES	Review of English Studies: A Quarterly Journal of English Literature and the English Language
Restant	Tijdschrift voor Recente Semiotische Teorievorming en de Analyse van Teksten/Review for Semiotic Theories and the Analysis of Texts
RevEL	The Review of English Literature
RevH	La Revue Hebdomadaire
RevP	La Revue de Paris
Revue de la Universidad de Costa Rica	
RFemI	Regionalism and the Female Imagination
RFL	Revista da Faculdade de Letras
RFULL	Revista de Filologia de la Universidad de La Laguna
RILA	Rassegna Italiana di Linguistica Applicata

RLAn	RLA: Romance Languages Annual
RLet	Revista Letras
RLetras	República de las Letras
RLC	Revue de Littérature Comparée
RLM	La Revue des Lettres Modernes: Histoire des Idées et des Littératures
RLMC	Rivista di Letterature Moderne e Comparate
RLV	Revue des langues vivantes
RMR	The Rocky Mountain Review of Language and Literature
RMS	Renaissance & Modern Studies
RO	Revista de Occidente
Romantist	The Romantist
RomN	Romance Notes
RPol	Review of Politics
RQ	The Riverside Quarterly
RRL	Revue Roumaine de Linguistique (*incorporates* Cahiers de Linguistique Théorique et Appliqée)
RSH	Revue des Sciences Humaines
RsSt	Research Studies
RT	The Round Table
RtSoCCEA	The Round Table of South Central College English Association
RUSEng	Rajasthau University Studies in English
RusL	Russkaia Literatura
RUSt	Rice University Studies
S&T	Sky & Telescope
Samtiden: Tidsskrift for Politikk, Litteratur og Samfunnssporsmål	
SAQ	The South Atlantic Quarterly
SARE	The Southeast Asian Review of English
SatR	The Saturday Review of Literature, Arts

Sayers Review	
SC	The Stendhal Club: Revue International Études Stendhaliennes. Nouvelle Série
Schlern	
SCL	Studies in Canadian Literature
ScLJ	The Scottish Literary Journal (*formerly* Scottish Literary Journal: A Review of Studies in Scottish Language and Literature)
SCRev	The South Central Review: The Journal of the South Central Modern Language Association
Scriobh	
Scrutiny	
SDR	The South Dakota Review
SECC	Studies in Eighteenth-Century Culture
SEEJ	Slavic and East European Journal
SEL	Studies in English Literature, 1500–1900
SELit	Studies in English Literature
SELL	Studies in English Language and Literature
SELL Chuo-ku	Studies in English Language and Literature (Chuo-ku)
SES	Sophia English Studies
Seven: An Anglo-American Literary Review	
SFic	Science Fiction: A Review of Speculative Literature
SFolkQ	Southern Folklore Quarterly
SFRB	The San Francisco Review of Books
SFS	Science Fiction Studies
SG	Survey Graphic
Shenandoah: The Washington & Lee University Review (*formerly* Shenendoah)	
ShHR	The Sherlock Holmes Review
Shiron	
SHR	The Southern Humanities Review

SHW	Studies in Hogg and His World
Signs	Journal of Women in Culture and Society
SiPC	Studies of Popular Culture
SIR	Studies in Romanticism
SJL	Southwest Journal of Linguistics
SJS	San Josè Studies
SLitI	Studies in the Literary Imagination
SLRev	Shoin Literature Review
SLRJ	Saint Louis University Research Journal of the Graduate School of Arts and Sciences
Smithsonian	Smithsonian Magazine
SMod	Spicilegio Moderno
SMy	Studia Mystica
SN	Studia Neophilologica: A Journal of Germanic and Romance Languages and Literature
SNNTS	Studies in the Novel
SoAB	The South Atlantic Bulletin
SoAR	The South Atlantic Review
SoCB	The South Central Bulletin
Social Theory and Practice	
Sociocriticism	
SoCR	The South Carolina Rview
SoQ	The Southern Quarterly: A Journal of the Arts in the South
SoR	The Southern Review: Literary and Interdisciplinary Essays
Soundings: An Interdisciplinary Journal	
Southerly: A Review of Australian Literature	
Sovremenost	Spisanie za Literatura, Umetnost i Opstestveni Prasanja
SP	Studies in Philology
SPAN	Journal of the South Pacific Association for Commonwealth Literature and Language Studies

Spectator

Spectrum

Sphinx	The Sphinx
SpL	Spiegel der Letteren: Tijdschrift voor Nederlandse Literatuurgeschiedenis en voor Literatuurwetenschap

Sprachkunst: Beiträge zur Literaturwissenschaft

SpSR	Springfield Sunday Republican
SPsyT	Studies in Psychoanalytic Theory
SR	The Sewanee Review
SRAZ	Studia Romanica et Anglica Zagrabiensia
SSEng	Sydney Studies in English
SSF	Studies in Short Fiction
SSHMB	Society of Social History Medical Bulletin

Standpoint

Standpunte

The Stanford Law Review

Steaua

SText	Social Text
StHum	Studies in the Humanities
StII	Studien zur Indologie und Iranistik
StIL	Studi dell'Istituto Linguistico
StIng	Studia Inglesi
StLU	Studiu de Literatura Universala

Streven

StSL	Studies in Scottish Literature
StTCL	Studies in the Twentieth Century Literature
StWF	Studies in Weird Fiction

Style

SubStance: A Review of Theory and Literary Criticism

SULLA Studi Urbinati, Serie B3: Linguistica, Letteraura, Arte

Suplemento Literario La Nacion, Buenos Aires

Symposium: A Quarterly Journal in Modern Literatures (*formerly* Symposium: A Quarterly Journal in Modern Foreign Literatures)

Synthésis: Bulletin du Comitéte National de Littérature Comparée et de l'Institut d'Historie et Théorie Littéraire "G. Cálinescu" de l'Académie de Roumanie

SZ Stimmen der Zeit

TbR La Table Ronde

Twentieth Century

TCL Twentieth Century Literature: A Scholarly and Critical Journal

Turn of the Century Women

Telegraph

TES Tampere English Studies

TexP Textual Practice

TexasQ The Texas Quarterly

TexasR The Texas Review

Textus: Annual of the Hebrew University Bible Project

THA The Thomas Hardy Annual

Thalia

Theology Today

Theoria Theoria: A Journal of Studies in the Arts, Humanities, and Social Sciences

THJ The Thomas Hardy Journal

Thoth

Thought

THY The Thomas Hardy Yearbook

Times The [London] Times

TimesES The [London] Times Educational Supplement

Tirade

TkR	Tamkang Review: A Quarterly of Comparative Studies between Chinese and Foreign Literatures
TLS	Times Literary Supplement
TM	Temps Modernes
	Today
TPB	The Tennessee Philological Bulletin: Proceedings of the Annual Meeting of the Tennessee Philological Association
Tradition: A Journal of Orthodox Jewish Thought	
Trimestre	
Trivium	
Trollopian	
TSLL	Texas Studies in Literature and Language
TStL	Tennessee Studies in Literature
Tsuda Review	
TSWL	Tulsa Studies in Women's Literature
TWN	The Thomas Wolfe Review
TYDS	Transactions of the Yorkshire Dialect Society
UCTStE	The University of Cape Town Studies in English
UDR	The University of Dayton Review
UeL	Uomini e Libri: Periodico Bimestrale di Critica ed Informazione Letteraria
UES	The Unisa English Studies: Journal of the Department of English
UKanR	The University of Kansas Review
UMSE	The University of Mississippi Studies in English
Unicorn	
UofE	Use of English
UPR	University of Portland Reivew
UR	The University Review
UtopSt	Utopian Studies: Journal of the Society for Utopian Studies

UTQ	The University of Toronto Quarterly
UWRev	University of Windsor Review
Vector	
Venture	
Verbatim: The Language Quarterly	
Versus: Quaderni di Studi Semiotici	
VIJ	The Victorian Institute Journal
The Village Voice	
The Village Voice Literary Supplement	
VirEB	The Virginia English Bulletin
Virginia Woolf Review	
Vladimir Nabokov Research Newsletter	
VMU	Vestnik Moskovskogo Universiteta
VN	The Victorian Newsletter
VPR	The Victorian Periodicals Review
VRev	The Victorian Review: The Journal of the Victorian Studies Association of Western Canada
VS	Victorian Studies
Vsesvit: Zhurnal Inozemnoi Literatury. Literaturno-Mystets'kyi ta	Hromads'ko-Politychnyi Misiachnyk
VQR	The Virginia Quarterly Review
VSPU	Vestnik Sankt-Peterburgskogo Universiteta. Seriia 2, Istoriia, Iazykoznanie, Literaturovedenie (*formerly* Vestnik Leningradskogo Universiteta, Seriia 2, Istoriia, Iazykoznanie, Literaturovedenie)
VWM	Virginia Woolf Miscellany
VWQ	The Virginia Woolf Quarterly
W&D	Works and Days: Essays in the Socio-Historical Dimensions of Literature and the Arts
W&I	Word and Image

W&L Women & Literature

Waiguoyu

Waiyu Jiaoxue Yu Yanjiu

Wake Wake Newsletter: Studies in James Joyce's :Finnegan's Wake"

WAL Western American Literature

WascanaR Wascana Review

WB Weimarer Beiträge: Zeitschrift für Literaturwissenschaft, Ästhetik und Kulturwissenschaften (*formerly* Weimarer Beiträge: Zeitschrift für Literaturwissenschaft, Ästhetik und Kulturtheorie)

WC The Wordsworth Circle

WCR The West Coast Review

WCSJ The Wilkie Collins Society Journal

Wellsian The Wellsian: The Journal of the H. G. Wells Society

Westerly: A Quarterly Review

Western Review

WestR The Westminster Review

WF Western Folklore

WHR The Western Humanities Review

Wind and the Rain

WinP Work in Progress

WitB The [Wichita] Bulletin

WLB The Wilson Library Bulletin

WLT World Literature Today: A Literary Quarterly of the University of Oklahoma

WLWE World Literature Written in English

Word WORD: Journal of the International Linguistics Association

WR The World Review

WRB The Women's Review of Books

WRev The Wiseman Review

Writer

WS	Women's Studies: An Interdisciplinary Journal
WSp	Western Speech
WStConL	The Wisconsin Studies in Contemporary Literature
WStL	The Wisconsin Studies in Literature
WUVPP	The West Virginia University Philological Papers
WWort	Wirkendes Wort: Deutsche Sprache und Literatur in Forschung und Lehre
WZUR	Wissenschaftliche Zeitschrift der Wilhelm-Pieck-Universitat Rostock Gesellschaftswissenschaftlich Reihe
Xanadu	Xanadu: A Literary Journal
YER	Yeats Eliot Review: A Journal of Criticism and Scholarship
YES	The Yearbook of English Studies
YFS	Yale French Studies
YJC	The Yale Journal of Criticism: Interpretation in the Humanities
YR	The Yale Review
ZAA	Zeitschrift für Anglistik und Amerikanistik
ZRL	Zagadnienia Rodzajów Literackich: Woprosy Literaturnych Zanrov/Les Problèmes des Genres Littéraires
ZS	Zeitschrift fòr Slavische Philologie American Imago: A Psychoanalytic Journal for Culture, Science, and the Arts 1985
ZSP	Zeitschrift für Slavische Philologie

Checklist of Interpretation

ACKROYD, PETER

Chatterton

Brian Finney, "Peter Ackroyd, Postmodernist Play and *Chatterton*," *TCL* 38 (Summer 1992): 240–61.

English Music

Edward T. Wheeler, "*English Music*," *Commonweal* 120 (26 March 1993): 25.

T. A. Shippey, "*English Music*," *TLS* (22 May 1992): 29.

Hawksmoor

Susana Onega Jaen, "Pattern and Magic in *Hawksmoor*," *Atlantis* 12 (November 1991): 31–43.

ADAMS, DOUGLAS (NOEL)

Dirk Gently's Holistic Detective Agency

Tom Easton, "*Dirk Gently's Holistic Detective Agency*," *Analog* 108 (February 1988): 187–88.

Last Chance to See

Susan Murphy, "*Last Chance to See*," *JRead* 35 (April 1992): 600–03

William Dieter, "*Last Chance to See*," *Smithsonian* 22 (June 1991): 140–41

The Long Dark Tea-Time of the Soul

Cathleen Schine, "*The Long Dark Tea-Time of the Soul*," *NYTBR* (12 March 1989): 11

Mostly Harmless

Tom Easton, "*Mostly Harmless*," *Analog* 113 (September 1993): 164–65

Nick Hornby, "*Mostly Harmless*," *TLS* (9 October 1992): 22

Bill Sharp, "*Mostly Harmless*," *NYTBR* (1 November 1992): 20

ALDISS, BRIAN

Brothers of the Head

Michael R. Collings, "*Brothers of the Head*: Brian W. Aldiss's Psychological Landscape," in *Spectrum of the Fantastic*, ed. Donald Palumbo (Westport, CT: Greenwood, 1988), 119–26.

Forgotten Life

L. R. Leavis, "*Forgotten Life*," *ES* 71 (April 1990): 135–36.

Ellen R. Weil, "The Secret You: Fantasy and Story in Brian Aldiss's Mainstream Fiction," *NYRB* 26 (October 1990): 1, 3–5.

Frankenstein Unbound

Sylvain Floc'h, "La Chute d'un ange, ou Le Monstrueux a travers le mythe de Frankenstein, de Shelley a Aldiss," in *Le Monstrueux dans la littérature et la pensée anglaises*, ed. Nadia J. Rigaud (Aix-en-Provence: Université de Provence, 1985), 133–44.

Helliconia

Denise Terrel, "Au coeur du labyrinthe: Le Phagor dans la trilogie de *Helliconia* de Brian Aldiss," *ÉA* 41 (July–September 1988): 307–18.

Last Orders

Philip E. Smith II, "*Last Orders* and First Principles for the Interpretation of Aldiss's Enigmas," in *Reflections on the Fantastic*, ed. Michael R. Collings (Westport, CT: Greenwood, 1986), 69–78.

Starswarm

David Leon Hidgon, "Conrad in Outer Space," *Conradian* 12 (May 1987): 74–77.

David Leon Higdon, "Samuel Beckett in Outer Space," *JBeckS* 11–12 (1989): 153–57.

AMBLER, ERIC

Cause for Alarm

Gavin Lambert, "Eric Ambler," in *The Dangerous Edge* (New York: Grossman, 1976), 109–12.

Dirty Story

Gavin Lambert, "Eric Ambler," in *The Dangerous Edge* (New York: Grossman, 1976), 125–27.

The Intercom Conspiracy

Gavin Lambert, "Eric Ambler," in *The Dangerous Edge* (New York: Grossman, 1976), 128–31.

Journey into Fear

Gavin Lambert, "Eric Ambler," in *The Dangerous Edge* (New York: Grossman, 1976), 116–21.

The Light of Day

Gavin Lambert, "Eric Ambler," in *The Dangerous Edge* (New York: Grossman, 1976), 123–25.

The Mask of Dimitrios
(U.S. title: *A Coffin for Dimitrios*)

Gavin Lambert, "Eric Ambler," in *The Dangerous Edge* (New York: Grossman, 1976), 112–16.

The Night-Comers

Julian Symons, "Confidential Agents," *Times*, 5 July 1956, 13. Reprinted in *Critical Occasions* (London: Hamish Hamilton, 1966), 168–73.

AMIS, KINGSLEY

Difficulties with Girls

Jeremy Treglown, "What Are Little Girls Made Of?" *GrandS* 9 (Autumn 1989): 249–57.

Ending Up

Dennis McCort, "The Dreadful Weight of Days: The Hilarious Heroism of Old Age in Kingsley Amis's *Ending Up*," *Sphinx* 4, no. 2 (1982): 101–8.

I Like It Here

Norman Macleod, "A Trip to Greeneland: The Plagiarizing Narrator of Kingsley Amis's *I Like It Here*," *SNNTS* 17 (Summer 1985): 203–17.

Lucky Jim

Robert H. Bell, "'True Comic Edge' in *Lucky Jim*," *AmH* 8 (Fall 1981): 1–7.

Mark Brady, “Funny Jim,” in *Four Fits of Anger: Essays on the Angry Young Men* (Udine: Campanotto, 1986), 70–99.

John K. Eastman, “Dissimilar Discourses: The Realism of Amis's Conversations in *Lucky Jim*,” *RAEI* 2 (November 1989): 43–51.

Old Devils

Jill Farringdon, “When You Come Home Again to Wales,” *AWR* 86 (Fall 1987): 87–92.

One Fat Englishman

John S. Batts, “Amis Abroad: American Occasions for English Humor,” *Humor* 5, no. 3 (1992): 251–66.

The Russian Girl

John Banville, “A Real Funny Guy,” *NYRB* 61 (9 June 1994): 29–30.

Stanislaw Baranczak, “*The Russian Girl*,” *NewR* 211 (3 October 1994): 36–39.

Thomas Mallon, “*The Russian Girl*,” *NatlR* 46 (1 August 1994): 62–63.

Christopher Buckley, “A Little Sex, a Little Dostoyevsky,” *NYTBR* (15 May 1994): 11–12.

We Are All Guilty

Nicholas Pyke, “Old Devil Seeks Young Souls,” *TES* 3896 (1 March 1991): 4.

AMIS, MARTIN

Dead Babies

Shanti Padhi, “Bed and Bedlam: The Hard–Core Extravangazas of Martin Amis,” *LHY* 23 (January 1982): 36–42.

London Fields

Catherine Bernard, “London Fields de Martin Amis: La Mimesis revisitee,” *ÉBC* 1 (December 1992): 1–15.

Money

Richard Todd, "The Intrusive Author in British Postmodernist Fiction: The Cases of Alasdair Gray and Martin Amis," in *Exploring Postmodernism*, ed. Matei Calinescu and Douwe Fokkema (Amsterdam: Benjamins, 1987), 123–30.

R. N. Leonard Ashley, "'Names Are Awfully Important': The Onomastics of Satirical Comment in Martin Amis' *Money*: 'A Suicide Note,'" *LOS* 14 (1987): 1–48.

ATWOOD, MARGARET

Bodily Harm

Marilyn Patton, "Tourists and Terrorists: The Creation of *Bodily Harm*," *PLL* 28 (Spring 1992): 150–73.

Cat's Eye

Stephen Ahern, "'Meat like you like it': The Production of Identity in Atwood's *Cat's Eye*" *CanL* 137 (Summer 1993): 8–17.

Nathalie Cooke, "Reading Reflections: The Autobiographical Illusion in *Cat's Eye*," in *Essays on Life Writing: From Genre to Critical Practice*, ed. Marlene Kadar (Toronto: University of Toronto Press, 1992), 162–70.

David Cowart, "Bridge and Mirror: Replicating Selves in *Cat's Eye*," in *Postmodern Fiction in Canada*, ed. Theo D'haen and Hans Bertens (Amsterdam: Rodopi, 1992), 125–36.

Earl G. Ingersoll, "Margaret Atwood's *Cat's Eye*: Re-viewing Women in a Postmodern World," *Ariel* 22 (October 1991): 17–27.

R. D. Lane, "Cordelia's 'nothing': The Character of Cordelia and Margaret Atwood's *Cat's Eye*," *ECW* 48 (Winter 1992): 73–88.

Judith McCombs, "Contrary Re-memberings: The Creating Self and Feminism in *Cat's Eye*," *CanL* 129 (Summer 1991): 9–23.

Carol Osborne, 'Constructing the Self Through Memory: *Cat's Eye* As a Novel of Female Development,' *Frontiers* 14 (Spring 1994): 95–112.

Martha Sharpe, "Margaret Atwood and Julia Kristeva: Space–time, The Dissident Woman Artist, and the Pursuit of Female Solidarity in *Cat's Eye*," *ECW* 50 (Fall 1993): 174–89.

The Diviners

Christian Bok, "Sibyls: Echoes of French Feminism in *The Diviners* and *Lady Oracle*," *CanL* 135 (Winter 1992): 80–93.

The Edible Woman

J. Brooks Bouson, "The Anxiety of Being Influenced: Reading and Responding to Character in Margaret Atwood's *The Edible Woman*," *Style* 24 (Summer 1990): 228–41.

David L. Harkness, "Alice in Toronto: the Carrollian Intertext in *The Edible Woman*," *ECW* 37 (Spring 1989): 103–11.

The Handmaid's Tale

Joseph Andriano, "*The Handmaid's Tale* as Scrabble Game," *ECW* 48 (Winter 1992): 89–97.

Raffaella Baccolini, "Breaking the Boundaries: Gender, Genre, and Dystopia," in *Per una definizione dell'utopia: Metodologie e discipline a confronto*, ed. Nadia Minerva and Vita Fortunati (Ravenna: Longo, 1992), 137–46.

Chinmoy Banerjee, "Alice in Disneyland: Criticism as Commodity in *The Handmaid's Tale*," *ECW* 41 (Summer 1990): 74–92.

Harriet F. Bergmann, "'Teaching them to read': A Fishing Expedition in *The Handmaid's Tale*," *CE* 51 (December 1989): 847–54.

Glenn Deer, "Rhetorical Strategies in *The Handmaid's Tale*: Dystopia and the Paradoxes of Power," *ESC 18 (June 1992): 215–33.*

Chris Ferns, "The Value/s of Dystopia: *The Handmaid's Tale* and The Anti-utopian Tradition," DR 69 (Fall 1989): 373–82.

Shannon Hengen, "'Metaphysical romance': Atwood's PhD Thesis and *The Handmaid's Tale," SFS* 18 (March 1991): 154–57.

David Ketterer, "Critical Misconceptions," *SFS* 17 (July 1990): 285–86.

David Ketterer, "Margaret Atwood's *The Handmaid's Tale:* A Contextual Dystopia," *SFS* 16 (July 1989): 209–17.

Madonne Miner, "'Trust Me': Reading the Romance Plot in Margaret Atwood's *The Handmaid's Tale," TCL* 37 (Summer 1991): 148–68.

Walter Pache, "Margaret Atwood: *The Handmaid's Tale*," in *Anglistentag 1991*, ed. Wilhelm G. Busse (Tubingen: Niemeyer, 1992), 386–400.

Karen F. Stein, "Margaret Atwood's *The Handmaid's Tale:* Scheherazade in Dystopia," *UTQ* 61 (Winter 1991): 269–79.

Charlotte Templin, "Atwood's *The Handmaid's Tale," Expl* 49 (Summer 1991): 255–56.

Sandra Tomc, "'The Missionary Position': Feminism and Nationalism in Margaret Atwood's *The Handmaid's Tale," CanL* 138–39 (Fall–Winter 1993): 73–87.

Lorraine M. York, "The Habits of Language: Uniform(ity), Transgression and Margaret Atwood," *CanL* 126 (Autumn 1990): 6–19.

Lady Oracle

Marilyn Patton, "*Lady Oracle*: The Politics of the Body," *Ariel* 22 (October 1991): 29–48.

John Thieme, "A Female Houdini: Popular Culture in Margaret Atwood's *Lady Oracle*," *Kunapipi* 14, no. 1 (1992): 71–80.

Life Before Man

Carol I. Beran, "The Canadian Mosaic: Functional Ethnicity in Margaret Atwood's *Life Before Man*," *ECW* 41 (Summer 1990): 59–73.

"Lives of the Poets"

Sandra Nelson, "Response to Margaret Atwood's 'Lives of the Poets,'" *MaRev* 12, no. 2 (1992): 111–15.

The Robber Bride

Gabriele Annan, "Donna Giovanna," *NYRB* 40 (16 December 1993): 14, 16.

Surfacing

Ronald Granofsky, "Fairy-tale Morphology in Margaret Atwood's *Surfacing*," *Mosaic* 23 (Fall 1990): 51–65.

Reingard M. Nischik, "'Ou maintenant? Quand maintenant? Qui maintenant?': Die namenlose Ich-Erzahlfigur im Roman," *Poetica* 23 no. 1–2 (1991): 257–75.

Christina Strobel, "On the Representation of Representation in Margaret Atwood's *Surfacing*," *ZAA* 40, no. 1 (1992): 35–43.

AUSTEN, JANE

Emma

Peter F. Alexander, "'Robin Adair' as a Musical Clue in Jane Austen's *Emma*, *RES* 39 (February 1988): 84–86.

Wayne C. Booth, "Emma, Emma, and the Question of Feminism," *Persuasions* 5 (December 1983): 29–40.

D. Dean Cantrell, "Porcine Tittle-Tattle," *Persuasions* 4 (16 December 1982): 14–15.

Richard Creese, "Austen's *Emma*," *Expl* 44 (Winter 1986): 21–23.

Christina Crosby, "Facing the Charms of *Emma*," *NOR* 16 (Spring 1989): 88–97.

J. M. Q. Davies, "*Emma* as Charade and the Education of the Reader," *PQ* 65 (Spring 1986): 231–42.

Patricia D. Davis, "Jane Austen's Use of Frank Churchill's Letters in *Emma*," *Persuasions* 10 (16 December 1988): 34–38.

Mary DeForest, "Mrs. Elton and the Slave Trade," *Persuasions* 9 (16 December 1987): 11–13.

Stephen Derry, "*Emma*, the Maple, and Spenser's Garden of Adonis," *N&Q* 40 (December 1993): 467.

Hiroshi Ebine, "*Emma* no Plot," *EigoS* 126 (1981): 554–58.

Hanquan Fang, "Comment on *Emma*," *Waiguoyu* 4 (July 1985): 71–75.

Casey Finch and Peter Bowen, "'The Tittle-Tattle of Highbury': Gossip and the Free Indirect Style in *Emma*," *Representations* 31 (Summer 1990): 1–18.

Avrom Fleishman, "Two Faces of *Emma*," *W&L* 3 (1983): 248–56.

Cathy Fried, "Some Notes on the 'Parish Business' in *Emma*," *Persuasions* 1 (December 1979): 17, 24.

Frank Gibbon, "Jane Austen and a Bleached Stain: The Case of Lady Bolton," *N&Q* 30 (June 1983): 217.

Gloria Sybil Gross, "Jane Austen and Psychological Realism: 'What Does a Woman Want?'" in *Reading and Writing Women's Lives: A Study of the Novel of*

Manners, ed. Bege K. Bowers and Barbara Brothers (Ann Arbor, MI: University Microfilms International Research Press, 1990), 19–33.

David Groves, "The Two Picnics in *Emma*," *Persuasions* 5 (December 1983): 6–7.

Grant I. Holly, "Emmagrammatology," *SECC* 19 (1989): 39–51.

Catherine Kenney, "The Mystery of *Emma*: Or, The Consummate Case of the Least Likely Heroine," *Persuasions* 13 (December 1991): 138–45.

Bo-won Kim, "Jane Austen and the Tradition of the Nineteenth Century English Novel: With Reference to the Marriages in *Emma*," *JELL* 36 (Autumn 1990): 455–69.

Yuri Kinashi, "*Emma*: Katari no Giho," in *Jane Austen: Shosetsu no Kenkyu* (Tokyo: Aratake, 1981), 167–88.

Edith Lank, "'The Word Was Blunder': Who Was Harriet Smith's Mother?" *Persuasions* 7 (December 1985): 14–15.

Joseph Litvak, "Reading Characters: Self, Society, and Text in *Emma*," *PMLA* 100 (October 1985): 763–73.

John P. McGowan, "Knowledge/Power and Jane Austen's Radicalism," *Mosaic* 18 (Summer 1985): 1–15.

Beatrice Marie, "*Emma* and the Democracy of Desire," *SNNTS* 17 (Spring 1985): 1–13.

Mary Millard, "Do You Not Dance, Mr. Elton?" *Persuasions* 5 (December 1983): 14.

Kimiko Miyamoto, "*Emma*: Chisei e no Yugana Chosen," in *Jane Austen: Shosetsu no Kenkyu* (Tokyo: Aratake, 1981), 189–207.

Wendy Moffat, "Identifying with Emma: Some Problems for the Feminist Reader," *CE* 53 (January 1991): 45–58.

Leland Monk, "Murder She Wrote: The Mystery of Jane Austen's *Emma*," *JNT* 20 (Fall 1990): 342–53.

Edward Neill, "Between Deference and Destruction: 'Situations' of Recent Critical Theory and Jane Austen's *Emma*," *CritQ* 29 (Autumn 1987): 39–54.

Alex Page, "'Straightforward Emotions and Zigzag Embarrassments' in Austen's *Emma*," in *Johnson and His Age*, ed. James Engell (Cambridge, MA: Harvard University Press, 1984), 559–74.

Mark Parker, “The End of *Emma*: Drawing the Boundaries of Class in Austen,” *JEGP* 91 (July 1992): 344–59.

Ruth Perry, “Interrupted Friendships in Jane Austen’s *Emma*,” *TSWL* 5 (Fall 1986): 185–202.

Paul Pickrel, “Lionel Trilling and *Emma*: A Reconsideration,” *NCF* 40 (December 1985): 297–311.

Gregory T. Polletta, “The Author’s Place in Contemporary Narratology,” in *Contemporary Approaches to Narrative*, ed. Anthony Mortimer (Tubingen: Narr, 1984), 109–23.

Anne Pradeilles, “Pour une information de l’analyse syntaxique des formes verbales en anglais scientifique et technique,” in *Actes du Congrès d’Amiens*, 1982, ed. Société des Anglicistes de l’Enseignement Superièur (Paris: Didier, 1987), 439–57.

Nicholas E. Preus, “Sexuality in *Emma*: A Case History,” *SNNTS* 23 (Summer 1991): 196–216.

Pat Rogers, “‘Caro Sposo’: Mrs. Elton, Burneys, Thrales, and Noels,” *RES* 45 (February 1994): 70–75.

Adena Rosmarin, “‘Misreading’ *Emma*: The Powers and Perfidies of Interpretative History,” *ELH* 51 (Summer 1984): 315–42.

John Peter Rumrich, “The Importance of Being Frank,” *ELWIU* 8 (Spring 1981): 97–104.

Luciana Sciullo, “Miss Bates, personaggio chiave di *Emma*,” *QLL* 2 (1977): 91–98.

Ralph Stewart, “Fairfax, Churchill, and Jane Austen’s *Emma*,” *HSL* 14 (September 1982): 96–100.

Barbara Z. Thaden, “Figure and Ground: The Receding Heroine in Jane Austen’s *Emma*,” *SAQ* 55 (January 1990): 47–62.

Beth Fowkes Tobin, “The Moral and Political Economy of Property in Austen’s *Emma*,” *ECF* 2 (April 1990): 229–54.

Mary–Elisabeth Fowkes Tobin, “Aiding Impoverished Gentlewomen: Power and Class in *Emma*,” *Criticism* 30 (Fall 1988): 413–30.

Joel Weinsheimer, “*Emma* and Its Critics: The Value of Tact,” *W&L* 3 (1983): 257–72.

G. A. Wilkes, “Unconscious Motives in Jane Austen’s *Emma*,” *SSEng* 13 (1987–88): 74–89.

Judith Wilt, "The Powers of the Instrument: Or Jane, Frank, and the Pianoforte," *Persuasions* 5 (December 1983): 41–47.

John Wiltshire, "The World of *Emma*," *CR* 27 (1985): 84–97.

Lady Susan

Beatrice Anderson, "The Unmasking of *Lady Susan*," in *Jane Austen's Beginnings: The Juvenilia and Lady Susan*, ed. J. David Grey (Ann Arbor, MI: University Microfilms International Research Press, 1989), 193–203.

Roger Gard, "*Lady Susan* and the Single Effect," *EIC* 39 (October 1989): 305–25.

Barbara J. Horwitz, "*Lady Susan*: The Wicked Mother in Jane Austen's Novels," *Persuasions* 9 (16 December 1987): 84–88. Reprinted as "*Lady Susan*: The Wicked Mother in Jane Austen's Work," in *Jane Austen's Beginnings: The Juvenilia and Lady Susan*, ed. J. David Grey (Ann Arbor, MI: University Microfilms International Research Press, 1989), 181–91.

Deborah Kaplan, "Female Friendship and Epistolary Form: *Lady Susan* and the Development of Jane Austen's Fiction," *Criticism* 29 (Spring 1987): 163–78.

A. Walton Litz, "*Lady Susan* and the Juvenilia," *Persuasions* 9 (16 December 1987): 59–63.

Hugh McKellar, "*Lady Susan*: Sport or Cinderella?" in *Jane Austen's Beginnings: The Juvenilia and Lady Susan*, ed. J. David Grey (Ann Arbor, MI: University Microfilms International Research Press, 1989), 205–14.

Patricia Meyer Spacks, "Female Resources: Epistles, Plot, and Power," *Persuasions* 9 (16 December 1987): 88–98.

Love and Friendship

Stephen Derry, "Sources of Jane Austen's *Love and Friendship*: A Note," *N&Q* 37 (March 1990): 18–19.

Mansfield Park

Nina Auerbach, "Janes Austen's Dangerous Charm: Feeling as One Ought about Fanny Price," *W&L* 3 (1983): 208–23.

C. Knatchbull Bevan, "Personal Identity in *Mansfield Park*: Forms, Fictions, Role-Play, and Reality," *SEL* 27 (Autumn 1987): 595–608.

Martha F. Bowden, "What Does Lady Bertram Do?" *ELN* 30 (December 1992): 30–33.

Maggie Hunt Cohn, "Suppressed Desires in *Mansfield Park*," *Persuasions* 2 (December 1980): 27–28.

Paula Marantz Cohen, "Stabilizing the Family System at *Mansfield Park*," *ELH* 54 (Fall 1987): 669–93.

F. T. Flahiff, "Place and Replacement in *Mansfield Park*," *UTQ* 54 (Spring 1985): 221–33.

Louise Flavin, "*Mansfield Park*: Free Indirect Discourse and the Psychological Novel," *SNNTS* 19 (Summer 1987): 137–59.

Pierre Gaubert, "La Position morale de Jane Austen dans *Mansfield Park*," *ÉA* 43 (January–March 1990):1–13.

Christina Marsden Gillis, "Garden, Sermon, and Novel in *Mansfield Park*: Exercises in Legibility," *Novel* 18 (Winter 1985): 117–25.

Giulia Giuffre, "Sex, Self and Society in *Mansfield Park*," *SSEng* 9 (1983–1984): 76–93.

Patrick Goold, "Obedience and Integrity in *Mansfield Park*," *Renascence* 39 (Summer 1987): 452–69.

J. David Grey, "Sibling Relationships in *Mansfield Park*," *Persuasions* 2 (December 1980): 28–29.

Robin Grove, "Jane Austen's Free Enquiry: *Mansfield Park*," *CR* 25 (1983): 132–50.

John Halperin, "The Novelist as Heroine in *Mansfield Park*: A Study in Autobiography," *MLQ* 33 (June 1983): 136–56.

Michael Heyns, "Shock and Horror: The Moral Vocabulary of *Mansfield Park*," *ESA* 29, no.1 (January 1986): 1–18.

Glenda A. Hudson, "Incestuous Relationships: *Mansfield Park* Revisited," *ECF* 4 (October 1991): 53–68.

Mizue Imaizumi, "*Mansfield Park*: 'Chin moku' to 'Joai,'" in *Jane Austen: Shosetsu no Kenkyu* (Tokyo: Aratake, 1981), 123–43.

W. A. M. Jarvis, "The Ships in *Mansfield Park*," *Persuasions* 10 (16 December 1988): 31–33.

Elaine Jordan, "Pulpit, Stage, and Novel: *Mansfield Park* and Mrs. Inchbald's Lovers' Vows," *Novel* 20 (Winter 1987): 138–48.

AUSTEN, JANE, *Mansfield Park*

David Kaufmann, "Closure in *Mansfield Park* and the Sanctity of the Family," *PQ* 65 (Spring 1986): 211–29.

J. A. Kearney, "Tumult of Feeling, and Restraint, in *Mansfield Park*," *Theoria* 71 (May 1988): 35–45.

Gary Kelly, "Reading Aloud in *Mansfield Park*," *NCF* 37 (June 1982): 29–49.

Gene Koppel, "The Role of Contingency in *Mansfield Park*: The Necessity of an Ambiguous Conclusion," *SoR* 15 (November 1982): 306–13.

Margaret Lenta, "Androgyny and Authority in *Mansfield Park*," *SNNTS* 15 (Fall 1983): 169–82.

Joseph Litvak, "The Infection of Acting: Theatricals and Theatricality in *Mansfield Park*," *ELH* 53 (Summer 1986): 331–55.

Oliver MacDonagh, "The Church in *Mansfield Park*: A Serious Call?" *SSEng* 12 (1986–1987): 36–55.

Jane McDonnell, "'A Little Spirit of Independence': Sexual Politics and the Bildungsroman in *Mansfield Park*," *Novel* 17 (Spring 1984): 197–214.

Alan T. McKenzie, "The Derivation and Distribution of 'Consequence' in *Mansfield Park*," *NCF* 40 (December 1985): 281–96.

David Marshall, "True Acting and the Language of Real Feeling: *Mansfield Park*," *YJC* 3 (Fall 1989): 87–106.

Kate Beaird Meyers, "Jane Austen's Use of Literary Allusion in the Sotherton Episode of *Mansfield Park*," *PLL* 22 (Winter 1986): 96–99.

Marylea Meyersohn, "What Fanny Knew: A Quiet Auditor of the Whole," *W&L* 3 (1983):224–30.

Mary Millard, "1807 and All That," *Persuasions* 8 (December 1986): 50–51.

Kenneth L. Moler, "'Only Connect': Emotional Strength and Health in *Mansfield Park*," *ES* 64 (April 1983): 144–52.

Kenneth L. Moler, "Miss Price All Alone: Metaphors of Distance in *Mansfield Park*," *SNNTS* 17 (Summer 1985): 189–93.

Susan Moore, "The Heroine of *Mansfield Park*," *ES* 63 (April 1982): 139–44.

Weixin Pan, "Appreciation of Literary Language in *Mansfield Park*," *Waiguoyu* 4 (August 1989): 52–56.

Atma Ram, "Frail and Weak: A Portrait of Fanny Price," *PURBA* 8 (April–October 1977): 27–34.

Erna Schwerin, "*Mansfield Park*: A Note on the Elopement of Henry and Maria," *Persuasions* 2 (December 1980): 22–23, 25.

Janice C. Simpson, "Fanny Price as Cinderella: Folk and Fairy–Tale in *Mansfield Park*," *Persuasions* 9 (16 December 1987): 25–30.

Martin Spence, "Austen's *Mansfield Park*," *Expl* 45 (Spring 1987): 22–25.

Johanna M. Smith, "'My Only Sister Now': Incest in *Mansfield Park*," *SNNTS* 19 (Spring 1987): 1–15.

Leroy W. Smith, "*Mansfield Park*: The Revolt of The 'Feminine' Woman," in *Jane Austen in a Social Context*, ed. David Monaghan (Totowa, NJ: Barnes & Noble, 1981), 143–58.

Rachel Trickett, "*Mansfield Park*," *WC* 17 (Spring 1986): 87–95.

Midori Uematsu, "*Mansfield Park*: Kiro ni Tatsu Onna," in *Jane Austen: Shosetsu no Kenkyu* (Tokyo: Aratake, 1981), 145–66.

Lorraine M. York, "'The pen of the contriver' and the Eye of the Perceiver: *Mansfield Park*, the Implied Author and the Implied Reader," *ESC* 13 (June 1987): 161–73.

Lesley Willis, "Religion in Jane Austen's *Mansfield Park*," *ESC* 13 (March 1987): 65–78.

Ruth Bernard Yeazell, "The Boundaries of *Mansfield Park*," *Representations* 7 (Summer 1984): 133–52.

Alma C. Zook, "Star-Gazing at *Mansfield Park*," *Persuasions* 8 (December 1986): 29–33.

Northanger Abbey

Joan Aiken, "How Might Jane Austen Have Revised *Northanger Abbey*?" *Persuasions* 7 (December 1985): 42–54.

Walter E. Anderson, "From Northanger to Woodston: Catherine's Education to Common Life," *PQ* 63 (Fall 1984): 493–509.

A. Banerjee, "Dr. Johnson's Daughter: Jane Austen and *Northanger Abbey*," *ES* 71 (April 1990): 113–24.

Patrick Bizzaro, "Global and Contextual Humor in *Northanger Abbey*," *Persuasions* 7 (December 1985): 82–88.

D. Dean Cantrell, "Her Passion for Ancient Edifices," *Persuasions* 7 (December 1985): 89–93.

AUSTEN, JANE, *Northanger Abbey*

Dean Cantrell, "Yes, There Is a Petty France," *Persuasions* 9 (16 December 1987): 13–17.

Jo Ann Citron, "Running the Basepaths: Baseball and Jane Austen," *JNT* 18 (Fall 1988): 269–77.

Stephen Derry, "The Northanger Hyacinths," *Persuasions* 11 (16 December 1989): 14.

Maggie Lane, "Blaise Castle," *Persuasions* 7 (December 1985): 78–81.

Maggie Lane, "Jane Austen's Bath," *Persuasions* 7 (December 1985): 55–57.

Mark Loveridge, "*Northanger Abbey*; or, Nature and Probability," *NCF* 46 (June 1991): 1–29.

Kenneth L. Moler, "Some Verbal Tactics of General Tilney," *Persuasions* 6 (December 1984): 10–12.

Paul Morrison, "Enclosed in Openness: *Northanger Abbey* and the Domestic Carceral," *TSLL* 33 (Spring 1991): 1–23.

Trudi Marais, "*Northanger Abbey* in the '80s," *CRUX* 14 (October 1980): 42–43.

F. B. Pinion, "Jane Austen and the Name 'Richard,' *N&Q* 40 (March 1993): 38.

Joan Pittock, "The Novelist in Search of a Fiction: *Northanger Abbey*," *ÉA* 40 (April–June 1987): 142–53.

Narelle Shaw, "Free Indirect Speech and Jane Austen's 1816 Revision of *Northanger Abbey*," *SEL* 30 (Autumn 1990): 591–601.

Amy Elizabeth Smith, "'Julias and Louisas': Austen's *Northanger Abbey* and the Sentimental Novel," *ELN* 30 (September 1992): 33–42.

Nelly Stephane, "Une Parodie de roman noir: *Northanger Abbey* de Jane Austen," *Europe* 659 (March 1984): 19–28.

Mitsuko Suzuki, "Bath ni okeru 'Chushin' to 'Shuen': *Northanger Abbey* no Toshi Ron teki Kosatsu," in *Muraoka Isamu Sensei Kiju Kinen Ronbunshu: Eibungaku Shiron* (Tokyo: Kinseido, 1983), 220–34.

Birthe Tandrup, "Free Indirect Style and the Critique of the Gothic in *Northanger Abbey*," in *The Romantic Heritage: A Collection of Critical Essays*, ed. Karsten Engelberg (Copenhagen: University of Copenhagen Press, 1983), 81–92.

Tara Ghoshal Wallace, "*Northanger Abbey* and the Limits of Parody," *SNNTS* 20 (Fall 1988): 262–73.

Michael Williams, "*Northanger Abbey*: Some Problems of Engagement," *UES* 25 (September 1987): 8–17.

Theodor Wolpers, "Schrecken und Vernunft: Die romanlesende Heldin in Jane Austens *Northanger Abbey*," in *Gelebte Literatur in der Literatur: Studien zu Erscheinungsformen und Geschichte eines literarischen Motivs*, ed. Theodor Wolpers (Gottingen: Vandenhoeck & Ruprecht, 1986), 168–84.

Haruko Yamada, "*Northanger Abbey*: Bungaku jo no Kanshu o koete," in *Jane Austen: Shosetsu no Kenkyu* (Tokyo: Aratake, 1981), 3–24.

Persuasion

John Adlard, "The Nothingness of Anne," *N&Q* 35 (September 1988): 319.

Ann W. Astell, "Anne Elliot's Education: The Learning of Romance in *Persuasion*," *Renascence* 40 (Fall 1987): 2–14.

K. K. Collins, "Prejudice, Persuasion, and the Puzzle of Mrs. Smith," *Persuasions* 6 (December 1984): 40–43.

Trevor Davison, "Jane Austen and the 'Process' of *Persuasion*," *DUJ* 77 (December 1984): 43–47.

Mariko Enomoto, "*Persuasion*: Charater no Miryoku," in *Jane Austen: Shosetsu no Kenkyu* (Tokyo: Aratake, 1981), 209–32.

Jennifer Fitzgerald, "Jane Austen's *Persuasion* and the French Revolution," *Persuasions* 10 (16 December 1988): 39–43.

Louise Flavin, "Austen's *Persuasion*," *Expl* 47 (Summer 1989): 20–23.

John E. Grant, "Shows of Mourning in the Text of Jane Austen's *Persuasion*," *MP* 80 (February 1983): 283–86.

David Groves, "Knowing One's Species Better: Social Satire in *Persuasion*," *Persuasions* 6 (December 1984): 13–15.

Daniel P. Gunn, "In the Vicinity of Winthrop: Ideological Rhetoric in *Persuasion*," *NFC* 41 (March 1987): 403–18.

Weirui Hou, "Explication of Text: A Passage from Jane Austen's *Persuasion*," *Waiyu Jiaoxue Yu Yanjiu* 2 (June 1982): 16–20.

Alice Hufstader, "Family Patterns in *Persuasion*," *Persuasions* 6 (December 1984): 21–23.

Judy Van Sickle Johnson, "The Bodily Frame: Learning Romance in *Persuasion*," *NFC* 38 (June 1983): 43–61.

Peter Knox-Shaw, "Persuasion, Byron, and the Turkish Tale," *RES* 44 (February 1993): 47–69.

AUSTEN, JANE, *Persuasion*

Gene Koppel, "The Mystery of the Self in *Persuasion*," *Persuasions* 6 (December 1984): 48–54.

P. Scott Marshall, "Techniques of Persuasion in *Persuasion*: A Lawyer's Viewpoint," *Persuasions* 6 (December 1984): 44–47.

Mary Millard, "The Fortune of the Misses Elliot," *Persuasions* 6 (December 1984): 34.

Ann Molan, "Persuasion in *Persuasion*," *CR* 24 (1982): 16–29.

Michael Orange, "Aspects of Narration in *Persuasion*," *SSEng* 15 (1989–1990): 63–71.

Adela Pinch, "Lost in a Book: Jane Austen's *Persuasion*," *SIR* 32 (Spring 1993): 97–117.

Mary Poovey, "'Persuasion' and the Promises of Love," in *The Representation of Women in Fiction*, ed. Carolyn G. Heilbrun and Margaret R. Higonnet (Baltimore: Johns Hopkins University Press, 1983), 152–79.

Charles J. Rzepka, "Making it in a brave new world: Marriage, Profession, and Anti-romantic Ekstasis in Austen's *Persuasion*," *SNNTS* 26 (Summer 1994): 99–120.

Gene Ruoff, "The Triumph of *Persuasion*: Jane Austen and the Creation of Woman," *Persuasions* 6 (December 1984): 54–61.

Noriko Sasaki, "*Persuasion*: Kofuku no Zahyo o Motomete," in *Jane Austen: Shosetsu no Kenkyu* (Tokyo: Aratake, 1981), 233–54.

Max Schott, "The Scene at the White Hart Inn," *Spectrum* 27, no. 1–2 (1985): 87–92.

Jon Spence, "The Abiding Possibilities of Nature in *Persuasion*," *SEL* 21 (Autumn 1981): 625–36.

Roselle Taylor, "Point of View and Estrangement in *Persuasion*," *PAPA* 15 (April 1989): 97–108.

Midori Uematsu, "Shizukanaur Jonetsu no Onna: J. Austen—Settoku," in *Igirisu Shosetsu no Joseitachi*, ed. Yaeko Sumi and Naomi Okamura (Tokyo: Keiso, 1983), 29–51.

Robyn Warhol, "The Look, the Body, and the Heroine: A Feminist-Narratological Reading of *Persuasion*," *Novel* 26 (Fall 1992): 5–19.

Cheryl Weissman, "Doubleness and Refrain in Jane Austen's *Persuasion*," *KR* 10 (Fall 1988): 87–91.

Pride and Prejudice

Edward Alexander, "A Biblical Source for *Pride and Prejudice*? The Bennet Girls and Zelophehad's Daughters," *ELN* 29 (June 1992): 57–58.

Dennis W. Allen, "No Love for Lydia: The Fate of Desire in *Pride and Prejudice*," *TSLL* 27 (Winter 1985): 425–43.

Lisa Altomari, "Jane Austen and Her Outdoors," *Persuasions* 12 (16 December 1990): 50–53.

Nancy Armstrong, "Inside Greimas's Square: Literary Characters and Cultural Constraints," in *The Sign in Music and Literature*, ed. Wendy Steiner (Austin: University of Texas Press, 1981), 52–66.

Lance Bertelsen, "A Portrait of Mrs. Bingley," *Persuasions* 8 (December 1986): 37–38.

C. Knatchbull Bevan, "The Rhetoric of Syntax in *Pride and Prejudice*," *Lang&S* 20 (Fall 1987): 396–410.

Carole O. Brown, "Dwindling into a Wife: A Jane Austen Heroine Grows Up," *IJWS* 5 (November–December 1982): 460–69.

Rachel M. Brownstein, "Jane Austen: Irony and Authority," *WS* 15, no.1–3 (1988): 57–70.

Katrin R. Burlin, "'Pictures of Perfection' at Pemberley: Art in *Pride and Prejudice*," *W&L* 3 (1983): 155–70.

Jean Ferguson Carr, "The Polemics of Incomprehension: Mother and Daughter in *Pride and Prejudice*," in *Tradition and the Talents of Women*, ed. Florence Howe (Urbana: University of Illinois Press, 1991), 68–86.

Jocelyn Creigh Cass, "An Amusing Study: Family Likenesses in *Pride and Prejudice*," *Persuasions* 9 (16 December 1987): 49–50.

Cynthia L. Caywood, "*Pride and Prejudice* and the Belief in Choice: Jane Austen's Fantastical Vision," in *Portraits of Marriage in Literature*, ed. Anne C. Hargrove and Maurine Magliocco (Macomb, IL: Essays in Literature, 1984), 31–37.

Stephen Derry, "Two Georgianas: The Duchess of Devonshire and Jane Austen's Miss Darcy," *Persuasions* 11 (16 December 1989): 15–16.

R. E. Ewin, "Pride, Prejudice and Shyness," *Philosophy* 65 (April 1990): 137–54.

Anna Falkenberg, "'Curious dialogues': Writers and Their Writing in *Pride and Prejudice*," *CCTEP* 53 (September 1988): 67–73.

AUSTEN, JANE, *Pride and Prejudice*

Susan Fraiman, "The Humiliation of Elizabeth Bennet," in *Refiguring the Father: New Feminist Readings of Patriarchy*, ed. Patricia Yaeger and Beth Kowaleski-Wallace (Carbondale: University of Illinois Press, 1989), 168–87.

Walker Gibson, "Contrarieties of Emotion: Or, Five Days with *Pride and Prejudice*," in *Conversations: Contemporary Critical Theory and the Teaching of Literature*, ed. Charles Moran and Elizabeth F. Penfield (Urbana: NCTE, 1990), 114–19.

Kathleen Glancy, "What Happened Next? Or, The Many Husbands of Georgiana Darcy," *Persuasions* 11 (16 December 1989): 110–16.

Donald Greene, "The Original of Pemberley," *ECF* 1 (October 1988): 1–23.

John Halperin, "Inside *Pride and Prejudice*," *Persuasions* 11 (16 December 1989): 7–45.

Fujiko Hatsugano, "*Pride and Prejudice*: Jane Austen no Heya," in *Jane Austen: Shosetsu no Kenkyu* (Tokyo: Aratake, 1981), 101–21.

James Heldman, "How Wealthy Is Mr. Darcy—Really? Pounds and Dollars in the World of *Pride and Prejudice*," *Persuasions* 12 (16 December 1990): 38–49.

Mark M. Hennelly, Jr., "*Pride and Prejudice*: The Eyes Have It," *W&L* 3 (1983): 187–207.

Jill Heydt, "'First Impressions' and Later Recollections: The Place of the Picturesque in *Pride and Prejudice*," *StHum* 12 (December 1985): 115–24.

Gordon Hirsch, "Shame, Pride and Prejudice: Jane Austen's Psychological Sophistication," *Mosaic* 25 (Winter 1992): 63–78.

Weirui Hou, "Austen's Literary Art as Seen in Her *Pride and Prejudice*," *Waiguoyu* 6 (November 1981): 1–8.

Glenda A. Hudson, "'Precious Remains of the Earliest Attachment': Sibling Love in Jane Austen's *Pride and Prejudice*," *Persuasions* 11 (16 December 1989): 125–31.

Charles Issawi, "Another Source for *Pride and Prejudice*," *Persuasions* 10 (16 December 1988): 43.

Setsu Ito, "Pride and Prejudice: Kodo to Jiritsu," in *Jane Austen: Shosetsu no Kenkyu* (Tokyo: Aratake, 1981), 75–99.

Gary Kelly, "The Art of Reading in *Pride and Prejudice*," *ESC* 10 (June 1984): 156–71.

Gene Koppel, "*Pride and Prejudice*: Conservative or Liberal Novel—Or Both? (A Gadamerian Approach)," *Persuasions* 11 (16 December 1989): 132–39.

Deborah J. Knuth, "Sisterhood and Friendship in *Pride and Prejudice*: Need Happiness Be 'Entirely a Matter of Chance'?" *Persuasions* 11 (16 December 1989): 99–109.

Claudia Brodsky Lacour, "Austen's *Pride and Prejudice* and Hegel's 'Truth in Art': Concept, Reference, and History," *ELH* 59 (Fall 1992): 597–623.

A. Walton Litz, "The Picturesque in *Pride and Prejudice*," *Persuasions* 1 (December 1979): 13–15, 20–24.

John McAleer, "The Comedy of Social Distinctions in *Pride and Prejudice*," *Persuasions* 11 (16 December 1989): 70–76.

Juliet McMaster, "Lady Catherine's Grammar," *Persuasions* 8 (December 1986): 26–27.

Joel Marcus, "Jane Austen's *Pride and Prejudice*: A Theological Reflection," *Theology Today* 46 (October 1989): 288–98.

Patricia Howell Michaelson, "Reading *Pride and Prejudice*," *ECF* 3 (October 1990): 65–76.

Kenneth L. Moler, "The Olive Branch Metaphor in *Pride and Prejudice*," *N&Q* 30 (June 1983): 214.

Kenneth L. Moler, "'Truth Universally Acknowledged,'" *Persuasions* 8 (December 1986): 25.

Anne Waldron Neumann, "Characterization and Comment in *Pride and Prejudice*: Free Indirect Discourse and 'Double-Voiced' Verbs of Speaking, Thinking, and Feeling," *Style* 20 (Fall 1986): 364–94.

Karen Newman, "Can This Marriage Be Saved: Jane Austen Makes Sense of an Ending," *ELH* 50 (Winter 1983): 693–710.

Stein Haugom Olsen, "Appreciating *Pride and Prejudice*," in *The Nineteenth-Century British Novel*, ed. Jeremy Hawthorn (Baltimore: Arnold, 1986), 1–16.

James Phelan, "Character, Progression, and the Mimetic-Didactic Distinction," *MP* 84 (February 1987): 282–99.

Luanne Bethke Redmond, "Land, Law and Love," *Persuasions* 11 (16 December 1989): 46–52.

Martha Satz, "An Epistemological Understanding of *Pride and Prejudice*: Humility and Objectivity," *W&L* 3 (1983): 171–86.

Matthew Schneider, "Card-playing and the Marriage Gamble in *Pride and Prejudice*," *DR* 73 (Spring 1993): 5–17.

Barbara Sherrod, "*Pride and Prejudice*: A Classic Love Story," *Persuasions* 11 (16 December 1989): 66–69.

Bruce Stovel, "'A Contrariety of Emotion': Jane Austen's Ambivalent Lovers in *Pride and Prejudice*," *IFR* 14 (Winter 1987): 27–33.

Bruce Stovel, "Secrets, Silence, and Surprise in *Pride and Prejudice*," *Persuasions* 11 (16 December 1989): 85–91.

Thorell Tsomondo, "Representation, Context and Cognition, and Jane Austen," *Theoria* 64 (May 1985): 65–75.

David Allen Ward, "Austen's *Pride and Prejudice*," *Expl* 51 (Fall 1992): 18–19.

Joseph Wiesenfarth, "The Case of *Pride and Prejudice*," *SNNTS* 16 (Fall 1984): 261–73.

Sara Wingard, "Reversal and Revelation: The Five Seasons of *Pride and Prejudice*," *Persuasions* 11 (16 December 1989): 92–98.

Dvora Zelicovici, "Reversal in *Pride and Prejudice*," *StHum* 12 (December 1985): 106–14.

Sanditon

John Halperin, "Jane Austen's Anti–Romantic Fragment: Somes Notes on *Sanditon*," *TSWL* 2 (Fall 1983): 183–91.

Oliver MacDonagh, "*Sanditon*: A Regency Novel," in *The Writer as Witness: Literature as Historical Evidence*, ed. Tom Dunne (Cork: Cork University Press, 1987), 114–32.

D. A. Miller, "The Late Jane Austen," *Raritan* 10 (Summer 1990): 55–79.

Irene Tayler, "Afterword: Jane Austen Looks Ahead," in *Fetter'd or Free? British Women Novelists, 1670–1815*, ed. Mary Anne Schofield and Cecilia Macheski (Athens: Ohio University Press, 1986), 426–33.

Sense and Sensibility

Yoko Abe, "*Sense and Sensibility*: Jiga no Tatakai," in *Jane Austen: Shosetsu no Kenkyu* (Tokyo: Aratake, 1981), 51–73.

Barbara M. Benedict, "Jane Austen's *Sense and Sensibility*: The Politics of Point of View," *PQ* 69 (Fall 1990): 453–70.

Zelda Boyd, "The Language of Supposing: Modal Auxiliaries in *Sense and Sensibility*," *W&L* 3 (1983): 142–54.

Eva Brann, “Whose Sense? Whose Sensibility? Jane Austen’s Subtlest Novel,” *Persuasions* 12 (16 December 1990): 131–33.

R. F. Brissenden, “The Task of Telling Lies: Candor and Deception in *Sense and Sensibility*,” in *Greene Centennial Studies: Essays Presented to Donald Greene in the Centennial Year of the University of Southern California*, ed. Paul J. Korshin and Robert R. Allen (Charlottesville: University Press of Virginia, 1984), 442–57.

Judith Warner Fisher, “All the ‘Write’ Moves; Or, Theatrical Gesture in *Sense and Sensibility*,” *Persuasions* 9 (16 December 1987): 17–23.

June M. Frazer, “The Apprenticeship of Elinor Dashwood,” *Persuasions* 3 (December 1981): 6, 8.

George E. Haggerty, “The Sacrifice of Privacy in *Sense and Sensibility*,” *TSWL* 7 (Fall 1988): 221–37.

Mary Hardenbrook, “Gunfight at the Combe Magna Corral,” *Persuasions* 9 (16 December 1987): 34–35.

D. W. Harding, “The Supposed Letter Form of *Sense and Sensibility*,” *N&Q* 40 (December 1993): 464–66.

Claudia L. Johnson, “The ‘Twilight of Probability’: Uncertainty and Hope in *Sense and Sensibility*,” *PQ* 62 (Spring 1983): 171–86.

Deborah Kaplan, “Achieving Authority: Jane Austen’s First Published Novel,” *NCF* 37 (March 1983): 531–51.

David Kaufmann, “Law and Propriety, *Sense and Sensibility*: Austen on the Cusp of Modernity,” *ELH* 59 (Summer 1992): 385–408.

Janice J. Kirkland, “Jane Austen and Bonomi,” *N&Q* 34 (March 1987): 24–25.

Noriko Kubota, “*Sense and Sensibility*: Kotoba, Kanjo, Shakai,” in *Jane Austen: Shosetsu no Kenkyu* (Tokyo: Aratake, 1981), 25–50.

Angela Leighton, “Sense and Silences: Reading Jane Austen Again,” *W&L* 3 (1983): 128–41.

Mary Millard, “The Extraordinary Fate of Marianne Dashwood,” *Persuasions* 8 (December 1981): 5.

P. Gila Reinstein, “Moral Priorities in *Sense and Sensibility*,” *Renascence* 35 (Summer 1983): 269–83.

Sharlene Roeder, “The Fall on High-Church Down in Jane Austen’s *Sense and Sensibility*,” *Persuasions* 12 (16 December 1990): 60.

Edward Joseph Shoben, Jr., “Impulse and Virtue in Jane Austen: *Sense and Sensibility* in Two Centuries,” *HudR* 35 (Winter 1982–83): 521–39.

Miwako Sonoda, "Sokeki to Jane Austen: Meian to Funbetsu to Takan no Baai," in *Jane Austen: Shosetsu no Kenkyu* (Tokyo: Aratake, 1981), 299–321.

Patricia Meyer Spacks, "The Difference It Makes," *Soundings* 64 (Winter 1981): 343–60.

James Thompson, "*Sense and Sensibility*: Finance and Romance; Essays in Honor of Jean H. Hagstrum," in *Sensibility in Transformation: Creative Resistance to Sentiment from the Augustans to the Romantics*, ed. Syndy McMillen Conger (Rutherford, NJ: Fairleigh Dickinson University Press, 1990), 147–71.

Inger Sigrun Thomsen, "Dangerous Words and Silent Lovers in *Sense and Sensibility*," *Persuasions* 12 (16 December 1990): 134–38.

Thorell Tsomondo, "Imperfect Articulation: A Saving Instability in *Sense and Sensibility*," *Persuasions* 12 (16 December 1990): 99–110.

Ian Watt, "Jane Austen and the Traditions of Comic Aggression: *Sense and Sensibility*," *Persuasions* 3 (December 1981): 14–15, 25–28.

The Watsons

James Heldman, "Where is Jane Austen in *The Watsons*?" *Persuasions* 8 (December 1986): 84–91.

Juliet McMaster, "'God Gave Us Our Relations': The Watson Family," *Persuasions* 8 (December 1986): 60–72.

Paul Pickrel, "*The Watsons* and the Other Jane Austen," *ELH* 55 (Summer 1988): 443–67.

Joseph Wiesenfarth, "*The Watsons* as Pretext," *Persuasions* 8 (December 1986): 101–11.

BALLARD, JAMES GRAHAM

The Concrete Island

Reinhart Lutz, "The Two Landscapes of J. G. Ballard's *The Concrete Island*," in *Mindscapes: The Geographies of Imagined Worlds*, ed. George Edgar Slusser and Eric S. Rabkin (Carbondale: Southern Illinois University Press, 1989), 185–94.

Crash!

Jean Baudrillard and Arthur B. Evans, "Ballard's *Crash!*," *SFS* 18 (November 1991): 313–30.

Terry Dowling, "Alternative Reality and Deviant Logic in J. G. Ballard's Second 'Disaster' Trilogy," *SFic* 1 (June 1977): 6–18.

David Pringle, "An Honest Madness," *Foundation* 6 (May 1974): 83–86.

Nicholas Ruddick, "Ballard/Crash/Baudrillard," *SFS* 19 (November 1992): 354–60.

The Crystal World

Michael Moorcock, "Landscape Without Time," *New Worlds* 50 (July 1966): 146–48.

Nick Perry and Roy Wilkie, "The Undivided Self: J. G. Ballard's *The Crystal World*," *RQ* 5 (April 1973): 268–77.

"Sums and Scrubbers," *TLS* (14 April 1966): 332.

The Drowned Giant

Emma Susana Speratti-Pinero, "De las fuentes y su utilizacion en 'El ahogado mas hermoso del mundo,'" in *Homenaje a Ana Maria Barrenechea*, ed. Lia Schwartz Lerner and Isaias Lerner (Madrid: Castalia, 1984), 549–55.

Empire of the Sun

Michael Hollington, "Great Books and Great Wars: J. G. Ballard's *Empire of the Sun*," *Meanjin* 44 (June 1985): 269–75.

The Drought
(Rev. edition of *The Burning World*)

Joe Milicia, "Dry Thoughts in a Dry Season," *RQ* 7 (December 1985): 208–21.

High Rise

Guido Eckhaut, "Hoogbouw in chaos: Sociale en morele entropie in J. G. Ballards *High Rise*," in *Just the Other Day: Essays on the Suture of the Future*, ed. Luk de Vos (Antwerp: EXA, 1985), 426–32.

Digby Durrant, "Squibs and Rockets: A Note on J. G. Ballard," *London Magazine* 15 (December 1975/January 1976): 69–73.

Francesco Marroni, "High-Rise: Avventura interiore e spazio della finzione," *Trimestre* 16 (July–December 1983): 197–207.

BALLARD, JAMES GRAHAM, *The Terminal Beach*

Francesco Marroni, "High-Rise: Interior Adventure and Fictional Space: Topology as a Metalanguage in J. G. Ballard's Fiction," *RCEI* 10 (April 1985): 81–93.

John Sutherland, "Return of the Native," *TLS* (5 December 1975): 1438.

Denise Terrel-Fauconnier, "*High Rise*, la cité dressée de J. G. Ballard," *Cycnos* 1 (1984): 109–17.

The Terminal Beach

Michael Moorcock, "No Short-Cuts," *New Worlds* 48 (September/October 1964): 119–20.

Peter White, "Ballard's *Terminal Beach*," *Vector* 31 (March 1965): 9–10. 14.

The Unlimited Dream Company

Malcolm Bradbury, "Fly Away," *NYTBR* (9 December 1979): 14–16.

Vermilion Sands

"Dusty Answer," *TLS* (30 November 1973): 1466.

The Voices of Time

Peter Brigg, "J.G. Ballard: Time Out of Mind," *Extrapolation* 35 (Spring 1994): 43–59.

BARING, MAURICE

Cat's Cradle

Emma Letley, "*Cat's Cradle*: Maurice Baring and the Novel," *CRev* 19 (February 1988): 25–33.

The Good High-Brow

Joseph Epstein, "Maurice Baring & *The Good High-Brow*," *NewC* 11 (June 1992): 10–19.

BARKER, ELSPETH

O Caledonia

Betty Abel, "*O Caledonia*," *ContempR* 260 (February 1992): 101–3.

Michael Steinberg, "*O Caledonia*," *NYTBR* (10 January 1993): 20.

BARKER, PAT

Blow Your House Down

Ann Ardis, "Political Attentiveness vs. Political Correctness: Teaching Pat Barker's *Blow Your House Down*," *CollL* 18 (October 1991): 44–54.

The Eye in the Door

Judy Cooke, "*The Eye in the Door*," *NewS&S* (10 September 1993): 40–41.

Jim Shepard, "Gentlemen in the Trenches," *NYTBR* (15 May 1994): 9.

The Ghost Road

Lavinia Greenlaw, "*The Ghost Road*," *NewR* 214 (29 April 1996): 38–41.

Charlotte Joll, "Back to the Front—*The Ghost Road*," *Spectator* 275 (30 September 1995): 44–45.

Peter Parker, "The War that Never Becomes the Past: *The Ghost Road*," *TLS* (8 September 1995): 4–5.

The Man Who Wasn't There

Nicci Gerrard, "Adolescent Angst," *NewS&S* 2 (3 March 1989): 45–46.

Regeneration, The Eye in the Door, The Ghost Way

Ben Shepard, "Digging Up the Past: Pat Barker's Great War Trilogy," *TLS* (22 March 1996): 12–13.

Rosemary Dinnage, "Death's Grey Land, *NYBR* 43 (15 February 1996): 29–31.

BARNES, JULIAN

Flaubert's Parrot

Jean-Pierre Salgas, "Julian Barnes n'en a pas fini avec Flaubert," *QL* 463 (16–31 May 1986): 10–13.

James B. Scott, "Parrot as Paradigms: Infinite Deferral of Meaning in *Flaubert's Parrot*," *Ariel* 21 (July 1990): 57–68.

Ramon Suarez, "Notas acerca de un loro famoso," *RChL* 29 (April 1987): 151–55.

A History of the World in 10 1/2 Chapters

Isabelle Raucq-Hoorickx, "Julian Barnes' *History of the World in 10 1/2 Chapters*: A Levinasian Deconstructionist Point of View," *Lang&H* 26 (March 1991): 47–54.

The Porcupine

Robert Stone, "The Cold Peace," *NYTBR* (13 December 1992): 3.

Staring at the Sun

Carlos Fuentes, "Dos veces, el sol: La nueva novela de Julian Barnes," *Suplemento Literario La Nacion* (27 March 1988): 6.

BATES, H. E.

A Month by the Lake and Other Stories

Brock Baker, "H. E. Bates, Storyteller," *NewC* 6 (March 1988): 72–73.

My Uncle Silas

Dean R. Baldwin, "*Uncle Silas*: H. E. Bates's Romantic Individualist," *WVUPP* 28 (1982): 132–39.

Larkin

Dean R. Baldwin, "H. E. Bates's Festive Comedies," *WVUPP* 29 (1983): 77–83.

BECKETT, SAMUEL

Babel of Silence

Barbara Trieloff, "*Babel of Silence*: Beckett's Post-Trilogy Prose Articulated," in *Rethinking Beckett: A Collection of Critical Essays*, ed. Lance St. John Butler and Robert Davis (London: Macmillan, 1990), 89–104.

Fingal

John Fletcher, "Joyce, Beckett, and the Short Story in Ireland," in *RE: Joyce 'n Beckett*, ed. Phyllis Carey and Ed Jewinski (New York: Fordham University Press, 1992), 20–30.

For an End Yet Again

Li-Ling Tseng, " Samuel Beckett's *For to End Yet Again*: A Conflict between 'Syntax of Energy' and 'Syntax of Weakness,'" *TCL* 38 (Spring 1992): 101–23.

How It Is

Ursula Heise, "Erzahlzeit and Postmodern Narrative: Text as Duration in Beckett's *How It Is*," *Style* 26 (Summer 1992): 245–69.

Ill Seen Ill Said

Adam Piette, "*Ill Seen Ill Said*: Allusion and Cultural Memory," in *Writing and Culture*, ed. Balz Engler (Zurich: Swiss Papers in English Language and Literature, 1992), 179–95.

Imagination Dead Imagine

James Hansford, "*Imagination Dead Imagine*: The Imagination and Its Context," in *The Beckett Studies Reader*, ed. S.E. Gontarski (Gainesville: University Press of Florida, 1987), 144–46.

Lessness

Mary Catanzaro, "Musical Form and Beckett's *Lessness*," *NMIL* 4 (1992): 45–51.

Molloy

Kevin J. H. Dettmar, "The Figure in Beckett's Carpet: *Molloy* and the Assault on Metaphor," in *Rethinking Beckett: A Collection of Critical Essays*, ed. Lance St. John Butler and Robert Davis (London: Macmillan, 1990), 68–88.

Brian Evenson, "Heterotopia and Negativity in Beckett's *Molloy(s)*," *Symposium* 46 (Winter 1992): 273–87

J. D. O'Hara, "Jung and the *Molloy* Narrative," in *The Beckett Studies Reader*, ed. S. E. Gontarski (Gainesville: University Press of Florida, 1987), 129–45.

Murphy

James Atchenson, "Murphy's Metaphysics," in *The Beckett Studies Reader*, ed. S. E. Gontarski (Gainesville: University Press of Florida, 1987), 78–93.

John Pilling, "From a W(horoscopy) to *Murphy*," in *The Ideal Core of the Onion: Reading Beckett Archives*, ed. John Pilling and Mary Bryden (Bristol: Beckett International Foundation, 1992), 1–20.

Watt

James Acheson, "A Note on the Ladder Joke in *Watt*," *JBeckS* 15 (Autumn 1992): 115–16.

Gottfried Buttner, "A New Approach to Watt," in *Rethinking Beckett: A Collection of Critical Essays*, ed. Lance St. John Butler and Robert Davis (London: Macmillan, 1990), 169–180.

Thomas Cousineau, "*Watt*: Language as Interdiction and Consolation," in *The Beckett Studies Reader*, ed., S. E. Gontarski (Gainesville: University Press of Florida, 1987), 64–67.

Michael E. Mooney, "*Watt*: Samuel Beckett's Sceptical Fiction," in *Rethinking Beckett: A Collection of Critical Essays*, ed. Lance St. John Butler and Robert Davis (London: Macmillan, 1990), 160–68.

What a Misfortune

Jeri Kroll, "Belacqua as Artist and Lover: *What a Misfortune*," in *The Beckett Studies Reader*, ed. S. E. Gontarski (Gainesville: University Press of Florida, 1987), 35–63.

Worstward Ho

Charles Krance, "*Worstward Ho* and On-Words: Writing to(wards) the Point," in *Rethinking Beckett: A Collection of Critical Essays*, ed. Lance St. John Butler and Robert Davis (London: Macmillan, 1990), 124–40.

Andrew Renton, "*Worstward Ho* and the End(s) of Representation," in *The Ideal Core of the Onion: Reading Beckett Archives*, ed. John Pilling and Mary Bryden (Bristol: Beckett International Foundation, 1992), 99–135.

SIR BEERBOHM, MAX

A Christmas Garland Woven by Max Beerbohm

Addison C. Bross, "Beerbohm's 'The Feast' and Conrad's Early Fiction," *NCF* 26 (December 1971): 329–36.

Terry Caesar, "Betrayal and Theft: Beerbohm, Parody, and Modernism," *Ariel* 17 (July 1986): 23–37.

The Mirror of the Past

Lawrence Danson, "Max Beerbohm and *The Mirror of the Past*," *PULC* 43 (Winter 1982): 77–153.

Ira Grushow, "Beerbohm's Lord Runcorn," *N&Q* 22 (May 1975): 207–08.

"Seven Men and Two Others"

Martin Maner, "Beerbohm's Seven Men and the Power of the Press," *ELT* 34, no. 2 (1991): 133–51.

Robert Viscusi, "Max And," *ELT* 27, no. 4 (1984): 304–19.

Zuleika Dobson; or, An Oxford Love Story

Christine Jordis, "Dandy consomme et parfait," *QL* 431 (1–15 January 1985): 9.

Michael Murphy, "Medieval Max and Zuleika Dobson," *ELT* 30, no.3 (1987): 303–7.

BENNETT, ARNOLD

Anna of the Five Towns

James Voss, "Arnold Bennett's Realism: Social Process and the Individual in *Anna of the Five Towns*," *OL* 38, no. 2 (1983): 168–84.

Clayhanger Trilogy: Clayhanger

Andrew Lincoln, "The Sociology of Bennett's *Clayhanger*," *ELT* 27, no. 3 (1984): 188–200.

"The Death of Simon Fuge"

John Wain, "Remarks on the Short Story," *CahiersN* 2 (January 1984): 49–66.

The Grim Smile of the Five Towns

Charles Swann, "A Bennett Debt to Hardy?" *N&Q* 39 (June 1992): 190–91.

"The Lion's Share"

Alain Blayac, " 'The Lion's Share': Essai sur le realisme d'Arnold Bennett," *CVE* 24 (October 1986): 47–61.

Lord Raingo

Robert F. Sheard, "The Manuscript Synopsis of *Lord Raingo*: A Picture of Bennett the Writer," *ELT* 34, no. 3 (1991): 310–21.

The Old Wives' Tale

Albert Denjean, "Euphorie et dysphorie dans *The Old Wives' Tale* d'A. Bennett," *CVE* 15 (April 1982): 79–86.

Tales of the Five Towns

Brian J. Hudson, "Bennett's *Five Towns*: A Prospect-refuge Analysis," *BJA* 33 (January 1993): 41–51.

Peter Preston, "'A Grim and Original Beauty': Arnold Bennett and the Landscape of the *Five Towns*," in *Geography and Literature: A Meeting of the Disciplines*, ed. William E. Mallory and Paul Simpson-Housley (Syracuse, NY: Syracuse University Press, 1987), 31–55.

Whom God Hath Joined

John Lucas, "The Marriage Question and *Whom God Hath Joined*," *CVE* 24 (October 1986): 31–45.

BENTLEY, E. C.

Trent's Case Book

Ben Ray Redman, "Introduction," in *Trent's Case Book* (New York: Knopf, 1964), v–xii.

Trent's Last Case

Jacques Barzun and Wendell Hertig Taylor, "Preface to *Trent's Last Case*," in *A Book of Prefaces to Fifty Classics of Crime Fiction, 1900–1950* (New York: Garland, 1976), 19–20.

E. C. Bentley, "Trent's Last Case," in *Those Days* (London: Constable, 1940), 249–61.

Howard Haycraft, "Trent's Last Case Reopened," *NYTBR* (15 December 1963): 18–19. Reprinted in *E. C. Bentley's "Trent's Last Case"* (San Diego: University Extension, University of California, 1977), 266–68.

LeRoy Panek, "E. C. Bentley," in *Watteau's Shepherds: The Detective Novel in Britain, 1914–1940*, LeRoy Panek (Bowling Green, OH: Bowling Green University Press, 1979), 29–37.

Erik Routley, *The Puritan Pleasures of the Detective Story: A Personal Monograph* (London: Gollancz, 1972), 119–23.

Dorothy L. Sayers, "Introduction," in *Trent's Last Case* (New York: Perennial Library, 1978), x–xiii.

Aaron Marc Stein, "Introduction," in *Trent's Last Case* (San Diego: University Extension, University of California, 1977), ix–xxv.

H. Douglas Thomas, "Mr. E. C. Bentley's *Trent's Last Case*," in *Masters of Mystery: A Study of the Detective Story* (London: Collins, 1931), 147–55.

BOWEN, ELIZABETH

"All Saints"

Edward Mitchell, "Themes in Elizabeth Bowen's Short Stories," in *Elizabeth Bowen*, ed Harold Bloom (New York: Chelsea House, 1987), 40–41.

"Ann Lee's"

Clare Hanson, "The Free Story," in *Elizabeth Bowen*, ed. Harold Bloom (New York: Chelsea House, 1987), 144–45.

Phyllis Lassner, *Elizabeth Bowen: A Study of Her Short Fiction* (New York: Twayne, 1991), 20–21.

David W. Meredith, "Authorial Detachment in Elizabeth Bowen's 'Ann Lee's,'" *MSE* 8, no. 2 (1982): 9–20.

George Brandon Saul, "The Short Stories of Elizabeth Bowen," *ArQ* 21 (Spring 1965): 55–59.

"The Apple Tree"

Phyllis Lassner, *Elizabeth Bowen: A Study of Her Short Fiction* (New York: Twayne, 1991), 50–52.

"Attractive Modern Homes"

Phyllis Lassner, *Elizabeth Bowen: A Study of Her Short Fiction* (New York: Twayne, 1991), 80–82, 85, 90, 99.

"The Cat Jumps"

Judith Bates, "Undertones of Horrow in Elizabeth Bowen's 'Look at All Those Roses' and 'The Cat Jumps,'" *JSSE* 8 (Spring 1987): 85–91.

Phyllis Lassner, *Elizabeth Bowen: A Study of Her Short Fiction* (New York: Twayne, 1991), 60–63.

"Charity"

Phyllis Lassner, *Elizabeth Bowen: A Study of Her Short Fiction* (New York: Twayne, 1991), 47–48, 51, 129.

"The Dancing Mistress"

Allen E. Austin, *Elizabeth Bowen* (New York: Twayne, 1971), 97–98.

Phyllis Lassner, *Elizabeth Bowen: A Study of Her Short Fiction* (New York: Twayne, 1991), 36–39.

Edward Mitchell, "Themes in Elizabeth Bowen's Short Stories," in *Elizabeth Bowen*, ed. Harold Bloom (New York: Chelsea House, 1987), 41–42.

"Dead Mabelle"

Phyllis Lassner, *Elizabeth Bowen: A Study of Her Short Fiction* (New York: Twayne, 1991), 59–60, 61, 62.

Edward Mitchell, "Themes in Elizabeth Bowen's Short Stories," in *Elizabeth Bowen*, ed. Harold Bloom (New York: Chelsea House, 1987), 43–44.

The Death of the Heart

Ann Ashworth, "'But Why Was She Called Portia?' Judgment and Feeling in Bowen's *The Death of the Heart*," *Critique* 28 (Spring 1987): 159–66.

Allen E. Austin, *Elizabeth Bowen* (New York: Twayne, 1971), 48–49, 59–66.

Andrew Bennett and Nicholas Royle, *Elizabeth Bowen and the Dissolution of the Novel: Still Lives* (New York: St. Martin's, 1995), 63–81.

John Coates, "In Praise of Civility: Conservative Values in Elizabeth Bowen's *The Death of the Heart*," *Renascence* 37 (Summer 1985): 248–65.

Alison Heinemann, "The Indoor Landscape in Bowen's *The Death of the Heart*," *Critique* 10, no.3 (1968): 5–12.

Phyllis Lassner, *Elizabeth Bowen* (New York: Macmillan, 1990), 97–119.

Phyllis Lassner, *Elizabeth Bowen: A Study of Her Short Fiction* (New York: Twayne, 1991), 63–64.

Alfred McDowell, "*The Death of the Heart* and the Human Dilemma," *MLS* 8, no. 2 (1978): 5–16.

Mona Van Duyn, in *Elizabeth Bowen*, ed. Harold Bloom (New York: Chelsea House, 1987), 13–25.

"The Demon Lover"

Elizabeth Bowen, "'The Demon Lover,'" in *The Mulberry Tree: Writings of Elizabeth Bowen*, ed. Hermione Lee (New York: Harcourt, Brace, 1958), 97–99.

Robert L. Calder, "'A More Sinister Troth': Elizabeth Bowen's 'The Demon Lover' as Allegory," *SSF* 31 (Winter 1994): 91–97.

Douglass A. Hughes, "Cracks in the Psyche: Elizabeth Bowen's 'The Demon Lover,'" *SSF* 10 (1973): 411–13.

The Demon Lover

Allen E. Austin, *Elizabeth Bowen* (New York: Twayne, 1971), 117–18.

Daniel V. Fraustino, "Elizabeth Bowen's *The Demon Lover*: Psychosis or Seduction?" *SSF* 17 (1980): 483–87.

Phyllis Lassner, *Elizabeth Bowen: A Study of Her Short Fiction* (New York: Twayne, 1991), 64–67, 131–36.

Reingard M. Nischik, "'. . . und für einmal statt der Texte die Kurzungen zu interpretieren': Beitrag zur Problematik von Textkurzungen anhand von Elizabeth Bowens *The Demon Lover*," *NsM* 36, no. 3 (1983): 143–49.

Henry Reed, "Review of *The Demon Lover*," *NewS&N* 30 (11 March 1945): 302–3.

Lotus Snow, "The Uncertain I: A Study of Elizabeth Bowen's Fiction," *WHR* 4 (Autumn 1950): 300–2.

"The Disinherited"

Allen E. Austen, *Elizabeth Bowen* (New York: Twayne, 1971), 102–5.

Phyllis Lassner, *Elizabeth Bowen: A Study of Her Short Fiction* (New York: Twayne, 1991), 97–101, 175–76.

Encounters; Early Fiction

A. C. Partridge, "Language and Identity in the Shorter Fiction of Elizabeth Bowen," in *Irish Writers and Society at Large*, ed. Masaru Sekine (Gerrards Cross, Buckinghamshire; Totowa, NJ: Smythe; Barnes & Noble, 1985), 169–80.

Eva Trout

Allen E. Austin, *Elizabeth Bowen* (New York: Twayne, 1971), 87–91.

Andrew Bennett and Nicholas Royle, *Elizabeth Bowen and the Dissolution of the Novel: Still Lives* (New York: St. Martin's, 1995), 140–57.

Phyllis Lassner, *Elizabeth Bowen: A Study of Her Short Fiction* (New York: Twayne, 1991), 162–63.

Hermione Lee, "The Bend Back: 'A World of Love' (1955), 'The Little Girls' (1964), and *Eva Trout* (1968)," in *Elizabeth Bowen*, ed. Harold Bloom (New York: Chelsea House, 1987), 118–22.

"Foothold"

Allen E. Austin, *Elizabeth Bowen* (New York: Twayne, 1971), 100–1.

Phyllis Lassner, *Elizabeth Bowen: A Study of Her Short Fiction* (New York: Twayne, 1991), 12–14.

"Green Holly"

Phyllis Lassner, *Elizabeth Bowen: A Study of Her Short Fiction* (New York: Twayne, 1991), 55–57.

"The Happy Autumn Fields"

Allen E. Austin, *Elizabeth Bowen* (New York: Twayne, 1971), 120–22.

Brad Hooper, "Elizabeth Bowen's 'The Happy Autumn Fields': A

Dream or Not?" *SSF* 21 (Spring 1984): 151–53.

Phyllis Lassner, *Elizabeth Bowen: A Study of Her Short Fiction* (New York: Twayne, 1991), 105–10, 168–69.

The Heat of the Day

Andrew Bennett and Nicholas Royle, *Elizabeth Bowen and the Dissolution of the Novel: Still Lives* (New York: St. Martin's, 1995), 82–103.

Barbara Brothers, "Pattern and Void: Bowen's Irish Landscape and *The Heat of the Day*," *Mosaic* 12 (Summer 1979): 129–38.

Robert L. Caserio, "*The Heat of the Day*: Modernism and Narrative in Paul de Man and Elizabeth Bowen," *MLQ* 54 (June 1993): 263–84.

John Coates, "The Rewards and Problems of Rootedness in Elizabeth Bowen's *The Heat of the Day*," *Renascence* 39 (Summer 1987): 484–501.

Angela G. Dorenkamp, "'Fall or Leap': Bowen's *The Heat of the Day*," *Critique* 10, no. 3 (1968): 13–21.

BOWEN, ELIZABETH, "Her Table Spread"

Phyllis Lassner, *Elizabeth Bowen* (New York: Macmillan, 1990), 120–40.

Barbara Bellow Watson, "Variations on an Enigma: Elizabeth Bowen's War Novel," *SHR* 15 (Spring 1981): 131–51. Reprinted in *Elizabeth Bowen*, ed. Harold Bloom (New York: Chelsea House, 1987), 81–101.

"Her Table Spread"

Allen E. Austin, *Elizabeth Bowen* (New York: Twayne, 1971), 107–8.

Margaret Church, "The Irish Writer, Elizabeth Bowen, 'Her Table Spread': Allusion and 'Anti-Roman,'" *Folio* 11 (August 1978): 17–20.

Alexander G. Gonzalez, "Elizabeth Bowen's 'Her Table Spread': A Joycean Irish Story," *SSF* 30 (Summer 1993): 343–48.

Phyllis Lassner, *Elizabeth Bowen: A Study of Her Short Fiction* (New York: Twayne, 1991), 14–16.

Sean O'Faolain, "'Her Table Spread,'" in *The Short Story* (New York: Devin-Adair, 1951), 202–4, 207–10, 229–31.

The Hotel

Allen E. Austin, *Elizabeth Bowen* (New York: Twayne, 1971), 29–37.

The House in Paris

Timothy Dow Adams, "'Bend Sinister': Duration in Elizabeth Bowen's *The House in Paris*," *IFR* 7, no. 1 (1980): 49–52.

Allen E. Austin, *Elizabeth Bowen* (New York: Twayne, 1971), 53–59.

Andrew Bennett and Nicholas Royle, *Elizabeth Bowen and the Dissolution of the Novel: Still Lives* (New York: St. Martin's, 1995), 42–62, 144–45, 163–64.

Harriet Blodgett, "The Necessary Child: 'The House in Paris,'" in *Elizabeth Bowen*, ed. Harold Bloom (New York: Chelsea House, 1987), 63–79.

John Coates, "Emotional Need and Cultural Codes in *The House in Paris*," *Renascence* 47 (Fall 1994): 1–19.

R. B. Kershner Jr., "Bowen's Oneiric House in Paris," *TSLL* 28 (Winter 1986): 407–23.

Phyllis Lassner, *Elizabeth Bowen* (New York: Macmillan, 1990), 73–96.

"The Inherited Clock"

Allen E. Austin, *Elizabeth Bowen* (New York: Twayne, 1971), 110–12.

Phyllis Lassner, *Elizabeth Bowen: A Study of Her Short Fiction* (New York: Twayne, 1991), 23–24.

"In The Square"

Allen E. Austin, *Elizabeth Bowen* (New York: Twayne, 1971), 116–17.

Phyllis Lassner, *Elizabeth Bowen: A Study of Her Short Fiction* (New York: Twayne, 1991), 79–81.

"Ivy Gripped the Steps"

Allen E. Austin, *Elizabeth Bowen* (New York: Twayne, 1971), 101–2.

Harold Bloom, "Introduction," in *Elizabeth Bowen* (New York: Chelsea House, 1987), 7–11.

Phyllis Lassner, *Elizabeth Bowen: A Study of Her Short Fiction* (New York: Twayne, 1991), 91–92.

"The Jungle"

Allen E. Austin, *Elizabeth Bowen* (New York: Twayne, 1971), 109–10.

Phyllis Lassner, *Elizabeth Bowen: A Study of Her Short Fiction* (New York: Twayne, 1991), 47–48.

The Last September

Allen E. Austin, *Elizabeth Bowen* (New York: Twayne, 1971), 30–31, 37–41.

Andrew Bennett and Nicholas Royle, *Elizabeth Bowen and the Dissolution of the Novel: Still Lives* (New York: St. Martin's, 1995), 14–22, 30–31.

John Coates, "Elizabeth Bowen's *The Last September*: The Loss of the Past and the Modern Consciousness," *DUJ* 51 (July 1990): 205–16.

Deirdre M. Laigle, "Images of the Big House in Elizabeth Bowen: *The Last September*," *CahiersI* 9 (1984): 61–80.

Phyllis Lassner, *Elizabeth Bowen* (New York: Macmillan, 1990), 26–47.

Phyllis Lassner, "The Past Is a Burning Pattern: Elizabeth Bowen's *The Last September*," *Éire* 21 (Spring 1986): 40–54.

The Little Girls

Allen E. Austin, *Elizabeth Bowen* (New York: Twayne, 1971), 82–87.

Andrew Bennett and Nicholas Royle, *Elizabeth Bowen and the Dissolution of the Novel: Still Lives* (New York: St. Martin's, 1995), 121–39, 162–63.

John Coates, "False History and True in *The Little Girls*," *Renascence* 44 (Winter 1992): 82–103.

Hermione Lee, "The Bend Back: 'A World of Love' (1955), *The Little Girls* (1964), and *Eva Trout* (1968)," in *Elizabeth Bowen*, ed. Harold Bloom (New York: Chelsea House, 1987), 112–18.

"The Little Girl's Room"

Allen E. Austin, *Elizabeth Bowen* (New York: Twayne, 1971), 96–97.

Clare Hanson, "The Free Story," in *Elizabeth Bowen*, ed. Harold Bloom (New York: Chelsea House, 1987), 145–48.

Phyllis Lassner, *Elizabeth Bowen: A Study of Her Short Fiction* (New York: Twayne, 1991), 49–50.

Edward Mitchell, "Themes in Elizabeth Bowen's Short Stories," in *Elizabeth Bowen*, ed. Harold Bloom (New York: Chelsea House, 1987), 42–43.

"Look at All Those Roses"

Judith Bates, "Undertones of Horror in Elizabeth Bowen's 'Look at All Those Roses' and 'The Cat Jumps,'" *JSSE* 8 (Spring 1987): 81–85.

Phyllis Lassner, *Elizabeth Bowen: A Study of Her Short Fiction* (New York: Twayne, 1991), 72–73, 158–59.

"A Love Story"

Allen E. Austin, *Elizabeth Bowen* (New York: Twayne, 1971), 99–100.

Phyllis Lassner, *Elizabeth Bowen: A Study of Her Short Fiction* (New York: Twayne, 1991), 85–86

"The Man of the Family"

Phyllis Lassner, *Elizabeth Bowen: A Study of Her Short Fiction* (New York: Twayne, 1991), 32–33.

Edward Mitchell, "Themes in Elizabeth Bowen's Short Stories," in *Elizabeth Bowen*, ed. Harold Bloom (New York: Chelsea House, 1987), 46–47.

"Mysterious Kor"

Allen E. Austin, *Elizabeth Bowen* (New York: Twayne, 1971), 118–20.

Harold Bloom, "Introduction," in *Elizabeth Bowen* (New York: Chelsea House, 1987), 4–7.

Clare Hanson, "The Free Story," in *Elizabeth Bowen*, ed. Harold Bloom (New York: Chelsea House, 1987), 149–51.

Phyllis Lassner, *Elizabeth Bowen: A Study of Her Short Fiction* (New York: Twayne, 1991), 93–95.

Edward Mitchell, "Themes in Elizabeth Bowen's Short Stories," in *Elizabeth Bowen*, ed. Harold Bloom (New York: Chelsea House, 1987), 45–46.

"The Parrot"

Sean O'Faolain, "The Parrot," in *Elizabeth Bowen; or, Romance Does Not Pay in the Vanishing Hero: Studies in Novelists of the Twenties* (London: Eyre & Spottiswoode, 1956), 169–73, 189–90.

"The Queer Heart"

Allen E. Austin, *Elizabeth Bowen* (New York: Twayne, 1971), 112–13.

Phyllis Lassner, *Elizabeth Bowen: A Study of Her Short Fiction* (New York: Twayne, 1991), 22–23.

"The Shadowy Third"

Phyllis Lassner, *Elizabeth Bowen: A Study of Her Short Fiction* (New York: Twayne, 1991), 13–15.

"Sunday Afternoon"

Harold Bloom, "Introduction," in *Elizabeth Bowen* (New York: Chelsea House, 1987), 2–4.

BOWEN, ELIZABETH, "Summer Night"

Phyllis Lassner, *Elizabeth Bowen: A Study of Her Short Fiction* (New York: Twayne, 1991), 3–4, 75–76.

"Summer Night"

Allen E. Austin, *Elizabeth Bowen* (New York: Twayne, 1971), 82–87.

Clare Hanson, "The Free Story," in *Elizabeth Bowen*, ed. Harold Bloom (New York: Chelsea House, 1987), 148–49.

Edward Mitchell, "Themes in Elizabeth Bowen's Short Stories," in *Elizabeth Bowen*, ed. Harold Bloom (New York: Chelsea House, 1987), 48–50.

"Telling"

Allen E. Austin, *Elizabeth Bowen* (New York: Twayne, 1971), 98–99.

Phyllis Lassner, *Elizabeth Bowen: A Study of Her Short Fiction* (New York: Twayne, 1991), 64–65.

To the North

Allen E. Austin, *Elizabeth Bowen* (New York: Twayne, 1971), 41–46.

Andrew Bennett and Nicholas Royle, *Elizabeth Bowen and the Dissolution of the Novel: Still Lives* (New York: St. Martin's, 1995), 23–29, 31–33, 35–41.

John Coates, "Moral Choice in Elizabeth Bowen's *To the North*," *Renascence* 43 (Summer 1991): 241–67.

William Heath, "The Jacobean Melodrama of *To the North*," in *Elizabeth Bowen*, ed. Harold Bloom (New York: Chelsea House, 1987), 27–37.

Phyllis Lassner, *Elizabeth Bowen: A Study of Her Short Fiction* (New York: Twayne, 1991), 55–72.

Hermione Lee, "The Placing of Loss: Elizabeth Bowen's *To the North*," *EIC* 28 (April 1978): 129–42.

A World of Love

Allen E. Austin, *Elizabeth Bowen* (New York: Twayne, 1971), 75–82.

Andrew Bennett and Nicholas Royle, *Elizabeth Bowen and the Dissolution of the Novel: Still Lives* (New York: St. Martin's, 1995), 104–20.

John Coates, "The Recovery of the Past in *A World of Love*," *Renascence* 40 (Summer 1988): 226–46.

Hermione Lee, "The Bend Back: *A World of Love* (1955), *The Little Girls* (1964), and *Eva Trout* (1968)," in *Elizabeth Bowen*, ed. Harold Bloom (New York: Chelsea House, 1987), 104–12.

Martha McGowan, "The Enclosed Garden in Elizabeth Bowen's *A World of Love*," *Éire* 16 (Spring 1981): 55–70.

BRADBURY, MALCOLM

The History Man

Richard Todd, "Malcolm Bradbury's *The History Man*: The Novelist as Reluctant Impresario," *DQR* 11, no.3 (1981): 162–82.

Rates of Exchange

Robert S. Burton, "A Plurality of Voices: Malcolm Bradbury's *Rates of Exchange*," *Critique* 28 (Winter 1987): 101–06.

Blake Morrison, "Stepping Eastward," *TLS* (8 April 1983): 345.

Blake Morrison, "On the Global Campus," *TLS* (23 March 1984): 293.

BRADDON, MARY ELIZABETH

Lady Audley's Secret

Norman Donaldson, "Introduction," in *Lady Audley's Secret*, ed. Norman Donaldson (New York: Dover, 1974), v–xiv.

"*Lady Audley's Secret*," *Nation* 100 (11 February 1915): 161–62.

Joel H. Kaplan, "Exhuming *Lady Audley*: Period Melodrama for the 1990s," in *Melodrama*, ed. James Redmond (Cambridge: Cambridge University Press, 1992), 143–60.

Audrey Peterson, "Some Minor Voices," in *Victorian Masters of Mystery: From Wilkie Collins to Conan Doyle* (New York: Ungar, 1984), 161–64.

C. S. Wiesenthal, "'Ghost haunted': A Trace of Wilkie Collins in Mary Elizabeth Braddon's *Lady Audley's Secret*," *ELN* 28 (June 1991): 42–44.

Birds of Prey

Audrey Peterson, "Some Minor Voices," in *Victorian Masters of Mystery: From Wilkie Collins to Conan Doyle* (New York: Ungar, 1984), 167–68.

Charlotte's Inheritance

Audrey Peterson, "Some Minor Voices," in *Victorian Masters of Mystery: From Wilkie Collins to Conan Doyle* (New York: Ungar, 1984), 167–68.

Henry Dunbar

Audrey Peterson, "Some Minor Voices," in *Victorian Masters of Mystery: From Wilkie Collins to Conan Doyle* (New York: Ungar, 1984), 164–67.

A Strange World

Audrey Peterson, "Some Minor Voices," in *Victorian Masters of Mystery: From Wilkie Collins to Conan Doyle* (New York: Ungar, 1984), 169–71.

BRETT, SIMON

An Amateur Corpse

Earl F. Bargainnier, "Simon Brett," in *Twelve Englishmen of Mystery* (Bowling Green, OH: Popular, 1984), 311–13, 319–21.

A Comedian Dies

Earl F. Bargainnier, "Simon Brett," in *Twelve Englishmen of Mystery* (Bowling Green, OH: Popular, 1984), 313–15.

The Death of Mike

Earl F. Bargainnier, "Simon Brett," in *Twelve Englishmen of Mystery* (Bowling Green, OH: Popular, 1984), 306–08, 324.

Situation Tragedy

Earl F. Bargainnier, "Simon Brett," in *Twelve Englishmen of Mystery* (Bowling Green, OH: Popular, 1984), 316–19, 321–23.

BRONTë, ANNE, *The Tenant of Wildfell Hall*

So Much Blood

Earl F. Bargainnier, "Simon Brett," in *Twelve Englishmen of Mystery* (Bowling Green, OH: Popular, 1984), 308–10.

BRONTË, ANNE

Agnes Grey

Janet H. Freeman, "Telling Over *Agnes Grey*," *CVE* 34 (October 1991): 109–26.

Midori Uematsu, "*Agnes Grey*," in *Bronte Kenkyu: Sakuhin to Haikei*, ed. Seiko Aoyama and Hiroshi Nakaoka (Tokyo: Kaibunsha, 1983), 175–94.

The Tenant of Wildfell Hall

Margaret Mary Berg, "*The Tenant of Wildfell Hall*: Anne Brontë's Jane Eyre," *VN* 71 (Spring 1987): 10–15.

W. A. Craik, "*The Tenant of Wildfell Hall*," in *The Brontës*, ed. Harold Bloom (New York: Chelsea House, 1987), 37–56.

Jan B. Gordon, "Gossip, Diary, Letter, Text: Anne Brontë's Narrative Tenant and the Problematic of the Gothic Sequel," *ELH* 51 (Winter 1984): 719–45.

Minoru Hirota, "Wildfell Yashiki no Junin," in *Bronte Kenkyu: Sakuhin to Haikei*, ed. Seiko Aoyama and Hiroshi Nakaoka (Tokyo: Kaibunsha, 1983), 195–225.

Arlene M. Jackson, "The Question of Credibility in Anne Brontë's *The Tenant of Wildfell Hall*," *ES* 63 (June 1982): 198–206.

Naomi Jacobs, "Gender and Layered Narrative in *Wuthering Heights* and *The Tenant of Wildfell Hall*," *JNT* 16 (Fall 1986): 204–12.

Edith Kostka, "Narrative Experience as a Means to Maturity in Anne Brontë's Victorian Novel *The Tenant of Wildfell Hall*," *ConnR* 14 (Fall 1992): 41–47.

Elizabeth Langland, "The Voicing of Feminine Desire in Anne Brontë's *The Tenant of Wildfell Hall*," in *Gender and Discourse in Victorian Literature and Art*, ed. Anthony Harrison and Beverly Taylor (Dekalb: Northern Illinois University Press, 1992), 111–23.

Catherine MacGregor, " 'I Cannot Trust Your Oaths and Promises: I Must Have a Written Agreement': Talk and Text in *The Tenant of Wildfell Hall*," *Dionysos* 3 (Fall 1992): 31–39.

Juliet McMaster, "'Imbecile Laughter' and 'Desperate Earnest' in *The Tenant of Wildfell Hall*," *MLQ* 43 (December 1982): 352–68.

Françoise Martin, "*The Tenant of Wildfell Hall*, portrait de l'artiste en jeune femme," *CVE* 34 (October 1991): 95–107.

Russell Poole, "Cultural Reformation and Cultural Reproduction in Anne Brontë's *The Tenant of Wildfell Hall*," *SELit* 33 (Autumn 1993): 859–64.

Carol A. Senf, "*The Tenant of Wildfell Hall*: Narrative Silences and Questions of Gender," *CE* 52 (April 1990): 446–56.

Linda Shires, "Of Maenads, Mothers, and Feminized Males: Victorian Readings of the French Revolution," in *Rewriting the Victorians: Theory History and the Politics of Gender*, ed. Linda Shires (New York: Routledge & Kegan Paul, 1992), 147–65.

Marianne Thormahlen, "The Villain of *Wildfell Hall*: Aspects and Prospects of Arthur Huntingdon," *MLR* 88 (October 1993): 831–41.

Maria Verch, "Die Brontes und Shakespeare," *Archiv* 223, no. 1 (1986): 45–63.

BRONTË, CHARLOTTE

Ashworth

Melodie Monahan, "*Ashworth*: An Unfinished Novel by Charlotte Brontë," *SP* 80 (Fall 1983): 1–33.

Jane Eyre

Seiko Aoyama, "*Jane Eyre*," in *Bronte Kenkyu: Sakuhin to Haikei*, ed. Seiko Aoyama and Hiroshi Nakaoka (Tokyo: Kaibunsha, 1983), 37–71.

Frederick L. Ashe, "*Jane Eyre*: The Quest for Optimism," *SNNTS* 20 (Summer 1988): 121–30.

Claire Bazin, "Ordre apparent et desordre cache dans *Jane Eyre*," *CVE* 27 (April 1988): 29–36.

Jerome Beaty, "*Jane Eyre* and Genre," *Genre* 10, no. 1 (1977): 619–54.

Jerome Beaty, "*Jane Eyre* at Gateshead: Mixed Signals in the Text and Context," in *Victorian Literature and Society: Essays Presented to Richard D. Altick*, ed. James R. Kincaid and Albert J. Kuhn (Columbus: Ohio State University Press, 1984), 168–96.

Peter J. Bellis, "In the Window-Seat: Vision and Power in *Jane Eyre*," *ELH* 54 (Fall 1987): 639–52.

Richard Benvenuto, "The Child of Nature, the Child of Grace, and the Unresolved Conflict of *Jane Eyre*," *ELH* 39 (1972): 620–38.

Susan D. Bernstein, "Madam Mope: The Bereaved Child in Brontë's *Jane Eyre*," in *Adolescents, Literature, and Work with Youth*, ed. J. Pamela Weiner and Ruth M. Stein (New York: Haworth, 1985), 117–29.

Gerd Birkner, "Charlotte Brontë's *Jane Eyre*—das Selbst als Pneuma," in *Radikalismus in Literatur und Gesellschaft des 19. Jahrhunderts*, ed. Gregory Claeys and Liselotte Glage (Frankfurt: Peter Lang, 1987), 183–200.

M. A. Blom, "*Jane Eyre*: Mind as Law Unto Itself," *Criticism* 15 (1973): 350–64.

Harold Bloom, "Introduction," in *Charlotte Brontë's "Jane Eyre,"* ed. Harold Bloom (New York: Chelsea House, 1987), 1–6.

Rosemarie Bodenheimer, "Jane Eyre in Search of Her Story," in *Charlotte Brontë's "Jane Eyre,"* ed. Harold Bloom (New York: Chelsea House, 1987), 97–112.

Karen Ann Butery, "Jane Eyre's Flights from Decision," *LitR* 24 (Winter 1981): 222–51. Reprinted as "Jane Eyre's Flights from Decision," in *Third Force Psychology and the Study of Literature*, ed. Bernard J. Paris (Rutherford, NJ: Fairleigh Dickinson University Press, 1986), 114–35.

Cynthia Carlton-Ford, "Intimacy without Immolation: Fire in *Jane Eyre*," *WS* 15 (December 1988): 375–86.

Maria-Jose Codaccioni, "L'Autre vie de Bertha Rochester," in *Societe des Anglicistes de l'Enseignement Superieur*, ed. Actes du Congrès de Poitiers (Paris: Didier, 1984), 107–14.

W. A. Craik, "The Shape of the Novel," in *Charlotte Brontë's "Jane Eyre,"* ed. Harold Bloom (New York: Chelsea House, 1987), 7–20.

Peter Allan Dale, "Charlotte Brontë's 'tale half-told': The Disruption of Narrative Structure in *Jane Eyre*," *MLQ* 47 (June 1986): 108–29.

R. J. Dingley, "Rochester as Slave: An Allusion in *Jane Eyre*," *N&Q* 31 (March 1984): 66.

Janay Downing, "Fire and Ice Imagery in *Jane Eyre*," *Punch* 26 (October 1966): 68–78.

Terry Eagleton, "*Jane Eyre*: A Marxist Study," in *Charlotte Brontë's "Jane Eyre,"* ed. Harold Bloom (New York: Chelsea House, 1987), 29–45.

BRONTË, CHARLOTTE, *Jane Eyre*

Angus Easson, "Jane Eyre's 'Three-Tailed Bashaw,' Again," *N&Q* 37 (December 1990): 425.

Connie L. Eberhart, "Jane Eyre—a Daughter of the Lady in Milton's 'Comus,'" *UMSE* 8 (1990): 80–91.

Donald H. Eriksen, "Imagery as Structure in *Jane Eyre*," *VN* 30 (Fall 1966): 18–22.

Janet H. Freeman, "Speech and Silence in *Jane Eyre*," *SEL* 24 (Autumn 1984): 683–700.

Sandra M. Gilbert and Susan Gubar, "A Dialogue of Self and Soul: Plain Jane's Progress," in *Charlotte Brontë's "Jane Eyre,"* ed. Harold Bloom (New York: Chelsea House, 1987), 63–95.

Mary Ellis Gibson, "The Seraglio or Suttee: Brontë's *Jane Eyre*," *PostS* 4 (1987): 1–8.

Gail B. Griffin, "The Humanization of Edward Rochester," *W&L* 2 (1982): 118–29.

Gail B. Griffin, "Once More to the Attic: Bertha Rochester and the Pattern of Redemption in *Jane Eyre*," in *Nineteenth-Century Women Writers of the English-Speaking World*, ed. Rhoda B. Nathan (New York: Greenwood, 1986), 90–97.

Peter Grudin, "Jane and the Other Mrs. Rochester: Excess and Restraint in *Jane Eyre*," *Novel* 10 (Winter 1977): 145–57.

John Hagen, "Enemies of Freedom in *Jane Eyre*," *Crotocos* 13 (Fall 1971): 351–76.

June Steffensen Hagen, "Jane Eyre at Fourteen, Twenty-Four and Forty-Four," *LitO* 1 (Fall 1987): 22–33.

Lynn Hamilton, "Nicknames, Forms of Address, and Alias in *Jane Eyre*," *LOS* 14 (1987): 69–80.

Minzhong Han, "Feminist Literary Criticism: The Mad Woman and *Jane Eyre*," *FLitS* 39 (March 1988): 22–27.

Barbara Hardy, "Providence Invoked: Dogmatic Form in *Jane Eyre* and 'Robinson Crusoe,' in *Charlotte Brontë's "Jane Eyre,"* ed. Harold Bloom (New York: Chelsea House, 1987), 21–28.

Jeremy Hawthorn, "Formal and Social Issues in the Study of Interior Dialogue: The Case of *Jane Eyre*," in *Narrative: From Malory to Motion Pictures*, ed. Jeremy Hawthorn (London: Arnold, 1985), 86–99.

Mark M. Hennelly, Jr., "Jane Eyre's Reading Lesson," *ELH* 51 (Winter 1984): 693–717.

Quentin Hogge and Penelope Hogge, "Conflict in *Jane Eyre*," *CRUX* 24 (February 1990): 13–15.

Margaret Homans, "Dreaming of Children: Literalization in *Jane Eyre* and *Wuthering Heights*," in *The Female Gothic*, ed. Julian E. Fleenor (Montreal: Eden, 1983), 257–79. Reprinted as "Dreaming of Children: Literalization in *Jane Eyre*" in *Charlotte Brontë's "Jane Eyre*," ed. Harold Bloom (New York: Chelsea House, 1987), 113–31.

Margot Horne, "From the Window-Seat to the Red Room: Innocence to Experience in *Jane Eyre*," *DQR* 10 (1980): 199–213.

Joseph Kestner, "Charlotte Brontë and Charlotte Elizabeth Tonna: A Possible Source for *Jane Eyre*," *PLL* 20 (Winter 1984): 96–98.

Naomi M. Jacobs, "A Possible Source for Charlotte Brontë's Thornfield in 'A Lyke-Wake Dirge,' " *BrN* 6 (1987): 2–3.

"The Last New Novel," *Mirror* 2 (December 1847): 376–80.

Kate Lawson, "Madness and Grace: Grace Poole's Name and Her Role in *Jane Eyre*," *ELN* 30 (September 1992): 46–50.

Laurence Lerner, "Bertha and the Critics," *NCF* 44 (December 1989): 273–300.

George Henry Lewes, "*Jane Eyre*," *WestR* 48 (January 1848): 581–84.

David Malcolm, "*Jane Eyre* and the Condition-of-England Question," *EigoS* 129 (1983): 218–21.

John Malham-Dembleby, "The Key to *Jane Eyre*," *SatR* (6 September 1902): 292–93.

Daniel Margoliath, "Passion and Duty: A Study of Charlotte Brontë's *Jane Eyre*," *HUSL* 7 (1979): 182–213.

Robert Martin, "*Jane Eyre* and the World of Faery," *Mosaic* 10 (Fall 1977): 85–95.

Robert James Merrett, "The Conduct of Spiritual Autobiography in *Jane Eyre*," *Renascence* 37 (Autumn 1984): 2–15.

Susan L. Meyer, "Colonialism and the Figurative Strategy of Jane Eyre," *VS* 33 (Winter 1990): 247–68.

Cynthia Miecznikowski, " 'Do you never laugh, Miss Eyre?': Humor, Wit and the Comic in *Jane Eyre*," *SNNTS* 21 (Winter 1989): 367–79.

Jane Millgate, "Narrative Distance in *Jane Eyre*: The Relevance of the Pictures," *MLR* 63 (April 1968): 315–19.

Helene Moglen, "The End of *Jane Eyre* and the Creation of a Feminist Myth," in *Charlotte Brontë's "Jane Eyre,"* ed. Harold Bloom (New York: Chelsea House, 1987), 47–61.

Melodie Monahan, "Heading Out Is Not Going Home: *Jane Eyre*," *SEL* 28 (Autumn 1988): 589–608.

Richard Moore, "*Jane Eyre*: Love and the Symbolism of Art," *CrSur* 3(1) (1991): 44–52.

Valerie Grosvenor Myer, "*Jane Eyre*: The Madwoman as Hyena," *N&Q* 35 (September 1988): 318.

Nancy Pell, "Resistance, Rebellion, and Marriage: The Economics of *Jane Eyre*," *NCF* 31 (December 1977): 397–420.

Joan D. Peters, "Finding a Voice: Towards a Woman's Discourse of Dialogue in the Narration of *Jane Eyre*," *SNNTS* 23 (Summer 1991): 217–36.

Paul Pickrel, "*Jane Eyre*: The Apocalypse of the Body," *ELH* 53 (Spring 1986): 165–82.

Murray G. H. Pittock, "John Wilmot and Mr. Rochester," *NCF* 41 (March 1987): 462–69.

Jina Politi, "*Jane Eyre* Class-ified," *L&H* 8 (Spring 1982): 56–66.

Mary Poovey, "The Anathematized Race: The Governess and Jane Eyre," in *Feminism and Psychoanalysis*, ed. Richard Feldstein and Judith Roof (Ithaca, NY: Cornell University Press, 1989), 230–254.

Joanne E. Rea, " Brontë's *Jane Eyre*," *Expl* 50 (Winter 1992): 75–78.

Joanne E. Rea, "Hair Imagery in *Jane Eyre*," *VIJ* 16 (1988): 19–26.

Mark Reger, "Brontë's *Jane Eyre*," *Expl* 50 (Summer 1992): 213–25.

Parama Roy, "Unaccommodated Woman and the Poetics of Property in *Jane Eyre*," *SEL* 29 (Autumn 1989): 713–27.

Karen E. Rowe, "'Fairy-born and human-bred': Jane Eyre's Education in Romance," in *The Voyage In: Fictions of Female Development*, ed. Elizabeth Abel, Marianne Hirsch, and Elizabeth Langland (Hanover, NH: University Press of New England for Dartmouth, 1983), 69–89.

Philip C. Rule, "The Function of Allusion in *Jane Eyre*," *MLS* 15 (Fall 1985): 165–71.

Nanko Saito, "Jiko Ninshiki eno Tabi: C. Brontë *Jane Eyre*," in *Igirisu Shosetsu no Joseitachi*, ed. Yaeko Sumi and Naomi Okamura (Tokyo: Keiso, 1983), 53–72.

Paul Schact, "Jane Eyre and the History of Self-Respect," *MLQ* 52 (December 1991): 423–53.

Edgar F. Shannon Jr., "The Present Tense in *Jane Eyre*," *NCF* 10 (June 1956): 141–45.

William R. Siebenschuh, "The Image of the Child and the Plot of *Jane Eyre*," *SNNTS* 8 (Fall 1976): 304–17.

Louise Simons, "Authority and *Jane Eyre*: A New Generic Approach," *CEA* 48 (Fall 1985): 45–53.

Peter A. Tasch, "Jane Eyre's 'Three-Tailed Bashaw,'" *N&Q* 29 (June 1982): 232.

Carolyn Williams, "Closing the Book: The Intertextual End of *Jane Eyre*," in *Victorian Connections*, ed. Jerome J. McGann (Charlottesville: University Press of Virginia, 1989), 60–87.

Nancy V. Workman, "Scheherazade at Thornfield: Mythic Elements in *Jane Eyre*," *ELWIU* 15 (Fall 1988): 177–92.

Ruth P. Yeazell, "More Truth than Real: Jane Eyre's 'Mysterious Summons,'" *NCF* 29 (June 1974): 127–43.

Bonnie Zare, "*Jane Eyre*'s Excruciating Ending," *CLAJ* 37 (December 1993): 204–20.

The Professor

Sue Ann Betsinger, "Charlotte Brontë's Archetypal Heroine," *BST* 19 (1989): 301–09.

Janet Butler, "Charlotte Brontë's *Professor*," *Expl* 44 (Spring 1986): 35–37.

Minoru Hirota, "*The Professor*: Charlotte Brontë's Narrative Technique and Its Limitations," *SELL* 31 (January 1981): 39–64.

Ruth D. Johnston, "*The Professor*: Charlotte Brontë's Hysterical Text: Or, Realistic Narrative and the Ideology of the Subject from a Feminist Perspective," *DSA* 18 (1989): 353–80.

Fiona Morphet, "Playing with *The Professor*," *CLAJ* 37 (March 1994): 348–57.

Theodore Watts-Dunton, "Introduction," in *"The Professor" by Charlotte Brontë: To Which Are Added the Poems of Charlotte, Emily and Anne Brontë* (London: Oxford University Press, 1906), v–xiv.

Shirley

Margaret J. Arnold, "Coriolanus Transformed: Charlotte Brontë's Use of Shakespeare in *Shirley*," in *Women's Re-Visions of Shakespeare: On the Responses of Dickinson, Woolf, Rich, H. D., George Eliot, and Others*, ed. Marianne Novy (Urbana: University of Illinois Press, 1990), 76–88.

Miriam Bailin, "'Varieties of Pain': The Victorian Sickroom and Brontë's *Shirley*," *MLQ* 48 (September 1987): 254–78.

BRONTË, CHARLOTTE, *Shirley*

Carol A. Bock, "Storytelling and the Multiple Audiences of *Shirley*," *JNT* 18 (Fall 1988): 226–42.

Louis Cazamian, "Charlotte Brontë: *Shirley*," in *Le Roman Social en Angleterre (1830–1850): Dickens—Disraeli—Mrs. Gaskell—Kingsley* (Paris: Société Nouvelle de Librairie et d'Edition, 1904), 419–26.

Joseph A. Dupras, "Charlotte Brontë's *Shirley* and Interpretive Engendering," *PLL* 24 (Summer 1988): 301–16.

Hiroshi Ebine, "*Shirley*," in *Bronte Kenkyu: Sakuhin to Haikei*, ed. Seiko Aoyama and Hiroshi Nakaoka (Tokyo: Kaibunsha, 1983), 73–106.

Mabel Ferrett, "*Shirley* by Charlotte Brontë: The Importance of Proper Names," *TYDS* 17(87) (1988): 9–16.

Janet Freeman, "Unity and Diversity in *Shirley*," *JEGP* 87 (October 1988): 558–75.

Sandra M. Gilbert and Susan Gubar, "The Genesis of Hunger According to *Shirley*," in *The Brontës*, ed. Harold Bloom (New York: Chelsea House, 1987), 109–30.

Suzanne Keen, "Narrative Annexes in Charlotte Brontë's *Shirley*," *JNT* 20 (Spring 1990): 107–19.

Elizabeth Langland, "Dialogic Plots and Chameleon Narrators in the Novels of Victorian Women Writers: The Example of Charlotte Brontë's *Shirley*," in *Narrative Poetics: Innovations, Limits, Challenges*, ed. James Phelan (Columbus: Center for Comparative Studies in Humanities, Ohio State University, 1987), 23–37.

Deirdre Lashgari, "What Some Women Can't Swallow: Hunger as Protest in Charlotte Brontë's *Shirley*," in *Disorderly Eaters: Texts in Self-Empowerment*, ed. Lilian Furst (University Park: Pennsylvania State University Press, 1992), 141–52.

Kate Lawson, "The Dissenting Voice: Shirley's Vision of Women and Christianity," *SEL* 29 (Autumn 1989): 729–43.

George Henry Lewes, "Currier Bell's *Shirley*," *EdinR* 91 (January 1850): 153–73.

Ken Edward Smith, "Yorkshire Dialect in Charlotte Brontë's *Shirley*," *TYDS* 17, no. 87 (1988): 17–23.

Yasuko Tanaka, "*Shirley*," in *Igirisu Bungaku: Kenkyu to Kansho 2*, ed. Yoshitsugu Uchida and Kishimoto Yoshitaka (Osaka: Sogensha, 1982), 17–27, 81–89.

Susan Zlotnick, "Luddism, Medievalism and Women's History in *Shirley*: Charlotte Brontë's Revisionist Tactics," *Novel* 24 (Spring 1991): 282–95.

"There Was Once a Little Girl"

Branwen Bailey Pratt, "Charlotte Brontë's 'There Was Once a Little Girl': The Creative Process," *AI* 39 (Spring 1982): 31–39.

Villette

Joseph A. Boone, "Depolicing *Villette*: Surveillance, Invisibility, and the Female Erotics of 'Heretic Narrative,'" *Novel* 26 (Fall 1992): 20–42.

Chiara Briganti, "Charlotte Brontë's *Villette*: The History of Desire," *WVUPP* 35 (1989): 8–20.

Janet Butler, "Brontë's *Villette*," *Expl* 47 (Spring 1989): 22–25.

Janice Carlisle, "The Face in the Mirror: *Villette* and the Conventions of Autobiography," in *The Brontës*, ed. Harold Bloom (New York: Chelsea House, 1987), 131–53.

Ailee Cho, "A Feminist Study on *Villette*," *JELL* 38 (Spring 1992): 91–112.

Rosemary Clark-Beattie, "Fables of Rebellion: Anti-Catholicism and the Structure of *Villette*," *ELH* 53 (Winter 1986): 821–47.

Christina Crosby, "Charlotte Brontë's Haunted Text," *SEL* 24 (Autumn 1984): 701–15.

Rodney Stenning Edgecombe, "Odic Elements in Charlotte Brontë's *Villette*," *MLR* 87 (October 1992): 817–26.

Luann McCracken Fletcher, "Manufactured Marvels, Heretic Narratives, and the Process of Interpretation in *Villette*," *SEL* 52 (Autumn 1992): 723–46.

Shirley Foster, "'A Suggestive Book': A Source for *Villette*," *ÉA* 35 (April–June 1982): 177–84.

Janet Freeman, "Looking on at Life: Objectivity and Intimacy in *Villette*," *PQ* 67 (Fall 1988): 481–511.

Charisse Gendron, "Harriet Martineau and Virginia Woolf Reading *Villette*," *VIJ* 11 (1982–1983): 13–21.

Lynn Hamilton, "The Function of Names in *Villette*," *OnomasticaC* 70 (December 1988): 71–78.

BRONTË, CHARLOTTE, *Villette*

Robert B. Heilman, "Tulip-Hood, Streaks, and Other Strange Bedfellows: Style in *Villette*," *SNNTS* 14 (Fall 1982): 223–47.

Margot Horne, "Portrait of the Artist as a Young Woman: The Dualism of Heroine and Anti-Heroine in *Villette*," *DQR* 6, no. 3 (1976): 216–32.

Linda C. Hunt, "*Villette*: The Inward and the Outward Life," *VIJ* 11 (1982–1983): 23–31.

Mary Jacobus, "The Buried Letter: Feminism and Romanticism in *Villette*," in *Women Writing and Writing About Women*, ed. Mary Jacobus (London: Croom Helm, 1984), 42–60.

Patricia E. Johnson, "'This Heretic Narrative': The Strategy of the Split Narrative in Charlotte Brontë's *Villette*," *SEL* 30 (Autumn 1990): 617–31.

Francesca Kazan, "Heresy, the Image, and Description: Or, Picturing the Invisible: Charlotte Brontë's *Villette*," *TSLL* 32 (Winter 1990): 543–66.

Mary Ann Kelly, "Paralysis and the Circular Nature of Memory in 'Villette,'" *JEGP* 90 (July 1991): 342–60.

Karen Lawrence, "The Cypher: Disclosure and Reticence in *Villette*," in *Tradition and the Talents of Women*, ed. Florence Howe (Urbana: University of Illinois Press, 1991), 87–101.

Kate Lawson, "Reading Desire: *Villette* as 'Heretic Narrative,'" *ESC* 17 (March 1991): 53–71.

Margaret Lenta, "The Tone of Protest: An Interpretation of Charlotte Brontë's *Villette*," *ES* 64 (October 1983): 422–32.

Joseph Litvak, "Charlotte Brontë and the Scene of Instruction: Authority and Subversion in *Villette*," *NCF* 42 (March 1988): 467–89.

Steven Milhauser, "*Villette*," *GrandS* 6 (Winter 1987): 176–84.

Gregory S. O'Dea, "Narrator and Reader in Charlotte Brontë's *Villette*," *SoAR* 53 (January 1988): 41–57.

Tang Soo Ping, "C. Brontë's *Villette*," *Expl* 42 (Fall 1983): 25–26.

Nancy Sorkin Rabinowitz, "'Faithful Narrator' or 'Partial Eulogist': First-Person Narration in Brontë's *Villette*," *JNT* 15 (Fall 1985): 244–55.

Yoshiaki Shirai, "*Villette* ni okeru 'Arashi' no Imeji," in *Muraoka Isamu Sensei Kiju Kinen Ronbunshu: Eibungaku Shiron* (Tokyo: Kinseido, 1983), 274–86.

Sally Shuttleworth, "'The Surveillance of a Sleepless Eye': The Constitution of Neurosis in *Villette*," in *One Culture: Essays in Science and Literature*, ed. George Levine and Alan Rauch (Madison: University of Wisconsin Press, 1987), 313–35.

Brenda R. Silver, "The Reflecting Reader in *Villette*," in *The Voyage In: Fictions of Female Development*, ed. Elizabeth Abel, Marianne Hirsch, and Elizabeth Langland (Hanover, NH: University Press of New England for Dartmouth, 1983), 90–111.

Syd Thomas, "'References to Persons Not Named, or Circumstances Not Defined' in *Villette*," *TSLL* 32 (Winter 1990): 567–83.

Krystyna Urbisz, "Charlotte Brontë's *Villette*: Outer Manifestations and Inner Truth," in *Litterae et Lingua: In Honorem Premislavi Mroczkowski*, ed. Jan Nowakowski (Wroclaw: Polish Akademi, Nauk, 1984), 123–28.

Athena Vrettos, "From Neurosis to Narrative: The Private Life of the Nerves in *Villette* and *Daniel Deronda*," *VS* 33 (Summer 1990): 551–62.

Paul Wotipka, "Ocularity and Irony: Pictorialism in *Villette*," *W&I* 8 (April–June 1992): 100–08.

Noriko Yamawaki, "*Villette*," in *Bronte Kenkyu: Sakuhin to Haikei*, ed. Seiko Aoyama and Hiroshi Nakaoka (Tokyo: Kaibunsha, 1983), 107–42.

BRONTË, EMILY

Wuthering Heights

Miriam Allott, "The Rejection of Heathcliff?" *EIC* 8 (January 1958): 27–47. Reprinted in *Emily Brontë: Wuthering Heights: A Casebook*, ed. Miriam Allott (London: Macmillan, 1970; rev. ed. 1992), 166–80. Reprinted in *Heathcliff*, ed. Harold Bloom (New York: Chelsea House, 1993), 57–69.

Walter E. Anderson, "The Lyrical Form of *Wuthering Heights*," *UTQ* 47 (1977–78): 112–34. Reprinted in *Heathcliff*, ed. Harold Bloom (New York: Chelsea House, 1993), 114–33.

Seiko Aoyama, "'Arashigaoka' Kenkyu no Shindoko," *EigoS* 133 (1987): 322–24.

Mieke Bal, "Notes on Narrative Embedding," *PoT* 2 (Winter 1981): 41–59.

Cates Baldridge, "Voyeuristic Rebellion: Lockwood's Dream and the Reader of *Wuthering Heights*," *SNNTS* 20 (Fall 1988): 274–87.

Regina Barreca, "The Power of Excommunication: Sex and the Feminine Text in *Wuthering Heights*," in *Sex and Death in Victorian Literature*, ed. Regina Barreca (Bloomington: Indiana University Press, 1990), 227–40.

Georges Batalille, "Emily Brontë," in *Literature and Evil*, tr. Alastair Hamilton (London: Calder & Boyars, 1973), 6–8. Reprinted in *Heathcliff*, ed. Harold Bloom (New York: Chelsea House, 1993), 19–21.

BRONTË, EMILY, *Wuthering Heights*

Judith Bates, "Lockwood et le refus de l'Eros dans *Wuthering Heights*," in *Romantisme Anglais et Eros*, pref. Christian La Cassagnere (Clermont-Ferrand: Université de Clermont-Ferrand II, 1982), 179–98.

Claire Bazin, " 'Is Mr Heathcliff a Man?' " *CVE* 34 (October 1991): 71–9.

Claire Bazin, "Les Rêves d'angoisse dans *Wuthering Heights*," in *Visages de l'angoisse*, ed. Christian La Cassagnere (Clermont-Ferrand: Publications de la faculte des lettres de Clermont, 1989), 249–60.

Claire Bazin, "Heathcliff ou l'amour de l'argent," *CVE* 35 (April 1992): 71–82.

Jeffrey Berman, "Attachment and Loss in *Wuthering Heights*," in *Narcissism and the Novel* (New York: New York University Press, 1990), 78–112.

John Beversluis, "Love and Self-Knowledge: A Study of *Wuthering Heights*," *Eng* 120 (Autumn 1975): 77–82. Reprinted in *Heathcliff*, ed. Harold Bloom (New York: Chelsea House, 1993), 106–13.

Michael Black, "*Wuthering Heights*: Romantic Self-Commitment," in *The Literature of Fidelity* (New York: Barnes & Noble, 1975), 125–51.

J. Blondel, "*Wuthering Heights*: Emily's Divided Allegiance to Scripture," in *Du verbe au geste: Melanges en l'honneur de Pierre Danchin* (Nancy: Publications de Université de Nancy, 1986), 173–78.

Harold Bloom, "Introduction," in *The Brontës*, ed. Harold Bloom (New York: Chelsea House, 1987), 6–11.

Harold Bloom, "Introduction," in *Heathcliff*, ed. Harold Bloom (New York: Chelsea House, 1993), 1–3.

Françoise Bolton, "Les Hauts de Hurlevent: Superposition de genres," in *Le Genre du roman—les genres de romans* (Paris: Publications de Université de France, 1980), 105–11.

Ronald A. Bosco, "Heathcliff: Societal Victim or Demon?" *GypS* 2 (Fall 1974): 21–39.

Allen R. Brick, "*Wuthering Heights*: Narrators, Audience and Message," *CE* 21 (November 1959): 80–86.

William E. Buckler, "Chapter VII of *Wuthering Heights*: A Key to Interpretation," *NCF* 7 (March 1952–1953): 51–55.

Vincent Buckley, "Passion and Control in *Wuthering Heights*," *SoR* 1 (Winter 1964): 5–23.

Mary Burgan, " 'Some Fit Parentage': Identity and the Cycle of Generations in *Wuthering Heights*," *PQ* 61 (Fall 1982): 395–413. Reprinted as "Identity and the Cycle of Generations in *Wuthering Heights*," in *Heathcliff*, ed. Harold Bloom (New York: Chelsea House, 1993), 134–48.

Marjorie Burns, "'The Shattered Prison': Versions of Eden in *Wuthering Heights*," in *The Nineteenth-Century British Novel*, ed. Jeremy Hawthorn (Baltimore: Arnold, 1986), 31–46.

Joan Carson, "Visionary Experience in *Wuthering Heights*," *PsyAR* 62 (1975–76): 131–51.

Lord David Cecil, "Emily Brontë," in *Early Victorian Novelists* (Indianapolis: Bobbs-Merril, 1935. Reprint. Chicago: University of Chicago Press, 1958), 174–77; 136–82. Reprinted in *Heathcliff*, ed. Harold Bloom (New York: Chelsea House, 1993), 14–16.

Larry A. Champion, "Heathcliff: A Study in Authorial Technique," *BSUF* 9 (Spring 1968): 19–25.

Roger Chazal, "Tropismes 5: *Wuthering Heights*: Et l'errance," in *L'Errance*, ed. Jean–Jacques Lecercle (Paris: Universite de Paris X, 1991), 107–42.

Jay Clayton, "*Wuthering Heights*," in *Romantic Vision and the Novel* (Cambridge: Cambridge University Press, 1987), 81–102.

Clifford Collins, "Theme and Conventions in *Wuthering Heights*," *Critic* 1 (Autumn 1947): 43–50.

Syndy McMillen Conger, "The Reconstruction of the Gothic Feminine Ideal in Emily Brontë's *Wuthering Heights*," in *The Female Gothic*, ed. Julian E. Fleenor (Montreal: Eden, 1983), 91–106.

Sheryl Craig, "Brontë's *Wuthering Heights*," *Expl* 52 (Spring 1994): 157–59.

Brian Crews, "*Wuthering Heights*: A Dionysiac Vision," *RAEI* 15 (November 1987): 169–79.

H. M. Daleski, "*Wuthering Heights*: The Whirl of Contraries," in *The Divided Heroine: A Recurrent Pattern in Six English Novels* (New York: Holmes & Meier, 1984), 25–46.

Vinni Marie D'Ambrosio, "'The Cat' at *Wuthering Heights*," *ABACJ* 12 (September–December 1992): 10–21.

Cecil W. Davies, "A Reading of *Wuthering Heights*," *EIC* 19 (October 1969): 254–72.

Stevie Davies, "Baby-Work: The Myth of Rebirth in *Wuthering Heights*," in *Emily Brontë's Wuthering Heights*, ed. Harold Bloom (New York: Chelsea House, 1987), 119–36.

Terence Dawson, "'An Oppression Past Explaining': The Structures of *Wuthering Heights*," *OL* 44, no. 1 (1989): 48–68.

Terence Dawson, "The Struggle for Deliverance from the Father: The Structural Principle of *Wuthering Heights*," *MLR* 84 (April 1989): 289–304.

BRONTË, EMILY, *Wuthering Heights*

Emilio De Grazia, "The Ethical Dimension of *Wuthering Heights*," *MidWQ* 19 (Winter 1978): 178–95.

Herbert Dingle, "The Origin of Heathcliff," *BST* 16 (Winter 1971–75): 131–38.

M. Hope Dodds, "Heathcliff's Country," *MLR* 39 (March 1944): 116–29.

Andrew P. Drew, "Emily Brontë and *Hamlet*," *N&Q* n.s. 1 (1954): 81–82.

François Durand, "Emily Bronte, ou l'art d'exploiter ses deficiences," *Licorne* 8 (1984): 59–73.

Terry Eagleton, "*Wuthering Heights*," in *Myths of Power* (New York: Barnes & Noble, 1975), 97–121.

Arthur Efron, "Reichian Criticism: The Human Body in *Wuthering Heights*," in *Psychological Perspectives on Literature: Freudian Dissidents and Non-Freudians: A Casebook*, ed. Joseph Natoli (Hamden, CT: Archon, 1984), 53–78.

Inga-Stina Ewbank, "Emily Brontë: The Woman Writer as Poet," in *Their Proper Sphere: A Study of the Brontë Sisters as Early-Victorian Female Novelists* (Cambridge, MA: Harvard University Press, 1966), 95–101. Reprinted in *Heathcliff*, ed. Harold Bloom (New York: Chelsea House, 1993), 24–29.

Ping Fang, "On the Narrative Devices of *Wuthering Heights*," *FLitS* 36 (June 1987): 9–13.

Ping Fang, "Who Is the Protagonist of *Wuthering Heights*?" *FLitS* 39 (March 1988): 3–9.

John P. Farrell, "Reading the Text of Community in *Wuthering Heights*," *ELH* 56 (Spring 1989): 173–208.

Annette R. Federico, "The Waif at the Window: Emily Brontë's Feminine Bildungsroman," *VN* 68 (Fall 1985): 26–28.

Francis Fike, "Bitter Herbs and Wholesome Medicines: Love as Theological Affirmation in *Wuthering Heights*," *NCF* 23 (March 1968–69): 127–49.

Ronald E. Fine, "Lockwood's Dreams and the Key to *Wuthering Heights*," *NCF* 24 (March 1969): 16–30.

Avrom Fleishman, "*Wuthering Heights*: The Love of a Sylph and a Gnome," in *Fiction and the Ways of Knowing: Essays on British Novels* (Austin: University of Texas Press, 1928), 44–48. Reprinted in *Heathcliff*, ed. Harold Bloom (New York: Chelsea House, 1993), 39–43.

Boris Ford, "*Wuthering Heights*," *Scrutiny* 7 (1938–39): 375–89. Reprinted in *A Centre of Excellence: Essays Presented to Seymour Betsky*, ed. Robert Druce (Amsterdam: Rodopi, 1987), 29–42.

John Fraser, "The Name of Action: Nelly Dean and *Wuthering Heights*," *NCF* 20 (September 1965): 223–36.

David Galef, "Keeping One's Distance: Irony and Doubling in *Wuthering Heights*," *SNNTS* 24 (Fall 1992): 242–50.

Heidemarie Ganner, "Emily Brontë s Roman *Wuthering Heights* in deutscher Ubersetzung," *ZAA* 29, no. 4 (1981): 307–12.

Barbara Gates, "Suicide and *Wuthering Heights*," *VN* 50 (Fall 1976): 15–19.

Carole Gerster, "The Reality of Fantasy: Emily Brontë's *Wuthering Heights*," in *Spectrum of the Fantastic: Selected Essays from Sixth International Conference on Fantastic in Arts*, ed. Donald Palumbo (Westport, CT: Greenwood, 1988), 71–80.

Sandra M. Gilbert and Susan Gubar, "Looking Oppositely: Catherine Earnshaw's Fall," in *The Madwoman in the Attic: The Woman Writer and the Nineteenth-Century Literary Imagination* (New Haven: Yale University Press, 1979), 293–98. Reprinted in *Emily Brontë's "Wuthering Heights,"* ed. Harold Bloom (New York: Chelsea House, 1987), 79–97. Reprinted in *Heathcliff*, ed. Harold Bloom (New York: Chelsea House, 1993), 43–47.

Robin Gilmour, "Scott and the Victorian Novel: The Case of *Wuthering Heights*," in *Scott and His Influence*, ed. J. H. Alexander, David Hewitt, and Thomas Crawford (Aberdeen: Association for Scottish Literary Studies, 1983), 363–71.

Lew Girdler, "*Wuthering Heights* and Shakespeare," *HLQ* 19 (1955–1956): 389–90.

Robert F. Gleckner, "Time in *Wuthering Heights*," *Criticism* 1 (Summer 1959): 328–38.

William R. Goetz, "Genealogy and Incest in *Wuthering Heights*," *SNNTS* 14 (Winter 1982): 359–76.

Barbara Munson Goff, "Between Natural Theology and Natural Selection: Breeding the Human Animal in *Wuthering Heights*," *VS* 27 (Summer 1984): 477–508.

Linda Gold, "Catherine Earnshaw: Mother & Daughter," *EJ* 74 (March 1985): 68–73.

Eugene Goodheart, "Family, Incest and Transcendence in *Wuthering Heights*," in *Explorations: The Nineteenth Century*, ed. Ann B. Dobie (Lafayette, LA: Levy Humanities Series, 1988), 34–50.

Marci M. Gordon, "Kristeva's Abject and Sublime in Brontë's *Wuthering Heights*," *L&P* 34 (Fall 1988): 44–58.

BRONTË, EMILY, *Wuthering Heights*

Elliott B. Gose, Jr. "*Wuthering Heights*: The Heath and the Hearth," *NCF* 21 (March 1966–67): 1–19.

Robin Grove, "*Wuthering Heights*," *CR* 8 (1965): 71–87.

Peter D. Grudin, "*Wuthering Heights*: The Question of Unquiet Slumbers," *SNNTS* 6 (Winter 1974): 389–407.

George E. Haggerty, "The Gothic Form of *Wuthering Heights*," *VN* 74 (Fall 1988): 1–6.

James Hafley, "The Villain in *Wuthering Heights*," *NCF* 13 (June 1958–59): 199–215.

John Hagan, "Control of Sympathy in *Wuthering Heights*," *NCF* 21 (December 1966–67): 305–23.

George E. Haggerty, "The Gothic Form of *Wuthering Heights*," *VN* 74 (Fall 1988): 1–6.

Barbara Hannah, "*Wuthering Heights*," in *Striving Towards Wholeness* (New York: Putnam, 1971), 208–57.

Geoffrey Falt Harpham, "Walking on Silence: The Lamination of Narratives in *Wuthering Heights*," in *On the Grotesque: Strategies of Contradiction in Art and Literature* (Princeton: Princeton University Press, 1982), 79–105.

Anne Leslie Harris, "Psychological Time in *Wuthering Heights*," *IFR* 7 (1980): 112–17.

Ronald B. Hatch, "Heathcliff's 'Queer End' and Schopenhauer's Denial of the Will," *CRCL* 1 (Winter 1974): 49–64. Reprinted in *Heathcliff*, ed. Harold Bloom (New York: Chelsea House, 1993), 106.

Hilda Mafud Haye, "La empatia y lo demoniaco en *Wuthering Heights*," *NRP* 19–20 (1981): 14–21.

Caroyln G. Heilbrun, "The Woman as Hero," in *Toward a Recognition of Androgyny* (New York: Knopf, 1973), 80–82. Reprinted in *Heathcliff*, ed. Harold Bloom (New York: Chelsea House, 1993), 35–36.

Baruch Hochman, "*Wuthering Heights*: Unity and Scope, Surface and Depth," in *The Test of Character: From the Victorian Novel to the Modern* (Rutherford, NJ: Fairleigh Dickinson University Press, 1983), 91–110.

A. J. Hoenselaars, "Emily Brontë, *Hamlet*, and 'Wilhelm Meister,'" *N&Q* 39 (June 1992): 177–78.

Margaret Homans, "Repression and Sublimation of Nature in *Wuthering Heights*," *PMLA* 93 (January 1978): 9–19. Reprinted and revised as "The Name of the Mother in *Wuthering Heights*," in *Bearing the Word: Language and Female Experience in Nineteenth-Century Women's Writing* (Chicago: University of

Chicago Press, 1986), 68–83. Reprinted in *Emily Brontë's "Wuthering Heights,"* ed. Harold Bloom (New York: Chelsea House, 1987), 61–78. Reprinted in *The Brontës*, ed. Harold Bloom (New York: Chelsea House, 1987), 91–108.

Kimitaka Ishii, "On the Theme of *Wuthering Heights*," *SELL* 26 (March 1986): 1–27.

Carol Jacobs, "*Wuthering Heights*: At the Threshold of Interpretation," *boundaryII* 7 (Spring 1979): 49–71. Reprinted in *Emily Brontë's Wuthering Heights*, ed. Harold Bloom (New York: Chelsea House, 1987), 99–118.

Douglas Jefferson, "Irresistible Narrative: The Art of *Wuthering Heights*," *BST* 17 (1980): 337–47.

James Justus, "Beyond Gothicism: *Wuthering Heights* and an American Tradition," *TStL* 5 (1960): 25–33.

Frank Kermode, "A Modern Way with the Classic," *NLH* 5 (1973–74): 415–34. Reprinted in *Emily Brontë's "Wuthering Heights,"* ed. Harold Bloom (New York: Chelsea House, 1987), 47–60.

G. D. Klingpoulos, "The Novel as Dramatic Poem (II): *Wuthering Heights*," *Scrutiny* 14 (1946–47): 269–86.

U. C. Knoepflmacher, "*Wuthering Heights*: A Tragicomic Romance," in *Laughter & Despair: Readings in Ten Novels of the Victorian Era* (Berkeley: University of California Press, 1971), 84–108.

Arnold Krupat, "The Strangeness of *Wuthering Heights*," *NCF* 25 (December 1970): 269–80.

Bette Landon, "*Wuthering Heights* and the Text between the Lines," *PLL* 24 (Winter 1988): 34–52.

F. H. Langman, "*Wuthering Heights*," *EIC* 15 (October 1965): 294–312.

Simone Lavabre, "Feminisme et liberté dans *Wuthering Heights*," *CVE* 34 (October 1991): 63–70.

Norman Lavers, "The Action of *Wuthering Heights*," *SAQ* 72 (Winter 1973): 43–52.

Pamela Law, "Reading *Wuthering Heights*," *SSEng* 7 (1981–1982): 49–54.

Q. D. Leavis, "A Fresh Approach to *Wuthering Heights*," in *Lectures in America*, ed. F. R. Leavis and Q. D. Leavis (New York: Pantheon, 1969), 88–93, 95–96. Reprinted in *Wuthering Heights*, ed. William M. Sale, Jr. (New York: Norton, 1972), 306–21. Reprinted in *Heathcliff*, ed. Harold Bloom (New York: Chelsea House, 1993), 29–31.

B. H. Lehman, "Of Material, Subject, and Form: *Wuthering Heights*," in *The Image of the Work*, ed. B. H. Lehman et al. (Berkeley: University of California Press, 1955), 3–17.

BRONTË, EMILY, *Wuthering Heights*

Margaret Lenta, "Capitalism or Patriarchy and Immoral Love: A Study of *Wuthering Heights*," *Theoria* 62 (May 1984): 63–76

Anita Levy, "Blood, Kinship, and Gender," *Genders* 5 (July 1989): 70–85.

Bette London, "*Wuthering Heights* and the Text between the Lines," *PLL* 24 (Winter 1988): 34–52.

Alan S. Loxterman, "*Wuthering Heights* as Romantic Poem and Victorian Novel," in *A Festschrift for Professor Marguerite Roberts*, ed. Frieda Elaine Penninger (Richmond, VA: University of Richmond Press, 1976), 87–100.

Terence McCarthy, "A Late Eighteenth-Century Ballad Community: *Wuthering Heights*," *SFolkQ* 43, no. 3–4 (1979): 241–51.

Terence McCarthy, "The Incompetent Narrator of *Wuthering Heights*," *MLQ* 42 (March 1981): 48–64.

Kathryn B. McGuire, "The Incest Taboo in *Wuthering Heights*: A Modern Appraisal," *AI* 45 (Summer 1988): 217–24.

Jean N. McIlwraith, "Introduction," in *Wuthering Heights* (New York: Doubleday, 1907), v–xi.

Robert C. McKibben, "The Image of the Book in *Wuthering Heights*," *NCF* 15 (September 1960): 159–69.

Susan Jaret McKinstry, "Desire's Dreams: Power and Passion in *Wuthering Heights*," *CollL* 12 (Spring 1985): 141–46.

Joy Ellis McLemore, "Edgar Linton: Master of Thrushcross Grange," *RE* 8 (Fall 1981): 13–26.

Juliet McMaster, "The Courtship and Honeymoon of Mr. and Mrs. Linton Heathcliff: Emily Brontë's Sexual Imagery," *VRev* 18 (Summer 1992): 1–12.

Michael S. Macovski, "*Wuthering Heights* and the Rhetoric of Interpretation," *ELH* 54 (Summer 1987): 363–84.

William A. Madden, "*Wuthering Heights*: The Binding of Passion," *NCF* 27 (June 1972–73): 127–54.

John T. Matthews, "Framing in *Wuthering Heights*," *TSLL* 27 (Spring 1985): 25–61. Reprinted in *Heathcliff*, ed. Harold Bloom (New York: Chelsea House, 1993), 149–62.

John K. Mathison, "Nelly Dean and the Power of *Wuthering Heights*," *NCF* 11 (September 1956): 106–29.

J. Hillis Miller, "Emily Brontë," in *The Disappearance of God: Five Nineteeth-Century Writers* (Cambridge, MA: Harvard University Press, 1963), 194–97.

Reprinted in *Heathcliff*, ed. Harold Bloom (New York: Chelsea House, 1993), 21–23.

J. Hillis Miller, "*Wuthering Heights*: Repetition and the 'Uncanny,'" in *Fiction and Repetition: Seven English Novels* (Cambridge, MA: Harvard University Press, 1982), 42–72. Reprinted in *The Brontës*, ed. Harold Bloom (New York: Chelsea House, 1987), 169–92.

Giles Mitchell, "Incest, Demonism, and Death in *Wuthering Heights*," *L&P* 23 (Spring–Summer 1973): 27–36.

Helene Moglen, "The Double Vision of *Wuthering Heights*: A Clarifying View of Female Development," *CentR* 15 (1971): 391–405.

Thomas Moser, "What Is the Matter with Emily Jane? Conflicting Impulses in *Wuthering Heights*," *NCF* 17 (June 1962): 1–19. Reprinted in *The Victorian Novel*, ed. Ian Watt (Oxford: Oxford University Press, 1971), 183–203.

Elizabeth R. Napier, "The Problem of Boundaries in *Wuthering Heights*," *PQ* 63 (Winter 1984): 95–107. Reprinted in *Heathcliff*, ed. Harold Bloom (New York: Chelsea House, 1993), 48–50.

Beth Newman, "'The Situation of the Looker-On': Gender, Narration, and Gaze in *Wuthering Heights*," *PMLA* 105 (October 1990): 1029–41.

Hidekatsu Nojima, "Arashigaoka, in *Bronte Kenkyu: Sakuhin to Haikei*, ed. Seiko Aoyama and Hiroshi Nakaoka (Tokyo: Kaibunsha 1983), 143–74.

Joyce Carol Oates, "The Magnanimity of *Wuthering Heights*," *CritI* 9 (December 1982): 435–49.

Bernard J. Paris, "'Hush, hush! He's a human being': A Psychological Approach to Heathcliff," *W&L* 2 (1982): 101–17.

Patricia Parker, "The (Self-)Identity of the Literary Text: Property, Propriety, Proper Place, and Proper Name in *Wuthering Heights*," in *Identity of the Literary Text*, ed. Mario J. Valdes and Owen Miller (Toronto: University of Toronto Press, 1985), 92–116.

Charles I. Patterson, Jr., "Empathy and the Daemonic in *Wuthering Heights*," in *The English Novel in the Nineteenth Century*, ed. George Goodin (Urbana: University of Illinois Press, 1972), 81–96.

Robert M. Polhemus, "The Passionate Calling: Emily Brontë's *Wuthering Heights*," in *Erotic Faith: Being in Love from Jane Austen to D. H. Lawrence* (Chicago: University of Chicago Press, 1990), 79–107. Reprinted as "The Passionate Calling: *Wuthering Heights*," in *Heathcliff*, ed. Harold Bloom (New York: Chelsea House, 1993), 163–89.

Linda Ray Pratt, "'I Shall Be Your Father': Heathcliff's Narrative of Paternity," *VIJ* 20 (1992): 13–38.

V. S. Pritchett, "Books in General," *NewS & N* (22 June 1946): 453. Reprinted in *Heathcliff*, ed. Harold Bloom (New York: Chelsea House, 1993), 16–18.

V. S. Pritchett, "Introduction to *Wuthering Heights*," in *Wuthering Heights*, ed. V. S. Pritchett (Boston: Houghton Mifflin, 1956), i–xiv.

Lyn Pykett, "The Male Part of the Poem," in *Emily Brontë* (Savage, MD: Barnes & Noble, 1989), 112–20. Reprinted in *Heathcliff*, ed. Harold Bloom (New York: Chelsea House, 1993), 51–56.

Joanne E. Rea, "A Note on Freudian Symbolism in *Wuthering Heights*," *CVE* 25 (April 1987): 25–27.

Joanne E. Rea, "Window Imagery and Suppressed Incest in *Wuthering Heights*," *JEP* 8 (August 1987): 262–68.

Walter L. Reed, "Brontë and Lermontov: The Hero in and out of Time," in *Mediations on the Hero: A Study of the Romantic Hero in Ninteenth-Century Fiction* (New Haven: Yale University Press, 1974), 85–119. Reprinted as "Heathcliff: The Hero Out of Time," in *Heathcliff*, ed. Harold Bloom (New York: Chelsea House, 1993), 70–91.

Mary Rohrberger, "The Merging of Antinomies: Surreality in *Wuthering Heights*," in *Reconciliations: Studies in Honor of Richard Harter Fogle*, ed. Mary Lynn Johnson and Seraphia D. Leyda (Salzburg: Inst. für Anglistik & Amerikanistik, Universite Salzburg, 1983), 177–93.

C. P. Sanger, "The Structure of *Wuthering Heights*," in *Twentieth-Century Interpretations of Wuthering Heights*, ed. Thomas A. Vogler (Englewood Cliffs, NJ: Prentice-Hall, 1968), 15–27.

E. San Juan, Jr., "Nature, History, and the Organizing Principle of *Wuthering Heights*" *DLSUGraJ* 13, no. 1 (1988): 67–82.

Barbara Schapiro, "The Rebirth of Catherine Earnshaw: Splitting and Reintegration of Self in *Wuthering Heights*," *NCS* 3 (1989): 37–51.

Carol A. Senf, "Emily Brontë's Version of Feminist History: *Wuthering Heights*," *ELWIU* 12 (Fall 1985): 201–14.

Edgar Shannon, "Lockwood's Dreams and the Exegesis of *Wuthering Heights*," *NCF* 14 (June 1959): 95–109.

Arnold Shapiro, "*Wuthering Heights* as a Victorian Novel," *SNNTS* 1 (1969): 284–96.

W. David Shaw, "'It Is Unutterable': The Burden of Signs in *Wuthering Heights* and *Villette*," in *Victorians and Mystery: Crises of Representation* (Ithaca, NY: Cornell University Press, 1990), 53–61. Reprinted as "The Burden of Signs in

Wuthering Heights," in *Heathcliff*, ed. Harold Bloom (New York: Chelsea House, 1993), 190–96.

Sheila Smith, "'At Once Strong and Eerie': The Supernatural in *Wuthering Heights* and Its Debt to the Traditional Ballad," *RES* 43 (November 1992): 498–517.

David Sonstroem, "*Wuthering Heights* and the Limits of Vision," *PMLA* 86 (January 1971): 51–62. Reprinted in *Emily Brontë's Wuthering Heights*, ed. Harold Bloom (New York: Chelsea House, 1987), 27–45.

Patricia Meyer Spacks, "The Adolescent as Heroine," in *The Female Imagination* (New York: Knopf, 1975), 136–38. Reprinted in *Heathcliff*, ed. Harold Bloom (New York: Chelsea House, 1993), 36–38.

W. Kera Stevens, "The Devil on the Moors and in the 'Sertao': Modes of Fantasy in *Wuthering Heights* and Grande Sertao: Veredas," *EAA* 12–13 (1988–1989): 134–39.

John Allen Stevenson, "'Heathcliff is me!': *Wuthering Heights* and the Question of Likeness," *NFC* 43 (June 1988): 60–81.

W. H. Stevenson, "*Wuthering Heights*: The Facts," *EIC* 35 (April 1985): 149–66.

Halliwell Sutcliffe, "The Spirit of the Moores," *BST* 2 (January 1903): 174–90.

Ronald R. Thomas, "Dreams and Disorders in *Wuthering Heights*," in *Dreams of Authority: Freud and the Fictions of the Unconscious* (Ithaca, NY: Cornell University Press, 1990), 112–35.

Wade Thompson, "Infanticide and Sadism in *Wuthering Heights*," *PMLA* 78 (January 1963): 69–74.

Derek Traversi, "*Wuthering Heights*: After a Hundred Years," *DubR* 449 (Spring 1949): 154–68.

Rachael Trickett, "*Wuthering Heights*: The Story of a Haunting," *BST* 16 (1971–72): 338–47.

James Twitchell, "Heathcliff as Vampire," *SHR* 11 (Fall 1977): 355–62.

Graeme Tytler, "Heathcliff's Monomania: An Anachronism in *Wuthering Heights*," *BST* 20, no. 6 (1992): 331–43.

Dorothy Van Ghent, "On *Wuthering Heights*," in *The English Novel: Form and Function* (New York: Holt, Rinehart, 1953), 163–65. Reprinted in *Emily Brontë's "Wuthering Heights,"* ed. Harold Bloom (New York: Chelsea House, 1987), 9–25. Reprinted in *Heathcliff*, ed. Harold Bloom (New York: Chelsea House, 1993), 18–19.

Thomas Vargish, "Revenge and *Wuthering Heights*," *SNNTS* 3 (Spring 1971): 7–17.

Thomas A. Vogler, "Story and History in *Wuthering Heights*," in *Twentieth-Century Interpretations of "Wuthering Heights,"* ed. Thomas A. Vogler (Englewood Cliffs, NJ: Prentice-Hall, 1968), 78–99.

Guoqin Wang, "Viewing *Wuthering Heights* from Emily's Biography," *FLitS* 39 (March 1988): 16–21.

Xiaoqin Wang, "*Wuthering Heights* in Terms of Emily Brontë's Poetic Creation," *FLitS* 31 (March 1986): 38–43.

Melvin R. Watson, "Tempest in the Soul: The Theme and Structure of *Wuthering Heights*," *NCF* 4 (June 1949–50): 87–100.

Judith Weissman, "'Like a Mad Dog': The Radical Romanticism of *Wuthering Heights*," *SP* 82 (Winter 1985): 104–27.

Colin Wilcockson, "'Fair(y) Annie's Wedding': A Note on *Wuthering Heights*," *EIC* 33 (July 1983): 259–61.

Mary E. Wilkins, "Emily Brontë and *Wuthering Heights*," *BM* 1 (May 1903): 514–19.

Anne Williams, "'The Child Is Mother of the Man': The 'Female' Aesthetic of *Wuthering Heights*," *CVE* 34 (October 1991): 81–94.

Anne Williams, "Natural Supernaturalism in *Wuthering Heights*," *SP* 82 (Winter 1985): 104–27.

Gordon Williams, "The Problem of Passion in *Wuthering Heights*," *Trivium* 7 (1972): 41–53.

Philip K. Wion, "The Absent Mother in Emily Brontë's *Wuthering Heights*," *AI* 42 (Summer 1985): 143–64.

Patricia Yaeger, "The Novel and Laughter: *Wuthering Heights*," in *Honey-Mad Women: Emancipatory Strategies in Women's Writing* (New York: Columbia University Press, 1988), 177–206.

Patricia Yeager, "Violence in the Sitting Room: *Wuthering Heights* and the Woman's Novel," *Genre* 21 (Summer 1988): 203–29.

Kathleen A. Yocum, "Brontë's *Wuthering Heights*," *Expl* 48 (Fall 1989): 21–22.

BROOKE-ROSE, CHRISTINE

Amalgamemnon

Susan E. Hawkins, "Innovation/History/Poltics: Reading Christine Brooke-Rose's *Amalgamemnon*," *ConL* 32 (Spring 1991): 58–74.

Judy Little, "*Amalgamemnon* and the Politics of Narrative," *RCF* 9 (Fall 1989): 134–37.

Richard Martin, "'Stepping-Stones into the Dark': Redundancy and Generation in Christine Brooke-Rose's *Amalgamemnon*," in *Breaking the Sequence: Women's Experimental Fiction*, ed. Ellen G. Friedman and Miriam Fuchs (Princeton: Princeton University Press, 1989), 177–87.

Between

Susan Rubin Suleiman, "Living Between: Or, The Loneliness of the Alleinstehende Frau," *RCF* 9 (Fall 1989): 124–27.

Stories, Theories and Things

Flora Alexander, "*Stories, Theories & Things*," *RES* 44 (May 1993): 301–3.

Steven Connor, "*Stories, Theories and Things*," *MLR* 89 (April 1994): 427–28.

Paul Hansom, "*Stories, Theories and Things*," *ConL* 34 (Winter 1993): 797–802.

David Seed, "*Stories, Theories and Things*," *RCF* 12 (Spring 1992): 142–44.

Thru

Hanjo Berressem, "Thru the Looking Glass: A Journey into the Universe of Discourse," *RCF* 9 (Fall 1989): 128–33.

Shlomith Rimmon-Kenan, "Ambiguity and Narrative Levels: Christine Brooke-Rose's *Thru*," *PoT* 3 (Winter 1982): 21–32.

Xorandor

Susan E. Hawkins, "Memory and Discourse: Fictionalizing the Present in *Xorandor*," *RCF* 9 (Fall 1989): 138–44.

BROOKNER, ANITA

A Start of Life

Gisele Marie Baxter, "Clothes, Men and Books: Cultural Experiences and Identity in the Early Novels of Anita Brookner," *English* 42 (Summer 1993): 125–39.

Dolly

Carol Kino, "She Married Well-Off Uncle Hugo," *NYTBR* (20 February 1994): 12.

A Family Romance

Aisling Foster, "*A Family Romance*," *TLS* (25 June 1993): 22.

Alison Light, "*A Family Romance*," *NewS&S* 6 (9 July 1993): 33–34.

Fraud

Ursula Hegi, "The Curse of Being a Good Woman," *NYTBR* (10 January 1993): 7.

Victoria Radin, "*Fraud*," *NewS&S* 5 (21 August 1992): 38.

Candice Rodd, "*Fraud*," *TLS* (21 August 1992): 17.

Hotel du Lac

Gisele Marie Baxter, "Clothes, Men and Books: Cultural Experiences and Identity in the Early Novels of Anita Brookner," *English* 42 (Summer 1993): 125–39.

Ansgar Nunning, "Formen und Funktionen der Auflosung von Geschlechts-stereotypen in ausgewahlten Romanen von Anita Brookner: Interpretationshinweise für eine Behandlung im Englischunterricht der Sekundarstufe II," *Die Neueren Sprachen* 92 (June 1993): 249–70.

Isabel Medrano, "La dimension espacio-temporal de 'Hotel du Lac,'" *Epos* 6 (1990): 411–22.

Incidents in the Rue Laugier

Hilary Mantel, "*Incidents in the Rue Langier*," *NYTBR* (14 January 1996): 13.

Teresa Waugh, "*Incidents in the Rue Langier*," *Spectator* (17 June 1995): 43.

Latecomers

Bruce Nawer, "Doubles and More Doubles," *NewC* 7 (April 1989): 67–74.

Rosemary Dinnage, "*Latecomers*," *NYRB* 36 (1 June 1989): 34–36.

David Leavitt, "*Latecomers*," *NYTRB* (2 April 1989): 3.

A Private View

Nicholas Clee, "*A Private View*," *TLS* (17 June 1994): 22.

Linda Simon, "*A Private View*," *NYTBR* (8 January 1995): 9.

Boyd Tonkin, "*A Private View*," *New S&S* 7 (24 June 1994): 40.

Providence

Gisele Marie Baxter, "Clothes, Men and Books: Cultural Experiences and Identity in the Early Novels of Anita Brookner," *English* 42 (Summer 1993): 125–39.

Small Expectations

Jan Zita Grover, "*Small Expectations*," *WRB* 11 (July 1994): 38–40.

BROPHY, BRIGID

The Finishing Touch

Corinne E. Blackmer, "*The Finishing Touch* and the Tradition of Homoerotic Girls' School Fiction," *RCF* 15 (Fall 1995): 32–39.

Hackenfeller Ape

Mark Axelrod, "Mozart, Moonshots, and Monkey Business in Brigid Brophy's *Hackenfeller Ape*," *RCF* 15 (Fall 1995): 18–22.

In Transit

Brooke Horvath, "Brigid Brophy's It's-All-Right-I'm-Only-Dying Comedy of Modern Manners: Notes on *In Transit*," *RCF* 15 (Fall 1995): 46–53.

Patricia Lee, "Communications Breakdown and the 'Twin Genius' of Brophy's *In Transit*," *RCF* 15 (Fall 1995): 62–67.

Annegret Mack, "Concordia Discors: Brigid Brophy's *In Transit*," *RCF* 15 (Fall 1995): 40–45.

The King of a Rainy Country

Patricia Juliana Smith, "Desperately Seeking Susan[na]: Closeted Quests and Mozartean Gender Bending in Brigid Brophy's *The King of a Rainy Country*," *RCF* 15 (Fall 1995): 23–31.

BROWN, GEORGE MACKAY

Greenvoe

David Robb, "*Greenvoe*: A Poet's Novel," *ScLJ* 19 (May 1992): 47–60.

Magnus

Elizabeth Huberman, "George Mackay Brown's *Magnus*," *StSL* 16 (1981): 122–34.

Time in a Red Coat

John Burns, "Myths and Marvels," in *The Scottish Novel Since the Seventies: New Visions, Old Dreams*, ed. Gavin Wallace (Edinburgh: Edinburgh University Press 1993), 71–81.

BUCHAN, JOHN

"The Company of the Marjolaine"

Susanne Hagemann, "More News of Bonnie Prince Charlie after the '45: A Myth Debunked and Reaffirmed," *FMLS* 25 (April 1989): 147–53.

Greenmantle

Gavin Lambert, "The Thin Protection," in *The Dangerous Edge* (London: Barrie & Jenkins, 1975), 92–95.

The Half-Hearted

William Greenslade, "Fitness and the Fin de Siecle," in *Fin de Siecle/Fin du Globe: Fears and Fantasies of the Late Nineteenth Century*, ed. John Stokes (New York: St. Martin's, 1992), 37–51.

John Macnab

Michael Young, "The Rules of the Game: Buchan's *John Macnab*," *StSL* 24 (1989): 194–211.

Mr. Standfast

Gavin Lambert, "The Thin Protection," in *The Dangerous Edge* (London: Barrie & Jenkins, 1975), 95–96.

Prester John

T. J. Couzens, "'The Old Africa of a Boy's Dream': Towards Interpreting Buchan's *Prester John*," *ESA* 24 (March 1981): 1–24.

David Daniell, "Buchan and 'The Black General,'" in *The Black Presence in English Literature*, ed. David Dabydeen (Manchester: Manchester University Press, 1985), 135–53.

Gavin Lambert, "The Thin Protection," in *The Dangerous Edge* (London: Barrie & Jenkins, 1975), 85–88.

Sick Heart River
(in U.S. *Mountain Meadow*)

Gavin Lambert, "The Thin Protection," in *The Dangerous Edge* (London: Barrie & Jenkins, 1975), 101–4.

The Thirty-Nine Steps

Gavin Lambert, "The Thin Protection," in *The Dangerous Edge* (London: Barrie & Jenkins, 1975), 88–92.

David Stafford, "John Buchan's Tales of Espionage: A Popular Archive of British History," *CJH* 18 (April 1983): 1–21.

The Three Hostages

Gavin Lambert, "The Thin Protection," in *The Dangerous Edge* (London: Barrie & Jenkins, 1975), 96–101.

BULWER-LYTTON, EDWARD GEORGE EARLE

Back to Methuselah

Werner Sedlak, "Utopie und Darwinismus," in *Alternative Welten*, ed. Manfred Pfister (Munich: Fink, 1982), 216–38.

The Coming Race

James L. Campbell, Sr., "Edward Bulwer-Lytton's *The Coming Race* as a Condemnation of Advanced Ideas," *EAS* 16 (May 1987): 55–63.

B. G. Knepper, "*The Coming Race*: Hell? or Paradise Foretasted?" in *No Place Else: Explorations in Utopian and Dystopian Fiction*, ed. Eric Rabkin, Martin H. Greenberg, and Joseph D. Olander (Carbondale: Southern Illinois University Press, 1983), 11–32.

Werner Sedlak, "Utopie und Darwinismus," in *Alternative Welten*, ed. Manfred Pfister (Munich: Fink; 1982), 216–38.

Godolphin

William E. Cragg, "Bulwer's *Godolphin*: The Metamorphosis of the Fashionable Novel," *SEL* 26 (Autumn 1986): 675–90.

Peter W. Graham, "Bulwer the Moraliste," *DSA* 9 (1981), 143–61.

The Last Days of Pompeii

Walter Gobel, "'Entertaining Knowledge': Systemreferenz in Bulwers *Last Days of Pompeii*," *GRM* 40, no. 4 (1990): 399–407.

Lucretia

L. Ciolkowski, "The Woman (in) Question: Gender, Politics, and Edward Bulwer-Lytton's *Lucretia*," *Novel* 26 (Fall 1992): 80–96.

Marius

Bernard Richards, "Stopping the Press in *Marius*," *ELT* 27, no. 2 (1984): 90–99.

Mephistophiles

Edwin M. Eigner and David Thomas, "The Authorship of *Mephistophiles* in England," *NCF* 39 (June 1984): 91–94.

Pelham; or, The Adventures of a Gentleman

Peter W. Graham, "Bulwer the Moraliste," *DSA* 9 (1981): 143–61.

Wolfgang Kissel, "Englischer Gentleman und russischer *Mann von Ehre*: Zu Puskins Rezeption des Gesellschaftsromans *Pelham; or, the Adventures of a Gentleman* von Lord Bulwer-Lytton," *ZS* 51, no. 1 (1991): 60–85.

J. W. Oakley, "The Reform of Honor in Bulwer's *Pelham*," *NCF* 47 (June 1992): 49–71.

Rienzi

Andrew Brown, "Metaphysics and Melodrama: Bulwer's *Rienzi*," *NCF* 36 (December 1981): 261–76.

A Strange Story

Noel Macainsh, "Queensland, Rosicrucians, and *A Strange Story*: Aspects of Literary Occultism," *LiNQ* 11, no. 3 (1983): 1–18.

Zanoni

John Coates, "*Zanoni* by Bulwer-Lytton: A Discussion of Its 'Philosophy' and Its Possible Influences," *DUJ* 76 (June 1984): 223–33.

BURGESS, ANTHONY

A Clockwork Orange

Ken Anderson, "A Note on *A Clockwork Orange*," *NConL* 2 (November 1972): 5–7.

Robert Bowie, "Freedom and Art in *A Clockwork Orange*: Anthony Burgess and the Christian Premises of Dostoevsky," *Thought* 56 (December 1981): 402–16.

Elizabeth Brophy, "*A Clockwork Orange*: English and Nadsat," *NConL* 2 (March 1972): 4–5.

Julie Carson, "Pronominalization in *A Clockwork Orange*," *PLL* 12 (Spring 1976): 200–05.

Julian Coleman, "Burgess' *A Clockwork Orange*," *Expl* 42 (Fall 1983): 62–63.

Wayne C. Connelly, "Optimism in Burgess' *A Clockwork Orange*," *Extrapolation* 14 (December 1972): 25–29.

John Cullinan, "Anthony Burgess' *A Clockwork Orange*: Two Versions," *ELN* 9 (June 1972): 287–92.

A. A. de Vitis, *Anthony Burgess* (New York: Twayne, 1972), 103–12.

A. Escuret-Bertrand, "*A Clockwork Orange*: Anthony Burgess; Actes du Congres de Saint-Etienne (1975), in *Autour de l'idée de Nature: Histoire des idées et civilisation: Pedagogie et divers* (Paris: Didier, 1977), 169–91.

Robert O. Evans, "Nadsat: The Argot and Its Implications in Anthony Burgess' *A Clockwork Orange*," *JLM* 1 (March 1971): 406–10.

James Guetti, "Voiced Narrative: *A Clockwork Orange*," in *Word-Music: The Aesthetic Aspect of Narrative Fiction* (New Brunswick, NJ: Rutgers University Press, 1980), 54–76.

Lars Hartveit, "Anthony Burgess, *A Clockwork Orange*. Impact and Form: The Limits of Persuasion," in *The Art of Persuasion: A Study of Six Novels* (Bergen: Universitetsforlaget, 1977), 117–31.

Rita K. Gladsky, "Schema Theory and Literary Texts: Anthony Burgess' Nadsat," *LangQ* 30 (Winter–Spring 1992): 39–46.

Michael Gorra, "The World of *A Clockwork Orange*," *GettR* 3 (Autumn 1990): 630–43.

Earl Ingersoll, "Burgess' *A Clockwork Orange*," *Expl* 45 (Fall 1986): 60–62.

Thomas L. Mentzer, "The Ethics of Behavior Modification: *A Clockwork Orange* Revisited," *EAS* 9 (May 1980): 93–105.

Esther Petix, "Linguistics, Mechanics, and Metaphysics: Anthony Burgess's *A Clockwork Orange*," in *Old Lines, New Forces: Essays on the Contemporary British Novels, 1960–1970*, ed. Robert K. Morris (Rutherford, NJ: Fairleigh Dickinson University Press, 1976), 38–52.

Rubin Rabinovitz, "Ethical Values in Anthony Burgess' *A Clockwork Orange*," *SNNTS* 11 (Spring 1979), 43–50.

Rubin Rabinovitz, "Mechanism vs. Organism: Anthony Burgess' *A Clockwork Orange*," *MFS* 24 (Winter 1978–79): 538–41.

Philip E. Ray, "Alex before and after: A New Approach to Burgess' *A Clockwork Orange*," *MFS* 27 (Autumn 1981): 479–87.

Trevor J. Saunders, "Plato's Clockwork Orange," *DUJ* 37 (June 1976): 113–17.

Bettina Stoll, "Die Russismen der 'Nasdat'-Sprache in *A Clockwork Orange*," *LWU* 20 (June 1987): 364–73.

John Wightman Tilton, "*A Clockwork Orange*: Awareness is All," in *Comic Satire in the Contemporary Novel* (Lewisburg, PA: Bucknell University Press, 1977), 21–42.

The Clockwork Testament; Or, Enderby's End

Geoffrey Aggeler, "Enderby Immolatus: Burgess' *The Clockwork Testament*," *MalR* 44 (October 1977): 22–46.

Michael Rudick, "Enderbyan Poetics: The Word in the Fallen World," in *Critical Essays on Anthony Burgess*, ed. Geoffrey Aggeler (Boston: G.K. Hall, 1986), 110–21.

Devil's Mode

Lou Lewis, "Holmes Murdered to Music," *BSJ* 40 (September 1990): 167–69.

Devil of State

A. A. de Vitis, *Anthony Burgess* (New York: Twayne, 1972), 86–95.

The Doctor Is Sick

A. A. de Vitis, *Anthony Burgess* (New York: Twayne, 1972), 79–86.

Earthly Powers

Geoffrey Aggeler, "Faust in the Labyrinth: Burgess' *Earthly Powers*," *MFS* 27 (Autumn 1981): 517–31.

M. Bronski, "Moce ciemnosci," *KulturaP* 6 (June 1983): 131–35.

Francis Sparshott, "The Case of the Unreliable Narrator," *P&L* 10 (October 1986): 145–67.

The End of the World News

Ellen McDaniel, "Anthony Burgess' End of the World Triptych," *NConL* 15 (November 1985): 7–8.

Marc Poree, "Le Roman des derniers jours: Anthony Burgess, *The End of the World News*," in *Age d'or et apocalypse*, ed. Robert Ellrodt and Bernard Brugiere (Paris: Publications de la Sorbonne, 1986), 273–92.

Michael Rutschky, "Literatur: Eine Kolumne," *Merkur* 38 (April 1984): 329–34.

Enderby Outside

Geoffrey Aggeler, "Mr. Enderby and Mr. Burgess," *MalR* 10 (April 1969): 104–10.

A. A. de Vitis, *Anthony Burgess* (New York: Twayne, 1972), 20–21, 130–33.

The Enemy in the Blanket

A. A. de Vitis, *Anthony Burgess* (New York: Twayne, 1972), 49–57.

Honey for the Bears

A. A. de Vitis, *Anthony Burgess* (New York: Twayne, 1972), 131–41.

Stanley Kauffmann, "Literature of the Early Sixties," *WLB* 39 (May 1965): 763–64.

MF

Geoffrey Aggeler, "Incest and the Artist: Anthony Burgess's *MF* as Summation," *MFS* 18 (Winter 1972–1973): 529–43.

Arnold Cassola, "*MF*: A Glossary of Anthony Burgess's Castitan Language," *ELN* 26 (June 1989): 72–79.

Jean Kennard, "*MF*: A Separable Meaning," *RQ* 6 (1975): 200–6.

Timothy R. Lucas, "The Old Shelley Game: Prometheus & Predestination in Burgess' Works," *MFS* 27 (Autumn 1981): 465–78.

"The Muse"

John Cullinan, "Anthony Burgess' 'The Muse': A Sort of SF Story," *SSF* 9 (Summer 1972): 213–20.

Napoleon Symphony

Jean Bessiere, "Le Roman de l'homme illustre ou l'incontestable de l'historique et du fictif: Cendrars, Savinio, Burgess," *Recit et histoire*, ed. Jean Bessiere (Paris: Publication Université de France, 1984), 75–91.

Manfred Beyer, "Anthony Burgess: *Napoleon Symphony*," in *Englische Literatur der Gegenwart*, ed. Hrsg. von Rainer Lengeler (Dusseldorf: August Bogek, 1977), 313–24.

Margaret S. Schoon, "*Napolean Symphony*," in *Magill's Literary Annual, 1977*, Vol. 2 (Englewood Cliffs, NJ: Salem, 1977), 525–28.

1985

John J. Stinson, "Better to Be Hot or Cold: *1985* and the Dynamic of the Manichaean Duoverse," *MFS* 27 (Autumn 1981): 505–16.

Arthur Whellens, "Anthony Burgess's *1985*," *StIL* 5 (1982): 223–44.

Nothing Like the Sun

Geoffrey Aggeler, "A Prophetic Acrostic in Anthony Burgess' *Nothing Like the Sun*," *N&Q* 21 (April 1974): 136.

Dennis Joseph Enright, "A Modern Disease: Anthony Burgess' Shakespeare," in *Man is an Onion* (London: Chatto & Windus, 1972), 39–43.

George Garrett, "*Nothing Like the Sun*," in *Survey of Contemporary Literature*, ed. Frank N. Magill (New York: Salem, 1971), 3323–25.

Samuel Schoenbaum, "Burgess and Gibson," in *Shakespeare's Lives* (Oxford: Clarendon, 1970), 765–68.

John J. Stinson, "*Nothing Like the Sun*: The Faces in Bella Cohen's Mirror," *JLM* 5 (February 1976): 131–47.

Tremor of Intent

Geoffrey Aggeler, "Between God and Notgod: Anthony Burgess' *Tremor of Intent*," *MalR* 17 (January 1971): 90–102. Reprinted in *Anthony Burgess: The Artist as Novelist* (University: University of Alabama Press, 1979), 185–94.

James I. Bly, "Sonata Form in *Tremor of Intent*," *MFS* 27 (Autumn 1981): 489–504.

François Camoin, "Speaking Himself in the Language of God: Burgess's *Tremor of Intent*" in *Critical Essays on Anthony Burgess*, ed. Geoffrey Aggeler (Boston: G.K. Hall, 1986), 152–58.

Charles F. Duffy, "From Espionage to Eschatology: Anthony Burgess' *Tremor of Intent*," *Renascence* 32 (Spring 1980): 79–88.

Ronald J. Palumbo, "Names and Games in *Tremor of Intent*," *ELN* 18 (September 1980): 48–51.

The Wanting Seed

Lila Chalpin, "Anthony Burgess's Gallows Humor in Dystopia," *TexasQ* 16 (Autumn 1973): 73–84.

John Cullinan, "Burgess' *The Wanting Seed*," *Expl* 31 (March 1973): 51.

A. A. de Vitis, *Anthony Burgess* (New York: Twayne, 1972), 112–18, 129, 140, 146.

John H. Dorenkamp, "Anthony Burgess and the Future of Man: *The Wanting Seed*," *UDR* 15 (Spring 1981): 107–11.

Paul Fussell, "Theater of War," in *The Great War and Modern Memory* (New York: Oxford University Press, 1975), 222–28.

George Kateb, "Politics and Modernity: The Strategies of Desperation," *NLH* 3 (Autumn 1971): 98–111.

Brian Murdoch, "The Overpopulated Wasteland: Myth in Anthony Burgess' *The Wanting Seed*," *RLV* 39, no. 3 (1973): 203–17.

The Worm and the Ring

Geoffrey Aggeler, "A Wagnerian Affirmation: *The Worm and the Ring*," *WHR* 27 (Autumn 1973): 401–10.

A. A. de Vitis, *Anthony Burgess* (New York: Twayne, 1972), 96–103, 124.

BUTLER, SAMUEL

The Authoress of the Odyssey

Alison Booth, "The Author of *The Authoress of the Odyssey*: Samuel Butler as a Paterian Critic," *SEL* 25 (Autumn 1985): 865–83.

Ralf Norrman, "Enantiomorphism and Samuel Butler's *The Authoress of the Odyssey*," *W&I* 2 (July–September 1986): 231–36.

Erewhon

Jurgen Klein and Klaus Zollner, "Samuel Butler: *Erewhon* (1872)," in *Die Utopie in der mangloamerikanischen Literatur: Interpretationen*, ed. Hartmut Heuermann and Bernd-Peter Lange (Dusseldorf: Bagel, 1984), 80–102.

M. Prum, "Hommes et machines chez Samuel Butler," *CVE* 31 (April 1990): 111–18.

Thomas J. Remington, "'The Mirror up to Nature': Reflections of Victorianism in Samuel Butler's *Erewhon*," in *No Place Else: Explorations in Utopian and Dystopian Fiction*, ed. Eric S. Rabkin, Martin H. Greenberg, and Joseph D. Olander (Carbondale: Southern Illinois University Press, 1983), 33–55.

Erewhon Revisited

Francesco Marroni, "*Erewhon Revisited*: Il ritorno del figlio del sole," in *Nel tempo del sogno: Le forme della narrativa fantastica dall'immaginario vittoriano all'utopia contemporanea*, ed. Carlo Pagetti (Ravenna: Longo, 1988), 35–53.

M. Prum, “Hommes et Machines Chez Samuel Butler,” *CVE* 31 (April 1990): 111–18.

“A Psalm of Montreal”

Josef Altholz, “Mr. Spurgeon’s Haberdasher,” *VPR* 18 (Winter 1985): 147–48.

The Way of All Flesh

Margaret Ganz, “Samuel Butler: Ironic Abdication and the Way to the Unconscious,” *ELT* 28, no. 4 (1985): 366–94.

David Guest, “Acquired Characters: Cultural vs. Biological Determinism in *The Way of All Flesh*,” *ELT* 34, no. 3 (1991): 283–92.

Claude Jolicoeur, “Mythologie chrétienne et structure narrative dans *The Way of All Flesh* de Samuel Butler,” in *Actes du Congrès de Poitiers*, ed. Société des Anglicistes de l’Enseignement Superièur (Paris: Didier Erudition, 1984), 91–101.

John B. Rosenman, “Evangelicalism in *The Way of All Flesh*,” *CLAJ* 26 (September 1982): 76-97.

Jurgen Schlaeger, “Ernst oder Unernst? Anmerkungen zu Samuel Butlers *The Way of All Flesh*,” in *Theorie und Praxis im Erzahlen des 19. und 20. Jahrhunderts: Studien zur englischen und amerikanischen Literatur zu Ehren von Willi Erzgraber*, ed. Winfried Herget, Klaus Peter Jochum, and Ingeborg Weber (Tubingen: Narr, 1986), 91–105.

Greg Sieminski, “Suited for Satire: Butler’s Re-Tailoring of ‘Sartor Resartus’ in *The Way of All Flesh*,” *ELT* 31, no. 1 (1988): 29–37.

Kaspar Spinner, “Samuel Butler und Der Weg allen Fleisches; Ringvorlesung der Philos,” Fakultat der RWTH Aachen im WS 1987/88 in *Von Augustinus bis Heinrich Mann: Meisterwerke der Weltliteratur, III*, ed. Helmut Siepmann and Frank-Rutger Hausmann (Bonn: Romantischer Verlag, 1989), 254–70.

BYATT, ANTONIA S.

The Game

Jane Campbell, “The Hunger of the Imagination in A. S. Byatt’s *The Game*,” *Critique* 29 (Spring 1988): 147–62.

Possession

“The Booker Prize 1990,” *UES* 29 (April 1991): 39.

BYATT, ANTONIA S., "Precipice-Encurled"

Jean Louis Chevalier, "Conclusion in *Possession* by Antonia Byatt," in *Fins de romans: Aspects de la conclusion dans la littérature anglaise*, ed. Lucien Le Bouille (Caen: Publication Université de Caen, 1993), 109–31.

C. E. Feiling, "La novela erudita," *SupLN* (27 October 1991): 6.

Jean Vache, "Fiction romanesque et poesie fictive dans *Possession* de A. S. Byatt," *ÉBC* 1 (December 1992): 73–81.

Louise Yelin, "Cultural Cartography: A. S. Byatt's *Possession* and the Politics of Victorian Studies," *VN* 81 (Spring 1992): 38–41.

"Precipice-Encurled"

Jane Campbell, "'The Somehow May Be Thishow': Fact, Ficton, and Intertextuality in Antonia Byatt's 'Precipice-Encurled,'" *SSF* 28 (Spring 1991): 115–23.

The Still Life

Marie Pascale Buschini, "Attrait du Sud et mise en abyme du processus de creation dans *Still Life* de A. S. Byatt," *Cycnos* 7 (1991): 97–111.

Michael Westlake, "The Hard Idea of Truth," *PNR* 15, no. 4 (1989): 33–37.

The Virgin in the Garden

Juliet Dusinberre, "Forms of Reality in A. S. Byatt's *The Virgin in the Garden*," *Critique* 24 (Fall 1982): 55–62.

CARROLL, LEWIS (CHARLES LUTWIDGE DODGSON)

Alice's Adventures in Wonderland

Nina Auerbach, "Alice and Wonderland: A Curious Child," *VS* 17 (September 1973): 31–47.

M. Brede and V. Gurtaja, "Skanu atveidojoso vardu fonetiska struktura," in *Valodas aktualitates 1988, I: III Valodas nedela; II: Vietvardi un personvardi*, ed. A. Blinkena, B. Laumane, and V. Skujina (Riga: Zinatne, 1989), 129–32.

Barbara Elpern Buchalter, "Logic of Nonsense," *MathT* (May 1962): 459–64.

Kenneth Burke, "The Thinking of the Body: Comments on the Imagery of Catharsis in Literature," *PsyAR* 50, no. 3 (1963): 25–67.

Robert W. Brockway, "The Descensus ad Inferos of Lewis Carroll," *DR* 62 (Spring 1982): 36–43.

Lothar Cerny, "Autor-Intention und dichterische Fantasie: Lewis Carroll und *Alice in Wonderland*," *Archiv* 224, no. 2 (1987): 286–303.

Morton N. Cohen, "Curiouser and curiouser! The Endurance of Little Alice," *NYTBR* (11 November 1990): 54.

Mark Conroy, "A Tale of Two Alices in Wonderland," *L&P* 37 (Fall 1991): 29–44.

A. Dwight Culler, "The Darwinian Revolution and Literary Form," in *The Art of Victorian Prose*, ed. George Levine and William Madden (London: Oxford University Press, 1968), 224–46.

Michael A. D'Ambrosio, "Alice for Adolescents," *EJ* 59 (November 1970): 1074–75, 1085

George Dimock, "Chilhood's End: Lewis Carroll and the Image of the Rat," *W&I* 8 (July–September 1992): 183–205.

Terry Eagleton, "Alice and Anarchy," *NewB* 53 (October 1972): 447–55.

Jacqueline Flescher, "The Language of Nonsense in Alice," *YFS* 43 (1969): 128–44.

Selwyn H. Goodacre, "On Alice's Changes of Size in Wonderland," *Jabberwocky* 6 (Winter 1977): 20–24.

Johannes Hedberg, "Dodgson, Charles Lutwidge=Lewis Carroll," *Artes* 6 (1983): 98–108.

Roger B. Henkle, "The Mad Hatter's World," *VQR* 49 (Winter 1973): 99–117.

Siriol Hugh-Jones, "A New Review of *Alice*," *Punch* 243 (24 October 1962): 596–98.

Don L. F. Nilsen, "The Linguistic Humor of Lewis Carroll," *Thalia* 10 (Spring–Summer 1988): 35–42.

Hugh O'Brien, "Alice's Journey *Through the Looking Glass*," *N&Q* n.s. 14 (October 1967): 380–382.

Terry Otten, "After Innocence: Alice in the Garden," in *Lewis Carroll: A Celebration: Essays on the Occasion of the 150th Anniversary of the Birth of Charles Lutwidge Dodgson*, ed. Edward Guiliano (New York: Potter, 1982), 50–61.

Donald Rackin, "Alice's Journey to the End of Night," *PMLA* 81 (October 1966): 313–326.

D. Sapire, "Alice in Wonderland: A Work of Intellect," *ESA* 15 (1972): 53–62.

Jeffrey Stern, "Lewis Carroll and 'Printing & the Mind of Man,'" *Jabberwocky* 10 (Winter 1980–1981): 17–19.

Jun Yan, "Lewis Carroll and Blending," *Waiguoyu* 5 (September 1985): 64–65.

The Hunting of the Snark

Denis Crutch, "The Hunting of the Snark: A Study in Fits and Starts," *Jabberwocky* 5 (Autumn 1976): 103–9.

T. F. Foss, "The Man They Called 'Ho,' Plus the Butcher Also," *BSJ* 35 (December 1985): 206–10.

Edward Guiliano, "A Time for Humor: Lewis Carroll, Laughter and Despair, and *The Hunting of the Snark*," in *Lewis Carroll: A Celebration: Essays on the Occasion of the 150th Anniverdary of the Birth of Charles Lutwidge Dodgson*, ed. Edward Guiliano (New York: Potter, 1982), 123–31.

Robert Higbie, "Lewis Carroll and the Victorian Reaction against Doubt," *Thalia* 3 (Spring–Summer 1980): 21–28.

Michael Holquist, "What is a Boojum? Nonsense and Modernism," *YFS* 43 (1969): 145–64.

R. Merrill Root, "Snark Hunting: Lewis Carroll on Collectivism," *AmO* 9 (April 1966): 73–82.

Brian Sibley, "End Game," *Jabberwocky* 5 (Autumn 1976): 119–24.

Dieter Stundel, "Phantastik bei Lewis Carroll: Realitat und Mechanismus," in *Phantastik in Literatur und Kunst*, ed. Christian W. Thomsen and Jens Malte Fischer (Darmstadt: Wissenschaftliche Buchgesellschaft, 1980), 237–54.

Sylvie and Bruno

Jan B. Gordon, "Lewis Carroll, the Sylvie and Bruno Books, and the Nineties: The Tyranny of Textuality," in *Lewis Carroll: A Celebration: Essays on the Occasion of the 150th Anniversary of the Birth of Charles Lutwidge Dodgson*, ed. Edward Guiliano (New York: Potter, 1982), 176–94.

Dieter Stundel, "Phantastik bei Lewis Carroll: Realitat und the Nineties: The Tyranny of Textuality," in *Phantastik in Literatur und Kunst*, ed. Christian W. Thomsen and Jens Malte Fischer (Darmstadt: Wissenschaftliche Buchgesellschaft, 1980), 237–54.

Sylvie and Bruno Concluded

Joe R. Christopher, "Lewis Carroll, Sciencefictionist (Pt 2)," *Mythlore* 9 (Winter 1983): 45–48.

Brian Sibley, "The Poems to Sylvie and Bruno," *Jabberwocky* 4 (Summer 1975): 51–58.

Through the Looking-Glass

Brigid Brophy, Michael Levey, and Charles Osbourne, in *Fifty Works of English Literature We Could Do Without* (London: Rapp & Carroll, 1967), 81–82.

G. K. Chesterton, "Both Sides of the Looking-Glass," in *The Spice of Life and Other Essays* (Beaconsfield: Darween Finlayson, 1964), 66–70

Ivor Davies, "Looking-Glass Chess," *AWR* 15 (Autumn 1970): 189–91.

Robert Dupree, "The White Knight's Whiskers and the Wasp's Wig in *Through the Looking-Glass*," in *Lewis Carroll: A Celebration: Essays on the Occasion of the 150th Anniversary of the Birth of Charles Lutwidge Dodgson*, ed. Edward Guiliano (New York: Potter, 1982), 112–22.

Ellis S. Hillman, "Tiny Earthquakes in the Looking-Glass," *Jabberwocky* 8 (Autumn 1971): 14–15.

Ellis S. Hillman, "The World of the Looking-Glass," *Jabberwocky* 1 (1969): 9–12.

Terry Otten, "After Innocence: Alice in the Garden," in *Lewis Carroll: A Celebration: Essays on the Occasion of the 150th Anniversary of the Birth of Charles Lutwidge Dodgson*, ed. Edward Guiliano (New York: Potter, 1982), 50–61.

Richard Reichertz, "Alice through the 'Looking-Glass Book': Carroll's Use of Children's Literature as a Ground for Reversal in *Through the Looking Glass and What Alice Found There*," *CLAQ* (Fall 1992): 23–27.

William Sacksteader, "Looking-Glass: A Treatise on Logic," *PPR* 27 (March 1967): 338–55.

Patricia Meyer Spacks, "Logical and Language in *Through the Looking-Glass*," *ETC* 18, no. 1 (1961): 91–100.

Jun Yan, "Lewis Carroll and Blending," *Waiguoyu* 5 (September 1985): 64–65.

CARTER, ANGELA

"Black Venus"

Jill Matus, "Blonde, Black and Hottentot Venus: Context and Critique in Angela Carter's 'Black Venus,'" *SSF* 28 (Fall 1991): 467–76.

CARTER, ANGELA, *The Bloody Chamber and Other Stories*

The Bloody Chamber and Other Stories

John Bayley, "*The Bloody Chamber and Other Stories*," *NYRB* 39 (23 April 1992): 9–11.

Patricia Duncker, "Re-Imagining the Fairy Tales: Angela Carter's *Bloody Chamber*," *L&H* 10 (Spring 1984): 3–14.

Lisa Jacobson, "Tales of Violence and Desire: Angela Carter's *The Bloody Chamber*," *Antithesis* 6, no. 2 (1993): 81–90.

Mary Kaiser, "Fairy Tale as Sexual Allegory: Intertextuality in Angela Carter's *The Bloody Chamber*," *RCF* 14 (Fall 1994): 30–36.

Kari E. Lokke, "Bluebeard and *The Bloody Chamber*: The Grotesque of Self-Parody and Self-Assertion," *Frontiers* 10 (Spring 1988): 7–12.

Avis Lewallen, "Wayward Girls but Wicked Women? Female Sexuality in Angela Carter's *The Bloody Chamber*," in *Perspectives on Pornography: Sexuality in Film and Literature*, ed. Gary Day and Clive Bloom (New York: St. Martin's, 1988), 144–58.

Merja Makinen, "Angela Carter's *The Bloody Chamber* and the Decolonization of Feminine Sexuality," *FemR* 42 (Autumn 1992): 2–15.

"The Erl-King"

Harriet Kramer Linkin, "Isn't It Romantic? Angela Carter's Bloody Revision of the Romantic Aesthetic in 'The Erl-King,'" *ConL* 35 (Summer 1994): 305–23.

"The Fall River Ax Murders"

Rikki Ducornet, "A Scatological and Cannibal Clock: Angela Carter's 'The Fall River Axe Murders,'" *RCF* 14 (Fall 1994): 37–42.

The Infernal Desire Machines of Dr. Hoffman

Cornel Bonca, "In Despair of the Old Adams: Angela Carter's *The Infernal Desire Machines of Dr. Hoffman*," *RCF* 14 (Fall 1994): 56–62.

Peter Christensen, "The Hoffman Connection: Demystification in Angela Carter's *The Infernal Desire Machines of Dr. Hoffman*," *RCF* 14 (Fall 1994): 63–70.

Robert Clark, "Angela Carter's Desire Machine," *WS* 14, no. 2 (1987): 147–61.

Ricarda Schmidt, "The Journey of the Subject in Angela Carter's Fiction," *TexP* 3 (Spring 1989): 56–75.

Lady of the House of Love

Robert Rawdon Wilson, "SLIP PAGE: Angela Carter, In/Out/In the Post-Modern Nexus," in *Past the Last Post: Theorizing Post-Colonialism and Post-Modernism*, ed. Ian Adam and Helen Tiffin (Calgary: University of Calgary Press, 1990), 109–23.

Love

Patricia Juliana Smith, "All You Need Is *Love*: Angela Carter's Novel of Sixties Sex and Sensibility," *RCF* 14 (Fall 1994): 24–29.

Nights at the Circus

Michael Bell, "Narration as Action: Goethe's 'Bekenntnisse einer schonen Seele' and Angela Carter's *Nights at the Circus*," *GL&L* 45, no. 1 (1992): 16–32.

Joanne M. Gass, "Panopticism in *Nights at the Circus*," *RCF* 14 (Fall 1994): 71–80.

Magali Cornier Michael, "Angela Carter's *Nights at the Circus*: An Engaged Feminism Via Subversive Postmodern Strategies," *ConL* 35 (Fall 1994): 492–521.

Ricarda Schmidt, "The Journey of the Subject in Angela Carter's Fiction," *TexP* 3 (Spring 1989): 56–75.

Carolyn Steedman, "New Time: Mignon and Her Meanings," in *Fin de Siecle/Fin du Globe: Fears and Fantasies of the Late Nineteenth Century*, ed. John Stokes (New York: St. Martin's, 1992), 102–16.

Rory P. B. Turner, "Subjects and Symbols: Transformations of Identity in *Nights at the Circus*," *FForum* 20, no. 1–2 (1987): 39–60.

The Passion of New Eve

Heather Johnson, "Textualizing the Double-Gendered Body: Forms of the Grotesque in *The Passion of New Eve*," *RCF* 14 (Fall 1994): 43–55.

Ricarda Schmidt, "The Journey of the Subject in Angela Carter's Fiction," *TexP* 3 (Spring 1989): 56–75.

A Private View

James Wood, "Aspic of the Novel: *A Private View*," *NR* 212 (24 April 1995): 41.

The Sadeian Woman

Hugo Claus, "Gender Matters in *The Sadeian Woman*," *RCF* 14 (Fall 1994): 18–23.

The Second Virago Book of Fairy Tales

Neil Philip, "*The Second Virago Book of Fairy Tales*," *TES* 26 (27 August 1993): 17.

Jenny Uglow, "*The Second Virago Book of Fairy Tales*," *TLS* 77 (20 November 1992): 22.

Wise Children

Beth A. Boehm, "*Wise Children*: Angela Carter's Swan Song," *RCF* 14 (Fall 1994): 84–93.

Scott Bradfield, "Remembering Angela Carter," *RCF* 14 (Fall 1994): 90–93.

Jeanne K. Gibbs, "*Wise Children*," *RCF* 12 (Summer 1992): 195–96.

Michael Hardin, "The Other Other: Self Definition Outside Patriachal Institutions in Angela Carter's *Wise Children*," *RCF* 14 (Fall 1994): 77–83.

Marilynne Robinson, "*Wise Children*," *YR* 80 (April 1992): 227–35.

Edmund White, "*Wise Children*," *TLS* 4601 (June 1991): 22.

CARY, JOYCE

The African Witch

"JuJu Woman," *TLS* (23 May 1936): 437–38.

Aissa Saved

Brian Downes, "'Almost a Fabulous Treatment': A Reading of Joyce Cary's *Aissa Saved*," *WinP* 3 (1980): 52–62.

An American Visitor

Warren G. French, "Joyce Cary's American Rover Girl," *TLSS* 2 (Autumn 1959): 281–91.

The Captive and the Free

Edwin Ernest Christian, "*The Captive and the Free*: Joyce Cary's Christianity," *C&L* 33 (Spring 1984): 11–21.

Richard Hugh Miller, "Faith Healing and God's Love in Joyce Cary's *The Captive and the Free*," *AntigR* 6 (Fall 1975): 71–73.

Charley Is My Darling

James Stern, "Beneath the Guilt Lay Innocence," *NYTBR* 24 (January 1959): 4, 32.

Bernice Larson Webb, "Animal Imagery and Juvenile Deliquents in Joyce Cary's *Charley Is My Darling*," *SoCB* 32 (Winter 1972): 19–22.

Anthony West, "Footloose and Fancy-Free," *NewY* 36 (30 April 1959): 170, 173–74, 176.

Cock Jarvis

Christopher Fyfe, "Imperial Slumbers," *TLS* (22 November 1974): 1308.

Charles R. Larson, "*Cock Jarvis* by Joyce Cary," *NewR* 173 (29 November 1975): 34–35.

Except the Lord

Doris Grumbach, "Final Wisdom," *Commonweal* 59 (4 December 1953): 234–35.

David E. Latane Jr., "A Blakean Reference in Joyce Cary's *Except the Lord*," *ELN* 24 (March 1987): 57–61.

A Fearful Joy

Malcolm Pittock, "Joyce Cary: *A Fearful Joy*," *EIC* 13 (October 1963): 428–32.

Harrison Smith, ". . . & Glad Eye," *SatR* 33 (7 October 1950): 23–24.

Herself Surprised

Catherine Meredith Brown, "Nature Girl," *SatR* 31 (9 October 1948): 38–39.

Helen B. Parker, "A Living Lady," *NYTBR* (3 October 1948): 34.

The Horse's Mouth

Robert H. Adams, "Freedom in *The Horse's Mouth*," *CE* 26 (March 1965): 451–60.

Donald Barr, "A Careful and Profound Thinker," *Adam* 18 (1950): 30–31. Reprinted as "For Gulley Jimson, Life was Fun," *NYTBR* (29 January 1950): 24.

Jeanne Garant, "Joyce Cary's Portrait of the Artist," *BRLV* 24 (1958): 476–86.

Oddvar Holmesland, "Freedom and Community in Joyce Cary's Fiction: A Study of *The Horse's Mouth*," *ES* 68 (April 1987): 160–70.

Edward H. Kelly, "The Meaning of *The Horse's Mouth*," *MLS* 1 (1971): 9–11.

Annette S. Levitt, " 'The Mental Traveller' in *The Horse's Mouth*: New Light on the Old Cycle," in *William Blake and the Moderns*, ed. Robert J. Bertholf and Annette S. Levitt (Albany: State University of New York Press, 1982), 186–211.

Annette S. Levitt, "The Miltonic Progression of Gulley Jimson," *Mosaic* 11 (Summer 1977): 77–91,

Ann P. Messenger, "A Painter's Prose: Similes in Joyce Cary's *The Horse's Mouth*," *RE* 3 (1970): 16–28.

Lucretia Petri, "A Tentative Analysis of 'Bourgeois' Substitutes and '. . . Colour' Compounds in Joyce Cary's *The Horse's Mouth*," *AnaU* 21 (1972): 39–44.

Peter J. Reed, "Getting Stuck: Joyce Cary's Gulley Jimson," *TCL* 16 (October 1970): 241–52.

Marjorie Ryan, "An Interpretation of Joyce Cary's *The Horse's Mouth*," *PCrit* 2 (Spring–Summer 1958): 29–38.

Alvin J. Seltzer, "Speaking Out of Both Sides of the Horse's Mouth: Joyce Cary vs. Gully Jimson," *ConL* 15 (Winter 1974): 488–502.

Harrison Smith, "The Artist as a Lusty Old Man," *SatR* 33 (28 January 1950): 9–10.

Romona Kelley Stamm, "A Further Note on the Blakean Connection in Joyce Cary's *The Horse's Mouth*," *NConL* 15 (September 1985): 4–5.

Romona Kelley Stamm, "Joyce Cary's Onomastic 'Orchestration': Name, Symbol, and Theme in *The Horse's Mouth*," *LOS* 15 (1988): 43–49.

A House of Children

Michael J. Echeruo, "Mood and Meaning in Joyce Cary's *A House of Children*," *PURBA* 6 (June 1975): 3–8.

Mister Johnson

Christopher Fyfe, "The Colonia Situation in *Mister Johnson*," *MFS* 9 (Autumn 1963): 257–62

Gerald Moore, "'Mister Johnson Reconsidered,'" *BO* 4 (October 1958): 16–23.

Juliet Okonkwo, "Joyce Cary, *Mister Johnson*, Penguin Modern Classics," *Okike* 13 (1979): 113–23.

A. G. Sandison, "Living Out the Lyric: *Mr. Johnson* and the Present Day," *Eng* 20 (1971): 11–16.

B. R. Smith, "Moral Evaluation in *Mister Johnson*," *Critique* 11 (Winter 1969): 101–10.

The Moonlight

Julie Fenwick, "Women, Sex, and Culture in *The Moonlight*: Joyce Cary's Response to D. H. Lawrence," *Ariel* 24 (April 1993): 27–42.

Malcolm Foster, "Fell of the Lion, Fleece of the Sheep," *MFS* 9 (Autumn 1963): 226–30.

Not Honour More

Francis Joseph Battaglia, "Spurious Armageddon: Joyce Cary's *Not Honour More*," *MFS* 13 (Winter 1967): 479–91.

The Prisoner of Grace

Ruth Chapin, "Portrait of a Demagogue," *CSM* (23 October 1952): 15.

Richard Hayes, "Felt in the Head and Felt Along the Heart," *Commonweal* 57 (17 October 1952): 42–43.

CARY, JOYCE, *To Be a Pilgrim*

Giles Mitchell, "Joyce Cary's *Prisoner of Grace*," *MFS 13 (October 1963): 263–75.*

To Be a Pilgrim

Richard S. Lyons, "Narrative Method in Cary's *To Be a Pilgrim*," *TSLL* 6 (Summer 1964): 269–79.

Benjamin Nyce, "Joyce Cary's Political Trilogy: The Atmosphere of Power," *MLQ* 32 (March 1971): 89–106.

Orville Prescott, "Outstanding Novels," *YR* 38 (Summer 1949): 765.

Peter J. Reed, "Joyce Cary's *To Be a Pilgrim*," *ContL* 10 (Winter 1969): 103–16.

Harrison Smith, "Old Invalid's Days," *SatR* 32 (30 April 1949): 16, 33.

Stephen A. Shapiro, "Joyce Cary's *To Be a Pilgrim*: Mr. Facing-Both–Ways," *TSLL* 8 (Spring 1966): 81–91.

CHESTERTON, G(ILBERT) K(EITH)

"The Ballad of the Battle of Gibeon"

Ian Boyd, "'The Ballad of the Battle of Gibeon,'" *CRev* 8 (May 1982): 95–100.

"The Ballad of the White Horse"

G. Emmett Carter, "Homily for the Mass of Anniversary of the Death of G. K. Chesterton" *CRev* 12 (November 1986): 439–43.

John LeVay, "The Whiteness of the Horse Apocalypticism in 'The Ballad of the White Horse,'" *CRev* 13 (February 1987): 73–82.

The Ball and the Cross

William Blissett, "*The Ball and the Cross* (1910)," *CRev* 8 (February 1982): 30–34.

John Coates, "*The Ball and the Cross* and the Edwardian Novel of Ideas," *CRev* 18 (Fall 1992): 49–81.

D. J. Dooley, "The Ball with or without the Cross: How the Great Debate Is Resolved in Chesterton and Orwell," *CRev* 12 (February 1986): 29–47.

Martin Gardner, "Levels of Allegory in *The Ball and the Cross*," *CRev* 18 (Fall 1992): 37–47.

Gerard Slevin, "Chesterton's Scottish Characters," *CRev* 18 (Fall 1992): 83–87.

John Wren-Lewis, "Joy without a Cause: An Anticipation of Modern 'Near-Death Experience' Research in G. K. Chesterton's Novel *The Ball and the Cross*," *CRev* 12 (February 1986): 49–61.

"The Blue Cross"

Aden W. Hayes and Khachig Tololyan, "The Cross and the Compass: Patterns of Order in Chesterton and Borges," *HR* 49 (Autumn 1981): 395–405.

G. K. Chesterton, "The God with the Golden Key," in *Autobiography* (London: Hutchinson, 1969), 326–28.

Gavin Lambert, "Final Problems," in *The Dangerous Edge* (London: Barrie & Jenkins, 1975), 68–72.

The Club of Queer Trades

William J. Scheick, "Ethical Romance and the Detecting Reader: The Example of *The Club of Queer Trades*," in *The Cunning Craft: Original Essays on Detective Fiction and Contemporary Literary Theory*, ed. Ronald G. Walker and June M. Frazer (Macomb: Western Illinois University Press, 1990), 86–97.

The Defendant

E. J. Oliver, "Paradise in Chesterton, Giraudoux, Ramon Gomez de la Serna," *CRev* 8 (February 1982): 10–29.

The Everlasting Man

Warren H. Carroll, "Chesterton's Christ-Centered View of History," *F&R* 12, no. 3–4 (1986): 299–312.

Leo A. Hetzler, "G. K. Chesterton and the Myth-Making Power," *Seven* 3 (March 1982): 72–82.

John LeVay, "Confronting Evil: *The Everlasting Man* versus the Ubiquitous Devil," *CRev* 13 (November 1987): 475–86.

Sylvere Monod, "The Uses and Varieties of Imagination in G. K. Chesterton's *The Everlasting Man*," *CRev* 13 (February 1987): 55–71.

John Sullivan, "*The Everlasting Man*: G. K. Chesterton's Answer to H. G. Wells," *Seven* 2 (March 1981): 57–65.

"A Fairy Tale"

Christiane D'Haussy, "Man's Leap into Space," *CRev* 13 (February 1987): 12–14.

Father Brown

Ernest Bramah, "*Father Brown*," *GKW* 24 (8 October 1936): 84–85.

Owen Dudley Edwards, "The Immortality of *Father Brown*," *CRev* 15 (August 1989): 295–325.

Anthony Grist, "*Father Brown* and Kenneth More," *CRev* 9 (February 1983): 85–87.

R. W. Hays, "The Private Life of Father Brown," *ArmD* 4 (April 1971): 13–39.

Robert A. W. Lowndes, "G. K. Chesterton's *Father Brown*," *ArmD* 9 (July 1976): 184–88, 235.

John J. Mulloy, "The Twilight or Daylight World of Father Brown? An Answer to Professor Scheick," *CRev* 4 (November 1978): 316–18.

W. W. Robson, "G. K. Chesterton's *Father Brown Stories*," *SoR* n.s. 5 (Summer 1969): 611–29.

William J. Scheick, "The Twilight Harlequinade of Chesterton's *Father Brown*," *CRev* 4 (February 1977–78): 104–14.

The Flying Inn

John Coates, "Malaise at the Heart of *The Flying Inn*," *Seven* 8 (January 1987): 25–41.

John Coates, "The Philosophy and Religious Background of *The Flying Inn*," *CRev* 12 (August 1986): 303–28.

The House of the Peacock

R. J. Dingley, "G. K. Chesterton and the Thirteen Club," *N&Q* 31 (December 1984): 516.

"The Invisible Man"

Jon L. Breen, "'The Invisible Man' Revisited," *ArmD* 4 (April 1971): 154.

The Man Who Was Thursday

Ian Boyd, "Sacramental Mysticism in Chesterton and Lewis," *BNYCSLS* 21 (November 1989): 1–2.

Louise Mausell Field, "*The Man Who Was Thursday*," *NYTBR* (10 December 1922): 10.

David J. Leigh, "Politics and Perspective in *The Man Who Was Thursday*," *CRev* 7 (November 1981): 329–36.

Witold Ostrowski, "*The Man Who Was Thursday*, or Detection Without Crime," in *Litterae et Lingua: In Honorem Premislavi Mroczkowski*, ed. Jan Nowakowski (Wroclaw: Polish Akademy Nauk, 1984), 141–52.

Matthias Worther, "Von Anarchisten und Polizisten: Uberlegungen zum Erzahlwerk G. K. Chestertons," *Inklings* 4 (1986): 147–59.

The Napoleon of Notting Hill

Bernard Bergonzi, "*The Napoleon of Notting Hill*: An Introduction," *CRev* 19 (Spring 1993): 515–31.

Denis J. Conlon, "'La Trahison des clercs' in Chesterton's Parables for Social Reformers," *Seven* 9 (1988): 29–46.

The Queer Feet

Rudolf Fabritius, "Das Bild des 'Gentleman' in G.K. Chesterson's Detektivgeschichte *The Queer Feet*," *NS* 14 (1965): 376–81.

The Return of Don Quixote

Denis J. Conlon, "'La Trahison des clercs' in Chesterton's Parables for Social Reformers," *Seven* 9 (1988): 29–46.

CHILDERS, ERSKINE

The Riddle of the Sands

David Seed, "The Adventure of Spying: Erskine Childers's *The Riddle of the Sands*," in *Spy Thrillers: From Buchan to le Carré*, ed. Clive Bloom (New York: St. Martins, 1990), 28–43.

David Seed, "Erskine Childers and the German Peril," *GL&L* 45 (Spring 1992): 66–73.

CHRISTIE, AGATHA

And Then There Were None
(British titles: *Ten Little Niggers; Ten Little Indians*)

Earl F. Bargainnier, *The Gentle Art of Murder: The Detective Fiction of Agatha Christie* (Bowling Green, OH: Popular, 1980), 2, 22, 111–12, 117, 124, 128, 146, 149–50.

Michael C. Gerald, *The Poisonous Pen of Agatha Christie* (Austin: University of Texas Press, 1993), 130–31.

Susan M. Hardesty, "A Literary Approach to Agatha Christie: An Analysis of *And Then There Were None*," *Clues* 3 (Spring–Summer 1982): 17–30.

Appointment with Death

Earl F. Bargainnier, *The Gentle Art of Murder: The Detective Fiction of Agatha Christie* (Bowling Green, OH: Popular, 1980), 115–16.

Michael C. Gerald, *The Poisonous Pen of Agatha Christie* (Austin: University of Texas Press, 1993), 14–15, 160–62, 186, 234–35.

Death on the Nile

Michael C. Gerald, *The Poisonous Pen of Agatha Christie* (Austin: University of Texas Press, 1993), 179–80.

Jerry Palmer, *Thrillers: Genesis and Structure of a Popular Genre* (New York: St. Martin's, 1979), 96–98.

The Hollow

Margaret Boe Birns, "Agatha Christie's Portrait of the Artist," *Clues* 1 (Fall–Winter 1980): 31–34.

Michael C. Gerald, *The Poisonous Pen of Agatha Christie* (Austin: University of Texas Press, 1993), 130, 139, 145, 172, 203, 226.

The Moving Finger

Robert Barnard and Louise Barnard, "The Case of the Two Moving Fingers," *ArmD* 18 (Summer 1985): 306–8.

The Murder of Roger Ackroyd

Daniel R. Barnes, “A Note on *The Murder of Roger Ackroyd*,” *M&DA* 1972 (Beverly Hills: Donald Adams, 1972), 254–55.

Earl F. Bargainnier, *The Gentle Art of Murder: The Detective Fiction of Agatha Christie* (Bowling Green, OH: Popular, 1980), 6, 25, 28, 50, 62, 65, 67, 110, 123, 124, 128, 129–30, 145, 151, 155, 156, 161, 171, 175, 180, 181, 201.

Sara Gesuato, “Textually Interesting Aspects of Agatha Christie’s *The Murder of Roger Ackroyd*,” *Versus* 57 (September–December 1990): 29–56.

Dario Gibelli, “Le Paradoxe du narrateur dans *Roger Ackroyd*,” *Poétique* 23 (November 1992): 387–97.

Robert R. Hodges, “The Secret of Roger Ackroyd: A Biographical Reading,” *Clues* 8 (Spring–Summer 1987): 127–36.

Carl R. Lovitt, “Controlling Discourse in Detective Fiction: Or, Caring Very Much Who Killed Roger Ackroyd,” in *The Cunning Craft: Original Essays on Detective Fiction and Contemporary Literary Theory*, ed. Ronald G. Walker and June M. Frazer (Macomb: Western Illinois University Press, 1990), 68–85.

Henry Douglas Thomson, “The Orthodox Detective Story,” in *Masters of Mystery* (New York: Dover, 1978), 193–211.

The Mysterious Affair at Styles

Michael C. Gerald, *The Poisonous Pen of Agatha Christie* (Austin: University of Texas Press, 1993), 50–53.

A. A. Milne, “Books and Writers,” *Spectator* 184 (30 June 1950): 893.

An Overdose of Death
(Alternate titles: *The Patriotic Murders; One, Two, Buckle My Shoe*)

John G. Cawelti, *Adventure, Mystery and Romance: Formula Stories as Art and Popular Culture* (Chicago: University of Chicago Press, 1976), 111–19

The Third Girl

John G. Cawelti, *Adventure, Mystery and Romance: Formula Stories as Art and Popular Culture* (Chicago: University of Chicago Press, 1976), 129–37.

CLARKE, ARTHUR C., *Childhood's End*

Michael C. Gerald, *The Poisonous Pen of Agatha Christie* (Austin: University of Texas Press, 1993), 63–64.

CLARKE, ARTHUR C(HARLES) PSEUDONYMS: E. G. O'BRIEN, CHARLES WILLIS

Childhood's End

Merritt Abrash, "Utopia Subverted: Unstated Messages in *Childhood's End*," *Extrapolation* 30 (Winter 1989): 372–79.

Bruce A. Beatie, "Arthur C. Clarke and the Alien Encounter: The Background of *Childhood's End*," *Extrapolation* 30 (Spring 1989): 53–69.

Stephen H. Goldman, "Immortal Man and Mortal Overlord: The Case for Intertextuality," in *Death and the Serpent: Immortality in Science Fiction and Fantasy*, ed. Carl B. Yoke and Donald M. Hassler (Westport, CT: Greenwood, 1985), 193–208.

Stephen H. Goldman, "Wandering in Mazes Lost; Or, The Unhappy Life of Arthur C. Clarke's *Childhood's End* in Academia," *Foundation* 41 (Winter 1987): 21–29.

Kenneth L. Golden, "Self, Overmind, and the Evolution of Consciousness: Jung, Myth, and Arthur C. Clarke's *Childhood's End*," *POMPA* (1984): 134–52.

Alan B. Howes, "Expectation and Surprise in *Childhood's End*," in *Arthur C. Clarke* (New York: Taplinger, 1977), 149–71.

Lucy Menger, "The Appeal of *Childhood's End*," in *Criticial Encounters: Writers and Themes in Science Fiction*, ed. Dick Riley (New York: Ungar, 1978), 87–108.

David N. Samuelson, "*Childhood's End*: A Median Stage of Adolescence," *SFS* 1 (Spring 1973): 4–17.

Robert H. Waugh, "The Lament of the Midwives: Arthur C. Clarke and the Tradition," *Extrapolation* 31 (Spring 1990): 36–52.

The City and the Stars

Jean Babrick, "The Possible Gods: Religion in Science Fiction," *ArEB* 15 (Fall 1972): 37–42.

Thomas P. Dunn and Richard D. Erlich, "Environmental Concerns in Arthur C. Clarke's *The City and the Stars*," in *Aspects of Fantasy: Selected Essays from the*

Second International Conference on the Fantastic in Literature and Film, ed. William Coyle (Westport, CT: Greenwood, 1986), 203–11.

Tom Moylan, "Ideological Contrdiction in Clarke's *The City and the Stars*," *SFS* 4 (July 1977): 150–57.

Jack Williamson, "*The City and the Stars*," in *Survey of Science Fiction Literature*, ed. Frank N. Magill (Englewood Cliffs, NJ: Salem, 1979), 374–77.

Gary K. Wolfe, "The Known and the Unknown: Structure and Image in Science Fiction," in *Many Futures, Many Worlds*, ed. Thomas D. Clareson (Kent, OH: Kent State University Press, 1978), 104–14.

"The Food of the Gods"

Peter Brigg, "Three Styles of Arthur C. Clarke: The Projector, the Wit, and the Mystic," in *Arthur C. Clarke*, ed. Joseph D. Olander and Martin Harry Greenberg (New York: Taplinger, 1977), 26–30.

"If I Forget Thee, O Earth"

Thomas D. Clareson, "'If I Forget Thee, O Earth': Notes," in *A Spectrum of Worlds*, ed. Thomas D. Clareson (Garden City, NY: Doubleday, 1972), 178–79.

Imperial Earth

Donald L. Lawler, "*Imperial Earth*," in *Survey of Science Fiction Literature*, ed. Frank N. Magill (Englewood Cliffs, NJ: Salem, 1979), 1019–125.

"A Meeting with Medusa"

Peter Brigg, "Three Styles of Arthur C. Clarke: The Projector, the Wit, and the Mystic," in *Arthur C. Clarke*, ed. Joseph D. Olander and Martin Harry Greenberg (New York: Taplinger, 1977), 21–22.

George Edgar Slusser, *The Space Odysseys of Arthur C. Clarke* (San Bernadino, CA: Borgo, 1978), 19–24.

Rendezvous with Rama

Gregory Feeley, "Partners in Plunder: Or, Rendezvous with Manna," *Foundation* 49 (Summer 1990): 58–63.

William H. Hardesty, IV, "*Rendezvous with Rama*," in *Survey of Science Fiction Literature*, ed. Frank N. Magill (Englewood Cliffs, NJ: Salem, 1979), 1759–63.

Martin Labar, "Arthur C. Clarke: Humanism in Science Fiction," *ChT* 22 (2 June 1978): 27.

Steven Lehman, "Ruddick on Rama: An Amplification," *SFS* 12 (July 1985): 237.

Nicholas Ruddick, "The World Turned Inside Out: Decoding Clarke's *Rendezvous with Rama*," *SFS* 12 (1985 March): 42–50.

"The Star"

Roger Bozzetto, "L'Image de Dieu dans la science-fiction: Analyse de L'Etoile de A. C. Clarke," in *Mythes, Images, Representations*, ed. Jean–Marie Grassin (Paris: Didier; Limoges: Trames Université de Limoges, 1981; 1981), 317–40.

Patricia Ferrara, "'Nature's Priest': Establishing Literary Criteria for Arthur C. Clarke's 'The Star,'" *Extrapolation* 28 (Summer 1987): 148–58.

George E. Slusser, *The Space Odysseys of Arthur C. Clarke* (San Bernadino, CA: Borgo, 1978), 14–19.

Thomas C. Sutton and Marilyn Sutton, "Science Fiction as Mythology," *WF* 28 (October 1979): 230–37.

2001: A Space Odyssey

Annette Goizet, "2001-2010: Les Odyssées de l'espace d'Arthur C. Clarke," *ÉA* 41 (July–September 1988): 328–34.

George Edgar Slusser, "*2001: A Space Odyssey*," in *Survey of Science Fiction Literature*, ed. Frank N. Magill (Englewood Cliffs, NJ: Salem, 1979), 2343–49.

2010: Odyssey Two

Annette Goizet, "2001-2010: Les Odyssées de l'espace d'Arthur C. Clarke," *ÉA* 41 (July–September 1988): 328–34.

Robert Plank, "1001 Interpretations of *2001*," *Extrapolation* 11 (December 1969): 23–24.

Robert Plank, "Sons and Fathers, A. D., *2001*," *HSL* 1 (March 1979): 26–33.

COLLINS, WILLIAM WILKIE

After Dark

H. Kirk Beetz, "Plots within Plots: Wilkie Collins's *After Dark*," *WCSJ* 4 (1984): 31–34.

Armadale

R. V. Andrew, *Wilkie Collins: A Critical Survey of his Prose Fiction with a Bibliography* (New York: Garland, 1979), 188–203

Audrey Peterson, "Wilkie Collins: Early Works," *Victorian Masters of Mystery: From Wilkie Collins to Conan Doyle* (New York: Ungar, 1984), 50–57.

Natalie Schroeder, "*Armadale*: 'A Book That Is Daring Enough to Speak the Truth,'" *WCSJ* 3 (1983): 5–9.

Jonathan Tutor, "Lydia Gwilt: Wilkie Collins's Satanic, Sirenic Psychotic," *UMSE* 10 (1992): 37–55.

Lisa M. Zeitz and Peter Thoms, "Collin's Use of the Strasbourg Clock in *Armadale*," *NCF* 45 (March 1991): 495–503.

Basil

Audrey Peterson, "Wilkie Collins: Early Works," in *Victorian Masters of Mystery: From Wilkie Collins to Conan Doyle* (New York: Ungar, 1984), 25–26.

Jonathan Craig Tutor, "Lydia Gwilt: Wilkie Collins's Satanic, Sirenic Psychotic," *UMSE* 10 (1992): 37–55.

"The Biter Bit"

Audrey Peterson, "Wilkie Collins: Early Works," in *Victorian Masters of Mystery: From Wilkie Collins to Conan Doyle* (New York: Ungar, 1984), 37–38.

Blind Love

R. V. Andrew, *Wilkie Collins: A Critical Survey of His Prose Fiction with a Bibliography* (New York: Garland, 1979), 312–16.

"The Captain's Last Love"

R. V. Andrew, *Wilkie Collins: A Critical Survey of His Prose Fiction with a Bibliography* (New York: Garland, 1979), 263–64.

"The Clergyman's Confession"

R. V. Andrew, *Wilkie Collins: A Critical Survey of His Prose Fiction with a Bibliography* (New York: Garland, 1979), 260–61.

The Dead Alive

Robert Ashley, "Wilkie Collins and a Vermont Murder Trial," *NEQ* 21 (September 1948): 368–73.

"The Dead Hand"

Audrey Peterson, "Wilkie Collins: Early Works," in *Victorian Masters of Mystery: From Wilkie Collins to Conan Doyle* (New York: Ungar, 1984), 35.

The Dead Secret

Robert Ashley, "A Second Look at *The Dead Secret*," *WCSJ* 3 (1983): 21–25.

Anne Lohrli, "Wilkie Collins and Household Words," *VPR* 15 (Fall 1982): 118–19.

Audrey Peterson, "Wilkie Collins: Early Works," in *Victorian Masters of Mystery: From Wilkie Collins to Conan Doyle* (New York: Ungar, 1984), 33–34.

"The Devil's Spectacles"

R. V. Andrew, *Wilkie Collins: A Critical Survey of His Prose Fiction with a Bibliography* (New York: Garland, 1979), 276–77.

"The Double-Bedded Room"

Anne Lohrli, "Wilkie Collins: Two Corrections," *ELN* 22 (September 1984): 50–53.

The Dream Woman

R. V. Andrew, *Wilkie Collins: A Critical Survey of His Prose Fiction with a Bibliography* (New York: Garland, 1979), 247–49.

Audrey Peterson, "Wilkie Collins: Early Works," in *Victorian Masters of Mystery: From Wilkie Collins to Conan Doyle* (New York: Ungar, 1984), 35.

"The Duel in the Herne Wood"

R. V. Andrew, *Wilkie Collins: A Critical Survey of His Prose Fiction with a Bibliography* (New York: Garland, 1979), 265.

The Evil Genius

R. V. Andrew, *Wilkie Collins: A Critical Survey of His Prose Fiction with a Bibliography* (New York: Garland, 1979), 300–03.

The Fallen Leaves

R. V. Andrew, *Wilkie Collins: A Critical Survey of His Prose Fiction with a Bibliography* (New York: Garland, 1979), 273–76.

Laura Hapke, "He Stoops To Conquer: Redeeming the Fallen Woman in the Fiction of Dickens, Gaskell and Their Contemporaries," *VN* 69 (Spring 1986): 16–22.

"The Family Secret"

Audrey Peterson, "Wilkie Collins: Early Works," in *Victorian Masters of Mystery: From Wilkie Collins to Conan Doyle* (New York: Ungar, 1984), 34.

"A Fatal Fortune"

R. V. Andrew, *Wilkie Collins: A Critical Survey of His Prose Fiction with a Bibliography* (New York: Garland, 1979), 246–47.

"Fauntleroy"

Audrey Peterson, "Wilkie Collins: Early Works," in *Victorian Masters of Mystery: From Wilkie Collins to Conan Doyle* (New York: Ungar, 1984), 34.

"The First Officer's Confession"

R. V. Andrew, *Wilkie Collins: A Critical Survey of His Prose Fiction with a Bibliography* (New York: Garland, 1979), 306–07.

"Gabriel's Marriage"

Audrey Peterson, "Wilkie Collins: Early Works," in *Victorian Masters of Mystery: From Wilkie Collins to Conan Doyle* (New York: Ungar, 1984), 31.

"The Guilty River"

R. V. Andrew, *Wilkie Collins: A Critical Survey of His Prose Fiction with a Bibliography* (New York: Garland, 1979), 305–06.

"The Haunted Hotel"

R. V. Andrew, *Wilkie Collins: A Critical Survey of His Prose Fiction with a Bibliography* (New York: Garland, 1979), 268–72.

Heart and Science

R. V. Andrew, *Wilkie Collins: A Critical Survey of His Prose Fiction with a Bibliography* (New York: Garland, 1979), 287–93.

Hide and Seek

Audrey Peterson, "Wilkie Collins: Early Works," in *Victorian Masters of Mystery: From Wilkie Collins to Conan Doyle* (New York: Ungar, 1984), 26–29.

"How I Married Him"

R. V. Andrew, *Wilkie Collins: A Critical Survey of His Prose Fiction with a Bibliography* (New York: Garland, 1979), 285–86.

"Jezebel's Daughter"

R. V. Andrew, *Wilkie Collins: A Critical Survey of His Prose Fiction with a Bibliography* (New York: Garland, 1979), 278–82.

"John Jago's Ghost"

R. V. Andrew, *Wilkie Collins: A Critical Survey of His Prose Fiction with a Bibliography* (New York: Garland, 1979), 242–43.

"The Lady of Glenwith Grange"

Audrey Peterson, "Wilkie Collins: Early Works," in *Victorian Masters of Mystery: From Wilkie Collins to Conan Doyle* (New York: Ungar, 1984), 32–33.

The Law and the Lady

R. V. Andrew, *Wilkie Collins: A Critical Survey of His Prose Fiction with a Bibliography* (New York: Garland, 1979), 249–60.

Audrey Peterson, "Wilkie Collins: Early Works," in *Victorian Masters of Mystery: From Wilkie Collins to Conan Doyle* (New York: Ungar, 1984), 68–69.

The Lazy Tour of Two Idle Apprentices
(with Charles Dickens)

P. L. Caracciolo and R. G. Hampson, "'Money Turned to Leaves': Conrad, Collins, Dickens, and the Barber's Fourth Brother," *N&Q* 36 (June 1989): 193–96.

The Leader

Kirk H. Beetz, "Wilkie Collins and *The Leader*," *VPR* 15 (Spring 1982): 20–29.

The Legacy of Cain

R. V. Andrew, *Wilkie Collins: A Critical Survey of His Prose Fiction with a Bibliography* (New York: Garland, 1979), 307–12.

"Love's Random Shot"

R. V. Andrew, *Wilkie Collins: A Critical Survey of His Prose Fiction with a Bibliography* (New York: Garland, 1979), 294–99.

"Mad Monkton"

Audrey Peterson, "Wilkie Collins: Early Works," in *Victorian Masters of Mystery: From Wilkie Collins to Conan Doyle* (New York: Ungar, 1984), 35–36.

Man and Wife

R. V. Andrew, *Wilkie Collins: A Critical Survey of His Prose Fiction with a Bibliography* (New York: Garland, 1979), 221–31.

COLLINS, WILLIAM WILKIE, "Mr Marmaduke and the Minister"

Robert Ashley, "Man and Wife: Collins, Dickens, and Muhammad Ali," *WCSJ* 5 (1985): 5–9.

"Mr Marmaduke and the Minister"

R. V. Andrew, *Wilkie Collins: A Critical Survey of His Prose Fiction with a Bibliography* (New York: Garland, 1979), 272–73.

The Moonstone

Patrick Anderson, "Detective Story," *Spectator* 217 (23 December 1966): 820.

R. V. Andrew, *Wilkie Collins: A Critical Survey of His Prose Fiction with a Bibliography* (New York: Garland, 1979), 204–20.

Robert Ashley, "Wilkie Collins and the Detective Story," *NCF* 6 (June 1951): 47–60.

Uwe Boker, "Wilkie Collins, Henry James und Dr. Carpenters 'Unconscious Cerebration,'" *GRM* 34, no. 3 (1984): 323–36.

Robert L. Caserio, "Story, Discourse, and Anglo-American Philosophy of Action," *JNT* 17 (Winter 1987): 1–11.

Robert Fleissner, "The Master Sleuth Accommodated," *ShHR* 2, no. 1 (n.d.): 15–20, 42.

Patricia Miller Frick, "Wilkie Collins's 'Little Jewel': The Meaning of *The Moonstone*," *PQ* 63 (Summer 1984): 313–21.

E. R. Gregory, "Murder in Fact," *NewR* 179 (22 July 1978): 33–34.

Mark M. Hennelly Jr., "Detecting Collins' Diamond: From Serpentstone to *Moonstone*," *NCF* 39 (June 1984): 25–47.

G. F. McCleary, "A Victorian Classic," *Fortnightly* 160 (August 1946): 137–41. Reprinted as "A Victorian Masterpiece: *The Moonstone*," in *On Detective Fiction and Other Things*, ed. G. F. McCleary (London: Hollis & Carter, 1960), 19–25.

Henry James Wye Milley, "The Eustace Diamonds and the Moonstone," *SP* 36 (October 1939): 651–63.

A. A. Milne, "Books and Writers," *Spectator* 86 (6 April 1951): 452.

Charles Muller, "*The Moonstone*: Victorian Detective Novel," *Communique* 5, no. 1 (1980): 1–24.

Ross C. Murfin, "The Art of Representation: Collins' *The Moonstone* and Dickens Example,'" *ELH* 49 (Fall 1982): 653–72.

Ira Bruce Nadel, "Science and *The Moonstone*," *DSA* 11 (1983): 239–59.

Bill Nelson, "Evil as Illusion in the Detective Story," *Clues* 1 (Spring 1980): 9–14.

Ian Ousby, "Wilkie Collins," in *Bloodhounds of Heaven: The Detective in English Fiction from Godwin to Doyle* (Cambridge, MA: Harvard University Press, 1976), 117–28.

Audrey Peterson, "Wilkie Collins: Early Works," in *Victorian Masters of Mystery: From Wilkie Collins to Conan Doyle* (New York: Ungar, 1984), 57–66.

V. S. Prichett, "The Roots of Detection," *BinG* (New York: Harcourt, 1953), 179–84.

John R. Reed, "English Imperialism and the Unacknowledged Crime of *The Moonstone*," *Clio* 2 (June 1973): 281–90.

"Review of *The Moonstone*," in *The Art of the Mystery Story*, ed. Howard Haycraft (New York: Simon & Schuster, 1946), 379–80.

Maurice Richardson, "Introduction," in *Novels of Mystery from the Victorian Age*, eds. Maurice Richardson and U. C. Knoepflmacher (London: Pilot, 1945), vii–xvi.

Ashish Roy, "The Fabulous Imperialist Semiotic of Wilkie Collins's *The Moonstone*," *NLH* 24 (Summer 1993): 657–81.

Charles Rycroft, "The Analysis of a Detective Story," in *Imagination and Reality: Psycho-Analytic Essays, 1951–1961*, ed. Charles Rycroft (London: Hogarth and the Institute of Psycho-Analysis, 1968), 114–28.

Muriel Smith, "The Jewel Theme in *The Moonstone*," *WCSJ* 5 (1985): 11–13.

Muriel Smith, "An Unnoticed Follower of Wilkie Collins," *N&Q* 35 (September 1988): 326.

Vincent Starrett, "Introduction," *Wilkie Collins's "The Moonstone"* (New York: Heritage, 1959), vii–xvi.

Peter Wolfe, "Point of View and Characterization in Wilkie Collins's *The Moonstone*," *Forum* 4 (Summer 1965): 27–29.

My Lady's Money

Audrey Peterson, "Wilkie Collins: Early Works," in *Victorian Masters of Mystery: From Wilkie Collins to Conan Doyle* (New York: Ungar, 1984), 67–68.

The New Magdalen

R. V. Andrew, *Wilkie Collins: A Critical Survey of His Prose Fiction with a Bibliography* (New York: Garland, 1979), 236–41.

"No Lady's Money"

R. V. Andrew, *Wilkie Collins: A Critical Survey of His Prose Fiction with a Bibliography* (New York: Garland, 1979), 266–68.

No Name

R. V. Andrew, *Wilkie Collins: A Critical Survey of His Prose Fiction with a Bibliography* (New York: Garland, 1979), 164–87.

Virginia Blain, "The Naming of *No Name*," *WCSJ* 4 (1984): 25–29.

Deirdre David, "Rewriting the Male Plot in Wilkie Collins's *No Name*: Captain Wragge Orders an Omelette and Mrs. Wragge Goes into Custody," in *Out of Bounds: Male Writers and Gender(ed) Criticism*, ed. Laura Claridge and Elizabeth Langland (Amherst: University of Massachusetts Press, 1990), 186–96.

Melynda Huskey, "*No Name*: Embodying the Sensation Heroine," *VN* 82 (Fall 1992): 5–13.

Audrey Peterson, "Wilkie Collins: Early Works," in *Victorian Masters of Mystery: From Wilkie Collins to Conan Doyle* (New York: Ungar, 1984), 50–57.

Valerie Purton, "Dickens and Collins: The Rape of the Sentimental Heroine," *Ariel* 16 (January 1985): 77–89.

Geoffrey Tillotson, "Wilkie Collins's *No Name*," in *Criticism and the Nineteenth Century* (New York: Barnes & Noble, 1951), 231–34.

"An Old Maid's Husband"

R. V. Andrew, *Wilkie Collin:. A Critical Survey of His Prose Fiction with a Bibliography* (New York: Garland, 1979), 304–05.

"The Parson's Scruple"

Audrey Peterson, "Wilkie Collins: Early Works," in *Victorian Masters of Mystery: From Wilkie Collins to Conan Doyle* (New York: Ungar, 1984), 34.

"Percy and the Prophet"

R. V. Andrew, *Wilkie Collins: A Critical Survey of His Prose Fiction with a Bibliography* (New York: Garland, 1979), 264–65.

“The Plot in Private Life”

Audrey Peterson, “Wilkie Collins: Early Works,” in *Victorian Masters of Mystery: From Wilkie Collins to Conan Doyle* (New York: Ungar, 1984), 38–39.

Poor Miss Finch

R. V. Andrew, *Wilkie Collins: A Critical Survey of His Prose Fiction with a Bibliography* (New York: Garland, 1979), 231–36.

A Rogue's Life

Robert Ashley, “*A Rogue's Life*: Who Ever Heard of Frank Softly?” *WCSJ* 6 (1986): 15–18.

“Royal Love”

R. V. Andrew, *Wilkie Collins: A Critical Survey of His Prose Fiction with a Bibliography* (New York: Garland, 1979), 299–300.

“A Shocking Story”

R. V. Andrew, *Wilkie Collins: A Critical Survey of His Prose Fiction with a Bibliography* (New York: Garland, 1979), 272.

“Sister Rose”

Audrey Peterson, “Wilkie Collins: Early Works,” in *Victorian Masters of Mystery: From Wilkie Collins to Conan Doyle* (New York: Ungar, 1984), 31–32

“A Stolen Letter”

Audrey Peterson, “Wilkie Collins: Early Works,” in *Victorian Masters of Mystery: From Wilkie Collins to Conan Doyle* (New York: Ungar, 1984), 30–31.

“A Terribly Strange Bed”

Nick Rance, “‘A Terribly Strange Bed’: Self-Subverting Gothic,” *WCSJ* 7 (1987): 5–12.

COLLINS, WILLIAM WILKIE, *The Two Destinies*

Audrey Peterson, "Wilkie Collins: Early Works," in *Victorian Masters of Mystery: From Wilkie Collins to Conan Doyle* (New York: Ugar, 1984), 29–30.

Graeme Watson, "A Rather Strange Proustian," *AJFS* 18 (January–April 1981): 35–38.

The Two Destinies

R. V. Andrew, *Wilkie Collins: A Critical Survey of His Prose Fiction with a Bibliography* (New York: Garland, 1979), 261–63.

"Who Killed Zebedee"

R. V. Andrew, *Wilkie Collins: A Critical Survey of His Prose Fiction with a Bibliography* (New York: Garland, 1979), 281–84.

The Woman in White

R. V. Andrew, *Wilkie Collins: A Critical Survey of His Prose Fiction with a Bibliography* (New York: Garland, 1979), 126–65.

Stephen Bernstein, "Reading Blackwater Park: Gothicism, Narrative, and Ideology in *The Woman in White*," *SNNTS* 25 (Fall 1993): 291–305.

Ann Cvetkovich, "Ghostlier Determinations: The Economy of Sensation and *The Woman in White*," *Novel* 23 (Fall 1989): 24–43.

J. D. Coates, "Techniques of Terror in *The Woman in White*," *DUJ* 73 (June 1981): 177–89.

Cyndy Hendershot, "A Sensation Novel's Appropriation of the Terror-Gothic: Wilkie Collins' *The Woman in White*," *Clues* 13 (Fall–Winter 1992): 127–33.

Clyde K. Hyder, "Wilkie Collins and *The Woman in White*," *PMLA* 54 (March 1939): 297–303.

U. C. Knoepflmacher, "The Counterworld of Victorian Fiction and *The Woman in White*," in *The Worlds of Victorian Fiction*, ed. Jerome H. Buckley (Cambridge, MA: Harvard University Press, 1975), 353, 360–69.

Laurie Langbauer, "Women in White, Men in Feminism," *YJC* 2 (Spring 1989): 219–43.

Barbara Fass Leavy, "Wilkie Collins' Cinderella: The History of Psychology and *The Woman in White*," *DSA* 10 (1982): 91–141.

Jonathan Loesberg, "The Ideology of Narrative Form in Sensation Fiction," *Representations* 13 (Winter 1986): 115–38.

Gloria-Jean Masciarotte, "The Madonna with Child, and Another Child, and Still Another Child . . .: Sensationalism and the Dysfunction of Emotions," *Discourse* 14 (Winter 1991–92): 88–125.

Jerome Meckier, "Wilkie Collins's *The Woman in White*: Providence Against the Evils of Propriety," *JBritS* 22 (Fall 1982): 104–26.

D. A. Miller, "Cage aux Folles: Sensation and Gender in Wilkie Collins's *The Woman in White*," in *The Nineteenth-Century British Novel*, ed. Jeremy Hawthorn (Baltimore: Arnold, 1986), 95–124.

D. A. Miller, "Cage aux folles: Sensation and Gender in Wilkie Collins's *The Woman in White*," in *Speaking of Gender*, ed. Elaine Showalter (New York: Routledge, 1989), 187–215.

Pamela Perkins and Mary Donaghy, "A Man's Resolution: Narrative Strategies in Wilkie Collins' *The Woman in White*," *SNNTS* 22 (Winter 1990): 392–402.

Audrey Peterson, "Wilkie Collins: Early Works," in *Victorian Masters of Mystery: From Wilkie Collins to Conan Doyle* (New York: Ungar, 1984), 39–50.

Vincent Starrett, "Introduction," *The Woman in White* (New York: Heritage, 1964), v–xii.

Harvey Peter Sucksmith, "Introduction," *The Woman in White* (New York: Oxford University Press, 1975), vii–xxii.

Julian Symons, "Introduction," *The Woman in White* (Harmondsworth: Penguin, 1974), 7–21.

Jenny Bourne Taylor, "Psychology and Sensation: The Narrative of Moral Management in *The Woman in White*," *CrSur* 2, no. 1 (1990): 49–56.

"The Yellow Mask"

Audrey Peterson, "Wilkie Collins: Early Works," in *Victorian Masters of Mystery: From Wilkie Collins to Conan Doyle* (New York: Ungar, 1984), 31.

"Your Money or Your Life"

R. V. Andrew, *Wilkie Collins: A Critical Survey of His Prose Fiction with a Bibliography* (New York: Garland, 1979), 284–85.

COMPTON-BURNETT, IVY

A Family and a Fortune

Mary Jane Hurst, "Speech Acts in Ivy Compton-Burnett's *A Family and a Fortune*," *Lang&S* 20 (Fall 1987): 342–58.

Men and Wives

Jurgen Manthey, "Komodie des kommunikativen Handelns: Zu Ivy Compton-Burnetts Roman *Manner und Frauen*," *Merkur* 41 (November 1987): 994–97

Pastors and Masters

A. W. Bellringer, "I. Compton-Burnett's *Pastors and Masters*: A 1920's Experiment," *ES* 72 (June 1991): 246–55.

CONRAD, JOSEPH (JÓZEF TEODOR KONRAD KORZENIOWSKI)

Almayer's Folly

Alan Heywood Kenny, "Almayer and the Upas Tree," *Conradian* 8 (Summer 1983): 12–13.

Claude Maisonnat, "*Almayer's Folly*: Ou, la question de la voix," *RANAM* 15 (1982): 21–38.

Claude Maisonnat, "Discursive Deception and the Quest for Meaning in *Almayer's Folly*," in *Conrad's Literary Career*, ed. Keith Carabine, Owen Knowles, and Wieslaw Krajka (Lublin: Maria Curie-Skldowska University Press, 1992), 3–20

Claude Maisonnat, "La Question de la langue dans *Almayer's Folly* de Joseph Conrad," *ÉA* 43 (July–September 1990): 270–83.

Ruth Nadelhaft, "Women as Moral and Political Alternatives in Conrad's Early Novels," in *Joseph Conrad*, ed. Harold Bloom (New York: Chelsea House, 1986), 151–56.

Sanford Pinsker, "Conrad's Curious 'Natives': Fatalistic Machiavellians/Cannibals with Restraint," *Conradiana* 14, no. 3 (1982): 199–204.

Allan H. Simmons, "Ambiguity as Meaning: The Subversion of Suspense in *Almayer's Folly*," *Conradian* 14 (December 1989): 1–18.

Cedric Watts, "The Covert Plot of *Almayer's Folly*: A Structural Discovery," *Conradiana* 15, no. 3 (1983): 227–30.

"Amy Foster"

Robert Andreach, "The Two Narrators of 'Amy Foster,'" *SSF* 2 (Spring 1965): 262–69.

Keith Carrabine, "'Irreconcilable Differences': England as an Undiscovered Country' in Conrad's 'Amy Foster'; 1876–1918," in *The Ends of the Earth*, ed. Simon Gatrell (London: Ashfield, 1992), 187–204.

Gail Fraser, "Conrad's Revisions to 'Amy Foster,'" *Conradiana* 20, no. 3 (1988): 181–93.

Wieslaw Krajka, "The Dialogue of Cultures in Joseph Conrad's 'Amy Foster,'" *NewComp* 9 (Spring 1990): 149–57.

Claude Maisonnat, "Exile, Betrayal and the Foreclosure of the Name–of–the–Father in 'Amy Foster,'" *EConr* 18 (1992): 103–24.

The Arrow of Gold

Daphna Erdinast-Vulcan, "Conrad's Double-Edged Arrow," *Conradiana* 20, no. 3 (1988): 215–28.

"The Black Mate"

Keith Carabine, "'The Black Mate': June–July 1886; January 1908," *Conradian* 13 (December 1988): 128–48.

Dale Kramer, "Maturity of Conrad's First Tale," *SSF* 20 (Winter 1983): 45–49.

"Certain Steamship"

J. H. Stape, "Conrad's 'Certain Steamship': The Background of 'Tradition,'" *Conradiana* 16, no. 3 (1984): 236–39.

Chance

Gail Fraser, "Mediating between the Sexes: Conrad's *Chance*," *RES* 43 (February 1992): 81–88.

Adam Gillon, "*Under Western Eyes*, *Chance*, and *Victory*," in *Joseph Conrad*, ed. Harold Bloom (New York: Chelsea House, 1986), 139–42.

Julie M. Johnson, "The Damsel and Her Knights: The Goddess and the Grail in Conrad's *Chance*," *Conradiana* 13, no. 3 (1981): 221–28.

Robert Siegle, "The Two Texts of *Chance*," *Conradiana* 16, no. 2 (1984): 83–101.

Jerome Zuckerman, "Contrapuntal Structure in Conrad's *Chance*," *MFS* 10 (1964): 49–54.

"The Crime of Partition"

J. H. Stape, "'The Crime of Partition': Conrad's Sources," *Conradiana* 15, no. 3 (1983): 219–26.

"The Duel"

J. H. Stape, "Conrad's 'The Duel': A Reconsideration," *Conradian* 11 (May 1986): 42–46.

"The End of the Tether"

François Lombard, "Rhétorique et symbole dans *The End of the Tether*, de Joseph Conrad," in *Rhétorique et communication* (Paris: Didier, 1979), 183–90.

François Lombard, "Joseph Conrad et la mer dans *The End of the Tether*," *CVE* 23 (April 1986): 147–55.

J. H. Stape, "Conrad's 'Unreal City': Singapore in *The End of the Tether*," in *Conrad's Cities: Essays for Hans van Marle*, ed. Gene M. Moore (Amsterdam: Rodopi, 1992), 85–96.

"Falk"

Walter E. Anderson, "'Falk': Conrad's Tale of Evolution," *SSF* 25 (Spring 1988): 101–8.

Redmond O'Hanlon, "Knife, 'Falk' and Sexual Selection," *EIC* 31 (April 1981): 127–41.

"Heart of Darkness"

P. K. Saha, "Conrad's 'Heart of Darkness,'" *Expl* 46 (Winter 1988): 21.

Heart of Darkness

Walter E. Anderson, "*Heart of Darkness*: The Sublime Spectacle," *UTQ* 57 (Spring 1988): 404–21.

Eiko Araki, "The Tiresias Consciousness," *SELit* 59 Eng. no. (1983): 33–48.

Radwa Ashour, "Significant Incongruities in Conrad's *Heart of Darkness*," *Neohelicon* 10, no. 2 (1983): 183–201.

John Batchelor, "*Heart of Darkness*, Source of Light," *RES* 43 (May 1992): 227–42.

Donald R. Benson, "The Crisis of Space: Ether, Atmosphere, and the Solidarity of Men and Nature in *Heart of Darkness*" in *Beyond the Two Cultures: Essays on Science, Technology, and Literature*, ed. Joseph W. Slade and Judith Yaross Lee (Ames: Iowa State University Press, 1990), 161–75.

Marjorie Berger, "Telling Darkness," *ELT* 25, no. 4 (1982): 199–210.

Susan L. Blake, "Racism and the Classics: Teaching *Heart of Darkness*," *CLAJ* 25 (June 1982): 396–404.

Ted Boyle, "Marlow's Choice in *Heart of Darkness*," in *The Modernists: Studies in a Literary Phenomenon: Essays in Honor of Harry T. Moore*, ed. Lawrence B. Gamache and Ian S. MacNiven (Rutherford, NJ: Fairleigh Dickinson University Press, 1987), 92–102.

Graham Bradshaw, "Mythos, Ethos, and the Heart of Conrad's Darkness," *ES* 72 (April 1991): 160–72.

Remi Brague, "Joseph Conrad et la dialectique des Lumières: Le Mal dans Coeur des ténèbres," *EP* 1 (January–March 1990): 21–36.

Patrick Brantlinger, "*Heart of Darkness*: Anti–Imperialism, Racism, or Impressionism?" *Criticism* 27 (Fall 1985): 363–85.

Peter Brooks, "An Unreadable Report: Conrad's *Heart of Darkness*," in *Joseph Conrad's "Heart of Darkness,"* ed. Harold Bloom (New York: Chelsea House, 1987), 105–27.

Robert Burden, "Conrad's *Heart of Darkness*: The Critique of Imperialism and the Post-Colonial Reader," *EConr* 18 (1992): 63–83.

Roland E. Bush, "Tragic Versus Comic Vision: Joseph Conrad's *Heart of Darkness* and Camara Laye's *Le Regard Du Roi*," *CLAJ* 34 (September 1990): 81–93.

George Cheatham, "The Absence of God in *Heart of Darkness*," *SNNTS* 18 (Fall 1986): 304–13.

CONRAD, JOSEPH, *Heart of Darkness*

Andrea Church, "Conrad's *Heart of Darkness*," *Expl* 45 (Winter 1987): 35–37.

Michael Clark, "Conrad's *Heart of Darkness*," *Expl* 39 (Spring 1981): 47–48.

Thomas R. Cleary and Terry G. Sherwood, "Women in Conrad's Ironical Epic: Virgil, Dante, and *Heart of Darkness*," *Conradiana* 16, no. 3 (1984): 183–94.

C. B. Cox, "*Heart of Darkness*: A Choice of Nightmares?" in *Joseph Conrad's "Heart of Darkness,"* ed. Harold Bloom (New York: Chelsea House, 1987), 29–43.

Barbara DeMille, "An Inquiry into Some Points of Seamanship: Narration as Preservation in *Heart of Darkness*," *Conradiana* 18, no. 2 (1986): 94–104.

Thomas Dilworth, "Listeners and Lies in *Heart of Darkness*," *RES* 38 (November 1987): 510–22.

Joseph Dobrinsky, "From Whisper to Voice: Marlow's 'Accursed Inheritance' in *Heart of Darkness*," *CVE* 16 (October 1982): 77–104.

Arturo Echavarria, "La confluencia de las aguas: La geografia como configuracion del tiempo en Los pasos perdidos de Carpentier y *Heart of Darkness* de Conrad," *NRFH* 35, no. 2 (1987): 531–41.

Samir Elbarbary, "*Heart of Darkness* and Late-Victorian Fascination with the Primitive and the Double," *TCL* 39 (Spring 1993): 113–26.

James Ellis, "Kurtz's Voice: The Intended as 'The Horror,'" *ELT* 19 (1976): 105–10.

Aaron Fogel, "Forceful Overhearing," in *Joseph Conrad's "Heart of Darkness,"* ed. Harold Bloom (New York: Chelsea House, 1987), 129–38.

Anthony Fothergill, "The Poetics of Particulars: Pronouns, Punctuation and Ideology in *Heart of Darkness*," in *Conrad's Literary Career*, ed. Keith Carabine, Owen Knowles, and Wieslaw Krajka (Lublin: Maria Curie-Skldowska University Press, 1992), 57–73.

David Galef, "On the Margin: the Peripheral Characters in Conrad's *Heart of Darkness*," *JML* 17 (Summer 1990): 117–38.

Francisco Anton Garcia, "*Heart of Darkness*: Una Reinterpretacion," *RCEI* 6 (April 1983): 27–45.

Barbara Gates, "Kurtz's Moral Insanity," *VIJ* 11 (1982–1983): 53–59.

J. P. Geise and L. A. Lange, "Deliberate Belief and Digging Holes: Joseph Conrad and the Problem of Restraint," *Interpretation* 16 (Winter 1988–1989): 193–209.

R. A. Gekoski, "*Heart of Darkness*," in *Joseph Conrad's "Heart of Darkness,"* ed. Harold Bloom (New York: Chelsea House, 1987), 57–75.

Ian Glenn, "Conrad's *Heart of Darkness*: A Sociological Reading," *L&H* 13 (Autumn 1987): 238–56.

Mary Golanka, "Mr. Kurtz, I Presume? Livingstone and Stanley as Prototypes of Kurtz and Marlow," *SNNTS* 17 (Summer 1985): 194–202.

Kenneth L. Golden, "Joseph Conrad's Mr. Kurtz and Jungian Enantiodromia," *Interpretations* 13 (Fall 1981): 31–38.

Jennifer Gribble, "The Fogginess of *Heart of Darkness*," *SSEng* 11 (1985–1986): 83–94.

Albert J. Guerard, "The Journey Within," in *Joseph Conrad's "Heart of Darkness,"* ed. Harold Bloom (New York: Chelsea House, 1987), 5–16.

James Guetti, "*Heart of Darkness*: The Failure of Imagination," in *Joseph Conrad's "Heart of Darkness,"* ed. Harold Bloom (New York: Chelsea House, 1987), 17–28.

Deborah Guth, "Conrad's *Heart of Darkness* as Creation Myth," *JES* 17 (September 1987): 155–66.

Duncan Hadfield, "Under the Volcano and Conrad's *Heart of Darkness*," *MLNew* 17–18 (Fall–Spring 1985–1986): 104–16.

Frantz Leander Hansen, "Conrads Clairobscur," *KuKl* 17, no. 3 (1990): 48–74.

Wilson Harris, "The Frontier on Which *Heart of Darkness* Stands," *RAL* 12 (Spring 1981): 86–93.

Hunt Hawkins, "Conrad and Congolese Exploitation," *Conradiana* 13, no. 2 (1981): 94–100.

Hunt Hawkins, "Conrad's Critique of Imperialism in *Heart of Darkness*," *PMLA* 94 (1979): 286–99.

Hunt Hawkins, "The Issue of Racism in *Heart of Darkness*," *Conradiana* 14, no. 3 (1982): 163–71.

Eloise Knapp Hay, "Cities Like Whited Sepulchres," in *Conrad's Cities: Essays for Hans van Marle*, ed. Gene M. Moore (Amsterdam: Rodopi, 1992), 125–37.

CONRAD, JOSEPH, *Heart of Darkness*

Bruce Henricksen, "The *Heart of Darkness* and the Gnostic Myth," *Mosaic* 11 (Summer 1978): 35–44. Reprinted in *Joseph Conrad's "Heart of Darkness,"* ed. Harold Bloom (New York: Chelsea House, 1987), 45–55.

Douglas Hewitt, "*Heart of Darkness* and Some 'Old and Unpleasant Reports,'" *RES* 38 (August 1987): 374–76.

David Leon Hidgon, "Conrad in Outer Space," *Conradian* 12 (May 1987): 74–77.

Edward H. Hoeppner, "*Heart of Darkness*: An Archeology of the Lie," *Conradiana* 20 (Summer 1988): 137–46.

Brigitta Holm, "Hjarta av morker: Om Orfeus, Eurydike och Joseph Conrads Roman," *BLM* 58 (November 1989): 281–92.

Reynold Humphries, "The Discourse of Colonialism: Its Meaning and Relevance for Conrad's Fiction," *Conradiana* 21 (Summer 1989): 107–33.

Peter Hyland, "The Little Woman in the *Heart of Darkness*," *Conradiana* 20 (Spring 1988): 3–11.

Phil Joffe, "Africa and Joseph Conrad's *Heart of Darkness*: The 'Bloody Racist' (?) as Demystifier of Imperialism," in *Conrad's Literary Career*, ed. Keith Carabine, Owen Knowles, and Wieslaw Krajka (Lublin: Maria Curie–Skldowska University Press, 1992), 75–90.

Frederick R. Karl, "Introduction to the Danse Macabre: Conrad's *Heart of Darkness*: Case Study in Contemporary Criticism," in *Joseph Conrad: "Heart of Darkness,"* ed. Ross C. Murfin (New York: St. Martin's, 1989), 123–36.

Donald M. Kartiganer, "The Divided Protagonist: Reading as Repetition and Discovery," *TSLL* 30 (Summer 1988): 151–78.

Mahmoud K. Kharbutli, "The Treatment of Women in *Heart of Darkness*," *DQR* 17, no. 4 (1987): 237–48.

Wolfgang Klooss, "Die Metaphorik des Kolonialismus: Joseph Conrad's *Heart of Darkness* als Problem literarischer Wirklichkeitsauffassung um die Jahrhundertwende," *GRM* 31, no. 1 (1981): 74–92.

Owen Knowles, "'Who's Afraid of Arthur Schopenhauer?': A New Context for Conrad's *Heart of Darkness*," *NCF* 49 (June 1994): 75–106.

Arnold Krupat, "Antonymy, Language, and Value in Conrad's *Heart of Darkness*," *MissR* 3 (Fall 1979): 63–85.

Olof Lagercrantz, "Den inre stationen: Ur Fard med Morkets hjarta: En studie i Joseph Conrads roman," *BLM* 56 (February 1987): 82–89.

Henry J. Laskowsky, "*Heart of Darkness*: A Primer for the Holocaust," *VQR* 58 (Winter 1982): 93–110.

Michael Levenson, "On the Edge of the *Heart of Darkness*," *SSF* 23 (Spring 1986): 153–57.

Michael Levenson, "The Value of Facts in the *Heart of Darkness*," *NCF* 40 (December 1985): 261–80.

Gerald Levin, "Victorian Kurtz," *JLM* 7 (1979): 433–40.

Peter Lindenbaum, "Hulks with One and Two Anchors: The Frame, Geographical Detail, and Ritual Process in *Heart of Darkness*," *MFS* 30 (Winter 1984): 703–10.

Ian Littlewood, "Conrad's *Heart of Darkness*: From the Monstrous to the Commonplace," in *Le Monstrueux dans la littérature et la pensée anglaises*, ed. Nadia J. Rigaud (Aix-en-Provence: Publications Université de Provence, 1985), 159–70.

Emilia Lodigiani, "Conrad e il mito: Un 'mistero' grottesco nel cuore dell'Africa," *Acme* 38 (September–December 1985): 115–36.

Thomas Loe, "*Heart of Darkness* and the Form of the Short Novel," *Conradiana* 20 (Spring 1988): 33–44.

Bette London, "Reading Race and Gender in Conrad's Dark Continent," *Criticism* 31 (Summer 1989): 235–52.

John A. McClure, "Late Imperial Romance," *Raritan* 11 (Spring 1991): 111–30.

Juliet McLauchlan, "Conrad's Heart of Emptiness: 'The Planter of Malata,'" *Conradiana* 18, no. 3 (1986): 180–92.

Juliet McLauchlan, "The 'Value' and 'Significance' of *Heart of Darkness*," *Conradiana* 15, no. 1 (1983): 3–21.

Nancy McNeal, "Joseph Conrad's Voice in *Heart of Darkness*: A Jungian Approach," *JEP* 1 (June 1979): 1–12.

Fred Madden, "Marlow and the Double Horror of *Heart of Darkness*," *MidWQ* 27 (Summer 1986): 504–17.

Miriam B. Mandel, "Significant Patterns of Color and Animal Imagery in Conrad's *Heart of Darkness*," *Neophil* 73 (April 1989): 305–19.

Darrel Mansell, "Trying to Bring Literature Back Alive: The Ivory in Joseph Conrad's *Heart of Darkness*," *Criticism* 33 (Spring 1991): 205–35.

W. R. Martin, "Conrad's Management of Narration," *Conradiana* 14, no. 1 (1982): 53–56.

Jerome Meckier, "The Truth about Marlow," *SSF* 19 (Fall 1982): 373–79.

Perry Meisel, "Decenter *Heart of Darkness*," *MLS* 8, no. 3 (1978): 20–28.

David Melnick, "The Morality of Conrad's Imagination: *Heart of Darkness* and *Nostromo*," in *Joseph Conrad*, ed. Harold Bloom (New York: Chelsea House, 1986), 117–20, 125–28.

Fred L. Milne, "Marlow's Lie and the Intended: Civilization as the Lie in *Heart of Darkness*," *ArQ* 44 (Spring 1988): 106–12.

L. J. Morrissey, "The Tellers in *Heart of Darkness*: Conrad's Chinese Boxes," *Conradiana* 13, no. 2 (1981): 141–48.

Susan J. Navarette, "The Anatomy of Failure in Joseph Conrad's *Heart of Darkness*," *TSLL* 35 (Fall 1993): 279–317.

Renn G. Neilson, "Conrad's *Heart of Darkness*," *Expl* 45 (Spring 1987): 41–42.

Walter J. Ong, S. J., "Truth in Conrad's Darkness," *Mosaic* 11, no. 1 (1977): 151–63.

Josiane Paccaud, "Speech and the Nature of Communication in Conrad's *Heart of Darkness*," *Conradian* 8 (Winter 1983): 41–48.

Patrick Parrinder, "*Heart of Darkness*: Geography as Apocalypse," in *Fin de Siecle/Fin du Globe: Fears and Fantasies of the Late Nineteenth Century*, ed. John Stokes (New York: St. Martin's, 1992), 85–101.

Vincent Pecora, "*Heart of Darkness* and the Phenomenology of Voice," *ELH* 52 (Winter 1985): 993–1015.

Sanford Pinsker, "Conrad's Curious 'Natives': Fatalistic Machiavellians/Cannibals with Restraint," *Conradiana* 14, no. 3 (1982): 199–204.

Charles Eric Reeves, "A Voice of Unrest: Conrad's Rhetoric of the Unspeakable," *TSLL* 27 (Fall 1985): 284–310.

Stanley Renner, "Kurtz, Christ, and the Darkness of *Heart of Darkness*," *Renascence* 28 (1976): 95–104.

J. A. Richardson, "James S. Jameson and *Heart of Darkness*," *N&Q* 40 (March 1993): 64–66.

Adena Rosmarin, "Darkening the Reader: Reader-Response Criticism and *Heart of Darkness*: Case Study in Contemporary Criticism," in *Joseph Conrad: "Heart of Darkness,"* ed. Ross C. Murfin (New York: St. Martin's, 1989), 148–69.

Richard Ruppel, "*Heart of Darkness* and the Popular Exotic Stories of the 1890s," *Conradiana* 21 (Winter 1989): 3–14.

Dieter Saalmann, "Effective Affinities: Christa Wolf's Storfall and Joseph Conrad's *Heart of Darkness*: The Curse of the 'Blind Spot,'" *CLS* 29 (Summer 1992): 238–57.

P. K. Saha, "Conrad's *Heart of Darkness*," *Expl* 46 (Winter 1988): 21–22.

P. K. Saha, "Conrad's *Heart of Darkness*," *Expl* 50 (Spring 1992): 155–59.

Larry Marshall Sams, "*Heart of Darkness*: The Meaning around the Nutshell," *IFR* 5 (1978): 129–33.

Peter Schotten, "Of Madness and Evil," *ModA* 33 (Summer 1991): 346–55.

Nina Schwartz, "The Ideologies of Romanticism in *Heart of Darkness*," *NOR* 13 (Spring 1986): 84–95.

Valerie F. Sedlak, "'A World of Their Own': Narrative Distortion and Fictive Exemplification in the Portrayal of Women in *Heart of Darkness*," *CLAJ* 32 (June 1989): 443–65.

Michael Seidel, "Defoe in Conrad's Africa," *Conradiana* 17, no. 2 (1985): 145–46.

Sandhya Shetty, "*Heart of Darkness*: Out of Africa Some New Thing Rarely Comes," *JLM* 15 (Spring 1989): 461–74.

John P. Sisk, "The Doubtful Pleasures of the Higher Agape," *SoR* 24 (Winter 1988): 134–44.

Johanna M. Smith, "'Too Beautiful Altogether': Patriarchal Ideology in Heart of Darkness; Case Study in Contemporary Criticism," in *Joseph Conrad: "Heart of Darkness,"* ed. Ross C. Murfin (New York: St. Martin's, 1989), 179–95.

Barry Stampfl, "Conrad's *Heart of Darkness*," *Expl* 49 (Spring 1991): 162–65.

Barry Stampfl, "Marlow's Rhetoric of (Self-)Deception in *Heart of Darkness*," *MFS* 37 (Summer 1991): 183–96.

Henry Staten, "Conrad's Mortal Word," *CritI* 12 (Summer 1986): 720–40.

Joan E. Steiner, "Modern Pharisees and False Apostles: Ironic New Testament Parallels in Conrad's *Heart of Darkness*," *NCF* 37 (June 1982): 75–96.

Nelly Stephane, "La Morale au coeur des ténèbres," *Europe* 70 (June–July 1992): 62–68.

Garrett Steward, "Lying as Dying in *Heart of Darkness*," *PMLA* 95 (1980): 319–31.

Nina Pelikan Straus, "The Exclusion of the Intended from Secret Sharing in Conrad's *Heart of Darkness*," *Novel* 20 (Winter 1987): 123–37.

CONRAD, JOSEPH, *Heart of Darkness*

John Tessitore, "Freud, Conrad, and *Heart of Darkness*," in *Joseph Conrad's "Heart of Darkness,"* ed. Harold Bloom (New York: Chelsea House, 1987), 91–103.

Brook Thomas, "Preserving and Keeping Order by Killing Time in *Heart of Darkness*: Case Study in Contemporary Criticism," in *Joseph Conrad: "Heart of Darkness,"* ed. Ross C. Murfin (New York: St. Martin's, 1989), 237–55.

Edwin Thumbo, "Some Plain Reading: Marlow's Lie in *Heart of Darkness*," *LCrit* 16, no. 3 (1981): 12–22.

Eric Trethewey, "Language, Experience, and Selfhood in Conrad's *Heart of Darkness*," *SHR* 22 (Spring 1988): 101–11.

Mark Troy, "A Wedge-Shaped Core of Darkness," in *Papers on Language and Literature: Presented to Alvar Ellegard and Erik Frykman*, ed. Sven Backman and Goran Kjellmer (Goteborg: ACTA Universite Gothoburgensis, 1985), 362–72.

Jan Verleun, "Conrad's *Heart of Darkness*: Marlow and the Intended," *Neophil* 67 (October 1983): 623–39.

Jan Verleun, "Marlow and the Harlequin," *Conradiana* 13, no. 3 (1981): 195–220.

Andre Viola, "Conrad et les autres: Les Écueils du langage dans Coeur des ténèbres," *Cycnos* 2 (Winter 1985–1986): 91–101.

Gunter Walch, "Literarisches Funktionsverstandnis und Werkstruktur bei Joseph Conrad," *ZAA* 28, no. 3 (1980): 226–36.

Ian Watt, "Conrad's *Heart of Darkness* and the Critics," *NDQ* 57 (Summer 1989): 5–15.

Ian Watt, "*Heart of Darkness* and Nineteenth-Century Thought," in *Joseph Conrad's "Heart of Darkness,"* ed. Harold Bloom (New York: Chelsea House, 1987), 77–89.

Ian Watt, "Impressionism and Symbolism in *Heart of Darkness*," in *Joseph Conrad*, ed. Harold Bloom (New York: Chelsea House, 1986), 83–99.

Ian Watt, "Marlow, Henry James, and *Heart of Darkness*," *NCF* 33 (June 1978): 159–74.

Roger West, "Conrad's *Heart of Darkness*," *Expl* 50 (Summer 1992): 222–23.

Michael Wilding, "*Heart of Darkness*," *SSEng* 10 (1984–1985): 85–102.

G. Peter Winnington, "Conrad and Cutcliffe Hyne: A New Source for *Heart of Darkness*," *Conradiana* 16, no. 3 (1984): 163–82.

G. Young, "Kurtz as a Narcissistic Megalomaniac in J. Conrad's *Heart of Darkness*," in *Working Papers in Linguistics and Literature*, ed. A. Kakouriotis and R. Parkin–Gounelas (Thessaloniki: Aristotle University, 1989), 253.

William Zak, "Conrad, F. R. Leavis, and Whitehead: *Heart of Darkness* and Organic Holism," *Conradiana* 4 (Winter 1972): 5–24.

Weiwen Zhang, "A Tentative Comment on Conrad's *Heart of Darkness*," *FLitS* 27 (March 1985): 39–45.

"The Informer"

Allan Hepburn, "Collectors in Conrad's 'The Informer,'" *SSF* 29 (Winter 1992): 103–12.

"Il Conde"

Gaetano D'Elia, "Sulle Rive del Golfo Amato: 'Il Conde' di Conrad," *Belfagor* 38 (31 July 1983): 395–414.

Daniel R. Schwartz, "The Self-Deceiving Narrator of Conrad's 'Il Conde,'" *SSF* 6 (Spring 1969): 187–93.

"Karain"

Michele Drouart, "'Gunrunning,' Theatre, and Cultural Attitude in Conrad's 'Karain,'" *SPAN* 33 (May 1992): 134–49.

Christopher Gogwilt, "The Charm of Empire Joseph Conrad's 'Karain: A Memory,'" *Mosaic* 24 (Winter 1991): 77–91.

"The Lagoon"

Ronald J. Nelson, "Conrad's 'The Lagoon,'" *Expl* 40 (Fall 1981): 39–41.

Donna Richardson, "Art of Darkness: Imagery in Conrad's 'The Lagoon,'" *SSF* 27 (Spring 1990): 247–55.

Lord Jim

Steven Barza, "Bonds of Empathy: The Widening Audience in *Lord Jim*," *MidWQ* 25 (Winter 1984): 220–32.

CONRAD, JOSEPH, *Lord Jim*

Todd K. Bender, "Definition of Style in Joseph Conrad," in *Proceedings of the International Conference on Literary and Linguistic Computing*, ed. Zvi Malachi (Tel Aviv: Tel Aviv University Faculty of Humanities, n.d.), 325–58.

Ernest Bevan, Jr., "Marlow and Jim: The Reconstructed Past," *Conradiana* 15, no. 3 (1983): 191–202.

Daniel Born, "Echoes of Kipling in Marlow's 'Privileged Man'?" *Conradiana* 24, no. 2 (1992): 100–15.

Daniel Cottom, "*Lord Jim*: Destruction through Time," *CentR* 27 (Winter 1983): 10–29.

Randall Craig, "Swapping Yarns: The Oral Mode of *Lord Jim*," *Conradiana* 13, no. 3 (1981): 181–93.

Arnold E. Davidson, "The Abdication of *Lord Jim*," *Conradiana* 13, no. 1 (1981): 19–34.

Joseph Dobrinsky, "Notes sur les Symbolismes de la Mer dans *Lord Jim*," *CVE* 23 (April 1986): 133–46.

Peter Ebersole, "Analysis of Conrad's Lord Jim's Life Meaning," *PsycholRep* 72 (February 1993): 31–34.

Nina Galen, "Stephen Crane as a Source for Conrad's Jim," *NCF* 38 (June 1983): 78–96.

Reynold Humphries, "'Wrecks, Maritime and Oedipal': The Patna, Jim and Gentleman Brown," *EConr* 18 (1992): 85–102.

Tony E. Jackson, "Turning into Modernism: *Lord Jim* and the Alteration of the Narrative Subject," *L&P* 39 (Winter 1993): 65–85.

V. M. K. Kelleher, "A Third Voice: The Dialectical Structure of *Lord Jim*," *UES* 25 (May 1987): 24–28.

Hans Lippe, "*Lord Jim*: Some Geographic Observations," *Conradian* 10 (November 1985): 135–38.

Hans Lippe, "Reconsidering the Patna Inquiry in *Lord Jim*," *Conradian* 15 (June 1990): 59–69.

Jakob Lothe, "Narrators and Characters in *Lord Jim*," in *Conrad's Literary Career*, ed. Keith Carabine, Owen Knowles, and Wieslaw Krajka (Lublin: Maria Curie-Skldowska University Press, 1992), 113–25.

Hans van Marle and Pierre Lefranc, "Ashore and Afloat: New Perspectives on Topography and Geography in *Lord Jim*," *Conradiana* 20 (Summer 1988): 109–35.

J. Hillis Miller, "*Lord Jim*: Repetition as Subversion of Organic Form," in *Joseph Conrad*, ed. Harold Bloom (New York: Chelsea House, 1986), 165–79.

Giles Mitchell, "Lord Jim's Death Fear, Narcissism, and Suicide," *Conradiana* 18, no. 3 (1986): 163–79.

Padmini Mongia, "Narrative Strategy and Imperialism in Conrad's *Lord Jim*," *SNNTS* 24 (Summer 1992): 173–86.

John Murawski, "Conrad's *Lord Jim*," *Expl* 48 (Summer 1990): 266–68.

Jean Paumen, "Une Lecture de *Lord Jim*," in *Philosophie et littérature*, ed. Gilbert Hottois (Brussels: Université de Bruxelles, 1985), 23–53.

Georges Piroue, "*Lord Jim* sous l'ombre du nuage," *Europe* 70 (June–July 1992): 37–42.

Martin Price, "The Limits of Irony: *Lord Jim* and *Nostromo*" in *Joseph Conrad*, ed. Harold Bloom (New York: Chelsea House, 1986), 181–90.

Ralph W. Rader, "*Lord Jim* and the Formal Development of the English Novel," in *Reading Narrative: Form, Ethics, Ideology*, ed. James Phelan (Columbus: Ohio State University Press, 1989), 220–35.

Christopher Ricks, "The Pink Toads in *Lord Jim*," *EIC* 31 (April 1981): 142–44.

Daniel W. Ross, "*Lord Jim* and the Saving Illusion," *Conradian* 20 (Spring 1988): 45–69.

Tracy Seeley, "Conrad's Modernist Romance: *Lord Jim*," *ELH* 59 (Summer 1992): 495–511.

Werner Senn, "Conradian Intertext in the Fiction of Randolph Stow: Tourmaline and *Lord Jim*," *Conradian* 15 (June 1990): 12–29.

Linda M. Shires, "The 'Privileged' Reader and Narrative Methodology in *Lord Jim*," *Conradiana* 17, no. 1 (1985): 19–30.

Carole Slade, "La Chute and *Lord Jim*," *RomN* 24 (Winter 1983): 95–99.

Michael Sprinker, "Fiction and Ideology: *Lord Jim* and the Problem of Literary History," in *Reading Narrative: Form, Ethics, Ideology*, ed. James Phelan (Columbus: Ohio State University Press, 1989), 236–49.

Rosa Shand Turner, "The Redemptive Act of Narrating: Reclaiming the Trace of *Lord Jim*," *BSUF* 21, no. 4 (1980): 53–57.

Joanne Wood, "*Lord Jim* and the Consequences of Kantian Autonomy," *P&L* 11 (April 1987): 57–74.

"The Mirror of the Sea"

Robert Foulke, "The Elegiac Structure of Conrad's 'The Mirror of the Sea,'" in *Literature and Lore of the Sea*, ed. Patricia Ann Carlson (Amsterdam: Rodopi, 1986), 154–60

Elaine L. Kleiner, "Conrad's 'The Mirror of the Sea,'" *Expl* 42 (Spring 1984): 33–35.

The Nigger of the Narcissus

Jeremy Hawthorn, "The Incoherences of *The Nigger of the Narcissus*," *Conradian* 11 (November 1986): 98–115.

Bruce Henricksen, "The Construction of the Narrator in *The Nigger of the Narcissus*," *PMLA* 103 (October 1988): 783–95.

Reynold Humphries, "How to Change the Subject: Narrative, Reader and Ideology in *The Nigger of the Narcissus*," *RANAM* 15 (1982): 39–50.

Arthur Kay, "Joseph Conrad's Use of Key Names in *The Nigger of the Narcissus*," *Names* 29 (June 1981): 178–80.

Jakob Lothe, "Variations of Narrative in *The Nigger of the Narcissus*," *Conradiana* 16, no. 3 (1984): 215–24.

David Manicom, "True Lies/False Truths: Narrative Perspective and the Control of Ambiguity in *The Nigger of the Narcissus*," *Conradiana* 18, no. 2 (1986): 105–18.

Brigita Shilina, "Some Aspects of the Artistic Structure in Joseph Conrad's *The Nigger of the Narcissus*," *WZUR* 33, no. 7 (1984): 28–31.

J. H. Stape, "'History' and Fiction: Composite Sources and *The Nigger of the Narcissus*," *Conradian* 10 (May 1985): 47–49.

Ian Watt, "Conrad Criticism and *The Nigger of the Narcissus*," in *Joseph Conrad*, ed. Harold Bloom (New York: Chelsea House, 1986), 9–28.

Cedric Watts, "'Solidarity' in *The Nigger of the Narcissus*: A Defence of Ian Watt," *Conradiana* 20 (Summer 1988): 165–66.

Todd G. Willy, "The Conquest of the Commodore: Conrad's Rigging of *The Nigger* for the Henley Regatta," *Conradiana* 17, no. 3 (1985): 163–82.

Nostromo

Paul B. Armstrong, "Conrad's Contradictory Politics: The Ontology of Society in *Nostromo*," *TCL* 31 (Spring 1985): 1–21.

Jacques Berthoud, "The Modernization of Sulaco," in *Conrad's Cities: Essays for Hans van Marle*, ed. Gene M. Moore (Amsterdam: Rodopi, 1992), 139–57.

Ted Billy, "A Curious Case of Influence: *Nostromo* and Alien(s)," *Conradiana* 21 (Summer 1989): 147–57.

Harold Bloom, "Introduction," in *Joseph Conrad's "Nostromo,"* ed. Harold Bloom (New York: Chelsea House, 1987), 1–6.

Ernest C. Bufkin, "Conrad, Grand Opera, and *Nostromo*," *NCF* 30 (June 1975): 206–14.

Peter L. Caracciolo, "Ancient Egypt, Old Sarmatia, and the New World Empires: Archaeology and Folklore in *Nostromo*," *EConr* 18 (1992): 41–62.

Richard C. Carpenter, "The Geography of Costaguana, or Where Is Sulaco?" *JLM* 5 (1976): 321–26.

Mark Conroy, "Lost in Azuera: The Fate of Sulaco and Conrad's *Nostromo*," *GlyphT* 8 (1981): 148–69.

Roger L. Cox, "Conrad's Nostromo as Boatswain," *MLN* 74 (March 1959): 303–06.

Mario Curreli, "Aspetti della tecnica narrativa nel *Nostromo* di Conrad," *StIL* 2 (1979): 153–85

Mario Curreli, "Fictional Suicide and Personal Rescue: The Case-History of *Nostromo*," *StIL* 4 (1981): 97–121.

Mario Curreli, "Gli schiavi dell'argento del *Nostromo* di Conrad," *StIL* 3 (1980): 61–86.

Pamela H. Demory, "*Nostromo*: Making History," *TSLL* 35 (Fall 1993): 316–31.

Hugh Epstein, "Trusting in Words of Some Sort: Aspects of the Use of Language in *Nostromo*," *Conradian* 12 (May 1987): 17–31.

Aaron Fogel, "Silver and Silence: Dependent Currencies in *Nostromo*," in *Joseph Conrad*, ed. Harold Bloom (New York: Chelsea House, 1986), 205–27. Reprinted in *Joseph Conrad's "Nostromo,"* ed. Harold Bloom (New York: Chelsea House, 1987), 103–25.

Eloise Knapp Hay, "*Nostromo* and the Ideologies of Revolution," *EConr* 18 (1992): 25–39.

Gareth Jenkins, "Conrad's *Nostromo* and History," *L&H* 6 (Summer 1977): 138–78.

Karen Klein, "The Feminine Predicament in Conrad's *Nostromo*," in *Brandeis Essays in Literature*, ed. John Hazel Smith (Waltham, MA: Department of English & American Literature, Brandeis University Press, 1983), 101–16.

CONRAD, JOSEPH, *Nostromo*

Michael C. Kotzin, "A Fairy-Tale Pattern in Conrad's *Nostromo*," *ModBL* 2 (1977): 200–14.

Stephen K. Land, "Four Views of the Hero," in *Joseph Conrad's "Nostromo,"* ed. Harold Bloom (New York: Chelsea House, 1987), 81–102.

T. McAlindon, "*Nostromo*: Conrad's Organicist Philosophy of History," *Mosaic* 15 (September 1982): 27–41. Reprinted in *Joseph Conrad's "Nostromo,"* ed. Harold Bloom (New York: Chelsea House, 1987), 57–68.

David Melnick, "The Morality of Conrad's Imagination: *Heart of Darkness* and *Nostromo*," in *Joseph Conrad*, ed. Harold Bloom (New York: Chelsea House, 1986), 120–24.

Joyce Carol Oates, "'The Immense Indifference of Things': The Tragedy of Conrad's *Nostromo*," *Novel* 9 (Fall 1975): 5–22.

Leonard Orr, "The Semiotics of Description in Conrad's *Nostromo*," in *Critical Essays on Joseph Conrad*, ed. Ted Billy (Boston: G. K. Hall, 1987), 113–28.

Martin Price, "The Limits of Irony: *Lord Jim* and *Nostromo*" in *Joseph Conrad*, ed. Harold Bloom (New York: Chelsea House, 1986), 190–204. Reprinted in *Joseph Conrad's "Nostromo,"* ed. Harold Bloom (New York: Chelsea House, 1987), 69–79.

Martin Ray, "Conrad and Decoud," *PolR* 29, no. 3 (1984): 53–64.

Andrew Roberts, "*Nostromo* and History: Remarkable Individuality and Historical Inevitability," *Conradian* 12 (May 1987): 4–16

Kiernan Ryan, "Revelation and Repression in Conrad's *Nostromo*," in *The Uses of Fiction: Essays on the Modern Novel in Honour of Arnold Kettle*, ed. Douglas Jefferson and Graham Martin (Milton Keynes, England: Open University Press, 1982), 69–82. Reprinted in *Joseph Conrad's "Nostromo,"* ed. Harold Bloom (New York: Chelsea House, 1987), 43–55.

Daniel R. Schwarz, "Conrad's Quarrel with Politics: The Disputed Family in *Nostromo*," *UTQ* 47 (Fall 1977): 37–55.

Sabah A. Shakury, "The Rise of Neo-Colonialism in Conrad's *Nostromo*," *PURB* 18 (October 1987): 3–22.

J. H. Stape, "Conrad's Classic Line: A Note on Sources for *Nostromo*," *Conradiana* 21, no. 1 (1989): 59–61.

I. S. Talib, "Conrad's *Nostromo* and the Reader's Understanding of Anachronic Narratives," *JNT* 20 (Winter 1990): 1–21.

Leona Toker, "A Nabokovian Character in Conrad's *Nostromo*," *RLC* 59 (January–March 1985): 15–29.

Dorothy Van Ghent, "Guardianship of the Treasure: *Nostromo*," in *Joseph Conrad's "Nostromo,"* ed. Harold Bloom (New York: Chelsea House, 1987), 223–37.

Nicholas Visser, "Crowds and Politics in *Nostromo*," *Mosaic* 23 (Spring 1990): 1–15.

David Allen Ward, "'An Ideal Conception': Conrad's *Nostromo* and the Problem of Identity," *ELT* 35, no. 3 (1992): 288–98.

Robert Penn Warren, "'The Great Mirage': Conrad and *Nostromo*," in *Selected Essays* (New York: Vintage, 1966), 31–58. Reprinted in *Joseph Conrad's "Nostromo,"* ed. Harold Bloom (New York: Chelsea House, 1987), 7–21.

An Outcast of the Islands

Heliena Krenn, "The Shadow of a Successful Man: Conrad's Hollow Man in *An Outcast of the Islands*," *FJS* 16 (1983): 33–48.

Ruth Nadelhaft, "Women as Moral and Political Alternatives in Conrad's Early Novels," in *Joseph Conrad*, ed. Harold Bloom (New York: Chelsea House, 1986), 156–63.

An Outpost of Progress

Martha Fodaski Black, "Irony in Joseph Conrad's *An Outpost of Progress*," *Conradian* 10 (November 1985): 132–34.

V. J. Emmett Jr., "*An Outpost of Progress*: Conrad, Zola, and Hobbes," *TexasR* 2 (Fall 1981): 5–9.

Gail Fraser, "Conrad's Irony: *An Outpost of Progress* and *The Secret Agent*," *Conradian* 11 (November 1986): 155–59.

Teresa Gibert, "*An Outpost of Progress*: La ironia imperial de Joseph Conrad," *Epos* 4 (1988): 469–82.

"The Planter of Malta"

Stanislaw Modrzewski, "The Consciousness of Cultural Models in 'The Planter of Malata,'" *Conradian* 13 (December 1988): 171–82.

"The Return"

Paul Kirschner, "Wilde's Shadow in Conrad's 'The Return,'" *N&Q* 40 (December 1993): 495–96.

CONRAD, JOSEPH, "The Rover"

Dale Kramer, "Conrad's Experiments with Language and Narrative in 'The Return,'" *SSF* 25 (Winter 1988): 1–11.

"The Rover"

Camille R. La Bossiere, "Pop Conrad and Child's Play: A Context for 'The Rover,'" *DR* 71 (Spring 1991): 5–24.

Claudine Lesage, "A Trip to Giens: An Imaginary Journey into Fiction," in *Conrad's Cities: Essays for Hans van Marle*, ed. Gene M. Moore (Amsterdam: Rodopi, 1992), 255–68.

Secret Agent

Jonathan Arac, "Romanticism, the Self, and the City: *The Secret Agent* in Literary History," *boundaryII* 9 (Fall 1980): 75–90.

Jack I. Biles, "Winnie Verloc: Agent of Death," *Conradiana* 13, no. 2 (1981): 101–8.

Lawrence Casler, "Images of Conrad's Father in *Secret Agent*," *IFR* 16 (Winter 1989): 39–41.

Fausto Ciompi, "I segni della morte, dell'ironia e del nuovo in *Secret Agent* di Joseph Conrad," *StIL* 7 (1984): 207–43.

Mark Conroy, "The Panoptical City: The Structure of Suspicion in *Secret Agent*," *Conradiana* 15, no. 3 (1983): 203–17.

Arnold E. Davidson, "The Sign of Conrad's *Secret Agent*," *CollL* 8 (Winter 1981): 33–41.

Gaetano D'Elia, "L'anarchico e l'acrobata in *Secret Agent*," in *Studi inglesi: Raccolta di saggi e ricerche*, ed. Agostino Lombardo (Bari: Adriatica, 1978), 211–43.

Paul Dolan, "The Plot in *Secret Agent*," *Conradiana* 16, no. 3 (1984): 225–35.

James T. English, "Scientist, Moralist, Humorist: A Bergsonian Reading of *Secret Agent*," *Conradiana* 19 (Summer 1987): 139–56.

Hugh Epstein, "A Pier-Glass in the Cavern: The Construction of London in *Secret Agent*," in *Conrad's Cities: Essays for Hans van Marle*, ed. Gene M. Moore (Amsterdam: Rodopi, 1992), 175–96.

Avrom Fleishman, "The Landscape of Hysteria in *Secret Agent*," in *Conrad Revisited: Essays for the Eighties*, ed. Ross C. Murfin (University: University of Alabama Press, 1985), 89–105.

James Hansford, "Reference and Figuration in *Secret Agent*," *Conradian* 10 (November 1985): 116–31.

George Held, "Conrad's Oxymoronic Imagination in *Secret Agent*," *Conradiana* 17, no. 2 (1985): 93–107.

Norman Holland, "Style and Character: *Secret Agent*," in *Joseph Conrad*, ed. Harold Bloom (New York: Chelsea House, 1986), 53–62.

Margarete Holubetz, "'Bad World for Poor People': Social Criticism in *Secret Agent*," *ArAA* 7, no. 1 (1982): 13–22.

William C. Houze, "*Secret Agent* from Novel to Play: The Implications of Conrad's Handling of Structure," *Conradiana* 13, no. 2 (1981): 109–22.

Tracey Jordan, "Conrad's *Secret Agent*: Kids, Chaos, and Cannibalism," *Conradiana* 19 (Spring 1987): 61–83.

Owen Knowles, "Fishy Business in Conrad's *Secret Agent*," *N&Q* 37 (December 1990): 433–34.

Peter Krahe, "Zur Psychologie des Erzahlers in Joseph Conrad's *Secret Agent*," *GRM* 31, no. 2 (1981): 156–72.

A. Robert Lee, "Cracked Bells and Really Intelligent Detonators: Dislocation in Conrad's *Secret Agent*," in *Spy Thrillers: From Buchan to le Carrè*, ed. Clive Bloom (New York: St. Martins, 1990), 12–27.

Graham McMaster, "Some Other Secrets in *Secret Agent*," *L&H* 12 (Autumn 1986): 229–42.

Dorothea Meihuizen, "Exploitation in *Secret Agent*," *CRUX* 19 (February 1985): 15–19.

Sylvère Monod, "Some Dickensian Echoes in Joseph Conrad's *Secret Agent*," in *Litterae et Lingua: In Honorem Premislavi Mroczkowski*, ed. Jan Nowakowski (Wroclaw: Polish Akademe Nauk, 1984), 153–60.

Zdzislaw Najder, "Joseph Conrad's *Secret Agent* or the Melodrama of Reality," *NYLF* 7 (1980): 159–66.

David W. Pitre, "Loss of Temper, Loss of Art: Narrative Inconsistency in Conrad's *Secret Agent*," *MidWQ* 26 (Autumn 1984): 95–109.

Martin Ray, "Conrad, Nordau, and Other Degenerates: The Psychology of *Secret Agent*," *Conradiana* 16, no. 2 (1984): 125–40.

Martin Ray, "Conrad's Invisible Professor," *Conradian* 11 (May 1986): 35–41.

Martin Ray, "The Landscape of *The Secret Agent*," in *Conrad's Cities: Essays for Hans van Marle*, ed. Gene M. Moore (Amsterdam: Rodopi, 1992), 197–206.

Robert Schultz, "*Secret Agent*: Conrad's 'Perfect Detonator,'" *MidWQ* 22 (Spring 1981): 218–29.

Teruaki Shimomoto, "*Secret Agent*—The Deficiency of Efficiency," *Lang&C* 22 (1992): 11–24.

Peter Stine, "Conrad's Secrets in *Secret Agent*," *Conradiana* 13, no. 2 (1981): 123–40.

E. W. M. Tillyard, "*Secret Agent* Reconsidered," *EIC* 11 (October 1961): 309–18.

Sue Tyley, "Time and Space in *Secret Agent*," *Conradian* 8 (Summer 1983): 32–38.

Hans Van Marle, "Of Lodgings, Landladies, and *Secret Agent*," *Conradian* 12 (November 1987): 138–49.

Jetty de Vries, "Stevie and Recent Criticism," *Conradiana* 17, no. 2 (1985): 119–30.

Daphna Erdinast Vulcan, "'Sudden holes in space and time': Conrad's Anarchist Aesthetics in *Secret Agent*," in *Conrad's Cities: Essays for Hans van Marle*, ed. Gene M. Moore (Amsterdam: Rodopi, 1992), 207–21.

The Secret Sharer

Sherlyn Abdoo, "Ego Formation and the Land/Sea Metaphor in Conrad's *Secret Sharer*," in *Poetics of the Elements in the Human Condition: The Sea: From Elemental Stirrings to Symbolic Inspiration, Language, and Life-Significance in Literary Interpretation and Theory*, ed. Anna–Teresa Tymieniecka (Dordrecht: Reidel, 1985), 67–76.

Louise K. Barnett, "'The Whole Circle of the Horizon': The Circumscribed Universe of *The Secret Sharer*," *StHum* 8 (March 1981): 5–9.

Michael Cohen, "Sailing through *The Secret Sharer*: The End of Conrad's Story," *MSE* 10 (Fall 1985): 102–09.

Mary Ann Dazey, "Shared Secret or Secret Sharing in Joseph Conrad's *The Secret Sharer*," *Conradiana* 18, no. 3 (1986): 201–03.

Joseph Dobrinsky, "The Two Lives of Joseph Conrad in *The Secret Sharer*," *CVE* 21 (April 1985): 33–49.

Roland Garrett, "Leadership and Knowledge in Joseph Conrad's *The Secret Sharer*," *L&FAR* 1 (July 1981): 1–9.

James Hansford, "Closing, Enclosure and Passage in *The Secret Sharer*," *Conradian* 15 (June 1990): 30–55.

Owen Knowles, "A Note on the Naming of Archbold in *The Secret Sharer*," *Conradian* 9 (April 1984): 25–27.

Jakob Lothe, "Conrad's Narrative in *The Secret Sharer*," *Conradian* 8 (Winter 1983): 22–29.

Jacky Martin, "A 'Topological' Re-Reading of *The Secret Sharer*," *RANAM* 15 (1982): 51–66.

Fred L. Milne, "Conrad's *The Secret Sharer*," *Expl* 44 (Spring 1986): 38–39.

Michael Murphy, "*The Secret Sharer*: Conrad's Turn of the Winch," *Conradiana* 18, no. 3 (1986): 193–200.

Josiane Paccaud, "Under the Other's Eyes: Conrad's *The Secret Sharer*," *Conradian* 12 (May 1987): 59–73.

Steve Ressler, "Conrad's *The Secret Sharer*: Affirmation of Action," *Conradiana* 16, no. 3 (1984): 195–214.

Pedro Santana, "*The Secret Sharer*: Una narracion triunfal y melacolica," in *Actas de las I jornadas de lengua y literatura inglesa y norteamericana* (Logrono: Publications del Colegio Universite de Logrono, 1990), 75–82.

Joan E. Steiner, "*The Secret Sharer*: Complexities of the Doubling Relationship," in *Joseph Conrad*, ed. Harold Bloom (New York: Chelsea House, 1986), 101–12.

Mark Troy, "'. . . Of No Particular Significance Except to Myself': Narrative Posture in Conrad's *The Secret Sharer*," *SN* 56, no. 1 (1984): 35–50.

James F. White, "The Third Theme in *The Secret Sharer*," *Conradiana* 21, no. 1 (1989): 37–46.

"The Shadow-Line"

Jeremy Hawthorn, "Conrad and Lintels: A Note on the Text of 'The Shadow-Line,'" *Conradian* 12 (November 1987): 178–79.

Robert Penn Warren, "Story and Idea in Conrad's 'The Shadow-Line,'" *CritQ* 2 (Summer 1960): 133–48.

"The Sisters"

Zdzislaw Najder and Henry Sikorski, "Conrad's 'The Sisters': A Grandiose Failure," *PolR* 29, no. 3 (1984): 25–34.

"A Smile of Fortune"

Daphna Erdinast-Vulcan, "'A Smile of Fortune' and the Romantic Paradox," *Conradian* 15 (June 1990): 1–11.

Cedric Watts, "The Narrative Enigma of Conrad's 'A Smile of Fortune,'" *Conradiana* 17, no. 2 (1985): 131–36.

Suspense

Ugo Mursia, "Notes on Conrad's Italian Novel: *Suspense*," trans. Mario Curreli in *Conrad's Cities: Essays for Hans van Marle*, ed. Gene M. Moore (Amsterdam: Rodopi, 1992), 269–81.

Tetsuo Yoshida, "Joseph Conrad's Napoleonic Fiction," *SELL* 33 (January 1983): 66–92.

"The Tale"

Gaetano D'Elia, "Let Us Make Tales, Not Love: Conrad's 'The Tale,'" *Conradian* 12 (May 1987): 50–58.

"Typhoon"

Joseph Kolupke, "Elephants, Empires, and Blind Men: A Reading of the Figurative Language in Conrad's 'Typhoon,'" *Conradiana* 20 (Spring 1988): 71–85.

Alain Chareyre Mejean, "L'Annulation par la tempete," *Europe* 70 (June–July 1992): 99–110.

Under Western Eyes

Keith Carabine, "Construing 'Secrets' and 'Diabolism' in *Under Western Eyes*: A Response to Frank Kermode," in *Conrad's Literary Career*, ed. Keith Carabine, Owen Knowles, and Wieslaw Krajka (Lublin: Maria Curie–Skldowska University Press, 1992), 187–210.

Thomas J. Cousineau, "The Ambiguity of Razumov's Confession in *Under Western Eyes*," *Conradiana* 18, no. 1 (1986): 27–40.

Adam Gillon, "Conrad's Satirical Stance in *Under Western Eyes*: Two Strange Bedfellows—Prince Roman and Peter Ivanovitch," *Conradiana* 18, no. 2 (1986): 119–28.

Adam Gillon, "*Under Western Eyes*, *Chance*, and *Victory*," in *Joseph Conrad*, ed. Harold Bloom (New York: Chelsea House, 1986), 131–39.

Allan Hepburn, "Above Suspicion: Audience and Deception in *Under Western Eyes*," *SNNTS* 24 (Fall 1992): 282–97.

Yves Hervouet, "Conrad's Debt to French Authors in *Under Western Eyes*," *Conradiana* 14, no. 2 (1982): 113–25.

David Leon Higdon, "Conrad, *Under Western Eyes*, and the Mysteries of Revision," *RES* 39 (May 1988): 231–54.

David Leon Higdon, "'The End Is the Devil': The Conclusions to Conrad's *Under Western Eyes*," *SNNTS* 19 (Summer 1987): 187–96.

David Leon Higdon and Robert F. Sheard, "Conrad's 'Unkindest Cut': The Canceled Scenes in *Under Western Eyes*," *Conradiana* 19 (Autumn 1987): 167–81.

Reynold Humphries, "The Representation of Politics and History in *Under Western Eyes*," *Conradiana* 20 (Spring 1988): 13–32.

Paul Kirschner, "Revolution, Feminism, and Conrad's Western 'I,'" *Conradian* 10 (May 1985): 4–25.

Paul Kirschner, "Topodialogic Narrative in *Under Western Eyes* and the Rasoumoffs of *La Petite Russie*," in *Conrad's Cities: Essays for Hans van Marle*, ed. Gene M. Moore (Amsterdam: Rodopi, 1992), 223–54.

Owen Knowles, "*Under Western Eyes*: A Note on Two Sources," *Conradian* 10 (November 1985): 154–61.

George Levine, "The Novel as Scientific Discourse: The Example of Conrad," *Novel* 21 (Winter–Spring 1988): 220–27. Reprinted in *Why the Novel Matters: A Postmodern Perplex*, ed. Mark Spilka and Caroline McCracken–Flesher (Bloomington: Indiana University Press, 1990), 238–45.

Deborah Lovely, "'But I Digress': The Teacher in *Under Western Eyes*," *WVUPP* 36 (1990): 30–37.

Anne Luyat, "Betrayal and Revelation: The Double Source of Tragedy in *Under Western Eyes*," *EConr* 18 (1992): 153–62.

Gene M. Moore, "Chronotopes and Voices in *Under Western Eyes*," *Conradiana* 18, no. 1 (1986): 9–25.

Gene M. Moore, "Conrad's *Under Western Eyes*," *Expl* 49 (Winter 1991): 103–05.

Josiane Paccaud, "Hypertextuality in Joseph Conrad's *Under Western Eyes*," *CVE* 29 (April 1989): 73–82.

Josiane Paccaud, "Mr. Razumov's 'Disease of Perversity': Of Artistic Lies in Conrad's *Under Western Eyes*," *FMLS* 24 (April 1988): 111–25.

Josiane Paccaud, "The Name–of–the–Father in Conrad's *Under Western Eyes*," *Conradiana* 18, no. 3 (1986): 204–18.

Josiane Paccaud, "Trahison, parole et vérité dans *Under Western Eyes* de Joseph Conrad: L'Oeuvre comme métaphore de l'avenement d'une sujet de la parole," *ÉA* 39 (October–December 1986): 400–10.

Dwight H. Purdy, "Peace That Passeth Understanding': The Professor's English Bible in *Under Western Eyes*," *Conradiana* 13, no. 2 (1981): 83–93.

Penn R. Szittya, "Metafiction: The Double Narration in *Under Western Eyes*," *ELH* 48 (Winter 1981): 817–40.

Victory

Janet Butler, "Conrad's *Victory*: Another Look at Axel Heyst," *L&P* 31, no. 3 (1981): 33–46.

Soo-Young Chon, "Conrad's *Victory*: An Elusive Allegory," *JELL* 35 (Spring 1989): 83–101.

Terry Collits, "Imperialism, Marxism, Conrad: A Political Reading of *Victory*," *TexP* 3 (Winter 1989): 303–22.

H. M. Daleski, "*Victory* and Patterns of Self-Division," in *Conrad Revisited: Essays for the Eighties*, ed. Ross C. Murfin (University: University of Alabama Press, 1985), 107–23.

Donald A. Dike, "The Tempest of Axel Heyst," *NCF* 17 (June 1962): 96–113.

Frederick R. Karl, "*Victory*: Its Origin and Development," *Conradiana* 15, no. 1 (1983): 23–51.

John F. Lewis, "Plain Mr. Jones and the Final Chapter of *Victory*," *Conradian* 9 (April 1984): 4–14.

R. W. B. Lewis, "The Current of Conrad's *Victory*," in *Joseph Conrad*, ed. Harold Bloom (New York: Chelsea House, 1986), 63–81.

Dorothea Meihuizen, "The Matriculant's Encounter with *Victory*," *CRUX* 18 (April 1984): 11–17.

Rose Orlich, "The Psychology of Love in Conrad's *Victory*," *Conradiana* 13, no. 1 (1981): 65–72.

Dwight H. Purdy, "Paul and The Pardoner in Conrad's *Victory*," *TSLL* 23 (Summer 1981): 197–213.

Narain Prasad Shukla, "The Theme of Escape in Conrad's *Victory*," *JDECU* 17, no. 1 (1981–82): 99–106.

Andre Viola, "La Symbolique du Mandala dans *Victory* de Joseph Conrad," *CVE* 16 (October 1982): 105–24.

Cedric Watts, "Reflections on *Victory*," *Conradiana* 15, no. 1 (1983): 73–79.

Tetsuo Yoshida, "On Captain Davidson," *SELL, Chuo-ku* 43 (February 1993): 49–58.

"Youth"

James Hansford, "Reflection and Self-Consumption in 'Youth,'" *Conradian* 12 (November 1987): 150–65.

Heliena Krenn, "Joseph Conrad's Polish Heritage of Hopefulness in 'Youth,'" *FJS* 15 (1982): 37–53.

Stanley Renner, "'Youth' and the Sinking Ship of Faith: Conrad's Miniature Nineteenth-Century Epic," *BSUF* 28 (Winter 1987): 57–73.

John Rothfork, "The Buddha Center in Conrad's 'Youth,'" *LE&W* 21 (January–December 1977): 121–29.

John Howard Wills, "A Neglected Masterpiece: Conrad's 'Youth,'" *TSLL* 4 (1963): 591–601.

CRISPIN, EDMUND (ROBERT BRUCE MONTGOMERY)

Buried for Pleasure

Mary Jean DeMarr, "Edmund Crispin," in *Twelve Englishmen of Mystery*, ed. Earl F. Bargainnier (Bowling Green, OH: Popular, 1984), 271–72.

The Case of the Gilded Fly

Mary Jean DeMarr, "Edmund Crispin," in *Twelve Englishmen of Mystery*, ed. Earl F. Bargainnier (Bowling Green, OH: Popular, 1984), 258–59, 264, 267

Frequent Hearses

Mary Jean DeMarr, "Edmund Crispin," in *Twelve Englishmen of Mystery*, ed. Earl F. Bargainnier (Bowling Green, OH: Popular, 1984), 265, 267, 269–70

The Glimpses of the Moon

Mary Jean DeMarr, "Edmund Crispin," in *Twelve Englishmen of Mystery,* ed. Earl F. Bargainnier (Bowling Green, OH: Popular, 1984), 255–57, 264, 268–69, 270–71

Holy Disorders

Mary Jean DeMarr, "Edmund Crispin," in *Twelve Englishmen of Mystery*, ed. Earl F. Bargainnier (Bowling Green, OH: Popular, 1984), 266–67

The Long Divorce

Mary Jean DeMarr, "Edmund Crispin," in *Twelve Englishmen of Mystery*, ed. Earl F. Bargainnier (Bowling Green, OH: Popular, 1984), 272–75.

The Moving Toyshop

Mary Jean DeMarr, "Edmund Crispin," in *Twelve Englishmen of Mystery*, ed. Earl F. Bargainnier (Bowling Green, OH: Popular, 1984), 260–64.

William A. S. Sargeant, "Obsequies about Oxford: The Investigations and Eccentricities of Gervase Fen," *ArmD* 14 (Summer 1981): 196–209.

CRONIN, ARCHIBALD JOSEPH

The Citadel

Edwin Francis Edgett, "A Novel by a Doctor about a Doctor," *BET* (11 September 1937): 1–2.

Alfred Kazin, "Dr. Cronin's Novel about the Medical Profession," *NYTBR* (12 September 1937): 6.

Mabel S. Ulrich, M.D., "Doctor's Dilemma," *SatR* 16 (11 September 1937): 5–6.

Grand Canary

Percy Hutchinson, "Dr. Cronin's Gift for Narrative," *NYTBR* (14 May 1933): 6.

The Green Years

William DuBois, "Scenes from a Frustrated Boyhood," *NYTBR* (12 November 1944): 3.

Hatter's Castle

Percy Hutchinson, "*Hatter's Castle*: A Novel in the Great Tradition," *NYTBR* (19 July 1931): 4.

The Keys of the Kingdom

Katherine Woods, "A Modern Saint Is the Hero of A. J. Cronin's Novel," *NYTBR* (20 July 1941): 5.

A Song of Sixpence

Robert Burns, "Another Key, Another Kingdom," *Critic* 23 (October 1964): 74–75.

The Spanish Gardener

Lon Tinkle, "Serpent in Eden," *SatR* 33 (9 September 1950): 20–21.

The Stars Look Down

Percy Hutchinson, "The Clash of Capital and Labor," *NYTBR* (22 September 1935): 1, 23.

Mary Ross, "Life Before the War," *SG* 24 (November 1935): 557–58.

Three Loves

Percy Hutchinson, "Dr. Cronin's Portrait of a Stubborn Woman," *NYTBR* (3 April 1933): 6.

DEIGHTON, LEN

Funeral in Berlin

Edward Lense, "They've Taken Away Your Name: Identity and Illusion in Len Deighton's Early Novels," *Clues* 12 (Fall–Winter 1991): 67–81.

The Ipcress File

Edward Lense, "They've Taken Away Your Name: Identity and Illusion in Len Deighton's Early Novels," *Clues* 12 (Fall–Winter 1991): 67–81.

London Game, Mexico Set, Berlin Match

Bernd Lenz, "*Game, Set & Match*: Konstanten und Varianten in Len Deightons geheimer Welt," *A&E* 37 (1989): 65–97.

Mamista

Peter Jukes, "*Mamista*," *NewS&S* 4 (6 September 1991): 35–36.

Yesterday's Spy

Edward Lense, "They've Taken Away Your Name: Identity and Illusion in Len Deighton's Early Novels," *Clues* 12 (Fall–Winter 1991): 67–81.

DICKENS, CHARLES

Barnaby Rudge

Jerome H. Buckley, "'Quoth the Raven': The Role of Grip in *Barnaby Rudge*," *DSA* 21 (1992): 27–35.

Alison Case, "Against Scott: The Antihistory of Dickens's *Barnaby Rudge*," *CLIO* 19 (Winter 1990): 127–45.

Robert L. Caserio, "Plot and the Point of Reversal," in *Charles Dickens*, ed. Harold Bloom (New York: Chelsea House, 1987), 161–80.

Richard J. Dunn, "In Pursuit of the Dolly Varden," *Dickensian* 74 (January 1978): 22–24.

Judith Flynn, "The Sexual Politics of *Barnaby Rudge*," *ESC* 16 (March 1990): 56–73.

Vanda Foster, "The Dolly Varden," *Dickensian* 73 (January 1977): 19–24.

Joan B. Friedberg, "Alienation and Integration in *Barnaby Rudge*," *DSN* 11 (March 1980): 11–15.

Thelma Grove, "Barnaby Rudge: A Case Study in Autism," *Dickensian* 83 (Autumn 1987): 139–48.

Eiichi Hara, "Dickens Kanibaru: *Barnaby Rudge* Saidoku," *EigoS* 129 (1984): 470–74.

Charles Hatten, "Disciplining the Family in *Barnaby Rudge*: Dickens's Professionalization of Fiction," *Mosaic* 25 (Fall 1992): 17–34.

John P. McGowan, "Mystery and History in *Barnaby Rudge*," *DSA* 9 (1981): 33–52.

Juliet McMaster, "'Better to be Silly': From Vision to Reality in *Barnaby Rudge*," *DSA* 13 (1984): 1–17.

Patricia Marks, "Light and Dark Imagery in *Barnaby Rudge*," *DSN* 9 (September 1978): 73–76.

Kim Ian Michasiw, "*Barnaby Rudge*: The Since of the Fathers," *ELH* 56 (Fall 1989): 571–92.

Samuel F. Pickering, "Protestantism in *Barnaby Rudge*," in *The Moral Tradition in English Fiction, 1785–1850* (Hanover, NH: Dartmouth University Press, 1976), 123–48.

Thomas J. Rice, "*Barnaby Rudge*: A Vade Mecum for the Theme of Domestic Government in Dickens," *DSA* 7 (1978): 81–102. Reprinted as "The Politics of Barnaby Rudge," in *The Changing World of Charles Dickens*, ed. Robert Giddings (London: Vision, 1983; Totowa, NJ: Barnes & Noble, 1983), 51–74.

Thomas J. Rice, "Dickens, Pie and the Time Scheme of *Barnaby Rudge*," *DSN* 7 (June 1976): 34–38.

Thomas J. Rice, "The End of Dickens's Apprenticeship: Variable Focus in *Barnaby Rudge*," *NCF* 30 (September 1975): 172–84.

Brian Rosenberg, "Physical Opposition in *Barnaby Rudge*," *VN* 67 (Spring 1985): 21–22.

Natalie Schroeder, "Jack Sheppard and Barnaby Rudge: Yet More 'Humbug' from a 'Jolter Head,'" *SNNTS* 18 (Spring 1986): 27–35.

Michael Steig, "'Ten Thousand a–Year' and the Political Content of *Barnaby Rudge*," *DSN* 4 (September 1973): 67–68.

Paul Stigant and Peter Widdowson, "*Barnaby Rudge*: A Historical Novel?" *L&H* 2 (October 1975): 2–44.

Barry Westbury, "How Poe Solved the Mystery of *Barnaby Rudge*," *DSN* 5 (June 1974): 38–40.

"The Battle of Life"

Philip V. Allingham, "'The Battle of Life' (1846) and the Prologue to 'The Patrician's Daughter' (1842)," *ANQ* 3 (October 1990): 165–68.

Katherine Carolan, "'The Battle of Life': A Love Story," *Dickensian* 69 (May 1973): 105–10.

Bleak House

Doris Alexander, "Dickens and the False True Story," *Dickensian* 86 (Summer 1990): 87–92.

Doris Alexander, "The Poet in Grandfather Smallweed," *Dickensian* 80 (Summer 1984): 67–73.

Richard D. Altick, "Borrioboola-Gha, Bushmen, and Brickmakers," *Dickensian* 74 (September 1978): 157–59.

Richard D. Altick, "Harold Skimpole Revisited," in *The Life and Times of Leigh Hunt*, ed. Robert A. McCown (Iowa City: Friends of the University of Iowa Libraries, 1985), 1–15.

M[artin] A[mis], "Charles Dickens: *Bleak House*: How Awful Goodness Is," *TES* (21 September 1973): 61.

Elisabeth Sanders Arbuckle, "Dickens and Harriet Martineau: Some New Letters and a Note on *Bleak House*," *Dickensian* 81 (Autumn 1985): 157–62.

G. D. Arms, "Reassembling *Bleak House*: 'Is there three of 'em then?'" *L&P* 39 (Spring–Summer 1993): 84–96.

William Axton, "The Trouble with Esther," *MLQ* 26 (1965): 545–57.

Jean-Marie Baissus, "Dickens' Spacemanship in *Bleak House*," *CVE* 20 (October 1984): 5–18.

Nicolae Balota, "Dickens si ceata," in *Umanitati: Eseuri* (Bucharest: Eminescu, 1973), 197–99.

Marc Beckwith, "Catabasis in *Bleak House*: Bucket as Sibyl," *Dickens Quarterly* 1 (March 1984): 2–6.

Anthony M. Belmont, Jr., "Qualitative Progression and the Dual Narrative in Dickens' *Bleak House*," *PAPA* 7 (Fall 1981): 1–8.

Alice N. Benston, "The Smallweeds and Trooper George: The Autochthony Theme in *Bleak House*," *Mosaic* 21 (Fall 1988): 99–110.

Virginia Blain, "Double Vision and the Double Standard in *Bleak House*: A Feminist Perspective," *L&H* 11 (Spring 1985): 31–46. Reprinted. in *Charles Dickens's Bleak House*, ed. Harold Bloom (New York: Chelsea House, 1987), 139–56.

Trevor Blount, "Dickens and Mr. Krook's Spontaneous Combustion," *DSA* 1 (1970): 183–211.

Trevor Blount, "Dickens's Ironmaster Again," *EIC* 21 (October 1971): 429–36.

Trevor Blount, "The Documentary Symbolism of Chancery in *Bleak House*," *Dickensian* 62 (1966): 50–52, 106–11, 167–74.

Trevor Blount, "Literature and Medicine: Disease and Graveyards in Dickens's *Bleak House*," *SSHMB* 8 (September 1972): 11.

James E. Boasberg, "Chancery as Megalosaurus: Lawyers, Courts, and Society in *Bleak House*," *HSL* 21 (1989): 38–60.

Christine van Boheemen–Saaf, "'The Universe Makes an Indifferent Parent': *Bleak House* and the Victorian Family Romance," in *Interpreting Lacan*, ed. Joseph H. Smith and William Kerrigan (New Haven: Yale University Press, 1983), 225–57.

Elizabeth Bowen, "A Novelist at *Bleak House*," *Dickensian* 71 (September 1975): 159–63.

Chiara Briganti, "The Monstrous Actress: Esther Summerson's Spectral Name," *DSA* 19 (1990): 205–30.

Alan R. Burke, "The Strategy and Theme of Urban Observation in *Bleak House*," *SELit* 9 (Autumn 1969): 659–76.

Brahma Chaudhuri, "Dickens and the Critic: 1852–53," *VPR* 21 (Winter 1988): 139–44.

Brahma Chaudhuri, "Dickens and the Women of England at Strafford House," *ELN* 25 (June 1988): 54–60.

DICKENS, CHARLES, *Bleak House*

Brahma Chaudhuri, "Dickens's Serial Structure in *Bleak House*," *Dickensian* 86 (Summer 1990): 66–84.

Brahma Chaudhuri, "The Interpolated Chapter in *Bleak House*," *Dickensian* 81 (Summer 1985): 103–04.

Brahma Chaudhuri, "Leonard Skimpole in *Bleak House*," *DSN* 6 (September 1975): 75–78.

Brahma Chaudhuri, "Speculation about the Plot of *Bleak House*," *DQu* 1 (June 1984): 57.

G. K. Chesterton, "Characters in *Bleak House*," in *Bleak House*, ed. George Ford and Sylvère Monod (New York: Norton, 1977), 942–46.

Jean–Louis Chevalier, "Le Mariage d'Esther," *CVE* 20 (October 1984): 29–38.

Jean–Louis Chevalier, "La Parente dans *Bleak House*," in *Home, Sweet Home or Bleak House? Art et littérature à l'époque Victorienne*, ed. Marie–Claire Hamard (Paris: Belles Lettres, 1985), 93–116.

A. O. J. Cockshut, "Order and Madness in *Bleak House*," in *Bleak House*, ed. George Ford and Sylvère Monod (New York: Norton, 1977), 960–63.

Steven Cohan, "'They Are All Secret': The Fantasy Content of *Bleak House*," *L&P* 26 (1976): 79–91.

Philip Collins, "Charles Dickens and Rockingham Castle," *NPP* 6 (1980): 133–40.

Philip Collins, *A Critical Commentary on Dickens's "Bleak House"* (London: Macmillan, 1971), 1–80.

Philip Collins, "Some Narrative Devices in *Bleak House*," *DSA* 19 (1990): 125–46.

Claudette Kemper Columbus, "The (Un)Lettered Ensemble: What Charley Does Not Learn about Writing in *Bleak House*," *SEL* 28 (Autumn 1988): 609–23.

Raymond Conlon, "*Bleak House*'s Miss Barbary: A Psychological Miniature," *DSN* 14 (September 1983): 90–92.

Don Richard Cox, "The Birds of *Bleak House*," *DSN* 11 (March 1980): 6–11.

Patrick J. Creevy, "In Time and Out: The Tempo of Life in *Bleak House*," *DSA* 12 (1983): 63–80.

Katherine Cummings, "*Bleak House*: Remarks on a Daughter's Da," *Style* 21 (Summer 1987): 237–38.

Richard A. Currie, "Surviving Maternal Loss: Transitional Relatedness in Dickens's Esther Summerson," *DQu* 6 (June 1989): 60–66.

Martin A. Danahay, "Housekeeping and Hegemony in *Bleak House*," *SNNTS* 23 (Winter 1991): 416–31.

Paul Delany, "*Bleak House* and Doubting Castle," *DSN* 3 (December 1972): 100–06.

Peter Denman, "Krook's Death and Dickens's Authorities," *Dickensian* 82 (Autumn 1986): 130–41.

James Diedrick, "Dickens's Alter-Ego in *Bleak House*: The Importance of Lawrence Boythorn," *DSN* 9 (June 1978): 37–40.

Joseph Dobrinsky, "L'Imagination bloquée ou l'ere des Philistins dans *Bleak House*," in *Home, Sweet Home or Bleak House? Art et littérature à l'époque Victorienne*, ed. Marie–Claire Hamard (Paris: Belles Lettres, 1985), 117–29.

Richard J. Dunn, "Dickens and Mayhew Once More," *NCF* 25 (December 1970): 348–53.

John L. Dusseau, "The *Bleak House* of Charles Dickens," *SR* 92 (Fall 1984): 574–98.

Paul Eggert, "The Real Esther Summerson," *DSN* 11 (September 1980): 74–81.

Patricia R. Eldredge, "The Lost Self of Esther Summerson: A Horneyan Interpretation of *Bleak House*," *LitR* 24 (Winter 1981): 252–78. Reprinted in *Third Force Psychology and the Study of Literature*, ed. Bernard J. Paris (Rutherford, NJ: Fairleigh Dickinson University Press, 1986), 136–55.

Donald H. Ericksen, "Harold Skimpole: Dickens and the Early 'Art for Art's Sake' Movement," *JEGP* 72 (January 1973): 48–59.

Aida Farrag, "Zola, Dickens, and Spontaneous Combustion Again," *RomN* 19 (Winter 1978): 190–95.

Anthony P. Farrow, "The Cosmic Point of View in *Bleak House*," *Cithara* 13 (May 1974): 34–45.

Peter Faulkner, "The Humanity of Dickens," *Humanist* 85 (July 1970): 198–99.

Monica Feinberg, "Family Plot: The Bleak House of Victorian Romance," *VN* 76 (Fall 1989): 5–17.

John J. Fenstermaker, "Language Abuse in *Bleak House*: The First Monthly Installment," in *Victorian Literature and Society: Essays Presented to Richard D. Altick*, ed. James R. Kincaid and Albert J. Kuhn (Columbus: Ohio State University Press, 1984), 240–57.

K. J. Fielding and A. W. Brice, "*Bleak House* and the Graveyard," in *Dickens the Craftsman: Strategies of Presentation*, ed. Robert B. Partlow, Jr. (Carbondale: Southern Illinois University Press, 1970), 115–39.

Claude Fierobe, "Les Inventaires de *Bleak House*," *CVE* 20 (October 1984): 19–28.

Robert F. Fleissner, "'Ah humanity!' Dickens and Bartleby Revisited," *RsSt* 50 (June 1982): 106–09.

Robert F. Fleissner, "Charles Dickens and His China: The Architecture of *Bleak House*," *TkR* 3 (October 1972): 159–70.

George H. Ford, "The Brass Bassoon in *Bleak House*," *Dickensian* 68 (May 1972): 104.

George H. Ford, "Light in Darkness: Gas, Oil, and Tallow in Dickens's *Bleak House*," in *From Smollett to James: Studies in the Novel and Other Essays Presented to Edgar Johnson*, ed. Samuel I. Mintz, Alice Chandler, and Christopher Mulvey (Charlottesville: University Press of Virginia, 1981), 183–201.

George H. Ford, "Self-Help and the Helpless in *Bleak House*," in *From Jane Austen to Joseph Conrad*, ed. Robert C. Rathburn and Martin Steinmann, Jr. (Minneapolis: University of Minnesota, 1958), 92–105.

Lawrence Frank, "'Through a Glass Darkly': Esther Summerson and *Bleak House*," *DSA* 4 (1975): 91–112.

John P. Frazee, "The Character of Esther and the Narrative Structure of *Bleak House*," *SNNTS* 17 (Fall 1985): 227–40.

Norman Friedman, "The Shadow and the Sun: Archetypes in *Bleak House*," in *Form and Meaning in Fiction* (Athens: University of Georgia Press, 1975), 21–41, 359–79.

Stanley Friedman, "English History and the Midpoint of *Bleak House*," *Dickensian* 83 (Summer 1987): 89–92.

E. Gaskell, "More About Spontaneous Combustion," *Dickens Studies* 69 (January 1973): 25–35.

Richard T. Gaughan, "'Their Places Are a Blank': The Two Narrators in *Bleak House*," *DSA* 21 (1992): 79–96.

Joel Gold, "Mrs. Jellyby: Dickens's Inside Joke," *Dickensian* 79 (Spring 1983): 35–38.

Russell M. Goldfarb, "The East Wind as Biblical Allusion in *Bleak House*," *DSN* 12 (March 1981): 14–15.

Russell M. Goldfarb, "John Jarndyce of *Bleak House*," *SNNTS* 12 (Summer 1980): 144–52.

Marcia Renee Goodman, "'I'll Follow the Other': Tracing the (M)Other in *Bleak House*," *DSA* 19 (1990): 147–67.

Elliott B. Gose, Jr., "*Bleak House*," in *Imagination Indulged: The Irrational in the Nineteenth–Century Novel* (Montreal: McGill-Queen's University Press, 1972), 73–97.

Barbara Gottfried, "Fathers and Suitors: Narratives Of Desire in *Bleak House*," *DSA* 19 (1990): 169–203.

Jenny Graham, "Two Characters in *Bleak House*," *DQu* 6 (June 1989): 43–52.

Suzanne Graver, "Writing in a 'Womanly' Way and the Double Vision of *Bleak House*," *DQu* 4 (March 1987): 3–15.

Muriel M. Green, "The Variety of Dickens's *Bleak House*," *Library Review* 22 (Autumn 1970): 363–67.

M. E. Grenander, "The Mystery and the Moral: Point of View in Dickens's *Bleak House*," *NCF* 9 (September 1956): 301–05.

Albert J. Guerard, "*Bleak House*: Structure and Style," *SR* n.s. 5 (April 1969): 332–49.

Michael S. Gurney, "Disease as Device: The Role of Smallpox in *Bleak House*," *L&M* 9 (1990): 79–92.

Douglas Hamer, "Dickens: The Old Court of Chancery," *N&Q* n.s. 17 (September 1970): 9–20.

W. J. Harvey, "The Double Narrative of *Bleak House*," in "*Bleak House*," ed. George H. Ford and Sylvère Monod (New York: Norton, 1977), 963–70.

Christopher Herbert, "The Occult in "*Bleak House*," *Novel* 17 (Winter 1984): 101–15. Reprinted in *Charles Dickens's "Bleak House,"* ed. Harold Bloom (New York: Chelsea House, 1987), 121–38.

James Hill, "Dickens's *Bleak House*," *Expli* 47 (Spring 1989): 21–22.

Gordon D. Hirsch, "The Mysteries in *Bleak House*: A Psychoanalytic Study," *DSA* 4 (1975): 132–52.

Charles C. Hobbs, "Skinning a Dickens of a Skimpole," *TPB* 10 (July 1973): 37–38.

Shifra Hochberg, "Onomastics, Topicality, and Dickens's Use of Etymology in *Bleak House*," *Dickensian* 86 (Summer 1990): 85–86.

Bert G. Hornback, "The Other Portion of *Bleak House*," in *The Changing World of Charles Dickens*, ed. Robert Giddings (London: Vision, 1983; Totowa, NJ: Barnes & Noble, 1983), 180–95.

Graham Hough, "Language and Reality in *Bleak House*," in *Realism in European Literature*, ed. Nicolas Boyle, Martin Swales, and Richard Brinkmann (Cambridge: Cambridge University Press, 1986), 50–67.

DICKENS, CHARLES, *Bleak House*

Camilla Humphreys, "Dickens's Use of Letters in *Bleak House*," *DQu* 6 (June 1989): 53–60.

A. Abott Ikeler, "The Philanthropic Sham: Dickens' Corrective Method in *Bleak House*," *CLAJ* 24 (June 1981): 497–512.

Karen Jahn, "Fit To Survive: Christian Ethics in *Bleak House*," *SNNTS* 18 (Winter 1986): 367–80.

D. W. Jefferson, "The Artistry of *Bleak House*," *E&S* n.s. 27 (1974): 37–51.

Diane L. Jolly, "The Nature of Esther," *Dickensian* 86 (Spring 1990): 29–40.

Luther S. Juedtke, "Harold Frederic's Satanic Soulsby: Interpretation and Sources," *NCF* 30 (June 1975): 82–105.

Michael S. Kearns, "'But I Cried Very Much': Esther Summerson as Narrator," *DQu* 1 (December 1984): 121–29.

Alice VanBuren Kelly, "The Bleak Houses of *Bleak House*," *MLQ* 30 (September 1969): 386–401.

Valerie Kennedy, "*Bleak House*: More Trouble With Esther?" *JWSLIT* 1 (Autumn 1979): 330–47.

Crawford Kilian, "In Defence of Esther Summerson," *DR* 54 (Summer 1974): 318–28.

Norma G. Kobzina, "*Bleak House* Revisited: Cela's La colmena," *Hispanófila* 28 (September 1984): 57–66.

John Kucich, "Endings," in *Charles Dickens's "Bleak House,"* ed. Harold Bloom (New York: Chelsea House, 1987), 111–19.

Dominick La Capra and D. A. Miller, "Ideology and Critique in Dickens's *Bleak House*," *Representations* 6 (Spring 1984): 116–23.

Janet L. Larson, "The Battle of Biblical Books in Esther's Narrative," *NCF* 38 (September 1983): 131–60.

Janet L. Larson, "Biblical Reading in the Later Dickens: The Book of Job according to *Bleak House*," *DSA* 13 (1984): 35–83.

Diane Wolfe Levy, "Dickens's *Bleak House*," *Expl* 38 (Spring 1980): 40–42.

Thomas M. Linehan, "Parallel Lives: The Past and Self-Retribution in *Bleak House*," *SNNTS* 20 (Summer 1988): 131–50.

Luther S. Luedtke, "System and Sympathy: The Structural Dialectic of Dickens's *Bleak House*," *Lit&L* 3, no. 1 (1970): 1–14.

Kevin McLauglin, "Losing Pine's Place: Displacement and Domesticity in Dickens's *Bleak House*," *MLN* 108 (December 1993): 875–90.

Maurice L. McCullen, "Turveydrop of *Bleak House*: Basis of Dickens's Redefinition of Dandyism," *DSN* 4 (March 1973): 15–21.

Jane A. McCusker, "The Games Esther Plays: Chapter Three of *Bleak House*," *Dickensian* 81 (Autumn 1985): 163–74.

Cynthia Northcutt Malone, "'Flight' and 'Pursuit': Fugitive Identity in *Bleak House*," *DSA* 19 (1990): 107–24.

Françoise Martin, "L'Image de Londres chez Dickens et Gustave Dore," *CVE* 28 (October 1988): 25–38.

Jerome Meckier, "Double Logic versus Double Vision," *DSN* 14 (March 1983; June 1983): 14–21; 51–57.

Nancy Aycock Metz, "Narrative Gesturing in *Bleak House*," *Dickensian* 77 (Spring 1981): 13–31.

Helena Michie, "'Who Is This in Pain?': Scarring, Disfigurement, and Female Identity in *Bleak House* and *Our Mutual Friend*," *Novel* 22 (Winter 1989): 199–205.

Tom Middlebro, "Esther Summerson: A Plea for Justice," *QQ* 77 (Summer 1970): 252–60.

D. A. Miller, "Discipline in Different Voices: Bureaucracy, Police, Family, and *Bleak House*," in *Charles Dickens*, ed. Harold Bloom (New York: Chelsea House, 1987), 197–228.

J. Hillis Miller, in "The Interpretive Dane in *Bleak House*," in *Charles Dickens's "Bleak House*," ed. Harold Bloom (New York: Chelsea House, 1987), 13–36.

Michael G. Miller, "The Bleak House Number Cover: Which Way Is the Wind Blowing?" *DQu* 3 (June 1986): 93–94.

Carolyn Misenheimer and James B. Misenheimer, "Structural Unities: Paired Parallel Chapters in Dickens's *Bleak House*," *Dickensian* 85 (Autumn 1989): 140–49.

Ellen Moers, "*Bleak House*: The Agitating Women," *Dickensian* 69 (1973): 13–29.

Padmini Mongia, "The Problem of the Female Voice in *Bleak House*," *WVUPP* 34 (1988): 31–37.

Sylvère Monod, "Esther Summerson, Charles Dickens and the Reader of *Bleak House*," *DSN* 5 (May 1969): 5–25.

Merritt Moseley, "The Ontology of Esther's Narrative in *Bleak House*," *SoAR* 50 (May 1985): 35–46.

Kenneth Muir, "*Bleak House* Revisited," *ACM* 2 (1989): 85–100.

Christopher Mulvey, "A Surreal Image in *Bleak House*: A Landlord and His Tenants," *DSN* 8 (September 1977): 68–72.

John M. Neary, "*Bleak House*: From Phenomena to Story," *MSE* 9 (1984): 13–31.

M. A. Nersesova, *Kholodnii dom Dikkensa* (Moscow: Khudozh, 1971), 1–112.

Ian Ousby, "The Broken Glass: Vision and Comprehension in *Bleak House*," *NCF* 29 (Spring 1975): 381–92. Reprinted in "*Bleak House*," ed. George Ford and Sylvère Monod (New York: Norton, 1977), 974–84.

David Parker, "A Phiz Tribute to Cruikshank," *Dickensian* 84 (Spring 1988): 7–8.

Dorothy Parker, "Allegory and the Extension of Mr. Bucket's Fore–finger," *ELN* 12 (September 1974): 31–35.

Roy Pascal, "Victorians: Dickens and Mimicry: *Bleak House*," in *The Dual Voice: Free Indirect Speech and Its Functioning in the Nineteenth–Century European Novel* (Manchester: Manchester University Press, 1977), 67–78.

Janet Pate, "Inspector Bucket," in *The Book of Sleuths* (London: New English Library, 1977), 33–35.

T. S. Pearce, "*Bleak House*," in *George Eliot* (London: Evans, 1973), 62–66.

Lowry Pei, "Mirrors, the Dead Child, Snagsby's Secret, and Esther," *ELN* 16 (December 1978): 144–56.

Timothy Peltason, "Esther's Will," *ELH* 59 (Fall 1992): 671–91.

Paul Pickrel, "*Bleak House*: The Emergence of Theme," *NCF* 42 (June 1987): 73–96.

Allan Pritchard, "The Urban Gothic of *Bleak House*," *NFC* 45 (March 1991): 432–52.

Eugene F. Quirk, "Tulkinghorn's Buried Life: A Study of Character in *Bleak House*," *JEGP* 72 (October 1973): 526–35.

Eric S. Rabkin, "The Comedy and the Melodrama," in *Narrative Suspense: "When Slim turned Sideways . . . "* (Ann Arbor: University of Michigan Press, 1973), 139–49.

Michael Ragussis, "The Ghostly Signs of *Bleak House*," *NCF* 34 (December 1979): 253–80.

John R. Reed, "Freedom, Fate, and the Future in *Bleak House*," *CLIO* 8 (Winter 1979): 175–94.

Heinz Reinhold, "Charles Dickens: *Bleak House*," in *Der Englische Roman im 19 Jahrhundrert: Interpretationen*, ed. Paul Goetsch, Horst Oppel, Heinz Kosk, and Kurt Otten (Berlin: Schmidt, 1973), 106–23.

Margaret Reynolds, " 'In Chancery' Again: Dickens and Prize-Fighting," *DSN* 14 (June 1983): 48–50.

Françoise Rives, "*Bleak House* Roman Picaresque?" *Caliban* 22 (1983): 51–60.

Adam Roberts, "Dickens's Megalosaurus," *N&Q* 40 (December 1993): 478–79.

Ann Ronald, "Dickens's Gloomiest Gothic Castle," *DSN* 6 (September 1975): 71–75.

Devra Braun Rosenberg, "Contrasting Pictorial Representations of Time: The Dual Narration of *Bleak House*," *VN* 51 (Spring 1977): 10–16.

Mary Rosner, "Drizzle, Darkness, and Dinosaurs: Defining the World of *Bleak House*," *DSN* 13 (December 1982): 99–108.

Mary Rosner, "A Note on the Title of Chapter 1 in *Bleak House*," *DSN* 12 (March 1981): 13.

Anny Sadrin, "Charlotte Dickens: The Female Narrator of *Bleak House*," *DQu* 9 (June 1992): 47–57.

Anny Sadrin, "Presence et fonction de l'art et de l'artiste dans *Bleak House*," in *Home, Sweet Home or Bleak House? Art et littérature à l'époque Victorienne*, ed. Marie-Claire Hamard (Paris: Belles Lettres, 1985), 131–50.

Joseph Sawicki, " 'The mere truth won't do': Esther as Narrator in *Bleak House*," *JNT* 17 (Spring 1987): 209–24.

Lance Schachterle, "*Bleak House* as a Serial Novel," *DSA* 1 (1970): 212–24.

Charles I. Schuster, "Style and Meaning in *Bleak House*," *Sphinx* 4 (1984): 166–74.

F. S. Schwarzbach, "*Bleak House*: The Social Pathology of Urban Life," *L&M* 9 (1990): 93–104.

F. S. Schwarzbach, " 'Deadly stains': Lady Dedlock's Death," *DQu* 4 (September 1987): 160–65.

F. S. Schwarzbach, "The Fever of *Bleak House*," *ELN* 20 (March–June 1983): 21–27.

Carol A. Senf, "*Bleak House*: Dickens, Esther, and the Androgynous Mind," *VN* 64 (Fall 1983): 21–27.

DICKENS, CHARLES, *Bleak House*

Ellen Serlen, "The Two Worlds of *Bleak House*," *ELH* 43 (Winter 1976): 551–66.

G. B. Shand, "Middleton's Phoenix and the Opening of *Bleak House*," *Dickensian* 78 (Summer 1982): 93–95.

Susan Shatto, "Lady Dedlock and the Plot of *Bleak House*," *DQu* 5 (December 1988): 185–91.

Yamamoto Shiro, "Chancery in *Bleak House*: A Metacritical Analysis," *SELit* 60 (September 1983): 61–73.

R. Ann Smalley, "Crossing the Gulfs: The Importance of the Master–Servant Relationship in Dickens's *Bleak House*," *Dickensian* 85 (Autumn 1989): 151–60.

Anne Smith, "The Ironmaster in *Bleak House*," *EIC* 21 (April 1971): 159–69.

Grahame Smith, *Charles Dickens:* Bleak House, (London: Edward Arnold, 1974), 1–64.

Mary Daehler Smith, "'All Her Fections Tarnished': The Thematic Function of Esther Summerson," *VN* 38 (Fall 1970): 10–14.

Eadgyth Sowter, "The Dark Lady of Dickens," *Dickensian* 25 (1929): 204–06.

Jorgen Spodsberg, *Familiens Dodskamp: En Analyse af Charles Dickens Roman Bleak House* (Grena: GMT, 1976), 1–170.

Michael Steig, "Structure and the Grotesque in Dickens: 'Dombey and Son,' *Bleak House*," *CentR* 14 (Summer 1970): 313–31.

Michael Steig and F. A. C. Wilson, "Hortense versus Bucket: The Ambiguity of Order in *Bleak House*," *MLQ* 33 (September 1972): 289–98.

Donald C. Stewart, "Dickens's *Bleak House*: A Novel for Our Time," in *Kansas English*, ed. Duane Nichols (Lawrence: University of Kansas Press, 1970), 84–88.

Garrett Stewart, "The New Morality in *Bleak House*," *ELH* 45 (Fall 1978): 443–87. Reprinted as "Epitaphic Chapter Titles and the New Morality of *Bleak House*," in *Charles Dickens's "Bleak House,"* ed. Harold Bloom (New York: Chelsea House, 1987), 81–109.

P. E. Strauss, "Dickens and the Law in *Bleak House*," *NULR* 1, no. 4 (1975): 142–46.

Harvey Peter Sucksmith, "Sir Leichester Dedlock, Wat Tyler, and the Chartists: The Role of the Ironmaster in *Bleak House*," *DSA* 4 (1975): 113–31.

Rodger L. Tarr, "Foreign Philanthropy and the Thematic Art of *Bleak House*," *DSN* 8 (December 1977): 100–04.

Rodger L. Tarr, "The 'Foreign Philanthropy Question' in *Bleak House*: A Carlylean Influence," *SNNTS* 3 (Fall 1971): 275–83.

Kathleen Tillotson, "*Bleak House* at a Seance," *Dickensian* 84 (Spring 1988): 3–5.

Thorell Tsomondo, "'A Habitable Doll's House': Beginning in *Bleak House*," *VN* 62 (Fall 1982): 3–7.

J. R. Tye, "Legal Caricature: Cruikshank Analogues to the *Bleak House* Cover," *Dickensian* 69 (January 1969): 39–41.

John C. Ward, "The Virtues of the Mothers: Powerful Women in *Bleak House*," *DSN* 14 (June 1983): 37–42.

Roger P. Wallins, "Dickens and Decomposition," *DSN* 5 (September 1974): 68–70.

Michele S. Ware, "'True Legitimacy': The Myth of the Foundling in *Bleak House*," *SNNTS* 22 (Spring 1990): 1–9.

Catherine Waters, "The Dilettante and the Artist in Dickens' *Bleak House*," *SoR* 17 (November 1984): 232–49.

Gilian West, "*Bleak House*: Esther's Illness," *ES* 73 (February 1992): 30–34.

Allon H. White, "Language and Location in Charles Dickens's *Bleak House*," *CritQ* 20 (Winter 1978): 73–89.

Gwen Whitehead, "The First Fictional English Detective," *RtSoCCEA* 27 (Fall 1987): 1–3.

Michael Wilkins, "Dickens's Portrayal of the Dedlocks," *Dickensian* 72 (May 1976): 67–74.

Philip James Wilson, "Notice on the Megalosaurus or Great Fossil Lizard of Stonefield: Observations on the Beginning of *Bleak House*," *Dickensian* 78 (Summer 1982): 97–104.

Judith Wilt, "Confusion and Consciousness in Dickens's Esther," *NCF* 32 (December 1977): 285–309. Reprinted in *Charles Dickens's "Bleak House,"* ed. Harold Bloom (New York: Chelsea House, 1987), 57–79.

Joan D. Winslow, "Esther Summerson: The Betrayal of the Imagination," *JNT* 6 (Winter 1976): 1–12.

Irene E. Woods, "On the Significance of Jarndyce and Jarndyce," *DQu* 1 (September 1984): 81–87.

George J. Worth, "Mr. Guppy: What Did He Know, and When Did He Know It?" *DQu* 1 (March 1984): 6–9.

Kay Hetherly Wright, "The Grotesque and Urban Chaos in *Bleak House*," *DSA* 21 (1992): 97–112.

Saundra K. Young, "Uneasy Relations: Possibilities for Eloquence in *Bleak House*," *DSA* 9 (1981): 67–85.

Alex Zwerdling, "Esther Summerson Rehabilitated," *PMLA* 88 (May 1973): 429–39. Reprinted in *Charles Dickens's "Bleak House,"* ed. Harold Bloom (New York: Chelsea House, 1987), 37–56.

The Chimes

Barbara T. Gates, "Suicide, *Bentley's Miscellany*, and Dickens's *Chimes*," *DSN* 8 (December 1977): 98–100.

Marilyn J. Kurata, "Fantasy and Realism: A Defense of *The Chimes*," *DSA* 13 (1984): 19–34.

James E. Marlow, "Memory, Romance, and the Expressive Symbol in Dickens," *NCF* 30 (June 1975): 20–32.

Michael Shelden, "Dickens, *The Chimes*, and the Anti-Corn Law League," *VS* 25 (Spring 1982): 328–53.

Michael Slater, "Dickens's Tract for the Times," in *Dickens* 1970 (London: Chapman & Hall, 1970), 99–123.

Rodger L. Tarr, "Dickens's Debt to Carlyle's 'Justice Metaphor' in *The Chimes*," *NCF* 27 (September 1972): 208–15.

Alexander Welsh, "Time and the City in *The Chimes*," *Dickensian* 73 (January 1977): 8–17.

A Christmas Carol

Philip V. Allingham, "The Naming of Names in *A Christmas Carol*," *DQu* 4 (March 1987): 15–20.

Salvatore V. Ambrosino, "Analysis of Scrooge, Child of the Earth," *NewYSJM* 71 (15 December 1971): 2884–885.

George Anastaplo, "Notes from Charles Dickens's 'Christmas Carol,'" *Interpretation* 7 (January 1978): 52–73.

Craig Buckwald, "Stalking the Figurative Oyster: The Excursive Ideal in *A Christmas Carol*," *SSF* 27 (Winter 1990): 1–14.

Donald R. Burleson, "Dickens's *A Christmas Carol*," *Expl* 50 (Summer 1992): 211–12.

R. D. Butterworth, "*A Christmas Carol* and the Masque," *SSF* 30 (Winter 1993): 63–69.

Lesley Conger, "Joy, Joy!—and Pull Out All the Stops!" *Writer* 85 (December 1972): 8, 43.

Warren G. French, "The Greening of London Town," *KanQ* 7 (Fall 1975): 99–102.

Elliot L. Gilbert, "The Ceremony of Innocence: Charles Dickens's *A Christmas Carol*," *PMLA* 90 (January 1975): 22–31.

Susan Hill, "The Ghost of 131 Christmases Past," *DTel* (17 December 1977): 7.

Margaret Hodges, "Dickens for Children," *HBM* 58 (December 1982): 626–35.

Graham Holderness, "Imagination in *A Christmas Carol*," *ÉA* 32 (January–March 1979): 28–45.

Audrey Jaffe, "Spectacular Sympathy: Visuality and Ideology in Dickens's *A Christmas Carol*," *PMLA* 109 (March 1994): 254–65.

John Jordan, "What the Dickens!" *Hibernia* (12 December 1975): 19.

Sue Poe and Hazel Jesse, "Staging a Literary Festival," *VirEB* 36 (Winter 1986): 149–52.

Laurina Levi Sr., "The Origin of Mr. Scrooge," *FDig* 30 (December 1974): 9–11.

Masaie Matsumura, "*Christmas Carol* no Yurei to Asmodius," *EigoS* 133 (1987): 426–28.

John Mortimer, "Whatever Became of Tiny Tim?" *NYTBR* (6 December 1992): 37–38.

Philip McM. Pittman, "Time, Narrative Technique, and the Theme of Regeneration in *A Christmas Carol*," *BWVACET* 2, no. 2 (1975): 34–49.

Stephen Prickett, "Christmas at Scrooge's," in *Victorian Fantasy* (Hassocks, Sussex: Harvester, 1979), 38–74.

Martin H. Sable, "The Day of Atonement in Charles Dickens' *A Christmas Carol*," *Tradition* 22 (Fall 1986): 66–76.

Natalie Shainess, "Charles Dickens: The First (Interpersonal) Psychoanalyst or—*A Christmas Carol*: A Literary Psychoanalysis," *AJP* 52 (December 1992): 351–62.

Harry Stone, "*A Christmas Carol*: The Ghost of Things to Come," *AngF* 4 (Fall–Spring 1978–1979): 48–54.

Harry Stone, "*A Christmas Carol*: 'Giving Nursery Tales a Higher Form,'" in *Charles Dickens*, ed. Harold Bloom (New York: Chelsea House, 1987), 153–60.

Nicholas Tucker, "Comfort and Joy," *TES* (24 December 1993): 18.

R. W. Zandvoort, "Mr. Fezziwig's Ball," in *Multiple Worlds, Multiple Words*, ed. Hena Maés–Jelinek, Pierre Michel, and Paulette Michel–Michot (Liege: Université de Liege, 1987), 303–9.

"Colonel Quagg's Conversion"

Lawrence Huff, "The Lamar-Dickens Connection," *MissQ* 40 (Spring 1987): 113–15.

David Copperfield

Arthus A. Adrian, "*David Copperfield*: A Century of Critical and Popular Acclaim," *MLQ* 11 (1950): 325–31.

Michael Allen, "The Dickens Family at Portsmough, 1807–1814," *Dickensian* 77 (Autumn 1981): 131–43.

Mary Anne Andrade, "Pollution of an Honest Home," *DQu* 5 (June 1988): 65–74.

Ruth Ashby, "David Copperfield's Story—Telling in the Dark," *DSN* 9 (September 1978): 80–83.

Phillip D. Atteberry, "The Fictions of *David Copperfield*," *VIJ* 14 (1986): 67–76.

Carl Bandelin, "*David Copperfield*: A Third Interesting Penitent," *SEL* 16 (Autumn 1976): 601–11. Reprinted in *Charles Dickens's "David Copperfield,"* Harold Bloom (New York: Chelsea House, 1987), 21–30.

Matthias Bauer, "Orpheus and the Shades: The Myth of the Poet in *David Copperfield*," *UTQ* 63 (Winter 1993): 308–27.

Murray Baumgarten, "Writing and *David Copperfield*," *DSA* 14 (1985): 39–59.

Peter Bayne, "*David Copperfield*," *LitW* (9 May 1979); (16 May 1979): 296–98; 312–14.

Vereen M. Bell, "The Emotional Matrix of *David Copperfield*," *SEL* 8 (Autumn 1968): 633–49.

Ronald Berman, "The Innocent Observer," *ChildL* 9 (1981): 40–50.

Michael Black, "David Copperfield: Self, Childhood and Growth," in *The Literature of Fidelity* (London: Chatto & Windus; New York: Barnes and Noble; Toronto: Clarke, Irwin, 1975), 82–102.

Harold Bloom, "Introduction," in "*David Copperfield*," ed. Harold Bloom (New York: Chelsea House, 1992), 1–4.

Arthur W. Brown, "*David Copperfield*," in *Sexual Analysis of Dickens' Props* (New York: Emerson, 1971), 232–36.

E. K. Brown, "*David Copperfield*," *YR* 37 (1947–48): 651–66.

Janet H. Brown, "The Narrator's Role in *David Copperfield*," *DSA* 2 (1972): 197–207.

Jerome H. Buckley, "The Identity of David Copperfield," in *Victorian Literature and Society: Essays Presented to Richard D. Altick*, ed. James R. Kincaid and Albert J. Kuhn (Columbus: Ohio State University Press, 1984), 225–39.

Keith Carabine, "Reading *David Copperfield*," in *Dickens: Hard Times, Great Expectations, and Our Mutual Friend Casebook*, ed. Norman Page (London: Macmillan, 1979), 150–67. Reprinted in *Reading the Victorian Novel: Detail into Form*, ed. Ian Gregor (London: Vision, 1980), 150–67.

Virginia Carmichael, "In Search of Beein': Nom/Non du père in *David Copperfield*," *ELH* 54 (Fall 1987): 653–67. Reprinted as "Nom/Non du père in *David Copperfield*" in "*David Copperfield*," ed. Harold Bloom (New York: Chelsea House, 1992), 211–22.

Joyce Cary, "Including Mr. Micawber," *NYTBR* (15 April 1951): 4, 21. Reprinted in *Selected Essays*, ed. A. G. Bishop (London: Michael Joseph, 1976), 172–75.

G. K. Chesterton, "David Copperfield," in *Appreciations and Criticisms of the Work of Charles Dickens* (London: Dent, 1911), 132–36. Reprinted in "*David Copperfield*," ed. Harold Bloom (New York: Chelsea House, 1992), 9–11.

Henry F. Chroley, "Review of *David Copperfield*," *Athenaeum* (23 November 1850): 1209–10. Reprinted in "*David Copperfield*," ed. Harold Bloom (New York: Chelsea House, 1992), 5–6.

A. O. J. Cockshut, "*David Copperfield*," in *The Imagination of Charles Dickens* (London: Collins, 1961), 114–26.

Philip Collins, *Charles Dickens: David Copperfield* (London: Arnold, 1977), 1–64.

Philip Collins, "*David Copperfield*: 'A Very Complicated Interweaving of Truth and Fiction,'" *E&S* 23 (1970): 71–86.

Philip Collins, "Dickens's Autobiographical Fragment and *David Copperfield*," *CVE* 20 (October 1984): 87–96.

Roland Corthell, "The Transformation of Mrs. Gummidge," *Dickensian* 16 (1920): 189.

C. B. Cox, "Realism and Fantasy in *David Copperfield*," *BJRL* 52 (Spring 1970): 267–83.

Ian Crawford, "Sex and Seriousness in *David Copperfield*," *JNT* 16 (Winter 1986): 41–54. Reprinted in "*David Copperfield*," ed. Harold Bloom (New York: Chelsea House, 1992), 159–72.

Brian Crick, " 'Mr. Peggotty's Dream Comes True': Fathers and Husbands; Wives and Daughters," *UTQ* 54 (Fall 1984): 38–55.

Amy Cruse, "*David Copperfield*," in *Famous English Books and Their Stories* (New York: Thomas Y. Crowell, 1926), 241–51.

Graham Daldry, "The Novel as Narrative: *David Copperfield*," in *Charles Dickens and the Form of the Novel: Fiction and Narrative in Dickens's Work* (Totowa, NJ: Barnes & Noble, 1987), 99–130.

Sidney Dark, "*David Copperfield*," in *Charles Dickens* (London: Nelson, 1919), 83–90.

Bernard Darwin, "In Defense of Dora," *Dickensian* 45 (1949): 91–96.

Mario L. D'Avanzo, "Mr. Creakle and His Prison: A Note on Craft and Meaning," *Dickensian* 64 (1968): 50–52.

Earle Davis, "The Creation of Dickens's "*David Copperfield*": A Study in Narrative Craft," *WitB* 16 (April 1941): 2–30.

Earle Davis, "First Person—*David Copperfield*," in *The Flint and the Flame: The Artistry of Charles Dickens* (Columbia: University of Missouri Press, 1963), 157–83.

Robert M. DeGraaff, "Self–Articulating Characters in *David Copperfield*," *JNT* 14 (Fall 1984): 214–22.

H. C. Dent, "Chapter X [*David Copperfield*]," in *The Life and Characters of Charles Dickens* (London: Odham's, 1933), 343–62.

Peter I. DeRose, "The Symbolic Sea of *David Copperfield*," *PCCTET* 41 (September 1976): 45.

Joseph Dobrinsky, "Tommy Traddles as a Dickensian Hero?" *CVE* 20 (October 1984): 55–64.

Albert A. Dunn, "Time and Design in *David Copperfield*," *ES* 59 (June 1978): 225–36.

Richard J. Dunn, "*David Copperfield*: All Dickens Is There," *EJ* 54 (December 1965): 789–94.

A. E. Dyson, "*David Copperfield*: The Favourite Child," in *The Inimitable Dickens: A Reading of the Novels* (London: Macmillan, 1970), 119–53.

Simon Edwards, "*David Copperfield*: The Decomposing Self," *CentR* 29 (Summer 1985): 328–52.

Edwin M. Eigner, "David Copperfield and the Benevolent Spirit," *DSA* 14 (1985): 1–15.

Edwin M. Eigner, "Death and the Gentleman: *David Copperfield* as Elegiac Romance," *DSA* 16 (1987): 39–60. Reprinted in "*David Copperfield*," ed. Harold Bloom (New York: Chelsea House, 1992), 192–210.

Edwin M. Eigner, "The Lunatic at the Window: Magic Casements of David Copperfield," *DQu* 2 (March 1985): 18–21.

Monroe Engel, "*David Copperfield*," in *The Maturity of Dickens* (Cambridge, MA: Harvard University Press, 1959), 148–56.

Norren Ferris, "Circumlocution in *David Copperfield*," *DSN* 9 (June 1978): 43–46. Reprinted in "*David Copperfield*," ed. Harold Bloom (New York: Chelsea House, 1992), 29–33.

Martin Fido, "*David Copperfield*, Ch. 61," in *Charles Dickens*: *Profiles in Literature* (London: Routledge & Kegan Paul, 1968), 58–62.

Brian Firth, "*David Copperfield* and Jeremy Diddler," *N&Q* 31 (December 1984): 489–90.

Herbert Foltinek, "Unsicherheit, die nach Gewissheit strebt: Der Verlust des kirschroten Bandes in *David Copperfield*," *GRM* 40, no. 3 (1990): 278–303.

Stanley Friedman, "Dickens's Mid–Victorian Theodicy: *David Copperfield*," *DSA* 7 (1978): 128–50.

Stanley Friedman, "Kotzebue's 'The Stranger' in *David Copperfield*," *DSN* 9 (June 1978): 49–50.

St. J. O. B. G., "Literary Allusions in Dickens's *David Copperfield*," *N&Q* n.s. 12 (1923): 155–56.

Roger Gard, "*David Copperfield*," *EIC* 15 (1965): 313–25.

DICKENS, CHARLES, *David Copperfield*

Marjorie Garson, "Inclusion and Exclusion: The Motif of the Copyist in *David Copperfield*," *ÉA* 36 (1983): 401–13.

Philip Gaskell, "Dickens, *David Copperfield*, 1850," in *From Writer to Reader Studies in Editorial Method* (Oxford: Clarendon, 1978), 142–55.

Robin Gilmour, "Memory in *David Copperfield*," *Dickensian* 71 (January 1975): 30–42. Reprinted in "*David Copperfield*," ed. Harold Bloom (New York: Chelsea House, 1992), 99–110.

Joseph Gold, "*David Copperfield*: The Disciplined Heart," in *Charles Dickens: Radical Moralist* (Minneapolis: University of Minneapolis Press, 1975), 175–84.

Michael Greenstein, "Between Curtain and Caul: David Copperfield's Shining Transparencies," *DQu* 5 (June 1988): 75–81.

Neil Grill, "Home and Homeless in *David Copperfield*," *DSN* 11 (December 1980): 108–11. Reprinted in "*David Copperfield*," ed. Harold Bloom (New York: Chelsea House, 1992), 41–46.

Barbara Hardy, "*David Copperfield*," in *The Moral Art of Dickens* (New York: Oxford University Press, 1970), 122–38. Reprinted as "The Moral Art of Dickens: *David Copperfield*," in *Charles Dickens's "David Copperfield*," Harold Bloom (New York: Chelsea House, 1987), 9–19.

Donald Hawes, "David Copperfield's Names," *Dickensian* 385 (March 1978): 81–87. Reprinted in *David Copperfield*, ed. Harold Bloom (New York: Chelsea House, 1992), 33–39.

Mark M. Hennelly, Jr., "*David Copperfield*" 'The Theme of This Incomprehensible Conundrum was the Moon,'" *SNNTS* 10 (Winter 1978): 375–96. Reprinted in "*David Copperfield*," ed. Harold Bloom (New York: Chelsea House, 1992), 126–44.

Gordon D. Hirsch, "A Psychoanalytic Rereading of *David Copperfield*," *VN* 58 (Fall 1980): 1–5.

Baruch Hochman, "Straw People, Hollow Men, and the Postmodernist Hall of Dissipating Mirrors: The Case of *David Copperfield*," *Style* 24 (Fall 1990): 392–407.

Bert G. Hornback, "Frustration and Resolution in *David Copperfield*," *SEL* 8 (Autumn 1968): 651–67. Reprinted in *"Noah's Arkitecture": A Study of Dickens's Mythology* (Athens: Ohio University Press, 1972), 63–82. Reprinted in "*David Copperfield*," ed. Harold Bloom (New York: Chelsea House, 1992), 86–98.

Felicity Hughes, "Narrative Complexity in *David Copperfield*," *ELH* 41 (Spring 1974): 89–105.

Edward Hurley, "Dickens's Portrait of the Artist," *VN* 38 (Fall 1970): 1–5.

Arlene M. Jackson, "Agnes Wickfield and the Church Leitmotif in *David Copperfield*," *DSA* 9 (1981): 53–65.

T. A. Jackson, "*David Copperfield*," in *Charles Dickens: The Progress of a Radical* (New York: International, 1938), 119–28.

Wendy S. Jacobson, "Brothers and Sisters in *David Copperfield*," *ESA* 25, no. 1 (1982): 11–28.

Sylvia L. Jarmuth, "An Outstanding Achievement: *David Copperfield*," in *Dickens' Use of Women in His Novels* (New York: Excelsior, 1967), 97–111.

Edgar Johnson, "His Favorite Child," in *Charles Dickens: His Tragedy and Triumph*, vol. 2 (New York: Simon & Schuster, 1952), 677–700.

John Jones, "*David Copperfield*," in *Dickens and the Twentieth Century*, ed. John Gross and Gabriel Pearson (London: Routledge & Kegan Paul, 1962), 133–44.

John O. Jordan, "The Social Sub-Text of *David Copperfield*," *DSA* 14 (1985): 61–92.

J. J. C. Kabel, "James Steerforth: Enkele opmerkingen bij Dickens's beeld van de romantiek," *DD* 6 (December 1976): 3–23.

Michio Kawai, "[On Micawberism]," in *Literature and Language of Dickens: Essays and Studies in Commemoration of the Centenary of the Death of Dickens*, ed. Michio Masui and Masami Tanabe (Tokyo: Sanseido, 1972), 139–52.

Shizuko Kawamoto, "[Micawber's innocence]," *EigoS* 120 (1974): 52–54.

Anthony Kearney, "The Storm Scene in *David Copperfield*," *Ariel* 9 (1978): 19–30.

Arnold Kettle, "Thoughts on *David Copperfield*," *RES* n.s. 2 (1961): 65–74.

J. M. Keyte and M. L. Robinson, "Mr. Dick the Schizophrenic," *Dickensian* 76 (Spring 1980): 37–39.

James R. Kincaid, "The Darkness of *David Copperfield*," *DS* 1 (May 1965): 65–75.

James R. Kincaid, "*David Copperfield*: Laughter and Point of View," in *Dickens and the Rhetoric of Laughter* (Oxford: Oxford University Press, 1971), 162–91. Reprinted in "*David Copperfield*," ed. Harold Bloom (New York: Chelsea House, 1992), 65–85.

James R. Kincaid, "Dickens's Subversive Humor: *David Copperfield*," *NCF* 22 (September 1968): 313–29.

James R. Kincaid, "The Structure of *David Copperfield*," *DS* 2 (May 1966): 74–95.

James R. Kincaid, "Symbol and Subversion in *David Copperfield*," *SNNTS* 1 (Summer 1969): 196–206.

U. C. Knoepflmacher, "From Outrage to Rage: Dickens's Bruised Femininity," in *Dickens and Other Victorians: Essays in Honor of Philip Collins*, ed. Joanne Shattock (New York: St. Martin's, 1988), 75–96.

Doris Langley–Levy, "The Fascination of Steerforth," *Dickensian* 18 (1922): 191–93.

William T. Lankford, "'The Deep of Time': Narrative Order in *David Copperfield*," *ELH* 46 (1979): 452–67.

Paciencia Ontanon de Lope, "Miro y Dickens: Una posible relacion," *NRFH* 36, no. 2 (1988): 1221–30.

Robert E. Lougy, "Remembrances of Death Past and Future: A Reading of *David Copperfield*," *DSA* 6 (1977): 72–101. Reprinted in *Charles Dickens's "David Copperfield*," Harold Bloom (New York: Chelsea House, 1987), 47–66.

John Lucas, "*David Copperfield*," in *The Melancholy Man: A Study of Dickens's Novels* (London: Methuen, 1970), 166–201.

Ned Lukacher, "Containing the Destructive Work of Remembrance" in *Charles Dickens's "David Copperfield*," Harold Bloom (New York: Chelsea House, 1987), 111–17.

Bruce McCullough, "The Comedy of Character: *David Copperfield*," in *Representative British Novelists: Defoe to Conrad* (New York: Harper, 1946), 136–51.

John P. McGowan, "*David Copperfield*: The Trail of Realism," *NCF* 34 (June 1979): 1–19. Reprinted in *Charles Dickens's "David Copperfield"*, ed. Harold Bloom (New York: Chelsea House, 1987), 67–82. Reprinted in "*David Copperfield*," ed. Harold Bloom (New York: Chelsea House, 1992), 145–58.

Juliet McMaster, "Dickens and David Copperfield on the Act of Reading," *ESC* 15 (September 1989): 288–304.

Leonard Manheim, "The Personal History of *David Copperfield*," *AI* 9 (Spring 1952): 21–43. Reprinted in *The Practice of Psychologianalytic Criticism*, ed. Leonard Tennenhouse (Detroit: Wayne State University Press, 1976), 75–94.

Sylvia Manning, "*David Copperfield* and Scheherazada: The Necessity of Narrative," *SNNTS* 14 (Winter 1982): 327–36.

William H. Marshall, "The Image of Steerforth and the Structure of *David Copperfield*," *TStL* 5 (1960): 57–65.

W. Somerset Maugham, "Charles Dickens and *David Copperfield*," in *The Art of Fiction: An Introduction to Ten Novels and Their Authors* (London: Heinemann, 1954), 159–61. Reprinted in "*David Copperfield*," ed. Harold Bloom (New York: Chelsea House, 1992), 14–16.

D. A. Miller, "Secret Subjects, Open Secrets," in *Charles Dickens's "David Copperfield*," ed. Harold Bloom (New York: Chelsea House, 1987), 89–109.

J. Hillis Miller, "*David Copperfield*," in *Charles Dickens: The World of His Novels* (Cambridge, MA: Harvard University Press, 1958), 150–59. Reprinted in "*David Copperfield*," ed. Harold Bloom (New York: Chelsea House, 1992), 17–23.

Michael G. Miller, "Murdstone, Heep, and the Structure of *David Copperfield*," *DSN* 11 (September 1980): 65–70.

Joachim Moller, "Beschreibung als Mittel der Kritik in Illustrationen zu *David Copperfield*," *Arcadia* 20, no. 3 (1985): 239–51.

Patricia Morris, "Some Notes on the Women in *David Copperfield*: Eleven Crude Categories and a Case of Miss Mowcher," *ESA* 21 (March 1978): 17–21.

Christopher E. Mulvey, "*David Copperfield*: The Folk–Story Structure," *DSA* 5 (1976): 74–94.

Rosemary Mundhenk, "David Copperfield and 'The Oppression of Remembrance,'" *TSLL* 29 (Fall 1987): 323–41.

Margaret Myers, "The Lost Self: Gender in *David Copperfield*," in *Gender Studies: New Directions in Feminist Criticism*, ed. Judith Spector (Bowling Green, OH: Popular, 1986), 120–32.

Gwendolyn B. Needham, "The Undisciplined Heart of *David Copperfield*," *NCF* 9 (September 1954): 81–107. Reprinted in "*David Copperfield*," ed. Harold Bloom (New York: Chelsea House, 1992), 47–64.

Richard L. Newby, "Dickensian Foibles," *ANQ* 15 (January 1977): 72–73.

Renate Noll–Wiemann, "Charles Dickens, *David Copperfield* (1849/50)," in *Der Kunstler im englischen Roman des 19. Jahrhunderts* (Heidelberg: Winter, 1977), 77–88.

Michio Ochi, "[Transfiguration and Micawber]," in *Literature and Language of Dickens: Essays and Studies in Commemoration of the Centenary of the Death of Dickens*, ed. Michio Masui and Masami Tanabe (Tokyo: Sanseido, 1972), 75–98.

DICKENS, CHARLES, *David Copperfield*

William Oddie, "Mr. Micawber and the Redefintion of Experience," *Dickensian* 65 (December 1967): 100–10.

David Parker, "Our Pew in Church," *Dickensian* 88 (June 1992): 41–42.

Janet Pate, "Uriah Heep," in *The Black Book of Villains* (London: David & Charles, 1975), 116–19.

Robert L. Pattern, "Autobiography into Autobiography: The Evolution of *David Copperfield*," in *Approaches to Victorian Autobiography*, ed. George P. Landow (Athens: Ohio University Press, 1979), 269–91.

E. Pearlman, "*David Copperfield* Dreams of Drowning," *AI* 28 (1971): 391–403.

E. Pearlman, "Two Notes on Religion in *David Copperfield*," *VN* 41 (Spring 1972): 18–20.

Torsten Pettersson, "The Maturity of *David Copperfield*," *ES* 70 (February 1989): 63–74.

Gwenhael Ponnau, "Le Héros du roman d'éducation et ses doubles: Le Cas de *David Copperfield*," *Litt* 16 (Spring 1987): 39–47.

Laurence Poston, "Uriah Heep, Scott, and a Note on Puritanism," *Dickensian* 71 (June 1975): 43–44.

J. B. Priestley, "Mr. Micawber," in *The English Comic Characters* (Staten Island: Phaeton, 1972), 211–41.

Nicholas Ranson, "Dickens and Disability: *David Copperfield*," *Kaleidoscope* (Summer–Fall 1986): 11–15.

J. M. Reibetanz, "Villain, Victim and Hero: Structure and Theme in *David Copperfield*," *DR* 59 (Spring 1979): 321–37.

Philip Rogers, "A Tolstoyan Reading of *David Copperfield*," *CL* 42 (Winter 1990): 1–28.

Rebecca Rodolff, "What David Copperfield Remembers of Dora's Death," *Dickensian* 77 (Spring 1981): 32–40.

Joseph Rosenblum, "Doctor Strong and Doctor Johnson Revisited," *DQu* 1 (June 1984): 54–56.

Dianne F. Sadoff, "Language Engenders: *David Copperfield* and *Great Expectations*," in *Charles Dickens*, ed. Harold Bloom (New York: Chelsea House, 1987), 181–95.

Narayan Saha, "Dickens's Treatment of Child-Psychology—and *David Copperfield*," *JBECU* 6 (1970–71): 26–28.

Nancy E. Schaumburger, "Partners in Pathology: David, Dora, and Steerforth," *Dickensian* 84 (Autumn 1988): 155–59.

Bernard N. Schilling, "Mr. Micawber's Difficulties" and "Mr. Micawber's Abilities," in *The Comic Spirit: Boccaccio to Thomas Mann* (Detroit: Wayne State University Press, 1965), 99–144.

Natalie E. Schroeder and Ronald A. Schroeder, "Betsey Trotwood and Jane Murdstone: Dickensian Doubles," *SNNTS* 21 (Fall 1989): 268–78.

Georg Seehase, "Eine 'englishche' Geschichte des jungen Menschen: Zur literaturgeschichtlichen Stellung des Romans *David Copperfield* (1849) von Charles Dickens," *ZAA* 32, no. 3 (1984): 220–29.

Roger D. Sell, "Projection Characters in *David Copperfield*," *SN* 55, no. 1 (1983): 19–30.

Marisa Sestitio, "David Copperfield: Due ipotesi di 'mise en scene,'" in *La performance del testo*, ed. Franco Marucci and Adriano Bruttini (Siena: Ticci, 1986), 187–94.

Alan Shelston, "Past and Present in *David Copperfield*," *CritQ* 27 (Autumn 1985): 17–33.

Irene Simon, "David Copperfield: A Kunstlerroman?" *RES* 43 (February 1992): 40–56.

Michael Slater, "David to Dora: A New Dickens Letter," *Dickensian* 68 (1972): 162.

Ronald Soetaert, "Godfried Bomans en Charles Dickens," *OnsE* 23 (November–December 1980): 725–32.

William C. Spengemann, "Poetic Autobiography: *David Copperfield*," in *The Forms of Autobiography: Episodes in the History of a Literary Genre* (New Haven: Yale University Press, 1980), 119–32.

Mark Spilka, "*David Copperfield* as Psychological Fiction," *CritQ* 1 (Winter 1959): 292–301.

Michael Steig, "*David Copperfield*: Progress of a Confused Soul," in *Dickens and Phiz* (Bloomington: Indiana University Press, 1978), 113–30.

Michael Steig, "The Iconography of *David Copperfield*," *HSL* 2 (1970): 1–18.

Harry Stone, "*David Copperfield*: The Fairy–Tale Method Perfected," in *Dickens and the Invisible World: Fairy Tales, Fantasy, and Novel-Making* (Bloomington: Indiana University Press, 1979), 193–278.

Harry Stone, "Dickens and Fantasy: The Case of Uriah Heep," *Dickensian* 75 (Summer 1975): 95–103.

DICKENS, CHARLES, *David Copperfield*

Harry Stone, "Fairy Tales and Ogres: Dickens' Imagination and *David Copperfield*," *Criticism* 6 (1964): 324–30.

L. A. G. Strong, "*David Copperfield*," *Dickensian* 46 (1950): 65–75.

Norman Talbot, "The Naming and the Namers of the Hero: A Study in *David Copperfield*," *SoR* 11 (1978): 267–82. Reprinted in "*David Copperfield*," ed. Harold Bloom (New York: Chelsea House, 1992), 111–25.

Angela Thirkell, "*David Copperfield* Reconsidered," *Dickensian* 45 (1949): 119–22.

Geoffrey Thurley, "David Copperfield," in *The Dickens Myth: Its Genesis and Structure* (New York: St. Martin's, 1976), 132–72.

Stanley Tick, "The Memorializing of Mr. Dick," *NCF* 24 (September 1969): 142–53.

Stanley Tick, "Toward Jaggers," *DSA* 5 (1976): 133–49.

Kathleen Tillotson, "Steerforth's Old Nursery Tale," *Dickensian* 79 (Spring 1983): 31–84.

Susan Shoenbauer Thurin, "The Relationship between Dora and Agnes," *DSN* 12 (December 1981): 103–8.

Chris R. Vanden Bossche, "Cookery, Not Rookery: Family and Class in *David Copperfield*," *DSA* 15 (1986): 87–109. Reprinted as "Family and Class in *David Copperfield*," in "*David Copperfield*," ed. Harold Bloom (New York: Chelsea House, 1992), 173–91.

J. Don Vann, "The Death of Dora Spenlow in *David Copperfield*," *VN* 22 (Fall 1972): 19–20.

Max Vega–Ritter, "Étude Psychocritique de *David Copperfield*," in *Studies in the Later Dickens*, ed. Jean–Claude Amalric (Montpellier: Université Paul Valéry, 1973), 11–70.

Philip M. Weinstein, "A Palimpsest of Motives in *David Copperfield*," in *The Semantics of Desire: Changing Models of Identity from Joyce to Dickens* (Princeton, NJ: Princeton University Press, 1984), 22–47.

Philip M. Weinstein, "Mr. Peggotty and Little Em'ly: Misassessed Altruism?" in *Charles Dickens's "David Copperfield*," ed. Harold Bloom (New York: Chelsea House, 1987), 83–88.

Alexander Welsh, "Young Man Copperfield,'" in *From Copyright to Copperfield: The Identity of Dickens* (Cambridge, MA: Harvard University Press, 1987),

156–72. Reprinted in "*David Copperfield*," ed. Harold Bloom (New York: Chelsea House, 1992), 223–36.

David M. Wilkes, "Dickens's *David Copperfield*," *Expl* 51 (Spring 1993): 157–60.

Angus Wilson, "David Copperfield," in *The World of Charles Dickens* (London: Martin Secker & Warburg, 1970), 211–16. Reprinted in "*David Copperfield*," ed. Harold Bloom (New York: Chelsea House, 1992), 25–28.

Virginia Woolf, "*David Copperfield*," *Nation&A* 37 (1925): 620–21. Reprinted in *The Moment and Other Essays* (London: Hogarth, 1947), 75–80.

George J. Worth, "The Control of Emotional Response in *David Copperfield*," in *The English Novel in the Nineteenth Century: Essays on the Literary Mediation of Human Values*, ed. George Goodin (Urbana: University of Illinois Press, 1972), 97–108. Revised and reprinted as "*David Copperfield*," in *Dickensian Melodrama: A Reading of the Novels* (Lawrence: University of Kansas Press, 1978), 97–110.

Dombey and Son

Richard D. Altick, "Varieties of Readers' Response: The Case of *Dombey and Son*," *YES* 10 (1980): 70–94.

Nina Auerbach, "Dickens and Dombey: A Daughter After All," *DSA* 7 (1978): 95–114.

Murray Baumgarten, "Railway/Reading/Time: *Dombey & Son* and the Industrial World," *DSA* 19 (1990): 65–89.

Terry J. Box, "Young Paul Dombey: A Case of Progeria," *RE* 9 (Spring 1983): 17–21.

Janice Carlisle, "*Dombey and Son*: The Reader and the Present Tense," *JNT* 1 (September 1971): 146–58.

Robert Clark, "Riddling the Family Firm: The Sexual Economy in *Dombey and Son*," *ELH* 51 (Spring 1984): 69–84.

Richard Currie, "Doubles, Self–Attack, and Murderous Rage in Florence Dombey," *DSA* 21 (1992): 113–29.

Denis Donoghue, "The English Dickens and *Dombey and Son*," *NCF* 24 (March 1970): 383–403. Reprinted in *Dickens Centennial Essays*, ed. Ada Nisbet and Blake Nevius (Berkeley and Los Angeles: University of California Press, 1971), 1–21.

A. E. Dyson, "The Case for Dombey Senior," *Novel* 2 (Winter 1969): 123–34.

Robert F. Fleissner, "Dickens's *Dombey and Son*, Chapter XXII," *Expl* 32 (December 1973): item 26.

Michael Green, "Notes on Fathers and Sons from *Dombey and Son*," in *1848: The Sociology of Literature*, ed. Francis Barker, et al. (Colchester: University of Essex, 1978), 256–64.

Michael Greenstein, "Measuring Time in *Dombey and Son*," *DQu* 9 (December 1992): 151–57.

Lewis Horne, "The Way of Resentment in *Dombey and Son*," *MLQ* 51 (March 1990): 44–62.

Anne Humpherys, "*Dombey and Son*: Carker the Manager," *NCF* 34 (March 1980): 397–413.

Patricia Ingham, "Speech and Non–Communication in *Dombey and Son*," *RES* n.s. 30 (May 1979): 144–53.

Arlene M. Jackson, "Reward, Punishment, and the Conclusion of *Dombey and Son*," in *DSA* 7 (1978): 103–27.

Gerhard Joseph, "Change and the Changeling in *Dombey and Son*," *DSA* 19 (1990): 179–95.

G. W. Kennedy, "The Two Worlds of *Dombey and Son*," *EngStColl* 1 (September 1976): 1–11.

Barbara Lecker, "Walter Gay and the Theme of Fancy in *Dombey and Son*," *Dickensian* 67 (January 1971): 21–30.

Laurence Lerner, "An Essay on *Dombey and Son*," in *The Victorians*, ed. Laurence Lerner (New York: Holmes & Meier, 1978), 195–208.

Laurence Lerner, "The Life and Death of Paul Dombey," in *Anglistentag 1981: Vortrage*, ed. Jorg Hasler (Frankfurt am Main: Lang, 1983), 95–110.

Patrick J. McCarthy, "*Dombey and Son*: Language and the Roots of Meaning," *DSA* 19 (1990): 91–106.

Frank McCombie, "Sexual Repression in *Dombey and Son*," *Dickensian* 88 (Spring 1992): 25–38.

Andrew McDonald, "The Preservation of Innocence in *Dombey and Son*: Florence's Identity and the Role of Walter Gay," *TSLL* 18 (Spring 1976): 1–19.

Shanta Mahalanobis, "The Adult World of *Dombey and Son*," in *CalUB* n.s. 6 (1970–71): 59–71.

David D. Marcus, "Symbolism and Mental Process in *Dombey and Son*," in *DSA* 6 (1977): 57–71.

Joss Lutz Marsh, "Good Mrs. Brown's Connections: Sexuality and Story–telling in 'Dealings with the Firm of Dombey and Son,'" *ELH* 58 (Summer 1991): 405–26.

N. P. Mikhal'skaia, "Nravstvenno–esteticheskii ideal i sistema avtorskikh otsenok v romane Dikkensa *Dombi i syn*," *FN* 107 (1978): 88–97.

Ian Milner, "The Dickens Drama: Mr. Dombey," in *Dickens Centennial Essays*, ed. Ada Nisbet and Blake Nevius (Berkeley: University of California Press, 1971), 155–65.

Helene Moglen, "Theorizing Fiction/Fictionalizing Theory: The Case of *Dombey and Son*," *VS* 35 (Winter 1992): 159–84.

Mary Montaut, "The Second Mrs. Dombey," *DQu* 4 (September 1987): 141–53.

Christopher Murray, "A Dickens Parallel," *SoR* 6 (1980): 42–44.

Kansuke Neki, "Cuttle Sencho no Detaramena Kaichudokei: Dombey Oyako Shokai no Tokei to Jukan," in *Kazugo: Ryokyoju Taikan Kinen Ronbunshu*, ed. Ogoshi Suga Yasuo (Kyoto: Apollonsha, 1980), 407–18.

Robert Newsom, "Embodying Dombey: Whole and in Part," *DSA* 18 (1989): 197–219.

Gabriel Pearson, "Towards a Reading of *Dombey and Son*," in *The Modern English Novel: The Reader, The Writer and the Work*, ed. Gabriel Josipovici (New York: Barnes & Noble, 1976), 54–76.

Suvendrini Perera, "Wholesale, Retail and for Exportation: Empire and the Family Business in *Dombey and Son*," *VS* 33 (Summer 1990): 603–20.

Samuel F. Pickering, "*Dombey and Son* and Dickens's Unitarian Period," *GaR* 26 (Winter 1972): 438–54. Revised and reprinted as "*Dombey and Son* and Unitarianism," in *The Moral Tradition in English Fiction, 1785–1850* (Hanover, NH: Dartmouth College Press, 1976), 149–68.

Lyn Pykett, "*Dombey and Son*: A Sentimental Family Romance," *SNNTS* 19 (Spring 1987): 16–30.

Margaret Reynolds, "'In Chancery' Again: Dickens and Prize-Fighting," *DSN* 14 (June 1983): 48–50.

Paul Schacht, "Dickens and the Uses of Nature," *VS* 34 (Autumn 1990): 77–102.

Roger D. Sell, "Dickens and the New Historians: The Polyvocal Audience and Discourse of Dombey and Son," in *The Nineteenth-Century British Novel*, ed. Jeremy Hawthorn (Baltimore: Arnold, 1986), 63–80.

Harry Stone, "The Novel as Fairy Tale: Dickens' *Dombey and Son*," *ES* 47 (1966): 1–27.

Martha Goffe–Stoner and S. P. Cerasano, "'She was very young and had no mother': An Unnoticed Browning Allusion in *Dombey and Son*," *DSN* 13 (December 1982): 97–99.

Anna Maria Stuby, "Die Allegorisierung der Zeit als Kapitalismuskritik in Dickens Roman *Dombey and Son*," *ZAA* 34, no. 2 (1986): 116–27.

Jeremy Tambling, "Death and Modernity in *Dombey and Son*," *EIC* 43 (October 1993): 308–29.

Stanley Tick, "The Unfinished Business of *Dombey and Son*," *MLQ* 36 (December 1975): 390–402.

Kathleen Tillotson, "Louisa King and Cornelia Blimber," *Dickensian* 74 (May 1978): 91–95.

Kathleen Tillotson, "New Readings in *Dombey & Son*," in *Imagined Worlds: Essays on Some English Novels and Novelists in Honour of John Butt*, ed. Maynard Mack and Ian Gregor (London: Methuen, 1968), 173–82.

Catherine Waters, "Ambiguous Intimacy: Brother and Sister Relationships in *Dombey and Son*," *Dickensian* 84 (Spring 1988): 9–26.

Louise Yelin, "Strategies for Survival: Florence and Edith in *Dombey and Son*," *VS* 22 (Spring 1979): 297–319.

Dvora Zelicovici, "Tema con variazioni in *Dombey and Son*," *MLS* 15 (Fall 1985): 270–80.

Lynda Zwinger, "The Fear of the Father: Dombey and Daughter," *NCF* 39 (March 1985): 420–40.

"George Silverman's Explanation"

R. D. Butterworth, "Hoghton Tower and the Picaresque of 'George Silverman's Explanation,'" *Dickensian* 86 (Summer 1990): 93–104.

Dudley Flamm, "The Prosecutor Within: Dickens's Final Explanation," *Dickensian* 66 (January 1970): 16–23.

Deborah A. Thomas, "The Equivocal Explanation of Dickens's George Silverman," *DSA* 3 (1974): 134–43.

Michael A. Ullman, "Where George Stopped Growing: Dickens's 'George Silverman's Explanation,'" *Ariel* 10 (January 1979): 11–23.

Great Expectations

Jean-Claude Amalric, "Some Reflections on *Great Expectations* as Allegory," in *Studies in the Later Dickens* (Montpellier: Université Paul Valéry, Centre d'Études et de Recherches Victoriennes et Edouardiennes, 1973), 127–33.

William F. Axton, "*Great Expectations* Yet Again," *DSA* 2 (1972): 278–93.

C. C. Barfoot, "*Great Expectations*: The Perception of Fate," *DQR* 6, no. 1 (1976): 2–33.

Robert Barnard, "Imagery and Theme in *Great Expectations*," *DSA* 1 (1970): 238–51.

Shuli Barzilai, "Dickens's *Great Expectations*: The Motive for Moral Masochism," *AI* 42 (Spring 1985): 45–67. Reprinted in *Charles Dickens*, ed. Harold Bloom (New York: Chelsea House, 1987), 263–79.

Murray Baumgarten, "Calligraphy and Code: Writing in *Great Expectations*," *DSA* 11 (1983): 61–72.

C. J. P. Beatty, "Charles Dickens's *Great Expectations* (1860–61) and the Probable Source of the Expression 'Brought Up by Hand,'" *N&Q* 38 (September 1991): 315.

Daniel Belden, "Dickens's *Great Expectations*, XXXI," *Expl* 35 (Summer 1977): 6–7.

Gavriel Ben–Ephraim, "The Imagination and Its Vicissitudes in *Great Expectations*," *HUSL* 13 (Spring 1985): 43–62.

W. Bronzwaer, "Implied Author, Extradiegetic Narrator and Public Reader: Gérard Genette's Narratological Mode and the Reading Version of *Great Expectations*," *Neophil* 62 (January 1978): 1–18.

Peter Brooks, "Repetition, Repression, and Return: *Great Expectations* and the Study of Plot," *NLH* 11 (Spring 1980): 503–26.

William Burgan, "Dickens and Kevin Lynch: Making Cities Make Sense," *NCS* 2 (1988): 19–26.

Max Byrd, "'Reading' in *Great Expectations*," *PMLA* 91 (March 1976): 259–65.

Rodolfo Cardona, "Mendizabal: Grandes esperanzas," in *Galdos y la Historia*, ed. Peter Bly (Ottawa: Dovehouse, 1988), 99–111.

T. J. Carney, *Great Expectations: Folen's Student Aids* (Dublin: Folens, 1977), 1–68.

Lois Chaney, "Pip and the Fairchild Family," *Dickensian* 79 (Autumn 1983): 162–63.

John Cloy, "Two Altered Endings—Dickens and Bulwer-Lytton," *USME* 10 (1992): 170–72.

William A. Cohen, "Manual Conduct in *Great Expectations*," *ELH* 60 (Spring 1993): 217–59.

C. Carter Colwell, "*Great Expectations*," in *The Tradition of British Literature* (New York: Putnam's Sons, 1971), 311–18.

DICKENS, CHARLES, *Great Expectations*

Patricia Corr, *Charles Dickens: Great Expectations* (Dublin: Gill & Macmillan, 1978), 1–27.

David M. Craig, "Origins, Ends, and Pip's Two Selves," *RsSt* 47 (March 1979): 17–26.

Iain Crawford, "Pip and the Monster: The Joys of Bondage," *SEL* 28 (Autumn 1988): 625–48.

John W. Crawford, "The Garden Imagery in *Great Expectations*," *RsSt* 39 (March 1971): 63–67. Reprinted in *Discourse: Essay* [sic] *on English and American Literature.* Costerrus n.s. 14 (Amsterdam: Rodopi, 1978), 109–15.

MacDonald Critchley, "The Miss Havisham Syndrome," *HofM* 1 (Summer 1969): 2–6.

E. A. Davids, "*Great Expectations*: Mrs. Joe and Estella: Reality and Fancy," *DD* 7 (December 1978): 49–62.

Mary Alice DeHaven, "Pip and the Fortunate Fall," *DSN* 6 (June 1975): 42–46.

Lawrence Jay Dessner, "*Great Expectations*: 'the ghost of a man's own father,'" *PMLA* 91 (May 1976): 436–49.

Lawrence Jay Dessner, "*Great Expectations*: The Tragic Comedy of John Wemmick," *Ariel* 6 (April 1975): 65–80.

G. D'Hangest, "Dickens et les personnages de *Great Expectations*," *ÉA* 24 (April–June 1971): 126–46.

A. F. Dilnot, "The Case of Mr. Jaggers," *EIC* 25 (October 1975): 437–43.

Ann B. Dobie, "Early Stream-of-Consciousness Writing: *Great Expectations*," *NCF* 25 (March 1971): 405–16.

Albert A. Dunn, "The Altered Ending of *Great Expectations*: A Note on Bibliography and First–Person Narration," *DSN* 9 (June 1978): 40–42.

Rodney Stenning Edgecombe, "Dickens, Hunt and the Dramatic Criticism in *Great Expectations*: A Note," *Dickensian* 88 (Summer 1992): 82–99.

Edwin M. Eigner, "The Absent Clown in *Great Expectations*," *DSA* 11 (1983): 115–33.

Edwin M. Eigner, "Bulwer–Lytton and the Changed Ending of *Great Expectations*," *NCF* 25 (June 1970): 104–08.

V. J. Emmett, Jr., "The Endings of *Great Expectations*," *NDQ* 41 (Autumn 1973): 5–11.

Donald H. Ericksen, "Demonic Imagery and the Quest for Identity in Dickens's *Great Expectations*," *IllQ* 33 (September 1970): 4–11.

Richard Fadem, "*Great Expectations* and the Mnemonics of Pain," in *Humanitas: Essays in Honor of Ralph Ross*, ed. Quincy Howe Jr. (Claremont, CA: Scripps, 1977), 34–53.

James Flynn, "Miss Havisham," *RecL* 1 (Fall 1972): 40–49.

Henri Fluchère, "Lecture et relecture de *Great Expectations*," in *Europe* 488 (December 1969): 62–77.

Scott Foll, "*Great Expectations* and the 'Uncommercial' Sketch Book," *Dickensian* 81 (Summer 1985): 109–16.

A. L. French, "Beating and Cringing: *Great Expectations*," *EIC* 24 (April 1974): 147–68.

A. L. French, "Old Pip: The Ending of *Great Expectations*," *EIC* 29 (October 1979): 357–60.

Stanley Friedman, "Another Possible Source for Dickens's Miss Havisham," *VN* 39 (Spring 1971): 24–25.

Stanley Friedman, "The Complex Origins of Pip and Magwitch," *DSA* 15 (1986): 221–31.

Stanley Friedman, "Echoes of *Hamlet* in *Great Expectations*," *HamSt* 9 (Summer–Winter 1987): 86–89.

Stanley Friedman, "Estella's Parentage and Pip's Persistence: The Outcome of *Great Expectations*," *SNNTS* 19 (Winter 1987): 410–21.

David Gervais, "The Prose and Poetry of *Great Expectations*," *DSA* 13 (1984): 85–114.

Elliot L. Gilbert, "'In Primal Sympathy': *Great Expectations* and the Secret Life," *DSA* 11 (1983): 89–113.

Andrea Gilchrist, "The Power of the Grotesque in *Great Expectations*," *Dickensian* 75 (Summer 1979): 75–83.

Michal Peled Ginsburg, "Dickens and the Uncanny: Repression and Displacement in *Great Expectations*," *DSA* 13 (1984): 115–24.

Robert A. Greenberg, "On Ending *Great Expectations*," *PLL* 6 (Spring 1970): 152–63.

Marshall W. Gregory, "Vales and Meanings in *Great Expectations*: The Two Endings Revisited," *EIC* 19 (October 1969): 402–09.

Jennifer Gribble, "Pip and Estella: Expectations of Love," *SSEng* 2 (1976–77): 197–214.

Michael Haig, "The Allegory of *Great Expectations*," *SSEng* 10 (1984–1985): 51–60.

DICKENS, CHARLES, *Great Expectations*

Eiichi Hara, "Name and No Name: The Identity of Dickensian Heroes," *SELit* 58 (Eng. no.) (1982): 21–42.

Eiichi Hara, "Stories Present and Absent in *Great Expectations*," *ELH* 53 (Fall 1986): 593–614.

Curt Hartog, "The Rape of Miss Havisham," *SNNTS* 14 (Fall 1982): 248–65.

Dick Hoefnagel, "An Early Hint of *Great Expectations*," *Dickensian* 82 (Summer 1986): 83–84.

Gail Turley Houston, "'Pip' and 'Property': The (Re)Production of the Self in *Great Expectations*," *SNNTS* 24 (Spring 1992): 13–25.

Albert D. Hutter, "Crime and Fantasy in *Great Expectations*," in *Psychoanalysis and Literary Process*, ed. Frederick Crews (Cambridge, MA: Winthrop, 1970), 25–65.

Paul Italia, "The Function of Expectations in Dickens's *Great Expectations*," *RCEI* 13–14 (April 1987): 231–39.

John O. Jordan, "The Medium of *Great Expectations*," *DSA* 11 (1983): 73–88.

Mary Ann Kelly, "The Functions of Wemmick of Little Britain and Wemmick of Walworth," *DSN* 14 (September 1983): 145–49.

Michael C. Kotzin, "Herbert Pocket as Pip's Double," *Dickensian* 79 (Summer 1983): 95–103.

Ivanka Koviloska–Poposka, "Carls Dikens: Golemite iscekwanja," *Sovremenost* 21 (1971): 724–38.

L. R. Leavis, "The Dramatic Narrator in *Great Expectations*," *ES* 68 (June 1987): 236–48.

Edward LeComte, "Rubinstein, the Lady in Spain, and Miss Havisham," *Greyfriar* 17 (1976): 13–19.

Alan Lelchuk, "Self, Family, and Society in *Great Expectations*," *SR* 78 (July–September 1970): 407–28.

Nils-Göran von Lempruch, "Some Grotesque Characters in Dickens's *Great Expectations*," *MSpr* 67, no. 4 (1973): 328–32.

Naomi Lightman, "The 'Vulcanic Dialect' of *Great Expectations*," *Dickensian* 82 (Spring 1986): 33–38.

Thomas Loe, "Gothic Plot in *Great Expectations*," *DQu* 6 (September 1989): 102–10.

W. J. Lohman Jr., "The Economic Background of *Great Expectations*," *VIJ* 14 (1986): 53–66.

Elizabeth MacAndrew, “A Second Level of Symbolism in *Great Expectations*,” *ELWIU* 2 (Spring 1975): 65–75.

Rowland McMaster, “Teaching the Novel: The Creative Word in *Great Expectations*,” in *The Creating Word: Papers from an International Conference on the Learning and Teaching of English in the 1980s*, ed. Patricia Demers (Edmonton: University of Alberta Press, 1986), 116–33.

Richard Martin, “Dickens’s Mr. Jaggers: A Process of Abstraction,” *LWU* 7 (October 1974): 142–53.

Jerome Meckier, “Dating the Action in *Great Expectations*: A New Chronology,” *DSA* 21 (1992): 157–94.

Jerome Meckier, “Dickens, *Great Expectations*, and the Dartmouth College Notes,” *PLL* 28 (Spring 1992): 111–32.

Jerome Meckier, “Charles Dickens’s *Great Expectations*: A Defense of the Second Ending,” *SNNTS* 25 (Spring 1993): 28–58.

Paulette Michel-Michot, “The Fire Motif in *Great Expectations*,” *Ariel* 8 (April 1977): 49–69.

Milton Millhauser, “*Great Expectations*: The Three Endings,” *DSA* 2 (1972): 267–77.

Christopher D. Morris, “The Bad Faith of Pip’s Bad Faith: Deconstructing *Great Expectations*,” *ELH* 54 (Winter 1987): 941–55.

Ian Ousby, “Language and Gesture in *Great Expectations*,” *MLR* 72 (October 1977): 784–93.

E. Pearlman, “Inversion in *Great Expectations*,” in *The Practice of Psychoanalytic Criticism*, ed. Leonard Tennenhouse (Detroit: Wayne State University Press, 1976), 190–202.

Evelyne Pieller, “Revez lecteur!” *QL* 316 (January 1980): 10–11.

Luz Aurora Pimentel y A., “El encuentro fortuito y la casualidad aparente como fuente de conocimiento interno en *Great Expectations*,” in *Charles Dickens 1812–1870: Homenaje en al primer centenario de su muerte*, ed. Padilla González (Mexico City: University Nacional Autònoma de México, 1971), 109–44.

Jack P. Rawlins, “Great Expiations: Dickens and the Betrayal of the Child,” *SEL* 23 (Autumn 1983): 667–83.

Jean Raimond, “Charles Dickens: *Great Expectations*,” in *Le roman anglais aux XIXe siècle*, ed. Pierre Coustillas, Jean–Pierre Petit, and Jean Raimond (Paris: Presses Université de France, 1978), 210–33.

Linda Raphael, "A Re–vision of Miss Havisham: Her Expectations and Our Responses," *SNNTS* 21 (Winter 1989): 400–13.

Jon B. Reed, "Astrophil and Estella: A Defense of Poesy," *SEL* 30 (Autumn 1990): 655–78.

Hugh Remash and James Flynn, "Letter and Reply (on *Great Expectations*)," *RecL* 1 (Winter 1972): 29–42.

Evelyn M. Romig, "Twisted Tale, Silent Teller: Miss Havisham in *Great Expectations*," *DQu* 5 (March 1988): 18–22.

Moshe Ron, "Autobiographical Narration and Formal Closure in *Great Expectations*," *HUSL* 5 (Spring 1977): 37–66.

Edgar Rosenberg, "Last Words on *Great Expectations*: A Textual Brief on the Six Endings," *DSA* 9 (1981): 87–115.

Edgar Rosenberg, "Wopsle's Consecration," *DSN* 8 (March 1977): 6–11.

J. S. Ryan, "'The Second Magwitch Fortune' and His Second Daughter," *Dickensian* 83 (Summer 1987): 106–09.

Dianne F. Sadoff, "Language Engenders: *David Copperfield* and *Great Expectations*," in *Charles Dickens*, ed. Harold Bloom (New York: Chelsea House, 1987), 181–95.

Roberta C. Schwartz, "The Moral Fable of *Great Expectations*," *NDQ* 47 (Winter 1979): 55–66.

Susan Shatto, "Miss Havisham and Mr. Mopes the Hermit: Dickens and the Mentally Ill," *DQu* 2;2 (June 1985; September 1985): 43–49; 79–84.

Lucille P. Shores, "The Character of Estella in *Great Expectations*," *MSE* 3 (Fall 1972): 91–99.

Amritjit Singh, "The Ending of *Great Expectations*," *IJESt* 18 (1978–79): 43–53.

Samuel M. Sipe, "Memory and Confession in *Great Expectations*," *ELWIU* 2 (Spring 1975): 53–64.

Claire Slagter, "Pip's Dreams in *Great Expectations*," *Dickensian* 83 (Autumn 1987): 180–83.

D. H. F. Smith, *Narrator and Protagonist in Dickens's "Great Expectations"* (Hitchin: North Herts College, 1979), 1–56.

John T. Smith, "The Two Endings of *Great Expectations*: A Re-Evaluation," *Thoth* 12 (Fall 1971): 11–17.

Stephen Sossaman, "Language and Communication in *Great Expectations*," *DSN* 5 (September 1974): 66–68.

James Leo Spenko, "The Return of the Repressed in *Great Expectations*," *L&P* 30, no. 3–4 (1980): 133–46.

G. Robert Stange, "Expectations Well Lost: Dickens's Fable for His Time," in *The Nineteenth–Century Novel: Critical Essays and Documents*, ed. Arnold Kettle (London: Heinemann, 1972), 127–39. Reprinted in *The Victorian Novel: Modern Essays in Criticsm*, ed. Ian Watt (Oxford: Oxford University Press, 1971), 110–22. Reprinted in *The Dickens Critics*, ed. George H. Ford and Lauriat Lane Jr. (Westport, CT: Greenwood, 1972), 294–308.

Robert A. Stein, "Pip's Poisoning Magwitch, Supposedly: The Historical Context and Its Implications for Pip's Guilt and Shame," *PQ* 67 (Winter 1988): 103–16.

Robert A. Stein, "Repetitions during Pip's Closure," *DSA* 21 (1992): 143–56.

Harry Stone, "Fire, Hand, and Gate: Dickens' *Great Expectations*," *KR* 24 (1962): 662–91.

Randolph Stow, "The Australian Miss Havisham," *ALS* 6 (October 1976): 418–19.

Henri Talon, "Space, Time, and Memory in *Great Expectations*," *DSA* 1 (1970): 122–33.

Anya Taylor, "Devoured Hearts in *Great Expectations*," *DSN* 13 (September 1982): 65–71.

Kurt von Rosador Tetzeli, "Charles Dickens: *Great Expectations*: Das Ende eines Ich–Romans," *NS* 18 (August 1969): 399–408.

Christian W. Thomsen, "Das Groteske in Charles Dickens's *Great Expectations*," *Anglia* 92, no. 1–2 (1974): 113–42.

David T. Thomson Jr., "Pip: The Divided Self," *PCulR* 1 (Winter 1977): 49–67.

Douglass H. Thomson, "The Passing of Another Shadow: A Third Ending to *Great Expectations*," *DQu* 1 (September 1984): 94–96.

Susan Schoenbauer Thurin, "The Seven Deadly Sins in *Great Expectations*," *DSA* 15 (1986): 201–20.

Susan Schoenbauer Thurin, "To Be Brought Up 'By Hand,'" *VN* 64 (Fall 1983): 27–29.

Stanley Tick, "Toward Jaggers," *DSA* 5 (1976): 133–49.

Kathleen Tillotson, "*Great Expectations* and the Dartmouth College Notes," *Dickensian* 83 (Spring 1987): 17–18.

Ashie Tsuneoka, "The Language of *Great Expectations*," *HSELL* 27 (March 1982): 76–77.

Susan Walsh, "Bodies of Capital: *Great Expectations* and the Climacteric Economy," *VS* 37 (Autumn 1993): 73–98.

Thomas P. Walsh, "Yet Another Comment on Dickens's Two Endings for *Great Expectations*," *PAPA* 3 (Fall 1976): 16.

Irwin Weiser, "Dickens' *Great Expectations*," *Expl* 39 (Summer 1981): 14–15.

Irwin Weiser, "Reformed, but Unrewarded: Pip's Progress," *DSN* 14 (September 1983): 143–45.

Cheryl Ann Weissman, "Empty Pockets and Illusory Prizes: Perceptions of Loss in Dicken's *Great Expectations*," in *Semiotics 1984*, ed. John Deely (Lanham, MD: University Press of America, 1985), 63–72.

William A. Wilson, "The Magic Circle of Genius: Dickens's Translations of Shakespearean Drama in *Great Expectations*," *NCF* 40 (September 1985): 154–74.

Anthony Winner, "Character and Knowledge in Dickens: The Enigma of Jaggers," *DSA* 3 (1974): 100–21.

Hana Wirth-Nesher, "The Literary Orphan as National Hero: Huck and Pip," *DSA* 15 (1986): 259–73.

Richard Witt, "The Death of Miss Havisham," *Dickensian* 80 (Autumn 1984): 151–56.

George J. Worth, "'The Uncommercial Traveller' and *Great Expectations*," *Dickensian* 83 (Spring 1987): 19–21.

Melanie Young, "Distorted Expectations: Pip and the Problems of Language," *DSA* 7 (1978): 203–20.

Hard Times

Philip V. Allingham, "Theme, Form, and the Naming of Names in *Hard Times* for These Times," *Dickensian* 87 (Spring 1991): 17–31.

Anne Hiebert Alton, "Education in Victorian Fact and Fiction: Kay Shuttleworth and Dickens's *Hard Times*," *DQu* 9 (June 1992): 67–80.

Richard J. Arneson, "Benthamite Utilitarianism and *Hard Times*," *P&L* 2 (Spring 1978): 60–75.

F. G. Atkinson, "*Hard Times*—Motifs and Meanings," *UofE* 4 (1963): 165–69.

John D. Baird, "'Divorce and Matrimonial Causes': An Aspect of *Hard Times*," *VS* 20 (Summer 1977): 401–12.

N. K. Banerjee, "*Hard Times*: A Note on the Descriptive Titles of Its Books," *IJEST* 13 (1972): 22–28.

Robert Barnard, "Imagery and Theme in *Hard Times*," in *Charles Dickens's "Hard Times,"* ed. Harold Bloom (New York: Chelsea House, 1987), 39–53.

Gorman Beauchamp, "Mechanomorphism in *Hard Times*," *SLitI* 22 (Spring 1989): 61–77.

Diane Dewhurst Belcher, "Dickens's Mrs. Sparsit and the Politics of Service," *DQu* 2 (September 1985): 92–98.

Margaret E. Belcher, "Bulwer's Mr. Bluff: A Suggestion for *Hard Times*," *Dickensian* 78 (Summer 1982): 105–09.

J. Miriam Benn, "A Landscape with Figures: Characterization and Expression in *Hard Times*," *DSA* 1 (1970): 168–82.

Helena Bergmann, "*Hard Times* (1854)," in *Between Obedience and Freedom: Woman's Role in the Mid–Nineteenth Century Industrial Novel* (Götheborg: Acta Universitatis Gothoburgensis, 1979), 40–44.

Ronald Berman, "Human Scale: A Note on *Hard Times*," *NCF* 22 (September 1967): 288–93.

Harold Bloom, "Introduction," in *Charles Dickens's "Hard Times,"* ed. Harold Bloom (New York: Chelsea House, 1987), 1–10.

Alain Bony, "Réalité et imaginaire dans *Hard Times*," *ÉA* 23 (April–June 1970): 168–82.

George Bornstein, "Miscultivated Field and Corrupted Garden: Imagery in *Hard Times*," *NCF* 26 (September 1971): 158–70.

Peter Bracher, "Muddle and Wonderful No–Meaning: Verbal Irresponsibility and Verbal Failures in *Hard Times*," *SNNTS* 10 (Fall 1978): 305–19. Reprinted in *Charles Dickens's "Hard Times,"* ed. Harold Bloom (New York: Chelsea House, 1987), 79–95.

Terence Brown, *Hard Times* (Dublin: Educational Company of Ireland, 1974), 1–34.

John Butt and Kathleen Tillotson, "*Hard Times*: The Problems of a Weekly Serial," in *Dickens at Work* (London: Methuen, 1957), 201–21.

R. D. Butterworth, "Dickens the Novelist: The Preston Strike and *Hard Times*," *Dickensian* 88 (Summer 1992): 91–102.

Joseph Butwin, "*Hard Times*: The News and the Novel," *NCF* 32 (September 1977): 166–87. Reprinted in *Charles Dickens's "Hard Times,"* ed. Harold Bloom (New York: Chelsea House, 1987), 61–78.

Jane Campbell, "'Competing Towers of Babel': Some Patterns of Language in *Hard Times*," *ESC* 10 (December 1984): 416–35.

Jean Ferguson Carr, "Writing as a Woman: Dickens, *Hard Times*, and Feminine Discourses," *DSA* 18 (1989): 161–78.

Jacques Carré, "Le prolétariat industriel dans *Hard Times* de Dickens," in *Hommage à Georges Fourrier* (Paris: Université de Besancon, 1973), 71–85.

Robert L. Caserio, "The Name of the Horse: *Hard Times*, Semiotics, and the Supernatural," *Novel* 20 (Fall 1986): 5–23.

Coles Editorial Board, *Dickens: Hard Times Notes* (Toronto: Coles, 1982), 1–94.

Nicholas Coles, "The Politics of *Hard Times*: Dickens the Novelist versus Dickens the Reformer," *DSA* 15 (1986): 145–79.

Steven Connor, "Deconstructing *Hard Times*," in *Charles Dickens's "Hard Times,"* ed. Harold Bloom (New York: Chelsea House, 1987), 113–27.

David Craig, "*Hard Times* and the Condition of England," in *The Real Foundation: Literature and Social Change* (London: Chatto & Windus; New York: Oxford University Press, 1974), 109–31.

Judith Crockett, "Theme and Metaphor in *Hard Times*," *Spectrum* 6 (1962): 80–81.

Dale W. Davis, "Charles Dickens and the Human Potential Movement: The Schooling of 'Soft Hearts' in *Hard Times*," *PAPA* 1 (Fall 1974): 23.

Daniel P. Deneau, "The Brother–Sister Relationship in *Hard Times*," *Dickensian* 60, no. 3 (1964): 173–77.

W. J. Doran, "*Hard Times* and These Times," *Dickensian* 15 (1919): 199–200.

Richard J. Dunn, "Dickens, Carlyle, and the *Hard Times* Dedication," *DSN* 2 (December 1971): 90–92.

A. E. Dyson, "*Hard Times*: The Robber Fancy," *Dickensian* 5 (1969): 67–79.

Angus Easson, *Charles Dickens's Hard Times: A Critical Commentary and Notes* (London: University of London Press, 1973), 7–48.

Angus Easson, "Dialect in Dickens's *Hard Times*," *N&Q* n.s. 23 (September 1976): 412–13.

Leszek Elektorowicz, "Dickens pesymista?" *Motywy Zachodnie* (Cracow: Wydawnictow, 1973), 130–34.

Eugenia Adams Ellison, "*Hard Times*: Victimized Childhood," in *The Innocent Child in Dickens and Other Writers* (Burnet, TX: Eakin, 1982), 154–66.

Mabel Evans, "The Gradgrind Philosophy," *Dickensian* 30 (1934): 247–48.

Richard Fabrizio, "Wonderful No–Meaning: Language and the Psychopathology of the Family in Dickens' *Hard Times*," *DSA* 16 (1987): 61–94.

K. J. Fielding, "*Hard Times* and Common Things," in *Imagined Worlds: Essays on Some English Novels and Novelists in Honour of John Butt*, ed. Maynard Mack and Ian Gregor (London: Methuen, 1968), 183–203.

K. J. Fielding, "Mill and Gradgrind," *NCF* 11 (June 1956): 148–51.

K. J. Fielding and Anne Smith, "*Hard Times* and the Factory Controversy: Dickens vs. Harriet Martineau," in *Dickens Centennial Essays*, ed. Ada Nisbet and Blake Nevius (Berkeley: University of California Press, 1971), 22–45.

Roger Fowler, "Polyphony and Problematic in *Hard Times*," in *The Changing World of Charles Dickens*, ed. Robert Giddings (London: Vision, 1983; Totowa, NJ: Barnes & Noble, 1983), 91–108. Reprinted in *Charles Dickens's "Hard Times,"* ed. Harold Bloom (New York: Chelsea House, 1987), 97–112.

Stanley Friedman, "Sad Stephen and Troubled Louisa: Paired Protagonists in *Hard Times*," *DQu* 7 (June 1990): 254–62.

Robert D. Garis, "*Hard Times*," in *The Dickens Theatre* (Oxford: Clarendon, 1965), 144–63.

Vanna Gentili, "*Hard Times*: Per questi tempi," in *Arte e letteratura: Scritti in ricordo di Gabriele Baldini* (Rome: Edizioni di Storia e Letteratura, 1972), 61–106.

John W. Gibson, "*Hard Times*: A Further Note," *DS* 1, no. 2 (1965): 90–101.

Joseph Gold, "'Aw a Muddle': *Hard Times*," in *Charles Dickens: Radical Moralist* (Minneapolis: University of Minnesota Press, 1972), 196–207.

Michael Goldberg, "The Critique of Utility: *Hard Times*," in *Carlyle and Dickens* (Athens: University of Georgia Press, 1972), 78–99.

David Goldknopf, "The Morality of Hypocrisy: The Structure of *Hard Times*," in *The Life of the Novel* (Chicago: University of Chicago Press, 1972), 143–58.

Robert Green, "*Hard Times*: The Style of a Sermon," *TSLL* 11 (Winter 1970): 1375–97.

Melvyn Haberman, "The Courtship of the Void: The World of *Hard Times*," in *The Worlds of Victorian Fiction*, ed. Jerome H. Buckley (Cambridge, MA: Harvard University Press, 1975), 37–55.

DICKENS, CHARLES, *Hard Times*

Edwin J. Heck, "*Hard Times*: The Handwriting on the Factory Wall," *EJ* 61 (January 1972): 23–27.

James P. Henderson, "Charles Dickens's *Hard Times* and the Industrial Revolution," *Cresset* 43 (March 1980): 13–17.

Thomas W. Hill, "Notes on *Hard Times*," *Dickensian* 48 (1952): 134–41, 177–85.

David M. Hirsch, "*Hard Times* and Dr. Leavis," *Criticism* 6 (Winter 1964): 1–16.

Claire Hirshfield, "*Hard Times* and the Teacher of History: An Interdisciplinary Approach," *DSN* 13 (June 1982): 33–38.

Shifra Hochberg, "Mrs. Sparsit's Coriolanus Eyebrows and Dickensian Approach to Topicality," *Dickensian* 87 (Spring 1991): 32–36.

Emma Hogan, *Charles Dickens' "Hard Times": A Critical Introduction* (Cork & Dublin: Mercier Educational, 1973), 1–48.

Michael Hollington, "Physiognomy in *Hard Times*," *DQu* 9 (June 1992): 58–66.

Felicity Horne, "Character and Theme in *Hard Times*," *CRUX* 22 (August 1988): 56–61.

Lewis B. Horne, "Hope and Memory in *Hard Times*," *Dickensian* 75 (Autumn 1979): 167–73.

Edward Hurley, "A Missing Childhood in *Hard Times*," *VN* 42 (Fall 1972): 11–16.

D. W. Jefferson, "Mr. Gradgrind's Facts," *EIC* 35 (July 1985): 197–212.

John Jennings, ed., *Hard Times* (Dublin: Helicon, 1977), 1–56.

Alan P. Johnson, "*Hard Times*: 'Performance' or 'Poetry'?" *DS* 5 (May 1969): 62–80.

Patricia E. Johnson, "*Hard Times* and the Structure of Industrialism: The Novel as Factory," *SNNTS* 21 (Summer 1989): 128–37.

Katherine Kearns, "A Tropology of Realism in *Hard Times*," *ELH* 59 (Winter 1992): 857–81.

William R. G. Kent, "*Hard Times* from a Socialist Standpoint," *Dickensian* 24 (1928): 293–96.

Joan E. Klingel, "Dickens's First Epistle to the Utilitarians," *DQu* 3 (September 1986): 124–28.

Janet Karsten Larson, "Identity's Fictions: Naming and Renaming in *Hard Times*," *DSN* 10 (March 1979): 14–19.

F. R. Leavis, "The Novel as Dramatic Poem (1): *Hard Times*," *Scrutiny* 14 (1947): 185–203.

Ingeborg Leimberg, "*Hard Times*: Zeitbezug und Uberzeitiche Bedeutung," *GRM* n.s. 21, no. 3 (1971): 269–96.

J. W. T. Ley, "The Case of *Hard Times*," *Dickensian* 24 (1928): 257–61.

J. F. Lincks, "The Close Reading of *Hard Times*," *EJ* 58 (1969): 212–18.

Thomas M. Linehan, "Rhetorical Technique and Moral Purpose in *Hard Times*," *UTQ* 47 (Fall 1977): 22–36.

David Lodge, "How Successful Is *Hard Times*?" in *Working With Structuralism* (Boston: Routledge & Kegan Paul, 1981), 37–45.

David Lodge, "The Rhetoric of *Hard Times*," in *The Language of Fiction* (London: Routledge & Kegan Paul, 1966), 145–63.

Ramón López Ortega, "*Hard Times* (1854), de Charles Dickens," in *Movimiento obrero y novela inglesa* (Salamanca: Universidad de Salamanca, 1976), 47–52.

Robert E. Lougy, "Dickens's *Hard Times*: The Romance as Radical Literature," *DSA* 2 (1979): 237–54. Reprinted in *Charles Dickens's "Hard Times,"* ed. Harold Bloom (New York: Chelsea House, 1987), 17–38.

I. C. McCormick, "A Defense for *Hard Times*," *Dickensian* 12 (1916): 89–91. Reprinted in *The Living Age* 290 (1916): 690–92.

Roderick F. McGillis, "Plum Pies and Factories: Cross Connections in *Hard Times*," *DSN* 11 (December 1980): 102–07.

Cynthia Northcutt Malone, "The Fixed Eye and the Rolling Eye: Surveillance and Discipline in *Hard Times*," *SNNTS* 21 (Spring 1989): 14–26.

Sylvia B. Manning, "*Hard Times*," in *Dickens as Satirist* (New Haven: Yale University Press, 1971), 132–54.

Augustine Martin, ed., *Charles Dickens: Hard Times* (Dublin: Gill & Macmillan, 1974), 1–37.

Mitsuharu Matsuoka, "On Dickens's Changed View of Society: Fancy and Affection in *Hard Times*," *HSELL* 27 (March 1982): 79–81.

B. W. Matz, "Dickens, Carlyle, and *Hard Times*," *Dickensian* 20 (1924): 32–33.

W. D. Maxwell-Mahon, "Charles Dickens: *Hard Times*," *CRUX* 5 (August 1971): 20–24.

Jerome Meckier, "*Hard Times*: A Seminal Distopia [sic]," *SoCB* 30 (October 1970): 112.

DICKENS, CHARLES, *Hard Times*

Ivan Melada, "*Hard Times*," in *The Capital of Industry in English Fiction, 1821–1871* (Albuquerque: University of New Mexico Press, 1970), 110–15.

Sylvère Monod, "*Hard Times*: An Undickensian Novel?" in *Studies in the Later Dickens*, ed. Jean–Claude Amalric (Montpellier: Université Paul Valéry, 1973), 71–92.

Charles H. Muller, "Dickens's *Hard Times*: The Gradgrind Educational System, Coketown, and the Circus," *CRUX* 9 (August 1975): 45–48, 52.

Sena Jeter Naslund, "Mr. Sleary's Lisp: A Note on *Hard Times*," *DSN* 12 (June 1981): 42–46.

Cynthia Northcutt–Malone, "The Fixed Eye and the Rolling Eye: Surveillance and Discipline in *Hard Times*," *SNNTS* 21 (Spring 1989): 14–26.

William Oddie, "*Hard Times*," in *Dickens and Carlyle: The Question of Influence* (London: Centenary Press, 1972), 41–60.

Dennis Organ, "Compression and Explosion: Pattern in *Hard Times*," *RE* 8 (Fall 1981): 29–37.

Ian Ousby, "Figurative Language in *Hard Times*," *DUJ* 74 n.s. (December 1981): 103–9.

William J. Palmer, "*Hard Times*: A Dickens' Fable of Personal Salvation," *DR* 52 (Spring 1972): 67–77.

Anna Maria Piglionica, "M'Choackumchild M'Choakumreader: I paradossi di Dickens," in *La performance del testo*, ed. Franco Marucci and Adriano Bruttini (Siena: Ticci, 1986), 203–13.

Edwin Pugh, "*Hard Times*," in *Charles Dickens, The Apostle of the People* (London: New Age, 1908), 191–207.

Walter B. Rodd, "Stephen Blackpool's Prayer," *Dickensian* 6 (1910): 186–87.

Stephen R. Rounds, "Naming People: Dickens's Technique in *Hard Times*," *DSN* 8 (June 1977): 36–40.

Geoffrey Johnston Sadock, "Dickens and Dr. Leavis: A Critical Commentary on *Hard Times*," *DSA* 2 (1972): 208–16.

Anny Sadrin, "The Perversion of Desire: A Study of Irony as a Structural Element in *Hard Times*," in *Studies in the Later Dickens*, ed. Jean–Claude Amalric (Montpellier: Université Paul Valéry, 1973), 93–117.

Anny Sadrin, "A Plea for Gradgrind," *YES* 3 (1973): 196–205.

Anny Sadrin," La Ville dans *Hard Times*," in *ÉA* 45 (1973): 151–62.

Kristin Flieger Samuelian, "Being Rid of Women: Middle–Class Ideology in *Hard Times*," *VN* 82 (Fall 1992): 58–61.

Paul Schacht, "Dickens and the Uses of Nature," *VS* 34 (Autumn 1990): 77–102.

F. S. Schwarzbach, "*Hard Times*: The Industrial City," in *Dickens and the City* (London: Athlone, 1979), 143–50.

Anne Sedgely, "*Hard Times*: Facts or Fantasy?" *CR* 6 (1973): 116–32.

Georg Seehase, "Hard Times," in *Charles Dickens, zu einer Besonderheit seines Realismus* (Halle: Niemeyer, 1961), 92–109.

David E. E. Sloane, "Phrenology in *Hard Times*: A Source for Bitzer," *DSN* 5 (March 1974): 9–12.

Anne Smith, "*Hard Times* and *The Times* Newspaper," *Dickensian* 69 (September 1973): 153–62.

Anne Smith, "The Martyrdom of Stephen in *Hard Times*," *JNT* 2 (September 1972): 159–70.

Frank Smith, "Perverted Balance: Expressive Form in *Hard Times*," *DSN* 6 (December 1977): 102–18.

Grahame Smith, "Comic Subversion and *Hard Times*," *DSA* 18 (1989): 145–60.

Grahame Smith, "'O Reason Not the Need': *King Lear*, *Hard Times* and Utilitarian Values," *Dickensian* 86 (Autumn 1990): 164–70.

David Sonstroem, "Fettered Fancy in *Hard Times*," *PMLA* 84 (1969): 520–29.

Stephen J. Spector, "Monsters of Metonymy: *Hard Times* and Knowing the Working Class," *ELH* 51 (Summer 1984): 365–84. Reprinted in *Charles Dickens*, ed. Harold Bloom (New York: Chelsea House, 1987), 229–44.

Peter T. Stapleton, "*Hard Times*: Dickens' Counter Cultures," *Clearing House* 47 (1973): 380–81.

John A. Stoler, "Dickens' Use of Names in *Hard Times*," *LOS* 12 (1985): 153–64.

Mary Rose Sullivan, "Black and White Characters in *Hard Times*," *VN* 38 (1970): 5–10.

Masami Tanabe, "A Study on [sic] *Hard Times*—As an Example of the Collapse of a Novel," *HirUS* 29, no. 2 (1970): 125–42.

Rodger L. Tarr, "Carlyle and the Problem of the *Hard Times* Dedication," *DSN* 3 (March 1972): 25–27.

Geoffrey Thurley, "*Hard Times*," in *The Dickens Myth: Its Genesis and Structure* (New York: St. Martin's, 1976), 203–24. Reprinted as "Gradgrind and

Bounderby: Character and Caricature," in *Charles Dickens's "Hard Times,"* ed. Harold Bloom (New York: Chelsea House, 1987), 55–60.

Stanley Tick, "*Hard Times*, Page One: An Analysis," *VN* 46 (1974): 20–22.

V. V. Tsybul'skaia, "Zhanrovoe svoeobrazie romana Ch. Dikkensa *Tiazhelye vremena*," *FN* 2, no. 158 (1987): 22–27.

Kensuke Ueki, "Charles Dickens: *Hard Times*—His Creative Power and Social Criticism," *HirUS* 33 (1974): 300–28.

A. E. Voss, "A Note on Theme and Structure in *Hard Times*," *Theoria* 23 (1964): 35–42.

A. J. A. Waldock, "The Status of *Hard Times*," *Southerly* 9 (1948): 33–39.

Bruce L. Wallis, "Dickens' *Hard Times*," *Expl* 44 (Winter 1986): 26–27.

Michael Wheeler, "Apocalypse in a Mechanical Age: *Hard Times*," in *The Art of Allusion in Victorian Fiction* (London: Macmillan; New York: Barnes & Noble, 1979), 61–77.

Raymond Williams, "The Industrial Novels: *Hard Times*," in *Charles Dickens's "Hard Times,"* ed. Harold Bloom (New York: Chelsea House, 1987), 11–15.

Meinhart Winkgens, "Das Problem der 'historischen Wahrheit' in dem Roman *Hard Times* von Charles Dickens," *Poetica* 12, no. 1 (1980): 24–58.

Warrington Winters, "Dickens's *Hard Times*: The Lost Childhood," *DSA* 2 (1972): 217–36.

Shiro Yamamoto, "*Hard Times*: Forms and Content—Dickens, Leavis, and Another Tradition?" *SELit* 28 (1988): 35–50.

Cecilia Zeiss, "*Hard Times*," *CRUX* 7 (August 1973): 19–23.

"The Haunted Man"

Ruth Glancy, "Dickens at Work on 'The Haunted Man,'" *DSA* 15 (1986): 65–85.

Jerry Herron, "'The Haunted Man' and the Two Scrooges," *SSF* 19 (Winter 1982): 45–50.

Walter H. Kemp, "'The Haunted Man' and Musical Meaning," *Dickensian* 74 (May 1978): 76–79.

Scott Moncrieff, "Remembrance of Wrongs Past in 'The Haunted Man,'" *SSF* 28 (Fall 1991): 535–41.

Lucien Potyhet, "'The Haunted Man' de Charles Dickens, ou: Les déguisements d'une confidence," in *Littérature-linguistique-civilisation-pédagogie* (Paris: Didier, 1976), 151–68.

"The House at Holly-Tree Inn"

Deborah A. Thomas, "The Chord of the Christmas Season: Playing 'House at the Holly-Tree Inn,'" *DSN* 11 (June 1980): 41–46.

"Hunted Down"

Philip V. Allingham, "Dickens's Unreliable Narrator in 'Hunted Down,'" *SSF* 29 (Winter 1992): 85–93.

"The Key of the Street"

Maurice Blackman, "Charles Dickens et Les Nuits d'octobre: Cles pour le réalisme nervalien," *AJFS* 19 (January–April 1982): 32–40.

Little Dorrit

Jacques-Pierre Aintette, "Un roman de Dickens," *NRF* n.s. 36 (November 1970): 72–75.

Robert Barnard, "The Imagery of *Little Dorrit*," in *ES* 52 (December 1971): 520–32.

Edward B. Barrett, "*Little Dorrit* and the Disease of Modern Life," *NCF* 25 (September 1970): 199–215.

Jerome Beaty, "The 'Soothing Songs' of *Little Dorrit*: New Light on Dickens's Darkness," in *Nineteenth-Century Literary Perspectives: Essays in Honor of Lionel Stevenson*, ed. Clyde de L. Ryals (Durham, NC: Duke University Press, 1974), 219–36.

Carol A. Bock, "Miss Wade and George Silverman: The Forms of Fictional Monologue," *DSA* 16 (1987): 113–26.

William Burgan, "Little Dorrit in Italy," *NCF* 29 (March 1975): 393–411.

William Burgan, "People in the Setting of *Little Dorrit*," *TSLL* 15 (Spring 1973): 111–28.

Janice Carlisle, "*Little Dorrit*: Necessary Fictions," *SNNTS* 7 (Summer 1975): 195–214.

Peter Christmas, "*Little Dorrit*: The End of Good and Evil," *DSA* 6 (1977): 134–53.

Philip Collins, "Arthur Clennam Arrives in London: A Note on *Little Dorrit*, Chapter III,'" *L&H* 8 (Autumn 1978): 214–22.

Philip Collins, "*Little Dorrit*: The Prison and the Critics," *TLS* (18 April 1980): 445–46.

Michael Cotsell, "The Stephen Family and Dickens's Circumlocution Office Satire," *DQu* 3 (December 1986): 175–78.

Iain Crawford, "'Machinery in Motion': Time in *Little Dorrit*," *Dickensian* 84 (Spring 1988): 30–41.

Richard A. Currie, "'As if she had done him a wrong': Hidden Rage and Object Protection in Dickens's Amy Dorrit," *ES* 72 (August 1991): 368–76.

H. M. Daleski, "Large Loose Baggy Monsters and *Little Dorrit*," *DSA* 21 (1992): 131–42.

Alistair M. Duckworth, "*Little Dorrit* and the Question of Closure," *NCF* 33 (June 1978): 110–30.

Wilfred P. Dvorak, "The Misunderstood Pancks: Money and the Rhetoric of Disguise in *Little Dorrit*," *SNNTS* 23 (Fall 1991): 339–48.

Angus Easson, "John Civery and the Wounded Strephon: A Pastoral Element in *Little Dorrit*," *DUJ* 67 (June 1975): 165–69.

Angus Easson, "Marshalsea Prisoners: Mr. Dorrit and Mr. Hemens," *DSA* 3 (1974): 77–86.

F. T. Flahiff, "'Mysteriously Come Together': Dickens, Chaucer, and *Little Dorrit*," *UTQ* 61 (Winter 1991): 250–68.

Avrom Fleishman, "Master and Servant in *Little Dorrit*," *SEL* 14 (Autumn 1974): 575–86. Revised and reprinted in *Fiction and the Ways of Knowing: Essays on British Novels* (Austin: University of Texas Press, 1978), 64–73. Reprinted in *Nineteenth–Century Literary Perspectives: Essays in Honor of Lionel Stevenson*, ed. Clyde de L. Ryals (Durham, NC: Duke University Press, 1974), 219–36.

William E. Gamble, "Retribution and Reward in Dickens's *Little Dorrit*," *TPB* 11 (July 1974): 25–26.

David Gervais, "The Poetry of *Little Dorrit*," *CQ* 4 (Winter 1969): 38–54.

Benny Green, "In the Pit," *Spectator* 230 (3 March 1973): 275.

Michael Greenstein, "Liminality in *Little Dorrit*," *DQu* 7 (June 1990): 275–83.

T. N. Grove, "The Psychological Prison of Arthur Clennam in Dickens's *Little Dorrit*," *MLR* 68 (October 1973): 750–55.

Morse Hamilton, "Nature and the Unnatural in *Little Dorrit*," *VIJ* 6 (January 1977): 9–20.

Dirk Den Hartog, "*Little Dorrit*: Dickens's Dialogue with Wordsworth," *CR* 23 (1981): 13–19.

Edward Heatley, "The Redeemed Feminine of *Little Dorrit*," *DSA* 4 (1975): 153–66.

Douglas Hewitt, "The Logical Prison: *Little Dorrit*," in *The Approach to Fiction: Good and Bad Readings of Novels* (London: Longman, 1972), 85–102.

Michael Hollington, "Time in *Little Dorrit*," in *The English Novel in the Nineteenth Century: Essays on the Literary Mediation of Human Values*, ed. George Goodin (Urbana: University of Illinois Press, 1972), 109–25.

George Holoch, "Consciousness and Society in *Little Dorrit*," *VS* 21 (Spring 1978): 335–51.

Lewis Horne, "*Little Dorrit* and the Region of Despair," *DR* 69 (Winter 1989): 533–48.

David Jarrett, "The Fall of the House of Clennam: Gothic Conventions in *Little Dorrit*," *Dickensian* 73 (September 1977): 154–61.

D. W. Jefferson, "The Moral Centre of *Little Dorrit*," *EIC* 26 (October 1976): 300–17.

Mary Ann Kelly, "Imagination, Fantasy, and Memory in *Little Dorrit*," *DSN* 13 (June 1982): 48–50.

Janet Larson, "Apocalyptic Style in *Little Dorrit*," *DQu* 1 (June 1984): 41–49.

George Levine, "*Little Dorrit* and Three Kinds of Science," in *Dickens and Other Victorians: Essays in Honor of Philip Collins*, ed. Joanne Shattock (New York: St. Martin's, 1988), 3–24.

Ronald S. Librach, "Burdens of Self and Society: Release and Redemption in *Little Dorrit*," *SNNTS* 7 (Winter 1975): 538–51.

Tom Linehan, "The Importance of Plot in *Little Dorrit*," *JNT* 6 (Spring 1976): 116–31.

Roger D. Lund, "Genteel Fictions: Character and Satirical Design in *Little Dorrit*," *DSA* 10 (1982): 45–66.

Loralee MacPike, "Dickens and Dostoevsky: The Technique of Reverse Influence," in *The Changing World of Charles Dickens*, ed. Robert Giddings (London: Vision, 1983; Totowa, NJ: Barnes & Noble, 1983), 196–215.

DICKENS, CHARLES, *Little Dorrit*

Glenn K. S. Man, "Affirmation in Dickens's *Little Dorrit*," *ELWIU* 6 (Spring 1979): 43–56.

Mary Mason, "Deixis: A Point of Entry to Little Dorrit," in *Language and Literature: An Introductory Reader in Stylistics*, ed. Ronald Carter (London: Allen & Unwin, 1982), 29–38.

Nancy Aycock Metz, "The Blighted Tree and the Book of Fate: Female Models of Storytelling in *Little Dorrit*," *DSA* 18 (1989): 221–41.

Nancy Aycock Metz, "Little Dorrit's London: Babylon Revisited," *VS* 33 (Spring 1990): 465–86.

Nancy Aycock Metz, "Physician as Cliché and as Character," *DSN* 13 (June 1982): 38–42.

Koichi Miyazaki, *Capsules in Space*—Little Dorrit (Tokyo: Seijo, 1973), 1–21.

Graham Mott, "Was There a Stain upon Little Dorrit?" *Dickensian* 76 (Spring 1980): 31–39.

Ira Bruce Nadel, "'Wonderful Deception': Art and the Artist in *Little Dorrit*," *Criticism* 19 (Winter 1977): 17–33.

Jeff Nunokawa, "Getting and Having: Some Versions of Possession in *Little Dorrit*," *Charles Dickens*, ed. Harold Bloom (New York: Chelsea, 1987), 317–35.

Carol Pagetti, "*Little Dorrit*: Dickens e il labirinto del linguaggio," *StIng* 2 (1975): 155–78.

Marie Peel, "*Little Dorrit*: Prison or Cage?" *B&B* 17 (September 1972): 38–42.

Simon Petch, "*Little Dorrit*: Some Visions of Pastoral," *SSEng* 7 (1981–82): 102–14.

Trey Philpotts, "'To Working Men' and 'The People': Dickens's View of Class Relations in the Months Preceding *Little Dorrit*," *DQu* 7 (June 1990): 262–75.

Kalyan B. Ray, "Nomenclature and Satire in *Little Dorrit*," *DQu* 1 (March 1984): 10–11.

Bette B. Roberts, "Travel versus Imprisonment: The 'Fellow Travelers' in *Little Dorrit*," *DSN* 13 (December 1982): 109–112.

Henry N. Rogers, III, "Shadows of Irony: The Comic Structure of *Little Dorrit*," *PAPA* 5 (Fall 1979): 58–63.

R. Rupert Roopnaraine, "Time and the Circle in *Little Dorrit*," *DSA* 3 (1974): 54–76.

Charlotte Rotkin, "The Athenaeum Reviews *Little Dorrit*," *VPR* 23 (Spring 1990): 25–28.

Dianne F. Sadoff, "Storytelling and the Figure of the Father in *Little Dorrit*," *PMLA* 95 (March 1980): 234–45.

Akira Sano, "[The Decline of the Father in *Little Dorrit*]," in *ISP* 3 (1972): 73–87.

J. G. Schippers, "So Many Characters, So Many Words: Some Aspects of the Language of *Little Dorrit*," *DQu* 8, no. 4 (1978): 242–65.

Vikotr Shklovsky, "The Mystery Novel: Dickens's *Little Dorrit*," trans. Guy Carter, in *Readings in Russian Poetics: Formalist and Structuralist Views*, ed. Ladislav Matejka and Krystyna Pomorska (Cambridge, MA: MIT Press, 1971): 220–26.

Elaine Showalter, "Guilt, Authority, and the Shadows of *Little Dorrit*," *NCF* 34 (June 1979): 20–40.

Randolph Splitter, "Guilt and the Trappings of Melodrama in *Little Dorrit*," *DSA* 6 (1977): 119–33.

Marlene Springer, "Teaching Dickens: A Note on *Little Dorrit*," *JETT* 10 (Summer 1980): 53–58.

Michael Squires, "The Structure of Dickens's Imagination in *Little Dorrit*," *TSLL* 30 (Spring 1988): 49–64.

Richard Stang, "*Little Dorrit*: A World in Reverse," in *Dickens the Craftsman: Strategies of Presentation*, ed. Robert B. Partlow Jr. (Carbondale: Southern Illinois University Press, 1970), 140–64.

Adela Styczynska, "The Shifting Point of View in the Narrative Design of *Little Dorrit*," *Dickensian* 82 (Spring 1986): 39–51.

Harvey Peter Sucksmith, "The Melodramatic Villain in *Little Dorrit*," *Dickensian* 71 (May 1975): 76–83.

Kathryn Sutherland, "A Guide through the Labyrinth: Dickens's *Little Dorrit* as Hypertext," *L&LC* 5, no. 4 (1990): 305–09.

Charles Swann, "Wainewright the Poisoner: A Source for Blandois/Rigaud?" *N&Q* 35 (September 1988): 321–22.

Akira Takeuchi, "The Structure of *Little Dorrit*," *KS* 21 (March 1973): 39–65.

Deborah A. Thomas, "Dickens and Indigestion: The Deadly Dinners of the Rich," *DSN* 14 (March 1983): 7–12.

Stanley Tick, "The Sad End of Mr. Meagles," *DSA* 3 (1974): 87–99.

Lionel Trilling, "*Little Dorrit*," in *The Opposing Self: Nine Essays in Criticism* (New York: Harcourt Brace, 1978), 44–57.

Barbara Weiss, "Secret Pockets and Secret Breasts: *Little Dorrit* and the Commercial Scandals of the Fifties," *DSA* 10 (1982): 67–76.

George Wing, "Mr. F's Aunt: A Laughing Matter," *ESC* 3 (Summer 1977): 677–87.

Sarah Winter, "Domestic Fictions: Feminine Deference and Maternal Shadow Labor in Dickens's *Little Dorrit*," *DSA* 18 (1989): 243–54.

M. R. Woodhead, "De Quincy and *Little Dorrit*," *N&Q* n.s. 19 (November 1972): 409.

Kathleen Woodward, "Passivity and Passion in *Little Dorrit*," *Dickensian* 71 (September 1975): 140–48.

Ruth Bernard Yeazell, "Do It or Dorrit," *Novel* 25 (Fall 1991): 33–49.

Dvora Zelicovici, "Circularity and Linearity in *Little Dorrit*," *DQu* 1 (June 1984): 50–53.

Dvora Zelicovici, "The First Chapter of *Little Dorrit*: Overture to the Novel," *Ariel* 13 (April 1982): 47–64.

James R. Zimmerman, "Sun and Shadow in *Little Dorrit*," *Dickensian* 83 (Summer 1987): 93–105.

E. J. Zinkhan, "Charles Rowcroft's Chronicles of 'The Fleet Prison': A Source for Amy Dorrit?" *Dickensian* 81 (Autumn 1985): 130–39.

Martin Chuzzlewit

Jerry C. Beasley, "The Role of Tom Pinch in *Martin Chuzzlewit*," *Ariel* 5 (April 1974): 77–89.

M. T. Beatty, "Dickens and the Good–Natured Man: Eating and Drinking in *Martin Chuzzlewit*," *UCTStE* 6 (October 1976): 24–32.

Katherine Carolan, "Dickens's American Secretary and *Martin Chuzzlewit*," *DSN* 7 (December 1976): 109.

Michael Coulson Berthold, "Ontological Insecurity in *Martin Chuzzlewit*," *DSN* 14 (September 1983): 135–42.

Alan R. Burke, "The House of Chuzzlewit and the Architectural City," *DSA* 3 (1972): 14–40.

Stuart Curran, "The Lost Paradises of *Martin Chuzzlewit*," *NCF* 25 (June 1970): 51–68.

Rodney Stenning Edgecombe, "Locution and Authority in *Martin Chuzzlewit*," *ES* 74 (April 1993): 143–53.

Rodney Stenning Edgecombe, "The Urban Idyll in *Martin Chuzzlewit*," *RES* 45 (August 1994): 370–83.

Edward J. Evans, "The Established Self: The American Episodes of *Martin Chuzzlewit*," *DSA* 5 (1976): 59–73.

Leslie A. Fiedler, "*Martin Chuzzlewit*: A Great Bad Book," *DQR* 16, no. 1 (1986): 16–21. Reprinted in *A Centre of Excellence: Essays Presented to Seymour Betsky*, ed. Robert Druce (Amsterdam: Rodopi, 1987), 43–48.

John Hildebidle, "Hail Columbia: *Martin Chuzzlewit* in America," *DSA* 15 (1986): 41–54.

Gerhard Joseph, "The Labyrinth and the Library: A View from the Temple in *Martin Chuzzlewit*," *DSA* 15 (1986): 1–22.

Gerhard Joseph and Jay Fellows, "Mixed Messages in Mr. Pecksniff's Grammar School: A Defense of That Celebrated though Much–Maligned Parasite's Architectural Principles, as Necessitated by a Universal Misunderstanding of Them, of Him, and of Chapter 35 of *Martin Chuzzlewit*, by Charles Dickens, the Drunken Architect of the House of Chuzzlewit: Or, The Rift in Pater's Lute," in *Perspectives on Perception: Philosophy, Art, and Literature*, ed. Mary Ann Caws (New York: Peter Lang, 1989), 224–59.

Robert E. Lougy, "Repressive and Expressive Forms: The Bodies of Comedy and Desire in *Martin Chuzzlewit*," *DSA* 21 (1992): 37–61.

Carol Hanbery MacKay, "The Letter–Writer and the Text in *Martin Chuzzlewit*," *SEL* 26 (Autumn 1986): 737–58.

Sylvère Monod, "Mr. Bevan," *DSA* 15 (1986): 23–40.

Norris Pope, "A View from the Monument: A Note on *Martin Chuzzlewit*," *DQu* 4 (September 1987): 153–60.

Branwen Bailey Pratt, "Dickens and Freedom: Young Bailey in *Martin Chuzzlewit*," *NCF* 30 (June 1975): 185–99.

Mary Rosner, "A Note on Two Allusions: *Martin Chuzzlewit*, Chapter 1," *DSN* 12 (March 1981): 12–13.

Mary Rosner, "Reading the Beasts of *Martin Chuzzlewit*," *DQu* 4 (September 1987): 131–41.

Steven Rubenstein, "Visual Aids, Mental Impediments; or, the Problem with Phiz," *DQu* 9 (March 1992): 19–25.

Barrie Saywood, "*Martin Chuzzlewit*: Language as Disguise," *Dickensian* 82 (Summer 1986): 86–97.

Anne Summers, "The Mysterious Demise of Sarah Gamp: The Domiciliary Nurse and Her Detractors, c. 1830–1860," *VS* 32 (Spring 1989): 365–86.

Kathleen Wales, "The Claims of Kinship: The Opening Chapter of *Martin Chuzzlewit*," *Dickensian* 83 (Autumn 1987): 167–79.

Master Humphrey's Clock

K. A. Chittick, "The Idea of a Miscellany: *Master Humphrey's Clock*," *Dickensian* 78 (Autumn 1982): 156–64.

Tony Giffone, "Putting Master Humphrey Back Together Again," *JNT* 17 (Winter 1987): 102–06.

Rosemary Mundhenk, "Creative Ambivalence in Dickens's *Master Humphrey's Clock*," *SEL* 32 (Autumn 1992): 645–61.

"Mrs. Lirriper's Lodgings"

Deborah A. Thomas, "Dickens' Mrs. Lirriper and the Evolution of a Feminine Stereotype," *DSA* 6 (1977): 154–66, 196–98.

The Mystery of Edwin Drood

Doris Alexander, "Solving the Mysteries of the Mind in *Edwin Drood*," *DQu* 9 (September 1992): 125–31.

John Beer, "Edwin Drood and the Mystery of Apartness," *DSA* 13 (1984): 143–91.

Everett F. Bleiler, "The Names in Drood," *DQu* 1 (September 1984; December 1984): 88–93; 137–42.

Albert I. Borowitz, "The Mystery of Edwin Drood," *ArmD* 10 (January 1977): 14–16, 82. Reprinted in *Innocence and Arsenic: Studies in Crime and Literature* (New York: Harper & Row, 1977), 53–62.

Gareth Cordery, "The Cathedral as Setting and Symbol in *The Mystery of Edwin Drood*," *DSN* 10 (December 1979): 97–103.

Arthur J. Cox, "Dickens's Last Book: More Mysteries Than One," *ArmD* 14 (Winter 1981): 31–36.

Arthur J. Cox, "The Haggard Woman," *M&DA* (1972): 65–77.

Don Richard Cox, "Shaw on Edwin Drood: Some Unpublished Letters," *Dickensian* 84 (Spring 1988): 27–29.

Jean-Louis Cupers, "Présence de la musique chez Dickens et Daudet: Le Mystère d'Edwin Drood et La Petite Paroisse," *RLC* 61 (July–September 1987): 295–303.

A. E. Dyson, "*Edwin Drood*: A Horrible Wonder Apart," *CritQ* 11 (Winter 1969): 138–57.

Benjamin Franklin Fisher, IV, "Edwin's Mystery and Its History: Or, Another Look at Datchery," *MFAN* 4 (March 1980): 6–8.

Benjamin Franklin Fisher, "Sunshine and Shadow in *The Mystery of Edwin Drood*," *MFAN* 11 (Fall 1989): 11–28.

Robert F. Fleissner, "A Drood Awakening," *DSN* 11 (March 1980): 17–19.

Robert F. Fleissner, "Drood Renominated," *Names* 40 (June 1992): 117–22.

Robert F. Fleissner. "*Drood* the Obscure: The Evidence of the Names," *ArmD* 13 (Winter 1980): 12–16.

Judith Prescott Flynn, "'Fugitive and Cloistered Virtue': Innocence and Evil in *Edwin Drood*," *ESC* 9 (September 1983): 312–25.

Charles Forsyte, "An Ancient English Cathedral Town?" *N&Q* 31 (March 1984): 66–69.

Charles Forsyte, "Children's Games in *Edwin Drood*," *N&Q* 34 (March 1987): 43–46.

Charles Forsyte, "Dickens and Dick Datchery," *Dickensian* 87 (Spring 1991): 50–57.

Charles Forsyte, "Drood and the Beanstalk," *Dickensian* 80 (Summer 1984): 74–88.

Charles Forsyte, "How Did Drood Die?" *Dickensian* 84 (Summer 1988): 81–95.

Charles Forsyte, "The Sapsea Fragment: Fragment of What?" *Dickensian* 82 (Spring 1986): 12–26.

Jeffrey Michael Gantz, "Notes on the Identity of Dick Datchery," *DSN* 8 (September 1977): 72–78.

Paul Gottschalk, "Time in *Edwin Drood*," *DSA* 1 (1970): 265–72.

Apryl Lea Denny Heath, "Who was Hiram Grewgious? A Further Study of Identity in Charles Dickens' *The Mystery of Edwin Drood*," *ArmD* 17 (Fall 1984): 402–03.

Lauriat Lane, Jr., "*The Mystery of Edwin Drood* in Contexts," *IFR* 16 (Winter 1989): 23–25.

Stefano Manferlotti, "Generi e parodia dei generi in *The Mystery of Edwin Drood* di C. Dickens," in *La performance del testo*, ed. Franco Marucci and Adriano Bruttini (Siena: Ticci, 1986), 195–202.

Evelyne Pieller, "Rêvez lecteur!" *QL* 316 (January 1980): 10–11.

Margaret Reynolds, "'In Chancery' Again: Dickens and Prize-Fighting," *DSN* 14 (June 1983): 48–50.

W. W. Robson, "*The Mystery of Edwin Drood*: The Solution," *TLS* (11 November 1983): 1246.

Nancy E. Schaumburger, "The 'Gritty Stages of Life': Psychological Time in *The Mystery of Edwin Drood*," *Dickensian* 86 (Autumn 1990): 158–63.

Nancy E. Schaumburger, "The 'Gritty Stages' of Life: Psychological Time in *The Mystery of Edwin Drood*," *UMSE* 8 (1990): 137–42.

Natalie Schroeder, "Echoes of *Paradise Lost* in *The Mystery of Edwin Drood*," *DSN* 13 (June 1982): 42–47.

Susan Shatto, "Dickens's Edwin Drood and Southey's 'Jaspar,'" *N&Q* 32 (September 1985): 359–60.

Marilyn Thomas, "Edwin Drood: A Bone Yard Awaiting Resurrection," *DQu* 2 (March 1985): 12–17.

Kathleen Wales, "Dickens and Interior Monologue: The Opening of *Edwin Drood* Reconsidered," *L&S* 17 (Summer 1984): 234–50.

Nicholas Nickleby

Carol A. Bock, "Violence and the Fictional Modes of *Nicholas Nickelby*," *MSE* 10 (Fall 1985): 87–101.

W. J. Carlton, "Janet Barrow's Portrait Miniatures: An Australian Epilogue," *Dickensian* 68 (May 1972): 100–03.

Francesco Casotti, "Lo sviluppo delle tematiche dickensiane in *Nicholas Nickelby*," *Misc* 1 (1971): 83–112.

Lois E. Chaney, "The Fives Court," *Dickensian* 81 (Summer 1985): 86–87.

Mary Cleopha Cipar, O.S.U., "Picaresque Characteristics in *Nicholas Nickelby*," *Dickensian* 84 (Spring 1988): 43–46.

Michael Cotsell, "*Nicholas Nickelby*: Dickens's First Young Man," *DQu* 5 (September 1988): 118–28.

Ashby Bland Crowder, "A Source for Dickens's Sir Mulberry," *PLL* 12 (Winter 1976): 105–09.

Gary H. Day, "The Relevance of the Nickleby Stories," *Dickensian* 81 (Spring 1985): 52–56.

Angus Easson, "Emotion and Gesture in *Nicholas Nickelby*," *DQu* 5 (September 1988): 136–51.

Margaret Ganz, "*Nicholas Nickelby*: The Victories of Humor," *Mosaic* 9 (Summer 1976): 131–48.

Robin Gilmour, "Between Two Worlds: Aristocracy and Gentility in *Nicholas Nickelby*," *DQu* 5 (September 1988): 110–18.

Ruth F. Glancy, "The Significance of the 'Nickleby' Stories," *Dickensian* 75 (Spring 1979): 12–15.

Beth F. Herst, "*Nicholas Nickelby* and the Idea of the Hero," *DQu* 5 (September 1988): 128–36.

Lewis Horne, "Covenant and Power in *Nicholas Nickelby*; Or, The Guidance of Newman Noggs," *PLL* 25 (Spring 1989): 165–77.

Carol Hanbery MacKay, "The Melodramatic Impulse in *Nicholas Nickelby*," *DQu* 5 (September 1988): 152–63.

Robert Simpson MacLean, "Another Note on Nickleby," *DSN* 9 (March 1978): 6–9.

Robert Simpson MacLean, "How 'the Infant Phenomenon' Began the World: The Managing of Jean Margaret Davenport (182?–1903)," *Dickensian* 88 (Fall 1992): 133–53.

Patricia Marks, "Time in *Nicholas Nickelby*," *VN* 55 (Spring 1979): 23–26.

Jerome Meckier, "The Faint Image of Eden: The Many Worlds of *Nicholas Nickelby*," *DSA* 1 (1970): 129–46.

John W. Noffsinger, "The Complexity of Ralph Nickleby," *DSN* 5 (December 1974): 112–14.

John K. Saunders, "The Case of Mrs. Nickleby: Humor and Negligent Parenthood," *DSN* 10 (June–September 1979): 56–58.

Paul Schlicke, "Crummles Once More," *Dickensian* 86 (Spring 1990): 3–16.

Michael Slater, "Appreciating Mrs. Nickleby," *Dickensian* 71 (September 1975): 136–39.

DICKENS, CHARLES, *The Old Curiosity Shop*

Nancy Jane Tyson, "A Dickens Line from Sheridan," *ANQ* 3 (July 1990): 106–07.

Terrence Whaley, "Dickensian Image of the School Teacher," in *From Socrates to Software: The Teacher as Text and the Text as Teacher*, ed. Philip W. Jackson and Sophie Haroutunian-Gordon (Chicago: National Society for Study of Education, 1989), 36–59.

The Old Curiosity Shop

Lynn C. Bartlett, "High Life Below Stairs or Cribbage in the Kitchen," *ELN* 23 (December 1985): 54–61.

Rachel Bennett, "Punch versus Christian in *The Old Curiosity Shop*," *RES* n.s. 22 (November 1971): 423–34.

Joel J. Brattin, "Some Curiosities from *The Old Curiosity Shop* Manuscript," *DQu* 7 (March 1990): 218–34.

Jean Dalby Clift, "Dickens's Little Nell and the Lost Feminine: An Archetypal Analysis of Projections in Victorian Culture," *Albion* 8 (Summer 1976): 180.

John J. Conlon, "Private Sphinx and Public Sphynx: Riddle and Revelation in *The Old Curiosity Shop*," *DQu* 7 (March 1990): 234–36.

G. Cordery, "The Gambling Grandfather in *The Old Curiosity Shop*," *L&P* 33, no. 1 (1987): 43–61.

Patrick Diskin, "The Literary Background of *The Old Curiosity Shop*," *N&Q* n.s. 21 (June 1974): 210–13.

Wilfred P. Dvorak, "Charles Dickens's *The Old Curiosity Shop*: The Triumph of Compassion," *PLL* 28 (Winter 1992): 52–71.

Wilfred P. Dvorak, "On the Knocking at the Gate in *The Old Curiosity Shop*," *SNNTS* 16 (Fall 1984): 304–13.

A. E. Dyson, "*The Old Curiosity Shop*: Innocence and Grotesque," *CritQ* 8 (1966): 111–30.

Angus Easson, "Dickens's Marchioness Again," *MLR* 65 (July 1970): 517–19.

Marcia Muelder Eaton, "Laughing at the Death of Little Nell: Sentimental Art and Sentimental People," *AmPQ* 26 (October 1989): 269–82.

R. S. Edgecombe, "A Note on *The Old Curiosity Shop* and the Eighteenth-Century Night Piece," *Theoria* 72 (October 1988): 53–61.

Monroe Engel, "A Kind of Allegory: *The Old Curiosity Shop*," in *The Interpretation of Narrative: Theory and Practice*, ed. Morton W. Bloomfield (Cambridge, MA: Harvard University Press, 1970), 135–49.

Monica L. Feinberg, "Reading Curiosity: Does Dick's *Shop* Deliver?" *DQu* 7 (March 1990): 200–211.

J. C. Field, "Fantasy and Flaw in *The Old Curiosity*," *RVL* 35, no. 6 (1969): 609–22.

Robert F. Fleissner and Loralee MacPike, "'Fancy's (K)Nell' Retolled,'" *DSN* 13 (September 1982): 76–79.

Michael Greenstein, "Lenticular Curiosity and *The Old Curiosity Shop*," *DQu* 4 (December 1987): 187–94.

Pat Hodgell, "Charles Dickens' *Old Curiosity Shop*: The Gothic Novel in Transition," *RQ* 8 (July 1990): 152–69.

Michael Hollington, "Adorno, Benjamin and *The Old Curiosity Shop*," *DQu* 6 (September 1989): 87–95.

Lewis Horne, "*The Old Curiosity Shop* and the Limits of Melodrama," *DR* 72 (Winter 1992): 494–518.

Susan R. Horton, "Swivellers and Snivellers: Competing Epistemologies in *The Old Curiosity Shop*," *DQu* 7 (March 1990): 212–17.

Audrey Jaffe, "'Never Be Safe but in Hiding': Omniscience and Curiosity in *The Old Curiosity Shop*," *Novel* 19 (Winter 1986): 118–34.

G. W. Kennedy, "Terror and Dream: Nell and *The Old Curiosity Shop*," *EngStColl* 1 (September 1976): 1–7.

John Kucich, "Death Worship among the Victorians: *The Old Curiosity Shop*," *PMLA* 95 (January 1980): 58–72.

Adriane LaPointe, "Little Nell Once More: Absent Fathers in *The Old Curiosity Shop*," *DSA* 18 (1989): 19–38.

Robert Simpson McLean, "Another Source for Quilp," *NCF* 26 (December 1971): 337–39.

Loralee MacPike, "*The Old Curiosity Shop*: Changing Views of Little Nell, Part II," *DSN* 12 (September 1981): 70–76.

Richard Maxwell, "Crowds and Creativity in *The Old Curiosity Shop*," *JEGP* 78 (January 1979): 49–71.

Jerome Meckier, "Suspense in *The Old Curiosity Shop*: Dickens's Contrapuntal Artistry," *JNT* 2 (September 1972): 199–207.

John W. Noffsinger, "Dream in *The Old Curiosity Shop*," *SoAB* 42 (May 1977): 23–34.

Anthony O'Keeffe, "*The Old Curiosity Shop*," *SoAR* 53 (November 1988): 39–55.

Robert L. Patton, "'The Story–Weaver at His Loom': Dickens and the Beginning of *The Old Curiosity Shop*," in *Dickens the Craftsman: Strategies of Presentation*, ed. Robert B. Partlow Jr. (Carbondale: Southern Illinois University Press, 1970), 44–64.

Ross Peters, "Imaginative Transformation and Moral Unity in *The Old Curiosity Shop*," *AUMLA* 78 (November 1992): 41–62.

Torsten Pettersson, "'Impostors and Deceptions': The Social Side of *The Old Curiosity Shop*," *SN* 64, no. 1 (1992): 81–87.

Torsten Pettersson, "'That Never–Ending Restlessness': The Revulsion from Life in *The Old Curiosity Shop*," *MSpr* 86, no. 2 (1992): 120–26.

Samuel F. Pickering, "*The Old Curiosity Shop*: A Religious Tract?" *IllQ* 36 (September 1973): 5–20. Reprinted as "*The Old Curiosity Shop* and Leigh Richmond's Tracts," in *The Moral Tradition in English Fiction, 1785–1850* (Hanover, NH: Dartmouth College Press, 1976), 107–22.

Branwen Bailey Pratt, "Sympathy for the Devil: A Dissenting View of Quilp," *HSL* 6, no. 2 (1974): 129–46.

Philip Rogers, "The Dynamics of Time in *The Old Curiosity Shop*," *NCF* 28 (September 1973): 127–44.

Michael Schiefelbein, "Little Nell, Catholicism, and Dickens's Investigation of Death," *DQu* 9 (September 1992): 115–25.

Paul Schlicke, "The True Pathos of *The Old Curiosity Shop*," *DQu* 7 (March 1990): 189–99.

Michael Steig, "The Central Action of *The Old Curiosity Shop* or Little Nell Revisited Again," *L&P* 15, no. 3 (1965): 163–70.

Thomas H. Stewart, "Bliss and Dickens: A Note on Little Nell and 'Little Willie,'" *UMSE* 1 (1980): 125–26.

E. Tate, "Dickens's Vanity Fair: The Show Image in *The Old Curiosity Shop*," *HKBCACJ* 4 (July 1977): 167–71.

G. M. Watkins, "A Possible Source for Quilp," *N&Q* n.s. 18 (November 1971): 411–13.

Isabella White, "The Uses of Death in *The Old Curiosity Shop*," *KPAB* (1982): 29–40.

Joan D. Winslow, "*The Old Curiosity Shop*: The Meaning of Nell's Fate," *Dickensian* 77 (Autumn 1981): 162–67.

Sue Zemka, "From the Punchmen to Pugin's Gothics: The Broad Road to a Sentimental Death in *The Old Curiosity Shop*," *NCF* 48 (December 1993): 291–319.

Oliver Twist

Roland F. Anderson, "Structure, Myth, and Rite in *Oliver Twist*," *SNNTS* 18 (Fall 1986): 238–57.

Mary Anne Andrade, "Wake into Dream," *Dickensian* 86 (Spring 1990): 17–28.

Zelda Austen, "*Oliver Twist*: A Divided View," *DSN* 7 (March 1976): 8–12.

Zelda Austen and Katherine T. Brueck, "'Poverty and Villainy in *Oliver Twist*: A Response," *DSN* 13 (December 1982): 113–14.

Cates Baldridge, "The Instabilities of Inheritance in *Oliver Twist*," *SNNTS* 25 (Summer 1993): 184–95.

André Becherand, "*Oliver Twist* et les lois sur les pauvres," *LM* 70, no. iv–v (1976): 369–81.

Sonia Bicanic, "The Function of Language in our Experience of Oliver Twist and Nancy," *SrRAZ* 37 (July 1974): 277–86.

Patrick Brantlinger, "How Oliver Twist Learned to Read, and What He Read," *BuR* 34, no. 2 (1990): 59–81.

Benjamin Brody, "Brainwashing and *Oliver Twist*," *HSL* 14, no. 2 (1982): 61–66.

Katherine T. Brueck, "Poverty and Villainy in *Oliver Twist*: Unravelling the Paradox," *DSN* 12 (September 1981): 66–70.

Mary Burgan, "Bringing up by Hand: Dickens and the Feeding of Children," *Mosaic* 24 (Summer–Fall 1991): 69–88.

Robert A. Colby, "Oliver's Progeny: Some Unfortunate Foundlings," *DQu* 4 (June 1987): 109–21.

Ian Crawford, "'Shades of the prison–house': Religious Romanticism in *Oliver Twist*," *DQu* 4 (June 1987): 78–90.

Larry Edgerton, "Dickens' *Oliver Twist*," *Expl* 40 (Fall 1981): 28–30.

Simon Edwards, "Anorexia Nervosa Versus the Fleshpots of London: Rose and Nancy in *Oliver Twist*," *DSA* 19 (1990): 49–64.

N. Elmalih, "Valeurs et récit: *Oliver Twist*," in *Récit et Roman: Formes du Roman Anglais du XVIe au XXe Siècle* (Paris: Didier, 1972), 53–61.

Christian Enzensberger, "Das Nützliche in Wirklichkeit: Charles Dickens's *Oliver Twist*," in *Leteratur und Interesse: Eine Politische Ästhetic mit zwei Beispielen aus der Englischen Literatur* (Munich and Vienna: Hanser, 1977), 91–158.

John Ferns, "*Oliver Twist*: Destruction of Love," *QQ* 79 (Spring 1972): 87–92.

K. J. Fielding, "Benthamite Utilitarianism and *Oliver Twist*: A Novel of Ideas," *DQu* 4 (June 1987): 49–65.

Robert F. Fleissner, "Dickens' *Oliver Twist*," *Expl* 41 (Spring 1983): 30–32.

Michal Peled Ginsburg, "Truth and Persuasion: The Language of Realism and of Ideology in *Oliver Twist*," *Novel* 20 (Spring 1987): 220–36.

Morris Golden, "Dickens, Oliver, and Boz," *DQu* 4 (June 1987): 65–77.

Richard Hannaford, "The Fairy World of *Oliver Twist*," *DSN* 8 (June 1977): 33–36.

Eiichi Hara, "Name and No Name: The Identity of Dickensian Heroes," *SELit* 58 (Eng. no.) (1982): 21–42.

Michael Hollington, "Dickens and Cruikshank as Physiognomers in *Oliver Twist*," *DQu* 7 (June 1990): 243–54.

Patricia Ingham, "The Name of the Hero in *Oliver Twist*," *RES* 33 (May 1982): 188–89.

Louis James, "The View from Brick Lane: Contrasting Perspectives in Working–Class and Middle–Class Fiction of the Early Victorian Period," *YES* 11 (1981): 87–101.

John O. Jordan, "The Purloined Handkerchief," *DSA* 18 (1989): 1–17.

Henryk Kellermann, "'Good, murderous melodrama': Die Harmonie von Aussage und Erzahltechnik im fruhen Dickens–Roman *Oliver Twist*," *GRM* 38, no. 4 (1988): 411–28.

William T. Lankford, "'The Parish Boy's Progress': The Evolving Form of *Oliver Twist*," *PMLA* 93 (January 1978): 20–32.

Juliet McMaster, "Diabolic Trinity in *Oliver Twist*," *DR* 61 (Summer 1981): 263–77.

Ya'ir Mazor, "Smolenskin ve–Dickens," *AlS* 17–18 (1983): 37–48.

J. Hillis Miller, "The Dark World of *Oliver Twist*," in *Charles Dickens*, ed. Harold Bloom (New York: Chelsea House, 1987), 29–69.

Steven O'Connor, "'They're All in One Story': Public and Private Narratives in *Oliver Twist*," *Dickensian* 85 (Spring 1989): 3–16.

David Paroissien, "'What's in a Name?' Some Speculations about Fagin," *Dickensian* 80 (Spring 1984): 41–45.

Torsten Pettersson, "Enough to Have Bodies? Two Incongruities in *Oliver Twist*," *OL* 45, no. 4 (1990): 341–50.

Michael Timko, "Dickens, Carlyle, and the Chaos of Being," *DSA* 16 (1987): 1–15.

Max Vega–Ritter, "Loi, innocence et crime dans *Oliver Twist*," *CVE* 29 (April 1989): 15–40.

Mary Rohrberger, "The Daydream and the Nightmare: Surreality in *Oliver Twist*," *StHum* 6 (March 1978): 21–28.

Brian Rosenberg, "The Language of Doubt in *Oliver Twist*," *DQu* 4 (June 1987): 91–98.

Joan St. Germain, "Dickens' *Oliver Twist*," *Expl* 46 (Spring 1988): 16–20.

Joseph Sawicki, "Oliver (Un)Twisted: Narrative Strategies in *Oliver Twist*," *VN* 73 (Spring 1988): 23–27.

Paul Schlicke, "Bumble and the Poor Law Satire of *Oliver Twist*," *Dickensian* 71 (September 1975): 149–56.

Michael Steig, "A Chapter of Noses: George Cruikshank's Psyconography of the Nose," *Criticism* 17 (Fall 1975): 308–25.

Michael Steig, "Cruikshank's Nancy," *Dickensian* 72 (May 1976): 87–92.

Michael Steig, "Cruikshank's Peacock Feathers in *Oliver Twist*," *Ariel* 4 (April 1973): 49–53.

Michael Steig, "George Cruikshank and the Grotesque: A Psychodynamic Approach," in *PULC* 35 (Autumn–Winter 1973–74): 189–211.

Harry Stone, "*Oliver Twist* and Fairy Tales," *DSN* 10 (June–September 1979): 34–39.

Nancy M. West, "Order in Disorder: Surrealism and *Oliver Twist*," *SoAR* 54 (May 1989): 41–58.

Burton M. Wheeler, "The Text and Plan of *Oliver Twist*," *DSA* 12 (1983): 41–61.

Daniel Whitmore, "Fagin, Effie Deans, and the Spectacle of the Courtroom," *DQu* 3 (September 1986): 132–34.

Garry Wills, "Love in the Lower Depths," *NYRB* 36 (26 October 1989): 60–67.

Our Mutual Friend

Richard D. Altick, "Education, Print, and Paper in *Our Mutual Friend*," in *Nineteenth–Century Literary Perspectives*, ed. Clyde de L. Ryals (Durham, NC: Duke University Press, 1974), 237–54.

Sally S. Andersen, "The De–Spiritualization of the Elements in *Our Mutual Friend*," *Discourse* 12 (1969): 423–33.

Robert S. Baker, "Imagination and Literacy in Dickens' *Our Mutual Friend*," *Criticism* 18 (1976): 57–72.

Judith Barbour, "Euphemism and Paternalism in *Our Mutual Friend*," *SSEng* 7 (1981–1982): 55–68.

Robert Barnard, "The Choral Symphony: *Our Mutual Friend*," *REL* 2 (July 1961): 89–99.

Robert Barnard, "*Our Mutual Friend*," in *Imagery and Theme in the Novels of Dickens* (Oslo: Universitetsforlaget, 1974), 120–33.

Bruce Beiderwell, "The Coherence of Our Mutual Friend," *JNT* 15 (Fall 1985): 234–43.

Joel Brattin, "Dickens' Creation of Bradley Headstone," *DSA* 14 (1985): 147–65.

Arthur Washburn Brown, "*Our Mutual Friend*," in *Sexual Analysis of Dickens' Props* (New York: Emerson, 1971), 242–49.

Richard Burton, "Maturity," in *Charles Dickens* (Indianapolis: Bobbs-Merrill, 1919), 230–43.

Eva M. Campbell, "On the Title, *Our Mutual Friend*," *MLN* 38 (1923): 250–51.

Lothar Cerny, "'All My Work'? Wirkungsbedingungen der Mimesis in *Our Mutual Friend*," *Anglia* 108, no. 102 (1990): 75–95.

Edwin Charles, "Lizzie Hexam," in *Some Dickens Women* (London: T. Werner Laurie, 1926), 259–95.

A. O. J. Cockshut," *Our Mutual Friend*," in *The Imagination of Charles Dickens* (London: Collins, 1961; New York: New York University Press, 1962), 170–82.

Angus Paul Collins, "Dickens and *Our Mutual Friend*: Fancy as Self-Preservation," *ÉA* 38 (July–September 1985): 257–65.

Angus Paul Collins, "A Rhetorical Use of the 'Fancy' in *Our Mutual Friend*," *DSN* 12 (December 1981): 108–10.

Michael Cotsell, "The Book of Insolvent Fates: Financial Speculation in *Our Mutual Friend*," *DSA* 13 (1984): 125–42.

Michael Cotsell, "'Do I Never Read in the Newspaper': Dickens's Last Attack on the Poor Law," *DSN* 14 (September 1983): 81–90.

Michael Cotsell, "Mr Venus Rises from the Counter: Dickens's Taxidermist and His Contribution to *Our Mutual Friend*," *Dickensian* 80 (Summer 1984): 105–13.

Michael Cotsell, "Secretary or Sad Clerk? The Problem with John Harmon," *DQu* 1 (December 1984): 130–36.

Michael Cotsell, "'The Sensational Williams': A Mutual Friend in 1864," *Dickensian* 81 (Summer 1985): 79–85.

W. Walter Crotch, "Poor Law Reform" and "The Curse of Usury," in *Charles Dickens: Social Reformer* (London: Chapman & Hall, 1913), 219–30, 273–87.

Ross H. Dabney, "*Our Mutual Friend*," in *Love and Property in the Novels of Dickens* (London: Chatto & Windus; Berkeley: University of California Press, 1967), 149–76.

H. M. Daleski, "*Our Mutual Friend*," in *Dickens and the Art of Analogy* (New York: Schocken, 1970), 270–336.

Margaret Flanders Darby, "Four Women in *Our Mutual Friend*," *Dickensian* 83 (Spring 1987): 24–39.

Sidney Dark, "*Our Mutual Friend*," in *Charles Dickens* (London: Nelson; Edinburgh: T. C. & E. C. Jack, 1919; reprint. New York: Haskell House, 1975), 115–20.

James A. Davies, "Boffin's Secretary," *Dickensian* 72 (September 1976): 148–57.

James A. Davies, "Forster and Dickens: The Making of Podsnap," *Dickensian* 70 (September 1974): 145–58.

Lawrence Jay Dessner, "A Possible Source for Dickens's Lammles," *Dickensian* 85 (Summer 1989): 105–07.

David Neil Dobrin, "A Note on Jenny Wren's Name," *DSN* 9 (June 1978): 48–49.

Wilfred P. Dvorak, "Charles Dickens' *Our Mutual Friend* and Frederick Somner Merryweather's 'Lives and Anecdotes of Misers,'" *DSA* 9 (1981): 117–41.

Wilfred P. Dvorak, "Dickens and Popular Culture: Silas Wegg's Ballads in *Our Mutual Friend*," *Dickensian* 86 (Autumn 1990): 142–57.

Wilfred P. Dvorak, "Noddy Boffin's Dutch Bottle," *DSN* 9 (March 1978): 19–23.

A. E. Dyson, "*Our Mutual Friend*: Poetry Comes Dearer," in *The Inimitable Dickens: A Reading of the Novels* (London: Macmillan, 1970), 248–66.

Mabel Evans, "The Tragedy of Gaffer Hexam," *Dickensian* 34 (1938): 171–74.

K. J. Fielding, "The Spirit of Fiction—The Poetry of Fact," *DSA* 13 (1984): 231–42.

Frank Foster, "Silas Wegg: The Forerunner of a Cult," *Dickensian* 20 (1924): 18–22.

DICKENS, CHARLES, *Our Mutual Friend*

Stanley Friedman, "A Loose Thread in *Our Mutual Friend*," *DSN* 1 (September 1970): 18–20.

Stanley Friedman, "The Motif of Reading in *Our Mutual Friend*," *NCF* 28 (June 1973): 38–61.

Howard W. Fulweiler, "'A Dismal Swamp': Darwin, Design, and Evolution in *Our Mutual Friend*," *NCF* 49 (June 1994): 5073.

Richard T. Gaughan, "Prospecting for Meaning in *Our Mutual Friend*," *DSA* 19 (1990): 231–46.

Frank Gibbon, "R. H. Horne and *Our Mutual Friend*," *Dickensian* 81 (Autumn 1985): 140–44.

Frank A. Gibson, "The 'Impossible' Riah," *Dickensian* 62 (1966): 118–19.

Joseph Gold, "A Matter of Feeling: *Our Mutual Friend*," in *Charles Dickens: Radical Moralist* (Minneapolis: University of Minnesota Press, 1972), 255–74.

Jennifer Gribble, "Depth and Surface in *Our Mutual Friend*," *EIC* 25 (April 1975): 197–214.

Eiichi Hara, "Name and No Name: The Identity of Dickensian Heroes," *SELit* 58 (Eng. no.) (1982): 21–42.

T. W. Hill, "Betty," *Dickensian* 43 (1974): 41–42.

T. W. Hill, "Notes to *Our Mutual Friend*," *Dickensian* 43 (1947): 85–90, 142–49, 206–12.

Phillip Hobsbaum, "*Our Mutual Friend* (1864–65)," in *A Reader's Guide to Charles Dickens* (London: Thames & Hudson, 1972), 243–67.

Lewis Horne, "*Our Mutual Friend* and the Test of Worthiness," *DR* 62 (Summer 1982): 292–302.

William Dean Howells, "Dickens's Later Heroines," in *Heroines of Fiction*, vol. 1 (New York: Harper, 1901), 155–60.

Albert D. Hutter, "Dismemberment and Articulation in *Our Mutual Friend*," *DSA* 11 (1983): 135–75.

G. W. Kennedy, "Naming and Language in *Our Mutual Friend*," *NCF* 29 (September 1973): 165–78.

Arnold Kettle, "*Our Mutual Friend*," in *Dickens and the Twentieth Century*, ed. John Gross and Gabriel Pearson (London: Routledge & Kegan Paul, 1962), 213–25.

James R. Kincaid, "*Our Mutual Friend*: Mr. Pickwick in Purgatory," in *Dickens and the Rhetoric of Laughter* (Oxford: Clarendon, 1971), 223–52.

U. C. Knoepflmacher, "*Our Mutual Friend*: Fantasy as Affirmation," in *Laughter and Despair: Readings in Ten Novels of the Victorian Era* (Berkeley: University of California Press, 1971), 137–67.

Frederick G. Jackson, "*Our Mutual Friend*," *Dickensian* 4 (1908): 48.

T. A. Jackson, "*Our Mutual Friend*," in *Charles Dickens: The Progress of a Radical* (London: Lawrence & Wishart, 1937; New York: International Publishers, 1938), 200–44.

Audrey Jaffe, "Omniscience in *Our Mutual Friend*," *JNT* 17 (Winter 1987): 91–101.

Mary Ann Kelly, "From Nightmare to Reverie: Continuity in *Our Mutual Friend*," *DUJ* 78 (December 1986): 45–50.

G. W. Kennedy, "Naming and Language in *Our Mutual Friend*," *NCF* 28 (June 1973): 165–78.

Robert Kiely, "Plotting and Scheming: The Design of Design in *Our Mutual Friend*," *DSA* 12 (1983): 267–83.

Owen Knowles, "Veneering and the Age of Veneer: A Source and Background for *Our Mutual Friend*," *Dickensian* 81 (Summer 1985): 88–96.

John Kucich, "Dickens' Fantastic Rhetoric: The Semantics of Reality and Unreality in *Our Mutual Friend*," *DSA* 14 (1985): 167–89.

T. S. Lascelles, "Railway Signal Puzzle in *Our Mutual Friend*," *Dickensian* 45 (1949): 213–16.

Lauriat Lane Jr., "Dickens' Archetypal Jew," *PMLA* 73 (1958): 94–100.

Richard A. Lanham, "*Our Mutual Friend*: The Birds of Prey," *VN* 24 (Fall 1963): 6–12.

Henry Leffman, "Allusions in *Our Mutual Friend*," *Dickensian* 18 (1922): 218.

Peter Lewis, "The Waste Land of *Our Mutual Friend*," *DUJ* 39 (December 1977): 15–28.

J. W. T. Ley, "The Songs of Silas Wegg," *Dickensian* 26 (1930): 111–17.

James T. Lightwood, "Silas Wegg's Effusions," in *Charles Dickens and Music* (London: Charles H. Kelly, 1912), 132–34.

John Lucas, "In Conclusion: *Our Mutual Friend*," in *The Melancholy Man: A Study of Dickens's Novels* (London: Methuen, 1970; Hassocks, Sussex: Harvester, 1980), 315–45.

Rowland D. McMaster, "Birds of Prey: A Study of *Our Mutual Friend*," *DR* 40 (Fall 1960): 372–81.

David MacRitchie, "Allusions in *Our Mutual Friend*," *Dickensian* 19 (1932): 47.

Sylvia Bank Manning, "Modified Satire: *Our Mutual Friend*," in *Dickens the Satirist* (New Haven: Yale University Press, 1971), 199–227.

Patricia Marks, "Storytelling as Mimesis in *Our Mutual Friend*," *DQu* 5 (March 1988): 23–30.

James Elliott Marlow, "The Solecism in *Our Mutual Friend*," *DSN* 5 (March 1974): 7–9.

Jerome Meckier, "Boffin and Podsnap in Utopia," *Dickensian* 77 (Autumn 1981): 154–61.

Nancy Aycock Metz, "The Artistic Reclamation of Waste in *Our Mutual Friend*," *NCF* 34 (June 1979): 59–72.

Helena Michie, "'Who Is This in Pain?': Scarring, Disfigurement, and Female Identity in *Bleak House* and *Our Mutual Friend*," *Novel* 22 (Winter 1989): 199–212.

J. Hillis Miller, "*Our Mutual Friend*," in *Charles Dickens: The World of His Novels* (Cambridge, MA: Harvard University Press, 1958), 279–327.

Michael G. Miller, "The Fellowship–Porters and the Veneerings: Setting, Structure, and Justice in *Our Mutual Friend*," *Dickensian* 85 (Spring 1989): 31–38.

Emilie M. Miniken, "Betty Higden," *Dickensian* 4 (1908): 229–33.

Koichi Miyazaki, "Disguise and Identity in *Our Mutual Friend*," *SELit* 50 (1973): 211–30.

Masao Miyoshi, "Resolution of Identity in *Our Mutual Friend*," *VN* 26 (Fall 1964): 5–9.

Robert Morse, "*Our Mutual Friend*," *PR* 16 (March 1949): 277–89. Reprinted in *The Dickens Critics*, ed. George H. Ford and Lauriat Lane, Jr. (Ithaca, NY: Cornell University Press, 1961), 197–213. Reprinted in *Dickens: Modern Judgements*, ed. A. E. Dyson (London: Macmillan, 1968; Nashville, TN: Aurora, 1970), 30–39; 258–69.

Rosemary Mundhenk, "The Education of the Reader in *Our Mutual Friend*," *NCF* 34 (June 1979): 41–58.

Kenneth Muir, "Image and Structure in *Our Mutual Friend*," in *Essays and Studies 1966*, ed. R. M. Wilson (London: John Murray, 1966), 92–105. Reprinted in *Dickens: "Hard Times," "Great Expectations," and "Our Mutual Friend,"* (London: Macmillan, 1979), 184–95.

S. J. Newman, "Decline and Fall Off? Towards an Appreciation of *Our Mutual Friend*," *Dickensian* 85 (Summer 1989): 99–104.

V. M. Newman, "The Most Human Heroine," *Dickensian* 38 (1942): 181–82.

Robert Newsom, "'To Scatter Dust': Fancy and Authenticity in *Our Mutual Friend*," *DSA* 8 (1980): 39–60.

Patrick O'Donnell, "'A Speeches of Chaff': Ventriloquy and Expression in *Our Mutual Friend*," *DSA* 19 (1990): 247–79.

Norman Page, "*Our Mutual Friend*," in *Speech in the English Novel* (London: Longman, 1973), 98–105, 139–42.

Norman Page, "Silas Wegg Reads Gibbon," *Dickensian* 68 (May 1972): 115.

William Joseph Palmer, "The Movement of History in *Our Mutual Friend*," *PMLA* 89 (May 1974): 487–95.

Annabel M. Patterson, "*Our Mutual Friend*: Dickens as the Compleat Angler," *DSA* 1 (1970): 252–64.

Mary L. Pendered, "Soul Drama," *Dickensian* 35 (1939): 243–49.

Mary L. Pendered, "Twemlow: Knight of the Simple Heart," *Dickensian* 24 (1928): 16–22.

Gilbert Phelps, "*Our Mutual Friend*," in *A Reader's Guide to Fifty British Novels 1600–1900* (London: Heinemann, 1979), 396–406.

Peter Quennell, "*Our Mutual Friend*," *NewS&L* (13 September 1941): 257. Reprinted in *The Singular Preference* (London: Collins, 1952), 152–58.

John M. Robson, "*Our Mutual Friend*: A Rhetorical Approach to the First Number," *DSA* 3 (1974): 198–213.

Andrew Sanders, "'Come Back and Be Alive': Living and Dying in *Our Mutual Friend*," *Dickensian* 74 (September 1978): 131–43.

F. S. Schwarzbach, "*Our Mutual Friend*: The Changing City," in *Dickens and the City* (London: Athlone, 1979), 194–212.

Peter James Malcolm Scott, "*Our Mutual Friend*: The Rhetoric of Disaffection," in *Reality and Comic Confidence in Charles Dickens* (London: Macmillan, 1979), 11–60.

Eve Kosofsky Sedgwick, "Homophobia, Misogyny, and Capital: The Example of *Our Mutual Friend*," in *Charles Dickens*, ed. Harold Bloom (New York: Chelsea House, 1987), 245–61.

G. A. Sekon and T. S. Lascelles, "Railway Signals in *Our Mutual Friend*," *Dickensian* 39 (1943): 206.

Ray J. Sherer, "Laughter in *Our Mutual Friend*," *TSLL* 13 (Fall 1971): 509–21.

Mabell S. C. Smith, "*Our Mutual Friend*," in *Studies in Dickens* (Chautauqua, NY: Chautauqua, 1910; New York: Haskell House, 1972), 234–39.

J. Fisher Solomon, "Realism, Rhetoric, and Reification: Or the Case of the Missing Detective in *Our Mutual Friend*," *MP* 86 (August 1988): 34–45.

Henry Steel, "Allusions in *Our Mutual Friend*," *Dickensian* 19 (1923): 47.

Olivier Cohen Steiner, "Riah: Enquête sur un juif au–dessus de tout soupçon," *ÉA* 42 (April–June 1989): 168–81.

James S. Stevens, "*Our Mutual Friend*," in *Quotations and References in Charles Dickens* (Boston: Christopher, 1929), 70–75.

Garrett Stewart, "The Golden Bower of *Our Mutual Friend*," in *Dickens and the Trails of Imagination* (Cambridge, MA: Harvard University Press, 1974), 198–221.

Taylor Stoehr, "*Our Mutual Friend*," in *Dickens: The Dreamer's Stance* (Ithaca, NY: Cornell University Press, 1965), 203–25.

Harvey Peter Sucksmith, "The Dust–Heaps in *Our Mutual Friend*," *EIC* 23 (1973): 206–12.

Deborah A. Thomas, "Dickens and Indigestion: The Deadly Dinners of the Rich," *DSN* 14 (March 1983): 7–12.

O. H. Thomas, "Greenwich Church," *Dickensian* 29 (1933): 325–26.

Leslie M. Thompson, "The Masks of Pride in *Our Mutual Friend*," *Dickensian* 60 (1964): 124–28.

Geoffrey Thurley, "*Our Mutual Friend*," in *The Dickens Myth: Its Genesis and Structure* (New York: St. Martin's, 1976), 305–28.

Kensuke Ueki, "The Significance of *Our Mutual Friend*—Ties of Human Relationship in *Our Mutual Friend*," *HSELL* 31 (1986): 75–90.

Angus Wilson, "*Our Mutual Friend*," in *The World of Charles Dickens* (London: Martin Secker & Warburg; New York: Viking, 1970), 276–83.

Warrington Winters, "Charles Dickens: *Our Mutual Friend*," *NDQ* 34 (Spring 1969): 96–99.

Austin Wright, "*Our Mutual Friend* A Century Later," *CarM* 39 (1965): 29–31.

Liang Zhi, "A Simple Comment on Dickens' *Our Mutual Friend*," *FLitS* 30 (December 1985): 59–65.

"A Passage in the Life of Mr. Watkins Tottle"

George Wing, "The First of the Singles: Watkins Tottle," *DQu* 6 (March 1989): 10–16.

Pickwick Papers

Robert Allbut, "Sam Weller: A Character Sketch," *Dickensian* 2 (1906): 89–92.

W. H. Auden, "Dingley Dell and the Fleet," in *The Dyer's Hand and Other Essays* (New York: Random House, 1962), 407–28.

William F. Axton, "Unity and Coherence in the *Pickwick Papers*," *SEL* 5 (1965): 663–76.

Florence E. Baer, "Wellerisms in *The Pickwick Papers*," *Folklore* 94, no. 2 (1983): 173–83.

Sir William H. Bailey, "Wellerisms and Wit," *Dickensian* 1 (1905): 31–34.

Lynn C. Bartlett, "High Life Below Stairs or Cribbage in the Kitchen," *ELN* 23 (December 1985): 54–61.

David M. Bevinton, "Seasonal Relevance in *The Pickwick Papers*," *NCF* 16 (September 1961): 219–30.

E. W. Bovill, "Tony Weller's Trade," *N&Q* 201 (1956): 324–28, 527–31; 202 (1957): 155–59, 260–63, 451–53.

Patrizia Calefato, "Maschere d'autore, nomi propri e 'abbassamento': Il circolo *Pickwick*," *LdProv* 18 (December 1987): 63–74.

Albert S. Canning, "The *Pickwick Papers*," in *Philosophy of Charles Dickens* (London: Smith, Edler, 1880), 27–53. Revised and reprinted in *Dickens and Thackery Studied in Three Novels* (London: Unwin, 1911), 33–59.

W. J. Carlton, "Serjeant Buzfuz," *Dickensian* 45 (1948–1949): 21–22.

Katherine A. Carolan, "The Dingley Dell Christmas," *DSN* 4 (June 1975): 41–48.

Katherine A. Carolan, "The Dingley Dell Christmas Continued: 'Rip Van Winkle' and 'The Tale of Gabriel Grub,'" *DSN* 5 (December 1974): 104–6.

J. L. Cheeseman, *Notes on Charles Dickens's "Pickwick Papers"* (London: Methuen, 1978), 1–70.

G. K. Chesterton, "Editor's Introduction," in *Pickwick Papers* (London: Dent, 1907), vii–xv. Reprinted in *Appreciations and Criticisms of the Works of Charles Dickens* (London: Dent, 1911), 13–35.

G. K. Chesterton, "*The Pickwick Papers*," in *Charles Dickens: The Last of the Great Men* (New York: The Readers Club, 1942), 53–72.

Logan Clendening, *A Handbook to Pickwick Papers* (New York: Knopf, 1936), 1–156.

V. C. Clinton–Baddeley, "Stiggins," *Dickensian* 50 (1953–54): 53–56.

DICKENS, CHARLES, *Pickwick Papers*

Mary Colwell, "Organization in *Pickwick Papers*," *DS* 3 (1967): 90–110.

Michael Cotsell, "*The Pickwick Papers* and Travel: A Critical Diversion," *DQu* 3 (March 1986): 5–17.

"Could Phunkey Have Demurred?" *LQR* 60 (1944): 321–24.

Steven V. Daniels, "Pickwick and Dickens: Stages of Development," *DSA* 4 (1975): 56–77.

Sidney Dark, "*The Pickwick Papers*," in *Charles Dickens* (London: Nelson, 1919), 46–50.

James A. Davies, "Negative Similarity: the Fat Boy in *The Pickwick Papers*," *DUJ* 39 (December 1977): 29–34.

Earle R. Davis, "Dickens and the Evolution of Caricature," *PMLA* 55 (1940): 231–40.

Frank R. Donovan, "Incidental Children Everywhere Underfoot," in *Dickens and Youth* (New York: Dodd, Mead, 1968), 165–67.

Arnold P. Drew, "*Pygmalion* and *Pickwick*," *N&Q* 200 (1955): 221–22.

Richard J. Dunn, "But We Grow Affecting: Let Us Proceed," *Dickensian* 62 (1966): 53–55.

Angus Easson, "Imprisonment for Debt in *Pickwick Papers*," *Dickensian* 64 (1968): 105–12.

Clifton Fadiman, "Pickwick Lives Forever," *AtM* 184 (December 1949): 23–29.

Mara H. Fein, "The Politics of Family in the *Pickwick Papers*," *ELH* 61 (Summer 1994): 363–79.

Martin Fido, "Exuberant Domestic Optimism: *Pickwick Papers*, Ch. 28," in *Charles Dickens: Profiles in Literature* (London: Routledge & Kegan Paul, 1968), 18–21.

K. J. Fielding, "*Pickwick Papers*, and After," in *Charles Dickens: A Critical Introduction* (London: Longmans, Green, 1965), 13–25.

George H. Ford, "The Prospering of Pickwick," in *Dickens and His Readers: Aspects of Novel–Criticism Since 1836* (Princeton: Princeton University Press, 1955; New York: Norton, 1965), 3–19.

John Forster, "First Book and Origin of Pickwick" and "Writing the *Pickwick Papers*," in *The Life of Charles Dickens* (London: Chapman & Hall, 1872), 86–119.

Margaret Ganz, "*Pickwick Papers*: Humor and the Refashioning of Reality," *DSA* 4 (1975): 36–55.

Stanley Gerson, "'I Spells it vith a "V,"'" *Dickensian* 62 (1966): 138–46.

Stephen C. Gill, "*Pickwick Papers* and the 'Chronicles by the Line': A Note on Style," *MLR* 63 (1968): 33–36.

Barbara Hardy, "*Pickwick Papers*," in *The Moral Art of Dickens* (New York: Oxford University Press, 1970), 81–99.

Jean Harris, "'But He Was His Father': The Gothic and the Impostorious in Dickens's *The Pickwick Papers*," in *Psychoanalytic Approaches to Literature and Film*, ed. Maurice Charney and Joseph Reppen (Rutherford, NJ: Fairleigh Dickinson University Press, 1987), 69–79.

Mark M. Hennelly, Jr., "Dickens's Praise of Folly: Play in *The Pickwick Papers*," *DQu* 3 (March 1986): 27–46.

Christopher Herbert, "Converging Worlds in *Pickwick Papers*," *NCF* 27 (June 1972): 1–20.

Tobey C. Herzog, "The Merry Circle of *The Pickwick Papers*: A Dickensian Paradigm," *SNNTS* 20 (Spring 1988): 55–63.

T. W. Hill, "Notes on the *Pickwick Papers*," *Dickensian* 44 (1947–48; 1948–49): 29–36, 81–88, 145–52, 193–98; 27–33, 110.

Gordon D. Hirsch, "Mr. Pickwick's Impotence," *Sphinx* 9 (1979): 28–35.

A. A. Hopkins, "Eating and Drinking in *Pickwick*," *Dickensian* 22 (1926): 228–29.

Ignoto, "*Pickwick*: Two Queries," *N&Q* 179 (1940): 137.

Edgar Johnson, "Introduction to *Pickwick Papers*," in *The Pickwick Papers* (New York: Dell, 1964), 31–36.

Edgar Johnson, "Knight of the Joyful Countenance," in *Charles Dickens: His Tragedy and Triumph* (New York: Simon & Schuster, 1952): 157–75.

Fred Kaplan, "Pickwick's 'Magnanimous Revenge': Reason and Responsibility in the *Pickwick Papers*," *VN* 37 (Spring 1970): 18–21.

Joseph Kestner, "Elements of Epic in *The Pickwick Papers*," *UDR* 9 (Summer 1972): 15–24.

John Killham, "*Pickwick*: Dickens and the Art of Fiction," in *Dickens and the Twentieth Century*, ed. John Gross and Gabriel Pearson (Toronto: University of Toronto Press, 1962), 35–47.

James R. Kincaid, "The Education of Mr. Pickwick," *NCF* 24 (June 1969): 127–41.

James R. Kincaid, "Fattening Up on Pickwick," *Novel* 25 (Spring 1992): 235–44.

James R. Kincaid, "The *Pickwick Papers*: The Vision from the Wheelbarrow," in *Dickens and the Rhetoric of Laughter* (Oxford: Claredon, 1971), 20–49.

Karl L. Klein, "Die interpolierten Geschichten in Charles Dickens's *The Pickwick Papers*: Überlegungen gegen eine Integration," in *Miscellanea Anglo–Americana: Festschrift für Helmut Viebrock*, ed. Kuno Schuhmann, Helmut Viebrock, Wilhelm Hortmann, and Armin Paul Franks (Munich: Pressler, 1974), 320–44.

Lauriat Lane Jr., "Mr. Pickwick and 'The Dance of Death,'" *NCF* 14 (September 1959): 171–72.

Herman M. Levy Jr. and William Ruff, "The Interpolated Tales in *Pickwick Papers*, a Further Note," *DS* 3 (1967): 122–25.

Herman M. Levy Jr. and William Ruff, "Who Tells the Story of a Queer Client?" *Dickensian* 64 (1968): 19–21.

E. A. Lewis, "A Defense of Mrs. Bardell," *Dickensian* 38 (1941–42): 208–9.

Robert E. Lougy, "Pickwick and 'The Parish Clerk,'" *NCF* 25 (June 1970): 100–04.

John Lucas, "*The Pickwick Papers*," in *The Melancholy Man: A Study of Dickens's Novels* (London: Methuen, 1970), 1–20.

H. N. MacLean, "Mr. Pickwick and the Seven Deadly Sins," *NCF* 8 (September 1953): 198–212.

Juliet McMaster, "Visual Design in *Pickwick Papers*," *SEL* 23 (Autumn 1983): 595–614.

Juliet McMaster, "Who Is Jack Bamber? More about the Old Man and the Queer Client," *Dickensian* 81 (Summer 1985): 105–08.

Wolf Mankowitz, "Pickwick Triumphant," in *Dickens of London* (New York: Macmillan, 1976), 58–62.

Steven Marcus, "Afterword," in *Pickwick Papers* (New York: Signet;, 1964), 864–86. Revised and reprinted as "The Blest Dawn," in *Dickens: From Pickwick to Dombey* (New York: Basic, 1965), 13–53.

Steven Marcus, "Language into Structure: *Pickwick* Revisited," *Daedalus* 101 (Winter 1972): 183–202. Reprinted in *Representations: Essays on Literature and Society* (New York: Random House, 1975), 214–46. Reprinted in *Charles Dickens*, ed. Harold Bloom (New York: Chelsea House, 1987), 129–51.

James E. Marlow, "Pickwick's Writing: Propriety and Language," *ELH* 52 (Winter 1985): 939–63.

James E. Marlow, “Popular Culture, Pugilism, and *Pickwick*,” *JPC* 15 (Spring 1982): 16–30.

J. Hillis Miller, “Pickwick Papers,” in *Charles Dickens: The World of His Novels* (Cambridge, MA: Harvard University Press, 1958), 1–35.

Sylvère Monod, “*Pickwick*, or Triumphant Improvisation,” in *Dickens the Novelist* (Norman: University of Oklahoma Press, 1968), 83–115.

Claude Mouchard, “L’ange de l’intime,” *QL* 316 (January 1980): 13–14.

Hector Munro, “Curious Affair of the Cognovit,” *Dickensian* 74 (May 1978): 88–90.

Volker Neuhaus, “Das Verhältnis des Herausgebers zum Archiv—Charles Dickens *The Pickwick Papers*,” in *Typen multiperspektevischen Erzählens* 13 (Cologne & Vienna: Bohlau, 1971), 93–96.

Constance Nicolas, “Mrs. Raddle and Mistress Quickly,” *Dickensian* 62 (1966): 55–56.

David Paroissien, “Mr. Jingle: Another Bell,” *DSN* 8 (September 1977): 79.

Robert L. Patten, “The Art of Pickwick’s Interpolated Tales,” *ELH* 34 (1967): 349–66.

Robert L. Patten, “Boz, Phiz, and Pickwick in the Pound,” *ELH* 36 (September 1969): 575–91.

Robert L. Patten, “The Interpolated Tales in *Pickwick Papers*,” *DS* 1 (1965): 86–89.

Robert L. Patten, “‘I Thought of Mr. Pickwick, and Wrote the First Number’: Dickens and the Evolution of Character,” *DQu* 3 (March 1986): 18–26.

Robert L. Patten, “Introduction,” in *Penguin Edition: Pickwick Papers* (New York: Penguin, 1972), 11–30.

Robert L. Patten, “Pickwick and the Development of Serial Fiction,” *RUSt* 61 (Winter 1975): 51–74.

Robert L. Patten, “Portraits of Pott: Lord Brougham and the *Pickwick Papers*,” *Dickensian* 66 (September 1970): 205–24.

Robert L. Patten, “The Unpropitious Muse: Pickwick’s ‘Interpolated Tales,’” *DSN* 1 (March 1970): 7–10.

Elizabeth Pochoda, “Sense and Sentimentality,” *Nation* 223 (18 December 1976): 661–63.

Roy L. Prange Jr., “The Case Against Mrs. Cluppins,” *DSN* 11 (December 1980): 112–14.

DICKENS, CHARLES, *Pickwick Papers*

Edward G. Preston, "Muggleton and the Muggletonians," *DQu* 3 (September 1986): 129–31.

J. B. Priestley, "The Two Wellers," in *The English Comic Characters* (New York: Dutton, 1966), 198–223.

V. R., "Dickens: Two Curious Idioms," *N&Q* 195 (1950): 279.

Heinz Reinhold, "'The Strollers Tale' in *Pickwick*," *Dickensian* 64 (1968): 141–51.

Kenneth Rexroth, "*Pickwick Papers*," in *The Elastic Retort: Essays in Literature and Ideas* (New York: Seabury, 1973), 98–102.

William R. Riddell, "Plaintiff's Attorneys, Bardell vs. Pickwick," *ABAJ* 8 (1922): 203–05.

Max Vega Ritter, "De quelques mécanismes de l'humour dans les *Pickwick Papers*," *CVE* 20 (October 1984): 39–53.

Phillip E. Rogers, "Mr. Pickwick's Innocence," *NCF* 27 (June 1972): 21–37.

Stan S. Rubin, "Spectator and Spectacle: Narrative Evasion and Narrative Voice in *Pickwick Papers*," *JNT* 6 (September 1976): 188–203.

Takao Saijo, "Unity and 'The Pickwick Papers,'" *HSELL* 16, no. 1–2 (1969): 30–40.

Senex, "*Pickwick*: Two Queries," *N&Q* 179 (1940): 302–03.

Jacqueline Simpson, "Urban Legends in *The Pickwick Papers*," *JAF* 96 (October–December 1983): 462–70.

Glyn A. Strange, "Paired Episodes in *Pickwick*," *DSN* 12 (March 1981): 6–8.

Harry Stone, "Dickens and the Naming of Sam Weller," *Dickensian* 56 (1960): 47–49.

Harvey Peter Sucksmith, "The Identity and Significance of the Mad Huntsman in *Pickwick Papers*," *Dickensian* 68 (May 1972): 109–14.

Takanobu Tanaka, "Benevolence and Laughter as the Predominant Qualities of *The Pickwick Papers*," *HSELL* 27 (March 1982): 77–79.

Kathleen Tillotson, "Dickens's Count Smorltork," *TLS* (22 November 1957): 712.

Kathleen Tillotson, "*Pickwick* and Edward Jesse," *TLS* (1 April 1960): 214.

Joyce S. Toomre, "Dining with Dickens," *HM* 81 (January–February 1978): 38–44.

Gwenllian L. Williams, "Sam Weller," *Trivium* 1 (1966): 88–101.

Angus Wilson, "Pickwick," in *The World of Charles Dickens* (New York: Viking, 1970), 115–24.

Frederick T. Wood, "Sam Weller's Cockneyisms," *N&Q* 190 (1946): 234–45.

"Poor Mercantile Jack"

R. D. Butterworth, "'Fire and Candle Aboard Ship': A Reference in Dickens's 'Poor Mercantile Jack,'" *N&Q* 37 (March 1990): 34–35.

Sketches by Boz

T. G. Bogolepova, "Izobrazhenie gorodskoi zhizni v 'Ocherkakh Boza,'" *VLU* 24, no. 4 (1969): 100–09.

Julian W. Breslow, "The Narrator in *Sketches by Boz*," *ELH* 44 (Spring 1977): 127–49.

Edward Costigan, "Drama and Everyday Life in *Sketches by Boz*," *RES* 27 (November 1976): 403–21.

Angus Easson, "Who Is Boz? Dickens and His Sketches," *Dickensian* 81 (Spring 1985): 13–22.

Eliot D. Engel, "'First Sprightly Runnings': The Comic Narration of *Sketches by Boz*," *BSUF* 23 (Summer 1982): 35–39.

Sylvère Monod, "Revisiting 'Sketches by Boz,'" in *Dickens and Other Victorians: Essays in Honor of Philip Collins*, ed. Joanne Shattock (New York: St. Martin's, 1988), 25–36.

S. C. Sen, "Dickens the Conjurer," *CalUB* n.s. 6, no. 2 (1970–71): 1–13.

R. G. Ussher, "Boz and the Character Tradition," *Hermathena* 120 (Summer 1976): 59–62.

Yves Warson, "De hekelutopie in de *Schetsen van Boz* door Charles Dickesn," *Dialoog* 14, no. 1–2 (1973–74): 367–73.

A Tale of Two Cities

Robert Alter, "The Demons of History in Dicken's 'Tale,'" *Novel* 2 (Winter 1969): 135–42. Reprinted in *Charles Dickens's "A Tale of Two Cities,"* ed. Harold Bloom (New York: Chelsea House, 1987), 13–22. Reprinted in *Charles Dickens*, ed. Harold Bloom (New York: Chelsea House, 1987), 93–102.

O. V. Ankudinova, "K voprosu o poetike povesti N. S. Leskova *Zaiachii remiz*: Literaturno–istoricheskii kommentarii k odnomu motivu," *RusL* 3 (1981): 150–53.

Cates Baldridge, "Alternatives to Bourgeois Individualism in *A Tale of Two Cities*," *SEL* 30 (Autumn 1990): 633–54.

Raimund Borgmeier, "Gegenbilder der Geschichte: Dickens' *A Tale of Two Cities* (1859)," *A&E* 22 (1984): 109–27.

Franklin E. Court, "Boots, Barbarism, and the New Order in Dickens's *Tale of Two Cities*," *VIJ* 9 (1980–81): 29–37.

Harry De Puy, "American Prisons and *A Tale of Two Cities*," *CVE* 25 (April 1987): 39–48.

Robert W. Duncan, "Madame Defarge's Knitting," *N&Q* 24 (July–August 1977): 365.

Richard J. Dunn, "A Tale for Two Dramatists," *DSA* 12 (1983): 117–24.

Edwin M. Eigner, "Charles Darnay and Revolutionary Identity," *DSA* 12 (1983): 147–59. Reprinted in *Charles Dickens's "A Tale of Two Cities,"* ed. Harold Bloom (New York: Chelsea House, 1987), 95–106.

Charles Forsyte, "*A Tale of Two Cities*: A New Source," *ÉA* 43 (July–September 1990): 298–302.

Lawrence Frank, "Dickens's *A Tale of Two Cities*: The Poetics of Impass," *AI* 36 (Fall 1979): 215–44.

Catherine Gallagher, "The Duplicity of Doubling in *A Tale of Two Cities*," *DSA* 12 (1983): 125–45. Reprinted in *Charles Dickens's "A Tale of Two Cities,"* ed. Harold Bloom (New York: Chelsea House, 1987), 73–94.

Jean–Pierre Garces, "Stryver, ou une autre expression de la violence dans *A Tale of Two Cities*," in *La Violence dans la littérature et la pensée anglaises*, ed. Nadia Rigaud and Paul Denisot (Aix-en-Provence: Universite de Provence, 1989), 85–96.

John Gross, "*A Tale of Two Cities*," in *Dickens and the Twentieth Century*, ed. John Gross and Gabriel Pearson (London: Routledge & Kegan Paul, 1962), 187–98.

Kathryn M. Grossman, "'Angleterre et France melées': Fraternal Visions in Quatre-vingt-treize and *A Tale of Two Cities*," in *Victor Hugo et la Grande–Bretagne*, ed. A. R. W. James (Liverpool: Cairns, 1986), 105–20.

Stirling Haig, "Frenglish in *A Tale of Two Cities*," *DSN* 14 (September 1983): 93–97.

Albert D. Hutter, "Nation and Generation in *A Tale of Two Cities*," *PMLA* 93 (May 1978): 448–62. Reprinted in *Charles Dickens's "A Tale of Two Cities,"* ed. Harold Bloom (New York: Chelsea House, 1987), 37–56.

Florence King, "Revenge on the Nerd," *NatlR* 44 (3 August 1992): 56.

John Kucich, "The Purity of Violence: *A Tale of Two Cities*," in *Charles Dickens's "A Tale of Two Cities,"* ed. Harold Bloom (New York: Chelsea House, 1987), 57–72.

Hy Won Kim, "The Author's Consciousness Represented in *A Tale of Two Cities*," *JELL* 39 (Summer 1993): 283–92.

Bernd–Peter Lange, "Dickens und der historische Roman: *A Tale of Two Cities*," *GRM* 20, no. 4 (1970): 427–42.

Jack Lindsay, "*A Tale of Two Cities*," *L&L&LM* 62 (1949): 191–204.

Tom Lloyd, "Language, Love and Identity in *A Tale of Two Cities*," *Dickensian* 88 (Fall 1992): 154–70.

Angela Lorent, "*A Tale of Two Cities*: Die Revolution als Mythischer Kampf zwischen Individuum und Kollektiv," in *Funktionen der Massenszene im viktorianischen Roman* (Frankfurt: Peter Lang, 1980), 78–99.

John P. McWilliams Jr., "Progress without Politics: *A Tale of Two Cities*," *CLIO* 7 (Fall 1977): 19–31.

Leonard Manheim, "A Tale of Two Characters: A Study in Multiple Projection," *DSA* 1 (1970): 225–37.

David D. Marcus, "The Carlylean Vision of *A Tale of Two Cities*," *SNNTS* 8 (Spring 1976): 56–68. Reprinted in *Charles Dickens's "A Tale of Two Cities,"* ed. Harold Bloom (New York: Chelsea House, 1987), 23–35.

James E. Marlow, "Dickens and Carlyle's 'Way,'" *VIJ* 1 (July 1972): 15–22.

Ewald Mengel, "The Poisoned Fountain: Dickens's Use of a Traditional Symbol in *A Tale of Two Cities*," *Dickensian* 80 (Spring 1984): 26–32.

Sylvère Monod, "Dickens' Attitudes in *A Tale of Two Cities*," in *Dickens Centennial Essays*, ed. Ada Nisbet and Blake Nevius (Berkeley and Los Angeles: University of California Press, 1971), 166–83

Sylvère Monod, "Some Stylistic Devices in *A Tale of Two Cities*," in *Dickens the Craftsman: Strategies of Presentation*, ed. Robert B. Partlow Jr. (Carbondale: Southern Illinois University Press, 1970), 165–86.

Sylvère Monod, "*A Tale of Two Cities*: A French View," *Dickensian* 66 (September 1970): 23–37.

Harland S. Nelson, "Shadow and Substance in *A Tale of Two Cities*," *Dickensian* 84 (Summer 1988): 97–106.

Joseph H. O'Mealy, "Dickens' *A Tale of Two Cities*," *Expl* 42 (Winter 1984): 10–12.

Frank M. Patterson, "Dickens's *A Tale of Two Cities*," *Expl* 47 (Summer 1989): 30–31.

Sue Poe and Hazel Jessee, "Staging a Literary Festival," *VirEB* 36 (Winter 1986): 149–52.

Nicolas Rance, "Charles Dickens: *A Tale of Two Cities* (1859)," in *The Historical Novel and Popular Politics in Nineteenth-Century England* (London: Vision; New York: Barnes & Noble, 1975), 83–101.

J. M. Rignall, "Dickens and the Catastrophic Continuum of History in *A Tale of Two Cities*," *ELH* 51 (Fall 1984): 575–87. Reprinted in *Charles Dickens's "A Tale of Two Cities,"* ed. Harold Bloom (New York: Chelsea House, 1987), 121–32.

Lisa Robson, "The 'angels' in Dickens's House: Representation of Women in *A Tale of Two Cities*," *DR* 72 (Fall 1992): 311–33.

Kurt Tetzeli von Rosador, "Geschichtsrhetorik und Geschichtsauffassung in Charles Dickens' *A Tale of Two Cities*," *GRM* 35, no. 3 (1985): 301–16.

Anny Sadrin, "*A Tale of Two Cities*, 'Theatre–roman,'" *CVE* 20 (October 1984): 65–85.

Andrew Sanders, "'Cartloads of Books': Some Sources for *A Tale of Two Cities*," in *Dickens and Other Victorians: Essays in Honor of Philip Collins*, ed. Joanne Shattock (New York: St. Martin's, 1988), 37–52.

Andrew Sanders, "Monsieur Heretofore the Marquis: Dickens's St. Evremonde," *Dickensian* 81 (Autumn 1985): 148–56.

Garrett Stewart, "Death by Water in A Tale of Two Cities," in *Charles Dickens's "A Tale of Two Cities,"* ed. Harold Bloom (New York: Chelsea House, 1987), 107–20.

Michael Timko, "Splendid Impressions and Picturesque Means: Dickens, Carlyle, and the French Revolution," *DSA* 12 (1983): 177–95.

Ling Zhang, "An Analysis of the Theme of *A Tale of Two Cities*," *FLitS* 40 (June 1988): 32–38, 22.

"To Be Read at Dusk"

Ruth Glancy, "'To Be Read at Dusk,'" *Dickensian* 83 (Spring 1987): 40–47.

"To Be Taken with a Grain of Salt"

Helmut Bonheim, "The Principle of Cyclicity in Charles Dickens' 'The Signalman,'" *Anglia* 106, no. 3–4 (1988): 380–92.

Gary Day, "Figuring Out the Signalman: Dickens and the Ghost Story," in *Nineteenth–Century Suspense: From Poe to Conan Doyle*, ed. Clive Bloom, Brian Docherty, Jane Gibb, and Keith Shand (New York: St. Martin's, 1988), 26–45.

Henri Justin, "The Signalman's Signal–Man," *JSSE* 7 (Autumn 1986): 9–16.

Ewald Mengel, "The Structure and Meaning of Dickens's 'The Signalman,'" *SSF* 20 (Fall 1983): 271–80.

The Uncommercial Traveller
(with Wilkie Collins)

Michael Cotsell, "*The Uncommerical Traveller* on the Commercial Road: Dickens's East End," *DQu* 3 (June 1986; September 1986): 75–83; 115–23.

Scott Foll, "Great Expectations and the *Uncommercial* Sketch Book," *Dickensian* 81 (Summer 1985): 109–16.

Masaie Matsumura, "*The Uncommercial Traveller* no East End," *EigoS* 134 (n.d.): 425–27.

Michael Slater, "How Many Nurses Had Charles Dickens? *The Uncommerical Traveller* and Dickensian Biography," *PSt* 10 (December 1987): 250–58.

George J. Worth, "*The Uncommerical Traveller* and *Great Expectations*," *Dickensian* 83 (Spring 1987): 19–21.

DISRAELI, BENJAMIN

Coningsby; or, The New Generation

M. Edelman, "A Political Novel: Disraeli sets a Lively Pace," *TLS* (7 August 1959): 495.

Endymion

James D. Merritt, "The Novelist St. Barbe in Disraeli's *Endymion*: Revenge on Whom?" *NCF* 23 (March 1968): 85–88.

Edmond Scherer, "*Endymion*," *ÉLC* 7 (1882): 70–83.

Lothair

Frederic Harrison, "The Romance of the Peerage: *Lothair*," in *Modern English Essays, 1870–1920, Vol. I*, ed. Ernest Rhys (London: Dent, 1922), 190–215.

Henry James, "*Lothair*," in *Literary Reviews and Essays on American, English, and French Literature*, ed. Albert Mordell (New York: Twayne, 1957), 303–08.

Sybil

Gary Handwerk, "Behind *Sybil's* Veil: Disraeli's Mix of Ideological Messages," *MLQ* 49 (December 1988): 321–40.

Tancred; or, The New Crusade

James Russell Lowell, "D'Israeli as a Novelist," *RT* (1913): 83–120.

Marie E. de Meester, "Disraeli's *Tancred*," in *Oriental Influence in English Literature of the Nineteenth Century* (Amsterdam: Swets & Zeitlunger, 1967), 58–60.

Vivian Grey

Martin Fido, "The Key to *Vivian Grey* of 1827," *N&Q* 210 (November 1965): 418–19.

R. Maitre, "Un point de critique Disraelienne: le lancement de la leuxième partie de *Vivian Grey*," *ÉA* 5 (1952): 227–31.

The Wonderous Tale of Alroy

A. Brandl, "Zur Quelle van Disraelis Alkroy," *Archiv* 148 (1925): 97–98.

G. Jean–Aubry, "Disraeli et le solitaire de Bath," *LeF* (5 December 1931): 5–6.

DOUGLAS, NORMAN

South Wind

Reed Way Dasenbrock, "Norman Douglas and the Denizens of Siren Land," *DL* 5 (June 1982): 1–9.

Heiko Postma, "'Could You Oblige Me with a Fairy-Tale?' Norman Douglas (1868–1952) und *South Wind*," *Horen* 31, no. 2 (1986): 128–41.

DOYLE, ARTHUR CONAN

"The Adventure of the Three Gables"

Steven Rothman, "How Come a Bull Ring? A Brief Investigation," *BSJ* 35 (September 1985): 170–71.

"The Beryl Coronet"

Tom McGee, "Reflections on 'The Beryl Coronet,'" *BSJ* 39 (December 1989): 214–17.

Kate Karlson Redmond, "The Literary and Factual Origins of 'The Adventure of the Beryl Coronet,'" *BSJ* 39 (December 1989): 209–13.

"Black Peter"

William D. Jenkins, "Have Sight of Proteus: Mythological Archetypes in the Sherlockian Canon," *BSJ* 34 (September 1984): 150–54.

Sheldon Wesson, "The Crimes of 'The Adventure of Black Peter,'" *BSJ* 32 (September 1982): 153–55.

"The Blanched Soldier"

Raymond L. Holly, "A Pythagorean Theory," *BSJ* 37 (June 1987): 81–86.

Richard S. Warner, "To Simpson—A Canonical Hero," *BSJ* 32 (March 1982): 16–18.

B. Dean Wortman, "The Two-Author Theory of 'The Blanched Soldier,'" *BSJ* 38 (September 1988): 158–59.

"The Blue Carbuncle"

George Fletcher, "That Bashful British Meiosis; Or, The Season of Forgetfulness," *BSJ* 36 (December 1986): 199.

Thomas S. Galbo, "The First Adventure of 'The Blue Carbuncle,'" *BSJ* 36 (December 1986): 203–06.

Gordon R. Speck, "Carbuncle, Christmas, and the Bloomsbury Tales: Holmes as Wise Man," *BSJ* 35 (December 1985): 228.

"The Boscombe Valley Mystery"

Robert C. Burr, "But What about the Blood, Holmes?" *BSJ* 39 (June 1989): 75, 78.

William C. Waterhouse, "Holmes and the Buffalo," *BSJ* 32 (March 1982): 48–49.

"The Bruce Partington Plans"

James Ludwig, "Who Is Cadogan West and What Is He to Mycroft?" *BSJ* 39 (June 1989): 102–07.

Thomas M. Sobottke, "Speculations on the Further Career of Mycroft Holmes," *BSJ* 40 (June 1990): 75–77.

Richard Warner, "St. Patrick's Lament," *BSJ* 39 (March 1989): 17–21.

Peter H. Wood, "An Automatic Self-Adjusting Solution: Bruce-Partington Dives Again," *BSJ* 34 (September 1984): 166–72.

"The Captain of the Polestar"

Dana Martin Batory, "The Rime of the Polestar," *RQ* 7 (December 1985): 222–27.

"The Cardboard Box"

Brad Keefauver, "Violin Conversations," *BSJ* 37 (June 1987): 76–77.

"A Case of Identity"

William C. Waterhouse, "The Case of the Persian Proverb," *BSJ* 40 (September 1990): 135–36.

"The Case of the Man Who Was Wanted"

Noelle F. Schulte, "The Case of 'The Case of the Man Who Was Wanted,'" *BSJ* 36 (September 1986): 166–67.

"The Casting of the Runes"

Robert A. Emery, "Dr. James and Dr. Watson," *BSJ* 38 (June 1988): 82–83.

"Charles Augustus Milverton"

Judy L. Buddle, "Playing Your Cards as Best You Can," *BSJ* 41 (June 1991): 97–99.

Bruce Harris, "Did Sherlock Holmes Kill Charles Augustus Milverton?" *BSJ* 32 (March 1982): 45–47.

Charles A. Meyer, "Lady Eva's Secret Revealed," *BSJ* 38 (September 1988): 168–70.

"The Copper Beeches"

Richard A. Wein, "The Real Mystery of 'The Copper Beeches,'" *BSJ* 39 (December 1989): 219–22.

"The Dancing Men"

Barbara Pearce, "Holmes Connects with an Infamous Chicagoan," *BSJ* 39 (December 1989): 223–25.

Dante M. Torrese, "Firearms in the Canon: 'The Adventure of the Dancing Men,'" *BSJ* 41 (March 1991): 39–43.

"The Devil's Foot"

Martin Arbagi, "Radix Linguae Cornubiensis: Holmes and the Chaldean Roots of Cornish," *BSJ* 32 (March 1982): 11–14.

Bob Jones, "A Missed Clue in 'The Devil's Foot,'" *BSJ* 41 (December 1991): 215–17.

James G. Ravin, "The Devil's–Foot Root Identified: Eserine," *BSJ* 32 (December 1982): 199–202.

Calvert Roszell, "'The Devil's Foot' and the Dweller at the Threshold," *BSJ* 41 (June 1991): 100–03.

Evan M. Wilson, "With Sherlock Holmes and Karl Baedeker in Farthest Cornwall," *BSJ* 32 (March 1982): 7–10.

"The Empty House"

Hans Uno Begtsson, "A Norwegian Named Sigerson," *BSJ* 37 (September 1987): 148–52.

DOYLE, ARTHUR CONAN, "The Engineer's Thumb"

Richard M. Caplan, "Why Coal-Tar Derivatives at Montpellier?" *BSJ* 39 (March 1989): 29–33.

William R. Cockran, "Re: Murray," *BSJ* 39 (June 1989): 76–78.

Thomas J. Farrell, "Deconstructing Moriarty: False Armageddon at the Reichenbach," in *The Cunning Craft: Original Essays on Detective Fiction and Contemporary Literary Theory*, ed. Ronald G. Walker and June M. Frazer (Macomb: Western Illinois University Press, 1990), 61–67.

R. F. Fleissner, "'No Ghosts Need Apply'? Or, 'The Adventure of the Empty House's Empty House,'" *StWF* 6 (Fall 1989): 28–30.

Irving Kamil, "The Search for Oscar Meunier," *BSJ* 38 (December 1988): 209–14.

Irving Kamil, "Sherlock Holmes and the Locked–Room Mystery," *BSJ* 32 (September 1982): 143–45.

Robert A. Moss, "A Research into the Coal–Tar Derivatives," *BSJ* 32 (March 1982): 40–42.

"The Engineer's Thumb"

Donovan H. McClain, "The Curious Affair of the Counterfeit Consultant; Or, Holmes Was No Engineer," *BSJ* 37 (June 1987): 101–06.

"The Final Problem"

Michael Atkinson, "Staging the Disappearance of Sherlock Holmes: The Aesthetics of Absence 'The Final Problem,'" *GettR* 4 (Spring 1991): 206–14.

Zachary Dundas, "A Look at 'The Final Problem,'" *BSJ* 38 (December 1988): 233–36.

Thomas J. Farrell, "Deconstructing Moriarty: False Armageddon at the Reichenbach," in *The Cunning Craft: Original Essays on Detective Fiction and Contemporary Literary Theory*, ed. Ronald G. Walker and June M. Frazer (Macomb: Western Illinois University Press, 1990), 55–61.

George Cleve Haynes, "My Decrepit Italian Friend: 'Il maestro di color che sanno,'" *BSJ* 37 (June 1987): 88–96.

Christine Kenyon and James Ravin, "The Great Fall: Holmes's Final Problem at Reichenbach," *BSJ* 41 (December 1991): 199–202.

"The Greek-Interpreter"

Michael W. McClure, "Re: 'Which art in whose blood?'" *BSJ* 38 (September 1988): 148–49.

Robert S. Pasley, "'The Greek Interpreter' Interpreted: A Revisionist Essay," *BSJ* 35 (June 1985): 106–11.

Thomas M. Sobottke, "Speculations on the Further Career of Mycroft Holmes," *BSJ* 40 (June 1990): 75–77.

"His Last-Bow"

John L. Benton, "Dr. Watson's Automobile," *BSJ* 39 (June 1989): 79–80.

Norman M. Davis, "The Adventure of the American Interlude," *BSJ* 33 (March 1983): 10–16.

David L. Hammer, "Sherlock Holmes: Secret Agent," *BSJ* 36 (December 1986): 231–34.

Jon L. Lellenberg, "The Magnum Opus of His Latter Years," *BSJ* 37 (June 1987): 71–74.

The Hound of the Baskervilles

Marshall S. Berdan, "Perversion in the Canon: Dementia a la Devonshire," *BSJ* 40 (September 1990): 149–55.

Paul F. Ferguson, "Narrative Vision in *The Hound of the Baskervilles*," *Clues* 1 (Fall–Winter 1980): 24–30.

Mark E. Levitt, "The Vatican File," *BSJ* 41 (December 1991): 212–14.

Thomas F. O'Brien and James F. O'Brien, "The Holmes–Baskerville Connection," *BSJ* 35 (December 1985): 219–21.

"The Illustrious Client"

Donald E. Curtis, "'The Illustrious Client': Loyal Friend and Chivalrous Gentleman," *BSJ* 38 (September 1988): 163–66.

Bob Jones, "'It Was from the Carlton Club,'" *BSJ* 33 (March 1983): 19–22.

"The Lion's Mane"

Allen H. Butler, "A Speculation: Did Holmes Have Photo-Processing Capability at the Villa?" *BSJ* 40 (September 1990): 159–60.

"The Lost Special"

Edward J. Vatza, "The Apocryphal Letters Revisited," *BSJ* 38 (June 1988): 85–87.

The Lost World

Dana Martin Batory, "Was Watson an Uncle?" *BSJ* 38 (June 1988): 78–81.

Howard Davies, "*The Lost World*: Conan Doyle and the Suspense of Evolution," in *Nineteenth–Century Suspense: From Poe to Conan Doyle*, ed. Clive Bloom, Brian Docherty, Jane Gibb, and Keith Shand (New York: St. Martin's, 1988), 107–19.

Juanjo Fernandez, "Sherlock Holmes va de craneo," *Quimera* 65 (n.d.): 50–57.

"The Man with the Twisted Lip"

Audrey Jaffe, "Detecting the Beggar: Arthur Conan Doyle, Henry Mayhew, and 'The Man with the Twisted Lip,'" *Representations* 31 (Summer 1990): 96–117.

Michael Neumann, "Sherlock Holmes in Sezuan: Eine unbeachtete Quelle zu Brechts Drama," *JDSG* 34 (1990): 343–48.

"The Man with the Watches"

Edward J. Vatza, "The Apocryphal Letters Revisited," *BSJ* 38 (June 1988): 84–85.

"The Mazarin Stone"

Charles M. Lavazzi, "Sherlock Holmes, High Fidelity Pioneer; Or, The Advent of a Shure Thing," *BSJ* 39 (March 1989): 36–38.

"The Missing Three-Quarter"

M. S. Berdan, "A Suggested Two-Thirds of 'The Missing Three-Quarter,'" *BSJ* 38 (September 1988): 151–55.

"The Musgrave Ritual"

Howard E. Burr, "Stuart Brows Encircled or Tudor Loins Embraced?" *BSJ* 35 (September 1985): 161–69.

Evan M. Wilson, "Sherlock Holmes in Eastern Asia: The Thirty–Six Steps; or, Vambery Again," *BSJ* 33 (June 1983): 86–87.

Evan M. Wilson, "Vambery, the So–Called Wine Merchant; Or, The Dervish of Windsor Castle," *BSJ* 32 (September 1982): 140–42.

Jim Zunic, "Some Reflections on Indoor Target Practice," *BSJ* 38 (September 1988): 161.

"The Naval Treaty"

Christopher F. Baum, "The Twice–Stained Treaty," *BSJ* 32 (September 1982): 146–48.

Lee R. Walters, "The Great Experiment," *BSJ* 38 (June 1988): 94–95.

"The Noble Bachelor"

T. F. Foss, "The Bounder and the Bigamist," *BSJ* 34 (March 1984): 8–11.

Fred Kramer, "A Revealing Buffet on Baker Street," *BSJ* 41 (September 1991): 158–60.

Gordon R. Speck, "'The Noble Bachelor' and Browning's Duchess," *BSJ* 35 (March 1985): 35–37.

"The Norwood-Builder"

Michael W. McClure, "Re: 'Which art in whose blood?'" *BSJ* 38 (September 1988): 149–50.

"Our Midnight Visitor"

Ruth Berman, "Uffa's Midnight Visitor," *BSJ* 33 (March 1983): 7–8.

The Parasite

Anne Cranny Francis, "Arthur Conan Doyle's 'The Parasite': The Case of the Anguished Author," in *Nineteenth–Century Suspense: From Poe to Conan Doyle*, ed. Clive Bloom, Brian Docherty, Jane Gibb, and Keith Shand (New York: St. Martin's, 1988), 93–106.

The Poison Belt

Dana Martin Batory, "*The Poison Belt* as a Morality Tale," *RQ* 7 (March 1982): 97–100.

"The Priory School"

Marshall S. Berdan, "The Great Derbyshire Duke–Out," *BSJ* 39 (June 1989): 81–95.

Irving Kamil, "The Priory School Map: A Re-Examination," *BSJ* 34 (March 1984): 12–16.

M. Haddon MacRoberts, "On Determining the Direction of Travel of a Bicycle from Its Tracks," *BSJ* 33 (September 1983): 144–45.

Robert S. Pasley, "Breaking the Entail," *BSJ* 39 (June 1989): 96–98.

William L. Russell, "'The Adventure of the Priory School': Its Biblical Genesis," *BSJ* 36 (December 1986): 211–15.

Philip Weller, "The Priority of 'The Priory School,'" *BSJ* 41 (December 1991): 203–6.

"The Red Circle"

Marshall S. Berdan, "Watson and Shaw: Subtle Echoes in the Canon," *BSJ* 39 (December 1989): 206–08.

Charles G. Inman, "Are There Really No Caves on Long Island?" *BSJ* 41 (December 1991): 218–19.

Sheldon Wesson, "Light upon the Candle," *BSJ* 38 (December 1988): 238–39.

"The Red-Headed League"

Greg Darak, "But Why Dissolve the League?" *BSJ* 39 (June 1989): 108–09.

W. W. Higgins, "Some Tunnel Inferences in 'The Red-Headed League,'" *BSJ* 41 (September 1991): 163–64.

Brad Keefauver, "Upon the Relative Reliability of Watson and Wilson," *BSJ* 33 (June 1983): 92–94.

John A. Lanzalotti, "Saxe-Coburg Square," *BSJ* 41 (December 1991): 207–11.

"The Resident Patient"

Charles A. Meyer, "The Curious Incident of the Doctor in the Night–Time," *BSJ* 38 (June 1988): 88–90.

Richard S. Warner, "A Chronological Look at 'The Resident Patient,'" *BSJ* 34 (June 1984): 93–95.

"A Scandal in Bohemia"

Michael Atkinson, "Virginity Preserved and the Secret Marriage of Sherlock Holmes: The Theory of Popular Romance Applied to a Detective Fiction," *Clues* 2 (Spring–Summer 1981): 62–69.

Ray Betzner, "Dylan Thomas and Sherlock Holmes," *BSJ* 37 (June 1987): 97.

Dalma H. Brunauer, "Sherlock Holmes and the Hungarian Connection," *BSJ* 34 (June 1984): 98–105.

William D. Jenkins, "A Hair-Raising Epilogue," *BSJ* 35 (June 1985): 90–93.

William D. Jenkins, "We Were Both in the Photographs: I. Adler and Adah I.," *BSJ* 36 (March 1986): 6–16.

Steven Rothman, "On the Identity of a Staff-Commander," *BSJ* 36 (September 1986): 162–65.

William P. Schweickert, "The Better Man," *BSJ* 39 (June 1989): 99–101.

Harlan L. Umansky, "Of Seeing and Perceiving," *BSJ* 41 (September 1991): 162.

Edward J. Vatza, "Scandalous Adlerian Musings," *BSJ* 35 (June 1985): 80–83.

Evan M. Wilson, "Sherlock Holmes in Eastern Asia: The Thirty-Six Steps; or, Vambery Again," *BSJ* 33 (June 1983): 87–88.

"The Second Stain"

Christopher F. Baum, "The Twice-Stained Treaty," *BSJ* 32 (September 1982): 146–48.

Aubrey C. Roberts, "The Real Second Stain: A Tarnished Idol," *BSJ* 32 (December 1982): 227–29.

"Selecting a Ghost"

Chris Redmond, "Mr. Dodd's Client and Mr. D'odd," *BSJ* 35 (June 1985): 99–100.

The Sign of Four

S. E. Dahlinger, "In Search of the Agra Treasure (or Gelt by Association)," *BSJ* 36 (December 1986): 217–19.

Kirby Farrell, "Heroism, Culture, and Dread in *The Sign of Four*," *SNNTS* 16 (Spring 1984): 32–51.

Robert F. Fleissner, "The Onomastics of Sherlock," *MFAN* 8 (May–June 1984): 21–24.

David L. Hammer, "The Singular Case of the Enigmatic Initials," *BSJ* 35 (September 1985): 139–42.

Karel van het Reve, "Sigmund Freud en Sherlock Holmes," *Tirade* 29 (September–December 1985): 687–93.

Edward J. Vatza, "An Analysis of the Tracing of Footsteps from Sherlock Holmes to the Present," *BSJ* 37 (March 1987): 16–21.

Evan M. Wilson, "*The Sign of the Four* Revisited: With Some Notes on the Andaman Islands," *BSJ* 34 (March 1984): 19–21.

"Silver Blaze"

Hans Uno Bengtsson, "'And the Calculation Is a Simple One,'" *BSJ* 39 (December 1989): 232–36.

Jaakko Hintikka, "Sherlock Holmes Formalized," in *The Sign of Three: Dupin, Holmes, Peirce*, ed. Umberto Eco and Thomas A. Sebeok (Bloomington: Indiana University Press, 1983), 170–78.

Rita C. Manning, "Why Sherlock Holmes Can't Be Replaced by an Expert System," *PhS* 51 (January 1987): 19–28.

Wayne B. Swift, "'Silver Blaze'—A Corrected Identification," *BSJ 41 (March 1991): 25–35.*

"The Speckled Band"

William D. Jenkins, "Hunting Down 'The Speckled Band,'" *BSJ* 41 (March 1991): 37–38.

Lionel Needleman, "Unravelling 'The Speckled Band,'" *BSJ* 34 (September 1984): 139–49.

Pierce Pratte, "The Uncelebrated Accomplice of 'The Speckled Band,'" *BSJ* 40 (September 1990): 144–48.

A Study in Scarlet

L. M. Anderson, "Jefferson Hope as Tragic Revenger," *BSJ* 39 (September 1989): 135–43.

Michael Atkinson, "Type and Text in *A Study in Scarlet*: Repression and the Textual Unconscious," *Clues* 8 (Spring–Summer 1987): 67–99.

Massimo A. Bonfantini and Giampaolo Proni, "To Guess or Not to Guess?" in *The Sign of Three: Dupin, Holmes, Peirce,* ed. Umberto Eco and Thomas A. Sebeok (Bloomington: Indiana University Press, 1983), 119–34.

Howard Brody, "The Placebo in *A Study in Scarlet*," *BSJ* 40 (September 1990): 156–57.

Jennifer Decker, "The Whiteness in *Scarlet*," *BSJ* 37 (December 1987): 228–37.

Lydia Alix Fillingham, "'The Colorless Skein of Life': Threats to the Private Sphere in Conan Doyle's *A Study in Scarlet*," *ELH* 56 (Fall 1989): 667–88.

Christine L. Huber, "The Sherlock Holmes Blood Test: The Solution to a Century–Old Mystery," *BSJ* 37 (December 1987): 215–20.

Lloyd A. Hutton, "Sherlock Holmes and the Resident Doctor," *BSJ* 41 (June 1991): 77–81.

H. Paul Jeffers, "'You Have Been in Peshawar, I Perceive,'" *BSJ* 41 (June 1991): 82–84.

Brad Keefauver, "Violin Conversations," *BSJ* 37 (June 1987): 78–79.

Oliver Klis, "*A Study in Scarlet*: Doyle und sein Vorbild Gaboriau," *Horen* 34, no. 2 (1989): 134–39.

Colin Loader, "Conan Doyle's *A Study in Scarlet*: A Study in Irony," *CLIO* 19 (Winter 1990): 147–59.

Raymond J. McGowan, "Sherlock Holmes and Forensic Chemistry," *BSJ* 37 (March 1987): 10–14.

Robert A. Moss, "Brains and Attics," *BSJ* 41 (June 1991): 93–95.

Ruthann H. Stetak, "Jefferson Hope: A Fairly Good Dispenser," *BSJ* 39 (September 1989): 144–47.

"The Sussex Vampire"

Robert S. Katz, "John H. Watson, M.D.: Pioneer Neuropathologist," *BSJ* 32 (September 1982): 150–52.

DOYLE, ARTHUR CONAN, "The Thor Bridge"

Chris Redmond, "Mr. Dodd's Client and Mr. D'odd," *BSJ* 35 (June 1985): 100–01.

"The Thor Bridge"

Diane Maginn, "Suicide Disguised as Murder: A Munchausen–Related Event at Thor Bridge," *BSJ* 39 (March 1989): 13–15.

"The Three Students"

R. F. Fleissner, "Dr. Moriarty, Mr. Holmes, and the Clues of Art," *CanH* 8 (Spring 1985): 5–9.

The Valley of Fear

T. F. Foss, "The Man They Called 'Ho,' Plus the Butcher Also," *BSJ* 35 (December 1985): 206–10.

"When the World Screamed"

Dana Martin Batory, "The Climax of 'When the World Screamed,'" *RQ* 8 (March 1988): 124–28.

"Wisteria Lodge"

Henry A. Dietz, "Murillo and San Pedro: An Excursion in Identification," *BSJ* 39 (September 1989): 153–69.

DRABBLE, MARGARET

A Case for Equality

Kenneth Minogue, "The Preoccupation with Equality," *Encounter* 71 (November 1988): 39–41.

"Crossing the Alps"

Suzanne H. Mayer, "Margaret Drabble's Short Stories: Worksheets for her Novels," in *Margaret Drabble: Golden Realms*, ed. Dorey Schmidt and Jan Seale (Edinburg, TX: School of Humanities, Pan American University Press, 1982), 82–83.

The Garrick Year

P. N. Furbank, "Novels," *Encounter* 23 (September 1964): 76–81.

William Hill, "*The Garrick Year*," *America* 112 (8 May 1965): 678.

"The Little Woman," *TLS* (23 July 1964): 645.

Dee Pruessner, "Patterns in *The Garrick Year*," in *Margaret Drabble: Golden Realms*, ed. Dorey Schmidt and Jan Seale (Edinburg, TX: School of Humanities, Pan American University Press, 1982), 117–27.

David Rees, "Reality Blues," *Spectator* 213 (17 July 1964): 90.

Judith Ruderman, "An Invitation to a Dinner Party: Margaret Drabble on Women and Food," in *Margaret Drabble: Golden Realm,* ed. Dorey Schmidt and Jan Seale (Edinburg, TX: School of Humanities, Pan American University Press, 1982), 104–6.

Nora Foster Stovel, "Staging a Marriage: Margaret Drabble's *The Garrick Year*," *Mosaic* 17 (Spring 1984): 161–74.

Robert Taubman, "The Modern Conscience," *NewS* 68 (17 July 1964): 93–94.

Irving Wardle, "How to Catch the Reader's Attention," *Observer* 19 July 1964): 23.

The Ice Age

Paul Bailey, "Of Prophecy and Puppetry," *SatR* 5 (7 January 1978): 39.

Pearl K. Bell, "The English Sickness," *Commentary* 64 (December 1977): 80–83.

E. S. Duvall, "*The Ice Age*," *AtM* 240 (December 1977): 108.

Margaret Hill Goss, "Birds in Margaret Drabble's *The Ice Age*," *NConL* 15 (November 1985): 10.

Margaret Hill Goss, "Housing in Margaret Drabble's *The Ice Age*," *POMPA* 11 (1986): 19–26.

Elaine Tuttle Hansen, "The Uses of Imagination: Margaret Drabble's *The Ice Age*," in *Critical Essays on Margaret Drabble*, ed. Ellen Cronan Rose (Boston: G. K. Hall, 1985), 151–69.

Michael F. Harper, "Margaret Drabble and the Resurrection of the English Novel," in *Critical Essays on Margaret Drabble*, ed. Ellen Cronan Rose (Boston: G. K. Hall, 1985), 52–54.

Lis Harris, "Hard Times," *NewY* 53 (26 December 1977): 66–68.

DRABBLE, MARGARET, *Jerusalem the Golden*

Maureen Howard, "Fiction Chronicle," *HR* 31 (Spring 1978): 184–85.

Michael Irwin, "This Island Now," *TLS* (2 September 1977): 1045.

D. A. N. Jones, "Age Concern," *Listener* 98 (1 September 1977): 282–83.

Jonathan Keates, "*Ice Age*," *NewS* 94 (9 September 1977): 343.

Ellen Cronan Rose, "*Ice Age*," *NaR* 29 (23 December 1977): 1504.

Nora Foster Stovel, "The Aerial View of Modern Britain," *Ariel* 15 (1984): 29–30.

Jerusalem the Golden

Lee R. Edwards, "*Jerusalem the Golden*: A Fable for Our Times," *WS* 6 (1979): 321–24.

David Galloway, "Milk and Honey," *Spectator* 218 (14 April 1967): 425–26.

David J. Gordon, "Trust and Treachery: Some Recent Novels," *YR* 57 (Autumn 1967): 105–15.

"*Jerusalem the Golden*," *NYTBR* (21 August 1977): 33.

D. A. N. Jones, "No Roots," *NewS* 73 (26 May 1967): 724.

Ellen Z. Lambert, "Margaret Drabble and the Sense of Possibility," *UTQ* 49 (Spring 1980): 228–51. Reprinted in *Critical Essays on Margaret Drabble*, ed. Ellen Cronan Rose (Boston: G. K. Hall, 1985), 40–44.

Jonathan Raban, *The Technique of Modern Fiction: Essays in Practical Criticism* (London: Edward Arnold, 1968; Notre Dame: University of Notre Dame Press, 1969), 166–68.

The Middle Ground

Richard Boston, "A Knight's Tale," *Punch* (9 July 1980): 144.

William Boyd, "Beyond the Exemplary," *TLS* (11 July 1980): 772.

Pamela S. Bromberg, "Narrative in Drabble's *The Middle Ground*: Relativity versus Teleology," *ConL* 24 (Winter 1983): 463–79.

Jane Campbell, "Reaching Outwards: Versions of Reality in *The Middle Ground*," *JNT* 14 (Winter 1984): 17–32.

Denis Donaghue, "You Better Believe It," *NYRB* 27 (20 November 1980): 20–21.

Gail Eifrig, "*The Middle Ground*," in *Margaret Drabble: Golden Realms*, ed. Dorey Schmidt and Jan Seale (Edinburg, TX: School of Humanities, Pan American University Press, 1982), 178–85.

Mary Jane Elkins, "Alenoushka's Return: Motifs and Movement in Margaret Drabble's *The Middle Ground*," in *Critical Essays on Margaret Drabble*, ed. Ellen Cronan Rose (Boston: G.K. Hall, 1985), 169–80.

Lorna Irvine, "No Sense of an Ending: Drabble's Continuous Endings," in *Critical Essays on Margaret Drabble*, ed. Ellen Cronan Rose (Boston: G. K. Hall, 1985), 82–84.

D. A. N. Jones, "Deliberate Mistakes," *Listener* 104 (3 July 1980): 24–25.

Francis King, "*The Middle Ground*," *Spectator* 245 (5 July 1980): 21.

John Lucas, "Endlessly," *NewS* 100 (11 July 1980): 55–56.

Beth Madison, "Mr. Bennett, Mrs. Woolf, and Mrs. Drabble," *WVUPP* 34 (1988): 118–127.

Ellen Cronan Rose, "Drabble's *The Middle Ground*: 'Mid-Life' Narrative Strategies," *Critique* 23 (Spring 1982): 69–82.

Phyllis Rose, "Margaret Drabble," in *The Writing of Women: Essays in Renaissance* (Middletown, CT: Wesleyan University Press, 1985), 109–14.

Phyllis Rose, "Our Chronicler of Britain," *NYTBR* 85 (7 September 1980): 1, 32–33.

Roberta Rubenstein, "From Detritus to Discovery: Margaret Drabble's *The Middle Ground*," *JNT* 14 (Winter 1984): 1–16.

Judith Ruderman, "An Invitation to a Dinner Party: Margaret Drabble on Women and Food," in *Margaret Drabble: Golden Realm*, ed. Dorey Schmidt and Jan Seale (Edinburg, TX: School of Humanities, Pan American University Press, 1982), 112–15.

Lynn Veach Sadler, "'The Society We Have': The Search for Meaning in Drabble's *The Middle Ground*," *Crit* 23 (Spring 1982): 83–94.

Lorna Sage, "A Heroine of Our Time," *Observer* (29 June 1980): 29.

The Millstone

"Ask Any Girl," *TLS* (23 September 1965): 820.

Colin Butler, "Margaret Drabble: *The Millstone* and Wordsworth," *ES* 59 (1978): 353–60.

Nancy Hardin, "Drabble's *The Millstone*: A Fable for Our Times," *Critique* 15, no. 1 (1973): 22–34.

F. W. J. Hemmings, "Longs and Shorts," *NewS* 70 (10 September 1965): 365–66.

Naomi Okamura, "Aratano Jiko no Kakuritsu: M. Drabble - Hikiusu," in *Igirisu Shosetsu no Joseitachi*, ed. Yaeko Sumi and Naomi Okamura (Tokyo: Keiso, 1983), 245–68.

Norbert Timm, "Apropos *The Millstone*," *NM* 37 (February 1984): 45–46.

Ruth Sherry, "Margaret Drabble's *The Millstone*: A Feminist Approach," *Edda* 79 (1979): 41–53.

Linda Richetts Sorbo, "The Way Contemporary Women Write: An Analysis of Margaret Drabble's *The Millstone*," *Edda* 81 (1981): 93–101.

Susan Spitzer, "Fantasy and Femaleness in Margaret Drabble's *The Millstone*," *Novel* 11 (Spring 1978): 227–45. Reprinted in *Critical Essays on Margaret Drabble*, ed. Ellen Cronan Rose (Boston: G. K. Hall, 1985), 86–105.

A Natural Curiosity

Roberta Rubenstein, "Severed Heads, Primal Crimes, Narrative Revisions: Margaret Drabble's *A Natural Curiosity*," *Crit* 33 (Winter 1992): 95–105.

The Needle's Eye

Arnold E. Davidson, "Parables of Grace in *The Needle's Eye*," in *Margaret Drabble: Golden Realms*, ed. Dorey Schmidt and Jan Seale (Edinburg, TX: School of Humanities, Pan American University Press, 1982), 66–74.

Barbara Dixon, "Patterned Figurative Language in *The Needle's Eye*," in *Margaret Drabble: Golden Realms*, ed. Dorey Schmidt and Jan Seale (Edinburg, TX: School of Humanities, Pan American University Press, 1982), 128–38.

Lawrence S. Friedman, "Puritan Self-fashioning in *The Needle's Eye*," *CLAJ* 34 (June 1991): 426–35.

Mary M. Lay, "Margaret Drabble's *The Needle's Eye*: Jamesian Perception of Self," *CLAJ* 28 (September 1984): 33–45.

Judy Little, "Imagining Marriage," in *Portraits of Marriage in Literature*, ed. Anne C. Hargrove and Maurine Magliocco (Macomb, IL: Essays in Literature, 1984), 171–84.

Laurie Quinn, "And the Camel's Back," *ASch* 42 (Winter 1972–1973): 173–74.

Ellen Cronan Rose, "A Farewell to Renunciations," *Nation* 215 (23 October 1972): 379–80.

Judith Ruderman, "An Invitation to a Dinner Party: Margaret Drabble on Women and Food," in *Margaret Drabble: Golden Realm*, ed. Dorey Schmidt and Jan Seale (Edinburg, TX: School of Humanities, Pan American University Press, 1982), 107–09.

Robert H. Sale, "Willians, Weesner, Drabble," in *On Not Being Good Enough: Writings of a Working Critic* (New York: Oxford University Press, 1982), 42–53.

Roger H. Sale, "Enemies, Foreigners and Friends," *HudR* 25 (Winter 1972–73): 708–10.

Rosalind Wade, "Quarterly Fiction Review," *ContempR* 220 (April 1972): 213–14.

The Radiant Way

Margaret Atwood, "Margaret Atwood Talks to Margaret Drabble," *Chatelaine* 60 (April 1987): 73, 124, 126, 130.

Pamela S. Bromberg, "Margaret Drabble's *The Radiant Way*: Feminist Metafiction," *Novel* 24 (Fall 1990): 5–25.

Anita Brookner, "Too Much of a Muchness," *Spectator* 258 (2 May 1987): 29–30.

Lindsay Duguid, "Icons of the Times," *TLS* (1 May 1987): 458.

Marjorie Hill Goss, "Murder and Martyrdom in Margaret Drabble's *The Radiant Way*," *NConL* 19 (May 1989): 2.

Ann Hulbert, "Maggiemarch," *NewR* 197 (14 December 1987): 38–41.

Roberta Rubenstein, "Sexuality and Intertextuality: Margaret Drabble's *The Radiant Way*," *ConL* 30 (Spring 1989): 95–112.

Linda Taylor, "Ghosts," *Listener* 117 (7 May 1987): 25–26.

Realms of Gold

Peter Ackroyd, "Per Ardua," *Spectator* 235 (27 September 1975): 412.

Pamela S. Bromberg, "Romantic Revisionism in Margaret Drabble's *The Realms of Gold*," in *Margaret Drabble: Golden Realms*, ed. Dorey Schmidt and Jan Seale (Edinburg, TX: School of Humanities, Pan American University Press, 1982), 48–65.

DRABBLE, MARGARET, *Realms of Gold*

Cynthia A. Davis, "Unfolding Form: Narrative Approach and Theme in *The Realms of Gold*," in *Critical Essays on Margaret Drabble*, ed. Ellen Cronan Rose (Boston: G. K. Hall, 1985), 141–50.

Cynthia A. Davis, "Unfolding Form: Narrative Approach and Theme in *The Realms of Gold*," *MLQ* 40 (December 1979): 390–402.

Jacqueline Eis, "The Omniscient Narrator in *The Realms of Gold*," *SJS* 8 (1982): 101–07.

Michael F. Harper, "Margaret Drabble and the Resurrection of the English Novel," in *Critical Essays on Margaret Drabble*, ed. Ellen Cronan Rose (Boston: G. K. Hall, 1985), 61–62, 66–69.

Carey Kaplan, "A Vision of Power in Margaret Drabble's *The Realms of Gold*," in *Critical Essays on Margaret Drabble*, ed. Ellen Cronan Rose (Boston: G. K. Hall, 1985), 133–40.

Ellen Z. Lambert, "Margaret Drabble and the Sense of Possibility," *UTQ* 49 (Spring 1980): 228–51. Reprinted in *Critical Essays on Margaret Drabble*, ed. Ellen Cronan Rose (Boston: G. K. Hall, 1985), 44–51.

Judy Little, "Humor and the Female Quest: Margaret Drabble's *The Realms of Gold*," *RFemI* 4 (Fall 1978): 44–52.

Judy Little, "Margaret Drabble and the Romantic Imagination: *The Realms of Gold*," *PSc* 55 (Spring–Summer 1981): 241–52.

Lorna Irvine, "No Sense of an Ending: Drabble's Continuous Fictions," in *Critical Essays on Margaret Drabble*, ed. Ellen Cronan Rose (Boston: G. K. Hall, 1985), 80–81.

Pamela Hansford Johnson, "Ivory Bower," *NewS* 90 (26 September 1975): 375–76.

Ruth Mathewson, "A Tangled Bank," *NewL* 59 (26 April 1976): 17–19.

Joyce Carol Oates, "Shabby, Golden Lives," *SatR* 3 (15 November 1975): 20–22.

Gerard C. Reedy, "*The Realms of Gold*," *Commonweal* 103 (18 June 1976): 408–09.

Christopher Ricks, "Lost Allusions," *NYRB* 22 (27 November 1975): 42–44.

Barbara Hill Rigney, *Lilith's Daughters: Women and Religion in Contemporary Fiction* (Madison: University of Wisconsin Press, 1982), 97–98.

Margaret M. Rowe, "The Uses of the Past in Margaret Drabble's *The Realms of Gold*," in *Margaret Drabble: Golden Realms*, ed. Dorey Schmidt and Jan Seale (Edinburg, TX: School of Humanities, Pan American University Press, 1982), 158–67.

Mariko Sakurai, "Margaret Drabble no Ogon no Ryoiki; Suzuki Yukio Sensei Kinen Ronbunshu Kanko Iinkai," in *Phoenix o Motomete: Eibei Shosetsu no Yukue* (Tokyo: Nan'undo, 1982), 229–40.

Patricia Sharpe, "On First Looking Into *The Realms of Gold*," *MQR* 16 (1977): 225–31.

Walter Sullivan, "Gifts, Prophecies, and Prestidigitations: Fictional Frameworks, Fictional Modes," *SR* 85 (January 1977): 116–20.

A Summer Bird-Cage

Walter Allen, "*A Summer Bird-Cage*," *NewS* 65 (29 March 1963): 466.

Arnold E. Davidson, "Pride and Prejudice in Margaret Drabble's *A Summer Bird-Cage*," *ArQ* 38 (Winter 1982): 303–10.

Michael F. Harper, "Margaret Drabble and the Ressurection of the English Novel," in *Critical Essays on Margaret Drabble*, ed. Ellen Cronan Rose, 58–60, 62–63.

Ellen Z. Lambert, "Margaret Drabble and the Sense of Possibility," *UTQ* 49 (Spring 1980): 228–51. Reprinted in *Critical Essays on Margaret Drabble*, ed. Ellen Cronon Rose (Boston: G. K. Hall, 1985), 44–51.

David Lodge, "Picaresque and Gawky," *Spectator* 210 (19 April 1963): 504.

The Waterfall

Harriet F. Bergmann, "'A Piercing Virtue': Emily Dickinson in Margaret Drabble's *The Waterfall*," *MFS* 36 (Summer 1990): 181–93.

Pamela S. Bromberg, "The Development of Narrative Technique in Margaret Drabble's Novels," *JNT* 16 (Fall 1986): 179–91.

Joanne V. Creighton, "The Reader and Modern and Post-Modern Fiction," *CollL* 9 (Fall 1982): 216–30.

Joanne V. Creighton, "Reading Margaret Drabble's *The Waterfall*," in *Critical Essays on Margaret Drabble*, ed. Ellen Cronan Rose (Boston: G. K. Hall, 1985), 106–18.

Caryn Fuoroli, "Sophistry or Simple Truth? Narrative Technique in Margaret Drabble's *The Waterfall*," *JNT* 11 (Spring 1981): 110–24.

Gayle Greene, "Margaret Drabble's *The Waterfall*: New System, New Morality," *Novel* 22 (Fall 1988): 45–65.

Richard Jones, "*The Waterfall*," *Listener* 81 (22 May 1969): 732.

Joyce Carol Oates, "Realism of Distance, Realism of Immediacy," *SoR* 7 (Winter 1971): 309–10.

Nancy S. Rabinowitz, "Talc on the Scotch: Art and Morality in Margaret Drabble's *The Waterfall*," *IJWS* 5 (May–June 1982): 236–45.

Ellen Cronan Rose, "Feminine Endings—and Beginnings; Margaret Drabble's *The Waterfall*," *ConL* 21 (Winter 1980): 81–99.

Roberta Rubenstein, "*The Waterfall*: The Myth of Psyche, Romantic Tradition, and the Female Quest," in *Margaret Drabble: Golden Realms*, ed. Dorey Schmidt and Jan Seale (Edinburg, TX: School of Humanities, Pan American University Press, 1982), 139–57.

S. B. Shurbutt, "Margaret Drabble's *The Waterfall*: 'The Writer as Fiction, or Overcoming the Dilemma of Female Authorship,'" *WS* 16 (October 1989): 283–92.

Eleanor Honig Skoller, "The Progress of a Letter: Truth, Feminism, and *The Waterfall*," in *Critical Essays on Margaret Drabble*, ed. Ellen Cronan Rose (Boston: G. K. Hall, 1985), 119–33.

Jean Wyatt, "Escaping Literary Designs: The Politics of Reading and Writing in Margaret Drabble's *The Waterfall*," *PConL* 11 (1985): 37–45.

DURRELL, LAWRENCE

The Alexandria Quartet

R. M. Albérès, "Lawrence Durrell ou le roman pentagonal," *RevP* 72 (1965): 102–12.

Ann Ashworth, "Durrell's Hermetic Puer and Senex in *The Alexandria Quartet*," *Critique* 26 (Winter 1985): 67–80.

Joseph A. Boone, "Mappings of Male Desire in Durrell's *Alexandria Quartet*," *SoAQ* 88 (Winter 1989): 73–106. Reprinted as "Mappings of Male Desire in Durell's *Alexandria Quartet*: Homoerotic Negotiations in the Colonial Narrative," in *Out of Bounds: Male Writers and Gender(ed) Criticism*, ed. Laura Claridge and Elizabeth Langland (Amherst: University of Massachusetts Press, 1990), 316–66.

Roger Bowen, "Closing the 'Toybox': Orientalism and Empire in *The Alexandria Quartet*," *StLI* 24 (Spring 1991): 9–18.

Jennifer L. Brewer, "Character and Psychological Place: The Justine/Sophia Relation," *DL* 5 (September 1981): 236–39.

R. T. Chapman, "Dead, or Just Pretending? Reality in *The Alexandria Quartet*," *CentR* 16 (1972): 408–18.

Peter G. Christensen, "Greece, Egypt, and the Quartet: Response," *DL* 7 (July 1984): 79–88.

Peter Cortland, "Durrell's Sentimentalism," *EngR* 14 (April 1964): 15–19.

Walter G. Creed, "Pieces of the Puzzle: The Multiple-Narrative Structure of *The Alexandria Quartet*," *Mosaic* 6 (Spring 1973): 19–35.

Walter G. Creed, " 'The Whole Pointless Joke'? Darley's Search for Truth in *The Alexandria Quartet*," *ÉA* 28 (1975): 165–73.

Pierre Debray–Ritzen, "A Sovereign Harmony," *DL* 7 (September 1984): 16–19.

Louis Fraiberg, "Durrell's Dissonant Quartet," in *Contemporary British Novelists*, ed. Charles Shapiro (Carbondale: Southern Illinois University Press, 1965), 16–35.

Robert Fricker, "Lawrence Durrell: *The Alexandria Quartet*," in *Der Moderne Englische Roman: Interpretationen*, ed. Horst Oppel (Berlin: Erich Schmidt Verlag, 1965), 399–416.

Terrence L. Grimes, "How Real Is the City? Townscape in *The Alexandria Quartet*," *DL* 7 (September 1984): 51–68.

John V. Hagopian, "The Resolution of *The Alexandria Quartet*," *Crit* 7 (1964): 97–106.

Donald P. Kaczvinsky, "When was Darley in Alexandria? A Chronology for *The Alexandria Quartet*," *JML* 17 (Spring 1991): 591–94.

Steven G. Kellman, "The Reader in/of *The Alexandria Quartet*," *SNNTS* 20 (Spring 1988): 78–85.

Justyna Kostkowska, "Physics and the *Alexandria Quartet* by Lawrence Durrell," *ZRL* 32, no. 2 (1989): 83–96.

Bala Kothandaraman, "The Comic Dimension in *The Alexandria Quartet*," *OJES* 9 (1972): 27–37.

Joseph E. Kruppa, "Durrell's *Alexandria Quartet* and the 'Implosion' of the Modern Consciousness," *MFS* 13 (1967): 401–16.

Gérard Lebas, "The Fabric of Durrell's *Alexandria Quartet*," *Caliban* 8 (1971): 139–50.

Nancy W. Lewis, "*The Alexandria Quartet* and the Motion of the Field: Drifting, Exploding, Regrouping," *DL* 7 (September 1984): 145–54.

Mark F. Lund, "Sackcloth to Cloth-of-Gold: Durrell's Alchemical Quartet," *DL* 1 (Spring 1992): 45–56.

Joan Mellard, "The Unity of Lawrence Durrell's *Alexandria Quartet*," *LingLit* 1, no. 1 (1975): 77–143.

Ray Morrison, "Mirrors and the Heraldic Universe in Lawrence Durrell's *The Alexandria Quartet*," *TCL* 33 (Winter 1987): 499–514.

J. R. Nichols, "The Paradise of Bitter Fruit: Lawrence Durrell's *Alexandria Quartet*," *DL* 5 (Fall 1981): 224–34.

Carol Peirce, "'A Lass Unparalled'd': The Memory of Shakespeare's Cleopatra in *The Alexandria Quartet*," *DL* 7 (Fall 1984): 173–82.

Carol Peirce, "'Intimations of Powers Within': Durrell's Heavenly Game of the Tarot," in *Critical Essays on Lawrence Durrell*, ed. Alan Warren Friedman (Boston: G. K. Hall, 1987), 200–13.

Carol Peirce, "'Wrinkled Deep in Time': *The Alexandria Quartet* as Many-Layered Palimpsest," *TCL* 33 (Winter 1987): 485–98.

Michel W. Pharand, "Eros Agonistes: The Decay of Loving in *The Alexandria Quartet*," *DL* 1 (Spring 1992): 61–71.

Jane Lagoudis Pinchin, "Durrell's Fatal Cleopatra," *MFS* 28 (Summer 1982): 229–36.

Jane Lagoudis Pinchin and Joan Rodman Goulianos, "Durrell's Fatal Cleopatra," *DL* 5 (Fall 1981): 24–39.

Linda S. Rashidi, "Complexity of Reality in Lawrence Durrell's *The Alexandria Quartet*," in *Systemic Perspectives on Discourse, II: Selected Applied Papers from the 9th International Systemic Workshop*, ed. James D. Benson and William S. Greaves (Norwood, NJ: Ablex, 1985), 204–25.

Linda S. Rashidi, "Linguistic Signals of Activeness and Passiveness in Lawrence Durrell's *The Alexandria Quartet*," in *The Ninth LACUS Forum 1982*, ed. John Morreall (Columbia, SC: Hornbeam, 1983), 405–12.

Anna Rieger-Pratt, "Lawrence Durrell's *Alexandria Quartet*: A 'Novelist's Novel'?" *KN* 28, no. 3–4 (1981): 357–67.

Douglas Robillard Jr., "The Alchemist of *The Alexandria Quartet*," *CaudaP* 8 (Fall 1989): 7–9.

W. R. Robinson, "Intellect and Imagination in *The Alexandria Quartet*," *Shenandoah* 18 (1967): 55–68.

Lisa Schwerdt, "Coming of Age in Alexandria: The Narrator," *DL* 5 (Fall 1981): 210–21.

Sharon Spencer, "Dialogues, Drifting, and Otto Rank: A Response," *DL* 7 (September 1984): 155–58.

Harry R. Stoneback, "Et in Alexandria Ego: Lawrence Durrell and the Spirit of Place," *MidHLS* 5 (1982): 115–28.

Robert L. Stromberg, "The Contribution of Relativity to the Inconsistency of Form in *The Alexandria Quartet*," *DL* 5 (Fall 1981): 246–56.

Chet Taylor, "Dissonance and Digression: The Ill-Fitting Fusion of Philosophy and Form in Lawrence Durrell's *Alexandria Quartet*," *MFS* 17 (1971): 167–79.

Warren Wedin, "The Artist as Narrator in *The Alexandria Quartet*," *TCL* 18 (1972): 175–80.

David M. Woods, "Love and Meaning in *The Alexandria Quartet*: Some Tantric Perspectives," in *On Miracle Ground: Essays on the Fiction of Lawrence Durrell*, ed. Michael H. Begnal (Lewisburg, PA: Bucknell University Press, 1990), 93–112.

Anne Ricketson Zahlan, "City as Carnival, Narrative as Palimpsest: Lawrence Durrell's *The Alexandria Quartet*," *JNT* 18 (Winter 1988): 34–46.

Anne Ricketson Zahlan, "The Destruction of the Imperial Self in Lawrence Durrell's *The Alexandria Quartet*," *PConL* 12 (1986): 3–12.

"Antrobus Complete"

Frank L. Kersnowski, "Durrell's Diplomats: Inertia Where Is Thy Sting?" in *Into the Labyrinth: Essays on the Art of Lawrence Durrell*, ed. Frank L. Kersnowski (Ann Arbor, MI: University Microfilms International Research Press, 1989), 51–62.

The Avignon Quintet

Michael H. Begnal, "The Mystery of the Templars in *The Avignon Quintet*," in *On Miracle Ground: Essays on the Fiction of Lawrence Durrell*, ed. Michael H. Begnal (Lewisburg, PA: Bucknell University Press, 1990), 155–65.

Susan Vander Closter, "Writer as Painter in Lawrence Durrell's *Avignon Quintet*," in *On Miracle Ground: Essays on the Fiction of Lawrence Durrell*, ed. Michael H. Begnal (Lewisburg, PA: Bucknell University Press, 1990), 166–78.

William L. Godshalk, "Lawrence Durrell's Game in *The Avignon Quintet*," in *On Miracle Ground: Essays on the Fiction of Lawrence Durrell*, ed. Michael H. Begnal (Lewisburg, PA: Bucknell University Press, 1990), 187–200.

John Noel Lenzi, "Myth and the Daimonic Voice in *The Avignon Quintet*," *DL* 1 (Spring 1992): 57–60.

Ian S. MacNiven, "The Quincunx Quiddified: Structure in Lawrence Durrell," in *The Modernists: Studies in a Literary Phenomenon: Essays in Honor of Harry T. Moore*, ed. Lawrence B. Gamache and Ian S. MacNiven (Rutherford, NJ: Fairleigh Dickinson University Press, 1987), 234–48.

The Avignon Quintet: Livia, or Buried Alive

Donald P. Kaczvinsky, "Classical and Medieval Sources for Lawrence Durrell's 'Livia,'" *NConL* 23 (March 1993): 11–12.

The Avignon Quintet: Monsieur

James P. Carley, "Lawrence Durrell and the Gnostics," *DL* 2 (Spring 1978): 3–10.

Lee T. Lemon, "The Imagination of Reality: The Reality of Imagination," *DL* 1 (Spring 1992): 37–44.

The Black Book

M.C. Captain H. Dare, "The Quest for Durrell's Scobie," *MFS* 10 (1964): 379–83.

Desmond Hawkins, "Lawrence Durrell: *The Black Book*," *Criterion* 18 (1939): 316–18.

Henry Miller, "A Boost for *The Black Book*," *Booster* 2 (1937): 18.

Clea

Maurice Cranston, "*Clea* by Lawrence Durrell," *LMag* 7 (1960): 69–71.

The Dark Labyrinth

James A. Brigham, "Initiatory Experience in *The Dark Labyrinth*," *DL* 7 (July 1984): 19–29.

Gregory Dickson, "The Narrator in *The Dark Labyrinth*," in *Into the Labyrinth: Essays on the Art of Lawrence Durrell*, ed. Frank L. Kersnowski (Ann Arbor, MI: University Microfilms International Research Press, 1989), 63–72.

Donald P. Kaczvinsky, "Durrell's *The Dark Labyrinth*," *Expl* 46 (Spring 1988): 42–44.

Mountolive

Eugene Hollahan, "Who Wrote *Mountolive*? The Same One Who Wrote *Swann in Love*," *SNNTS* 20 (Summer 1988): 167–85.

Prospero's Cell

Harry R. Stoneback, "Et in Alexandria Ego: Lawrence Durrell and the Spirit of Place," *MidHLS* 5 (1982): 115–28.

The Revolt of Aphrodite

Gregory Dickson, "Setting and Character in *The Revolt of Aphrodite*," *TCL* 33 (Winter 1987): 528–35.

Sebastian

William L. Godshalk, "*Sebastian*: Or, Ruling Passions: Searches and Failures," *TCL* 33, no. 4 (Winter 1987): 536–49.

Tunc-Nunquam

Donald P. Kaczvinsky, "'The True Birth of Free Man': Culture and Civilization in *Tunc-Nunquam*," in *On Miracle Ground: Essays on the Fiction of Lawrence Durrell*, ed. Michael H. Begnal (Lewisburg, PA: Bucknell University Press, 1990), 140–52.

Tone Rugset, "*Tunc-Nunquam*: The Quest for Wholeness," *Labrys* 5 (1979): 155–62.

Two Cities

Jean Fanchette, "Lawrence Durrell and *Two Cities*," in *Into the Labyrinth: Essays on the Art of Lawrence Durrell*, ed. Frank L. Kersnowski (Ann Arbor, MI: University Microfilms International Research Press, 1989), 91–100.

The Village of the Turtle-Doves

Shelley Cox, "The Road Not Taken: Durrell's Unpublished Novel *The Village of the Turtle-Doves*," *StLI* 24 (Spring 1991): 19–27.

DURRELL, LAWRENCE, *White Eagles over Serbia*

White Eagles over Serbia

Michael J. Cartwright, "*White Eagles over Serbia*: Durrell's Transcendental Connection," *DL* 7 (July 1984): 31–33.

EDGEWORTH, MARIE

Belinda

Beth Kowaleski-Wallace, "Home Economics: Domestic Ideology in Maria Edgeworth's *Belinda*," *ECent* 29 (Fall 1988): 242–62.

Heather Macfadyen, "Lady Delacour's Library: Maria Edgeworth's *Belinda* and Fashionable Reading," *NCF* 48 (March 1994): 423–39.

Castle Rackrent

Bernard Escarbelt, "'We Lifts Him Up': Fait de langue et effet de style dans *Castle Rackrent*," *ÉI* 10 (December 1985): 25–30.

Anthony Mortimer, "*Castle Rackrent* and Its Historical Contexts," *ÉI* 9 (December 1984): 107–23.

Daithi O hOgain, "'Said an Elderly Man . . .': Maria Edgeworth's Use of Folklore in *Castle Rackrent*," in *Family Chronicles: Maria Edgeworth's "Castle Rackrent*," ed. Coilin Owens (Dublin: Wolfhound; Totowa, NJ: Barnes & Noble, 1987), 62–70.

Coilin Owens, "Irish Bulls in *Castle Rackrent*," in *Family Chronicles: Maria Edgeworth's "Castle Rackrent*," ed. Coilin Owens (Dublin: Wolfhound; Totowa, NJ: Barnes & Noble, 1987), 70–78.

Harrington

Twila Yates Papay, "A Near-Miss on the Psychological Novel: Maria Edgeworth's *Harrington*," in *Fetter'd or Free? British Women Novelists, 1670–1815*, ed. Mary Anne Schofield and Cecilia Macheski (Athens: Ohio University Press, 1986), 359–69.

Michael Ragussis, "Representation, Conversion, and Literary Form: *Harrington* and the Novel of Jewish Identity," *CritI* 16 (Autumn 1989): 113–43.

Ormond

Pamela Reilly, "The Influence of *Waverley* on Maria Edgeworth's *Ormond*," in *Scott and His Influence: Papers of the Aberdeen Scott Conference*, 1982, ed. J. H. Alexander and David Hewitt, (Aberdeen: Association for Scottish Literature Studies, 1983), 290–97.

The Wild Irish Girl

J. Th. Leerssen, "How *The Wild Irish Girl* Made Ireland Romantic," in *The Clash of Ireland: Literary Contrasts and Connections*, ed. C. C. Barfoot and Theo D'haen (Amsterdam: Rodopi, 1989), 98–117.

ELIOT, GEORGE (MARIAN EVANS)

Adam Bede

Ian Adam, "The Structure of Realisms in *Adam Bede*," *NCF* 30 (September 1975): 127–49.

D. R. Beeton, "Aspects of *Adam Bede*," *ESA* 14 (January 1971): 13–36.

Loren C. Bell, "A Kind of Madness: Hetty Sorrel's Infanticide," *PVR* 11 (Spring 1983): 82–87.

Monika Brown, "Dutch Painters and British Novel–Readers: *Adam Bede* in the Context of Victorian Cultural Literacy," *VIJ* 18 (1990): 113–33.

Beth Burch, "Eliot's *Adam Bede*," *Expl* 40 (Fall 1981): 27–28.

Alison Byerly, "'The Language of the Soul': George Eliot and Music," *NCF* 44 (June 1989): 1–17.

Alicia Carroll, "Tried by Earthly Fires: Hetty Wesley, Hetty Sorrel, and *Adam Bede*," *NCF* 44 (September 1989): 218–24.

Patricia E. Connors, "Arthurian Legend as a Source for George Eliot's *Adam Bede*," *RTSoCCEA* 28 (Spring 1989): 4–7.

Mary Jean Corbett, "Representing the Rural: The Critique of Loamshire in *Adam Bede*," *SNNTS* 20 (Fall 1988): 288–301.

ELIOT, GEORGE, *Adam Bede*

George R. Creeger, "An Interpretation of *Adam Bede*," *ELH* 23 (Fall 1956): 218–38.

Daniel Pierre Deneau, "Inconsistencies and Inaccuracies in *Adam Bede*," *NCF* 14 (March 1959): 71–75.

Elizabeth Deeds Ermarth, "Common Ground: *Scenes of Clerical Life*, *Adam Bede*, *The Mill on the Floss*," in *George Eliot* (Boston: Twayne, 1985), 68–77.

Albert J. Fyfe, "The Interpretation of *Adam Bede*," *NFC* (June 1954): 134–39.

Jean-Pierre Garces, "L'Implicite chez George Eliot: L'Exemple du traitement de Hetty Sorrel dans *Adam Bede*," in *L'Implicite dans la littérature et la pensée anglaises*, ed. Nadia J. Rigaud (Aix-en-Provence: Publications Université de Provence, 1984), 99–112.

Ian Gregor, "The Two Worlds of *Adam Bede*," in *The Moral and The Story, Ian Gregor and Brian Nichols* (London: Faber & Faber, 1962), 13–32.

Daniel P. Gunn, "The Dutch Painting and the Simple Truth in *Adam Bede*," *SNNTS* 24 (Winter 1992): 366–80.

Mason Harris, "Infanticide and Respectability: Hetty Sorrel as Abandoned Child in *Adam Bede*," *ESC* 9 (June 1983): 177–96.

W. J. Harvey, "The Treatment of Time in *Adam Bede*," *Anglia* 75 (1957): 429–40.

Elsie B. Holmes, "George Eliot's Wesleyan Madonna," *GEFR* 18 (1987): 52–59.

Elizabeth Holtze, "Aristotle and George Eliot: Hamartia in *Adam Bede*," in *Hamartia: The Concept of Error in the Western Tradition: Essays in Honor of John M. Crossett*, ed. Donald V. Stump, James A. Arieti, Lloyd Gerson, and Eleonore Stump (New York: Mellen, 1983), 267–80.

Cynthia Huggins, "Adam Bede: Author, Narrator and Narrative," *GEFR* 23 (1992): 35–39.

Maurice Hussey, "Structure and Imagery in *Adam Bede*," *NCF* 10 (March 1955): 115–29.

Peggy Fitzhugh Johnstone, "Self–Disorder and Aggression in *Adam Bede*: A Kohutian Analysis," *Mosaic* 22 (Fall 1989): 59–70.

Elaine J. Lawless, "The Silencing of the Preacher Woman: The Muted Message of George Eliot's *Adam Bede*," *WS* 18 (September 1990): 249–68.

F. R. Leavis, "*Adam Bede*," in *Anna Karenina and Other Essays* (London: Chatto & Windus, 1967), 49–58.

Lori Lefkovitz, "Delicate Beauty Goes Out: *Adam Bede*'s Transgressive Heroines," *KR* 9 (Summer 1987): 84–96.

Oliver Lovesey, "The Clerical Character in the Victorian Novel: George Eliot's *Adam Bede*," *NVSAWC* 13 (Fall 1987): 1–14.

David Malcolm, "*Adam Bede* and the Unions: 'A . . . Proletarian Novel,'" *ZAA* 31, no. 1 (1983): 5–16.

Ian Milner, "The Structure of Values in *Adam Bede*," *PhPr* 9 (1966): 281–91.

Susan Morgan, "Paradise Reconsidered: Edens without Eve," in *Historical Studies and Literary Criticism*, ed. Jerome J. McGann (Madison: University of Wisconsin Press, 1985), 266–82.

Kathleen Porter, "*Adam Bede*: George Eliot's First Symphony," *GEFR* 13 (1982): 52–54.

Clyde De L. Ryals, "The Thorn Imagery in *Adam Bede*," *VN* 22 (Fall 1962): 12–13.

Hans Ulrich Seeber, "Idylle und Realismus im England des 19. Jahrhunderts: Anmerkungen zu George Eliots Roman *Adam Bede*," in *Idylle und Modernisierung in der europaischen Literatur des 19. Jahrhunderts*, ed. Hans Ulrich Seeber and Paul Gerhard Klussmann (Bonn: Bouvier, 1986), 107–23.

Michael Squires, "*Adam Bede* and the Locus Amoenus,'" *SELit* 13 (Autumn 1973): 670–76.

Bruce S. Thornton, "A Rural Singing Match: Pastoral and Georgic in *Adam Bede*," *VN* 74 (Fall 1988): 6–11.

Dorothy Van Ghent, "*Adam Bede*," in *The English Novel: Form and Function* (New York: Rinehart, 1953), 171–81.

Orlo Williams, "*Adam Bede*," in *Some Great English Novels: Studies in the Art of Fiction* (London: Macmillan, 1926), 179–204.

"Armgart"

Rebecca A. Pope, "The Diva Doesn't Die: George Eliot's 'Armgart,'" *Criticism* 32 (Fall 1990): 469–83.

"Brother Jacob"

James Diedrick, "George Eliot's Experiments in Fiction: 'Brother Jacob' and the German Novelle," *SSF* 22 (Fall 1985): 461–68.

Susan de Sola Rodstein, "Sweetness and Dark: Geoge Eliot's 'Brother Jacob,'" *MLQ* 52 (September 1991): 295–313.

J. S. Szirotny, "Two Confectioners the Reverse of Sweet: The Role of Metaphor in Determining George Eliot's Use of Experience," *SSF* 21 (Spring 1984): 127–44.

"The Choir Invisible"

A. G. van den Broek, "'The Choir Invisible': Paul, Hamlet, George Eliot," *GEGHLN* 11 (September 1987): 7–10.

Martha S. Vogeler, "'The Choir Invisible': The Poetics of Humanist Piety," in *George Eliot: A Centenary Tribute*, ed. Gordon S. Haight and Rosemary T. Van-Arsdel (Totowa, NJ: Barnes & Noble, 1982), 64–81.

Daniel Deronda

Jean-Claude Amalric, "The Opening of *Daniel Deronda*," *CVE* 26 (October 1987): 111–19.

Nina Auerbach, "Alluring Vacancies in the Victorian Character," *KR* 8 (Summer 1986): 36–48.

William Baker, "F. R. Leavis as a Reader of *Daniel Deronda*," *GEGHLN* 14–15; 16–17 (September 1989; September 1990): 15–19; 7–14.

Richard Bates, "Gwendolyn Harleth: Character Creation or Character Analysis?" *CQ* 16, no. 1 (1987): 30–52.

Jerome Beaty, "*Daniel Deronda* and the Question of Unity in Fiction," *VN* 15 (Fall 1959): 16–20.

Maurice Beebe, "Visions are Creators: The Unity of *Daniel Deronda*," *BUSE* 1 (Autumn 1955): 166–77.

D. R. Beeton, "George Eliot's Greatest and Poorest Novel: An Appraisal of *Daniel Deronda*," *ESA* 9 (1966): 8–27.

Roslyn Belkin, "What George Eliot Knew: Women and Power in *Daniel Deronda*," *IJWS* 4 (November–December 1981): 472–83.

Harriet Blodgett, "Through the Labyrinth with Daniel: The Mythic Structure of George Eliot's *Daniel Deronda*," *JEP* 9 (March 1988): 164–79.

Dario Calimani, "*Daniel Deronda* tra Novel e Romance," in *Studi inglesi: Raccolta di saggi e ricerche*, ed. Agostino Lombardo (Bari: Adriatica, 1978), 125–64.

Colette Caraes, "La Peur dans *Daniel Deronda* de G. Eliot," *CVE* 15 (April 1982): 63–70.

James Caron, "The Rhetoric of Magic in *Daniel Deronda*," *SNNTS* 15 (Spring 1983): 1–9.

Mary Wilson Carpenter, "'A bit of her flesh': Circumcision and 'The Signification of the Phallus' in *Daniel Deronda*," *Genders* 1 (March 1988): 1–23.

Mary Wilson Carpenter, "The Apocalypse of the Old Testament: *Daniel Deronda* and the Interpretation of Interpretation," *PMLA* 99 (January 1984): 56–71.

David R. Carroll, "The Unity of *Daniel Deronda*," *EIC* 9 (December 1959): 369–80.

Joan M. Chard, "'A Lasting Habitation': The Quest for Identity and Vocation in *Daniel Deronda*," *GEFR* 15 (1984): 38–44.

Rupert Christiansen, "The Identity of Klesmer in *Daniel Deronda*," *GEFR* 17 (1986): 84–85.

Albert R. Cirillo, "Salvation in *Daniel Deronda*: The Fortunate Overthrow of Gwendolen Harleth," *Literary Monographs* 1 (Madison: University of Wisconsin Press, 1967): 203–45, 315–18.

Israel Cohen, "Comments on *Daniel Deronda*," *TLS* (23 August 1947): 427.

Peter Dale, "Symbolic Representation and the Means of Revolution in *Daniel Deronda*," *VN* 59 (Spring 1981): 25–30.

Joanne Long Demaria, "The Wondrous Marriages of *Daniel Deronda*: Gender, Work, and Love," *SNNTS* 22 (Winter 1990): 403–17.

Elizabeth Deeds Ermarth, "Secrecy and Confession: *Middlemarch* and *Daniel Deronda*," in *George Eliot*, ed. Herbert Sussman (Boston: Twayne, 1985), 121–31.

D. F., "*Daniel Deronda*: 'Organ Stop,'" *N&Q* 169 (March 1935): 175–76.

Robin Riley Fast, "Getting to the Ends of *Daniel Deronda*," *JNT* 7 (1977): 200–17.

Harold Fisch, "*Daniel Deronda* or 'Gwendolen Harleth'?" *NCF* 19 (September 1965): 345–56.

Sandra K. Fischer, "Eliot's *Daniel Deronda*," *Expl* 37 (Spring 1979): 21–22.

Jean–Paul Forster, "Beyond Reticence: The Power Politics Relationship in George Eliot," *ÉtL* 1 (1983): 13–29.

Vittorio Gabrieli, "A Quotation in *Daniel Deronda*," *N&Q* 37 (December 1990): 426.

Catherine Gallagher, "George Eliot and *Daniel Deronda*: The Prostitute and the Jewish Question," in *Sex, Politics, and Science in the Nineteenth–Century Novel*, ed. Ruth Bernard Yeazell (Baltimore: Johns Hopkins University Press, 1986), 39–62.

Hannah Goldberg, "George Henry Lewes and Daniel Deronda," *N&Q* 4 (December 1957): 356–58.

Leon Gottfried, "Structure and Genre in *Daniel Deronda*," in *The English Novel in the Nineteenth Century*, ed. George Goodwin (Urbana: University of Illinois Press, 1972), 164–75.

Gordon S. Haight, "George Eliot's Klesmer," in *Imagined Worlds: Essays on Some English Novels and Novelists in Honour of John Butt* (London: Methuen, 1968), 205–14.

Graham Handley, "A Missing Month in *Daniel Deronda*," *TLS* (3 February 1961): 73.

Graham Handley, "A Note on *Daniel Deronda*," *N&Q* 7 (March 1960): 147–48.

Graham Handley, "Reclaimed," *GEFR* 20 (1989): 38–40.

James Harrison, "The Root of the Matter with *Daniel Deronda*," *PQ* 68 (Fall 1989): 509–23.

Deborah Heller, "George Eliot's Jewish Feminist," *Atlantis* 8 (Spring 1983): 37–43.

Erwin Hester, "George Eliot's Use of Historical Events in *Daniel Deronda*," *ELN* 4 (March 1966): 115–18.

Shifra Hochberg, "Onomastics and the German Literary Ancestry of Daniel Deronda's Mother," *ELN* 28 (September 1990): 4650.

Eugene Hollahan, "Therapist or the Rapist? George Eliot's *Daniel Deronda* as a Pre–Freudian Example of Psychoanalysis in Literature," *JEP* 5 (March 1984): 55–68.

Peggy Ruth Fitzhugh Johnstone, "The Pattern of the Myth of Narcissus in *Daniel Deronda*," *HSL* 19, no. 2–3 (1987): 45–60.

Alain Jumeau, "Heritiers et heritages dans *Daniel Deronda*," *ÉA* 38 (January–March 1985): 24–35.

Alain Jumeau, "Le Gentleman anglais dans *Daniel Deronda*: Critique d'un modele artificiel," *CVE* 26 (October 1987): 89–99.

H. S. Kakar, "Gwendolen Harleth and the Growth of Conscience," *GEFR* 15 (1984): 49–54.

Masayuki Kato, "*Daniel Deronda* and Romance," *Shiron* 24 (1985): 43–58.

John Kearney, "Time and Beauty in *Daniel Deronda*," *NCF* 26 (December 1971): 286–306.

Missy Dehn Kubitschek, "Eliot as Activist: Marriage and Politics in *Daniel Deronda*," *CLAJ* 28 (December 1984): 176–89.

Michiko Kurisu, "*Daniel Deronda* ni okeru Gwendolyn Harleth no Kyofu," in *Eigakuronso: Ishii Shonosuke Sensei Kokikines Ronbunshu*, ed. Osamu Fukushima et. al (Tokyo: Kinseido, 1982), 147–56.

F. R. Leavis, "George Eliot: *Daniel Deronda* and *The Portrait of a Lady*," *Scrutiny* 14 (1946): 102–31.

Laurence Lerner, "The Education of Gwendolen Harleth," *CritQ* 7 (Winter 1965): 355–64.

Rolf Lessenich, "Jew, Artist, Providential Leader: Neoromantic Aspects in George Eliot's *Daniel Deronda*," *LJGG* 30 (1989): 123–40.

Shirley Frank Levenson, "The Use of Music in *Daniel Deronda*," *NCF* 24 (December 1969): 317–34.

Herbert J. Levine, "The Marriage of Allegory and Realism in *Daniel Deronda*," *Genre* 15 (Winter 1982): 421–45.

Katherine Bailey Linehan, "Mixed Politics: The Critique of Imperialism in *Daniel Deronda*," *TSLL* 34 (Fall 1992): 323–46.

E. A. McCobb, "*Daniel Deronda* as Will and Representation: George Eliot and Schopenhauer," *MLR* 80 (July 1985): 533–49.

E. A. McCobb, "The Morality of Musical Genius: Schopenhauerian Views in *Daniel Deronda*," *FMLS* 19 (October 1983): 321–30.

Kathleen McCormack, "George Eliot and Victorian Science Fiction: *Daniel Deronda* as Alternate History," *Extrapolation* 27 (Fall 1986): 185–96.

Carol A. Martin, "Contemporary Critics and Judaism in *Daniel Deronda*," *VPR* 21 (Fall 1988): 90–107.

Gail Marshall, "Actresses, Statues and Speculation in *Daniel Deronda*," *EIC* 44 (April 1994): 117–39.

Susan Meyer, "'Safely to Their Own Borders': Proto–Zionism, Feminism, and Nationalism in *Daniel Deronda*," *ELH* (Fall 1993): 733–58.

David Moldstad, "The Dantean Purgatorial Metaphor in *Daniel Deronda*," *PLL* 19 (Spring 1983): 183–98.

K. M. Newton, "*Daniel Deronda* and Circumcision," *EIC* 31 (October 1981): 313–27.

Marianne Novy, "*Daniel Deronda* and George Eliot's Female (Re)Vision of Shakespeare," *SEL* 28 (Autumn 1988): 671–92.

Nancy Nystul, "*Daniel Deronda*: A Family Romance," *Enclitic* 7 (Spring 1983): 45–53.

Nancy Pell, "The Fathers' Daughters in *Daniel Deronda*," *NCF* 36 (March 1982): 424–51.

Virgil A. Peterson, "Forgotten Bastards: A Note on *Daniel Deronda*," *VN* 15 (Spring 1959): 29.

Xavier Pons, "*Daniel Deronda*: A 'Silly Novel by a Lady Novelist?'" *CVE* 26 (October 1987): 101–09.

Adrian Poole, "'Hidden Affinities' in *Daniel Deronda*," *EIC* 33 (October 1983): 294–311.

Robert Preyer, "Beyond the Liberal Imagination: Vision and Unreality in *Daniel Deronda*," *VS* 4 (Spring 1960): 33–54.

Sara M. Putzell, "The Importance of Being Gwendolen: Contexts for George Eliot's *Daniel Deronda*," *SNNTS* 19 (Spring 1987): 31–45.

Sara M. Putzell–Korab, "The Role of the Prophet: The Rationality of Daniel Deronda's Idealist Mission," *NCF* 37 (September 1982): 170–87.

Lyn Pykett, "Typology and the End(s) of History in *Daniel Deronda*," *L&H* 9 (Spring 1983): 62–73.

Badri Raina, "*Daniel Deronda*: A View of Grandcourt," *SNNTS* 17 (Winter 1985): 371–82.

Linda K. Robertson, "Education and *Daniel Deronda*: Three of Eliot's Key Concepts," *GEFR* 14 (1983): 56–60.

Carole Robinson, "The Severe Angel: A Study of *Daniel Deronda*," *ELH* 31 (Fall 1964): 278–300.

Ellen B. Rosenman, "Women's Speech and the Roles of the Sexes in *Daniel Deronda*," *TSLL* 31 (Summer 1989): 237–56.

Margaret Moan Rowe, "Melting Outlines in *Daniel Deronda*," *SNNTS* 22 (Spring 1990): 10–18.

Carol de Saint Victor, "Acting and Action: Sexual Distinctions in *Daniel Deronda*," *CVE* 26 (October 1987): 77–88.

Sally Shuttleworth, "The Language of Science and Psychology in George Eliot's *Daniel Deronda*," in *Victorian Science and Victorian Values: Literary Perspectives*, ed. James Paradis and Thomas Postlewait (New York: New York Academy of Sciences, 1981), 269–98.

William R. Steinhoff, "The Metaphorical Texture of *Daniel Deronda*," *BkA* 35 (1961): 220–24.

Garrett Stewart, "'Beckoning Death': *Daniel Deronda* and the Plotting of Reading," in *Sex and Death in Victorian Literature*, ed. Regina Barreca (Bloomington: Indiana University Press, 1990), 69–109.

Judith Still, "Rousseau in *Daniel Deronda*," *RLC* 56 (January–March 1982): 62–77.

Jean Sudrann, "*Daniel Deronda* and the Landscape of Exile," *ELH* 37 (Fall 1970): 433–55.

Brian Swann, "Eyes in the Mirror: Imagery and Symbolism in *Daniel Deronda*," *NCF* 23 (December 1969): 434–45.

Jerome Thale, "*Daniel Deronda*: The Darkened World," *MFS* 3 (Spring 1957): 119–26.

Jerome Thale, "River Imagery in *Daniel Deronda*," *NCF* 7 (September 1954): 300–06.

John L. Tucker, "Prophecy, Originality, and Authority in *Daniel Deronda*," *ELWIU* 17 (Fall 1990): 190–203.

Carroll Viera, "A Neglected Parallel in *Daniel Deronda*," *GEGHLN* 3 (September 1983): 3–5.

Susan Ostrov Weisser, "Gwendolen's Hidden Wound: Sexual Possibilities and Impossibilities in *Daniel Deronda*," *MLS* 20 (Summer 1990): 3–13.

Judith Wilt, "'He Would Come Back': The Fathers of Daughters in *Daniel Deronda*," *NCF* 42 (December 1987): 313–38.

Meinhard Winkgens, "Die kulturelle Symbolik von Mundlichkeit und Schriftlichkeit in George Eliots Roman *Daniel Deronda*," in *Anglistentag* 1988 Gottingen: Vortrage, ed. Heinz–Joachim Mullenbrock and Renate Noll–Wiemann (Tubingen: Niemeyer, 1989), 163–78.

Rivkah Zim, "Awakened Perceptions in *Daniel Deronda*," *EIC* 36 (July 1986): 210–34.

Bonnie Zimmerman, "George Eliot and Feminism: The Case of *Daniel Deronda*," in *Nineteenth–Century Women Writers of the English-Speaking World*, ed. Rhoda B. Nathan (Westport, CT: Greenwood, 1986), 231–37.

Felix Holt, the Radical

Geoffrey D. M. Block, "George Eliot and the 1832 Election," *GEFR* 17 (1986): 30–37.

Alison Booth, "Not All Men Are Selfish and Cruel: *Felix Holt* as a Feminist Novel," in *Gender and Discourse in Victorian Literature and Art*, ed. Antony H. Harrison and Beverly Taylor (DeKalb: Northern Illinois University Press, 1992), 143–60.

David R. Carroll, "*Felix Holt*: Society as Protagonist," *NCF* 17 (December 1962): 237–52.

Elizabeth Deeds Ermath, "Sympathy: *Silas Marner, Felix Holt*," in *George Eliot*, ed. Herbert Sussman (Boston: Twayne, 1985), 101–07.

Liselotte Glage, "Was ist radikal an George Eliots Roman *Felix Holt, the Radical*?'" in *Radikalismus in Literatur und Gesellschaft des 19. Jahrhunderts*, ed. Gregory Claeys and Liselotte Glage (Frankfurt: Peter Lang, 1987), 219–42.

Lynn Blin Hetherington, "Mrs. Transome or the Absence of Pardon," *MCRel* 7 (1989): 50–60.

Shifra Hochberg, "Nomenclature and the Historical Matrix of *Felix Holt*," *ELN* 31 (December 1993): 46–56.

Lenore Horowitz, "George Eliot's Vision of Society in *Felix Holt, the Radical*,'" *TSLL* 17 (Spring 1975): 175–91.

H. S. Kakar, "Mrs. Transome and 'Desecrated Sanctities,'" *GEFR* 18 (1987): 66–73.

L. R. Leavis, "George Eliot's Creative Mind: *Felix Holt* as the Turning–Point of Her Art," *ES* 67 (August 1986): 311–26.

Ian Milner, "*Felix Holt, the Radical*' and Realism in George Eliot," *CMF* 37 (1955): 96–104.

W. F. T. Myers, "Politics and Personality in *Felix Holt*," *RMS* 10 (1966): 5–33.

Lyn Pykett, "George Eliot and Arnold: The Narrator's Voice and Ideology in *Felix Holt, the Radical*," *L&H* 11 (Autumn 1985): 229–40.

Bruce Robbins, "The Butler Did It: On Agency in the Novel," *Representations* 6 (Spring 1984): 85–97.

Philip Rogers, "Lessons for Fine Ladies: Tolstoi and George Eliot's *Felix Holt, the Radical*," *SEEJ* 29 (Winter 1985): 379–92.

Florence Sandler, "The Unity of *Felix Holt*," in *George Eliot: A Centenary Tribute*, ed. Gordon S. Haight and Rosemary T. VanArsdel (Totowa, NJ: Barnes & Noble, 1982), 137–52.

Robin Sheets, "*Felix Holt*: Language, the Bible, and the Problematic of Meaning," *NCF* 37 (September 1982): 146–69.

Andrew Thompson, "George Eliot, Dante, and Moral Choice in *Felix Holt, the Radical*," *MLR* 86 (July 1991): 553–66.

Fred C. Thomson, "*Felix Holt* as Classic Tragedy," *NCF* 16 (March 1961): 47–58.

Fred C. Thomson, "The Legal Plot in *Felix Holt*," *SEL* 7 (Autumn 1967): 691–704.

Judith Wilt, "Felix Holt, the Killer: A Reconstruction," *VS* 35 (Autumn 1991): 51–70.

"Janet's Repentance"

J. W. Bennett, "The Apprenticeship of George Eliot: Characterization as Case Study in 'Janet's Repentance,'" *L&M* 9 (1990): 50–68.

Mary B. Coney, "The Meaning of Milby in 'Janet's Repentance,'" *GEFR* 13 (1982): 19–24.

Stephanie Demetrakopoulos, "George Eliot's 'Janet's Repentance': The First Literary Portrait of a Woman Addict and Her Recovery," *MidWQ* 35 (Autumn 1993): 95–108.

Peter Fenves, "Exiling the Encyclopedia: The Individual in 'Janet's Repentance,'" *NCF* 41 (March 1987): 419–44.

J. Clinton McCann Jr., "Disease and Cure in 'Janet's Repentance': George Eliot's Change of Mind," *L&M* 9 (1990): 69–78.

A. G. van den Broek, "Shakespearean Allusions in 'Janet's Repentance,'" *GEFR* 18 (1987): 27–39.

"The Lifted Veil"

James M. Decker, "Interpreting Latimer: Wordsworthian Martyr or Textual Alchemist?" *GEGHLN* 20–21 (September 1992): 58–62.

Terry Eagleton, "Power and Knowledge in 'The Lifted Veil,'" *L&H* 9 (Spring 1983): 52–61.

Annie Escuret, "G. Eliot: 'The Lifted Veil' ou le scandale de la mémoire trouée," *CVE* 26 (October 1987): 21–35.

Middlemarch

Harriet Farwell Adams, "Dorothea and 'Miss Brooke' in *Middlemarch*," *NCF* 39 (June 1984): 69–90.

Sophia Andres, "The Germ and the Picture in *Middlemarch*," *ELH* 55 (Winter 1988): 853–68.

Mary A. Arnold, "The Unity of *Middlemarch*," *HusR* 1 (1968): 137–41.

Rosemary Ashton, "The Intellectural 'Medium' of *Middlemarch*," *RES* 30 (May 1979): 154–68.

David Ball, "Triangular Patterns in *Middlemarch*," *GEFR* 19 (1988): 23–25.

Richard Bates, "The Italian with White Mice in *Middlemarch*," *N&Q* 31 (December 1984): 497.

Jerome Beaty, "The Forgotten Past of Will Ladislaw," *NCF* 13 (June 1957): 159–63.

Jerome Beaty, "History by Indirection: The Era of Reform in *Middlemarch*," *VS* 1 (December 1957): 173–79.

Calvin Bedient, "*Middlemarch*: Touching Down," *HudR* 22 (1969): 70–84.

Gillian Beer, "Circulatory Systems: Money and Gossip in *Middlemarch*," *CVE* 26 (October 1987): 47–62.

Alan W. Bellringer, "The Study of Provincial Life in *Middlemarch*," *Eng* 28 (1979): 219–47.

James R. Bennett, "Scenic Structure of Judgement in *Middlemarch*," *E&S* 37 (1984): 62–74.

Kathleen Blake, "Materials," in *Approaches to Teaching Eliot's Middlemarch*, ed. Kathleen Blake (New York: MLA, 1990), 9–19.

Kathleen Blake, "*Middlemarch* and the Woman Question," in *George Eliot's "Middlemarch,"* ed. Harold Bloom (New York: Chelsea House, 1987), 49–70.

David–Everett Blythe, "Eliot's *Middlemarch*," *Expl* 48 (Fall 1989): 22–23.

Felicia Bonaparte, "*Middlemarch*: The Genesis of Myth in the English Novel: The Relationship between Literary Form and the Modern Predicament," *NDEJ* 8 (Summer 1981): 107–54.

Bege K. Bowers, "George Eliot's *Middlemarch* and the 'Text' of the Novel of Manners," in *Reading and Writing Women's Lives: A Study of the Novel of Manners*, ed. Bege K. Bowers and Barbara Brothers (Ann Arbor, MI: University Microfilms International Research Press, 1990), 105–17.

Selma B. Brody, "Dorothea Brooke and Henry James's Isabel Archer," *GEGHLN* 20–21 (September 1992): 63–66.

Selma B. Brody, "Origins of George Eliot's 'Pier-Glass' Image," *ELN* 22 (December 1984): 55–58.

Selma B. Brody, "Physics in *Middlemarch*: Gas Molecules and Ethereal Atoms," *MP* 85 (August 1987): 42–53.

Selma B. Brody, "Physics in *Middlemarch*: Gas Molecules and Ethereal Atoms," *MP* 85 (August 1987): 42–53.

Valerie Bystrom and Michael Kischner, "Really Reading *Middlemarch* in a Community College," in *Approaches to Teaching Eliot's "Middlemarch,"* ed. Kathleen Blake (New York: MLA, 1990), 154–61.

Elizabeth A. Campbell, "Relative Truths: Character in *Middlemarch*," in *Approaches to Teaching Eliot's "Middlemarch,"* ed. Kathleen Blake (New York: MLA, 1990), 117–22.

Colette Caraes, "Du comique dans *Middlemarch*," *CVE* 26 (October 1987): 63–76.

Janice Carlisle, "Reading *Middlemarch*, Then and Now," in *Approaches to Teaching Eliot's "Middlemarch,"* ed. Kathleen Blake (New York: MLA, 1990), 98–108.

David Carroll, "Unity through Analogy: An Interpretation of *Middlemarch*," *VS* 2 (June 1959): 305–16.

Rosemary Clark–Beattie, "*Middlemarch*'s Dialogic Style," *JNT* 15 (Fall 1985): 199–218.

Robert A. Colby, "*Middlemarch*: Dorothea Brooke and the Emancipated Woman; or The Heroine of the Nineteenth Century," in *Fiction With a Purpose: Major and Minor Nineteenth Century Novels* (Bloomington: Indiana University Press, 1967), 256–302.

Franklin E. Court, "The Image of St. Theresa in *Middlemarch* and Positive Ethics," *VN* 63 (Spring 1983): 21–25.

Martha Curry, R.S.C.J., "*Middlemarch*: Unity and Diversity," *BarRev* 5 (1970): 83–92, 101–3.

David Daiches, *George Eliot: "Middlemarch"* (London: Arnold, 1962), 1–69.

Jill Durey, "*Middlemarch*: The Role of the Functional Triad in the Portrayal of Hero and Heroine," in *Functions of Style*, ed. David Birch and Michael O'Toole (London: Pinter, 1988), 234–48.

Lee Edwards, "Women, Energy, and *Middlemarch*," *MR* 13 (1972): 223–38.

Elizabeth Deeds Ermarth, "Secrecy and Confession: *Middlemarch* and *Daniel Deronda*," in *George Eliot*, ed. Herbert Sussman (Boston: Twayne, 1985), 108–21.

Elizabeth Deeds Ermarth, "Teaching *Middlemarch* as Narrative," in *Approaches to Teaching Eliot's "Middlemarch,"* ed. Kathleen Blake (New York: MLA, 1990), 30–38.

Monica L. Feinberg, "Scenes of Marital Life: The Middle March of Extratextual Reading," *VN* 77 (Spring 1990): 16–26.

N. N. Feltes, "One Round of a Long Ladder: Gender, Profession, and the Production of *Middlemarch*," *ESC* 12 (June 1986): 210–28.

Sumner J. Ferris, "*Middlemarch*, George Eliot's Masterpiece," in *From Jane Austen to Joseph Conrad*, ed. Robert C. Rathburn and Martin Steinmann Jr. (Minneapolis: University of Minnesota Press, 1958), 194–207.

John Forrester, "Lydgate's Research Project in *Middlemarch*," *GEGHLN* 16–17 (September 1990): 2–6.

Hilary Fraser, "St. Theresa, St. Dorothea, and Miss Brooke in *Middlemarch*," *NCF* 40 (March 1986): 400–11.

A. L. French, "A Note on *Middlemarch*," *NCF* 26 (December 1971): 339–47.

Michal Peled Ginsburg, "Pseudonym, Epigraphs, and Narrative Voice: *Middlemarch* and the Deceit of Authorship," *ELH* 47 (1980): 542–58.

Russell M. Goldfarb, "Rosamond Vincy of *Middlemarch*," *CLAJ* 30 (September 1986): 83–101.

Jan B. Gordon, "Origins, *Middlemarch*, Endings: George Eliot's Crisis of the Antecedent," in *George Eliot's "Middlemarch,"* ed. Harold Bloom (New York: Chelsea House, 1987), 91–112.

Carol S. Gould, "Plato, George Eliot, and Moral Narcissism," *P&L* 14 (April 1990): 24–39.

Suzanne Graver, "'Incarnate History': The Feminisms of *Middlemarch*," in *Approaches to Teaching Eliot's "Middlemarch,"* ed. Kathleen Blake (New York: MLA, 1990), 64–74.

Robert A. Greenberg, "The Heritage of Will Ladislaw," *NCF* 15 (December 1961): 355–58.

Robert A. Greenberg, "Plexuses and Ganglia: Scientific Allusion in *Middlemarch*," *NCF* 30 (March 1975): 33–52.

Mildred S. Greene, "Another Look at Dorothea's Marriages," *GEFR* 15 (1984): 33–37.

Mildred S. Greene, "Another Look at Dorothea's Marriages," *L&P* 33, no. 1 (1987): 30–42.

Mildred Sarah Greene, "G. Eliot's *Middlemarch*," *Expl* 42 (Spring 1984): 26–28.

Robert P. Griffin, "Image and Intent: Some Observations on Style in *Middlemarch*," *BSUF* 10, no. 3 (1969): 60–63.

John Hagan, "*Middlemarch*: Narrative Unity in the Story of Dorothea Brooke," *NCF* 16 (March 1961): 17–32.

Barbara Hardy, "Implication and Incompleteness: George Eliot's *Middlemarch*," in *The Appropriate Form: An Essay on the Novel* (London: Athlone, 1964), 105–31.

Barbara Hardy, "*Middlemarch*: Public and Private Worlds," *English* 25 (Spring 1976): 5–26. Reprinted in *George Eliot's "Middlemarch,"* ed. Harold Bloom (New York: Chelsea House, 1987), 27–47.

Marie Paul Hastert and Jean Jacques Weber, "Power and Mutuality in *Middlemarch*," in *Language, Text, and Context: Essays in Stylistics*, ed. Michael Toolan (London: Routledge, 1992), 163–78.

Cicely Palser Havely, "Authorization in *Middlemarch*," *EIC* 40 (October 1990): 303–21.

Robert B. Heilman, "'Stealthy Convergence' in *Middlemarch*," in *George Eliot: A Centenary Tribute*, ed. Gordon S. Haight and Rosemary T. VanArsdel (Totowa, NJ: Barnes & Noble 1982), 47–54.

Neil Hertz, "Recognizing Casaubon," in *George Eliot's "Middlemarch,"* ed. Harold Bloom (New York: Chelsea House, 1987), 71–89.

James Hill, "G. Eliot's *Middlemarch*," *Expl* 45 (Winter 1987): 26–27.

Baruch Hochman, "Recon/Decon/Structing *Middlemarch*," in *Approaches to Teaching Eliot's "Middlemarch,"* ed. Kathleen Blake (New York: MLA, 1990), 39–50.

Eugene Hollahan, "The Concept of 'Crisis' in *Middlemarch*," *NCF* 28 (March 1974): 450–57.

Joy W. Hooton, "*Middlemarch* and Time," *SoR* 13 (November 1980): 188–202.

Bert G. Hornback, "The Organization of *Middlemarch*," *PLL* 2 (1966): 169–75.

John F. Hulcoop, "'This Petty Medium': In the Middle of *Middlemarch*," in *George Eliot: A Centenary Tribute*, ed. Gordon S. Haight and Rosemary T. VanArsdel (Totowa, NJ: Barnes & Noble, 1982), 153–66.

ELIOT, GEORGE, *Middlemarch*

Virginia Hyde, "George Eliot's Arthuriad: Heroes and Ideology in *Middlemarch*," *PLL* 24 (Fall 1988): 404–11.

Neil D. Isaacs, "*Middlemarch*: Crescendo of Obligatory Drama," *NCF* 18 (March 1963): 21–34.

Henry James, "George Eliot's *Middlemarch*," *NCF* 8 (September 1953): 161–70.

Judith Johnston, "*Middlemarch*: Medieval Discourses and Will Ladislaw," *SSEng* 15 (1989–90): 125–39.

Judith Johnston, "*Middlemarch*'s Dorothea Brooke and Medieval Hagiography," *GEFR* 23 (1992): 40–45.

Robert Kiely, "The Limits of Dialogue in *Middlemarch*," in *The Worlds of Victorian Fiction: Harvard English Studies 6*, ed. Jerome H. Buckley (Cambridge, MA: Harvard University Press, 1975), 103–23.

Shigeko Kimura, "*Middlemarch* ni okeru Ba ni tsuite," in *Yamakawa Kozo Kyoju Taikan Kinen Ronbunshu* (Toyonaka: N.p., 1981), 277–91.

U. C. Knoepflmacher, "*Middlemarch*: Affirmation through Compromise," in *Laughter and Despair: Readings in Ten Novels of the Victorian Era* (Berkeley: University of California Press, 1971), 168–201.

U. C. Knoepflmacher, "*Middlemarch*: An Avuncular View," *NCF* 30 (March 1975): 53–81.

Norbert Kohl, "George Eliot, *Middlemarch*: 'Prelude'—eine Interpretation," *DVLG* 42 (1968): 182–201.

John Kucich, "Repression and Dialectical Inwardness in *Middlemarch*," *Mosaic* 18 (Winter 1985): 45–63.

Olli Lagerspetz, "Dorothea and Casaubon," *Philosophy* 67 (April 1992): 211–32.

Sister Jane Marie Luecke, "Ladislaw and the *Middlemarch* Vision," *NCF* 19 (March 1964): 55–64.

Patricia Lorimer Lundberg, "George Eliot: Mary Ann Evans's Subversive Tool in *Middlemarch*," *SNNTS* 18 (Fall 1986): 270–82.

Richard S. Lyons, "The Method of *Middlemarch*," *NCF* 21 (June 1966): 35–48.

Kathleen McCormack, "*Middlemarch*: Dorothea's Husbands in the Vatican Museums," *VIJ* 20 ((1992): 75–91.

Bruce McCullough, "The Psychological Novel: George Eliot's *Middlemarch*," in *Representative English Novelists: Defoe to Conrad* (New York: Harper, 1946), 197–214.

Barbara McGovern, "Pier Glasses and Sympathy in Eliot's *Middlemarch*," *VN* 72 (Fall 1987): 6–8.

Patricia McKee, "Power as Partiality in *Middlemarch*," in *George Eliot's "Middlemarch*," ed. Harold Bloom (New York: Chelsea House, 1987), 141–49.

Juliet McMaster, "'A Microscope Directed on a Water–Drop': Chapter 19," in *Approaches to Teaching Eliot's "Middlemarch*," ed. Kathleen Blake (New York: MLA, 1990), 109–16.

Juliet McMaster, "Will Ladislaw and Other Italians with White Mice," *VRev* 16 (Winter 1990): 1–7.

David Malcolm, "What Is a Pole Doing in *Middlemarch*?" *GEFR* 17 (1986): 63–69.

Kenny Marotta, "*Middlemarch*: The Home Epic," *Genre* 15 (Winter 1982): 403–20.

Bruce K. Martin, "Fred Vincy and the Unravelling of *Middlemarch*," *PLL* 30 (Winter 1994): 3–24.

Carol A. Martin, "Reading *Middlemarch* in Installments as Victorian Readers Did," in *Approaches to Teaching Eliot's "Middlemarch,"* ed. Kathleen Blake (New York: MLA, 1990), 85–97.

Michael York Mason, "*Middlemarch* and History," *NCF* 25 (December 1971): 417–31.

Michael York Mason, "*Middlemarch* and Science: Problems of Life and Mind," *RES* 22 (1971): 151–69.

Jill L. Matus, "Saint Teresa, Hysteria, and *Middlemarch*," *JHS* 1 (October 1990): 215–40.

Jerome Meckier, "'That Arduous Invention': *Middlemarch* Versus the Modern Satirical Novel," *Ariel* 4, no. 9 (1978): 31–68.

J. Hillis Miller, "Optic and Semiotic in *Middlemarch*," in *The Worlds of Victorian Fiction*, *Harvard English Studies* 6 (1975), 125–45. Reprinted in *George Eliot's "Middlemarch*," ed. Harold Bloom (New York: Chelsea House, 1987), 9–25.

J. Hillis Miller, "Teaching *Middlemarch*: Close Reading and Theory," in *Approaches to Teaching Eliot's "Middlemarch*," ed. Kathleen Blake (New York: MLA, 1990), 51–63.

JoAnna Stephens Mink, "The Emergence of Woman as Hero in the Nineteenth Century," in *Heroines of Popular Culture*, ed. Pat Browne (Bowling Green, OH: Popular, 1987), 5–22.

ELIOT, GEORGE, *Middlemarch*

David Moldstad, "Old Age in *Middlemarch*," in *Approaches to Teaching Eliot's "Middlemarch*," ed. Kathleen Blake (New York: MLA, 1990), 123–28.

Timothy Morris, "The Dialogic Universe of *Middlemarch*," *SNNTS* 22 (Fall 1990): 282–95.

Merritt Moseley, "A Fuller Sort of Companionship: Defending Old–Fashioned Qualities," in *Approaches to Teaching Eliot's "Middlemarch*," ed. Kathleen Blake (New York: MLA, 1990), 75–84.

Catherine Neale, "Torpedoes, Tapirs and Tortoises: Scientific Discourse in *Middlemarch*," *CrSur* 2, no. 1 (1990): 57–62.

Vincent Newey, "Dorothea's Awakening: The Recall of Bunyan in *Middlemarch*," *N&Q* 31 (December 1984): 497–99.

Joseph Nicoles, "Dorothea in the Moated Grange: Millais's Mariana & the *Middlemarch* Window–Scenes," *VIJ* (1992): 93–124.

Joseph Nicoles, "Vertical Context in *Middlemarch*: George Eliot's Civil War of the Soul," *NCF* 45 (September 1990): 144–75.

A. D. Nuttall, "Realistic Convention and Conventional Realism in Shakespeare," *HEI* 1, no. 3 (1981): 237–48.

Derek Oldfield, "The Language of the Novel, the Character of Dorothea," in *"Middlemarch": Critical Approaches*, ed. Barbara Hardy (New York: Oxford University Press, 1967), 63–86.

David Parker, "'Bound in Charity': George Eliot, Dorothea and Casaubon," *CR* 26 (1984): 69–83.

Thomas Pinney, "Another Note on the Forgotten Past of Will Ladislaw," *NCF* 17 (June 1962): 69–73.

Kathleen Porter, "The *Middlemarch* Collection," *GEFR* 12 (1981): 32–33.

Sara M. Putzell–Korab and Martine Watson Brownley, "Dorothea and Her Husbands: Some Autobiographical Sources for Speculation," *VN* 68 (Fall 1985): 15–19.

Ann M. Ridler, "George Eliot and George Borrow—a Note on *Middlemarch*," *GEGHLN* 5 (September 1984): 3–4.

Ellin Ringler, "*Middlemarch*: A Feminist Perspective," *SNNTS* 15 (Spring 1983): 55–61.

Larry Robbins, "Mill and *Middlemarch*: The Progress of Public Opinion," *VN* 31 (Spring 1967): 37–39.

John M. Robson, "Narrative Transitions in *Middlemarch*," *HumAR* 31 (Winter–Spring 1980): 97–120.

Edward Sackville–West, "*Middlemarch*," in *Inclinations* (London: Secker & Warburg, 1949), 27–32.

James F. Scott, "George Eliot, Positivism, and the Social Vision of *Middlemarch*," *VS* 16 (1972): 59–76.

Carol A. Senf, "The Vampire in *Middlemarch* and George Eliot's Quest for Historical Reality," *NOR* 14 (Spring 1987): 87–97.

Alan Shelston, "What Rosy Knew: Language, Learning and Lore in *Middlemarch*," *CritQ* 35 (Winter 1993): 2130.

Otice C. Sircy, "'The Fashion of Sentiment': Allusive Technique and the Sonnets of *Middlemarch*," *SP* 84 (Spring 1987): 219–44.

Jane S. Smith, "The Reader as Part of the Fiction: *Middlemarch*," *TSLL* 19 (1977): 188–203.

Katherine M. Sorensen, "Evangelical Doctrine and George Eliot's Narrator in *Middlemarch*," *VN* 74 (Fall 1988): 18–26.

Martin Spence, "C. Brontë's *Jane Eyre* and G. Eliot's *Middlemarch*," *Expl* 43 (Spring 1985): 10–11.

Newton P. Stallknecht, "Resolution and Independence: A Reading of *Middlemarch*," in *Twelve Original Essays on Great English Novels*, ed. Charles Shapiro (Detroit: Wayne State University Press, 1960), 125–52.

F. George Steiner, "A Preface to *Middlemarch*," *NCF* 9 (September 1955): 262–79.

Eve Marie Stwertka, "The Web of Utterance: *Middlemarch*," *TSLL* 19 (1977): 179–87.

Brian Swann, "*Middlemarch* and Myth," *NCF* 28 (September 1973): 210–14.

Brian Swann, "*Middlemarch*: Realism and Symbolic Form," *ELH* 39 (1972): 279–308.

Jeremy Tambling, "*Middlemarch*, Realism and The Birth of the Clinic," *ELH* 57 (Winter 1990): 939–60.

Jeanie Thomas, "A Novel 'Written for Grown–Up People': *Middlemarch* in the Undergraduate Classroom," in *Approaches to Teaching Eliot's "Middlemarch,"* ed. Kathleen Blake (New York: MLA, 1990), 162–70.

Jeanie G. Thomas, "An Inconvenient Indefiniteness: George Eliot, *Middlemarch*, and Feminism," *UTQ* 56 (Spring 1987): 392–415.

Stanley Tick, "'The Very Nature of a Conclusion,'" in *Approaches to Teaching Eliot's "Middlemarch,"* ed. Kathleen Blake (New York: MLA, 1990), 146–53.

Shigeko Tomita, "Kansei eno Kiseki: G. Eliot—*Middlemarch*," in *Igirisu Shosetsu no Joseitachi*, ed. Yaeko Sumi and Naomi Okamura (Tokyo: Keiso, 1983), 93–117.

Marianna Torgovnick, "Closure and the Victorian Novel," *VN* 71 (Spring 1987): 4–6.

John L. Tucker, "George Eliot's Reflexive Text: Three Tonalities in the Narrative Voice of *Middlemarch*," *SEL* 31 (Autumn 1991): 773–80.

Rosemary T. VanArsdel, "*Middlemarch* and the Modern American Student: Making the Cultural Leap," in *Approaches to Teaching Eliot's "Middlemarch,"* ed. Kathleen Blake (New York: MLA, 1990), 138–45.

Chull Wang, "George Eliot's Moral Aesthetics in *Middlemarch*," *JELL* 38 (Summer 1992): 283–94.

Robyn R. Warhol, "Before We Go in Depth: A Narratogical Approach," in *Approaches to Teaching Eliot's "Middlemarch,"* ed. Kathleen Blake (New York: MLA, 1990), 23–29.

Alexander Welsh, "Knowledge in *Middlemarch*," in *George Eliot's "Middlemarch,"* ed. Harold Bloom (New York: Chelsea House, 1987), 113–39.

Joseph Wiesenfarth, "The Greeks, the Germans, and George Eliot," *BIS* 10 (1982): 91–104.

Katharina M. Wilson, "The Key to All Mythologies: A Possible Source of Inspiration," *VN* 61 (Spring 1982): 27–28.

Margaret Wolfit, "Octavia Hill and George Eliot: Coincidences," *GEFR* 17 (1986): 72–77.

T. R. Wright, "*Middlemarch* as a Religious Novel, or Life without God," in *Images of Belief in Literature*, ed. David Jasper (New York: St. Martin's, 1984), 138–54.

The Mill on the Floss

Ian Adam, "The Ambivalence of *The Mill on the Floss*," in *George Eliot: A Centenary Tribute*, ed. Gordon S. Haight and Rosemary T. VanArsdel (Totowa, NJ: Barnes & Noble, 1982), 122–36.

Kathleen Adams, "A View of St. Ogg's," *GEFR* 13 (1982): 43–47.

Edward Alexander, "A Little Toryism by the Sly: *The Mill on the Floss*," *WHR* 39 (Summer 1985): 97–118.

Jonathan Arac, "Rhetoric and Realism in Nineteenth–Century Fiction: Hyperbole in *The Mill on the Floss*," *ELH* 46 (1979): 673–92.

Nina Auerbach, "The Power of Hunger: Demonism and Maggie Tulliver," in *George Eliot's "The Mill on the Floss*," ed. Harold Bloom (New York: Chelsea House, 1988), 43–60.

C. C. Barfoot, "Life Divided, Death Undivided in *The Mill on the Floss*," in *Essays on English and American Literature and a Sheaf of Poems*, ed. J. Bakker, J. A. Verleun, and J. Vriesenaerde (Amsterdam: Rodopi, 1987), 81–99.

Gillian Beer, "'The Dark Woman Triumphs': Passion in *The Mill on the Floss*," in *George Eliot's "The Mill on the Floss*," ed. Harold Bloom (New York: Chelsea House, 1988), 123–41.

A. W. Bellringer, "Education in *The Mill on the Floss*," *RevEL* 6, no. 3 (1966): 52–61.

Ernest Bevan, "Maggie Tulliver and the Bonds of Time," *VIJ* 12 (1984): 63–76.

Jacques Blondel, "Morale, psychologie, destinée dans *La Moulin sur la Floss*," *LM* 59 (1965): 342–48.

Jerome H. Buckley, "George Eliot's Double Life: *The Mill on the Floss* as a Bildungsroman," in *From Smollett to James: Studies in the Novel and Other Essays Presented to Edgar Johnson*, ed. Samuel I. Mintz, Alice Chandler, and Christopher Mulvey (Charlottesville: University Press of Virginia, 1981), 211–36.

John P. Bushnell, "Maggie Tulliver's 'Stored–Up Force': A Re–Reading of *The Mill on the Floss*," *SNNTS* 16 (Winter 1984): 378–95.

Janice Carlisle, "The Mirror in *The Mill on the Floss*: Toward a Reading of Autobiography as Discourse," *StLI* 23 (Fall 1990): 177–96.

Robert A. Colby, "*The Mill on the Floss*: Maggie Tulliver and the Child of Nature," in *Fiction With a Purpose: Major and Minor Nineteenth-Century Novels* (Bloomington: Indiana University Press, 1967), 213–55.

Keith Cushman, "Dabbling in the Tradition: *The Waterfall* and *The Mill on the Floss*," in *The Modernists: Studies in a Literary Phenomenon: Essays in Honor of Harry T. Moore*, ed. Lawrence B. Gamache and Ian S. MacNiven (Rutherford, NJ: Fairleigh Dickinson University Press, 1987), 275–87.

James Diedrick, "The 'Grotesque Body': Physiology in *The Mill on the Floss*," *Mosaic* 21 (Fall 1988): 27–43.

ELIOT, GEORGE, *The Mill on the Floss*

Elizabeth Deeds Ermarth, "Common Ground: *Scenes of Clerical Life*, *Adam Bede*, *The Mill on the Floss*," in *George Eliot* (Boston: Twayne, 1985), 77–89.

Elizabeth Deeds Ermarth, "Maggie Tulliver's Long Suicide," *SELit* 14 (Fall 1974): 587–601.

Preston Fambrough, "Ontogeny and Phylogeny in *The Mill on the Floss*," *VN* 74 (Fall 1988): 46–51.

Monika Fludernik, "Subversive Irony: Reflectorization, Trustworthy Narration and Dead–Pan Narrative in *The Mill on the Floss*," *REAL* 9 (1992): 157–82.

Susan Fraiman, "*The Mill on the Floss*, The Critics, and the Bildungsroman," *PMLA* 108 (January 1993): 136–50.

Eva Fuchs, "Eliot's *The Mill on the Floss*," *Expl* 52 (Winter 1994): 79–81.

Eva Fuchs, "The Pattern's All Missed: Separation/Individuation in *The Mill on the Floss*," *SNNTS* 19 (Winter 1987): 422–34.

S. L. Goldberg, "'Poetry' as Moral Thinking: *The Mill on the Floss*," *CR* 24 (1982): 55–79.

Beryl Gray, "The Seduction of Maggie Tulliver," *GEFR* 19 (1988): 10–17.

Barbara Guth, "Philip: The Tragedy of *The Mill on the Floss*," *SNNTS* 15 (Winter 1983): 356–63.

Margaret Homans, "Eliot, Wordsworth, and the Scenes of the Sisters' Instruction," *Critical Inquiry* 8 (Winter 1981): 223–41. Reprinted in *George Eliot's "The Mill on the Floss*," ed. Harold Bloom (New York: Chelsea House, 1988), 89–122.

Mary Ann Kelly, "The Narrative Emphasis on the Power of the Imagination in *The Mill on the Floss*," *GEFR* 14 (1983): 86–93.

John Kucich, "George Eliot and Objects: Meaning as Matter in *The Mill on the Floss*," *DSA* 12 (1983): 319–40.

Mary Jacobus, "The Question of Language: Men of Maxims and *The Mill on the Floss*," *CritI* 8 (Winter 1981): 207–22. Reprinted in *George Eliot's "The Mill on the Floss*," ed. Harold Bloom (New York: Chelsea House, 1988), 61–76.

Peggy Ruth Fitzhugh Johnstone, "Narcissistic Rage in *The Mill on the Floss*," *L&P* 36, no. 1–2 (1990): 90–109.

U. C. Knoepflmacher, "Tragedy and the Flux: *The Mill on the Floss*," in *George Eliot's "The Mill on the Floss*," ed. Harold Bloom (New York: Chelsea House, 1988), 23–42.

Jose Angel Garcia Landa, "The Chains of Semiosis: Semiotics, Marxism, and the Female Stereotype in *The Mill on the Floss*," *PLL* 27 (Winter 1991): 32–49.

Jules Law, "Water Rights and the 'crossing o' breeds': Chiastic Exchange in *The Mill on the Floss*," in *Rewriting the Victorians: Theory, History, and the Politics of Gender*, ed. Linda M. Shires (New York: Routledge, 1992), 52–69.

A. Robert Lee, "*The Mill on the Floss*: Memory and the Reading Experience," in *Reading the Victorian Novel: Detail into Form*, ed. Ian Gregor (New York: Barnes & Noble, 1980), 72–91.

John LeVay, "Maggie as Muse: The Philip–Maggie Relationship in *The Mill on the Floss*," *ESC* 9 (March 1983): 69–79.

George Levine, "Intelligence as Deception: *The Mill on the Floss*," *PMLA* 80 (September 1965): 402–9. Reprinted in *George Eliot's "The Mill on the Floss*," ed. Harold Bloom (New York: Chelsea House, 1988), 9–21.

Oliver Lovesey, "Maggie's Sisters: Feminist Readings of *The Mill on the Floss*," *GEFR* 19 (1988): 47–49.

Jane McDonnell, "'Perfect Goodness' or 'the Wider Life': *The Mill on the Floss* as Bildungsroman," *Genre* 15 (Winter 1982): 379–402.

Juliet McLaughlan, "*The Mill on the Floss*: Fiction or Autobiography?" *CVE* 27 (April 1988): 127–39.

Kerry McSweeney, "The Ending of *The Mill on the Floss*," *ESC* 12 (March 1986): 55–68.

David Malcolm, "*The Mill on the Floss* and Contemporary Social Values: Tom Tulliver and Samuel Smiles," *CVE* 26 (October 1987): 37–45.

Carl D. Malmgren, "Reading Authorial Narration: The Example of *The Mill on the Floss*," *PoT* 7, no. 3 (1986): 471–94.

Carol A. Martin, "Pastoral and Romance in George Eliot's *The Mill on the Floss*," *CLAJ* 28 (September 1984): 78–101.

Rosemary Mundhenk, "Patterns of Irresolution in Eliot's *The Mill on the Floss*," *JNT* 13 (Winter 1983): 20–30.

Ian Milner, "The Quest for Community in *The Mill on the Floss*," *PraSE* 12 (1967): 77–92.

Bernard J. Paris, "The Inner Conflicts of Maggie Tulliver: A Horneyan Analysis," *CentR* 13 (1969): 166–99.

Bernard J. Paris, "Toward a Revaluation of George Eliot's *The Mill on the Floss*," *NCF* 11 (March 1956): 18–31.

Ranjini Philip, "Maggie, Tom and Oedipus: A Lacanian Reading of *The Mill on the Floss*," *VN* 82 (Fall 1992): 35–40.

Diana Postlethwaite, "Of Maggie, Mothers, Monsters, and Madonnas: Diving Deep in *The Mill on the Floss*," *WS* 20, no. 3 (1992): 303–19.

Sara M. Putzell, "'An Antagonism of Valid Claims': *The Mill on the Floss*," *TSLL* 13 (1971): 111–24.

Lynne Tidaback Roberts, "Perfect Pyramids: *The Mill on the Floss*," *TSLL* 13 (1971): 111–24.

J. S. Ryan, "God's Children Are Not Mocked; Or, King Swegen in *The Mill on the Floss*," *N&Q* 34 (December 1987): 495–97.

Dianne F. Sadoff, "George Eliot: The Law and the Father," in *George Eliot's "The Mill on the Floss*," ed. Harold Bloom (New York: Chelsea House, 1988), 77–88.

Gerard Salviati, "Le Diable et le bon dieu dans l'âme de Maggie Tulliver," *MCRel* 3 (1985): 135–52.

Elaine Showalter, "The Greening of Sister George," *NCF* 35 (September 1980): 292–311.

Jonathan Smith, "The 'Wonderful Geological Story': Uniformitarianism and *The Mill on the Floss*," *PLL* 27 (Fall 1991): 430–52.

Michael Steig, "Anality in *The Mill on the Floss*," *SNNTS* 5 (Fall 1970): 42–53.

William R. Steinhoff, "Intent and Fulfillment in the Ending of *The Mill on the Floss*," in *The Image of the Work: Essays in Criticism*, ed. Bertrand Evans, Josephine Miles, and William R. Steinhoff (Berkeley: University of California Press, 1955), 231–51.

Jerome Thale, "Image and Theme: *The Mill on the Floss*," *UKanR* 23 (1957): 227–34.

Renata R. Mautner Wassermann, "Narrative Logic and the Form of Tradition in *The Mill on the Floss*," *SNNTS* 14 (Fall 1982): 266–79.

G. A. Wilkes, "*The Mill on the Floss* as Moral Fable?" *SSEng* 11 (1985–86): 69–82.

Wendy Woodward, "The Solitariness of Selfhood: Maggie Tulliver and the Female Community at St. Ogg's," *ESA* 28, no. 1 (1985): 47–55.

Margaret Wolfit, "Dearly Beloved Scott," *GEFR* 23 (1992): 49–52.

"Mr. Gilfil's Love Story"

Andre DeCuir, "Italy, England, and the Female Artist in George Eliot's 'Mr. Gilfil's Love Story,'" *SSF* 29 (Winter 1992): 67–75.

Elizabeth Deeds Ermarth, "Common Ground: *Scenes of Clerical Life*, *Adam Bede*, *The Mill on the Floss*" in *George Eliot*, ed. Herbert Sussman (Boston: Twayne, 1985), 63–64.

Ranthorpe

Graham Handley, "*Ranthorpe* and George Eliot," *GEGHLN* 3 (September 1983): 1–3.

Romola

Henry Alley, "*Romola* and the Preservation of Household Gods," *Cithara* 23 (May 1984): 25–35.

Steve Bamlett, "'A Way–Worn Ancestry Returning': The Function of the Representation of Peasants in the Novel," in *Peasants and Countrymen in Literature*, ed. Kathleen Parkinson and Martin Priestman (London: Roehampton Institute, 1982), 153–82.

Karen Chase, "The Modern Family and the Ancient Image in *Romola*," *DSA* 14 (1985), 303–26.

Serge Cottereau, "Le *Romola* de George Eliot: Trop d'histoire, ou trop peu?" *Caliban* 28 (1991): 101–7.

Mary Gosselink De Jong, "*Romola*: A Bildungsroman for Feminists," *SoAR* 49 (November 1984): 75–90.

Mary De Jong, "Tito: A Portrait of Fear," *GEFR* 14 (1983): 18–22.

David J. DeLaura, "*Romola* and the Origin of the Paterian View of Life," *NCF* 21 (September 1966): 225–33.

Elizabeth Deeds Ermarth, "Sympathy: *Romola*, *Silas Marner*, *Felix Holt*" in *George Eliot*, (Boston: Twayne, 1985), 93–97.

Jan B. Gordon, "Affiliation as (Dis)semination: Gossip and Family in George Eliot's European Novel," *JES* 15 (September 1985): 155–89.

Edward Hurley, "Piero di Cosimo: An Alternate Analogy for George Eliot's Realism," *VN* 31 (Spring 1976): 54–58.

John A. Huzzard, "The Treatment of Florence and Florentine Characters in George Eliot's *Romola*," *Italica* 34 (1957): 158–65.

Nancy L. Paxton, "Feminism and Positivism in George Eliot's *Romola*," in *Nineteenth-Century Women Writers of the English-Speaking World*, ed. Rhoda B. Nathan (Westport, CT: Greenwood, 1986), 143–50.

Lawrence Sanford Poston, "Setting and Theme in *Romola*," *NCF* 20 (March 1966): 355–66.

Bernhard Reitz, "'Veracious Imagination' und 'Aesthetic Teaching': Die historisch-didaktische Konzeption von George Eliots' *Romola* (1862–63)," *A&E* 22 (1984): 143–60.

R. J. Schork, "Ti To Melema?" *N&Q* 35 (September 1988): 324–25.

William J. Sullivan, "Piero di Cosimo and the Higher Primitivism in *Romola*," *NCF* 26 (March 1972): 390–405.

Seiko Tomita, "Romola ni Egakareta Renaissance," *EigoS* 134 (n.d.): 177–79.

The Sad Fortunes of the Rev. Amos Barton

Marcia Wilson Lebow, "Choir Invisible: A Music Gloss for *The Sad Fortunes of the Rev. Amos Barton*," *GEFR* 13 (1982): 30–33.

Timothy Pace, "*The Sad Fortunes of the Rev. Amos Barton*: George Eliot and Displaced Religious Confession," *Style* 20 (Spring 1986): 75–89.

Michael Wolff, "George Eliot's First Family: The Bartons of Shepperton," *GEFR* 23 (1992): 46–48.

Scenes of Clerical Life

Nancy Cervetti, "The Resurrection of Milly Barton: At the Nexus of Production, Text, and Re-Production," *WS* 21, no. 3 (1992): 339–59.

Elizabeth Deeds Ermarth, "Common Ground: *Scenes of Clerical Life*, *Adam Bede*, *The Mill on the Floss*," in *George Eliot*, (Boston: Twayne, 1985), 60–68.

Alain Jumeau, "Images de la femme dans les *Scenes of Clerical Life* de George Eliot," *CVE* 31 (April 1990): 51–61.

Alexandra M. Norton, "The Seeds of Fiction: George Eliot's *Scenes of Clerical Life*," *JNT* 19 (Spring 1989): 217–32.

Kathleen Porter, "Study Group Notes," *GEFR* 13 (1982): 50–52.

Silas Marner

Henry Alley, "*Silas Marner* and the Balance of Male and Female," *VIJ* 16 (1988): 65–73.

Alain Barrat, "George Eliot's Mixed Vision of Human Progress in *Silas Marner*: A Pessimistic Reading of the Novel," *CVE* 35 (April 1992): 193–200.

Felicia Bonaparte, "Carrying the Word of the Lord to the Gentiles: *Silas Marner* and the Translation of Scripture into a Secular Text," *R&L* 23 (Summer 1991): 39–60.

David R. Carroll, "*Silas Marner*: Reversing the Oracles of Religion," *Literary Monographs* 1 (Madison: University of Wisconsin Press, 1967), 165–200, 312–14.

Susan R. Cohen, "'A History and a Metamorphosis': Continuity and Discontinuity in *Silas Marner*," *TSLL* 25 (Fall 1983): 410–26.

Terence Dawson, "'Light Enough to Trusten by': Structure and Experience in *Silas Marner*," *MLR* 88 (January 1993): 26–45.

Elizabeth Deeds Ermarth, "Sympathy: *Silas Marner*, *Felix Holt*" in *George Eliot* (Boston: Twayne, 1985), 97–102.

Harold Fisch, "Biblical Realism in *Silas Marner*," in *Identity and Ethos: Festschrift for Sol Liptzin on Occasion of His 85th Birthday*, ed. Mark Gelber (New York: Peter Lang, 1986), 343–60.

J. H., "The Schoolteacher's Novel: *Silas Marner*," *SatR* 15 (20 March 1937): 13.

Donald Hawes, "Chance in *Silas Marner*," *Eng* 31 (Autumn 1982): 213–18.

Liliana Ionescu-Matache, "Studiu tipologic asupra lui *Silas Marner*," *StLU* 15 (1970): 79–90.

Ming Jing, "The Right Angle Coordinate System of the Character Structure in *Silas Marner*," *FLitS* 28 (June 1985): 130–36.

Peggy Fitzhugh Johnstone, "Loss, Anxiety and Cure: Mourning and Creativity in *Silas Marner*," *Mosaic* 25 (Fall 1992): 35–47.

James McLaverty, "Comtean Fetishism in *Silas Marner*," *NCF* 36 (December 1981): 318–36.

Ian Milner, "Structure and Quality in *Silas Marner*," *SELit* 16 (Autumn 1966): 717–29.

Peter New, "Chance, Providence and Destiny in George Eliot's Fiction," *Eng* 34 (Autumn 1985): 191–208.

Jeff Nunokawa, "The Miser's Two Bodies: *Silas Marner* and the Sexual Possibilities of the Commodity," *VS* 36 (Spring 1993): 273–42.

Coleman O. Parsons, "Background Material Illustrative of *Silas Marner*," *N&Q* 191 (1946): 266–70.

John Preston, "The Community of the Novel: *Silas Marner*," *CCrit* 2 (1980): 109–30.

John Preston, "*Silas Marner*: The Community of the Novel," *GEFR* 11 (1980): 8–10.

Meri–Jane Rochelson, "The Weaver of Raveloe: Metaphor as Narrative Persuasion in *Silas Marner*," *SNNTS* 15 (Spring 1983): 35–43.

Sally Shuttleworth, "Fairy Tale or Science? Physiological Psychology in *Silas Marner*," in *Languages of Nature: Critical Essays on Science and Literature*, ed. L. J. Jordanova (New Brunswick, NJ: Rutgers University Press, 1986), 244–88.

Brian Swann, "*Silas Marner* and the New Mythus," *Criticism* 18 (Spring 1976): 101–21.

Fred C. Thomson, "The Theme of Alienation in *Silas Marner*," *NCF* 20 (March 1965): 69–84.

FORD, FORD MADOX

The Fifth Queen

William Gass, "The Neglect of *The Fifth Queen*," in *The Presence of Ford Madox Ford: A Memorial Volume of Essays, Poems, and Memoirs*, ed. Sondra J. Stang (Philadelphia: University of Pennsylvania Press, 1981), 24–43.

Judie Newman, "Ford Madox Ford's *Fifth Queen* Trilogy: Mythical Fiction and Political Letters," *ÉA* 38 (October–December 1985): 397–410.

The Good Soldier

James T. Adams, "Discrepancies in the Time-Scheme of *The Good Soldier*," *ELT* 34, no. 2 (1991): 153–64.

Miriam Bailin, "'An Extraordinarily Safe Castle': Aesthetics as Refuge in *The Good Soldier*," *MFS* 30 (Winter 1984): 621–36.

Bruce Bassoff, "Oedipal Fantasy and Arrested Development in *The Good Soldier*," *TCL* 34 (Spring 1988): 40–47.

Diane Stockmar Bonds, "The Seeing Eye and the Slothful Heart: The Narrator of Ford's *The Good Soldier*," *ELT* 25, no. 1 (1982): 21–27.

Vincent J. Cheng, "A Chronology of *The Good Soldier*," *ELN* 24 (September 1986): 91–97.

Vincent J. Cheng, "Religious Differences in *The Good Soldier*: The 'Protest' Scene," *Renascence* 37 (Summer 1985): 238–47.

Vincent J. Cheng, "The Spirit of *The Good Soldier* and The Spirit of the People," *ELT* 32, no. 3 (1989): 303–16.

Charles Daughady, "Cubist Viewing with the Comic Spirit in Ford's *The Good Soldier*," *KPAB* (1984): 14–24.

Avrom Fleishman, "The Genre of *The Good Soldier*: Ford's Comic Mastery," in *British Novelists since 1900*, ed. Jack I. Biles (New York: AMS, 1987), 41–53.

Dewey Ganzel, "What the Letter Said: Fact and Inference in *The Good Soldier*," *JML* 11 (July 1984): 277–90.

Richard A. Hood, "'Constant reduction': Modernism and the Narrative Structure of *The Good Soldier*," *JML* 14 (Spring 1988): 445–64.

Carol Jacobs, "The (Too) Good Soldier: 'A Real Story,'" *Glyph* 3 (Spring 1978): 32–51.

Michael Levenson, "Character in *The Good Soldier*," *TCL* 30 (Winter 1984): 373–87.

Brian May, "Ford Madox Ford and the Politics of Impressionism," *ELWIU* 21 (Spring 1994): 82–96.

Frank Nigro, "Who Framed *The Good Soldier*? Dowell's Story in Search of a Form," *SNNTS* 24 (Winter 1992): 381–91.

Roger Poole, "The Real Plot Line of Ford Madox Ford's *The Good Soldier*: An Essay in Applied Deconstruction," *TexP* 4 (Winter 1990): 390–427.

John Reichert, "Poor Florence Indeed! or: *The Good Soldier* Retold," *SNNTS* 14 (Summer 1982): 161–79.

Dilvo I. Ristoff, "Class Orientations in Ford Madox Ford's *The Good Soldier*," *EAA* 9–11 (1985–87): 60–67.

C. Ruth Sabol, "Reliable Narration in *The Good Soldier*," in *Literary Computing and Literary Criticism: Theoretical and Practical Essays on Theme and Rhetoric*, ed. Rosanne G. Potter (Philadelphia: University of Pennsylvania Press, 1989), 207–23.

James B. Scott, "Coincidence or Irony? Ford's Use of August 4th in *The Good Soldier*," *ELN* 30 (June 1993): 53–58.

James M. Swafford, "A Rossetti Allusion in Ford's *The Good Soldier*," *N&Q* 31 (March 1984): 76–77.

The Last Post

Bruce Thornton, "Pastoral or Georgic? Ford Madox Ford's *The Last Post*," *ELN* 26 (September 1988): 59–66.

No More Parades

Michela Calderaro, "*No More Parades*: Le opposizioni elementari e la (bi)partizone del mondo," *ACF* 22, no. 1–2 (1983): 183–92.

Parade's End

Andrew Nelson Lytle, "A Partial Reading of *Parade's End*; or, the Hero as an Old Furniture Dealer," in *The Presence of Ford Madox Ford: A Memorial Volume of Essays, Poems, and Memoirs*, ed. Sondra J. Stang (Philadelphia: University of Pennsylvania Press, 1981), 77–95.

Eric Meyer, "Ford's War and (Post)Modern Memory: *Parade's End* and National Allegory," *Criticism* 32 (Winter 1990): 81–99.

Gene M. Moore, "The Tory in a Time of Change: Social Aspects of Ford Madox Ford's *Parade's End*," *TCL* 28 (Spring 1982): 49–68.

Norman Page, "Living as Ritual in Parade's End," in *British Novelists since 1900*, ed. Jack I. Biles (New York: AMS, 1987), 55–63.

Brindusa Popescu, "Continut si tehnica narativa in Sfirsitul paradei (*Parade's End*) de Ford Madox Ford," *ASUI* 33 (1987): 21–28.

War and the Mind

Sondra J. Stang, "*War and the Mind*," *YR* 78 (Summer 1989): 497–510.

When the Wicked Man

Martien Kappers, "Leer om leer: 'Quartet' en *When the Wicked Man*," *Maatstaf* 2 (1989): 51–65.

Zepplin Nights

Vincent J. Cheng, "The *Zeppelin Nights* of Ford Madox Ford," *JML* 15 (Spring 1989): 595–97.

Michael Dooley, "Readers and Writers: Ford's Narrative Technique in Stories from the Past: *Zeppelin Nights*," *JSSE* 13 (Autumn 1989): 39–55.

FORSTER, E[DWARD] M[ORGAN]

"Albergo Empedocle"

James S. Malek, "Forster's 'Albergo Empedocle': A Precursor of *Maurice*," *SSF* 11 (Fall 1974): 427–30.

Artic Summer

Elizabeth Ellem, "E. M. Forster's *Artic Summer*," *TLS* (21 September 1973): 1087–089.

"The Celestial Omnibus"

Leonard R. N. Ashley and Stuart L. Astor, "E. M. Forster," in *British Short Stories: Classics and Criticism*, ed. Leonard R. N. Ashley and Stuart Astor (Englewood Cliffs, NJ: Prentice-Hall, 1968), 174, 189–90.

W. B. Baroody, "E. M. Forster's "The Celestial Omnibus": All the Way for Boy and Teacher," *ArEB* 16 (April 1974): 129–31.

James Nagel, "The Celestial Omnibus," in *Suggestions for Teaching Vision and Value: A Thematic Introduction to the Short Story* (Belmont, CA: Dickenson, 1970), 2–3.

"The Curate's Friend"

Susan Grove Hall, "Among E. M. Forster's Idylls: 'The Curate's Friend,'" *CML* 3 (Winter 1983): 99–105.

"Dr. Woolacott"

James S. Malek, "Salvation in Forster's 'Dr. Woolacott,'" *SSF* 18 (Summer 1981): 319–20.

Goldsworthy Lowes Dickinson

Frederick P.W. McDowell, "E. M. Forster and *Goldsworthy Lowes Dickinson*," *SNNTS* 5 (Winter 1973): 441–56.

Richard Shone, "A Quiet Life," *Spectator* 231 (18 August 1973): 219–20.

Beatrice Webb, "Appendix G, Beatrice Webb on 'Goldsworthy Lowes Dickinson,'" in *"Goldsworthy Lowes Dickinson" and Related Writings*, ed. Oliver Stallybrass (London: Edward Arnold, 1973), 223–24.

The Hill of Devi

J. B. Appaswamy, "*The Hill of Devi*," in *A Garland for E. M. Forster*, ed. H. H. Anniah Gowda (Mysore, India: The Literary Half-Yearly, 1969), 51–53.

R. K. Kapur, "The Other India," *NewR* 129 (2 November 1953): 28–29.

Hugh N. Maclean, "Forster's India," *UTQ* 24 (January 1955): 208–10.

Steven Marcus, "Forster's India," *PR* 21 (January–February 1954): 115–19.

Ashish Roy, "Framing the Other: History and Literary Verisimilitude in E. M. Forster's *The Hill of Devi*," *Criticism* 36 (Spring 1994): 265–89.

Howards End

Walter Allen, "Reassessments—*Howards End*," *NewS&N* 49 (19 March 1955): 407–08.

Paul B. Armstrong, "E. M. Forster's *Howards End*: The Existential Crisis of the Liberal Imagination," *Mosaic* 8 (Fall 1974): 183–99.

Elizabeth Barrett, "The Advance beyond Daintiness: Voice and Myth in *Howards End*," in *E. M. Forster: Centenary Revaluations*, ed. Judith Scherer Herz and Robert K. Martin (Toronto: University of Toronto Press, 1982), 155–66.

Alice R. Bensen, "E. M. Foster's Dialectic: *Howards End*," *MFS* 1 (November 1955): 17–22.

Joseph L. Blotner, "E. M. Forster: The Problem of Imperialism," in *The Political Novel* (Garden City, NY: Doubleday, 1955), 22–23.

Daniel Born, "Private Gardens, Public Swamps: *Howards End* and the Revaluation of Liberal Guilt," *Novel* 25 (Winter 1992): 141–59.

Surabhi Chakrabarty, "Bi–Tonality in Fiction: Leonard Bast in E. M. Forster's *Howards End*," *JDECU* 17, no. 2 (1981–82): 1–25.

Surabhi Chakrabarty, "Forster's *Howards End*: Character of Margaret," *JDECU* 17, no. 1 (1981–82): 54–74.

Thomas Churchill, "Place and Personality in *Howards End*," *Critique* 5 (Spring–Summer 1962): 61–73.

John Colmer, "*Howards End* Revisted," in *A Garland for E. M. Forster*, ed. H. H. Anniah Gowda (Mysore, India: The Literary Half-Yearly, 1969), 9–22.

George B. Dutton, "*Howards End* Shows Up Disjointed Living," *SpSR* (1 January 1922): 11A. Reprinted in *E. M. Forster: The Critical Heritage*, ed. Philip Gardner (London; Boston: Routledge & Kegan Paul, 1973), 165–67.

J. R. Ebbatson, "The Schlegels' Family Tree," *ELT* 18, no. 3 (1975): 195–201.

M. J. C. Echeruo, "E. M. Forster and the 'Underdeveloped Heart'," *ESA* 5 (September 1962): 151–55.

Robert Friend, "The Rainbow Bridge: Forster's Failure in *Howards End*," in *Further Studies in English Language and Literature*, ed. A. A. Mendilow (Jerusalem: The Hebrew University, 1973), 227–39.

Francis Gillen, "*Howards End* and the Neglected Narrator," *Novel* 3 (Winter 1970): 139–52.

John V. Hagopian and Martin Dolch, "E. M. Forster," in *Insight II: Analysis of Modern British Literature* (Frankfurt am Main: Hirschgraben, 1964), 117–40.

John Edward Hardy, "*Howards End*: The Sacred Center," in *Man in the Modern Novel* (Seattle: University of Washington Press, 1964), 34–51.

Neil Heims, "Forsters *Howards End*," *Expl* 42 (Fall 1983): 39–41.

Suzette A. Henke, "*Howards End*: E. M. Forster without Marx or Sartre," *MSpr* 80, no. 2 (1986): 116–20.

Frederick J. Hoffman, "*Howards End* and the Bogey of Progress," *MFS* 7 (Autumn 1961): 243–57. Revised and reprinted in *The Mortal No Death and the Modern Imagination* (Princeton: Princeton University Press, 1964), 64–87.

Cyrus Hoy, "Forster's Metaphysical Novel," *PMLA* 75 (March 1960): 126–36.

Pat C. Hoy, III, "The Narrow, Rich Staircase in Forster's *Howards End*," *TCL* 31 (Summer–Fall 1985): 221–35.

Alfred Kazin, "*Howards End* Revisited," *PR* 59 (Winter 1992): 27–41.

Elizabeth Langland, "Gesturing toward an Open Space: Gender, Form, and Language in E. M. Forster's *Howards End*," in *Out of Bounds: Male Writers and Gender(ed) Criticism*, ed. Laura Claridge and Elizabeth Langland (Amherst: University of Massachusetts Press, 1990), 252–67.

Michael Levenson, "Liberalism and Symbolism in *Howards End*," *PLL* 21 (Summer 1985): 295–316.

Alastair A. MacDonald, "Class-Consciousness in E. M. Forster," *UKanR* 27 (March 1961): 235–40.

Frederick P. W. McDowell, "'The Mild, Intellectual Light': Idea and Theme in *Howard's End*," *PMLA* 74 (September 1959): 453–63. Reprinted as "'Glimpses of the Diviner Wheels': *Howards End*," in *E. M. Forster* (New York: Twayne, 1969), 64–80.

E. Barry McGurk, "Gentlefolk in Philistia: The Influence of Matthew Arnold on E. M. Forster's *Howards End*," *ELT* 15, no. 3 (1972): 213–19.

FORSTER, E. M., *Howards End*

Robert Bernard Martin, "Notes toward a Comic Fiction," in *The Theory of the Novel: New Essays*, ed. John Halperin (New York: Oxford University Press, 1974), 71–90.

James Missey, "The Connected and the Unconnected in *Howards End*," *WStL* 6 (1969): 72–89.

Edwin Moseley, "A New Correlative for *Howards End*: Demeter and Persephone," *LockHB* 1, no. 3 (1961): 1–6.

Heinz-Joachim Mullenbrock, "Gesellschaftliche Thematik in E. M. Forster's *Howards End*," *Anglia* 87, no. 3/4 (1969): 367–91.

Thomas Mulvey, "A Paraphrase of Nietzsche in Forster's *Howards End*," *N&Q* 19 (February 1972): 52.

Jeane N. Olson, "E. M. Forster's Prophetic Vision of the Modern Family in *Howards End*," *TSLL* 35 (Fall 1993): 347–62.

Takeshi Onodera, "Works: *Howards End*," in *E. M. Forster*, ed. Ineko Kondo (Toyko: Kentyusha, 1967), 93–112.

Mary Pinkerton, "Ambiguous Connections: Leonard Bast's Role in *Howards End*," *TCL* 31 (Summer–Fall 1985): 236–46.

Tariq Rahman, "The Use of the Millenarian Myth in E. M. Forster's *Howards End*," *SELit* (1987): 33–60.

W. G. L. Randles, "The Symbols of the Sacred in E. M. Forster's *Howards End*," *RFL* 3, no. 3 (1959): 89–102.

Paul R. Rivenberg, "The Role of the Essayist-Commentator in *Howards End*," in *E. M. Forster: Centenary Revaluations*, ed. Judith Scherer Herz and Robert K. Martin (Toronto: University of Toronto Press, 1982), 167–76.

Kinley E. Roby, "Irony and the Narrative Voice in *Howards End*," *JNT* 2 (May 1972): 116–24.

Dionsia Rola, "On E. M. Forster's *Howards End*: Some Generalizations," *DilR* 14 (July 1966): 285–86.

Vasant A. Shahane, "Beethoven's Fifth Symphony in *Howards End*," *IJES* 1 (December 1960): 100–03.

Kathryn Stubbs Smith, "Melville's Moby Dick in E. M. Forster's *Howards End*," *Expl* 46 (Fall 1987): 20–22.

Douglass H. Thomson, "From Words to Things: Margaret's Progress in *Howards End*," *SNNTS* 15 (Summer 1983): 122–34.

George H. Thomson, "Theme and Symbol in *Howards End*," *MFS* 7 (Autumn 1961): 229–42.

Andrea K. Weatherhead, "*Howards End*: Beethoven's Fifth," *TCL* 31 (Summer–Fall 1985): 247–64.

Barry R. Westburg, "Forster's Fifth Symphony: Another Aspect of *Howards End*," *MFS* 10 (Winter 1964–65): 359–65.

Anne M. Wyatt-Brown, "*Howards End*: Celibacy and Stalemate," *PsyHR* 12 (Fall 1983): 26–33.

The Longest Journey

Yoshio Abe, "Works: *The Longest Journey*," in *E. M. Forster*, ed. Ineko Kondo (Toyoka: Kenkyusha, 1967), 69–82.

Tony Brown, "E. M. Forster's Parsifal: A Reading of *The Longest Journey*," *JES* 12 (March 1982): 30–54.

Frederick C. Crews, "*The Longest Journey* and the Perils of Humanism," *ELH* 26 (December 1959): 575–96. Revised and reprinted in *Modern British Fiction*, ed. Mark Schorer (New York: Oxford University Press, 1961), 176–94; revised and reprinted as "*The Longest Journey*" in *E. M. Forster and the Perils of Humanism* (Princeton: Princeton University Press, 1962), 50–70.

M. D. Faber, "E. M. Forster's *The Longest Journey*: Doubled Offspring and Ambivalent Mothers," *HSL* 17, no. 1 (1985): 19–35.

John Harvey, "Imagination and Moral Theme in E. M. Forster's *The Longest Journey*," *EIC* 6 (October 1956): 418–33. Reprinted in *Forster: A Collection of Critical Essays*, ed. Malcolm Bradbury (Englewood Cliffs, NJ: Prentice-Hall, 1966), 112–27.

Peter L. Hays, "*The Longest Journey*," in *The Limping Hero: Grotesques in Literature* (New York: New York University Press, 1971), 141–42, 144.

Elizabeth Heine, "Rickie Elliot and the Cow: The Cambridge Apostles and *The Longest Journey*," *ELT* 15, no. 2 (1972): 116–34.

Thomas L. Jeffers, "Forster's *The Longest Journey* and the Idea of Apprenticeship," *TSLL* 30 (Summer 1988): 179–97.

Carola M. Kaplan, "Absent Father, Passive Son: The Dilemma of Rickie Elliott in *The Longest Journey*," *TCL* 33 (Summer 1987): 196–210.

Yoshihisa Kawaguchi, "Reality in *The Longest Journey*," in *Yamakawa Kozo Kyoju Taikan Kinen Ronbunshu*, (Toyonaka: N.p., 1981), 363–73.

Frank Kermode, "A Queer Business," *AtM* 227 (November 1971): 140–42, 144.

Hedwige Louis-Chevrillon, "Revue des Livres," *Études* 273 (June 1952): 427–28.

Frederick P. W. McDowell, "Forster's Many-Faceted Universe: Idea and Paradox in *The Longest Journey*," *Critique* 4 (Fall–Winter, 1960–61): 41–63. Revised and reprinted as "'The Union of Shadow and Adamant': *The Longest Journey*," in *E. M. Forster* (New York: Twayne, 1969), 64–80.

David Paul, "Time and the Novelist," *PR* 21 (November–December 1954): 636–49.

Tariq Rahman, "Alienation and Homosexuality in E. M. Forster's *The Longest Journey*," *LHY* 27 (January 1986): 44–65.

Tariq Rahman, "The Under-Plot in E. M. Forster's *The Longest Journey*," *DUJ* 83 (January 1991): 59–67.

Vasant A. Shahane, "E. M. Forster's *The Longest Journey*: A Moral Fable," *LCrit* 4 (December 1960): 1–8.

Rae H. Stoll, "'Aphrodite with a Janus Face': Language, Desire, and History in Forster's *The Longest Journey*," *Novel* 20 (Spring 1987): 237–59.

"The Machine Stops"

W. H. G. Armytage, "The Disenchanted Mechanophobes in Twentieth Century England," *Extrapolation* 9 (May 1968): 29–41, 44, 46, 53–59.

Charles Elkins, "E. M. Forster's 'The Machine Stops': Liberal-Humanist Hostility to Technology," in *Clockwork Worlds: Mechanized Environments in SF*, ed. Richard D. Erlich and Thomas P. Dunn (Westport, CT: Greenwood, 1983), 47–61.

Mark E. Hillegas, *The Future as Nightmare: H. G. Wells and the Anti-Utopians* (New York: Oxford University Press, 1967), 85–95.

Irving Howe, "Introduction to 'The Machine Stops,'" in *Classics of Modern Fiction*, 2nd ed., ed. Irving Howe (New York: Harcourt, Brace, 1972), 233–40.

Maurice

J. Birje-Patil, "The Way of All Sterility," *Quest* 77 (July–August 1972): 77–80.

Douglass Bolling, "The Distanced Heart: Artistry in E. M. Forster's *Maurice*," *MFS* 20 (Summer 1974): 157–68.

John Cronin, "'Publishable—but Worth It?" *Irish Press* (9 October 1971): 12. Reprinted in *E. M. Forster: The Critical Heritage*, ed. Philip Gardner (London: Routledge & Kegan Paul, 1973), 456–58.

Nigel Dennis, "The Lovel that Levels," *Telegraph* (10 October 1971): 16. Reprinted in *E. M. Forster: The Critical Heritage*, ed. Philip Gardner (London: Routledge & Kegan Paul, 1973), 465–68.

Elaine Feinstein, "Loving," *LMag* 11 (January 1972): 154–57.

E. M. Forster, "Terminal Note," *Maurice* (London: Edward Arnold, 1971), 235–41.

Philip Gardner, "The Evolution of E. M. Forster's *Maurice*," in *E. M. Forster: Centenary Revaluations*, ed. Judith Scherer Herz and Robert K. Martin (Toronto: University of Toronto Press, 1982), 204–23.

Kathleen Grant, "*Maurice* as Fantasy," in *E. M. Forster: Centenary Revaluations*, ed. Judith Scherer Herz and Robert K. Martin (Toronto: University of Toronto Press; 1982), 191–203.

Jon Harned, "Becoming Gay in E. M. Forster's *Maurice*," *PLL* 29 (Winter 1993): 49–66.

C. J. D. Harvey, "*Maurice*: E. M. Forster's 'Homosexual Novel,'" *Standpoint* 97 (1971): 29–33.

Joyce Hotchkiss, "Romance and Reality: The Dualistic Style of E. M. Forster's *Maurice*," *JNT* 4 (September 1974): 163–74.

Anne Lohrli, "Chapman and Hall," *N&Q* 32 (September 1985): 377–78.

Frederick P. W. McDowell, "Second Thoughts on E. M. Forster's *Maurice*," *VWQ* 1 (Fall 1972): 46–59.

Ira Bruce Nadel, "Moments in the Greenwood: *Maurice* in Context," in *E. M. Forster: Centenary Revaluations*, ed. Judith Scherer Herz and Robert K. Martin (Toronto: University of Toronto Press; 1982), 177–90.

Cynthia Ozick, "Forster as Homosexual," *Commentary* 52 (December 1971): 81–85.

V. S. Pritchett, "The Upholstered Prison," *NewS* 72 (8 October 1971): 479–80. Reprinted in *E. M. Forster: The Critical Heritage*, ed. Philip Gardner (London: Routledge & Kegan Paul, 1973), 447–50.

Meenakshi Puri, "Private Activity," *Thought* 24 (12 February 1972): 17–18.

Tariq Rahman, "A Study of Alienation in E. M. Forster's *Maurice*," *DUJ* 51 (January 1990): 81–87.

Michael Ratcliffe, "The Undeveloped Heart," *Times* (7 October 1971): 10. Reprinted in *E. M. Forster: The Critical Heritage*, ed. Philip Gardner (London: Routledge & Kegan Paul, 1973), 441–44.

C. Rising, "E. M. Forster's *Maurice*: A Summing Up," *TexasQ* 17 (Spring 1974): 84–96.

Stephen Spender, "Forster's Queer Novel," *PR* 39, no. 1 (1972): 113–17.

George Steiner, "Under the Greenwood Tree," *NewY* 47 (9 October 1971): 158, 160, 163–66, 169. Reprinted in *E. M. Forster: The Critical Heritage*, ed. Philip Gardner (London: Routledge & Kegan Paul, 1973), 475–82.

Jack Theogood, "Worlds Apart: Apropos E. M. Forster's *Maurice*," *RecL* 12 (1984): 41–50.

Philip Toynbee, "Forster's Love Story," *Observer* (10 October 1971): 32. Reprinted in "Books," *Critic* 30 (January–February 1972): 71–72. Reprinted in *E. M. Forster: The Critical Heritage*, ed. Philip Gardner (London: Routledge & Kegan Paul, 1973), 462–65.

Dieter Zeh, "'No Other of My Books Has Started Off in This Way': E. M. Forster's *Maurice*," in *Theorie und Praxis im Erzahlen des 19. und 20. Jahrhunderts: Studien zur englischen und amerikanischen Literatur zu Ehren von Willi Erzgraber*, ed. Winfried Herget, Klaus Peter Jochum, and Ingeborg Weber (Tubingen: Narr, 1986), 153–65.

The Other Boat

D. S. Kesava Rao, "E. M. Forster's *The Other Boat*," *LitE* 4, no. 3–4 (1984): 15–21.

A Passage to India

Ahmed Ali, "E. M. Forster and India," in *E. M. Forster: Centenary Revaluations*, ed. Judith Scherer Herz and Robert K. Martin (Toronto: University of Toronto Press, 1982), 278–82.

Glen O. Allen, "Structure, Symbol, and Theme in E. M. Foster's *A Passage to India*," *PMLA* 70 (December 1955): 934–54. Reprinted in *Perspectives on E. M. Forster's "A Passage to India,"* ed. Vasant A. Shahane (New York: Barnes & Noble, 1968), 121–41.

Masahito Ara, "Works: *A Passage to India*," in *E. M. Forster*, ed. Ineko Kondo (Toyko: Kentyusha, 1967), 113–45.

Paul B. Armstrong, "Reading India: E. M. Forster and the Politics of Interpretation," *TCL* 38 (Winter 1992): 365–85.

Edgar A. Austin, "Rites of Passage in *A Passage in India*," *OrientW* 9 (May–June 1964): 64–72.

Robert Barratt, "Marabar: The Caves of Deconstruction," *JNT* 23 (Spring 1993): 127–35.

Elizabeth Barrett, "Comedy, Courtesy, and *A Passage to India*," *ESC* 10 (March 1984): 77–93.

Gillian Beer, "'But Nothing in India Is Identifiable': Negation and Identification in *A Passage to India*," in *Approaches to E. M. Forster: A Centenary Volume*, ed. Vasant A. Shahane (New Delhi: Arnold-Heinemann; Atlantic Highlands, NJ: Humanities, 1981), 9–23.

John Beer, "Chapter VI: The Undying Worm," in *E. M. Forster: "A Passage to India" A Casebook*, ed. Malcolm Bradbury (London: Macmillan, 1970), 186–215.

John Beer, "Conclusion: *A Passage to India* and the Versatility of the Novel," in *A Passage to India: Essays in Interpretation*, ed. John Beer (Totowa, NJ: Barnes & Noble, 1986), 132–54.

John Beer, "Echoes, Reflections, Correspondences: Some Central Romantic Themes and *A Passage to India*," in *Approaches to E. M. Forster: A Centenary Volume*, ed. Vasant A. Shahane (New Delhi: Arnold-Heinemann; Atlantic Highlands, NJ: Humanities, 1981), 70–99.

John Beer, "*A Passage to India*, the French New Novel and English Romanticism," in *E. M. Forster: Centenary Revaluations*, ed. Judith Scherer Herz and Robert K. Martin (Toronto: University of Toronto Press, 1982), 124–52.

D. R. Beeton, "The Message beyond the Marabar: Some Aspects of E. M. Forster's *A Passage to India*," *UES* 7 (November 1970): 20–26.

Vereen M. Bell, "Comic Seriousness in *A Passage to India*," *SoAQ* 66 (Winter 1967): 606–17.

Rosemarie Bodenheimer, "The Romantic Impasse in *A Passage to India*," *Criticism* 22 (Winter 1980): 40–56.

Ted. E. Boyle, "Adela Quested's Delusion: The Failure of Rationalism in *A Passage to India*," *CE* 26 (March 1965): 478–80. Reprinted in *Perspectives on E. M. Forster's "A Passage to India*," ed. Vasant A. Shahane (New York: Barnes & Noble, 1968), 73–75.

FORSTER, E. M., *A Passage to India*

Laurence Brander, "Aspects of E. M. Forster," in *A Garland for E. M. Forster*, ed. H. H. Anniah Gowda (Mysore, India: The Literary Half–Yearly, 1969), 95–104

Laurence Brander, "E. M. Forster and India," *RevEL* 2 (October 1962): 76–84.

Reuben Arthur Brower, "The Twilight of the Double Vision: Symbol and Irony in *A Passage to India*," in *The Fields of Light* (New York: Oxford University Press, 1951), 182–98. Reprinted in *Modern British Fiction: Essays in Criticism*, ed. Mark Schorer (New York: Oxford University Press, 1961), 210–24 and in *E. M. Forster: "A Passage to India": A Casebook*, ed. Malcolm Bradbury (London: Macmillan, 1970), 114–31.

E. K. Brown, "Rhythm in E. M. Forster's *A Passage to India*," in *Rhythm in the Novel* (Toronto: University of Toronto Press, 1950), 89–115. Reprinted in *Forster: A Collection of Critical Essays*, ed. Malcolm Bradbury (Englewood Cliffs, NJ: Prentice-Hall, 1966), 134–59 and in *E. M. Forster "A Passage to India": A Casebook*, ed. Malcolm Bradbury (London: Macmillan, 1970), 93–113.

Kenneth Burke, "Social and Cosmic Mystery: *A Passage to India*," *LugR* 1 (Summer 1966): 140–55. Reprinted in *Language as Symbolic Action* (Los Angeles: University of California Press, 1968), 223–39.

Richard S. Cammarota, "Musical Analogy and Internal Design in *A Passage to India*," *ELT* 18, no. 1 (1975): 38–46.

Francis A. de Caro, "'A Mystery Is a Muddle': Gnomic Expressions in *A Passage to India*," *MJLF* 12 (Spring 1986): 15–23.

A. K. Chanda, "The Failure of Humanism—A Study of the Structure of E. M. Forster's *A Passage to India*," *CalUB* 5, no. 2 (1969–1970): 2–19.

Nird C. Chaudhuri, "Passage To and From India," *Encounter* 2 (June 1954): 19–24. Reprinted in *Perspectives on E. M. Forster's "A Passage to India,"* ed. Vasant A. Shahane (New York: Barnes & Noble, 1968), 115–20. Reprinted in *Twentieth Century Interpretations of "A Passage to India": A Collection of Critical Essays*, ed. Andrew Rutherford (Englewood Cliffs, NJ: Prentice-Hall, 1970), 68–77.

Roger L. Clubb, "*A Passage to India*: The Meaning of the Marabar Caves," *CLAJ* 6 (March 1963): 184–93.

Frederick C. Crews, "Chapter 10: *A Passage to India*," in *Twentieth Century Interpretations of "A Passage to India": A Collection of Critical Essays*, ed. Andrew Rutherford (Englewood Cliffs, NJ: Prentice–Hall, 1970), 78–89.

H. M. Daleski, "Rhythmic and Symbolic Patterns in *A Passage to India*," in *Studies in English Language and Literature*, ed. Alice Shalvi and A. A. Mendilow (Jerusalem: Hebrew University Press, 1966), 259–79.

Bikram K. Das, "A Stylistic Analysis of the Speech of the Indian Characters in Forster's *A Passage to India*," *IJES* 12 (December 1971): 42–54.

G. K. Das, "*A Passage to India*: A Socio–Historical Study," in *"A Passage to India": Essays in Interpretation*, ed. John Beer (Totowa, NJ: Barnes & Noble; 1986), 1–15.

G. K. Das, "Shonfield and Forster's India: A Controversial Exchange," *Encounter* 30 (June 1968): 95.

Louise Dauner, "What Happened in the Cave? Relfections on *A Passage to India*," *MFS* 7 (Autumn 1961): 258–70. Reprinted in *Perspectives on E. M. Forster's "A Passage to India,"* ed. Vasant A. Shahane (New York: Barnes & Noble, 1968), 52–64.

Doreen D'Cruz, "Emptying and Filling Along the Existential Coil in *A Passage to India*," *SNNTS* 18 (Summer 1986): 193–205.

Andrew Deacon, "*A Passage to India*: Forster's Confidence," *CR* 14 (1971): 125–36.

Roger Decap, "Un Roman Pascalien: *A Passage to India* de E. M. Forster," *Caliban* 5 (January 1968): 103–28.

Gerald Doherty, "White Circles/Black Holes: Worlds of Difference in *A Passage to India*," *OL* 46, no. 2 (1991): 105–22.

Kieran Dolin, "Freedom, Uncertainty, and Diversity: *A Passage to India* as a Critique of Imperialist Law," *TSLL* 36 (Fall 1994): 328–52.

Steven Doloff, "Forster's Use of Names in *A Passage to India*," *ELN* 28 (June 1991): 61–63.

David Dowling, "*A Passage to India* through 'The Spaces between the Words.'" *JNT* 15 (Fall 1985): 256–66.

John Drew, "The Spirit behind the Frieze?" in *"A Passage to India": Essays in Interpretation*, ed. John Beer (Totowa, NJ: Barnes & Noble, 1986), 81–103.

V. J. Emmett, Jr., "Verbal Truth and Truth of Mood in E. M. Forster's *A Passage to India*," *ELT* 15, no. 3 (1972): 199–212.

Francisco Fernandez, "*A Passage to India*: El lenguaje artistico y simbolico de E. M. Forster," *RAEI* 1 (November 1988): 33–79.

Gail Fincham, "Arches and Echoes: Framing Devices in *A Passage to India*," *Pretexts* 2 (Winter 1990): 52–67.

Avrom Fleishman, "Being and Nothing in *A Passage to India*," *Criticism* 15 (Spring 1973): 109–25.

FORSTER, E. M., *A Passage to India*

Robert F. Fleissner, "A Passage from 'Kubla Khan' in Forster's *India*," *ILit* 14 (September 1971): 79–84.

Robert Friend, "The Quest for Rondure: A Comparison of Two Passages of India," *HUSL* 1 (Spring 1973): 76–85.

Paul Fussell, Jr., "E. M. Forster's Mrs. Moore: Some Suggestions," *PQ* 32 (October 1953): 388–95.

Stephen M. Gill, "Forster's Message in *A Passage to India*," *CalRev* 2 (January–March 1971): 321–23.

Robert Gish, "Forster as Fabulist: Proverbs and Parables in *A Passage to India*," *ELT* 15, no. 4 (1972): 245–56.

H. H. Anniah Gowda, "'To the Caves,'" in *A Garland for E. M. Forster*, ed. H. H. Anniah Gowda (Mysore, India: The Literary Half-Yearly, 1969), 23–34.

K. W. Grandsden, "Chapter 7: The Last Movement of the Symphony," in *E. M. Forster* (Edinburgh: Oliver & Boyd, 1962), 101–06. Revised and reprinted in *Perspectives on E. M. Forster's "A Passage to India*," ed. Vasant A. Shahane (New York: Barnes & Noble, 1968), 167–72.

Nancy Hale, "A Passage to Relationship," *AR* 20 (Spring 1960): 19–30. Revised and reprinted as "The Novel: A Passage to Relationship" in *The Realities of Fiction: A Book About Writing* (Boston: Little, Brown, 1962), 67–84.

Wilson Harris, "A Comment on *A Passage to India*," in *A Garland for E. M. Forster*, ed. H. H. Anniah Gowda (Mysore, India: The Literary Half-Yearly, 1969), 35–39.

Hunt Hawkins, "Forster's Critique of Imperialism in *A Passage to India*," *SoAR* 48 (January 1983): 54–65.

Jeffrey Heath, "A Voluntary Surrender: Imperialism and Imagination in *A Passage to India*," *UTQ* 59 (Winter 1990): 287–309.

Judith Scherer Herz, "Listening to Language," in *"A Passage to India": Essays in Interpretation*, ed. John Beer (Totowa, NJ: Barnes & Noble; 1986), 59–70.

Keith Hollingsworth, "*A Passage to India*: The Echoes in the Marabar Caves," *Criticism* 4 (Summer 1962): 210–24. Reprinted in *Perspectives on E. M. Forster's "A Passage to India*," ed. Vasant A. Shahane (New York: Barnes & Noble, 1968), 36–50.

E. A. Horne, "Mr. Forster's *A Passage to India*," *NewS* 23 (16 August 1924): 543–44. Reprinted as "An Anglo-Indian View" in *E. M. Forster: The Critical Heritage*, ed. Philip Gardner (London: Routledge & Kegan Paul, 1973), 246–51.

Ellen Horowitz, "The Communal Ritual and the Dying God in E. M. Forster's *A Passage to India*," *Criticism* 6 (Winter 1964): 70–88.

John Dixon Hunt, "Muddle and Mystery in *A Passage to India*," *ELH* 33 (December 1966): 497–517.

Paul G. Italia, "On Miss Quested's Given Name, in E. M. Forster's *A Passage to India*," *ELN* 11 (December 1973): 118–20.

Paul G. Italia, "Under the Rules of Time: Story and Plot in E. M. Forster's *A Passage to India*," *ELN* 27 (March 1990): 58–62.

Richard M. Kain, "Vision and Discovery in E. M. Forster's *A Passage to India*," in *Twelve Original Essays on Great English Novels*, ed. Charles Shapiro (Detroit: Wayne State University Press, 1960), 253–75.

Francesca Kazan, "Confabulations in *A Passage to India*," *Criticism* 29 (Spring 1987): 197–214.

W. A. S. Keir, "*A Passage to India* Reconsidered," *CamJ* 5 (April 1952): 426–35. Reprinted in *Twentieth Century Interpretations of "A Passage to India": A Collection of Critical Essays*, ed. Andrew Rutherford (Englewood Cliffs, NJ: Prentice-Hall, 1970), 33–44.

Frank Kermode, "Mr. E. M. Forster as Symbolist," *Listener* 59 (2 January 1958): 17–18. Reprinted as "The One Orderly Product: E. M. Forster," in *Puzzles and Epiphanies: Essays and Reviews, 1958–1961* (London: Routledge & Kegan Paul, 1962), 79–85; as "Mr. E. M. Forster as Symbolist" in *Forster: A Collection of Critical Essays*, ed. Malcolm Bradbury (Englewood Cliffs, NJ: Prentice-Hall, 1966), 90–95; as "The One Orderly Product," in *E. M. Forster: "A Passage to India": A Casebook*, ed. Malcolm Bradbury (London: Macmillan, 1970), 216–23.

Arnold Kettle, "E. M. Forster: *A Passage to India*," in *An Introduction to the English Novel, II: Henry James to the Present* (London: Hutchinson, 1953), 152–63. Reprinted in part in *Twentieth Century Interpretations of "A Passage to India": A Collection of Critical Essays*, ed. Andrew Rutherford (Englewood Cliffs, NJ: Prentice-Hall, 1970), 45–49.

G. Kilner, "Some Questions of Interpretation in *A Passage to India*," *UofE* 16 (Summer 1965): 302–07.

A. G. Krasil'nikov, "Obshchestvenno-politicheskaia problematika romana E. M. Forstera *Poezdka v Indiiu*," *FN* 6, no. 156 (1986): 32–37.

Françoise Lafourçade, "Symbole, Symbolisme et Prophe/tie dans *A Passage to India*," *Caliban* 9 (1972): 122–34.

FORSTER, E. M., *A Passage to India*

Naomi Lebowitz, "*A Passage to India*: History as Humanist Humor," in *Humanism and the Absurd in the Modern Novel* (Evanston, IL: Northwestern University Press, 1971), 67–83.

E. F. C. Ludowyk, "Return to *A Passage to India*," in *A Garland for E. M. Forster*, ed. H. H. Anniah Gowda (Mysore, India: The Literary Half-Yearly, 1969), 41–47.

Hugh Maclean, "The Structure of *A Passage to India*," *UTQ* 22 (January 1953): 157–71. Reprinted in *Perspectives on E. M. Forster's "A Passage to India*," ed. Vasant A. Shahane (New York: Barnes & Noble, 1968), 19–33.

James McConkey, "The Prophetic Novel: *A Passage to India*, in *Perspectives on E. M. Forster's "A Passage to India*," ed. Vasant A. Shahane (New York: Barnes & Noble, 1968), 77–90. Reprinted in *E. M. Forster, "A Passage to India*," ed. Malcolm Bradbury (London: Macmillan, 1970), 154–64.

Walter R. McDonald, "Forster's *A Passage to India*," *Expl* 25 (March 1967): Item 54.

Walter R. McDonald, "The Unity of *A Passage to India*," *CEA* 36 (November 1973): 38–42.

M. M. Mahood, "Amritsar to Chandrapore: E. M. Forster and the Massacre," *Encounter* 41 (September 1973): 26–29.

John S. Martin, "Mrs. Moore and the Marabar Caves: A Mythological Reading," *MFS* 11 (Winter 1965–66): 429–33.

Sena Jeter Maslund, "Fantasy, Prophecy, and Point of View in *A Passage to India*," *SNNTS* 7 (Summer 1975): 258–76.

A. A. Mendilow, "The Triadic World of E. M. Forster," in *Studies in English Language and Literature*, ed. Alice Shalvi and A. A. Mendilow (Jerusalem: Hebrew University, 1966), 280–91.

Robert James Merrett, "E. M. Forster's Modernism: Tragic Faith in *A Passage to India*," *Mosaic* 17 (Summer 1984): 71–86.

Jeffrey Meyers, "The Politics of *Passage to India*," *JML* 1 (March 1971): 329–38. Reprinted as "E. M. Forster: *A Passage to India*," in *Fiction and the Colonial Experience* (Totawa, NJ: Rowman & Littlefield; Ipswich: Boydell, 1973), 29–54.

Marc Meyet, "*A Passage to India*: Notes on Forster's Scepticism," *EA&A* 2 (1964): 149–54.

Wendy Moffat, "*A Passage to India* and the Limits of Certainty," *JNT* 20 (Fall 1990): 331–41.

Jo Ann Hoeppner Moran, "E. M. Forster's *A Passage to India*: What Really Happened in the Caves," *MFS* 34 (Winter 1988): 596–604.

Ronald Moran, "'Come, Come,' 'Boum, Boum,' 'Easy' Rhythm in E. M. Forster's *A Passage to India*," *BSUF* 9 (Spring 1968): 3–9.

A. L. Morton, "An Englishman Discovers India," in *The Matter of Britain: Essays on a Living Culture* (London: Laurence & Wishart, 1966), 150–54.

Edwin M. Moseley, "Christ as One Avatar: Forster's *Passage to India*," in *Pseudonyms of Christ in the Modern Novel: Motifs and Methods* (Pittsburgh: University of Pittsburgh Press, 1962), 153–63.

Meenakshi Mukherjee, "The Poem for Mr. Bhattacharya," *LCrit* 16, no. 1 (1981): 33–41.

Sujit Mukherjee, "The Marabar Mystery: An Addition to the Case-Book on the Caves," *CE* 27 (March 1966): 501–03.

K. Natwar-Singh, "Only Connect. . .E. M. Forster and India," in *Aspects of E. M. Forster*, ed. Oliver Stallybrass (New York: Harcourt, Brace, 1969), 37–50. Revised and reprinted in *A Garland for E. M. Forster*, ed. H. H. Anniah Gowda (Mysore, India: The Literary Half-Yearly, 1969), 105–14. Reprinted and abridged. as "The Face of a Friend," *'Magazine'* (19 April 1969): 1. Reprinted as "Only Connect . . . : Forster and India," in *E. M. Forster's "A Passage to India,"* ed. Harold Bloom (New York: Chelsea House, 1987), 45–56.

Harland Nelson, "Shonfield and Forster's India: A Controversial Exchange," *Encounter* 30 (June 1968): 95.

Edwin Nierenberg, "The Withered Priestess: Mrs. Moore's Incomplete Passage to India," *MLQ* 25 (June 1964): 198–204. Reprinted in *Perspectives on E. M. Forster's "A Passage to India,"* ed. Vasant A. Shahane (New York: Barnes & Noble, 1968), 66–72.

Bhagwanjee Ojha, "*A Passage to India*: Beyond the 'Personal' Parlour," in *Modern Studies and Other Essays in Honour of Dr. R. K. Sinha*, ed. R. C. Prasad and A. K. Sharma (New Delhi: Vikas, 1987), 80–88.

Benita Parry, "Passage to More than India," in *Forester: A Collection of Critical Essays*, ed. Malcolm Bradbury (Englewood Cliffs, NJ: Prentice-Hall, 1966), 106–16. Reprinted in *Perspectives on E. M. Forster's "A Passage to India,"* ed. Vasant A. Shahane (New York: Barnes & Noble, 1968), 151–68.

Benita Parry, "The Politics of Representation in *A Passage to India*," in *A Passage to India: Essays in Interpretation*, ed. John Beer (Totowa, NJ: Barnes & Noble, 1986), 27–43.

Glenn Pederson, "Forster's Symbolic Form," *KR* 21 (Spring 1959): 231–49.

FORSTER, E. M., *A Passage to India*

Alice Hall Petry, "Fantasy, Prophesy, and *A Passage to India*," *DQR* 12, no. 2 (1982): 99–112.

K. J. Phillips, "Hindu Avatars, Moslem Martyrs, and Primitive Dying Gods in E. M. Forster's *A Passage to India*," *JML* 15 (Summer 1988): 121–40.

Ann Piroelle, "A Mutual Gift of Love: Forster and India," *CE&S* 11 (Autumn 1988): 32–45.

Ann Piroelle, "Order through Creation in a World of Chaos: E. M. Forster's Fiction," *CVE* 27 (April 1988): 63–71.

Nicholas Potter, "*A Passage to India*: The Crisis of 'Reasonable Form,'" *DUJ* 83 (July 1991): 209–13.

S. V. Pradhan, "Anglo-Indian Fiction and E. M. Forster," in *English and India: Essays Presented to Professor Samuel Mathai on His Seventieth Birthday*, ed. M. Manuel and K. Ayyappa Paniker (Madras, India: Wasani for Macmillan, 1978), 42–61.

S. V. Pradhan, "*A Passage to India*: Realism versus Symbolism, A Marxist Analysis," *DR* 60 (Summer 1980): 300–17.

S. V. Pradhan, "A 'Song' of Love: Forster's *A Passage to India*," *CentR* 17 (Summer 1973): 297–320.

Martin Price, "People of the Book: Character in Forster's *A Passage to India*," *CritI* 1 (March 1975): 605–22.

Kalimur Rahman, "Race Relations in *A Passage to India*," *Venture* 2 (March 1961): 56–59.

Shaista Rahman, "Onomastic Devices in Forster's *A Passage to India*," *LOS* 10 (1983): 55–74.

Tariq Rahman, "The Homosexual Aspect of Forster's *A Passage to India*," *SELit* Eng. no. (1984): 37–54.

Tariq Rahman, "Syed Ross Masood and E.M. Forster's *A Passage to India*," *ANQ* 4 (April 1991): 78–82.

M. L. Raina, "Imagery of *A Passage to India*: A Further Note," *ELT* 10, no. 1 (1967): 8–9.

M. L. Raina, "Traditional Symbolism and Forster's *Passage to India*," *N&Q* 13 (November 1966): 416–17.

J. A. Ramsaran, "An Indian Reading of E. M. Forster's Classic," *IbSE* 1 (1969): 48–55.

B. Syamal Rao, "E. M. Forster—*A Passage to India*," *Century* (4 July 1970): 9, 12.

Frances L. Restuccia, "'A Cave of My Own': E.M. Forster and Sexual Politics," *Raritan* 9 (Fall 1989): 110–19.

Barbara Rosecrance, "*A Passage to India*: Forster's Narrative Vision," in *E. M. Forster's "A Passage to India,"* ed. Harold Bloom (New York: Chelsea House, 1987), 75–90.

Barbara Rosecrance, "*A Passage to India*: The Dominant Voice," in *E. M. Forster: Centenary Revaluations*, ed. Judith Scherer Herz and Robert K. Martin (Toronto: University of Toronto Press, 1982), 234–43.

Chaman L. Sahni, "E. M. Forster's *A Passage to India*: The Islamic Dimension," *CVE* 17 (April 1983): 73–88.

Chaman L. Sahni, "The Marabar Caves in the Light of Indian Thought," in *Focus on Forster's "A Passage to India,"* ed. Vasant A. Shahane (Madras: Orient Longman, 1975), 105–14.

Paul Scott, "India: A Post-Forsterian View," in *Essays by Divers Hands* (London: Oxford University Press, 1970), 113–32.

Vasant A. Shahane, "Echoes of Plotinus in Forster's *A Passage to India,*" in *Approaches to E. M. Forster: A Centenary Volume*, ed. Vasant A. Shahane (New Delhi: Arnold-Heinemann; Atlantic Highlands, NJ: Humanities, 1981), 162–77.

Vasant A. Shahane, "Forster's *A Passage to India*, Chapter VII," *Expl* 26 (December 1967): Item 36.

Vasant A. Shahane, "Forster's Inner Passage to India," in *E. M. Forster: Centenary Revaluations*, ed. Judith Scherer Herz and Robert K. Martin (Toronto: University of Toronto Press, 1982), 267–77.

Vasant A. Shahane, "Mrs. Moore's Experience in the Marabar Caves: A Zen Buddhist Reading," *TCL* 31 (Summer–Fall 1985): 279–86.

Vasant A. Shahane, "A Note on the Marabar Caves in E. M. Foster's *A Passage to India,*" *OJES* 2 (1962): 67–75. Revised and reprinted as "The Marabar Caves: Fact and Fiction," *ANQ* 5 (September, October, November, December, 1966): 3–4, 20–21, 36–37, 54–55.

Vasant A. Shahane, "Search for a Synthesis," in *Focus on Forster's "A Passage to India,"* ed. Vasant A. Shahane (Madras: Orient Longman, 1975), 114–32.

Jenny Sharpe, "The Unspeakable Limits of Rape: Colonial Violence and Counter-Insurgency," *Genders* 10 (Spring 1991): 25–46.

Andrew Shonfield, "The Politics of Forster's India," *Encounter* 30 (January 1968): 62–69.

Andrew Shonfield, "Shonfield and Forster's India: A Controversial Exchange," *Encounter* 30 (June 1968): 95.

FORSTER, E. M., *A Passage to India*

David Shusterman, "The Curious Case of Professor Godbole: *A Passage to India* Re-examined," *PMLA* 76 (September 1961): 426–35. Reprinted in *Perspectives on E. M. Forster's "A Passage to India,"* ed. Vasant A. Shahane (New York: Barnes & Noble, 1968), 91–100. Revised and reprinted in *The Quest for Certitude in E. M. Forster's Fiction* (Bloomington: Indiana University Press, 1965), 182–202.

Brenda R. Silver, "Periphrasis, Power, and Rape in *A Passage to India,*" *Novel* 22 (Fall 1988): 86–105.

Brijraj Singh, "Mrs. Moore, Prof. Godbole and the Supernatural: Some Comments on *A Passage to India,*" *LCrit* 15, no. 2 (1980): 44–53.

Frances B. Singh, "*A Passage to India*, the National Movement, and Independence," *TCL* 31 (Summer–Fall 1985): 265–78.

M. Sivaramkrishna, "Epiphany and History: The Dialectic of Transcendence and *A Passage to India,*" in *Approaches to E. M. Forster: A Centenary Volume*, ed. Vasant A. Shahane (New Delhi: Arnold-Heinemann; Atlantic Highlands, NJ: Humanities, 1981), 148–61.

M. Sivaramkrishna, "Marabar Caves Revisited," in *Focus on Forster's "A Passage to India,"* ed. Vasant A. Shahane (Madras: Orient Longman, 1975), 5–17.

Lyle H. Smith, Jr. "What Fielding Missed: 'Special Effects' in Forster's *A Passage to India,*" *SMy* 8 (Fall 1985): 32–41.

Michael Spencer, "Hinduism to E. M. Forster's *A Passage to India,*" *JASt* 27 (February 1968): 281–95.

Gerhard Stebner, "E. M. Forster: *A Passage to India,*" in *Der Moderne Englische Roman, Interpretationen*, ed. Horst Oppel (Berlin: Eric Schmidt, 1965), 135–59.

Frederick C. Stern, "Never Resemble M. de Lesseps: A Note on *A Passage to India,*" *ELT* 14, no. 2 (1971): 119–21.

Douglas Alexander Stewart, "Irreconcilable India," in *The Flesh and the Spirit: An Outlook on Literature* (Sydney: Angus & Roberton, 1948), 17–24.

Wilfred Stone, "The Caves of *A Passage to India,*" in *A Passage to India: Essays in Interpretation*, ed. John Beer (Totowa, NJ: Barnes & Noble, 1986), 16–26.

Sara Suleri, "The Geography of *A Passage to India,*" in *E. M. Forster's "A Passage to India,"* ed. Harold Bloom (New York: Chelsea House, 1987), 107–13.

M. P. Taraporewala, "*A Passage to India*: Symphonic Symmetry," in *Siddha III*, ed. Frank D'Souza and Jagdish Shivpuri (Bombay: Siddarth College of Arts and Sciences, 1968), 58–86.

Roy Thomas and Howard Erskine–Hill, "*A Passage to India*: Two Points of View," *AWR* 15 (Summer 1965): 44–50.

George H. Thomson, "A Note on the Snake Imagery of *A Passage to India*," *ELT* 9, no. 2 (1966): 108–10.

George H. Thomson, "Thematic Symbol in *A Passage to India*," *TCL* 7 (July 1961): 51–63. Reprinted in *Perspectives on E. M. Forster's "A Passage to India*," ed. Vasant A. Shahane (New York: Barnes & Noble, 1968), 101–14.

Edwin Thumboo, "E. M. Forster's *A Passage to India*: From Caves to Court," *SoR* 10 (December 1978): 386–404.

Midori Uematsu, "Dokutsu no Naka no Hakken: E. M. Forster-Indo en Michi," in *Igirisu Shosetsu no Joseitachi*, ed. Yaeko Sumi and Naomi Okamura (Tokyo: Keiso, 1983), 199–218.

T. G. Vaidyanathan, "In Defense of Professor Godbole," in *Focus on Forster's "A Passage to India*," ed. Vasant A. Shahane (Madras: Orient Longman, 1975), 42–62.

Sarala Van Dover, "Beyond Words: Language and Its Limits in *A Passage to India*," *MidHLS* 11 (1988): 56–64.

K. Viswanatham, "Forster: *A Passage to India* (The Desperate View," in *India in English Fiction* (Waltair, India: Andhra University Press, 1971), 90–120.

C. Roland Wagner, "The Excremental and the Spiritual in *A Passage to India*," *MLQ* 21 (September 1970): 359–71.

Donald Watt, "E. M. Forster's Quarrel with the God–State," *PQ* 60 (Fall 1981): 523–37.

Donald Watt, "Mohammed el Adl and *A Passage to India*," *JML* 10 (June 1983): 311–26.

Hélène L. Webner, "E. M. Forster's Divine Comedy," *Renascence* 23 (Winter 1971): 98–110.

Richard R. Werry, "Rhythm in Forster's *A Passage to India*," in *Studies in Honor of John Wilcox*, ed. A. Dayle Wallace and Woodburn O. Ross (Detroit: Wayne State University Press, 1958), 227–37.

Gertrude M. White, "*A Passage to India*: Analysis and Revaluation," *PMLA* 68 (September 1953): 641–57. Reprinted in *Perspectives on E. M. Forster's "A Passage to India*," ed. Vasant A. Shahane (New York: Barnes & Noble, 1968), 1–17; Reprinted in *E. M. Forster's "A Passage to India": A Casebook*, ed. Malcolm Bradbury (London: Macmillan, 1970), 132–53. Reprinted in *Twentieth Century Interpretations of "A Passage to India": A Collection of Critical Essays*, ed. Andrew Rutherford (Englewood Cliffs, NJ: Prentice-Hall, 1970), 50–67.

"The Point of It"

Robert Friend, "The Theme of Salvation in 'The Point of It,'" in *Studies in English Language and Literature*, ed. Alice Shalvi and A. A. Mendilow (Jerusalem: The Hebrew University, 1966), 243–57.

"The Road from Colonus"

Steven Doloff, "Forster's 'The Road from Colonus,'" *Expl* 48 (Fall 1989): 20–21.

Robert Gordon, "Questions for Discussion: 'The Road from Colonus,'" in *The Expanded Moment: A Short Story Anthology* (Boston: Heath, 1963), 301–02.

Michael L. Storey, "Forster's 'The Road from Colonus,'" *Expl* 49 (Spring 1991): 170–73.

A Room with a View

Yoshio Abe, "Works: *A Room with a View*," in *E. M. Forster*, ed. Ineko Kondo (Toyko: Kenkyusha, 1967), 83–92.

Bonnie Blumenthal Finkelstein, "Forster's Women: *A Room with a View*," *ELT* 16, no. 4 (1973): 275–87. Revised and reprinted in *Forster's Women: Eternal Differences* (New York: Columbia University Press, 1973), 65–88.

David Leon Higdon, "Opus 3 or Opus 111 in Forster's *A Room with a View?*" *ELN* 28 (June 1991): 57–60.

Jeffrey Meyers, "'Vacant Heart and Hand and Eye': The Homosexual Theme in *A Room with a View*," *ELT* 13, no. 3 (1970): 181–92.

Tarq Rahman, "The Double-Plot in E. M. Forster's *A Room with a View*," *CVE* 33 (April 1991): 43–62.

Claude J. Summers, "The Meaningful Ambiguity of Giotto in *A Room with a View*," *ELT* 30, no. 2 (1987): 165–76.

Philip C. Wagner, Jr., "Phaethon, Persephone, and *A Room with a View*," *CLS* 27 (Fall 1990): 275–84.

Gerda van Woudenberg, "'Van Orlando's viooltjes' en E. M. Forster's roman: *A Room with a View*," *NTg* 75 (May 1982): 254–56.

Where Angels Fear to Tread

Yoshio Abe, "Works: *Where Angels Fear to Tread*," in *E. M. Forster*, ed. Ineko Kondo (Toyko: Kenkyusha, 1967), 58–68.

Tariq Rahman, "A Study of the Under-Plot in E. M. Forster's *Where Angels Fear To Tread*," *SELit* (1988): 51–69.

Alan Wilde, "The Aesthetic View of Life: *Where Angels Fear to Tread*," *MFS* 7 (Autumn 1961): 207–16. Reprinted in *Art and Order: A Study of E. M. Forster* (New York: New York University Press, 1964), 16–27.

FOWLES, JOHN

The Aristos

Peter Brandt, "In Search of the Eighth Man: A Study of John Fowles," *RCEI* 7 (November 1983): 39–59.

"The Cloud"

Arnold E. Davidson, "The Barthesian Configuration of John Fowles's 'The Cloud,'" *CentR* 28–29 (Fall–Winter 1984–85): 80–93.

Raymond J. Wilson, III, "Allusion and Implication in John Fowles's 'The Cloud,'" *SSF* 20 (Winter 1983): 17–22.

The Collector

Syhamal Bagchee, "*The Collector*: The Paradoxical Imagination of John Fowles," *JML* 8, no. 2 (1980–81): 219–34.

Patricia V. Beatty, "John Fowles' Clegg: Captive Landlord of Eden," *Ariel* 13 (July 1982): 73–81.

David Leon Higdon, "The Epigraph to John Fowles's *The Collector*," *MFS* 32 (Winter 1986): 568–72.

"Miranda Removed," *TLS* (17 May 1963):353.

John M. Neary, "John Fowles's Clegg: A Metaphysical Rebel," *ELWIU* 15 (Spring 1988): 45–61.

Perry Nodelman, "John Fowles's Variations in *The Collector*," *ConL* 28 (Fall 1987): 332–46.

Oriana Palusci, "*The Collector* di John Fowles: 'We Are Such Stuff as Media Are Made On,'" in *La Performance del Testo*, ed. Franco Marucci and Adriano Bruttini (Siena: Ticci, 1986), 349–58.

Laurence Vincent–Durroux, "Points de vue et changements de points de vue dans *The Collector* de John Fowles," *BACLA* 11 (Spring 1989): 65–70.

Daniel Martin

Robert Alter, "*Daniel Martin* and the Mimetic Task," *Genre* 14 (Spring 1981): 65–78.

Robert Arlett, "*Daniel Martin* and the Contemporary Epic Novel," *MFS* 31 (Spring 1985): 173–85.

Carol Barnum, "John Fowles's *Daniel Martin*: A Vision of Whole Sight," *LitR* 25 (Fall 1981): 64–79.

Patricia J. Boomsma, "'Whole Sight': Fowles, Lukacs and *Daniel Martin*," *JML* 8, no. 2 (1980–81): 325–36.

Kathryn A. Chittick, "The Laboratory of Narrative and John Fowles's *Daniel Martin*," *ESC* 11 (March 1985): 70–81.

Ina Ferris, "Realist Intention and Mythic Impulse in *Daniel Martin*," *JNT* 12 (Spring 1982): 146–53.

Paul H. Lorenz, "Epiphany among the Ruins: Etruscan Places in John Fowles's *Daniel Martin*," *TexasR* 11 (Spring–Summer 1990): 78–86.

Kerry McSweeney, "Withering into the Truth: John Fowles and *Daniel Martin*," *CritQ* 20 (Winter 1978): 31–38.

Sue Park, "John Fowles, *Daniel Martin*, and Simon Wolfe," *MFS* 31 (Spring 1985): 165–71.

Sue Park, "Time and Ruins in John Fowles's *Daniel Martin*," *MFS* 31 (Spring 1985): 157–63.

The Ebony Tower

Timothy C. Alderman, "The Enigma of *The Ebony Tower*: A Genre Study," *MFS* 31 (Spring 1985): 135–47.

Carol M. Barnum, "The Quest Motif in John Fowles's *The Ebony Tower*; Theme and Variations," *TSLL* 23 (Spring 1981): 138–57.

Arnold E. Davidson, "Eliduc and *The Ebony Tower*: John Fowles's Variation on a Medieval Lay," *IFR* 11 (Winter 1984): 31–36.

Frederick M. Holmes, "Fictional Self-Consciousness in John Fowles's *The Ebony Tower*," *Ariel* 16 (July 1985): 21–38.

John B. Humma, "John Fowles' *The Ebony Tower*: In the Celtic Mood," *SoHR* 17 (Winter 1983): 33–47.

Frank Kersnowski, "John Fowles' *The Ebony Tower*: A Discourse with Critics," *JSSE* 13 (Autumn 1989): 57–64.

Ellen McDaniel, "Fowles as Collector: The Failed Artists of *The Ebony Tower*," *PLL* 23 (Winter 1987): 70–83.

Kerry McSweeney, "John Fowles's Variations in *The Ebony Tower*," *JML* 8, no. 2 (1980–81): 303–24.

Rimgaila Salys, "The Medieval Context of John Fowles's *The Ebony Tower*," *Critique* 25 (Fall 1983): 11–24.

James W. Sollisch, "The Passion of Existence: John Fowles's *The Ebony Tower*," *Critique* 25 (Fall 1983): 1–9.

Raymond J. Wilson, III, "Ambiguity in John Fowles' *The Ebony Tower*," *NConL* 12 (November 1982): 6–8.

Raymond J. Wilson, III, "John Fowles's *The Ebony Tower*: Unity and Celtic Myth," *TCL* 28 (Fall 1982): 302–18.

"The Enigma"

Ulrich Broich, "John Fowles, 'The Enigma' and the Contemporary British Short Story," in *Modes of Narrative: Approaches to American, Canadian and British Fiction*, ed. Reingard M. Nischik and Barbara Korte (Wurzburg: Konigshausen & Neumann, 1990), 179–89.

David Brownell, "John Fowles' Experiments with the Form of the Mystery Story," *ArmD* 10 (April 1977): 184–86.

Thomas D. O'Donnell, "Generic Discontinuity in Fowles' 'Enigma,'" Paper read at the session entitled "Fowles's Games" at the University of Louisville Conference on Twentieth-Century Literature, February 1979.

The French Lieutenant's Woman

Ian Adam, Patrick Brantlinger, and Sheldon Rothblatt, "*The French Lieutenant's Woman*: A Discussion," *VS* 15 (March 1972): 339–56.

I. V. Arnol'd and N. Ia. D'iakonova, "Avtorskii kommentarii v romane Dzhona Faulza Zhenshchina frantsuzskogo leitenanta," *IAT* 44 (September–October 1985): 393–405.

Judith Barnoin, "Quand le miroir se fend: Identite et alterite dans *The French Lieutenant's Woman* de John Fowles," *Cycnos* 2 (Winter 1985–1986): 41–49.

FOWLES, JOHN, *The French Lieutenant's Woman*

Mirella Billi, "Dialogismo testuale e parodia in *The French Lieutenant's Woman* di John Fowles," *RLMC* 41 (April–June 1988): 165–80.

M. Keith Booker, "What We Have Instead of God: Sexuality, Textuality and Infinity in *The French Lieutenant's Woman,*" *Novel* 24 (Winter 1991): 178–98.

Lucien le Bouille, "L'oeuvre de John Fowles: Esquisse de Quelques Grandes Lignes," in *Études sur "The French Lieutenant's Woman" de John Fowles* (Caen: Centre National de Documentation Pédagogique, 1977), 9–14.

Jerome Bump, "The Narrator as Protoreader in *The French Lieutenant's Woman,*" *VN* 74 (Fall 1988): 16–18.

Deborah Byrd, "The Evolution and Emancipation of Sarah Woodruff: *The French Lieutenant's Woman* as a Feminist Novel," *IJWS* 7 (September–October 1984): 306–21.

Jean-Claude Castangt and Rene Gallet, "La Symbolique Spatiale," in *Études sur "The French Lieutenant's Woman" de John Fowles* (Caen: Centre National de Documentation Pédagogique, 1977), 43–50.

Jean-Claude Castangt and Rene Gallet, "Quelques Aspects des Relations entre Personnages," in *Études sur "The French Lieutenant's Woman" de John Fowles* (Caen: Centre National de Documentation Pédagogique, 1977), 25–33.

Dominique Catherine and Ginette Emprin, "Aspects de la Technique Narrative: Les Relatonsh Narrateur/Lecteur/Personages," in *Études sur "The French Lieutenant's Woman" de John Fowles* (Caen: Centre National de Documentation Pédagogique, 1977), 15–23.

Philip Cohen, "Postmodernist Technique in *The French Lieutenant's Woman,*" *WHR* 38 (Summer 1984): 148–61.

Richard Hauer Costa, "Trickery's Mixed Bag: The Perils of Fowles' *French Lieutenant's Woman,*" *RMR* 29 (Spring 1975): 1–9.

Gerald Doherty, "The Secret Plot of Metaphor: Rhetorical Designs in John Fowles's *The French Lieutenant's Woman,*" *Paragraph* 9 (March 1987): 49–68.

Walter Gobbers, "John Fowles en de deconstructie van de historische roman," *Restant* 15, no. 2 (1987): 315–33.

Margaret Bozenna Goscilo, "John Fowles's Pre–Raphaelite Woman: Interart Strategies and Gender Politics," *Mosaic* 26 (Spring 1993): 63–84.

Patricia L. Hagen, "Revision Revisited: Reading (and) *The French Lieutenant's Woman,*" *CE* 53 (April 1991): 439–51.

John V. Hagopian, "Bad Faith in *The French Lieutenant's Woman,*" *ConL* 23 (Spring 1982): 190–201.

Elisabeth Hellegouarc'h and Sylviane Troadec, "L'image du Victorianisme," in *Études sur "The French Lieutenant's Woman" de John Fowles* (Caen: Centre National de Documentation Pédagogique, 1977), 35–42.

Ken Hogan, "Fowles' Narrative Style in *The French Lieutenant's Woman*," *CCTEP* 48 (September 1983): 54–63.

Frederick M. Holmes, "The Novel, Illusion, and Reality: The Paradox of Omniscience in *The French Lieutenant's Woman*," *JNT* 11 (Fall 1981): 184–98.

Sung Joo Hong, " A Study of Multiple Ending in *The French Lieutenant's Woman*: A Trace of Fowles' Disconcerting Voice," *JELL* 38 (Fall 1992): 571–84.

Linda Hutcheon, "The 'Real World(s)' of Fiction: *The French Lieutenant's Woman*," *ESC* 4 (Spring 1978): 81–94.

K. R. Ireland, "Towards a Grammar of Narrative Sequence: The Model of *The French Lieutenant's Woman*," *PoT* 7, no. 3 (1986): 397–420.

Susana Onega Jaen, "Form and Meaning in *The French Lieutenant's Woman*," *RCEI* 13–14 (April 1987): 77–107.

A. J. B. Johnson, "Realism in *The French Lieutenant's Woman*," *JML* 8, no. 2 (1980–81): 287–302.

Douglas B. Johnstone, "The 'Unplumb'd, Salt Estranging' Tragedy of *The French Lieutenant's Woman*," *AI* 42 (Spring 1985): 69–83.

Steven G. Kellman, "Fictive Freedom through *The French Lieutenant's Woman*," *UMSE* 4 (1983): 159–67.

Brunilda Reichmann Lemos, "Fowles' Godgame: Characters and Conclusions in *The French Lieutenant's Woman*," *RLet* 32 (1983): 85–93.

Magali Cornier Michael, " 'Who Is Sarah?' A Critique of *The French Lieutenant's Woman*'s Feminism," *Critique* 28 (Summer 1987): 225–36.

Nan Miller, "Christina Rossetti and Sarah Woodruff: Two Remedies for a Divided Self," *PreRR* 3 (November 1982): 68–77.

William Nelles, "Problems for Narrative Theory: *The French Lieutenant's Woman*," *Style* 18 (Spring 1984): 207–17.

Byung joo Park, "*The French Lieutenant's Woman*: A Parody of Victorian Fiction," *JELL* 38 (Fall 1992): 315–39.

Luisa Pontrandolfo, "Alcune osservazioni sul romanzo metanarrativo *The French Lieutenant's Woman* di John Fowles," in *La performance del testo*, ed. Franco Marucci and Adriano Bruttini (Siena: Ticci, 1986), 245–51.

Elizabeth D. Rankin, "Cryptic Coloration in *The French Lieutenant's Woman*," *JNT* 3 (September 1973): 193–207.

Charles Scruggs, "The Two Endings of *The French Lieutenant's Woman*," *MFS* 31 (Spring 1985): 95–113.

Evelyn Sweet–Hurd, "Victorian Echoes in John Fowles's *The French Lieutenant's Woman*," *NConL* 13 (March 1983): 2–5.

Yuan-huang Ts'ai, "Fa kuo chung wei te nu jen—tso che yu tso p'in te cheng ho," *CWLM* 13 (January 1985): 138–59.

A Maggot

Jacques Chouleur, "John Fowles et les Shakers," *MCRel* 7 (1989): 61–71.

David Essex, "Review of John Fowles' *A Maggot*: The Novel as Koan," *ECLife* 10 (January 1986): 80–81.

Frederick M. Holmes, "History, Fiction, and the Dialogic Imagination: John Fowles's *A Maggot*," *ConL* 32 (Summer 1991): 229–43.

Pierre E. Monnin, "Cumulative Strangeness Without and Within *A Maggot* by J. Fowles," in *On Strangeness*, ed. Margaret Bridges (Tubingen: Narr, 1990), 151–62.

The Magus

Michael H. Begnal, "A View of John Fowles' *The Magus*," *ModBL* 3 (Fall 1978): 67–72.

Michael Boccia, "Feminism in *The Magus* by John Fowles," *NHCL* 6 (Spring 1989): 59–70.

Jean-Louis Chevalier, "Ailleurs, autrefois, autrement: L'Utopie du 'plan du conduite' dans *The Magus* de John Fowles," in *De William Shakespeare à William Golding: Mélanges dediés à la mémoire de Jean-Pierre Vernier*, preface by Sylvére Monod (Rouen: Université de Rouen, 1984), 27–43.

John A. Fossa, "Through Seeking to Mystery: A Reappraisal of John Fowles' *The Magus*," *OL* 44, no. 2 (1989): 161–80.

Dominique Gauthier, "Le Sourire du Kouros, ou: La Grece, le beau et le vrai dans *The Magus* de John Fowles," *Cycnos* 7 (1991): 85–95.

Frederick M. Holmes, "Art, Truth, and John Fowles's *The Magus*," *MFS* 31 (Spring 1985): 45–56.

Frederick M. Holmes, "The Novelist as Magus: John Fowles and the Function of Narrative," *DR* 68 (Fall 1988): 288–301.

Barbara L. Hussey, "John Fowles's *The Magus*: The Book and the World," *IFR* 10 (Winter 1983): 19–26.

Ellen McDaniel, "*The Magus*: Fowles's Tarot Quest," *JML* 8, no. 2 (1980–81): 247–60.

Ellen McDaniel, "Tarot Cards and Games in *The Magus*," Paper delivered at the session entitled "Tarot And Literature" at the University of Louisville Conference on Twentieth-Century Literature, February 1979.

Robert L. Nadeau, "Fowles and Physics: A Study of *The Magus*: A Revised Version," *JML* 8, no. 2 (1980–81): 261–74.

Robert D. Newman, "'An Anagram Made Flesh': The Transformation of Nicholas Urfe in Fowles' *The Magus*," *NConL* 12 (September 1982): 9.

George H. Nilsen, "Games and Fowles' *The Magus*," Paper read at the session enbtitled "Fowles's Games," at the University of Louisville Conference on Twentieth-Century Literature, February 1979.

Frank G. Novak Jr., "The Dialectics of Debasement in *The Magus*," *MFS* 31 (Spring 1985): 71–82.

Barry N. Olshen, "John Fowles's *The Magus*: An Allegory of Self-Realization," *JPC* 9 (Spring 1977): 916–25.

William J. Palmer, "Fowles' *The Magus*: The Vortex as Myth, Metaphor, and Masque," in *The Power of Myth in Literature and Film*, ed. Victor Carrabino (Tallahassee: University Press of Florida, 1980), 66–76.

Delma E. Presley, "The Quest of the Bourgeois Hero: An Approach ot Fowles' *The Magus*," *JPC* 6 (Fall 1972): 394–98.

Julius Rowan Raper, "John Fowles: The Psychological Complexity of *The Magus*," *AI* 45 (Spring 1988): 61–83.

Wolfgang Steuhl, "Der Roman als Romankritik: John Fowles' *The Magus*," *Sprachkunst* 16, no. 1 (1985): 74–97.

Yoshiko Takakuwa, "John Fowles no Sekai: Majutsushi o chushin ni," *EigoS* 130 (1984): 314–18.

J. A. Wainwright, "The Illusion of 'Things as they are': *The Magus*: versus *The Magus: A Revised Version*," *DR* 63 (Spring 1983): 107–19.

Mantissa

H. W. Fawkner, "The Neurocognitive Significance of John Fowles's *Mantissa*," *SN* 56, no. 1 (1984): 51–59.

FOWLES, JOHN, *Poor Koko*

John Haegert, "Memoirs of a Deconstructive Angel: The Heroine as *Mantissa* in the Fiction of John Fowles," *ConL* 27 (Summer 1986): 160–81.

Poor Koko

Michele Hita, "The Social Function of Literature and the 'Literatured': *Poor Koko*, a Novella by John Fowles," *Caliban* 27 (1990): 27–33.

Paulette Michel-Michot, "Fowles's *Poor Koko:* A Metaphor of the Quest," in *Multiple Worlds, Multiple Words: Essays in Honour of Irene Simon,* ed. Hena Maes-Jelinek, Pierre Michel, and Paulette Michel-Michot (Liege: Université de Liege, 1987), 203–11.

The Tree

Jamie Dopp, "Fathers and Sons: Fowles's *The Tree* and Autobiographical Theory," *Mosaic* 22 (Fall 1989): 31–44.

FRANCIS, DICK

Banker

Elaine Bander, "The Least Likely Victim in Dick Francis's *Banker*," *Clues* 13 (Spring–Summer 1992): 11–19.

Blood Sport

Melvyn Barnes, "The Hero as Reluctant Peer, Weary Agent," in *Dick Francis* (New York: Ungar, 1986), 59–64.

Dead Cert

Melvyn Barnes, "The Hero as Jockey, Hate Object, and Spy," in *Dick Francis* (New York: Ungar, 1986), 9–21.

Forfeit

Melvyn Barnes, "The Hero as Reluctant Peer, Weary Agent," in *Dick Francis* (New York: Ungar, 1986), 65–71.

For Kicks

Melvyn Barnes, "The Hero as Jockey, Hate Object, and Spy," in *Dick Francis* (New York: Ungar, 1986), 29–36.

Flying Finish

Melvyn Barnes, "The Hero as Reluctant Peer, Weary Agent," in *Dick Francis* (New York: Ungar, 1986), 53–56.

Albert E. Wilhelm, "Finding the True Self: Rites of Passage in Dick Francis's *Flying Finish*," *Clues* 9 (Fall–Winter 1988): 1–8.

Nerve

Melvyn Barnes, "The Hero as Jockey, Hate Object, and Spy," in *Dick Francis* (New York: Ungar, 1986), 22–28.

Odds Against

Melvyn Barnes, "The Hero as Halley," in *Dick Francis* (New York: Ungar, 1986), 37–44.

Proof

Albert E. Wilhelm, "Fathers and Sons in Dick Francis' *Proof*," *Critique* 32 (Spring 1991): 169–78.

Whip Hand

Melvyn Barnes, "The Hero as Halley," in *Dick Francis* (New York: Ungar, 1986), 45–52.

GALSWORTHY, JOHN

The Forsyte Saga

Adele M. Dalsimer, "A Not So Simple Saga: Kate O'Brien's Without My Cloak," *EI* 21 (Fall 1986): 55–71.

GALSWORTHY, JOHN, *The Forsyte Saga: The Man of Property*

Ia. I. Ts'ovkh, "Esteticheskaia funktsiia kolorita v Forsaitovskom Tsikle Dzh," *Golsuorsi* 4, no. 130 (1982): 32–37.

The Forsyte Saga: The Man of Property

M. I. Chizhevskaia, "O rechevoi kharakteristike literaturnogo personazha: Na materiale romana Dzhona Golsuorsi Sobstvennik," *FN* 1, no. 145 (1985): 36–40.

Pu Shi, "On *The Forsyte Saga*," *FLitS* 34 (December 1986): 3–10.

Meiyun Yue, "Linguistic Features and Author's Message," *Waiguoyu* 3 (May 1986): 68-71.

"The Japanese Quince"

Nathan Cervo, "Galsworthy's 'The Japanese Quince,'" *Expl* 47 (Winter 1989): 38–42.

Doris Lanier, "The Blackbird in John Galsworthy's 'The Japanese Quince,'" *ELN* 30 (December 1992): 57–62.

GALT, JOHN

The Ayrshire Legatees

Keith M. Costain, "The Epistolary Novel and John Galt's *The Ayrshire Legatees*," in *John Galt: Reappraisals*, ed. Elizabeth Waterston (Guelph: University of Guelph, 1985), 72–96.

Bogle Corbet

Martin Bowman, "*Bogle Corbet* and the Sentimental Romance," in *John Galt: Reappraisals*, ed. Elizabeth Waterson (Guelph: University of Guelph, 1985), 63–71.

Robert J. Graham, "John Galt's *Bogle Corbet*: A Parable of Progress," *ScLJ* 13 (November 1986): 31–47.

Elizabeth Waterston, "*Bogle Corbet* and the Annals of New World Parishes," in *John Galt: Reappraisals*, ed. Elizabeth Waterson (Guelph: University of Guelph, 1985), 57–62.

The Entail

J. D. McClure, "The Language of *The Entail*," *SclJ* 8 (May 1981): 30–51.

The Last of the Lairds

H. B. de Groot, "The Narrative Perspective of *The Last of the Lairds*," in *John Galt: Reappraisals*, ed. Elizabeth Waterston (Guelph: University of Guelph, 1985), 97–108.

The Provost

R. H. Carnie, "Names in John Galt's *The Provost*," in *Scott and His Influence*, ed. J. H. Alexander and David Hewitt (Aberdeen: Association for Scottish Literary Studies, 1983), 293–311.

Ringan Gilhaize

Patricia J. Wilson, "*Ringan Gilhaize*: The Product of an Informing Vision," *ScLJ* 8 (May 1981): 52–68.

GASKELL, ELIZABETH CLEGHORN

Cousin Phillis

Pearl Brown, "The Pastoral and Anti-Pastoral in Elizabeth Gaskell's *Cousin Phillis*," *VN* 82 (Fall 1992): 22–27.

Wendy Craik, "Lore and Learning in *Cousin Phillis*, I," *GSJ* 3 (Summer 1989): 68–80.

Cranford

Vincent J. Bowes, "The Issue of Centrality in Elizabeth Gaskell's *Cranford*," *DR* 69 (Fall 1989): 366–73.

Wendy K. Carse, "A Penchant for Narrative: 'Mary Smith' in Elizabeth Gaskell's *Cranford*," *JNT* 20 (Fall 1990): 318-30.

Martin Dodsworth, "Women Without Men at Cranford," *EIC* 13 (1963): 132–45.

Rowena Fowler, "*Cranford*: Cow in Grey Flannel or Lion Couchant?" *SEL* 24 (Autumn 1984): 717–29.

Eileen Gillooly, "Humor as Daughterly Defense in *Cranford*," *ELH* 59 (Winter 1992): 883–910.

George V. Griffith, "What Kind of Book Is *Cranford*?" *Ariel* 14 (April 1983): 53–65.

Andrew H. Miller, "Subjectivity Ltd: The Discourse of Liability in The Joint Stock Companies Act of 1856 and Gaskell's *Cranford*," *ELH* 61 (Spring 1994): 139–57.

James Mulvihill, "Economies of Living in Mrs. Gaskell's *Cranford*," *NCF* 50, no. 3 (December 1995): 337–66.

Thomas E. Recchio, "*Cranford* and 'the Lawe of Kynde,'" *GSJ* 1 (Summer 1987): 10–26.

Hilary M. Schor, "Affairs of the Alphabet: Reading, Writing and Narrating in *Cranford*," *Novel* 22 (Spring 1989): 288–304.

John Scotton, "Rev. John Jenkyns in *Cranford*," *N&Q* 12 (1965): 194.

Margaret Tarratt, "*Cranford* and 'the Strict Code of Gentility,'" *EIC* 18 (1968): 152–63.

Seiko Tsuda, "*Cranford*: Gaskell Fujin to Amazon tachi," in *Igirisu no Katari to Shiten no Shosetsu*, ed. Takeshi Uchida (Tokyo: Tokai Daigaku; 1983), 125–64.

Patricia A. Wolfe, "Structure and Movement in *Cranford*," *NCF* 23 (Spring 1968): 161–78.

Edgar Wright, "Mrs. Gaskell and the World of *Cranford*," *RevEL* 6, no. 1 (1965): 68–79.

P. J. Yarrow, "The Chronology of *Cranford*," *GSJ* 1 (Summer 1987): 27–29.

"The Grey Woman"

Maureen T. Reddy, "Gaskell's 'The Grey Woman': A Feminist Palimpsest," *JNT* 15 (Spring 1985): 183–93.

"Lizzie Leigh"

Joanne Thompson, "Faith of Our Mothers: Elizabeth Gaskell's 'Lizzie Leigh,'" *VN* 78 (Fall 1990): 22–26.

Mary Barton

Rudolf Beck, "'Romance' und 'Truth': Mrs. Gaskells Schwierigkeiten beim Schreiben der Wahrheit," *Anglia* 108, no. 1–2 (1990): 50–74.

Suzann Bick, "'Take Her Up Tenderly': Elizabeth Gaskell's Treatment of the Fallen Woman," *EAS* 18 (May 1989): 17–27.

D. S. Bland, "*Mary Barton* and Historical Accuracy," *RES* 1 (1950): 58–60.

Rosemarie Bodenheimer, "Private Grief and Public Acts in *Mary Barton*," *DSA* 9 (1981): 195–216.

John C. Hawley, S.J., "*Mary Barton*: The Inside View from Without," *NCS* 3 (Winter 1989): 23–30.

Annette B. Hopkins, "*Mary Barton*: A Victorian Best Seller," *Trollopian* 3 (1948): 1–18.

Elaine Jordan, "Spectres and Scorpians: Allusion and Confusion in *Mary Barton*," *L&H* 7 (Spring 1981): 48–61.

James Ogden, "Allusions to Shakespeare in *Mary Barton*," *N&Q* 31 (December 1984): 488-89.

Arthur Pollard, "Faith and Family: Fundamental Values in *Mary Barton*," *GSJ* 3 (Summer 1989): 1–5.

Thomas E. Recchio, "The Problem of Form in Mrs. Gaskell's *Mary Barton*: A Study of Mythic Patterning in Realistic Fiction," *SEL* (1984): 19–35.

Kathleen Tillotson, "*Mary Barton*," in *Novels of the Eighteen-Forties* (Oxford: Clarendon, 1954), 202–23.

Michael Wheeler, "The Writer as Reader in *Mary Barton*," *DUJ* 67 (1974): 92–102.

My Lady Ludlow

Christine L. Krueger, "The 'Female Paternalist' as Historian: Elizabeth Gaskell's *My Lady Ludlow*," in *Rewriting the Victorians: Theory History and the Politics of Gender*, ed. Linda M. Shires (New York: Routledge, 1992), 166–83.

Edgar Wright, "*My Lady Ludlow*: Forms of Social Change and Forms of Fiction, I," *GSJ* 3 (Summer 1989): 29–41.

North and South

Elizabeth Bowen, "Introduction to *North and South*," in *North and South* (London: John Lehmann, 1951), v–viii. Revised and reprinted in Elizabeth Bowen, *Seven Winters Memories of a Dublin Childhood & Afterthoughts: Pieces on Writing* (New York: Knopf, 1951), 139–47.

J. A. V. Chapple, "*North and South*: A Reassessment," *EIC* 17 (1965): 461–72.

Françoise Defromont, "Amour, machine dans *North and South*," *CVE* 31 (April 1990): 93–101.

Dorice Williams Elliott, "The Female Visitor and the Marriage of Classes in Gaskell's *North and South*," *NCL* 49 (June 1994): 21–49.

P. N. Furbank, "Mendacity in Mrs. Gaskell," *Encounter* 40, no. 6 (1973): 5155.

Barbara Leah Harman, "In Promiscuous Company: Female Public Appearance in Elizabeth Gaskell's *North and South*," *VS* 31 (Spring 1988): 351–74.

Shizuko Kawamoto, "*North and South*: A Victorian 'Pride and Prejudice,'" *Tsuda Review* 12 (November 1967): 43–54.

Carol A. Martin, "Gaskell, Darwin, and *North and South*," *SNNTS* 15 (Summer 1983): 91–107.

Jo Pryke, "The Treatment of Political Economy in *North and South*," *GSJ* 4 (Spring 1990): 28–39.

Nanko Saito, "Shakai to Kojin no Stten: Gaskell Funin—Kita to Minami," in *Igirisu Shosetsu no Joseitachi*, ed. Yaeko Sumi and Naomi Okamura (Tokyo: Keiso, 1983), 73–91.

Akira Usuda, "Elizabeth Gaskell: *North and South*," in *Eikoku Shosetsu Kenkyu Dai 13 satsu* (Tokyo: Shinozaki, 1981), 42–55.

Valerie Wainwright, "Discovering Autonomy and Authenticity in *North and South*: Elizabeth Gaskell, John Stuart Mill, and the Liberal Ethic," *CLIO* 23 (Winter 1994): 149–65.

"The Poor Clare"

Maureen T. Reddy, "Female Sexuality in 'The Poor Clare': The Demon in the House," *SSF* 21 (Summer 1984): 259–65.

Ruth

Herve Abalain, "Le Refus de la marginalite: Le Combat d'Elizabeth Gaskell pour la reinsertion et la rehabilitation de la femme dechue dans la societe," in *La Marginalite dans la littérature et la pensée anglaises*, ed. Nadia-J. Rigaud (Aix-en-Provence: Université de Provence, 1983), 105-23.

Jeanette Eve, "A Misdated Gaskell Letter and the Background Story to *Ruth*," *N&Q* 34 (March 1987): 36–39.

Sylvia's Lovers

Graham Handley, "The Chronology of *Sylvia's Lovers*," *N&Q* 12 (1965): 302–03.

Andrew Sanders, "Varieties of Religious Experience in *Sylvia's Lovers*," *GSJ* 6 (Spring 1992): 15–24.

Stephen Lee Schwartz, "Sea and Land Symbolism in Mrs. Gaskell's *Sylvia's Lovers*," *EAA* 7–8 (1983–84): 1–15.

Wives and Daughters

Eva Ashberg, "Maria Edgeworth, Fredrika Bremer and Elizabeth Gaskell: Sources for *Wives and Daughters*," *GSJ* 6 (Summer 1992): 73–76.

Laurie Buchanan, "Mothers and Daughters in Elizabeth Gaskell's *Wives and Daughters*: In a Woman's World," *MidWQ* 31 (Summer 1990): 499–513.

Maureen T. Reddy, "Men, Women, and Manners in *Wives and Daughters*," in *Reading and Writing Women's Lives: A Study of the Novel of Manners*, ed. Bege K. Bowers and Barbara Brothers (Ann Arbor, MI: University Microfilms International Research Press, 1990), 68–85.

Anna Unsworth, "Some Social Themes in *Wives and Daughters*, I: Education, Science and Heredity," *GSJ* 4 (Spring 1990): 40–51.

GISSING, GEORGE

Born in Exile

M. D. Allen, "Charles Lamb and *Born in Exile*," *GissingJ* 24 (October 1988): 1–7.

Janice Deledalle-Rhodes, "La Dramatisation du conflit entre la science et la religion dans *Born in Exile* de George Gissing," *MCRel* 7 (1989): 85–98.

GISSING, GEORGE, "Comrades in Arms"

Charles Swann, "Sincerity and Authenticity: The Problem of Identity in *Born in Exile*," *L&H* 10 (Autumn 1984): 165–88.

"Comrades in Arms"

Lawless Bean, "Gissing's 'Comrades in Arms': New Women, Old Attitudes," *TCW* 1 (Winter 1984): 40–42.

Demos

P. F. Kropholler, "Additional Notes to *Demos*," *GissingJ* 24 (July 1988): 30–34.

Denzil Quarrier

Clifford Brook, "References to Wakefield in *Denzil Quarrier*," *GissingJ* 17 (July 1981): 11–19.

Adeline R. Tintner, "*Denzil Quarrier*: Gissing's Ibsen Novel," *ES* 64 (June 1983): 225–32.

Brian Robert Walker, "Gissing out of Context: *Denzil Quarrier*," *GissingJ* 19 (July 1983): 1–16.

Eve's Ransom

Pierre Coustillas, "George Gissing, *Eve's Ransom*," *GissingJ* 17 (July 1981): 28–30.

Terry Spaise, "*Eve's Ransom* and the Mutability of Freedom and Repression," *GissingJ* 25 (October 1989): 2–15.

"Fleet-Footed Hester"

Adeline R. Tintner, "Gissing's 'Fleet-Footed Hester': The Atalanta of Hackney Downs," *ÉA* 34 (October–December 1981): 443–47.

The House of Cobwebs and Other Stories

P. F. Kropholler, "Notes on *The House of Cobwebs*," *GissingJ* 17 (October 1981): 23–25.

Kazuo Mizokawa, "A Japanese View of *The House of Cobwebs*," *GissingJ* 24 (July 1988): 27–30.

In the Year of Jubilee

Alison Cotes, "Gissing and Camberwell," *GissingJ* 21 (April 1985): 11–16.

Barbara Leah Harman, "Going Public: Female Emancipation in George Gissing's *In the Year of Jubilee*," *TSLL* 34 (Fall 1992): 347–74.

John Sloan, "The 'Worthy' Seducer: A Motif under Stress in George Gissing's *In the Year of Jubilee*," *ELT* 28 no. 4 (1985): 354–65.

"The Invincible Curate"

Clifford Brook, "'The Invincible Curate' and Penny Readings at Wakefield Mechanics' Institution," *GissingJ* 23 (January 1987): 15–27.

Isabel Clarendon

John Sloan, "Prisoners of Illusion: *Isabel Clarendon* and the Ideal of 'Literature,'" *GissingJ* 22 (April 1986): 1–15.

"Joseph"

Pierre Coustillas, "'Joseph': A Forgotten Gissing Story of the Mid-Nineties," *GissingJ* 24 (January 1988): 1–14.

A Life's Morning

G. O. Morse, "An Appreciation of *A Life's Morning*," *GissingJ* 18 (October 1982): 1–24.

The Nether World

Pierre Coustillas, "*The Nether World*: A Centenary," *GissingJ* 25 (October 1989): 15–26.

P. F. Kropholler, "Notes to *The Nether World*," *GissingJ* 22 (April 1986): 21–25.

Diana L. Theman, "Continuing the Debate," *GissingJ* 22 (January 1986): 31–40.

New Grub Street

Eugene M. Baer, "Authorial Intrusion in Gissing's *New Grub Street*," *GissingJ* 21 (January 1985): 14–25.

Pierre Coustillas, "Some Personal Observations on Realism and Idealism in *New Grub Street*," *CVE* 24 (October 1986): 63–78.

David B. Eakin, "The Unmaking of the Artist: Woman and Economics in Gissing's *New Grub Street*," *CVE* 13 (April 1981): 43–52.

Hans Magnus Enzensberger, "Introduction," *GissingJ* 22 (April 1986): 31–34.

Claude Jolicoeur, "L'Ecrivain, grand-prêtre de la littérature ou *New Grub Street*, allegorie de l'âme de l'artiste," *CVE* 15 (April 1982): 71–78.

M. A. Makinen, "The Three Points of View in *New Grub Street*," *GissingJ* 17 (January 1981): 8–14.

Jean-Paul Michaux, "Names in *New Grub Street*," in *George Gissing: Critical Essays*, ed. Jean-Paul Michaux (Totowa, NJ: Barnes & Noble; London: Vision, 1981), 204–11.

Lewis D. Moore, "The Triumph of Mediocrity: George Gissing's *New Grub Street*," *GissingJ* 23 (January 1987): 1–15.

Robert L. Selig, "Gissing's Benefactor at the Chicago Tribune: An Identification from a Passage in *New Grub Street*," *ÉA* 38 (October–December 1985): 434–41.

The Odd Women

Karen Chase, "The Literal Heroine: A Study of Gissing's *The Odd Women*," *Criticism* 26 (Summer 1984): 231–44.

Deirdre David, "Ideologies of Patriarchy, Feminism, and Fiction in *The Odd Women*," *FemS*1 10 (Spring 1984): 117–39.

George E. Kennedy, "Gissing's Narrative of Change: *The Odd Women*," *GissingJ* 18 (April 1982): 12–27.

Wendy Lesser, "Even–Handed Oddness: George Gissing's *The Odd Women*," *HudR* 37, no. 2 (1984): 209–20.

Carolyn J. Perry, "A Voice of the Past: Ruskin's Pervasive Presence in Gissing's *The Odd Women*," *POMPA* 3 (1988): 63–70.

Akira Sano, "Mi o Yorou Onna Rhoda Nunn," *EigoS* 132 (1987): 482–83.

Christina Sjoholm, "The Haunting Headmistress: Fredrika Bremer's Hertha and Gissing's *The Odd Women*," *GissingJ* 25 (April 1989): 5–14.

Our Friend the Charlatan

Anthony Petyt, "Wakefield Associations in *Our Friend the Charlatan*," *GissingJ* 23 (October 1987): 19–24.

The Private Papers of Henry Ryecroft

Lowell T. Frye, "'An Author of Grass': Ironic Intent in Gissing's *The Private Papers of Henry Ryecroft*," *ELT* 24, no. 1 (1981): 41–51.

Andrew Hassam, "Crossing the Adriatic: A Cautionary Tale," *GissingJ* 22 (July 1986): 32–36.

P. F. Kropholler, "Notes on *The Private Papers of Henry Ryecroft*," *GissingJ* 26 (January 1990): 27–30.

The Unclassed

Constance D. Harsh, "Gissing's *The Unclassed* and the Perils of Naturalism," *ELH* 59 (Winter 1992): 911–38.

Alice B. Markow, "George Gissing's *The Unclassed*: A Problematic Variation of the Dissociative Pattern," *L&P* 30, no. 3–4 (1980): 182–91.

Veranilda

David Dowling, "*Veranilda*: A Revaluation," *GissingJ* 18 (April 1982): 27–31.

P. F. Kropholler, "Archaisms in *Veranilda*," *GissingJ* 21 (October 1985): 10–17.

"Whirlpool"

William Greenslade, "Women and the Disease of Civilization: George Gissing's 'The Whirlpool,'" *VS* 32 (Summer 1989): 507–23.

Workers in the Dawn

P. F. Kropholler, "Notes on *Workers in the Dawn*," *GissingJ* 17 (July 1981): 19–28.

Andrew Whitehead, "'Against the Tyranny of Kings and Princes': Radicalism in *Workers in the Dawn*," *GissingJ* 22 (October 1986): 13–28.

GOLDING, WILLIAM

Darkness Visible

Carmen Gago Alvarez, "The Gita and Golding—A Study of *Darkness Visible*," *EAA* 9–11 (1985–87): 103–09.

Gunnel Cleve, "Some Elements of Mysticism in William Golding's Novel *Darkness Visible*," *NM* 83, no. 4 (1982): 457–70.

Hetty Clews, "*Darkness Visible*: William Golding's Parousia," *ESC* 10 (September 1984): 317–29.

John Coates, "Religious Quest in *Darkness Visible*," *Renascence* 39 (Fall 1986): 272–91.

Donald W. Crompton, "Biblical and Classical Metaphor in *Darkness Visible*," *TCL* 28 (Summer 1982): 195–215.

Gillian Stead Eilersen, "A Password for the Darkness: Systems, Coincidences and Visions in William Golding's *Darkness Visible*," *Critique* 28 (Winter 1987): 107–18.

John Mills, "William Golding: *Darkness Visible*," *WCR* 15 (Winter 1981): 70–72.

Henri Petter, "Golding's *Darkness Visible*," in *Modes of Interpretation: Essays Presented to Ernst Leisi on the Occasion of His 65th Birthday*, ed. Richard J. Watts and Urs Weidmann (Tubingen: Narr, 1984), 159–66.

Philip Redpath, "Tricks of the Light: William Golding's *Darkness Visible*," *Ariel* 17 (January 1986): 3–16.

Free Fall

Ushe Bande, "Why Does Miss Pringle Hate Sammy? A Horneyan Interpretation," *NConL* 20 (September 1990): 11–12.

B. R. Johnson, "Golding's First Argument: Theme and Structure in *Free Fall*," in *Critical Essays on William Golding*, ed. James R. Baker (Boston: G. K. Hall, 1988), 61–72.

Jurgen Kamm, "Narrative Cross-References as a Structural Device in William Golding's *Free Fall*," *Anglia* 107, no. 1–2 (1989): 89–92.

Sylvére Monod, "William Golding's View of the Human Condition or 'Predicament' in *Free Fall*," in *The Uses of Fiction: Essays on the Modern Novel in Honour of Arnold Kettle*, ed. Douglas Jefferson and Graham Martin (Milton Keynes, England: Open University Press, 1982), 249–60.

The Inheritors

L. L. Dickson, "H. G. Wells Upside Down: Fantasy as Allegory in William Golding's *Inheritors*," in *The Scope of the Fantastic: Theory, Technique, Major*

Authors, ed. Robert A. Collins and Howard D. Pearce (Westport, CT: Greenwood, 1985), 151–57.

Thomas Dilworth, "Golding's *Inheritors*," *Expl* 42 (Summer 1984): 46.

Michael A. K. Halliday, "Sprachfunktion und literarischer Stil: Eine Untersuchung uber die Sprache von William Goldings *Inheritors*," in *Literatur und Konversation: Sprachsoziologie und Pragmatik in der Literaturwissenschaft*, ed. Ernest W. B. Hess–Luttich (Wiesbaden: Athenaion, 1980), 311–40.

James Harrison, "Golding's *Inheritors*," *Expl* 43 (Winter 1985): 47–48.

Ted Hughes, "Baboons and Neanderthals: A Rereading of *Inheritors*," in *William Golding: The Man and His Books: A Tribute on His 75th Birthday*, ed. John Carey (London: Faber, 1986; New York: Farrar, Straus, 1987), 161–68.

B. R. Johnson, "William Golding's *The Inheritors*: Dualism and Synthesis," *SoR* 19 (July 1986): 173–83.

Marie Nelson, "Two Narrative Modes, Two Modes of Perception: The Use of the Instrumental in Golding's *Inheritors*," *Neophil* 70 (April 1986): 307–15.

Robert H. O'Connor, "The Deracination of Man in Golding's *Inheritors*," *NConL* 14 (January 1984): 2–5.

Philip Redpath, "'Dogs would find an arid space round my feet': A Humanist Reading of *Inheritors*," in *Critical Essays on William Golding*, ed. James R. Baker (Boston: G. K. Hall, 1988), 31–41.

Jeanne Murray Walker, "Reciprocity and Exchange in William Golding's *Inheritors*," *SFS* 8 (November 1981): 297–310.

Lord of the Flies

Ivica Dzeparoski, "Od onaa strana na dobroto," *Razgledi* 10 (December 1983): 1136–149.

John Fitzgerald and John Kayser, "Golding's *Lord of the Flies*: Pride as Original Sin," *SNNTS* 24 (Spring 1992): 78–88.

Joao Almeida Flor, "Reencontro com William Golding," *Colóquio* 77 (January 1984): 74–75.

Candido Perez Gallego, "William Golding: El triste concierto de la vida," *CHA* 431 (May 1986): 142–48.

Jens-Peter Green and Doris Veith, "Kartenskizzen als Hilfsmittel bei der Erarbeitung von Goldings *Lord of the Flies*," *NSM* 37 (May 1984): 87–94.

Leah Hadomi, "Imagery as a Source of Irony in Golding's *Lord of the Flies*," *HUSL* 9, no. 1 (1981): 126–38.

Gerard Klaus, "Jeu et sacre dans *Lord of the Flies* de William Golding," *ÉA* 37 (October–December 1984): 424–36.

Shaodan Luo, "William Golding and his *Lord of The Flies*," *FLitS* 23 (March 1984): 119–21.

Ian McEwan, "Schoolboys," in *William Golding: The Man and His Books*, ed. John Carey (London: Faber, 1986; New York: Farrar, Straus, 1987), 157–60.

Gilles Mathis, "En tête à tête avec l'étrange: La Metamorphose de Jack dans *Lord of the Flies*," in *L'Etranger dans la littérature et la pensée anglaises*, ed. N. J. Rigaud (Aix-en-Provence: Université de Provence, 1989), 247–78.

Jose Oviedo, "Leyendo al Premio Nobel: Golding y la construccion del poder y el mito," *CdP* 1 (January–April 1984): 22–31.

J. F. Galvan Reula, "El misterio en la estructura de *Lord of the Flies*," *RCEI* 3 (November 1981): 66–73.

Hans-George Ruprecht, "Réalités romanesques d'un monde possible: Essai sur William Golding, *Lord of the Flies*," in *Roman, Réalités, Réalismes*, ed. Jean Bessiere (Paris: Publications Université de France, 1989), 179–88.

Keith Selby, "Golding's *Lord of the Flies*," *Expl* 41 (Spring 1983): 57–59.

Leo Tanzman, "The Murder of Simon in Golding's *Lord of the Flies*," *NConL* 17 (November 1987): 2–3.

Kathleen Woodward, "On Aggression: William Golding's *Lord of the Flies*," in *No Place Else: Explorations in Utopian and Dystopian Fiction*, ed. Eric S. Rabkin, Martin H. Greenberg, and Joseph D. Olander (Carbondale: Southern Illinois University Press, 1983), 199–224.

Tetsuo Yoshida, "The Reversal of Light and Dark in *Lord of the Flies*," *SELL* 35 (March 1985): 63–84.

Man at an Extremity

Ronald Granofsky, "*Man at an Extremity*: Elemental Trauma and Revelation in the Fiction of William Golding," *MLS* 20 (Spring 1990): 50–63.

The Paper Man

Blake Morrison, "In Death as in Life," *TLS* (2 March 1984): 215.

The Paper Men

E. C. Bufkin, "The Nobel Prize and the *Paper Men*: The Fixing of William Golding," *GaR* 39 (Spring 1985): 55–65.

Jeanne Delbaere–Garant, "The Artist as Clown of God: Golding's *The Paper Men*," in *Multiple Worlds, Multiple Words*, ed. Hena Maes–Jelinek, Pierre Michel, and Paulette Michel–Michot (Liege: Université de Liege, 1987), 39–49.

Solomiia Pavlychko, "Paperovi liudy Anhliis'kyi filosofs'kyi roman 80–kh rokiv," *Vsesvit* 7 (July 1986): 133–40.

Irene Simon, "Vision or Dream? The Supernatural Design in William Golding's *The Paper Men*," in *Elizabethan and Modern Studies*, ed. J. P. Vander Motten (Ghent: Seminarie voor English & American Literature, Rijksuniversitéit Gent, 1985), 235–46.

Pincher Martin

Christoph Bode, "Goldings verachtlicher Sisyphos: Text und Autorenintention in *Pincher Martin*," *GRM* 38, no. 1–2 (1988): 151–67.

Minoru Hirota, "*Pincher Martin* as a Modern Metamorphosis of Greek Tragedy," *SELL* 39 (February 1989): 29–50.

Vijay Lakshmi, "Entering the Whirlpool: The Movement towards Self–Awareness in William Golding's *Pincher Martin*," *LCrit* 17, no. 3 (1982): 25–36.

Eleanor Wikborg, "The Control of Sympathy in William Golding's *Pincher Martin*," in *Studies in English Philology, Linguistics and Literature Presented to Alarik Rynell, 7 March 1978*, ed. Mats Ryden and Lennart A. Bjork (Stockholm: Almqvist & Wiksell, 1978), 179–87.

The Pyramid

Rebecca S. Kelly, "The Tragicomic Mode: William Golding's *The Pyramid*," *PConL* 7 (1981): 110–16.

Jacques Leclaire, "William Golding: *The Pyramid* as a Study in Mediocrity," in *De William Shakespeare à William Golding: Mélanges dediés à la memoire de Jean–Pierre*, ed. Sylvère Monod (Vernier. Rouen: Université de Rouen, 1984), 143–54.

Rites of Passage

Peter Krahe, "Die Linientaufe und ihre Folgen in William Goldings *Rites of Passage*," *LWU* 18, no. 1 (1985): 13–31.

Jean-Jacques Mayoux, "Un Darwinien noir," *QL* 405 (15–30 November 1983): 5–6.

V. V. Subba Rao, "Sin and Shame: A Note on Colley's Fall in Golding's *Rights of Passage*," *LitE* 9, no. 1–4 (1987–88): 71–78.

Irene Simon, "The Theatre Motif in William Golding's *Rites of Passage*," in *Communiquer et traduire: Hommages a Jean Dierickx/ Communicating and Translating: Essays in Honour of Jean Dierickx*, ed. Gilbert Debusscher and Jean–Pierre Van Noppen (Brussels: Eds. de l'Université de Bruxelles, 1985), 261–67.

Virginia Tiger, "William Golding's 'Wooden World': Religious Rites in *Rites of Passage*," *TCL* 28 (Summer 1982): 216–31.

Tetsuo Yoshida, "Word of Passage in *Rites of Passage*," *SELL* 40 (February 1990): 1–17.

The Spire

Usha Bande, "Jocelin's Glorified Self: A Horneyan Interpretation of Golding's *The Spire*," *NConL* 21 (November 1991): 9–10.

Gordon Campbell and Jeanina Umana Aguiar de Ramirez, "Constable y La aguja de Golding," *Káñina* 4 (January–June 1980): 97–100.

L. L. Dickson, "Modern Allegory: The Cathedral Motif in William Golding's *The Spire*," *WVUPP* 27 (1981): 98–105.

Richard Humphrey, "Der historische Roman und die Kathedrale: Zwei Weltbucher: Zu William Goldings *The Spire*," *A&E* 24 (1984): 117–33.

Laurence Lerner, "Jocelin's Folly; or, Down with the *Spire*," *CQ* 24 (Autumn 1982): 3–15.

Sue Thomas, "Some Religious Icons and Biblical Allusions in William Golding's *The Spire*," *AUMLA* 64 (November 1985): 190–97.

Sur la Sea Trilogy

Frederic Regard, "Polyphonie de voix narratives et autorité enonciative: *Sur la Sea Trilogy* de William Golding," *Poétique* 23 (February 1992): 7–58.

To the End of the Earth

J. H. Stape,""Fiction in the Wild, Modern Manner': Metanarrative Gesture in William Golding's *To the End of the Earth Trilogy*," *TCL* 38 (Summer 1992): 226–39.

GRAHAME, KENNETH

The Wind in the Willows

Mary DeForest, "*The Wind in the Willows*: A Tale for Two Readers," *CML* 10 (Fall 1989): 81–87.

Bonnie Gaarden, "The Inner Family of *The Wind in the Willows*," *ChildL* 22 (1994): 43–56.

Sarah Gilead, "Grahame's *The Wind in the Willows*," *Expl* 46 (Fall 1987): 33–36.

Sarah Gilead, "The Undoing of Idyll in *The Wind in the Willows*," *ChildL* 16 (1988): 145–58.

Richard Gillin, "Romantic Echoes in the *Willows*," *ChildL* 16 (1988): 169–74.

Lois R. Kuznets, "Kenneth Grahame and Father Nature; Or, Whither Blows *The Wind in the Willows*?" *ChildL* 16 (1988): 175–81.

Roderick McGillis, "Utopian Hopes: Criticism beyond Itself," *CLAQ* 9 (Winter 1984–85): 184–86.

Kenneth McLeish, "The Rippingest Yarn of All," *J. R. R. Tolkien: This Far Land*, ed. Robert Giddings (London: Vision; Totowa, NJ: Barnes & Noble, 1983), 125–36.

Cynthia Marshall, "Bodies and Pleasures in *The Wind in the Willows*," *ChildL* 22 (1994): 58–70.

Michael Mendelson, "*The Wind in the Willows* and the Plotting of Contrast," *ChildL* 16 (1988): 127–44.

John David Moore, "Pottering about in the Garden: Kenneth Grahame's Version of Pastoral in *The Wind in the Willows*," *JMMLA* 23 (Spring 1990): 45–60.

Michael Steig, "At the Back of *The Wind in the Willows*: An Experiment in Biographical and Autobiographical Interpretation," *VS* 24 (Spring 1981): 303–23.

Reinbert Tabbert, "Lockende Kinderbucheingange," *WWort* 36 (November–December 1986): 421–39.

Maureen Thum, "Exploring 'The Country of the Mind': Mental Dimensions of Landscape in Kenneth Grahame's *The Wind in the Willows*," *CLAQ* 17 (Fall 1992): 27–32.

Tony Watkins, "'Making a Break for the Real England': The River- Bankers Revisited," *CLAQ* 9 (Spring 1984): 34–35.

Lesley Willis, "'A sadder and a wiser rat/He rose the morrow morn': Echoes of the Romantics in Kenneth Grahame's *The Wind in the Willows*," *CLAQ* 13 (Fall 1988): 108–11.

GREEN, ANNA KATHERINE

The Golden Slipper

Audrey Peterson, "Some Minor Voices," in *Victorian Masters of Mystery: From Wilkie Collins to Conan Doyle* (New York: Ungar, 1984), 195–96.

Hand and Ring

Audrey Peterson, "Some Minor Voices," in *Victorian Masters of Mystery: From Wilkie Collins to Conan Doyle* (New York: Ungar, 1984), 192–94.

The Leavenworth Case

Audrey Peterson, "Some Minor Voices," in *Victorian Masters of Mystery: From Wilkie Collins to Conan Doyle* (New York: Ungar, 1984), 187–92.

That Affair Next Door

Audrey Peterson, "Some Minor Voices," in *Victorian Masters of Mystery: From Wilkie Collins to Conan Doyle* (New York: Ungar, 1984), 194–95.

GREEN, HENRY

Blindness

Barbara Brothers, "*Blindness*: The Eye of Henry Green," *TCL* 29 (Winter 1983): 403–21.

Angus Wilson, "Living and Loving," *TCL* 29 (Winter 1983): 384–86.

Concluding

Mark A. R. Facknitz, "The Edge of Night: Figures of Change in Henry Green's *Concluding*," *TCL* 36 (Spring 1990): 10–22.

Loving

Fiona McPhail, "Echanges et paradoxes: Deux aspects du roman de Henry Green, *Loving* (1945)," in *Echanges: Actes du Congrês de Strasbourg*, ed. Société des Anglicistes de l'Enseignement Supérieur (Paris: Didier, 1982), 255–70.

"The Lull"

Rod Mengham, "Reading 'The Lull,'" *TCL* 29 (Winter 1983): 455–64.

GREENE, GRAHAM

"Across the Bridge"

M. M. Liberman, "The Uses of Anti–fiction: Greene's 'Across the Bridge,'" *GaR* 27 (1973): 321–28.

"The Basement Room"

Robert B. Heilman, "'The Basement Room,'" in *Modern Short Stories: A Critical Anthology*, ed. Robert B. Heilman (New York: Harcourt, Brace, 1950), 264–66.

Arthur W. Pitts, Jr., "Greene's 'The Basement Room,'" *Expl* 23 (October 1964): no. 17.

Gerald E. Silveira, "Greene's 'The Basement Room,'" *Expl* 25 (December 1965): no. 13

Charles L. Willig, "Greene's 'The Basement Room,'" *Expl* 31 (February 1973): no. 48.

Brighton Rock

Jean Cayrol, "Autour de l'oeuvre de Graham Greene," *RPenF* 10 (April 1951): 69–72.

Dominick P. Consolo, "Music as Motif: The Unity of *Brighton Rock*," *Renascence* 15 (Fall 1962): 12–20. Reprinted in *Graham Greene*, ed. Harry J. Cargas (St. Louis, MO: B. Herder, 1969), 75–87.

Gerald H. Cox, III, "Graham Greene's Mystical Rose in Brighton," *Renascence* 23 (Autumn 1970): 21–30.

Basil Davenport, "Religious Melodrama," *SatR* 18 (25 June 1938): 6–7.

Brian Diemert, "Ida Arnold and the Detective Story: Reading *Brighton Rock*," *TCL* 38 (Winter 1992): 386–403.

Angelo Antony De Vitis, "Allegory in *Brighton Rock*," *MFS* 3 (Autumn 1957): 216–24.

Robert O. Evans, "The Satanist Fallacy of *Brighton Rock*," in *Graham Greene: Some Critical Considerations*, ed. Robert O. Evans (Lexington: University of Kentucky Press, 1963), 151–69.

Alan Warren Friedman, "'The Dangerous Edge': Beginning with Death," in *Graham Greene: A Revaluation*, ed. Jeffrey Meyers (New York: St. Martin's, 1990), 142–47.

David Leon Higdon, "'I Try To Be Accurate': The Text of Greene's *Brighton Rock*," in *Essays on Graham Greene*, ed. Peter Wolfe (Greenwood, FL: Penkevill, 1987), 169–87.

Robert Hoskins, "Hale, Pinkie, and the Pentecost Theme in *Brighton Rock*," *ModBL* 3 (Spring 1978): 56–66.

Robert Hoskins, "The Napoleonic Strategist of *Brighton Rock*," *CollL* 12 (Winter 1985): 11–17.

David L. Kubal, "Graham Greene's *Brighton Rock*: The Political Theme," *Renascence* 23 (Autumn 1970): 46–54.

Dan McCall, "*Brighton Rock*: The Price of Order," *ELN* 4 (June 1966): 290–94.

F. A. McGowan, "Symbolism in *Brighton Rock*," *Renascence* 8 (Autumn 1955): 25–35.

Claude-Edmonde Magny, "De Benito Cereno au Rocher de Brighton," *Guilde du Livre* 16 (July 1951): 150–53.

Charles H. Muller, "Graham Greene and the Justification of God's Ways," *UES* 10, no. 1 (1972): 23–35.

Michael Routh, "The Race-Gang Beating in *Brighton Rock*," *NConL* 15 (November 1985): 2.

Jean–H Roy, "L'oeuvre de Graham Greene ou un Christianisme de la damnation," *TM* 5 (February 1950): 1513–519.

Lucio P. Ruotolo, "*Brighton Rock*'s Absurd Heroine," *MLQ* 25 (December 1964): 425–33.

Trevor L. Williams, "History over Theology: The Case for Pinkie in Greene's *Brighton Rock*," *SNNTS* 24 (Spring 1992): 67–77.

David G. Wright, "Greene's *Brighton Rock*," *Expl* 41 (Summer 1983): 52–53.

"Brother"

John Bayley, "Graham Greene: The Short Stories," in *Graham Greene: A Revaluation: New Essays*, ed. Jeffrey Meyers (New York: St. Martin's, 1990), 101–03.

A Burnt-Out Case

Christine De Vinne, "Truth and Falsehood in the Metaphors of *A Burnt-Out Case*," *ES* 74 (October 1993): 445–50.

D. J. Dooley, "*A Burnt-Out Case* Reconsidered," *WRev* 237 (Summer 1963): 168–78.

D. J. Dooley, "The Suspension of Disbelief: Greene's *A Burnt-Out Case*," *DR* 43 (Autumn 1963): 343–52.

Maurits Engelborghs, "Graham Greene: *A Burnt-Out Case*," *KultuurL* 28 (October 1961): 610–15.

Robert M. Hanlon, S. J., "The Ascent to Belief in Graham Greene's *A Burnt-Out Case*," *C&L* 26 (Summer 1977): 20–26.

M. Whitcomb Hess, "Graham Greene's Travesty on *The Ring and the Book*," *CatW* 194 (October 1961): 37–42.

Frank Kermode, "Mr. Greene's Eggs and Crosses," *Encounter* 16 (April 1961): 69–75. Reprinted in *Puzzles and Epiphanies: Essays and Reviews: 1958–1961* (London: Routledge & Kegan Paul, 1962), 176–88. Reprinted in *Graham Greene: A Collection of Critical Essays*, ed. Samuel Hynes (Englewood Cliffs, NJ: Prentice-Hall, 1973), 126–38.

James Noxon, "Kierkegaard's Stages and *A Burnt-Out Case*," *RevEL* 3 (January 1962): 90–101.

S. J. Peters, "*A Burnt-Out Case*, Een mislukte roman," *Streven* (November 1961): 161–66.

Herman Servotte, "Bedenkingen bij *A Burnt-Out Case*," Graham Greene's jongste roman," *DWB* 106 (June 1961): 371–75.

Ira Neil Shor, "Greene's Later Humanism:*A Burnt-Out Case*," *LitR* 16 (Summer 1973): 397–411.

John K. Simon, "Off the 'Voie Royale': The Failure of Greene's *A Burnt-Out Case*," *Symposium* 18 (1964): 163–69.

Francis J. Smith, "The Anatomy of *A Burnt-Out Case*," *America* 105 (9 September 1961): 711–12.

Philip Stratford, "Greene's Hall of Mirrors," *KR* 23 (Summer 1961): 527–31.

Adrian van Kaam and Kathleen Healy, "Querry in Greene's *A Burnt-Out Case*," in *The Demon and the Dove: Personality Growth Through Literature* (Pittsburgh: Duquesne University Press, 1967), 259–85.

Tetsuo Yamaguchi, "*Moetsukita Ningen*" in tsuite no Moetsukita Shiron (Tokyo: Seium Shobo, 1971), 3–19.

The Captain and the Enemy

John Mills, "The Dog in the Perambulator," *WCR* 23 (Fall 1988): 77–91.

The Comedians

Walter Allen, "*The Comedians*," *LMag* 5 (March 1966): 73–80.

M. K. Chaudhury, "The Significance of Caricature in Graham Greene's *The Comedians*," *PURB* 5, no. 2 (1974): 51–56.

Randall Craig, "Good Places and Promised Lands in *The Comedians*," *Renascence* 39 (Fall 1986): 312–24.

Doreen D'Cruz, "Comedy and Moral Stasis in Greene's *The Comedians*," *Renascence* 40 (Fall 1987): 53–63.

Angelo Antony De Vitis, "Greene's *The Comedians*: Hollower Men," *Renascense* 18 (Spring 1966): 129–36, 146.

C. S. Ferns, "'Brown Is Not Greene': Narrative Role in *The Comedians*," *CollL* 12 (Winter 1985): 60–67.

Roland Hill, "Graham Greene, Die Stunde der *Komödianlen*," *Hochland* 59 (1966): 90–94.

Gavin Lambert, "The Double Agent Graham Greene," in *The Dangerous Edge* (London: Barrie & Jenkins, 1975), 164–66.

Michael Larson, "Laughing till the Tears Come: Greene's Failed Comedian," *Renascence* 41 (Spring 1989): 177–87.

Antoine Lauras, "Sommes-nous des comédiens?" *Études* 324 (April 1966): 510–13.

David Lodge, "Graham Greene's *Comedians*," *Commonweal* 83 (25 February 1966): 604–6.

M. M. Mahood, "The Possessed: Greene's 'The Comedians,'" in *The Colonial Encounter: A Reading of Six Novels* (London: Rex Collings, 1976), 115–41.

Alice Mayhew, "*The Comedians*," *MFS* 3 (Autumn 1957): 225–34. Reprinted in *Graham Greene*, ed. Harry J. Cargas (St. Louis, MO: Herder, 1969), 101–14.

Michael Routh, "Greene's Parody of Farce and Comedy in *The Comedians*," *Renascence* 26 (Spring 1974): 138–51.

The Confidential Agent

Gavin Lambert, "The Double Agent Graham Greene," in *The Dangerous Edge* (London: Barrie & Jenkins, 1975), 148–52.

"A Day Saved"

Steven E. Colburn, "Graham Greene's 'A Day Saved': A Modern Tale of Time and Modernity," *SSF* 29 (Summer 1992): 377–84.

"The Destructors"

Peter P. Clarke, "Graham Greene's 'The Destructors': An Anarchist Parable," *ELN* 23 (March 1986): 60–63.

Hans Feldman, "The Idea of History in Graham Greene's 'The Destructors,'" *SSF* 19 (Summer 1982): 241–45.

Jesse F. McCartney, "Politics in Graham Greene's 'The Destructors,'" *SoHR* 12 (1978): 31–41.

Tim McNamara, "Graham Greene's 'The Destructors': The Tragic World of 'Just Things,'" *ABR* 40 (September 1989): 304–22.

John Ower, "Dark Parable: History and Theology in Graham Greene's 'The Destructors,'" *Cithara* 15 (November 1975): 69–78.

The End of the Affair

G. L. A[rnold], "Adam's Tree," *TC* 154 (October 1951): 337–42. Reprinted in *Collected Essays* (New York: Viking, 1973), 477–82.

Neville Braybrooke, "Graham Greene and the Double Man: An Approach to *The End of the Affair*," *DubR* 226 (First Quarter, 1952): 61–73. Reprinted in *TC* 23 (1969): 293–304. Reprinted in *Graham Greene*, ed. Harry J. Cargas (St. Louis, MO: B. Herder, 1969), 114–30. Reprinted as "Graham Greene—The Double Man: An Approach to His Novel, *The End of the Affair*," *QQ* 77 (Spring 1970): 29–39. Reprinted in *Arbor* 303 (1971): 57–68.

Alan Warren Friedman, "The Dangerous Edge: Beginning with Death," in *Graham Greene: A Revaluation,* ed. Jeffrey Meyers (New York: St. Martin's, 1990), 147–55.

Ian Gregor, *"The End of the Affair,"* in *The Moral and the Story* (London: Faber & Faber, 1962), 192–206. Reprinted in *Graham Greene: A Collection of Critical Essays*, ed. Samuel Hynes (Englewood Cliffs, NJ: Prentice-Hall, 1973), 110–26.

Robert Hoskins, "Through a Glass Darkly: Mirrors in *The End of the Affair*," *NConL* 9, no. 3 (1979): 3–5.

Rita Isaacs, "Three Levels of Allegory in Graham Greene's *The End of the Affair*," *Lit&Ling* 1, no. 1 (1975): 29–52.

David Lodge, "Use of Key Words in the Novels of Graham Greene: Love, Hate, and *The End of the Affair*," *Blackfriars* 42 (November 1961): 468–74.

Julia McElhattan, "Bendrix's Descent in Greene's *End of the Affair*," *Lang&Lit* 8, no. 1–3 (1983): 55–68.

Makoto Manabe, "An Essay on *The End of the Affair*," *SELL* 27 (December 1986): 1–21.

Lucy S. Pake, "Courtly Love in Our Own Time: Graham Greene's *The End of the Affair*," *LJHum* 8 (Fall 1982): 36–43.

Gweneth Schwab, "Graham Greene's Pursuit of God," *BuR* 26, no. 2 (1982): 45–57.

Ray Snape, "Plaster Saints, Flesh and Blood Sinners: Graham Greene's *The End of the Affair*," *DUJ* 74 (June 1982): 241–50.

Ursula Spier, "Melodrama in Graham Greene's *The End of the Affair*," *MFS* 3 (Autumn 1957): 235–40.

Ronald G. Walker, "World without End: An Approach to Narrative Structure in Greene's *The End of the Affair*," *TSLL* 26 (Summer 1984): 218–41.

England Made Me

Robert Hoskins, "'Those Dreadful Clothes': The Meaning of Modern Sculpture and the Genesis of Greene's *England Made Me*," *SoAR* 57 (May 1992): 73–91.

The Fallen Idol

Stuart Y. McDougal, "Visual Tropes: An Analysis of *The Fallen Idol*," *Style* 9 (1975): 502–13.

A Gun for Sale

Gavin Lambert, "The Double Agent Graham Greene," in *The Dangerous Edge* (London: Barrie & Jenkins, 1975), 143–48.

Ivan Melada, "Graham Greene and the Munitions Makers: The Historical Context of *A Gun for Sale*," *SNNTS* 13 (Fall 1981): 303–21.

The Heart of the Matter

Robert J. Baker, "'The Space of an Upturned Coffin': Tragedy in *The Heart of the Matter*," *L&B* 12 (1992): 43–52.

Harold Barratt, "Adultery as Betrayal in Graham Greene," *DR* 45 (Autumn 1965): 324–32.

Werner Barzel, S. J., "Sunder aus Liebe? Zu Graham Greene *Das Herz aller Dinge*," *SZ* 146 (April 1950): 24–28

Jacques Blondel, "*The Heart of the Matter*: Le cas de Scobie," *LM* 65 (1971): 51–55.

Jacques Blondel, "*The Heart of the Matter*: Roman Catholique," *LM* 65 (1971): 56–60.

Angelo Antony De Vitis, "The Church and Major Scobie," *Renascence* 10 (Spring 1958): 115–20.

Teresita Fay and Michael G. Yetman, "Scobie the Just: A Reassessment of *The Heart of the Matter*," *Renascence* 29 (Spring 1977): 142–56.

Ingelborg Prytz Fougner, "Sjelens 'obotliga ansamhet,'" *KuKl* 74 (1971): 355–60.

Richard Freis, "Scobie's World," *R&L* 24 (Autumn 1992): 57–78.

Elizabeth Hardwick, "Loveless Love," *PR* 15 (1948): 937–39.

Bruce Harkness, "Greene's Old-Fashioned Remedy in *The Heart of the Matter*," *ANQ* 20 (March–April 1982): 115–16.

Eugene Hollahan, "'Of Course the Whole Thing Was Coueism': *The Heart of the Matter* as a Critique of Emile Coue's Psychotherapy," *SNNTS* 21 (Fall 1989): 320–31.

Joseph Hynes, "The Facts at *The Heart of the Matter*," *TSLL* 13 (Winter 1972): 711–26.

Mary Evelyn Jefferson, "*The Heart of the Matter*: The Responsible Man," *CarQ* 9 (Summer 1957): 23–31. Reprinted in *Graham Greene*, ed. Harry J. Cargas (St. Louis, MO: Herder, 1969), 88–100.

Thorsten Georg Jonsson, "Ett Portratt av Scobie," *Tva Essayer om Graham Greene* (Stockholm: Norstedts, 1950), 3–8.

Raymond Jouve, "La Damnation de Scobie?" *Études* 263 (November 1949): 164–77.

Arnold Kettle, "Graham Greene: *The Heart of the Matter*," in *An Introduction to the English Novel*, vol. 2 (London: Hutchinson University Library, 1953), 153–59.

Kai Laitinen, "The Heart of the Novel: The Turning Point in *The Heart of the Matter*," in *Graham Greene: Some Critical Considerations*, ed. Robert O. Evans (Lexington: University of Kentucky Press, 1963), 169–81.

Albert William Levi, "Chapter VII," in *Literature, Philosophy and the Imagination* (Bloomington: Indiana University Press, 1962), 266–72.

Gerald Levin, "The Rhetoric of Graham Greene's *The Heart of the Matter*," *Renascence* 23 (Autumn 1970): 14–20.

Irma Maini, "The Theme of Grace in *The Heart of the Matter*," *LCrit* 17, no. 3 (1982): 51–59.

Elliott Malamet, "Penning the Police/Policing the Pen: The Case of Graham Greene's *The Heart of the Matter*," *TCL* 39 (Fall 1993): 283–305.

Vida E. Mazkovic, "Major Scobie," in *The Changing Face: Disintegration of Personality in the Twentieth-Century British Novel, 1900–1950*, ed. Harry T. Moore (Carbondale: Southern Illinois University Press, 1970), 82–97.

Marcel Moré, "Les deux holocaustes de Scobie," *Dieu Vivant* 16 (1950): 77–105. Reprinted as "The Two Holocausts of Scobie," *Crosscurrents* 1 (Winter 1951): 44–63. Reprinted in *Cross Currents of Psychiatry and Catholic Morality*, ed. William Birmingham and Joseph E. Cunneen (New York: Pantheon, 1964), 274–99

W. R. Mueller, "Theme of Love: Graham Greene's *The Heart of the Matter*," in *Prophetic Voice in Modern Fiction* (New York: Association Press, 1959; Doubleday, 1966), 135–58.

Seán O'Fáolain, "The Novels of Graham Greene: *The Heart of the Matter*," *Britain Today* 148 (August 1948): 32–36.

Ronald G. Walker, "Seriation as Stylistic Norm in Graham Greene's *The Heart of the Matter*," *L&S* 6 (1973): 161–75.

Andrzej Weselinski, "Irony and Melodrama in *The Heart of the Matter*," *SAP* 8 (1975): 167–73.

"The Hint of an Explanation"

John Bayley, "Graham Greene: The Short Stories," in *Graham Greene: A Revaluation: New Essays*, ed. Jeffrey Meyers (New York: St. Martin's, 1990), 93–98.

A. R. Coulthard, "Graham Greene's 'The Hint of an Explanation': A Reinterpretation," *SSF* 8 (Fall 1971): 601–05.

Nikolaus Happel, "Forbetrachtung an Graham Greens Short Story 'The Hint of an Explanation,'" *DNS* 9 (1960): 81–86.

Brother Joseph, "Greene's 'The Hint of an Explanation,'" *Expl* 19 (January 1961): no. 21.

Barbara Sewell, "Graham Greene: A Hint of an Explanation," *Western Review* 22 (Winter 1958): 83–95.

The Honorary Consul

Miriam Allott, "Surviving the Course, Or a Novelist for All Seasons: Graham Greene's *The Honorary Consul*," in *The Uses of Fiction: Essays on the Modern Novel in Honour of Arnold Kettle*, ed. Douglas Jefferson and Graham Martin (Milton Keynes, England: Open University Press, 1982), 237–48.

Justo Leopoldo Duran, "A Priest Reads *The Honorary Consul*," *ClR* 61 (September 1976): 343–49.

Gavin Lambert, "The Double Agent Graham Greene," in *The Dangerous Edge* (London: Barrie & Jenkins, 1975), 166–70.

David J. Leigh, "The Structures of Greene's *The Honorary Consul*," *Renascence* 38 (Autumn 1985): 13–24.

Elliott Malamet, "'Art in a Police Station': Detection, Fatherhood, and Textual Influence in Greene's *The Honorary Consul*," *TSLL* 34 (Spring 1992): 106–28.

Peter Wolfe, "*The Honorary Consul*," *StT* 14 (Fall 1974): 117–20.

The Human Factor

Daphrna Endenart-Vulcan, "A Priest without a Church: *The Human Factor*," in *Graham Greene's Childless Fathers* (London: Macmillan, 1988), 100–14.

Dean Flower, "The Way We Live Now," *HudR* 31 (Summer 1978): 352–54.

Robert M. Hanlon, S.J., "Pity of Treachery: Graham Greene's *The Human Factor*," *America* 136 (17 June 1978): 486–88.

Judie Newman, "Games in Greeneland: *The Human Factor*," *DQR* 14, no. 4 (1984): 250–68.

Georg Seehase, "Horizonte des kunstlerischen Bildes in Graham Greenes Roman *The Human Factor* (1978)," *ZAA* 32, no. 1 (1984): 19–31.

Gary P. Storhoff, "To Choose a Different Loyalty: Greene's Politics in *The Human Factor*," *EL* 11 (Spring 1984): 59–66.

It's a Battlefield

L. Adinaryana, "A Reading of Greene's *It's a Battlefield*," *LitE* 3 (July–December 1981): 54–64.

Frances C. McInherny, "*It's a Battlefield*—A World in Chaos," in *Gleanings from Greeneland*, ed. J. S. Ryan (Biddeford, ME: University of New England, 1972), 20–30.

Walter Paznar, "Graham Greene's *It's a Battlefield*: A Center That Will Not Hold," *WascanaR* 18 (Spring 1983): 3–12.

The Man Within

S. N. Filyushkina, "Roman Grema Grina *Chelovek Vnutri*," *Permskii Universitét* 188 (1968): 3–18.

"Graham Greene: The Man Within," *TLS* (17 September 1971): 1101–102. Reprinted in *Graham Greene: A Collection of Critical Essays*, ed. Samuel L. Hynes (Englewood Cliffs, NJ: Prentice-Hall, 1973), 8–16.

"Men at Work"

Rowland Smith, "A People's War in Greeneland," in *Graham Greene: A Revaluation*, ed. Jeffrey Meyers (New York: St. Martin's, 1990), 114–15.

The Ministry of Fear

W. H. Auden, "The Heresy of Our Time," *Renascence* 1 (Spring 1949): 23–24. Reprinted as "A Note on Graham Greene," *The Wind and the Rain* 6 (Summer 1949): 53–54. Reprinted in *Renascence* 25 (Summer 1973): 181–82. Reprinted in *Graham Greene: A Collection of Critical Essays*, ed. Samuel Hynes (Englewood Cliffs, NJ: Prentice-Hall, 1973), 93–95.

Joseph M. Duffy, Jr., "The Lost World of Graham Greene," *Thought* 33 (Summer 1958): 229–47.

Gavin Lambert, "The Double Agent *Graham Greene*," in *The Dangerous Edge* (London: Barrie & Jenkins, 1975), 152–56.

Robert Hoskins, "Greene and Wordsworth: *The Ministry of Fear*," *SoAR* 48 (November 1983): 32–42.

Rowland Smith, "A People's War in Greeneland," in *Graham Greene: A Revaluation*, ed. Jeffrey Meyers (New York: St. Martin's, 1990), 109–30.

Morton Dauwen Zabel, "Graham Greene," *Nation* 157 (3 July 1943): 18–20. Revised and reprinted in *Forms of Modern Fiction*, ed. William van O'Connor (Minneapolis: University of Minnesota Press, 1948), 287–93. Reprinted in *Critiques and Essays of Modern Fiction, 1920–1951*, ed. John W. Wldridge (New York: Ronald, 1952), 518–25. Revised and reprinted as "Graham Greene: The Best and the Worst," in *Craft and Character: Texts, Method and Vocation in Modern Fiction* (London: Gollancz, 1957), 276–96. Reprinted in *Graham Greene: A Collection of Critical Essays*, ed. Samuel Hynes (Englewood Cliffs, NJ: Prentice-Hall, 1973), 30–49.

Monsignor Quixote

John F. Desmond, "The Heart of (the) Matter: The Mystery of the Real in *Monsignor Quixote*," *R&L* 22 (Spring 1990): 59–78.

Patrick Henry, "Doubt and Certitude in *Monsignor Quixote*," *CollL* 12 (Winter 1985): 68–79.

The Quiet American

Miriam Allott, "The Moral Situation in *The Quiet American*," in *Graham Greene: Some Critical Considerations*, ed. Robert O. Evans (Lexington: University of Kentucky Press, 1963), 188–206.

Robert O. Evans, "Existentialism in Graham Greene's *The Quiet American*," *MFS* 3 (Autumn 1957): 241–48.

Ralph Freedman, "Novel of Contention: *The Quiet American*," *Western Review* 21 (Autumn 1956): 76–81.

R. E. Hughes, "*The Quiet American*: The Case Reopened," *Renascence* 12 (Autumn 1959): 41–42, 49. Reprinted in *Graham Greene*, ed. Harry J. Cargas (St. Louis, MO: Herder, 1969), 130–33.

Gavin Lambert, "The Double Agent *Graham Greene*," in *The Dangerous Edge* (London: Barrie & Jenkins, 1975), 159–64.

Niels Bugge Hansen, "The Unquiet Englishman: A Reading of Graham Greene's *The Quiet American*," in *Occasional Papers 1976–1977*, ed. Graham D. Caie, Michael Chesnutt, Lis Christensen, and Claus Faerch (Copenhagen: Universiti-forl. i Kobenhavn, 1978), 188–201.

J. McMahon, "Graham Greene and *The Quiet American*," *J&KUR* 1 (November 1958): 64–73.

Eric Solomon, "Notes toward a Definition of the Colonial Novel," *NDQ* 57 (Summer 1989): 16–23.

Our Man in Havana

L. Adinarayana, "Greene's *Our Man in Havana*: A Study of Its Narrative Structure," *LitE* 4, no. 3–4 (1984): 22–29.

Henry L. Shapiro, "The Infidel Greene: Radical Ambiguity in *Our Man in Havana*," in *Essays on Graham Greene*, ed. Peter Wolfe (Greenwood, FL: Penkevill, 1987), 83–103.

The Power and the Glory

John Atkins, "Altogether Amen: A Reconsideration of *The Power and the Glory*," in *Graham Greene: Some Critical Considerations*, ed. Robert O. Evans (Lexington: University of Kentucky Press, 1963), 181–88.

D. Hayward Brock and James M. Welsh, "Graham Greene and the Structure of Salvation," *Renascence* 27 (Autumn 1974): 31–39.

Frank de Caro, "Proverbs in Graham Greene's *The Power and the Glory*: Framing Thematic Concerns in a Modern Novel," *Proverbium* 6 (1989): 1–7.

Lawrence Cunningham, "The Alter Ego of Greene's 'Whiskey Priest,'" *ELN* 8 (September 1970): 50–52.

Daniel Horton Davies, "Chapter IV: The Confessional and the Altar," in *A Mirror of the Ministry in Modern Novels* (New York: Oxford University Press, 1959), 100–10.

Daniel Diephouse, "The Sense of Ends in Graham Greene and *The Power and the Glory*," *JNT* 20 (Winter 1990): 22–41.

Robert DuParc, "Saint ou Maudit? Le Prêtre dans *La Puissance et la Glorie*," *Études* 260 (March 1949): 368–81.

Leopoldo Duran, "*El poder y la gloria* de Graham Greene. Parabola metafisica," *Arbor* 387 (1978): 101–08.

Fred M. Fetrow, "The Function of Geography in *The Power and the Glory*," *Descant* 23, no. 3 (1979): 40–48.

Alan Warren Friedman, "'The Dangerous Edge': Beginning with Death," in *Graham Greene: A Revaluation*, ed. Jeffrey Meyers (New York: St. Martin's, 1990), 135–38.

Karl Heinz Göller, "Graham Greene: *The Power and the Glory*," *Der Moderne Englische Roman* 51 (1966): 245–61.

A. Grob, "*Power and the Glory*: Graham Greene's Argument from Design," *Criticism* 11 (Winter 1969): 1–30.

Franz Hillig, "Die Draft und die Herrlichkeit: zu dem Priesterroman von Graham Greene," *SZ* 143 (February 1949): 354–66.

Josandra Janisch, "*The Power and the Glory* by Graham Greene," *CRUX* 14 (June 1980): 30–37.

Charles W. Leland, CSB., "The Whiskey-Priest—Lamb of God?" *Basilian* 8 (1963): 52–58.

Patricia E. Rudin Monge, "Elementos descriptivos evocadores de muerte en *The Power and the Glory*," *Revista de la Universidad de Costa Rica* 41 (1975): 193–98.

Edgar Neis, "Zum Sprachstil Graham Greenes," *NS* 25 (April 1957): 166–73.

Karl Patten, "The Strucutre of *The Power and the Glory*," *MFS* 3 (August 1957): 225–34. Reprinted in *Graham Greene*, ed. Harry J. Cargas (St. Louis, MO: Herder, 1969), 101–13.

Patricia E. Monge Rudín, "Elementos Descriptivos Evocadores de Muerte en *The Power and the Glory*," *Revista de la Universidad de Costa Rica* 41 (1975): 193–98.

John Sprott Ryan, "Structure, Imagery and Theme in *The Power and the Glory*," in *Gleanings from Greeneland*, ed. J. S. Ryan (Biddeford, ME: University of New England, 1972), 44–69.

L. O. Smykalova, "Stylistychna funktsiia khudozhnoho porivniannia v romani Gr. Grina Vlada i slava," *InozF* 61 (1981): 20–26.

Joe Straub, "A Psychological View of Priesthood, Sin, and Redemption in Graham Greene's *The Power and the Glory*," in *Third Force Psychology and the Study of Literature*, ed. Bernard J. Paris (Rutherford, NJ: Fairleigh Dickinson University Press, 1986), 191–205.

D. P. Thomas, "Mr. Tench and Secondary Glory in *The Power and the Glory*," *ELN* 7 (December 1969): 129–33.

Gerald Vann, OP, "*The Power and the Glory*," *Blackfriars* 21 (May 1940): 339–40.

Hector J. Vila, "Crisis in the Church: The Element of Irony in *The Power and the Glory*," *JEP* 8 (August 1987): 195–200.

W. D. White, "*The Power and the Glory*: An Apology to the Church," *UPR* 21 (September 1969): 14–22.

Theodore Ziolkowski, "The Power and the Glory," in *Fictional Transfigurations of Jesus* (Princeton: Princeton University Press, 1972), 214–325.

The Quiet American

Hubert Becher, "Der Stille Amerikaner," *SZ* 160 (April 1957): 68–72.

Ralph O. Evans, "Existentialism in Graham Greene's *The Quiet American*," *MFS* 3 (Autumn 1957): 241–48.

Ralph Freedman, "Novel of Contention: *The Quiet American*," *Western Review* 21 (Autumn 1956): 76–81.

G. M. Gaston, "The Structure of Salvation in *The Quiet American*," *Renascence* 31 (Winter 1979): 93–106.

Riley E. Hughes, "*The Quiet American*: The Case Reopened," *Renascence* 12 (Fall 1959): 41–42, 49. Reprinted in *Graham Greene*, ed. Harry J. Cargas (St. Louis, MO: Herder, 1969), 130–33.

J. McMahon, "Graham Greene and *The Quiet American*," *JKUR* 1 (November 1958): 64–73.

Harry W. Rudman, "Clough and Graham Greene's *The Quiet American*," *VN* 19 (1961): 14–15.

Peter Zimmermann, Graham Greene's Auseinandersetzung mit der imperialistischen Vietnamaggression in dem Roman *The Quiet American*," *ZAA* 21 (1973): 34–49.

The Tenth Man

Richard I. Smyer, "*The Tenth Man*: Graham Greene's French Connection," *ELWIU* 15 (Fall 1988): 193–206.

The Third Man

Lawrence Alloway, "Symbolism in *The Third Man*," *WldR* 13 (March 1950): 57–60.

Norman Macleod, "'This strange, rather sad story': The Reflexive Design of Graham Greene's *The Third Man*," *DR* 63 (Summer 1983): 217–41.

Travels with My Aunt

Marilena Avvisati, "Graham Greene contra se," *RLMC* 24 (1973): 221–30.

M. K. Chaudhury, "Graham Greene's *Travels with My Aunt*: A Picaresque Novel," *PURB* 3, no. 2 (1972): 79–85.

Jerome Thale and Rose Marie Thale, "Greene's Literary Pilgrimage: Allusion in *Travels with My Aunt*," *PLL* 13 (Spring 1977): 207–12.

Peter Wolfe, "*Travels with My Aunt*," *StTCL* 6 (Fall 1970): 119–23.

"Under the Garden"

Gwenn Rosina Boardman, "Greene's 'Under the Garden': Aesthetic Explorations," *Renascence* 17 (Summer 1965): 180–90, 194.

Masaya Iwasaki, "Graham Greene no 'Niwa no Shite' ni tsuite; Suzuki Yukio Sensei Kinen Ronbunshu Kanko Iinkai," *Phoenix o Motomete: Eibei Shosetsu no Yukue* (Tokyo: Nan'undo, 1982), 169–82.

"A Visit to Morin"

John Bayley, "Graham Greene: The Short Stories," in *Graham Greene: A Revaluation: New Essays*, ed. Jeffrey Meyers (New York: St. Martin's, 1990), 98–101.

Justo Leopoldo Duran, "Graham Greene's 'A Visit to Morin,'" *ClR* 59 (October 1974): 643–47.

Thomas A. Wassmer, "Faith and Belief: A Footnote to Greene's 'Visit to Morin,'" *Renascence* 11 (1959): 84–88.

HARDY, THOMAS

"The Burghers"

Charles S. Kraszewski, "Hardy's 'The Burghers,'" *Expl* 52 (Winter 1994): 86–90.

"The Convergence of the Twain"

John Tyree Fain, "Hardy's 'The Convergence of the Twain,'" *Expl* 41 (Spring 1983): 34–36.

Desperate Remedies

Kevin Z. Moore, "The Poet within the Architect's Ring: *Desperate Remedies*, Hardy's Hybrid Detective-Gothic Narrative," *SNNTS* 14 (Spring 1982): 31–42.

Motoko Ono, "Hardy–saku *Desperate Remedies* to Taishu Bungaku," *EigoS* 131 (1985): 456–58.

Ian Ousby, "Class in *Desperate Remedies*," *DUJ* 76 (June 1984): 217–22.

Patrick Roberts, "Patterns of Relationship in *Desperate Remedies*," *THJ* 8 (May 1992): 50–57.

R. J. Schork, "A Virgilian Allusion in Hardy's *Desperate Remedies*," *ANQ* 24 (May–June 1986): 145–46.

G. Glen Wickens, "Romantic Myth and Victorian Nature in *Desperate Remedies*," *ESC* 8 (June 1982): 154–73.

Judith Bryant Wittenberg, "Thomas Hardy's First Novel: Women and the Quest for Autonomy," *CLQ* 18 (March 1982): 47–54.

Far from the Madding Crowd

Susan Beegel, "Bathsheba's Lovers: Male Sexuality in *Far from the Madding Crowd*," *TStL* 27 (1984): 108–27.

J. B. Bullen, "Thomas Hardy's *Far from the Madding Crowd*: Perception and Understanding," *THJ* 3 (May 1987): 38–61.

Michael Goss, "Aspects of Time in *Far from the Madding Crowd*," *THJ* 6 (October 1990): 43–53.

Lewis Horne, "Passion and Flood in *Far from the Madding Crowd*," *Ariel* 13 (July 1982): 39–49.

William Mistichelli, "Androgyny, Survival, and Fulfillment in Thomas Hardy's *Far from the Madding Crowd*," *MLS* 18 (Summer 1988): 53–64.

Roy Morrell, "*Far from the Madding Crowd* as an Introduction to Hardy's Novels," in *Critical Essays on Thomas Hardy: The Novels*, ed. Dale Kramer (Boston: G. K. Hall, 1990), 123–33.

Tomoko Nakano, "Hardy's New Conception of Nature in *Far from the Madding Crowd*," *SES* 7 (1982): 47–61.

E. M. Nollen, "The Loving Look in *Far from the Madding Crowd*," *THY* 13 (1986): 69–73.

Linda M. Shires, "Narrative, Gender, and Power in *Far from the Madding Crowd*" in *The Sense of Sex: Feminist Perspectives on Hardy*, ed. Margaret R. Higonnet (Urbana: University of Illinois Press, 1993), 49–65.

Charles Swann, Sybil Crerar, and Catherine Crerar, "*Far from the Madding Crowd*: How Good a Shepherd is Gabriel Oak?" *N&Q* 39 (June 1992): 2, 189.

Carroll Viera, "The Name Levi in *Far from the Madding Crowd*," *THY* 14 (1987): 63.

Judith Bryant Wittenberg, "Angles of Vision and Questions of Gender in *Far from the Madding Crowd*," *CentR* 30 (Winter 1986): 25–40.

"Fellow–Townsmen"

Toby C. Herzog, "Hardy's 'Fellow–Townsmen': A Primer for the Novels," *CLQ* 18 (December 1982): 231–40.

The Hand of Ethelberta

Penny Boumelha, "'A Complicated Position for a Woman': *The Hand of Ethelberta*," in *The Sense of Sex: Feminist Perspectives on Hardy*, ed. Margaret R. Higonnet (Urbana: University of Illinois Press, 1993), 242–59

Jude the Obscure

Sherlyn Abdoo, "Hardy's Jude: The Pursuit of the Ideal as Tragedy," in *The Existential Coordinates of the Human Condition: Poetic—Epic—Tragic: The Literary Genre*, ed. Anna–Teresa Tymieniecka (Dordrecht: Reidel, 1984), 307–18.

Patricia Alden, "A Short Story Prelude to *Jude the Obscure*: More Light on the Genesis of Hardy's Last Novel," *CLQ* 19 (March 1983): 45–52.

Jeffrey Berman, "Infanticide and Object Loss in *Jude the Obscure*," in *Compromise Formations: Current Directions in Psychoanalytic Criticism*, ed. Vera J. Camden (Kent, OH: Kent State University, 1989), 155–81.

Kathleen Blake, "Sue Bridehead: 'The Woman of the Feminist Movement,'" *SEL* 18 (Autumn 1978): 720–21, 726.

Richard Dellamora, "Male Relations in Thomas Hardy's *Jude the Obscure*," *PLL* 27 (Fall 1991): 453–72.

Ronald P. Draper, "Hardy's Comic Tragedy: *Jude the Obscure*," in *Critical Essays on Thomas Hardy: The Novels*, ed. Dale Kramer (Boston: G. K. Hall, 1990), 243–54.

Carol Edwards and Duane Edwards, "*Jude the Obscure*: A Psychoanalytic Study," *HSL* 13, no. 1 (1981): 78–90.

Suzanne Edwards, "A Shadow from the Past: Little Father Time in *Jude the Obscure*," *CLQ* 23 (March 1987): 32–38.

Alexander Fischler, "An Affinity for Birds: Kindness in Hardy's *Jude the Obscure*," *SNNTS* 13 (Fall 1981): 250–65.

Alexander Fischler, "Gins and Spirits: The Letter's Edge in Hardy's *Jude the Obscure*," *SNNTS* 16 (Spring 1984): 1–19.

Alexander Fischler, "A Kinship with Job: Obscurity and Remembrance in Hardy's *Jude the Obscure*," *JEGP* 84 (October 1985): 515–33.

William R. Goetz, "The Felicity and Infelicity of Marriage in *Jude the Obscure*," *NCF* 38 (September 1983): 189–213.

Eleanor C. Guetzloe and Ralph M. Cline, "*Jude the Obscure*: A Pathway to Suicide," in *Youth Suicide Prevention: Lessons from Literature*, ed. Sara Munson Deats and Lagretta Tallent Lenker (New York: Plenum, 1989), 115–34.

Andrew Hamer, "Marygreen," in *KM 80: A Birthday Album for Kenneth Muir, Tuesday, 5 May 1987* (Liverpool: Liverpool University Press, n.d.), 62–65.

Robert E. Heilman, "Hardy's Sue Bridehead," *NCF* 20 (December 1966): 307–23.

Julie Henigan, "Hardy's Emblem of Futility: The Role of Christminster in *Jude the Obscure*," *THY* 14 (1987): 12–14.

Hiroyuki Ide, "Orokamonotachi no Junan–Kyoku: Thomas Hardy: *Jude the Obscure*," *EigoS* 132 (1987): 488–89.

Julie A. Karsten, "Jude Fawley and Little Father Time: Hardy's 'New Men," *POMPA* (1985): 91–97.

Mary Ann Kelly, "Individuation and Consummation in Hardy's *Jude the Obscure*: The Lure of the Void," *VN* 82 (Fall 1992): 62–64.

Mary Ann Kelly, "Schopenhauer's Influence on Hardy's *Jude the Obscure*," in *Schopenhauer: New Essays in Honor of His 200th Birthday*, ed. Eric von der Luft (Lewiston, NY: Mellen, 1988), 232–46.

James R. Kincaid, "Girl–Watching, Child–Beating and Other Exercises for Readers of *Jude the Obscure*," in *The Sense of Sex: Feminist Perspectives on Hardy*, ed. Margaret R. Higonnet (Urbana: University of Illinois Press, 1993), 132–48.

Monique Labbe, "Symbolisme judeo-chrétien, mythe personnel et pessimisme à travers les figures feminines de *Jude the Obscure*," *CVE* 15 (April 1982): 119–29.

Elizabeth Langland, "Becoming a Man in *Jude the Obscure*," in *The Sense of Sex: Feminist Perspectives on Hardy*, ed. Margaret R. Higonnet (Urbana: University of Illinois Press, 1993), 32–48.

John LeVay, "Hardy's *Jude the Obscure*," *Expl* 49 (Summer 1991): 219–23.

Joyce C. H. Liu, "Journey and Landmark: The Merged Temporal and Spatial Perspectives in Thomas Hardy's *Jude the Obscure*," *FJS* 20 (1987): 1–18.

Peggy A. McCormack, "The Syntax of Quest in *Jude the Obscure*," *NOR* 8 (Winter 1981): 42–48.

Frederick P. W. McDowell, "Hardy's 'Seemings or Personal Impressions': The Symbolic Use of Image and Contrast in *Jude the Obscure*," *MFS* 6 (1960): 233–50.

Arthur Mizener, "*Jude the Obscure* as Tragedy," *SoR* 55 (1947): 283–96. Reprinted as "The Novel of Doctrine in the Nineteenth Century: Hardy's *Jude the Obscure*," in *The Sense of Life in the Modern Novel* (Boston: Houghton Mifflin, 1964), 55–77.

Paul Pickrel, "*Jude the Obscure* and the Fall of Phaethon," *HudR* 39 (Summer 1986): 231–50.

Ramon Saldivar, "*Jude the Obscure*: Reading and the Spirit of the Law," *ELH* 50 (Fall 1983): 607–25.

Kurt Schlueter, "The Obscure Birthday of Jude and the Duration of Action in Hardy's *Jude the Obscure*," in *Theorie und Praxis im Erzahlen des 19. und 20. Jahrhunderts: Studien zur englischen und amerikanischen Literatur zu Ehren von Willi Erzgraber*, ed. Winfried Herget, Klaus Peter Jochum, and Ingeborg Weber (Tubingen: Narr, 1986), 81–89.

Michio Seimiya, "Taisei kara no Jiritsu: T. Hardy—Hikagemono Jude," in *Igirisu Shosetsu no Joseitachi*, ed. Yaeko Sumi and Naomi Okamura (Tokyo: Keiso, 1983), 147–68.

Robert C. Slack, "The Text of Hardy's *Jude the Obscure*," *NFC* 22 (September 1957): 261–75.

David Sonstroem, "Order and Disorder in *Jude the Obscure*," *ELT* 24, no. 1 (1981): 6–15.

Julian N. Wasserman, "A Note on the Church of St. Thomas in *Jude the Obscure*," *THY* 14 (1987): 9–12.

Philip M. Weinstein, "'The Spirit Unappeassed and Peregrine': *Jude the Obscure*," in *The Semantics of Desire: Changing Models of Identity from Dickens to Joyce* (Princeton: Princeton University Press, 1984), 125–42. Reprinted in *Critical Essays on Thomas Hardy: The Novels*, ed. Dale Kramer (Boston: G. K. Hall, 1990), 228–42.

A Laodicean

Linda M. Austin, "Hardy's Laodicean Narrative," *MFS* 35 (Summer 1989): 211–22.

Paul Ward, "*A Laodicean*," *THY* 11 (1984): 28–30.

The Mayor of Casterbridge

Roger Bromley, "The Boundaries of Hegemony: Thomas Hardy and *The Mayor of Casterbridge*," in *Literature, Society and the Sociology of Literature*, ed. Francis Barker, et al. (Colchester: University of Essex Press, 1970), 30–40.

Raymond Chapman, "The Reader as Listener: Dialect and Relationships in *The Mayor of Casterbridge*," in *The Pragmatics of Style*, ed. Leo Hickey (London: Routledge, 1989), 159–87.

Karen Davis, "A Deaf Ear to Essence: Music and Hardy's *The Mayor of Casterbridge*," *JEGP* 89 (April 1990): 181–201.

W. Eugene Davis, "Comparatively Modern Skeletons in the Garden: A Reconsideration of *The Mayor of Casterbridge*," *ELT* 3 (1985): 108–20.

D. A. Dike, "A Modern Oedipus: *The Mayor of Casterbridge*," *EIC* 2 (April 1952): 169–79.

R. P. Draper, "*The Mayor of Casterbridge*," *CritQ* 25 (Spring 1983): 57–70.

Duane D. Edwards, "*The Mayor of Casterbridge* and Aeschylean Tragedy," *SNNTS* 4 (1972): 608–18.

Leonora Epstein, "Sale and Sacrament: The Wife Auction in *The Mayor of Casterbridge*," *ELN* 24 (June 1987): 50–56.

William Greenslade, "Hardy's 'Facts' Notebook: A Further Source for *The Mayor of Casterbridge*," *THJ* 2 (January 1986): 33–35.

Juliet M. Grindle, "Compulsion and Choice in *The Mayor of Casterbridge*," in *The Novels of Thomas Hardy*, ed. Anne Smith (London: Vision, 1979), 91–106.

Stirling Haig, "'By the Rivers of Babylon': Water and Exile in *The Mayor of Casterbridge*," *THY* 11 (1984): 55–62.

Robert B. Heilman, "Hardy's *Mayor*: Notes on Style," *NCF* 18 (December 1964): 307–29.

Earl Ingersoll, "Writing and Memory in *The Mayor of Casterbridge*," *ELT* 3, no. 3 (1990): 299–309.

Frederick R. Karl, "*The Mayor of Casterbridge*: A New Fiction Defined," *MFS* 6 (1960): 195–213.

Jeannette King, "*The Mayor of Casterbridge*: Talking about Character,'" *THJ* 8 (October 1992): 42–46.

George Levine, "Thomas Hardy's 'The Mayor of Casterbridge': Reversing the Real," in *Critical Essays on Thomas Hardy: The Novels*, ed. Dale Kramer (Boston: G. K. Hall, 1990), 169–90.

Kevin Z. Moore, "Death against Life: Hardy's Mortified and Mortifying 'Man of Character' in *The Mayor of Casterbridge*," *BSUF* 24, no. 3 (1983): 13–25.

Michael Valdez Moses, "Agon in the Marketplace: *The Mayor of Casterbridge* as Bourgeois Tragedy," *SoAQ* 87 (Spring 1988): 219–41.

John Paterson, "*The Mayor of Casterbridge* as Tragedy," *VS* 3 (1959): 151–71.

Elaine Showalter, "The Unmanning of the *Mayor of Casterbridge*," in *Critical Approaches to the Fiction of Thomas Hardy*, ed. Dale Kramer (London: Macmillan, 1979), 99–115.

Lawrence J. Starzyk, "Hardy's *Mayor*: The Antitradtional Basis of Tragedy," *SNNTS* 4 (1972): 592–607.

Michael Taft, "Hardy's Manipulation of Folklore and Literary Imagination: The Case of the Wife Sale in *The Mayor of Casterbridge*," *SNNTS* 13 (Winter 1981): 399–407.

Guruo Zhang, "Thomas Hardy and *The Mayor of Casterbridge*," *Waiguoyu* 1 (February 1990): 31–34, 61.

A Pair of Blue Eyes

Stevie Anne Bolduc, "The Imperative for Individuation: Thomas Hardy's *A Pair of Blue Eyes*," *JEP* 4 (August 1983): 196–206.

Peter W. L. Clough, "Hardy's Trilobite," *THJ* 4 (May 1988): 29–31.

Lawrence Jay Dessner, "Space, Time, and Coincidence in Hardy," *SNNTS* 24 (Summer 1992): 154–72.

Jo Devereux, "Thomas Hardy's *A Pair of Blue Eyes*: The Heroine as Text," *VN* 81 (Spring 1992): 20–23.

Annie Escuret, "*A Pair of Blue Eyes*: La Mer et la falaise," *CVE* 23 (April 1986): 111–31.

Lawrence Jones, "Thomas Hardy and the Cliff without a Name," in *Geography and Literature: A Meeting of the Disciplines*, ed. William E. Mallory and Paul Simpson-Housley (Syracuse, NY: Syracuse University Press, 1987), 169–84.

Mary Rimmer, "Club Laws: Chess and the Construction of Gender in *A Pair of Blue Eyes*," in *The Sense of Sex: Feminist Perspectives on Hardy*, ed. Margaret R. Higonnet (Urbana: University of Illinois Press, 1993), 203–20.

Yasunori Sugimura, "Repetition and Relativity: The Inner Structure of *A Pair of Blue Eyes*," *Shiron* 25 (1986): 69–88.

The Return of the Native

Richard Benvenuto, "*The Return of the Native* as Tragedy," *NCF* 26 (March 1971): 83–93.

Sandy Cohen, "Blind Clym, Unchristian Christian and the Redness of the Reddleman: Character Correspondences in Hardy's *The Return of the Native*," *THY* 11 (1984): 49–55.

Robert Evans, "The Other Eustacia," *Novel* 1 (1968): 251–59.

Avrom Fleishman, "The Buried Giant of Egdon Heath," in *Critical Essays on Thomas Hardy: The Novels*, ed. Dale Kramer (Boston: G. K. Hall, 1990), 140–55.

Lois Groner Gadek, "Tragic Potential and Narrative Perspective in Hardy's *The Return of the Native*: A Study in Tone," *THY* 14 (1987): 25–35.

Wilhelm Gauger, "Ordnung und Unordnung in *The Return of the Native*," in *Anglistentag 1981: Vortrage*, ed. Jorg Hasler (Frankfurt am Main: Lang, 1983), 190–205.

Leslie Grinsell, "Rainbarrows and Thomas Hardy," *THJ* 2 (May 1986): 59–61.

John Jewell, "Hardy's *The Return of the Native*," *Expl* 49 (Spring 1991): 159–62.

Mary Ellen Jordan, "Thomas Hardy's Return of the Native: Clym Yeobright and Melancholia," *AI* 39 (Summer 1982): 101–18.

Tianliang Liao, "The Root Cause of the Tragedy in *The Return of the Native*," *FLitS* 29 (September 1985): 140–42.

Charles E. May, "The Magic of Metaphor in *The Return of the Native*," *CLQ* 22 (June 1986): 111–18.

J. Hillis Miller, "Topography in *The Return of the Native*," *ELWIU* 8 (Fall 1981): 119–34.

John Paterson, "The 'Poetics' of *The Return of the Native*," *MFS* 6 (1960): 214–22. Reprinted in *Critical Essays on Thomas Hardy: The Novels*, ed. Dale Kramer (Boston: G. K. Hall, 1990), 133–40.

Martin Ray, "Hardy's Borrowing from Shakespeare: Eustacia Vye and Lady Macbeth," *THY* 14 (1987): 64.

Dieter Riesner, "Uber die Genesis von Thomas Hardys *The Return of the Native*," *Archiv* 200 (1963): 53–59.

Robert Squillace, "Hardy's Mummers," *NCF* 41 (September 1986): 172–89.

Katsuya Taki, "Kikyo," in *Igirisu Bungaku: Kenkyu to Kansho 2*, ed. Yoshitsugu Uchida and Kishimoto Yoshitaka (Osaka: Sogensha, 1982), 40–52; 97–106.

Otis B. Wheeler, "Four Versions of *The Return of the Native*," *NCF* 14 (March 1959): 27–44.

Bryant N. Wyatt, "Poetic Justice in *The Return of the Native*," *MTJ* 21 (Fall 1983): 56–57.

Tess of the D'Urbervilles

Jane Adamson, "Tess, Time and Its Shapings," *CR* 26 (1984): 18–36.

John A. Anonby, "Hardy's Handling of Biblical Allusions in His Portrayal of Tess of the d'Urbervilles," *C&L* 30, no. 3 (Spring 1981): 13–26.

Kathleen Blake, "Pure Tess: Hardy on Knowing a Woman," *SEL, 1500–1900* 22 (1982): 689–705. Reprinted in *Critical Essays on Thomas Hardy: The Novels*, ed. Dale Kramer (Boston: G. K. Hall, 1990), 204–19. Reprinted in *Thomas Hardy's "Tess of the d'Urbervilles*," ed. Harold Bloom (New York: Chelsea House, 1987), 87–102.

Paula C. Blank, "*Tess of the D'Urbervilles*: The English Novel and the Foreign Plot," *MidHLS* 12, no. 1 (1989): 62–71.

Charlotte Bonica, "Nature and Paganism in Hardy's *Tess of the D'Urbervilles*," *ELH* 49 (Winter 1982): 849–62.

William Bonnell, "Broken Communion in *Tess of the D'Urbervilles*," *ELN* 31 (June 1994): 63–71.

Allan Brick, "Paradise and Consciousness in Hardy's *Tess*," *NCF* 17 (June 1962): 115–34.

Suzanne Hunter Brown, "'Tess' and 'Tess': An Experiment in Genre," *MFS* 28 (1982): 25–44.

Jerome H. Buckley, "*Tess and the D'Urbervilles*," *VIJ* 20 (1992): 1–12.

HARDY, THOMAS, *Tess of the D'Urbervilles*

Elizabeth Campbell, "*Tess of the D'Urbervilles*: Misfortune Is a Woman," *VN* 76 (Fall 1989): 1–5.

Byron Caminero-Santangelo, "A Moral Dilemma: Ethics in *Tess of the D'Urbervilles*," *ES* 75 (January 1994): 46–61.

Laura Claridge, "Tess: A Less Than Pure Woman Ambivalently Presented," *TSLL* 28 (Fall 1986): 324–38.

Pierre Coustillas, "*Tess of the d'Urbervilles* ou le dernier vol de la pureté," *Fabula* 6 (1985): 107–27.

Julian Meldon D'Arcy, "Idolatry in Hardy's *Tess of the D'Urbervilles*," in *Proceedings from the Second Nordic Conference for English Studies*, ed. Haken Ringbom and Matti Rissanen (Abo: Abo Akademi, 1984), 519–28.

William A. Davis Jr., "'But He Can Be Prosecuted for This': Legal and Sociological Backgrounds of the Mock Marriage in Hardy's Serial Tess," *CLQ* 25 (March 1989): 28–41.

J. R. Ebbatson, "The Darwinian View of *Tess*: A Reply," *SoR* 8 (1975): 247–53.

Roger Ebbatson, "The Plutonic Master: Hardy and the Steam Threshing–Machine," *CrSur* 2, no. 1 (1990): 63–69.

Joseph J. Egan, "The Fatal Suitor: Early Foreshadowings in *Tess of the D'Urbervilles*," *TStL* 15 (1970): 161–64.

Robert F. Fleissner, "*Tess of the D'Urbervilles* and George Turberville," *Names* 37 (March 1989): 65–68.

Janet Freeman, "Ways of Looking at Tess," *SP* 79 (Summer 1982): 311–23.

Paul Goetsch, "Mundlichkeit und Schriftlichkeit in Hardys regionalem Roman *Tess of the D'Urbervilles*," in *Theorie und Praxis im Erzahlen des 19. und 20. Jahrhunderts: Studien zur englischen und amerikanischen Literatur zu Ehren von Willi Erzgraber*, ed. Winfried Herget, Klaus Peter Jochum, and Ingeborg Weber (Tubingen: Narr, 1986), 63–80.

Elliott B. Gose, Jr., "Psychic Evolution: Darwinism and Initiation in *Tess of the D'Urbervilles*," *NCF* 18 (December 1963): 261–72. Reprinted in *Critical Essays on Thomas Hardy: The Novels*, ed. Dale Kramer (Boston: G. K. Hall, 1990), 219–28.

Julie Grossman, "Hardy's *Tess* and 'The Photograph': Images to Die for," *Criticism* 35 (Fall 1993): 609–30.

Ali A. al-Hejazi, "The Symmetrical and Asymmetrical Elements in Hardy's *Tess of the D'Urbervilles*," *JKSUA* 11, no. 2 (1984): 149–59.

Margaret R. Higonnet, "Fictions of Feminine Voice: Antiphony and Silence in Hardy's *Tess of the D'Urbervilles*," in *Out of Bounds: Male Writers and Gender(ed) Criticism*, ed. Laura Claridge and Elizabeth Langland (Amherst: University of Massachusetts Press, 1990), 197–218.

Margaret R. Higonnet, "Tess and the Problem of Voice," in *The Sense of Sex: Feminist Perspectives on Hardy*, ed. Margaret R. Higonnet (Urbana: University of Illinois Press, 1993), 14–31.

Thomas Hinde, "Accident and Coincidence in *Tess of the D'Urbervilles*," in *The Genius of Thomas Hardy*, ed. Margaret Drabble (London: Weidenfeld, 1976), 74–79.

Lewis B. Horne, "The Darkening Sun of Tess Durbeyfield," *TSLL* 13 (1970): 299–311.

John B. Humma, "Language and Disguise: The Imagery of Nature and Sex in Tess," *SAR* 54 (November 1989): 63–83.

Mary Jacobus, "Tess: The Making of a Pure Woman," in *Thomas Hardy's "Tess of the d'Urbervilles,"* ed. Harold Bloom (New York: Chelsea House, 1987), 45–60.

Bruce Johnson, "'The Perfection of Species' and Hardy's Tess," in *Nature and the Victorian Imagination*, ed. G. B. Tennyson and U. C. Knoepflmacher (Berkeley: University of California Press, 1977), 259–77. Reprinted in *Thomas Hardy's "Tess of the d'Urbervilles,"* ed. Harold Bloom (New York: Chelsea House, 1987), 25–43.

James Kincaid, "'You Did Not Come': Absence, Death and Eroticism in *Tess*," in *Sex and Death in Victorian Literature*, ed. Regina Barreca (Bloomington: Indiana University Press, 1990), 9–31.

Henry Kozicki, "Myths of Redemption in Hardy's *Tess of the D'Urbervilles*," *PLL* 10 (1974): 150–58.

Marilyn J. Kurata, "Hardy's *Tess of the D'Ubervilles*," *Expl* 42 (Fall 1983): 34–35.

J. T. Laird, "New Light on the Evoluion of *Tess of the D'Urbervilles*," *RES* 31, no. 124 (1980): 414–35.

J. J. Lecercle, "La Question du style chez Thomas Hardy," *BSSA* 7 (1985): 161–71.

So–young Lee, "An Essay on Tess's Androgynous Vision: Hardy's Yin–Yang Principle in *Tess of the D'Urbervilles*," *JELL* 35 (Winter 1989): 651–69.

Jakob Lothe, "Hardy's Authorial Narrative Methods in *Tess of the D'Urbervilles*," in *The Nineteenth–Century British Novel*, ed. Jeremy Hawthorn (Baltimore: Arnold, 1986), 157–70.

Tetsuo Maekawa, "D'Urberville–ke no Tess no Ketsumatsu," in *Suga Yasuo, Ogoshi Kazugo: Ryokyoju Taikan Kinen Ronbunshu* (Kyoto: Apollonsha, 1980), 437–48.

Phillip Mallett, "'Smacked, and Brought to Her Senses': Hardy and the Clitheroe Abduction Case," *THJ* 8 (May 1992): 70–73.

J. Hillis Miller, "Fiction and Repetition: *Tess of the D'Urbervilles*," in *Forms of Modern British Fiction*, ed. Alan Waren Friedman (Austin: University of Texas Press, 1975), 32–71. Reprinted as "*Tess of the D'Urbervilles*: Fiction as Immanent Design," in *Thomas Hardy's "Tess of the d' Urbervilles,"* ed. Harold Bloom (New York: Chelsea House, 1987), 61–86.

R. Moers, "Tess as a Cultural Stereotype," in "Hardy Perennial," *NYRB* (9 November 1967): 31–33.

Rosemarie Morgan, "Passive Victim? *Tess of the D'Urbervilles*," *THJ* 5 (January 1989): 31–54.

Peter R. Morton, "*Tess of the D'Urbervilles*: A Neo–Darwinian Reading," *SoR* 7 (1974): 38–50.

Kazu Nagamori, "*Tess of the D'Urbervilles* ni okeru Higeki," *EL&L* 19 (1983): 73–97.

K. R. Narayanaswamy, "Archetypal Myths in *Tess of the D'Urbervilles*," *PURB* 13 (October 1982): 53–63.

Jeff Nunokawa, "Tess, Tourism, and the Spectacle of the Woman," in *Rewriting the Victorians: Theory History and the Politics of Gender*, ed. Linda M. Shires (New York: Routledge, 1992), 70–86.

Norman Page, "Hardy and Brazil," *N&Q* 30 (August 1983): 319–20.

Bernard J. Paris, "'A Confusion of Many Standards': Conflicting Value Systems in *Tess of the D'Urbervilles*," *NCF* 24 (March 1969): 57–79.

Lynn Parker, "'Pure Woman' and Tragic Heroine? Conflicting Myths in Hardy's *Tess of the D'Urbervilles*," *SNNTS* 24 (Fall 1992): 273–81.

P. J. Perry, "William Dewy, John Small, and the Musical Bull," *THY* 8 (1978): 34–35.

T. D. Pokhylevych, "Rol' pryrody v psykholohizatsii obrazu Tess: Roman T. Hardi *Tess iz rodu D'Erbervilliv*," *InozF* 64 (1981): 119–25.

Michael Ponsford, "Thomas Hardy's Control of Sympathy in *Tess of the D'Urbervilles*," *MQ* 27 (Summer 1986): 487–503.

Adrian Poole, "'Men's Words' and Hardy's Women," *EIC* 31 (October 1981): 328–45.

Atma Ram, "Morality in Tess: An Adjustment of Images," *PURB* 15 (April 1984): 65–72.

Meera Ramachandran, "Optimism in *Tess of the D'Urbervilles*," *PURB* 17 (October 1986): 67–71.

Annie Ramel, "L'Un Distinct ou l'indistinct? Le Destin Tragique de Tess," *CVE* 35 (April 1992): 201–16.

Adena Rosmarin, "The Narrativity of Interpretive History," in *Reading Narrative: Form, Ethics, Ideology*, ed. James Phelan (Columbus: Ohio State University Press, 1989), 12–26.

Robert C. Schweik, "Moral Perspective in *Tess of the D'Urbervilles*," *CE* 24 (1962): 14–18.

Janie Senechal, "*Tess of the D'Urbervilles*: Analyse d'un paragraphe," *Fabula* 6 (1985): 129–37.

Kaja Silverman, "History, Figuration and Female Subjectivity in 'Tess of the d'Urbevilles," *Novel* 18 (Fall 1984): 5–28.

Jeffrey Sommers, "Hardy's Other Bildungsroman: *Tess of the D'Urbervilles*," *ELT* 25, no. 3 (1982): 159–68.

Jack Stevens, "Literary and Biographical Allusion in *Tess of the D'Urbervilles*," *THY* 14 (1987): 20–25.

Tony Tanner, "Colour and Movement in Hardy's *Tess of the D'Urbervilles*," in *Thomas Hardy's "Tess of the d'Urbervilles*," ed. Harold Bloom (New York: Chelsea House, 1987), 9–23.

Charlotte Thompson, "Language and the Shape of Reality in *Tess*," *ELH* 50, no. 4 (1983): 729–62.

T. B. Tomlinson, "Hardy's Universe: *Tess of the D'Urbervilles*," *CR* 16 (1973): 19–38.

Dorothy Van Ghent, "On *Tess of the D'Urbervilles*," in *The English Novel: Form and Function* (New York: Holt, Rinehart, 1953), 195–209.

Duane Leroy Vorhees, "Hardy, Tess, and Psychic Scotoma," *JELL* 35 (Winter 1989): 671–75.

Leon Waldoff, "Psychological Determinism in *Tess of the D'Urbervilles*," in *Critical Approaches to the Fiction of Thomas Hardy*, ed. Dale Kramer (London: Macmillan, 1979), 135–54.

Philip M. Weinstein, "Hardy: 'Full–Hearted Evensong,'" in *Thomas Hardy's "Tess of the d'Urbervilles*," ed. Harold Bloom (New York: Chelsea House, 1987), 103–17.

G. Glen Wickens, "Hardy and the Aesthetic Mythographers: The Myth of Demeter and Persephone in *Tess of the D'Urbervilles*," *UTQ* 53 (Fall 1983): 85–106.

G. Glen Wickens, "'Sermons in stones': The Return to Nature in *Tess of the D'Urbervilles*," *ESC* 14 (June 1988): 184–203.

G. Glen Wickens, "Victorian Theories of Language and *Tess of the D'Urbervilles*," *Mosaic* 19 (Winter 1986): 99–115.

George Wing, "Tess and the Romantic Milkmaid," *RevEL* 3 (1962): 22–30.

Terence Wright, "Rhetoric and Lyrical Imagery in *Tess of the D'Urbervilles*," *DUJ* 34 (1973): 79–85.

The Trumpet Major

Simon Gatrell, "Middling Hardy," in *Critical Essays on Thomas Hardy: The Novels*, ed. Dale Kramer (Boston: G. K. Hall, 1990), 155–69.

Annie Escuret, "*Le Trompette-Major* ou l'histoire du Perroquet et de l'Agami," *CVE* 17 (April 1983): 1–20.

Two on a Tower

John Bayley, "The Love Story in *Two on a Tower*," *THA* 1 (1982), 60–70.

Martin Beech, "Thomas Hardy: Far from the Royal Observatory, Greenwich?" *THJ* 8 (May 1992): 74–78.

Joan Grundy, "*Two on a Tower* and 'The Duchess of Malfi,'" *THJ* 5 (May 1989): 55–60.

Glenn Irvin, "High Passion and High Church in Hardy's *Two on a Tower*," *ELT* 3 (1985): 121–29.

David H. Levy, "StarTrails," *S&T* 80 (July 1990): 84–85.

Rosemary Summer, "The Experimental and the Absurd in *Two on a Tower*," *THA* 1 (1982), 71–81.

Paul Ward, "*Two on a Tower*: A Critical Revaluation," *THY* 8 (1978): 29–34.

George Wing, "Hardy's Star–Cross'd Lovers in *Two on a Tower*," *THY* 14 (1987): 35–44.

Under the Greenwood Tree

Duane Edwards, "The Ending of *Under the Greenwood Tree*," *THY* 8 (1978): 21–22.

Timothy Hands, "Arthur Shirley (Vicar of Stinsford, 1837–1891)," *THA* 2 (1984): 171–86.

Glenn Irvin, "Hardy's Comic Archetype: *Under the Greenwood Tree*," *THJ* 6 (October 1990): 54–58.

Kensuke Morimatsu, "Hardy no Shoki–Shosetsu to Pastoral no Henyo: Ryokuju no Kage de no Chushin ni," in *Eikoku Shosetsu Kenkyu Dai 13 satsu* (Tokyo: Shinozaki, 1981), 56–95.

Stephen J. Spector, "Flight of Fancy: Characterization in Hardy's *Under the Greenwood Tree*," *ELH* 55 (Summer 1988): 469–85.

The Well-Beloved

Yoshiko Takakuwa, "*The Well-Beloved*: Hardy's 'Slight' Novel," *SELit* 59 (Eng. no.) (1983): 19–32.

"The Withered Arm"

Romey T. Keys, "Hardy's Uncanny Narrative: A Reading of 'The Withered Arm,'" *TSLL* 27 (Spring 1985): 106–23.

The Woodlanders

Norman Arkans, "Hardy's Novel Impression–Pictures," *CLQ* 22 (September 1986): 153–64.

David Ball, "Tragic Contradiction in Hardy's *The Woodlanders*," *Ariel* 18 (January 1987): 17–25.

John Bayley, "A Social Comedy? On Re–Reading *The Woodlanders*," *THA* 5 (1987), 3–21. Reprinted in *Critical Essays on Thomas Hardy: The Novels*, ed. Dale Kramer (Boston: G. K. Hall, 1990), 190–204.

Brandon B. Bennett, "Hardy's Noble Melancholics," *Novel* 27 (Fall 1993): 24–39.

Jeffrey S. Cramer, "The Grotesque in Thomas Hardy's *The Woodlanders*," *THY* 8 (1978): 25–29.

Marilyn Stall Fontane, "Hardy's Best Story," *THY* 11 (1984): 37–41.

"'A Forlorn Hope?' Grace Melbury and *The Woodlanders*," *THY* 10 (1980): 72–76.

Frank R. Giordano Jr., "The Martyrdom of Giles Winterborne," *THA* 2 (1984): 61–78.

Jonathan C. Glance, “The Problem of the Man–Trap in Hardy’s *The Woodlanders*,” *VN* 78 (Fall 1990): 26–29.

Louis K. Greiff, “Symbolic Action in Hardy’s *The Woodlanders*: An Application of Burkian Theory,” *THY* 14 (1987): 52–62.

William P. Hanson, “New Realities: Common Concerns in Raabe and Hardy,” in *Wilhelm Raabe: Studien zu seinem Leben und Werk*, ed. Leo A. Lensing and Hans–Werner Peter (Braunschweig: Verl, 1981), 255–65.

Lesley Higgins, “Pastoral Meets Melodrama in Thomas Hardy’s *The Woodlanders*,” *THJ* 6 (2 June 1990): 111–25.

Lesley Higgins, “‘Strange Webs of Melancholy’: Shelleyan Echoes in *The Woodlanders*,” *THA* 5 (1987): 38–46.

R. H. Hutton, “*The Woodlanders*,” *Spectator* (26 March 1887): 419.

Glenn Irvin, “Structure and Tone in *The Woodlanders*,” *THA* 2 (1984): 79–90.

Mary Jacobus, “Tree and Machine: *The Woodlanders*,” in *Critical Approaches to the Fiction of Thomas Hardy*, ed. Dale Kramer (London: Macmillan, 1979), 116–34.

Robert Kiely, “The Menace of Solitude: The Politics and Aesthetics of Exclusion in *The Woodlanders*,” *The Sense of Sex: Feminist Perspectives on Hardy*, ed. Margaret R. Higonnet (Urbana: University of Illinois Press, 1993), 188–202.

John Peck, “Hardy’s *The Woodlanders*: The Too Transparent Webb,” *ELT* 24, no. 3 (1981): 147–54.

M. R. Skilling, “Investigations into the Country of *The Woodlanders*,” *THJ* 8 (October 1992): 62–67.

Ralph Stewart, “Hardy’s *Woodlanders*,” *Expl* 48 (Spring 1990): 195–96.

William B. Thesing, “ ‘The Question of Matrimonial Divergence’: Distorting Mirrors and Windows in Hardy’s *The Woodlanders*,” *THY* 14 (1987): 44–52.

HARTLEY, LESLIE POLES

The Go–Between

K. E. Learmont-Batley, “‘The Past Is a Foreign Country: They Do Things Differently There’: Some Views on Teaching L. P. Hartley’s *The Go–Between*,” *CRUX* 19 (December 1985): 3–17.

Fiona MacArthur, "Miscommunication, Language Development and Enculturation in L. P. Hartley's *The Go–Between*," *Style* 24 (Spring 1990): 103–12.

Alan Radley, "Psychological Realism in L. P. Hartley's *The Go–Between*," *L&P* 33 (1987): 1–10.

Eustace and Hilda

Robert C. Petersen, "The Expanding Symbol as Narrative Device in the *Eustace and Hilda* Trilogy of L. P. Hartley," *ELWIU* 17 (Spring 1990): 43–51.

HILL, SUSAN

In the Springtime of the Year

K. R. Ireland, "Rite at the Center: Narrative Duplication in Susan Hill's *In the Springtime of the Year*," *JNT* 13 (Fall 1983): 172–80.

Mary Jane Reed, "Recommended: Susan Hill," *EJ* 72 (April 1983): 75–76.

Michele Thery, "Chant d'innocence ou chant d'expérience: l'itinéraire de la douleur dans *In the Springtime of the Year*, de Susan Hill," *ÉBC* (December 1992): 83–97.

HOGG, JAMES

The Brownie of Bodsbeck

Margaret Elphinstone, "*The Brownie of Bodsbeck*: History or Fantasy?" *SHW* 3 (1992): 31–41.

A Father's New-Year's Gift

David Groves, "James Hogg's New Year's Gift: New Information, and a Correction," *N&Q* 38 (September 1991): 313.

"Odd Characters"

Elaine Petrie, "'Odd Characters,'" *SHW* 1 (1990): 136–52.

The Private Memoirs and Confessions of a Justified Sinner

Pierre Arnaud, "Les Réverbérations de l'angoisse dans *The Private Memoirs & Confessions of a Justified Sinner*: Du narcissisme de Hogg au narcissisme du texte," in *Visages de l'angoisse*, ed. Christian La Cassagnere (Clermont-Ferrand: Publications de la faculté des lettres de Clermont, 1989), 231–47.

Williston R. Benedict, "A Story Replete with Horror," *PULC* 44 (Spring 1983): 246-51.

John Bligh, "The Doctrinal Premises of Hogg's *Confessions of a Justified Sinner*," *StSL* 19 (1984): 148-64.

David Groves, "Allusions to Dr. Faustus in James Hogg's *A Justified Sinner*," *StSL* 18 (1983): 157–65.

David Groves, "James Hogg's Confessions: New Information," *RES* 40 (May 1989): 240-42.

David Groves, "Parallel Narratives in Hogg's *Justified Sinner*," *ScLJ* 9 (December 1982): 37–44.

Douglas Jones, "Double Jeopardy and the Chameleon Art in James Hogg's *Justified Sinner*," *StSL* 23 (1988): 164–85.

Magdalene Redekop, "Beyond Closure: Buried Alive with Hogg's *Justified Sinner*," *ELH* 52 (Spring 1985): 159–84.

Philip Rogers, "'A name which may serve your turn': James Hogg's Gil-Martin," *StSL* 21 (1986): 89–98.

The Three Perils of Man

Barbara Blode, "The Gothic Antecedents of *The Three Perils of Man*," *SHW* 3 (1992): 76–78.

H. B. de Groot, "The Imperilled Reader in *The Three Perils of Man*," *SHW* 1 (1990): 114–25.

Douglas S. Mack, "James Hogg's Second Thoughts on *The Three Perils of Man*," *StSL* 21 (1986): 167–75.

W. G. Sheperd, "Fat Flesh: The Poetic Theme of *The Three Perils of Man*," *SHW* 3 (1992): 1–9.

The Three Perils of Woman

Barbara Bloede, "*The Three Perils of Woman* and the Edinburgh Prostitution Scandal of 1823: A Reply to Dr. Groves," *SHW* 3 (1992): 88–94.

Valentina Bold, "Traditional Narrative Elements in *The Three Perils of Woman*," *SHW* 3 (1992): 42–56.

David Groves, "Myth and Structure in James Hogg's *The Three Perils of Woman*," *WC* 13 (Autumn 1982): 203–10.

Emma Letley, "Some Literary Uses of Scots in *The Three Perils of Woman*," *SHW* 1 (1990): 46–56.

Douglas Mack, "Gatty's Illness in *The Three Perils of Woman*," *SHW* 1 (1990): 133–35.

The Spy

Roger Leitch, "Hogg, Scott, and the Gaick Catastrophe," *SHW* 1 (1990): 126–28.

HUGHES, RICHARD

A High Wind in Jamaica

Susanne M. Dumbleton, "Animals and Humans in *A High Wind in Jamaica*," *AWR* 68 (Summer 1981): 51–61.

Ian Milligan, "Richard Hughes and Michael Scott: A Further Source for *A High Wind in Jamaica*," *N&Q* 33 (June 1986): 192–93.

Paul Bennett Morgan, "Richard Hughes's *A High Wind in Jamaica*: A Misattributed Edition," *N&Q* 37 (March 1990): 67.

The Human Predicament

Richard Humphrey, "Der historische Roman und das Feindbild: Zu Richard Hughes' unvollendeter Faschismus-Trilogie *The Human Predicament* (1961–73)," *A&E* 29–30 (1986): 157–72.

A Moment of Time

Paul Bennett Morgan, "*A Moment of Time*: The Short Stories of Richard Hughes," *NewWR* (Autumn 1988): 57–63.

HUGHES, THOMAS

Tom Brown's School Days

Samuel Pickering, Jr., "The 'Race of Real Children' and Beyond in *Tom Brown's School Days*," *Arnoldian* 11 (Spring 1984): 36–46.

Ian Watson, "Victorian England, Colonialism and the Ideology of *Tom Brown's Schooldays*," *ZAA* 29, no. 2 (1981): 116–29.

George J. Worth, "Of Muscles and Manliness: Some Reflections on Thomas Hughes," in *Victorian Literature and Society: Essays Presented to Richard D. Altick*, ed. James R. Kincaid and Albert J. Kuhn (Columbus: Ohio State University Press, 1984), 300–13.

HUXLEY, ALDOUS

Antic Hay

James Hall, *The Tragic Comedians: Seven Modern British Novelists*, (Bloomington: Indiana University Press, 1963), 31–44.

Frederick R. Karl, "The Play Within the Novel in *Antic Hay*," *Renascence* 13 (Winter 1961): 59–68.

Marion Montgomery, "Aldous Huxley's Incomparable Man in *Antic Hay*," *Discourse* 3 (October 1960): 227–32.

Brave New World

Richard V. Chase, "The Huxley-Herd Paradise," *PR* 10 (March–April, 1943): 143–58.

Willi Erzgraber, "Aldous Huxley: *Brave New World* (1932)," in *Die Utopie in der angloamerikanischen Literatur: Interpretationen*, ed. Hartmut Heuermann and Bernd–Peter Lange (Dusseldorf: Bagel, 1984), 198–218.

Peter Firchow, "The Satire of Huxley's Brave New World," *MFS* 12 (Winter 1966): 260–78.

Koon–ki T. Ho, "Spatial and Temporal Ramifications in Modern Chinese and English Dystopias," in *II: Space and Boundaries in Literature/Espace et frontières dans la littérature*, ed. Roger Bauer, Douwe Fokkema, Michael de Graat, John Boening, Gerald Gillespie, Maria Moog–Grunewald, Virgil Nemoianu, Joseph Ricapito, Manfred Schmeling, Joachim von der Thusen, and Claus Uhlig (Munich: Iudicium, 1990), 473–77.

Irving Howe, “The Fiction of Anti–Utopia,” *NewR* 146 (23 April 1962): 13–16.

William M. Jones, “The Iago of *Brave New World*,” *WHR* 15 (Summer 1961): 275–78.

Almeda King, “Christianity Without Tears: Man Without Humanity,” *EJ* 57 (July 1968):820–824.

Peter M. Larsen, “Synthetic Myths in Aldous Huxley’s *Brave New World*: A Note,” *ES* 62 (December 1981): 506–8.

Edward Lobb, “The Subversion of Drama in Huxley’s *Brave New World*,” *IFR* 11 (Summer 1984): 94–101.

William Matter, “On *Brave New World*,” in *No Place Else: Explorations in Utopian and Disutopian Fiction*, ed. Eric S. Rabkin, Martin H. Greenberg, and Joseph D. Olander (Carbondale: Southern Illinois University Press, 1983), 94–109.

James D. Mulvihill, “A Source for Huxley’s ‘Savage Reservation,’” *NQ* 31 (March 1984): 83–84.

M. D. Petre, “Bolshevist Ideals and the *Brave New World*,” *HibJ* 31 (October 1932): 61–71.

I. Seehase, “Karel Capeks Umgang mit Huxleys *Brave New World*,” *ZS* 35, no. 1 (1990): 56–65.

James Sexton, “Aldous Huxley’s Bokanovsky,” *SFS* 16 (March 1989): 85–89.

James Sexton, “*Brave New World* and the Rationalization of Industry,” *ESC* 12 (December 1986): 424–39.

Malinda Snow, “The Gray Parody in *Brave New World*,” *PLL* 13 (1977): 85–88.

Douglass H. Stewart, “Significant Modern Writers: Aldous Huxley,” *ExTimes* 71 (January 1960): 100–03.

Pierre Vitoux, “Le Conflit idéologique dans *Brave New World*,” in *Autour de l’idée de Nature: Histoire des idées et civilisation: Pédagogie et divers* (Paris: Didier, 1977), 211–14.

George Wing, “The Shakespearean Voice of Conscience in *Brave New World*,” *DR* 51 (1971): 28–41.

Crome Yellow

Margaret Moran, “Bertrand Russell as Scogan in Aldous Huxley’s *Crome Yellow*,” *Mosaic* 17 (Summer 1984): 117–32.

Raymond Mortimer, "Bombination: Review of *Crome Yellow*," *Dial* 72 (June 1922): 631–33.

Kirpal Singh, "Denis Stone and the Problem of Integrated Living: An Essay on Aldous Huxley's *Crome Yellow*," *LCrit* 20, no. 2 (1985): 1–7.

Eyeless in Gaza

S. Krishnamoorthy Aithal, "Huxley's *Eyeless in Gaza*," *Expl* 42 (Spring 1984): 46–49.

M. M. Kirkwood, "The Thought of Aldous Huxley," *UTQ* 6 (January 1937): 189–98.

Susan Venter, "The 'Dog Episode' in Aldous Huxley's *Eyeless in Gaza*: An Exegesis," *Standpunte* 24 (August 1971): 16–19.

Island

Milton Birnbaum, "Aldous Huxley's Animadversions Upon Sexual Love," *TSLL* 8 (Summer 1966): 285–96.

Nora S. Choudhary, "The Huxley–Hero," *RUSEng* 6 (1972): 70–84.

Nora S. Choudhary, "Island: Huxley's Attempt at Practial Philosophy," *LE&W* 16 (1972): 1155–167.

John W. Crawford, "The Utopian Dream, Alive and Well," *CuyahogaR* 2 (Spring–Summer 1984): 27–33.

Jerome Mechier, "Cancer in Utopia: Positive and Negative Elements in Huxley's *Island*," *DR* 54 (1974–75): 619–33.

Yoshikuni Miura, "Huxley no Shima: Risokyo Pala ni tsuite," in *Yamakawa Kozo Kyoju Taikan Kinen Ronbunshu* (Toyonaka: n.p., 1981), 445–57.

Douglass H. Stewart, "Aldous Huxley's *Island*," *QQ* 70 (Autumn 1963): 326–35.

Point Counter Point

Milton Birnbaum, "Politics and Character in *Point Counter Point*," *SNNTS* 9 (1977): 468–87.

Zack Bowen, "Allusions to Musical Works in *Point Counter Point*," *SNNTS* 9 (1977): 488–508.

Peter Bowering, "'The Source of Light': Pictorial Imagery and Symbolism in *Point Counter Point*," *SNNTS* 9 (1977): 389–405.

Graziella Englaro, "*Punto contro punto*," *UeL* 17 (January–February 1981): 30.

Sisir Kumar Ghosh, "*Point Counter Point*: Looking Back," *AJES* 6, no. 1 (1981): 76–88.

Kulwant Singh Gill, "Aldous Huxley: The Quest for Identity," *PURBA* 8 (April–October 1977): 11–26.

Carlanda Green, "Huxley's Cosmic Dandy," *DR* 62 (Summer 1982): 303–14.

Arnold Kettle, *An Introduction to the English Novel*, vol. 2 (London: Hutchinson, 1953): 167–73.

Raymond G. McCall, "Huxley's *Point Counter Point*," *Expl* 42 (Fall 1983): 49–51.

André Maurois, "Aldous Huxley," *RevH* 44 (4 May 1935): 60–82.

André Maurois, "Aldous Huxley's Progress," *LA* 339 (September 1930): 52–55.

Jerome Meckier, "Fifty Years of Counterpoint," *SNNTS* 9 (Winter 1977): 367–72.

Peter R. Morton, "Huxley's *Point Counter Point*," *Expl* 37 (Summer 1979): 10–11.

James Quina, "The Mathematical–Physical Universe: A Basis for Multiplicity and the Quest for Unity in *Point Counter Point*," *SNNTS* 9 (Winter 1977): 428–44.

Murray Roston, "The Technique of Counterpoint," *SNNTS* 9 (Winter 1977): 378–88.

Donald J. Watt, "The Criminal–Victim Pattern in Huxley's *Point Counter Point*," *SNNTS* 2 (Spring 1970): 42–51.

Donald J. Watt, "The Fugal Construction of *Point Counter Point*," *SNNTS* 9 (Winter 1977): 509–17

Harold Watts, "The Viability of *Point Counter Point*," *SNNTS* 9 (Winter 1977): 406–17.

Those Barren Leaves

Francesca Bardazzi, "Antonio Maraini e Aldous Huxley: Due intellettuali nella Firenze del ventennio," *ASNSP* 13, no. 4 (1983): 1139–150.

Richard D. Charques, "The Bourgeois Novel," in *Contemporary Literature and Social Revolution* (London: Secker, 1933), 99–107.

Jerome Meckier, "Aldous Huxley: Satire and Structure," *WStConL* 7 (1966): 284–94.

JAMES, P. D.

The Black Tower

Norma Siebenheller, "Four Novels of the Seventies," in *P. D. James* (New York: Ungar, 1981), 44–49.

The Children of Men

Ralph C. Wood, "Rapidly Rises the Morning Tide: An Essay on P. D. James's *The Children of Men*," *ThT* 51 (July 1994): 277–88.

Cover Her Face

Norma Siebenheller, "Three Novels of the Sixties," in *P. D. James* (New York: Ungar, 1981), 7–11.

Death of an Expert Witness

Elaine Budd, "P. D. James," in *13 Mistresses of Murder* (New York: Ungar, 1986), 68–74.

Norma Siebenheller, "Four Novels of the Seventies," in *P. D. James* (New York: Ungar, 1981), 50–59.

Innocent Blood

Norma Siebenheller, "Into the Eighties," in *P. D. James* (New York: Ungar, 1981), 61–71.

A Mind to Murder

Norma Siebenheller, "Three Novels of the Sixties," in *P. D. James* (New York: Ungar, 1981), 12–18.

A Shroud for a Nightingale

Norma Siebenheller, "Four Novels of the Seventies," in *P. D. James* (New York: Ungar, 1981), 30–34.

The Skull Beneath the Skin

SueEllen Campbell, "The Detective Heroine and the Death of Her Hero: Dorothy Sayers to P. D. James," *MFS* 29 (Autumn 1983): 5–10.

A Taste for Death

Betty Richardson, "'Sweet Thames, run softly': P. D. James's Waste Land in *A Taste for Death*," *Clues* 9 (Fall–Winter 1988): 105–18.

Unnatural Causes

Norma Siebenheller, "Three Novels of the Sixties," in *P. D. James* (New York: Ungar, 1981), 19–27.

An Unsuitable Job for a Woman

Milagros Sanchez Arnosi, "El crimen o la fascinacion por el enigma," *CHA* 464 (February 1989): 125–28.

Jane S. Bakerman, "Cordelia Gray: Apprentice and Archetype," *Clues* 5 (Spring–Summer 1984): 101–14.

SueEllen Campbell, "The Detective Heroine and Death of Her Hero: Dorothy Sayers to P. D. James," in *Feminism in Women's Detective Fiction*, ed. Glenwood Irons (Toronto: University of Toronto Press, 1995), 12–28.

Norma Siebenheller, "Four Novels of the Seventies," in *P. D. James* (New York: Ungar, 1981), 35–43.

JOHNSON, BRYAN S.

Albert Angelo

Johan Thielmans, "*Albert Angelo* or B. S. Johnson's Paradigm of Truth," *RCF* 5 (Summer 1985): 81–87.

JOHNSON, BRYAN S., *Travelling People*

Nicolas Tredell, "The Truths of Lying: *Albert Angelo*," *RCF* 5 (Summer 1985): 64–70.

Travelling People

C. Kanaganayakam, "Artifice and Paradise in B. S. Johnson's *Travelling People*," *RCF* 5 (Summer 1985): 87–93.

Trawl

Andrew Hassam, "True Novel or Autobiography? The Case of B. S. Johnson's *Trawl*," *PSt* 9 (May 1986): 62–72.

The Unfortunates

Nicolas Tredell, "Telling Life, Telling Death: *The Unfortunates*," *RCF* 5 (Summer 1985): 34–42.

JOYCE, JAMES

"After the Race"

James Fairhall, "Big–power Politics and Colonial Economics: The Gordon Bennett Cup Race and 'After the Race,'" *JJQ* 28 (Winter 1991): 387–97.

"Araby"

Judith Barisonzi, "Who Eats Pigs' Cheeks?: Food and Class in 'Araby,'" *JJQ* 28 (Winter 1991): 518–20.

A. R. Coulthard, "Joyce's 'Araby,'" *Expl* 52 (Winter 1994): 97–99.

Steven Doloff, "On the Road with Loyola: St. Ignatius' Pilgrimage as Model for James Joyce's 'Araby,'" *JJQ* 28 (Winter 1991): 515–17.

H. George Hahn, "Tarsicius: A Hagiographical Allusion in Joyce's 'Araby,'" *PLL* 27 (Summer 1991): 381–85.

Jerome Mandel, "Medieval Romance and the Structure of 'Araby,'" *JJQ* 13 (Winter 1976): 234–37.

"The Boarding-House"

Earl G. Ingersoll, "The Stigma of Femininity in James Joyce's 'Eveline' and 'The Boarding House,'" *SSF* 30 (Fall 1993): 506–10.

Barbara McLean, "'The (Boar)ding House': Mrs. Mooney as Circe and Sow," *JJQ* 28 (Winter 1991): 520–22.

Fritz Senn, "'The Boarding House' Seen as a Tale of Misdirection," in *James Joyce's "Dubliners,"* ed. Harold Bloom (New York: Chelsea House, 1988), 121–29.

"Clay"

M. Hubert McDermott, "'Clay' and Cle in *Dubliners*," *JJQ* 20 (Winter 1983): 227–28.

Margot Norris, "Narration under a Blindfold: Reading Joyce's 'Clay,'" in *James Joyce's "Dubliners,"* ed. Harold Bloom (New York: Chelsea House, 1988), 143–60.

Coilin Owens, "'Clay' (2): The Myth of Irish Sovereignty," *JJQ* 27 (Summer 1990): 603–14.

Coilin Owens, "'Clay' (3): The Mass of Mary and All the Saints," *JJQ* 28 (Fall 1990): 257–67.

Florence L. Walzl, "Joyce's 'Clay': Fact and Fiction," *Renascence* 35 (Winter 1983): 119–37.

"Counterparts"

William Bysshe Stein, "'Counterparts': A Swine Song," *JJQ* 1 (Fall 1964): 30–32.

"The Dead"

Kelly Anspaugh, "Three Mortal Hour/i," *SSF* 31 (Winter 1994): 1–12.

Bruce Avery, "Distant Music: Sound and the Dialogics of Satire in 'The Dead,'" *JJQ* 28 (Winter 1991): 473–83.

Paul Barolsky, "Gretta's Name," *JJQ* 28 (Winter 1991): 519–20.

Samuel N. Bogorad, "Gabriel Conroy as 'Whited Sepulchre': Prefiguring Imagery in 'The Dead,'" *BSUF* 14, no. 1 (1973): 52–58.

JOYCE, JAMES, "The Dead"

John D. Boyd and Ruth A. Boyd, "The Love Triangle in Joyce's 'The Dead,'" *UTQ* 42 (Spring 1973): 202–17.

Ross Chambers, "Gabriel Conroy Sings for His Supper, or Love Refused ('The Dead') in *James Joyce's "Dubliners,"* ed. Harold Bloom (New York: Chelsea House, 1988), 97–119.

Vincent J. Cheng, "Empire and Patriarchy in 'The Dead,'" *JSA* 4 (Summer 1993): 16–42.

Tom Dilworth, "Sex and Politics in 'The Dead,'" *JJQ* 23 (Winter 1986): 157–71.

Gerald Doherty, "Shades of Difference: Tropic Transformations in James Joyce's 'The Dead,'" *Style* 23 (Summer 1989): 225–37.

Tilly Eggers, "What is a Woman . . . a Symbol Of?" in *Modern Critical Interpretations of "The Dubliners,"* ed. Harold Bloom (New York: Chelsea House, 1988), 23–38.

John Feeley, "Joyce's 'The Dead' and the Browning Quotation," *JJQ* 20 (Fall 1982): 87–96.

John W. Foster, "Passage through 'The Dead,'" *Criticism* 15 (Spring 1973): 91–108.

Roland Garrett, "Six Theories in the Bedroom of 'The Dead,'" *P&L* 16 (April 1992): 115–27.

William T. Going, "Joyce's Gabriel Conroy and Robert Browning: The Cult of 'Broadcloth,'" *PLL* 13 (1977): 202–07.

John Harty, "Joyce's 'The Dead,'" *Expl* 46 (Winter 1988): 23–24.

John Harty, "Joyce's 'The Dead,'" *Expl* 47 (Spring 1989): 35–37.

Earl G. Ingersoll, "The Gender of Travel in 'The Dead,'" *JJQ* 30 (Fall 1992): 41–50.

John V. Kelleher, "Irish History and Mythology in James Joyce's 'The Dead,'" *RPol* 27 (July 1965): 414–33.

Garry Leonard, "Joyce and Lacan: 'The Woman' as a Symptom of 'Masculinity' in 'The Dead,'" *JJQ* 28 (Winter 1991): 451–71.

Garry Leonard, "Power, Pornography, and the Problem of Pleasure: The Semerotics of Desire and Commodity Culture in Joyce," *JJQ* 30 (Summer–Fall 1993): 615–65.

Thomas Loe, "'The Dead' as Novella," *JJQ* 28 (Winter 1991): 485–97.

Gregory L. Lucente, "Encounters and Subtexts in 'The Dead': A Note on Joyce's Narrative Technique," *SSF* 20 (Fall 1983): 281–87.

Adrienne Auslander Munich, "Form and Subtext in Joyce's 'The Dead,'" *MP* 82 (November 1984): 173–84.

Kenneth Nilsen, "Down Among the Dead: Elements of Irish Language and Mythology in James Joyce's 'Dubliners,'" *CJIS* 12 (June 1986): 12–34.

Margot Norris, "Stifled Back Answers: The Gender Politics of Art in Joyce's 'The Dead,'" *MFS* 35 (Autumn 1989): 479–503.

Coilin Owens, "The Mystique of the West in Joyce's 'The Dead,'" *IUR* 22 (Spring 1992): 80–91.

Vincent D. Pecora, "'The Dead' and the Generosity of the Word," *PMLA* 101 (March 1986): 233–45.

Thomas Jackson Rice, "Dante . . . Browning. Gabriel . . . Joyce: Allusion and Structure in 'The Dead,'" *JJQ* 30 (Fall 1992): 29–40.

Michael W. Shurgot, "Windows of Escape and the Death Wish in Man: Joyce's 'The Dead,'" *Éire* 17, no. 4 (1982): 58–71.

Michael Sperber, "Shame and James Joyce's 'The Dead,'" *L&P* 37 (Spring–Summer 1991): 62–71.

Donald T. Torchiana, "The Ending of 'The Dead': I Follow Saint Patrick" *JJQ* 18 (1981): 122–32.

Florence L. Walzl, "Gabriel and Michael: The Conclusion of 'The Dead,'" *JJQ* 4 (1964): 17–31.

Dubliners

Morris Beja, "One Good Look at Themselves: Epiphanies in *Dubliners*," in *Work in Progress: Joyce Centenary Essays*, ed. Richard F. Peterson, Alan M. Cohn, and Edmund L. Epstein (Carbondale: Southern Illinois University Press, 1983), 3–14.

Bernard Benstock, "The Gnomonics of *Dubliners*," *MFS* 34 (Winter 1988): 519–39.

Bernard Benstock, "The L.S.D. of *Dubliners*," *TCL* 34 (Summer 1988): 191–210.

Bernard Benstock, "Narrative Strategies: Tellers in Dubliners Tales," *JML* 15 (Spring 1989): 541–59.

Zack Bowen, "Joyce's Prophylactic Paralysis: Exposure in *Dubliners*," *JJQ* 19 (Spring 1982): 257–73.

Terence Brown, "The Dublin of *Dubliners*," in *James Joyce: An International Perspective*, ed. Suheil Badi Bushrui and Bernard Benstock (Gerrards Cross, England: Colin Smythe, 1982; Totowa, NJ: Barnes & Noble, 1982), 11–18.

Sheila C. Conboy, "Exhibition and Inhibition: The Body Scene in *Dubliners*," *TCL* 37 (Winter 1991): 405–19.

Gary Davenport, "Joyce's Self–Conceivers," *SoR* 27 (Autumn 1991): 756–70.

Gerald Doherty, "Undercover Stories: Hypodiegetic Narration in James Joyce's *Dubliners*," *JNT* 22 (Winter 1992): 35–47.

Michael Faherty, "Heads and Tails: Rhetoric and Realism in *Dubliners*," *JJQ* 28 (Winter 1991): 377–85.

James Fairhall, "Joyce's *Dubliners*," *Expl* 43 (Winter 1985): 28–30.

James Fairhall, "Joyce's *Dubliners*," *Expl* 45 (Fall 1986): 32–34.

Therese Fischer-Seidel, "'The Story of the Injured Lady': Gender and the Anglo–Irish Tradition in James Joyce's *Dubliners*," in *Frauen und Frauendarstellung in der englischen und amerikanischen Literatur*, ed. Therese Fischer-Seidel (Tubingen: Narr, 1991), 319–55.

Gustave Flaubert, "A Book of Many Uncertainties: Joyce's *Dubliners*," *Style* 25 (Fall 1991): 351–77.

Wilhelm Fuger, "Crosslocution in *Dubliners*," *JJQ* 27 (Fall 1989): 87–99.

Blanche Gelfant, "A Frame of Her Own: Joyce's Women in *Dubliners* Re-Viewed: Introduction," in *James Joyce: The Augmented Ninth: Proceedings of Ninth International James Joyce Symposium*, Frankfurt, 1984, ed. Bernard Benstock (Syracuse, NY: Syracuse University Press, 1988), 263–66.

Michael Patrick Gillespie, "Aesthetic Evolution: The Shaping Forces behind *Dubliners*," *L&S* 19 (Spring 1986): 149–63.

Lia Guerra, "Fragmentation in *Dubliners* and the Reader's Epiphany," in *Myriad-minded Man: Jottings on Joyce*, ed. Rosa Maria Bosinelli, Paola Pugliatti, and Romana Zacchi (Bologna: Cooperativa Librari Universiti Educational Bologna, 1986), 41–49.

Robert Haas, "Music in *Dubliners*," *CLQ* 28 (March 1992): 19–33.

Johannes Hedberg, "Some Notes on Language and Atmosphere in *Dubliners*," *MSpr* 75, no. 2 (1981): 113–32.

Suzette A. Henke, "Through a Cracked Looking–Glass: Sex–Role Stereotypes in *Dubliners*," in *International Perspectives on James Joyce*, ed. Gottlieb Gaiser (Troy, NY: Whitston, 1986), 2–31.

Toni O'Brien Johnson, "Prescription and Proscription in *Dubliners*," *ÉLT* 4 (1987): 69–80.

Tomaso Kemeny, "The 'Unreal' Effect in *Dubliners*," in *Myriadminded Man: Jottings on Joyce,* ed. Rosa Maria Bosinelli, Paola Pugliatti, and Romana Zacchi (Bologna: Cooperativa Librari Universiti Educational Bologna, 1986), 19–40.

James Leigh, "The Gnomonic Principle in *Dubliners*," *LJHum* 9 (Spring 1983): 35–40.

J. B. Lyons, "Diseases in *Dubliners*: Tokens of Disaffection," *IRA* 2 (1981): 185–203.

John McGahern, "*Dubliners*," *CJIS* 17 (July 1991): 31–37.

John McNiff, "James Joyce's *Dubliners*: A Study of Stagnation and Entrapment," *DLSUDia* 23, no. 2 (1988): 29–43.

Augustine Martin, "Joyce's Narrative Strategies in the Central Stories of *Dubliners*," in *Joyce Centenary Offshoots: James Joyce, 1882–1892*, ed. Karl-Heinz Westarp (Aarhus, Denmark: Seklos, Department of English, University of Aarhus, 1983), 27–46.

Jacky Martin, "Pessimisme et fonctionnements textuels dans *Dubliners* de James Joyce," *CVE* 15 (August 1982): 87–90.

Giorgio Melchiori, "The Rev. John Flynn and Buck Mulligan," *JJQ* 27 (Fall 1989): 124–26.

Harold F. Mosher, Jr., "The Narrated and its Negatives: The Nonnarrated and the Disnarrated in Joyce's *Dubliners*," *Style* 27 (Fall 1993): 407–27.

Kenneth Nilsen, "Irish Language and Mythology in *Dubliners*," *CJIS* 12 (June 1986): 23–34.

Seong Soo Park, "A Rhetoric Gripped in Paralysis: James Joyce's Narrative Strategies in *Dubliners*," *JELL* 38 (Spring 1992): 71–89.

Ales Pogacnik, "*Dubliners*," *Problemi* 25, no. 6 (1987): 151–63.

Jean-Michel Rabate, "Silence in *Dubliners*," in *James Joyce: New Perspectives*, ed. Colin MacCabe (Brighton, England: Harvester, 1982; Bloomington: Indiana University Press, 1982), 45–72.

Joanne E. Rea, "Norwegian Wood: A Camusian Encounter with Joyce," *RLC* 64 (July–September 1990): 548–49.

Mary T. Reynolds, "The Dantean Design of Joyce's *Dubliners*," in *The Seventh of Joyce*, ed. Bernard Benstock (Bloomington: Indiana University Press, 1982; Brighton: Harvester, 1982), 124–30.

Franca Ruggieri, "Forms of Silence in *Dubliners*," in *Myriadminded Man: Jottings on Joyce,* ed. Rosa Maria Bosinelli, Paola Pugliatti, and Romana Zacchi (Bologna: Cooperativa Librari Universiti Educational Bologna, 1986), 51–58.

Fritz Senn, "Naming in *Dubliners* (a First Methermeneutic Fumbling)," *JJQ* 24 (Summer 1987): 465–68.

Annette Sisson, "Constructing the Human Conscience in Joyce's *Dubliners*," *MidWQ* 30 (Summer 1989): 492–514.

Jon Thompson, "Joyce and Dialogism: Politics of Style in *Dubliners*," *W&D* 5 (Fall 1987): 79–95.

Theresa Vichy, "Modernité esthétique des *Dubliners*," in *Home, Sweet Home or Bleak House? Art et littérature à l'époque Victorienne,* ed. Marie-Claire Hamard (Paris: Belles Lettres, 1985), 83–91.

Joseph C. Voelker, "'Chronicles of Disorder': Reading the Margins of Joyce's *Dubliners*," *CLQ* 18 (June 1982): 126–44.

Florence L. Walzl, "*Dubliners*," in *A Companion to Joyce Studies,* ed. Zack Bowen and James F. Carens (Westport, CT: Greenwood, 1984), 155–228.

Florence L. Walzl, "*Dubliners*: Women in Irish Society," in *Women in Joyce,* ed. Suzette Henke and Elaine Unkeless (Urbana: University of Illinois Press, 1982), 31–56.

David Weir, "Gnomon is an Island: Euclid and Bruno in Joyce's Narrative Practice," *JJQ* 28 (Winter 1991): 343–60.

Doris T. Wight, "Vladimir Propp and Dubliners," *JJQ* 23 (Summer 1986): 415–33.

Trevor L. Williams, "Resistance to Paralysis in *Dubliners*," *MFS* 35 (Autumn 1989): 437–57.

Hana Wirth–Nesher, "Reading Joyce's City: Public Space, Self, and Gender in *Dubliners*," in *James Joyce: The Augmented Ninth: Proceedings of Ninth International James Joyce Symposium*, Frankfurt, 1984, ed. Bernard Benstock (Syracuse, NY: Syracuse University Press, 1988), 282–92.

Lloyd Worley, "Joyce, Yeats, Tarot, and the Structure of *Dubliners*," in *The Shape of the Fantastic: Selected Essays from the Seventh International Conference on the Fantastic in the Arts*, ed. Olena H. Saciuk (New York: Greenwood, 1990), 181–91.

"An Encounter"

James P. Degnan, "The Encounter in Joyce's 'An Encounter,'" *TCL* 35 (Spring 1989): 89–93.

"Eveline"

Harold Bloom, "Introduction," in *James Joyce's "Dubliners"* (New York: Chelsea House, 1988), 1–3.

Joseph Florio, "Joyce's 'Eveline,'" *Expl* 51 (Spring 1993): 181–84.

Earl G. Ingersoll, "The Stigma of Femininity in James Joyce's 'Eveline' and 'The Boarding House,'" *SSF* 30 (Fall 1993): 501–06.

Garry M. Leonard, "Wondering Where All the Dust Comes From: Jouissance in 'Eveline,'" *JJQ* 29 (Fall 1991): 23–41.

John Paul Riquelme, "Metaphors of the Narration/Metaphors in the Narration: 'Eveline,'" in *James Joyce's "Dubliners,"* ed. Harold Bloom (New York: Chelsea House, 1988), 73–87.

Finnegans Wake

Charles Altieri, "*Finnegans Wake* as Modernist Historiography," *Novel* 21 (Winter–Spring 1988): 238–50.

Richard Beckman, "Panangelic Voices in *Finnegans Wake*," *JML* 17 (Spring 1991): 491–518.

Bernard Benstock, "Comic Seriousness and Poetic Prose," in *James Joyce: A Collection of Critical Essays*, ed. Mary T. Reynolds (Englewood Cliffs, NJ: Prentice Hall, 1993), 171–79.

Shari Benstock, "Apostrophizing the Feminine in *Finnegans Wake*," *MFS* 35 (Autumn 1989): 587–604.

Sheldon Brivic, "The Terror and Pity of Love: ALP's Soliloquy," *JJQ* 29 (Fall 1991): 145–71.

Vincent J. Cheng, "'Goddinpotty': James Joyce and the Language of Excrement," in *The Languages of Joyce: Selected Papers from the 11th International James Joyce Symposium*, ed. Rose Maria Bollettieri Bosinelli, C. Marengo Vaglio, and Christine van Boheemen (Philadelphia: Benjamins, 1992), 85–99.

Hilary Clark, "Networking in *Finnegans Wake*," *JJQ* 27 (Summer 1990): 745–58.

James A. Connor, "Radio Free Joyce: *Wake* Language and the Experience of Radio," *JJQ* 30 (Summer–Fall 1993): 825–43.

Marion Cumpiano, "Joyce's *Finnegans Wake*," *Expl* 48 (Fall 1989): 48–51.

Robert Frumkin, "Zen in *Finnegans Wake*: Joyce's Prankquean–Koan," *Rag* 11 (Winter 1992–1993): 7–67.

Edvige Giunta, "Dear Reverend: 'Lewis Carroll and the Boston Girls,'" *JJQ* 30 (Spring 1993): 488–92.

J. Carnero Gonzalez, "Leafyspeafing. Lpf!" *RAEI* 5 (November 1992): 47–55.

John Gordon, "Joyce's *Finnegans Wake*," *Expl* 50 (Winter 1992): 96–98.

John Gordon, "Marconimasts," *JJQ* 27 (Summer 1990): 852–53.

John Gordon, "Waalworth and Capapole," *JJQ* 27 (Summer 1990): 850–52.

Judith Harrington, "Whose E When E Is Turned?" *JJQ* 29 (Summer 1992): 847.

Clive Hart, "*Finnegans Wake* in Adjusted Perspective," in *Critical Essays on James Joyce's "Finnegans Wake*," ed. Patrick McCarthy (New York: G. K. Hall, 1992), 15–33.

David Hayman, "Transiting the Wake: A Response to Danis Rose," *JJQ* 29 (Winter 1992): 411–19.

Herman van der Heide, "On the Contribution of Umberto Eco to Joyce Criticism," *Style* 26 (Summer 1992): 327–39.

Thomas Hofheinz, "'Group Drinkards Maaks Grope Thinkards': Narrative in the 'Norwegian Captain' Episode of *Finnegans Wake*," *JJQ* 29 (Spring 1992): 643–58.

Morton P. Levitt, "The New Midrash: *Finnegans Wake*," *JSA* 3 (Summer 1992): 57–76.

Janet E. Lewis, "'The Cat and the Devil' and *Finnegans Wake*," *JJQ* 29 (Summer 1992): 805–14.

Mary Lowe–Evans, "'The Commonest of all Cases': Birth Control on Trial in the *Wake*," *JJQ* 27 (Summer 1990): 803–14.

Patrick A. McCarthy, "The Last Epistle of *Finnegans Wake*," *JJQ* 27 (Summer 1990): 725–33.

Laurent Milesi, "The Perversions of 'Aerse' and the Anglo–Irish Middle Voice in *Finnegans Wake*," *JSA* 4 (Summer 1993): 98–118.

Gino Moliterno, "The Candlebearer at the *Wake*: Bruno's 'Candelaio' in Joyce's Book of the Dark," *ComL* 30 (Summer 1993): 269–94.

Marguerite Quintelli Neavy, "*Finnegans Wake*: Imitating Sources," *JIL* 21 (May 1992): 24–40.

Arthur Nestrovski, "Punic Judgeship in *Finnegans Wake*," *JJQ* 27 (Summer 1990): 853–56.

Margot Norris, "*Finnegan's Wake*," in *The Cambridge Companion to James Joyce*, ed. Derek Attridge (Cambridge: Cambridge University Press; 1990), 161–84.

Andrew Peik, "Bbyrdwood de Trop Blogg," *JJQ* 27 (Summer 1990): 867–69.

Susan Shaw Sailer, "Conjunctions: Commentary and Text in *Finnegans Wake* II.2.," *JJQ* 27 (Summer 1990): 793–802.

Susan Shaw Sailer, "A Methodology of Reading *Finnegans Wake*," *TCL* 35 (Summer 1989): 195–203.

Talia Schaffer, "Letters to Biddy: About That Original Hen," *JJQ* 29 (Spring 1992): 623–42.

R. J. Schork, "Apollinaire and Tiresias in the *Wake*," *JML* 17 (Summer 1990): 166–72.

R. J. Schork, "Barnum at the *Wake*," *JJQ* 27 (Summer 1990): 759–66.

R. J. Schork, "The Latimers at the *Wake*," *N&Q* 39 (June 1992): 197.

R. J. Schork, "Sheep, Goats, and the 'Figura Etymologica' in *Finnegans Wake*," *JEGP* 92 (April 1993): 200–11.

Fritz Senn, "Ovid's Not–yet–Icity," *JJQ* 29 (Winter 1992): 401–03.

Scott Simkins, "The Agency of the Title: *Finnegans Wake*," *JJQ* 27 (Summer 1990): 735–43.

Kathleen M. Hewett Smith, "Anglo–Saxon in the 'Mutt and Jute' Episode of *Finnegans Wake*," *JJQ* 29 (Spring 1992): 679–80.

Jack Vespa, "Another Book at the 'Wake': Indian Mysticism and the *Bhagavad–Gita* in I.4 of *Finnegans Wake*," *JJQ* 31 (Winter 1994): 81–87.

James Walton, "A Chiliad of Perihelygangs," *JJQ* 30 (Spring 1993): 459–65.

Jennie Wang, "'To wielderfight his penisolate war': 'The Lover's Discourse' in Postmodern Fiction," *Critique* 34 (Fall 1992): 63–79.

"Grace"

Robert Boyle, "Swiftian Allegory and Dantean Parody in Joyce's 'Grace,'" *JJQ* 7 (Fall 1969):11–21.

Richard M. Kain, "Grace," in *James Joyce's "Dubliners,"* ed. Clive Hart (London: Faber & Faber, 1969), 134–52.

Corinna del Greco Lobner, "Quincunxial Sherlockholmesing in 'Grace,'" *JJQ* 28 (Winter 1991): 445–50.

Mark Osteen, "Serving Two Masters: Economics and Figures of Power in Joyce's 'Grace,'" *TCL* 37 (Spring 1991): 76–91.

"Ivy Day in the Committee Room"

Sylvia Huntley Horowitz, "More Christian Allegory in 'Ivy Day in the Committee Room,'" *JJQ* 21 (Winter 1984): 145–54.

Thomas B. O'Grady, "'Ivy Day in the Committee Room': The Use and Abuse of Parnell," in *James Joyce's "Dubliners,"* ed. Harold Bloom (New York: Chelsea House, 1988), 131–41.

Frederick C. Stern, "'Parnell is Dead': 'Ivy Day in the Committee Room,'" *JJQ* 10 (Winter 1973): 228–39.

"A Little Cloud"

Thomas B. O'Grady, "Little Chandler's Song of Experience," *JJQ* 28 (Winter 1991): 399–405.

"A Mother"

Ben L. Collins, "Joyce's Use of Yeats and Irish History: A Reading of 'A Mother,'" *Éire* 5 (Spring 1970): 45–66.

Jane E. Miller, "'O, she's a nice lady!": A Rereading of 'A Mother,'" *JJQ* 28 (Winter 1991): 407–26.

"Oxen of the Sun"

Bernard Benstock, "Decoding in the Dark in 'Oxen of the Sun,'" *JJQ* 28 (Spring 1991): 637–41.

"A Painful Case"

J. Mark Heumann, "Writing—and Not Writing—in Joyce's 'A Painful Case,'" *Éire* 16 (Fall 1981): 81–97.

R. B. Kershner, "Mr. Duffy's Apple," *JJQ* 29 (Winter 1992): 406–7.

Marvin Magalaner, "Joyce, Nietzache, and Hauptmann in James Joyce's 'A Painful Case,'" *PMLA* 68 (March 1953): 95–102.

Lindsay Tucker, "Duffy's Last Supper: Food, Language and the Failure of Integrative Processes in 'A Painful Case,'" in *James Joyce's "Dubliners,"* ed. Harold Bloom (New York: Chelsea House, 1988), 89–96.

Joseph C. Voelker, "'He Lumped the Emancipates Together': More Analogues for Joyce's Mr. Duffy," *JJQ* 18 (Fall 1980): 23–34.

A Portrait of the Artist as a Young Man

Jeonh Soot Ahn, "Stephen Dedalus' Essentialism in *A Portrait of the Artist as a Young Man,*" *JELL* 38 (Fall 1992): 495–508.

Lourdes S. Alviar, "The Stream–of–Consciousness Technique in James Joyce, *Portrait of the Artist as a Young Man,*" *SLRJ* 15 (June 1984): 46–54.

Nehama Aschkenasy, "Biblical Females in a Joycean Episode: The 'Strange Woman' Scene in James Joyce's *A Portrait of the Artist as a Young Man,*" *MLS* 15 (Fall 1985): 28–39.

Eugene R. August, "Father Arnall's Use of Scripture in *A Portrait,*" *JJQ* 4 (1967): 275–79.

Michel Bariou, "Le Vent paraclet: Quelques aspects de l'inspiration dans *Le Portrait,*" *CCEI* 7 (1982): 9–20.

Maurice Beebe, "The Portrait as Portrait: Joyce and Impressionism," *IRA* 1 (1980): 13–31.

Juan Domingo Moyano Benitez, "La poetica epifanica de Joyce en el Retrato del artista adolescente," *Insula* 37 (September 1982): 1, 12, 13.

Sheldon Brivic, "The Father in Joyce," in *The Seventh of Joyce*, ed. Bernard Benstock (Bloomington: Indiana University Press, 1982; Brighton: Harvester, 1982), 74–80.

Richard Brown, "The Purloined Letter," *JJB* 17 (June 1985): 4.

Anthony Burgess, "Martyr and Maze–maker," in *James Joyce's "A Portrait of the Artist as a Young Man,"* ed. Harold Bloom (New York: Chelsea House, 1988), 43–54.

Joseph A. Buttigieg, "Aesthetics and Religion in *A Portrait of the Artist as a Young Man,*" *C&L* 28, no. 4 (1979): 44–56.

James Carens, "The Motif of Hands in *A Portrait of the Artist as a Young Man,*" *IRA* 2 (1981): 139–57.

James F. Carens, "*A Portrait of the Artist as a Young Man*," in *A Companion to Joyce Studies*, ed. Zack Bowen and James F. Carens (Westport, CT: Greenwood, 1984), 255–359.

Steven R. Centola, "'The White Peace of the Altar': White Imagery in James Joyce's *A Portrait of the Artist as a Young Man*," *SoAR* 50 (November 1985): 93–106.

Nathan Cervo, "Joyce's *A Portrait of the Artist as a Young Man*," *Expl* 49 (Winter 1991): 114–16.

Nathan Cervo, "'Seeing' as Being: The Blind Apotheosis of Stephen Dedalus," *NNER* 10 (1983): 52–65.

Renato Chierici, "Variation Parameters in Joyce's *A Portrait of the Artist as a Young Man*," in *Myriadminded Man: Jottings on Joyce*, ed. Rosa Maria Bosinelli, Paola Pugliatti, and Romana Zacchi (Bologna: Cooperativa Librari Universiti Educational Bologna, 1986), 111–19.

Margaret Church, "The Adolescent Point of View toward Women in Joyce's *A Portrait of the Artist as a Young Man*," *IRA* 2 (1981): 158–65.

Diane Collinson, "The Aesthetic Theory of Stephen Dedalus," *BJA* 23 (Winter 1983): 61–73.

Bruce Comens, "Narrative Nets and Lyric Flights in Joyce's *A Portrait*," *JJQ* 29 (Winter 1992): 297–14.

Thomas E. Connolly, "Kinesis and Stasis: Structural Rhythm in Joyce's *Portrait*," *IRA* 2 (1981): 166–84.

Claudia Corti, "'Contrahit orator, variant in carmine vates': Allusioni e intrusioni poetiche nel *Portrait* di Joyce," *RLMC* 42 (July–September 1989): 275–95.

Alan Magalhaes Costa, "*A Portrait of the Artist as a Young Man*: A Study on Immortality," *EAA* 7–8 (1983–1984): 131–38.

Robert Crooks, "Triptych Vision: Voyeurism and Screen Memories in Joyce's *Portrait*," *MFS* 38 (Summer 1992): 377–401.

James Dauphine, "*A Portrait of the Artist as a Young Man* et le problème de l'autobiographie," *Europe* 657–658 (January–February 1984): 83–96.

Robert Adams Day, "How Stephen Wrote His Vampire Poem," *JJQ* 17 (1980): 183–97.

Robert Adams Day, "The Villanelle Perplex: Reading Joyce," *JJQ* 25 (Fall 1987): 69–85.

Jerry Allen Dibble, "Stephen's Esthetic and Joyce's Art: Theory and Practice of Genre in *A Portrait of the Artist as a Young Man*," *JNT* 6 (1976): 29–40.

Rita di Giuseppe, "The Mythos of Irony and Satire in Joyce's *Portrait*," *QLL* 6 (1981): 33–48.

Gerald Doherty, "From Encounter to Creation: The Genesis of Metaphor in *A Portrait of the Artist as a Young Man*," *Style* 21 (Summer 1987): 219–36.

James H. Druff, Jr., "The Romantic Complaint: The Logical Movement of Stephen's Aesthetics in *A Portrait of the Artist as a Young Man*," *SNNTS* 14 (Summer 1982): 180–88.

Bernard Duyfhuizen, "'Words [mis'taken': The Opening Sentence of the Retreat Sermons," *JJQ* 16 (1979): 488–90.

Kitti Carriker Eastman, "Joyce's *A Portrait of the Artist as a Young Man*," *Expl* 42 (Summer 1984): 29–30.

Samir Elbarbary, "The Image of the Goat in *Portrait of the Artist as a Young Man*," *CollL* 16 (Fall 1989): 261–73.

Maud Ellmann, "Disremembering Dedalus: *A Portrait of the Artist as a Young Man*," in *Untying the Text: A Post–Structuralist Reader*, ed. Robert Young (New York: Routledge, 1981), 189–201.

Julienne H. Empric, "The Mediation of the Woman and the Interpretation of the Artist in Joyce's *Portrait*," in *James Joyce and His Contemporaries*, ed. Diana A. Ben–Merre and Maureen Murphy (Westport, CT: Greenwood, 1989), 11–16.

Willi Erzgraber, "Motive und Leitmotive in James Joyces *A Portrait of the Artist as a Young Man*," in *Motive and Themen in englischsprachiger Literatur als Indikatoren literaturgeschichtlicher Prozesse: Festschrift zum 65. Geburtstag von Theodor Wolpers*, ed. Heinz–Joachim Mullenbrock and Alfons Klein (Tubingen: Niemeyer, 1990), 343–59.

Claude Fierobe, "Consonantia: Harmonie et esthétique dans *A Portrait of the Artist as a Young Man*," in *Visages de l'harmonie dans la littérature anglo-américaine* (Reims: Centre de Recherche sur l'Imaginaire dans les Littératures de Langue Anglaise, Université de Reims, 1982), 113–25.

Diane Fortuna, "The Labyrinth as Controlling Image in Joyce's *A Portrait of the Artist as a Young Man*," *BNYPL* 76 (1972): 120–80.

Peter J. Gillett, "James Joyce's Infernal Clock," *MFS* 34 (Summer 1988): 203–06.

D. M. E. Gilliam and R. W. McConchie, "Joyce's *A Portrait of the Artist as a Young Man*," *Expl* 44 (Spring 1986): 43–46.

Elliott B. Gose, "Destruction and Creation in *A Portrait of the Artist as a Young Man*," *JJQ* 22 (Spring 1985): 259–70.

Janet Grayson, "'Do You Kiss Your Mother?' Stephen Dedalus' Sovereignty of Ireland," *JJQ* 19 (Winter 1982): 119–26.

JOYCE, JAMES, *A Portrait of the Artist as a Young Man*

Donald Gutierrez, "James Joyce's *Portrait* as Maze: A Critique," *NAMM* 24 (Fall 1986): 30–34.

Angela Habermann, "The Joycean Faun," *IFR* 10 (Winter 1983): 44–47.

John Hannay, "Confessions of Love in Joyce's *Portrait*," *UDR* 17 (Winter 1985–86): 77–82.

Marguerite Harkness, "The Separate Roles of Language and Word in James Joyce's *Portrait*," *IRA* 4 (1983): 94–109.

Hunt Hawkins, "Joyce as Colonial Writer," *CLAJ* 35 (June 1992): 400–10.

David Hayman, "The Fractured *Portrait*," in *Myriadminded Man: Jottings on Joyce*, ed. Rosa Maria Bosinelli, Paola Pugliatti, and Romana Zacchi (Bologna: Cooperativa Librari Universiti Educational Bologna, 1986), 79–88.

David Hayman, "The Joycean Inset," *JJQ* 23 (Winter 1986): 137–55.

Suzette Henke, "Stephen Dedalus and Women: *A Portrait of the Artist* as a Young Misogynist," in *Women in Joyce*, ed. Suzette Henke and Elaine Unkeless (Urbana: University of Illinois Press, 1982), 82–107. Reprinted in *James Joyce's "A Portrait of the Artist as a Young Man*," ed. Harold Bloom (New York: Chelsea House, 1988), 55–75.

Carl G. Herndl, "The Epiphany in *A Portrait of the Artist* as a Romantic Moment," *UDR* 17 (Winter 1985–86): 69–75.

Barbara Stevens Heusel, "The Problems of Figure and Ground in *A Portrait of the Artist as a Young Man*," *CentR* 26 (Spring 1982): 180–98.

Rudiger Hillgartner, "Zum Einsatz der Verfremdungstechnik in James Joyces *A Portrait of the Artist as a Young Man*," in *Verfremdung in der Literatur*, ed. Hermann Helmers (Darmstadt: Wissenschaftliche Buchgesellschaft, 1984), 428–54.

David Jauss, "Indirect Interior Monologue and Subjective Narration in *A Portrait of the Artist as a Young Man*," *ParR* 3–4 (1980–81): 45–52.

Koichi Kanno, "Wakakihi no Geijutsuka no Shozo," in *Joyce kara Joyce e*, ed. Yukio Suzuki (Tokyo: Tokyodo Shuppan, 1982), 107–23.

Hugh Kenner, "The Portrait in Perspective," in *James Joyce's "A Portrait of the Artist as a Young Man*," ed. Harold Bloom (New York: Chelsea House, 1988), 5–30.

R. B. Kershner Jr., "The Artist as Text: Dialogism and Incremental Repetition in Joyce's *Portrait*," *ELH* 53 (Winter 1986): 881–94.

R. B. Kershner Jr., "Time and Language in Joyce's *A Portrait of the Artist as a Young Man*," *ELH* 43 (1976): 604–19.

Donald Lateiner, "The Epigraph to Joyce's *Portrait*," *CML* 4 (Winter 1984): 77–84.

Lee T. Lemon, "*A Portrait of the Artist as a Young Man*: Motif as Motivation and Structure," *MFS* 12 (1966): 439–50.

Michael Levenson, "Stephen's Diary in Joyce's *Portrait*—The Shape of Life," *ELH* 52 (Winter 1985): 1017–035.

Elsa Linguanti, "Towards the Basketness of It: Readings into *A Portrait of the Artist as a Young Man*," in *Myriadminded Man: Jottings on Joyce*, ed. Rosa Maria Bosinelli, Paola Pugliatti, Romana Zacchi (Bologna: Cooperativa Librari Universiti Educational Bologna, 1986), 89–94.

James F. Loucks, "'What an Awful Power, Stephen!': Simony and Joyce's Medieval Sources in *A Portrait*," *PLL* 28 (Spring 1992): 133–49.

Mary Lowe–Evans, "Joyce's *Portrait of the Artist as a Young Man*," *Expl* 48 (Summer 1990): 275–77.

Ian MacArthur, "Stephen's Sexual Aesthetics," *JJQ* 25 (Winter 1988): 268–69.

Michael Bruce McDonald, "The Strength and Sorrow of Young Stephen: Toward a Reading of the Dialectic of Harmony and Dissonance in Joyce's *Portrait*," *TCL* 37 (Winter 1991): 361–88.

F. C. McGrath, "Laughing in His Sleeve: The Sources of Stephen's Aesthetics," *JJQ* 23 (Spring 1986): 259–75.

Dominic Manganiello, "Joyce's 'Third Gospel': The Earthbound Vision of *A Portrait of the Artist*," *Renascence* 35 (Summer 1983): 219–34.

Carolyn L. Mathews, "Joyce's *A Portrait of the Artist as a Young Man*," *Expl* 50 (Fall 1991): 38–40.

Jerry Leath Mills, "Joyce's *A Portrait of the Artist as a Young Man*," *Expl* 42 (Summer 1984): 30–32.

Kathleen O'Gorman, "The Performativity of Utterance in *A Portrait of the Artist as a Young Man*," *JJQ* 30 (Spring 1993): 419–506.

Thomas B. O'Grady, "Conception, Gestation, and Reproduction: Stephen's Dream of Parnell," *JJQ* 27 (Winter 1990): 293–301.

B. Paliwal, "The Artist as Creator in *A Portrait of the Artist as a Young Man*," *LCrit* 10 (1971): 44–49.

Patrick Parrinder, "Joyce's *Portrait* and the Proof of the Oracle," in *James Joyce's "A Portrait of the Artist as a Young Man,"* ed. Harold Bloom (New York: Chelsea House, 1988), 109–45.

Richard F. Peterson, "Stephen and the Narrative of *A Portrait of the Artist as a Young Man,*" in *Work in Progress: Joyce Centenary Essays*, ed. Richard F. Peterson, Alan M. Cohn, and Edmund L. Epstein (Carbondale: Southern Illinois University Press, 1983), 15–29.

Willard Potts, "Stephen Dedalus and 'Irrland's Split Little Pea,'" *JJQ* 27 (Spring 1990): 559–75.

Martin Price, "The Beauty of Mortal Conditions: Joyce's *A Portrait of the Artist,*" in *James Joyce's "A Portrait of the Artist as a Young Man,"* ed. Harold Bloom (New York: Chelsea House, 1988), 77–86.

F. L. Radford, "Dedalus and the Bird Girl: Classical Text and Celtic Subtext in *A Portrait,*" *JJQ* 24 (Spring 1987): 253–74.

Harish Raizada, "Two Voices in *A Portrait of the Artist as a Young Man,*" *AJES* 7, no. 2 (1982): 125–46.

Bryan Reddick, "The Importance of Tone in the Structural Rhythm of Joyce's *Portrait,*" *JJQ* 6 (1969): 201–17.

Grant A. Redford, "The Role of Structure in Joyce's *Portrait,*" *MFS* 4 (1958): 21–30.

B. L. Reid, "Gnomon and Order in Joyce's *Portrait,*" *SR* 92 (Summer 1984): 397–420.

Shlomith Rimmon–Kenan, "Identity and Identification: Joyce's *A Portrait of the Artist as a Young Man,*" *HUSL* 9, no. 1 (1981): 107–25.

John Paul Riquelme, "Pretexts for Reading and for Writing: Title, Epigraph, and Journal in *A Portrait of the Artist as a Young Man,*" *JJQ* 18 (Spring 1981): 301–21. Reprinted in *James Joyce's "A Portrait of the Artist as a Young Man,"* ed. Harold Bloom (New York: Chelsea House, 1988), 87–107.

Dorothy Dodge Robbins, "'Coming Down Along the Road': The Journey Motif in *A Portrait of the Artist,*" *MidWQ* 35 (Spring 1994): 261–76.

David W. Robinson, "'What Kind of a Name Is That?': Joyce's Critique of Names and Naming in *A Portrait,*" *JJQ* 27 (Winter 1990): 325–35.

K. E. Robinson, "The Stream of Consciousness Technique and the Structure of Joyce's *Portrait,*" *JJQ* 9 (1971): 63–84.

Anthony Roche, "'The Strange Light of Some New World': Stephen's Vision in *A Portrait,*" *JJQ* 25 (Spring 1988): 323–32.

Ellen Cronan Rose, "Dancing Daedalus: Another Source for Joyce's *Portrait of the Artist*," *MFS* 28 (Winter 1982–83): 596–603.

Robert Scholes, "Stephen Dedalus: Eiron and Alazon," *TSLL* 3 (1961): 8–15.

Robert Scholes, "Stephen Dedalus: Poet or Aesthete?" *PMLA* 79 (1964): 484–89.

Michael Seidel, "Monte Cristo's Revenge and Joyce's *A Portrait of the Artist*," in *James Joyce's "A Portrait of the Artist as a Young Man*," ed. Harold Bloom (New York: Chelsea House, 1988), 147–62.

Fritz Senn, "*A Portrait*: Temporal Foreplay," *ÉI* 12 (December 1987): 65–73.

Alan Shepard "From Aristotle to Keats: Stephen's Search for 'The Good Life' in *A Portrait of the Artist as a Young Man*," *ES* 74 (February 1993): 105–12.

Thomas C. Singer, "Riddles, Silence and Wonder: Joyce and Wittgenstein Encountering the Limits of Language," *ELH* 57 (Summer 1990): 459–84.

Dirk Stratton, "Figs: Cranly as Precursor," *ELN* 24 (March 1987): 51–56.

Theoharis C. Theoharis, "Unveiling Joyce's *Portrait*: Stephen Dedalus and The Encyclopaedia Britannica," *SoR* 20 (Spring 1984): 286–99.

Calvin Thomas, "Stephen in Process/Stephen on Trial: The Anxiety of Production in Joyce's *Portrait*," *Novel* 23 (Spring 1990): 282–302.

James R. Thrane, "Joyce's Sermon on Hell: Its Sources and Background," *MP* 57 (1960): 172–98.

Michael Toolan, "Analysing Conversation in Fiction: The Christmas Dinner Scene in Joyce's *Portrait of the Artist as a Young Man*," *PoT* 8 (Summer 1987): 393–416.

Rita di Giuseppe Trivellato, "James Joyce's *Portrait*: A Case of Applied Mythology," *QLL* 2 (1977): 59–67.

Therese Vichy, "Rhetorique et crise du sujet dans *A Portrait of the Artist as a Young Man*," *ÉA* 37 (July–September 1984): 283–92.

Cordell D. K. Yee, "St. Thomas Aquinas as Figura of James Joyce: A Medieval View of Literary Influence," *JJQ* 22 (Fall 1984): 25–38.

Richard Wall, "Fleming's Unfinished Inscription," *JJQ* 19 (Spring 1982): 348–49.

Doris T. Wight, "Stephen's Villanelle: From Passive to Active Creation," *CLQ* 22 (December 1986): 215–24.

Dana Wilde, "A Note on Stephen's Shapeless Thoughts from Swedenborg in *A Portrait of the Artist*," *JML* 16 (Summer 1989): 179–81.

Nancy G. Wilds, "Style and Auctorial Presence in *A Portrait of the Artist as a Young Man*," *Style* 7 (1973): 39–55.

Trevor L. Williams, "Dominant Ideologies: The Production of Stephen Dedalus," in *James Joyce: The Augmented Ninth: Proceedings of Ninth International James Joyce Symposium*, ed. Bernard Benstock (Syracuse, NY: Syracuse University Press, 1988), 312–22.

Boxiang Zhang, "A Brief Comment on *A Portrait of the Artist as a Young Man*," *FLitS* 34 (December 1986): 16–20, 34.

"The Sisters"

Leonard Albert, "Gnomonology: Joyce's 'The Sisters,'" *JJQ* 27 (Winter 1990): 353–64.

Robert Bierman, "Joyce's 'The Sisters,'" *Expl* 48 (Summer 1990): 274–75.

M. Keith Booker, "History and Language in Joyce's 'The Sisters,'" *Criticism* 33 (Spring 1991): 217–23.

Joseph Chadwick, "Silence in 'The Sisters,'" *JJQ* 21 (Spring 1984): 245–56.

Thomas E. Connolly, "Joyce's 'The Sisters': A Pennyworth of Snuff," *CE* 27 (December 1965): 189–95.

Claudia Crawford, "James Joyce's 'The Sisters': A Letter-L-Analysis," *AI* 41 (Summer 1984): 181–200.

Edward Duffy, "'The Sisters' as an Introduction to *Dubliners*," *PLL* 22 (Fall 1986): 417–28.

David R. Fabian, "Joyce's 'The Sisters': Gnomon, Gnomic, Gnome," *SSF* 5 (Winter 1968): 187–89.

Edward A. Geary, "Undecidability in Joyce's 'The Sisters,'" *SSF* 26 (Summer 1989): 305–10.

John Harty, "The Doubling of Dublin Messages in 'The Sisters,'" *NMIL* 4 (1992): 42–44.

Phillip Herring, "Structure and Meaning in Joyce's 'The Sisters,'" in *Modern Critical Interpretations of "The Dubliners,"* ed. Harold Bloom (New York: Chelsea House, 1988), 39–50.

Garry M. Leonard, "The Free Man's Journal: The Making of his/s," *MFS* 36 (Winter 1990): 455–72.

J. B. Lyons, "Animadversions on Paralysis as Symbol in 'The Sisters,'" *JJQ* 11 (Spring 1974): 257–65.

John V. McDermott, "Joyce's 'The Sisters,'" *Expl* 51 (Summer 1993): 236–37.

L. J. Morrissey, "Joyce's Revision of 'The Sisters' from Epicleti to Modern Fiction," *JJQ* 24 (Fall 11986): 33–54.

R. Joseph Schork, "Liturgical Irony in Joyce's 'The Sisters,'" *SSF* 26 (Spring 1989): 193–97.

Fritz Senn, "'He Was Too Scrupulous Always': Joyce's 'The Sisters,'" *JJQ* 2 (Winter 1965): 66–72.

Thomas F. Staley, "A Beginning: Signification, Story and Discourse in Joyce's 'The Sisters,'" *Genre* 12 (Winter 1979): 533–49.

Burton A. Waisbren and Florence L. Walzl, "Paresis and the Priest: James Joyce's Symbolic Use of Syphilis in 'The Sisters,'" *AIM* 80 (June 1974): 758–62.

Florence L. Walzl, "Joyce's 'The Sisters': A Development," *JJQ* 10 (Summer 1973): 375–421.

A. James Wohlpart, "Laughing in the Confession-box: Vows of Silence in Joyce's 'The Sisters,'" *JJQ* 30 (Spring 1993): 409–17.

"Two Gallants"

Robert Adams Day, "Joyce's Gnomons, Lenehan, and the Persistence of an Image," in *James Joyce's "Dubliners,"* ed. Harold Bloom (New York: Chelsea House, 1988), 5–21.

Donald T. Torchiana, "Joyce's 'Two Gallants': A Walk through the Ascendency," *JJQ* 6 (1968): 115–27.

Ulysses

Eyal Amiran, "Bloom and Disraeli: On the Side of the Angels?" *ELN* 27 (March 1990): 53–57.

Eyal Amiran, "Proofs of Origin: Stephen's Intertexual Art in *Ulysses*," *JJQ* 29 (Summer 1992): 775–89.

Walter E. Anderson, "Byron's *Don Juan* and Joyce's *Ulysses*," *JJQ* 29 (Summer 1992): 829–32.

Derek Attridge, "Molly's Flow: The Writing of 'Penelope' and the Question of Women's Language," *MFS* 35 (Autumn 1989): 543–65.

Joseph Bentley, "The Stylistic Regression in *Ulysses*," in *James Joyce and His Contemporaries*, ed. Diana A. Ben-Merre and Maureen Murphy (Westport, CT: Greenwood, 1989), 31–35.

Carlo Bigazzi, "Imago canis nella 'Telemachia,'" in *Joyce Studies in Italy, II*, ed. Carla de Petris (Rome: Bulzoni, 1988), 137–48.

Christine van Boheemen, "'The Language of Flow': Joyce's Dispossession of the Feminine in *Ulysses*," in *Joyce, Modernity, and Its Mediation*, ed. Christine van Boheemen (Amsterdam: Rodopi, 1989), 63–77.

M. Keith Booker, "From the Sublime to the Ridiculous: Dante's Beatrice and Joyce's Bella Cohen," *JJQ* 29 (Winter 1992): 357–68.

M. Keith Booker, "Joyce, Planck, Einstein, and Heisenberg: A Relativistic Quantum Mechanical Discussion," *JJQ* 27 (Spring 1990): 577–86.

Joseph A. Boone, "Representing Interiority: Spaces of Sexuality in *Ulysses*," in *The Languages of Joyce: Selected Papers from the 11th International James Joyce Symposium*, ed. Rose Maria Bollettieri Bosinelli, C. Marengo Vaglio, and Christine van Boheemen (Philadelphia: Benjamins, 1992), 69–84.

John Bormanis, "'In the First Bloom of Her New Motherhood': The Appropriation of the Maternal and the Representation of Mothering in *Ulysses*," *JJQ* 29 (Spring 1992): 593–606.

Zack Bowen, "And the Music Goes Round and Round: A Couple of New Approaches to Joyce's Use of Music in *Ulysses*," in *Coping with Joyce: Essays from the Copenhagen Symposium*, ed. Morris Beja and Shari Benstock (Columbus: Ohio State University Press, 1989), 137–44.

Sheldon Brevic, "Images of a Lacanian Gaze in *Ulysses*," in *Coping with Joyce: Essays from the Copenhagen Symposium*, ed. Morris Beja and Shari Benstock (Columbus: Ohio State University Press, 1989), 157–67.

Sheldon Brevic, "The Veil of Signs: Perception as Language in Joyce's *Ulysses*," *ELH* 57 (Fall 1990): 737–55.

Austin Briggs, "'Roll Away the Reel World, the Reel World': 'Circe' and Cinema," in *Coping with Joyce: Essays from the Copenhagen Symposium*, ed. Morris Beja and Shari Benstock (Columbus: Ohio State University Press, 1989), 145–56.

Marius Buning, "History and Modernity in Joyce's *Ulysses*," in *Joyce, Modernity, and Its Mediation*, ed. Christine van Boheemen (Amsterdam: Rodopi, 1989), 127–37.

Michelle Burnham, "'Dark lady and fair man': The Love Triangle in Shakespeare's *Sonnets* and *Ulysses*," *SNNTS* 22 (Spring 1990): 43–56.

Robert Byrnes, "Agendath Netaim Discovered: Why Bloom Isn't a Zionist," *JJQ* 29 (Summer 1992): 833–38.

Robert Byrnes, "Bloom's Sexual Tropes: Stigmata of the 'Degenerate Jew,'" *JJQ* 27 (Winter 1990): 303–23.

Heather Cook Callow, "Joyce's Female Voices in *Ulysses*," *JNT* 22 (Fall 1992): 151–63.

Heather Cook Callow, "Leopold Bloom as Hebrew or 'Apiru,'" *JJQ* 31 (Winter 1994): 104–05.

Heather Cook Callow, "'Marion of the Bountiful Bosoms': Molly Bloom and the Nightmare of History," *TCL* 36 (Winter 1990): 464–76.

Brian G. Caraher, "A Question of Genre: Generic Experimentation, Self-Composition, and the Problem of Egoism in *Ulysses*," *ELH* 54 (Spring 1987): 183–214.

James Van Dyck Card, "Molly Bloom, Soprano," *JJQ* 27 (Spring 1990): 595–602.

Martha Celeste Carpentier, "Eleusinian Archetype and Ritual in 'Eumaeus' and 'Ithaca,'" *JJQ* 28 (Fall 1990): 221–38.

Gregory Castle, "'I Am Almosting It'; History, Nature, and the Will to Power in 'Proteus,'" *JJQ* 29 (Winter 1992): 281–96.

Gregory Castle, "Ousted Possibilities: Critical Histories in James Joyce's *Ulysses*," *TCL* 39 (Fall 1993): 306–28.

Bryan Cheyette, "'Jewgreek Is Jewgreek': The Disturbing Ambivalence of Joyce's Semitic Discourse in *Ulysses*," *JSA* 3 (Summer 1992): 32–56.

Sheon-Joo Chin, "The Death of Rudy: James Joyce's Use of the Doctrine of Prenatal Influence in *Ulysses*," *JELL* 35 (Spring 1989): 115–30.

Sheon-Joo Chin, "Joyce's Use of Embryological Concept and Structure of *Ulysses*," *JELL* 29 (May 1988): 117–36.

David Chinitz, "All the Dishevelled Wandering Stars: Astronomical Symbolism in 'Ithaca,'" *TCL* 37 (Winter 1991): 432–41.

Claudia Corti, "'Circe': Il comico onirico di Joyce," *RLMC* 39 (January–March 1986): 45–64.

J. Benjamin Cosgrove, "Macintosh and the Old Testament Character Joseph," *JJQ* 29 (Spring 1992): 681–84.

Michael Crumb, "Sweets of Sin: Joyce's *Ulysses* and Swinburne's 'Dolores,'" *JJQ* 28 (Fall 1990): 239–45.

H. M. Daleski, "Joyce's 'Circe': A Tale of Dragons," in *Essays on English and American Literature and a Sheaf of Poems*, ed. J Bakker, J. A. Verleun, and J. van der Vriesenaerde (Amsterdam: Rodopi, 1987), 151–63,

Palmira De Angelis, "'The radiant image': Note sul dannunzianesimo di Stephen Dedalus," in *Joyce Studies in Italy, II*, ed. Carla de Petris (Rome: Bulzoni, 1988), 93–110.

Daniel Dervin, "Bloom Again? Questions of Aggression and Psychoanalytic Reconstructions," *AI* 47 (Fall–Winter 1990): 249–69.

Kimberly J. Devlin, "Castration and Its Discontents: A Lacanian Approach to *Ulysses*," *JJQ* 29 (Fall 1991): 117–44.

Kimberly J. Devlin, "Pretending in "Penelope": Masquerade, Mimicry and Molly Bloom," *Novel* 25 (Fall 1991): 71–89.

Thomas Dilworth, "A.E.I.O.U.: Plato and Rimbaud in 'Scylla and Charybdis,'" *JJQ* 28 (Fall 1990): 298301.

Andrew Enda Duffy, "Parnellism and Rebellion: The Irish War of Independence and Revisions of the Heroic in *Ulysses*," *JJQ* 28 (Fall 1990): 179–95.

Jacqueline F. Eastman, "The Language of Flowers: A New Source for 'Lotus Eaters,'" *JJQ* 26 (Spring 1989): 379–96.

Maud Ellmann, "The Ghosts of *Ulysses*," in *The Languages of Joyce: Selected Papers from the 11th International James Joyce Symposium*, ed. Rose Maria Bollettieri Bosinelli, C. Marengo Vaglio, and Christine van Boheemen (Philadelphia: Benjamins, 1992), 103–19.

Maud Ellman, "To Sing or to Sign," in *James Joyce: A Collection of Critical Essays*, ed. Mary T. Reynolds (Englewood Cliffs, NJ: Prentice-Hall, 1993), 159–62.

James Fairhall, "*Ulysses*, the Great War, and the Easter 1916 Rising," in *Literature and War*, ed. David Bevan (Amsterdam: Rodopi, 1990), 25–38.

Charles Ford, "Dante's Other Brush: *Ulysses* and the Irish Revolution," *JJQ* 29 (Summer 1992): 751–61.

Cheryl Fox, "Absolutely: Redefining the Word Known to All Men," *JJQ* 29 (Summer 1992): 799–804.

Christine Froula, "History's Nightmare, Fiction's Dream: Joyce and the Psychohistory of *Ulysses*," *JJQ* 28 (Summer 1991): 857–71.

Robert Frumkin, "*Ulysses*: Stephen's Parable of the Plums," *CLQ* 28 (March 1992): 5–18.

David Galef, "The Fashion Show in *Ulysses*," *TCL* 37 (Winter 1991): 420–31.

David Galef, "Joyce, The Viconian Cyclist," *N&Q* 40 (December 1993): 496–97.

John Gordon, "Haines and the Black Panther," *JJQ* 27 (Spring 1990): 587–94.

John Gordon, "Love in Bloom, by Stephen Dedalus," *JJQ* 27 (Winter 1990): 241–55.

John Gordon, "The M'Intosh Mystery: II," *TCL* 38 (Summer 1992): 214–25.

John Gordon, "Obeying the Boss in 'Oxen of the Sun,'" *ELH* 58 (Spring 1991): 233–59.

Daniel P. Gunn, "The Name of Bloom," in *Joycean Occasions: Essays from the Milwaukee James Joyce Conference*, ed. Janet E. Dunleavy, Melvin J. Friedman, and Michael Patrick Gillespie (Newark: University of Delaware Press, 1991), 33–45.

Gail Hall, "'Plots and Plans': Molly Bloom's Fiction," *MR* 31 (Winter 1990): 582–98.

John Harty, "'Grave Morrice' (*Ulysses* 2.155): The Morris Dances," *NMIL* 2 (1990): 29–33.

Diana E. Henderson, "Joyce's Modernist Woman: Whose Last Word?" *MFS* 35 (Autumn 1989): 517–28.

Suzette Henke, "Joyce's New Womanly Man: Sexual Signatures of Androgynous Transformation in *Ulysses*," in *Joycean Occasions: Essays from the Milwaukee James Joyce Conference*, ed. Janet E. Dunleavy, Melvin J. Friedman, and Michael Patrick Gillespie (Newark: University of Delaware Press, 1991), 46–58.

Cheryl Herr, "'Penelope' as Period Piece," *Novel* 22 (Winter 1989): 130–42.

Michael Higgins, "A Note on 'Time or Setdown' in *Ulysses*," *N&Q* 36 (June 1989): 200–01.

Marylu Hill, "'Amor Matris': Mother and Self in the Telemachiad Episode of *Ulysses*," *TCL* 39 (Fall 1993): 329–43.

Patrick Colm Hogan, "Molly Bloom's Lacanian Firtree: Law, Ambiguity, and the Limits of Paradise," *JJQ* 29 (Fall 1991): 103–16.

Duk-Seon Hong, "James Joyce's Use of History in *Ulysses*," *JELL* 36 (Winter 1990): 679–90.

JOYCE, JAMES, *Ulysses*

Tony E. Jackson, "'Cyclops', 'Nausicaa', and Joyce's Imaginary Irish Couple," *JJQ* 29 (Fall 1991): 63–83.

Frederic R. Jameson, "*Ulysses* in History," in *James Joyce: A Collection of Critical Essays*, ed. Mary T. Reynolds (Englewood Cliffs, NJ: Prentice Hall, 1993), 145–58.

Robert Janusko, "Another Anthology for 'Oxen': Barnett and Dale," *JJQ* 27 (Winter 1990): 257–81.

Robert Janusko, "From Seymour to Amby to Bannon and Out: A Metamorphosis in Draft," *JJQ* 29 (Winter 1992): 393–97.

Robert Janusko, "Grave Beauty: Newman in 'Oxen,'" *JJQ* 28 (Spring 1991): 617–21.

Robert Janusko, "More on J. A. Dowie (& Son)," *JJQ* 29 (Spring 1992): 607–13.

Manuel Almagro Jimenez, "Modernismo yo postmodernismo en *Ulysses*," *RAEI* 5 (November 1992): 23–33.

Jeri Johnson, "'Beyond the Veil': *Ulysses*, Feminism, and the Figure of Woman," in *Joyce, Modernity, and Its Mediation*, ed. Christine van Boheemen (Amsterdam: Rodopi, 1989), 201–28.

Ralph Robert Joly, "Simchath Torah and the 'Wandering Rocks' Episode: A Festival of Readings," *JJQ* 28 (Fall 1990): 303–6.

Ellen Carol Jones, "Commodious Recirculation: Commodity and Dream in Joyce's *Ulysses*," *JJQ* 30 (Summer–Fall 1993): 739–56.

R. B. Kershner, "More Evidence on Breen's Telegram," *JJQ* 29 (Winter 1992): 407–8.

Declan Kiberd, "Bloom the Liberator; The Androgynous Anti–hero of *Ulysses* as the Embodiment of Joyce's Utopian Hopes," *TLS* (3 January 1992): 3–6.

Jean Kimball, "Love in the Kidd Era: An Afterword," *JJQ* 29 (Winter 1992): 369–77.

Scott W. Klein, "Speech Lent by Males: Gender, Identity, and the Example of Stephen's Shakespeare," *JJQ* 30 (Spring 1993): 439–49.

Susan Kurjiaka, "The Hypnagogic State in *Ulysses*," *MOR* 3 (Spring 1989): 50–58.

Jules David Law, "'Pity They Can't See Themselves': Assessing the 'Subject' of Pornography in 'Nausicaa,'" *JJQ* 27 (Winter 1990): 219–39.

Karen R. Lawrence, "'Beggaring Description': Politics and Style in Joyce's 'Eumaeus,'" *MFS* 38 (Summer 1992): 355–76.

Karin Lawrence, "*Ulysses*: The Narrative Norm," in *James Joyce: A Collection of Critical Essays*, ed. Mary T. Reynolds (Englewood Cliffs, NJ: Prentice-Hall, 1993), 118–29.

Garry M. Leonard, "Women on the Market: Commodity Culture, 'Femininity,' and 'Those Lovely Seaside Girls' in Joyce *Ulysses*," *JSA* 2 (1991): 27–68.

Jennifer Levine, "*Ulysses*," in *Cambridge Companion to James Joyce*, ed. Derek Attridge (Cambridge: Cambridge University Press, 1990), 131–59.

Benjamin Levitan, "Stephen Dedalus 'Prone,'" *JJQ* 28 (Spring 1991): 687–88.

Annette Shandler Levitt, "The Pattern out of the Wallpaper: Luce Irigaray and Molly Bloom," *MFS* 35 (Autumn 1989): 507–16.

A. Walton Litz, "The Genre of *Ulysses*," in *James Joyce: A Collection of Critical Essays*, ed. Mary T. Reynolds (Englewood Cliffs, NJ: Prentice-Hall, 1993), 109–17.

Ars Longa and Vita Brevis, "Towards an Interpretation of *Ulysses*: Metonymy and Gastronomy: A Bloom with a Stew," *Nabokovian* 20 (Spring 1988): 5–6.

Jay Losey, "Joyce's 'New Realism' in *Ulysses*," *NMIL* 2 (1990): 19–24.

Mark Loveridge, "Joycean Narrators Report the Ascot Gold Cup in 'The Times,'" *JJQ* 28 (Spring 1991): 679–82.

Mary Lowe-Evans, "Joyce's Bed-time Stories," *JJQ* 30 (Summer–Fall 1993): 813–23.

Patrick A. McCarthy, "Reading in *Ulysses*," in *Joycean Occasions: Essays from the Milwaukee James Joyce Conference*, ed. Janet E. Dunleavy, Melvin J. Friedman, and Michael Patrick Gillespie (Newark: University of Delaware Press, 1991), 15–32.

Brian McHale, "Constructing (post)modernism: The Case of *Ulysses*," *Style* 24 (Spring 1990): 1–21.

James H. Maddox, "Mockery in *Ulysses*," in *James Joyce: A Collection of Critical Essays*, ed. Mary T. Reynolds (Englewood Cliffs, NJ: Prentice-Hall, 1993), 130–44.

Tess Marsh, "Is There More to 'Photo Bits' Than Meets the Eye?" *JJQ* 30 (Summer–Fall 1993): 877–93.

Wendell Mayo, "Joyce's *Ulysses*," *Expl* 50 (Spring 1992): 164–66.

Giorgio Melchiori, "Mr. Bloom in Venice," *JJQ* 27 (Fall 1989): 121–24.

Robert Merritt, "Faith and Betrayal: The Potato in *Ulysses*," *JJQ* 28 (Fall 1990): 269–76.

Jeffrey Meyers, "'Cyclops' and the Ashanti War," *JJQ* 29 (Winter 1992): 408–10.

David Mikics, "History and the Rhetoric of the Artist in 'Aeolus,'" *JJQ* 27 (Spring 1990): 533–58.

Nicholas A. Miller, "Beyond Recognition: Reading the Unconscious in the "Ithaca" Episode of *Ulysses*," *JJQ* 30 (Winter 1993): 209–19.

J. Lawrence Mitchell, "Joyce and Boxing: Famous Fighters in *Ulysses*," *JJQ* 31 (Winter 1994): 21–20.

Mark Morrisson, "Stephen Dedalus and the Ghost of the Mother,'" *MFS* 39 (Summer 1993): 345–68.

Donald E. Morse, "Source Book or Book of Conduct: Changing Perpsectives on Reading Joyce's *Ulysses*," *HSE* 21 (December 1990): 67–71.

Mark Nair, "Joyce's *Ulysses*," *Expl* 50 (Summer 1992): 237–38.

Hiroaki Natsume, "*Ulysses*: Bunritsu no Shirabe," *EigoS* 135 (n.d.): 210–14.

Robert D. Newman, "'Eumaeus' as Sacrificial Narrative," *JJQ* 30 (Spring 1993): 451–58.

Robert D. Newman, "Narrative Transgression and Restoration: Hermetic Messengers in *Ulysses*," *JJQ* 29 (Winter 1992): 315–37.

Anne Nolan, "Father Charles of Mount Argus, 1821–1893," *JJQ* 29 (Summer 1992): 841–45.

Peggy Ochoa, "Joyce's 'Nausicaa': The Paradox of Advertising Narcissism," *JJQ* 30 (Summer–Fall 1993): 783–93.

Dorith Ofri-Scheps, "Intervenor's Questions on 'Quasisensations of Concealed Identities' (U 17.782)," *JJQ* 26 (Summer 1989):'561–72.

William O'Neill, "The Rout of the Suitors, the Making of an Artist: The Meaning of Parallel and Parody in *Ulysses*," *MidWQ* 27 (Summer 1986): 401–21.

Michael J. O'Shea, "Eumaeans Helvetically Wandered" *JJQ* 28 (Spring 1991): 688–91.

Mark Osteen, "The Intertextual Economy in 'Scylla and Charybdis,'" *JJQ* 28 (Fall 1990): 197–208.

Mark Osteen, "The Money Question at the Back of Everything: Clichés, Counterfeits and Forgeries in Joyce's 'Eumaeus,'" *MFS* 38 (Winter 1992): 821–43.

Mark Osteen, "Narrative Gifts: 'Cyclops' and the Economy of Excess," *JSA* 1 (1990): 162–96.

Mark Osteen, "Seeking Renewal: Bloom, Advertising, and the Domestic Economy," *JJQ* 30 (Summer–Fall 1993): 717–37.

Caroline Patey, "La logica di *Ulysses*: Musica, mito, metonimia," in *Joyce Studies in Italy, II*, ed. Carla de Petris (Rome: Bulzoni, 1988), 173–94.

William Pencak, "The Operatic *Ulysses*," *OQ* 7 (Spring 1990): 12–30.

Erwin Pfrang, "Circe Drawings," *PRev* 35 (Summer 1993): 145–59.

David J. Piwinski, "The Image of the Bleeding Horse in James Joyce's *Ulysses*," *PLL* 26 (Spring 1990): 285–88.

David J. Piwinski, "Tomatoes as 'Love Apples' in *Ulysses*," *ANQ* 4 (October 1991): 188–89.

L. H. Platt, "The Buckeen and the Dogsbody: Aspects of History and Culture in 'Telemachus,'" *JJQ* 27 (Fall 1989): 77–86.

L. H. Platt, "The Voice of Esau: Culture and Nationalism in 'Scylla and Charybdis,'" *JJQ* 29 (Summer 1992): 737–50.

Mary Power, "Molly Bloom and Mary Anderson: The Inside Story," in *Joyce, Modernity, and Its Mediation*, ed. Christine van Boheemen (Amsterdam: Rodopi, 1989), 113–18.

Jonathan Quick, "Molly Bloom's Mother," *ELH* 57 (Spring 1990): 223–40.

Ralph W. Rader, "Why Stephen's Hand Hurts: Joyce as Narcissus in *Ulysses*," *JJQ* 26 (Spring 1989): 440–45.

Thomas Jackson Rice, "*Ulysses*, Chaos, and Complexity," *JJQ* 31 (Winter 1994): 41–14.

Margaret Rogers, "Decoding the Fugue in 'Sirens,'" *JJLS* 4 (Spring 1990): 15–20.

Louis D. Rubin Jr., "Leopold Bloom's Prodigious Leap," *SR* 101 (Winter 1993): 85–97.

Ju-Hyun Ryu, "Author and His Experience: Scylla and Charybdis in *Ulysses*," *JELL* 35 (Autumn 1989): 445–62.

Mario Salvadori and Myron Schwartzman, "Musemathematics: The Literary Use of Science and Mathematics in Joyce's *Ulysses*," *JJQ* 29 (Winter 1992): 339–55.

R. J. Schork, "The Emperor's Butterfly," *JJQ* 29 (Winter 1992): 403–5.

R. J. Schork, "'Nodebinding Ayes': Milton, Blindness, and Egypt in the Wake," *JJQ* 30 (Fall 1992): 69–83.

R. J. Schork, "Plautus and Martial in Joyce," *N&Q* 36 (June 1989): 198–200.

R. J. Schork, "Tha Lassy! Tha Lassy!" *JJQ* 28 (Fall 1990): 293–96.

Thomas G. Schrand, "Authority and Catechesis: Narrative and Knowledge in *Ulysses*," *JJQ* 28 (Fall 1990): 209–20.

Daniel R. Schwarz, "'Tell Us in Plain Words': An Introduction to Reading Joyce's *Ulysses*," *JNT* 17 (Winter 1987): 25–38.

Jeffrey Segall, "Thirteen Ways of Looking at an Ad-Canvasser: Bloom and the Politics of Joyce Criticism," *JSA* 2 (1991): 69–85.

Fritz Senn, "Bucolic Strands in 'Aeolus,'" *JJQ* 27 (Fall 1989): 129–32.

Fritz Senn, "Cold Comfort," *JJQ* 27 (Fall 1989): 126–28.

Fritz Senn, "Habent Sua Fata," *JJQ* 27 (Fall 1989): 132–34.

Fritz Senn, "Intellectual Nodality of the Lisible: Genus Omne," *RLM* 953–958 (1990): 173–88.

Fritz Senn, "Invisible Strandentwining," *JJQ* 31 (Winter 1994): 101–4.

Fritz Senn, "Met Whom What?" *JJQ* 30 (Fall 1992): 109–12.

Fritz Senn, "Micro-Cycloptics," *JJQ* 27 (Fall 1989): 134–36.

Fritz Senn, "On Not Finding Places," *JJQ* 29 (Winter 1992): 397–401.

Fritz Senn, "Ovidian Roots of Gigantism in Joyce's *Ulysses*," *JML* 15 (Spring 1989): 561–77.

Fritz Senn, "'A Rump and Dozen,'" *NMIL* 1 (1989): 4–6.

Fritz Senn, "Sequential Close-Ups in Joyce's *Ulysses*," in *Modes of Narrative: Approaches to American, Canadian and British Fiction*, ed. Reingard M. Nischik and Barbara Korte (Wurzburg: Konigshausen & Neumann, 1990), 252–64.

Dennis M. Shanahan, "The Eucharistic Aesthetics of the Passion: The Testament of Blood in *Ulysses*," *JJQ* 27 (Winter 1990): 373–86.

Vincent Sherry, "Distant Music: 'Wandering Rocks' and the Art of Gratuity," *JJQ* 31 (Winter 1994): 31–40.

Carol Shloss, "Molly's Resistance to the Union: Marriage and Colonialism in Dublin, 1904," *MFS* 35 (Autumn 1989): 529–41.

Stephen Sicari, "Bloom in Purgatory: 'Sirens' and 'Purgatorio II,'" *TCL* 36 (Winter 1990): 47788.

Carol Siegel, "'Venus Metempsychosis'" and Venus in Furs: Masochism and Fertility in *Ulysses*," *TCL* 33 (Summer 1987): 179–95.

Peter Sims, "A Pocket Guide to *Ulysses*," *JJQ* 26 (Winter 1989): 239–58.

John P. Sisk, "Taking History Personally," *AR* 46 (Fall 1988): 428–37.

Craig S. Smith, "Joyce's *Ulysses*: Dimensions of the Sacred at Sandymount," *ELN* 27 (June 1990): 57–62.

Craig S. Smith, "Joyce's *Ulysses* 13.633,'" *Expl* 50 (Fall 1991): 37–38.

Craig S. Smith, "Twilight in Dublin: A Look at Joyce's 'Nausicaa,'" *JJQ* 28 (Spring 1991): 631–35.

Craig S. Smith and M.C. Bisch, "Joyce's *Ulysses* 11.1–4," *Expl* 48 (Spring 1990): 206.

Craig S. Smith and Matthew L. Jockers, "Joyce's *Ulysses*," *Expl* 50 (Summer 1992): 235–37.

John Somer, "The Self-reflexive Arranger in the Initial Style of Joyce's *Ulysses*," *JJQ* 31 (Winter 1994): 65–79.

Robert Spoo, "Reading Leopold Bloom/1904 in 1989," *JJQ* 26 (Spring 1989): 397–416.

Robert Spoo, "Teleology, Monocausality, and Marriage in *Ulysses*," *ELH* 56 (Summer 1989): 439–62.

Robert Spoo, "'Usurper': A Word on the Last Word in 'Telemachus,'" *JJQ* 26 (Spring 1989): 450–51.

Erwin R. Steinberg, "'Persecuted'sold'in Morocco like Slaves,'" *JJQ* 29 (Spring 1992): 615–22.

Cristina M. T. Stevens, "The Mock-Hero in Joyce's *Ulysses*," *EAA* 12–13 (1988–1989): 144–49.

Constance V. Tagopoulos, "Joyce and Homer: Return, Disguise, and Recognition in 'Ithaca,'" *Joyce in Context*, ed. Vincent J. Cheng and Timothy Martin (Cambridge: Cambridge University Press, 1992), 184–200.

Barbara Temple-Thurston, "The Reader as Absentminded Beggar: Recovering South Africa in *Ulysses*," *JJQ* 28 (Fall 1990): 247–56.

Grace Tiffany, "*Our Mutual Friend* in 'Eumaeus': Joyce Appropriates Dickens," *JML* 16 (Spring 1990): 643–46.

Wim Tigges, "An Analogue to Bloom's Mythical Potato," *JJQ* 29 (Summer 1992): 846.

Wim Tigges, "A Source for 'Old Fish . . . Young Flesh' (U8.867)," *JJQ* 29 (Summer 1992): 846–47.

Andre Topia, "The Matrix and the Echo: Intertextuality in *Ulysses*," in *Post–Structuralist Joyce: Essays from the French*, ed. Derek Attridge and Daniel Ferrer (Cambridge: Cambridge University Press, 1988), 103–26.

Michael Tratner, "Sex and Credit: Consumer Capitalism in *Ulysses*," *JJQ* 30 (Summer–Fall 1993): 695–716.

Gordon Tweedie, "'Common Sense': James to Joyce and the Pragmatic L. Bloom," *JJQ* 26 (Spring 1989): 351–66.

Bjorn Tysdahl, "Joyce's *Ulysses*—en roman som handler om noe," *Vinduet* 45, no. 3 (1991): 42–45.

Andras P. Ungar, "Among the Hapsburgs: Arthur Griffith, Stephen Dedalus, and the Myth of Bloom," *TCL* 35 (Winter 1989): 480–501.

Andras P. Ungar, "Joyce's Hungarian in *Ulysses*," *JJQ* 27 (Spring 1990): 648–50.

Joseph Valente, "Who Made the Tune: Becoming-woman in 'Sirens,'" *JJQ* 30 (Winter 1993): 191–208.

Joe Voelker and Thomas Arner, "Bloomian Pantomine: J. A. Dowie and the 'Messianic Scene,'" *JJQ* 27 (Winter 1990): 283–91.

Kathleen Wales, "The 'Oxen of the Sun' in *Ulysses*: Joyce and Anglo-Saxon," *JJQ* 26 (Spring 1989): 319–32.

Stephen Watt, "Brief Exposures: Commodification, Exchange Value, and the Figure of Woman in 'Eumaeus,'" *JJQ* 30 (Summer–Fall 1993): 757–82.

Wolfgang Weber, "Irrfelsen fur den Leser: Zur Erzahltechnik des Kapitels 'Wandering Rocks' in James Joyces *Ulysses*," in *Theorie und Praxis im Erzahlen des 19. und 20. Jahrhunderts: Studien zur englischen und amerikanischen Literatur zu Ehren von Willi Erzgraber*, ed. Winfried Herget, Klaus Peter Jochum, and Ingeborg Weber (Tubingen: Narr, 1986), 107–16.

David Weir, "Sophomore Plum(p)s for Old Man Moses," *JJQ* 28 (Spring 1991): 657–61.

David Weir, "What "Mn" Means," *JJQ* 30 (Spring 1993): 480–82.

Jennifer Wicke, "Lingerie and (Literary) History: Joyce's *Ulysses* and Fashionability," *CritQ* 36 (Summer 1994): 25–41.

Jennifer Wicke, "'Who's She When She's at Home?' Molly Bloom and the Work of Consumption," *JJQ* 28 (Summer 1991): 749–63.

Joan Parisi Wilcox, "Joyce, Euclid, and 'Ithaca,'" *JJQ* 28 (Spring 1991): 643–49.

Andrew P. Williams, "Hero Bloom: The Development of Character in the Calypso Chapter of Joyce's *Ulysses*," *MidWQ* 33 (Summer 1992): 420–29.

Trevor L. Williams, "'As It Was in the Beginning': The Struggle for History in the 'Nestor' Episode of *Ulysses*," *CJIS* 16 (December 1990): 36–46.

Trevor L. Williams, "'Conmeeism' and the Universe of Discourse in 'Wandering Rocks,'" *JJQ* 29 (Winter 1992): 267–79.

Trevor L. Williams, "Demystifying the Power of the Given: The 'Telemachus' Episode of *Ulysses*," *TCL* 37 (Spring 1991): 38–53.

Trevor L. Williams, "Hungry Man is an Angry Man': A Marxist Reading of Consumption in Joyce's *Ulysses*," *Mosaic* 26 (Winter 1993): 87–108.

Romana Zacchi, "Quoting Words and Worlds: Discourse Strategies in *Ulysses*," *JJQ* 27 (Fall 1989): 101–9.

Ewa Ziarek, "'Circe': Joyce's Argumentum ad Feminam," *JJQ* 30 (Fall 1992): 51–68.

KEANE, MOLLY NESTA

Good Behaviour

Alice Adams, "Coming Apart at the Seams: *Good Behaviour* as an Anti-Comedy of Manners," *JIL* 20 (September 1991): 27–35.

KEANE, MOLLY NESTA, *Time After Time*

Time After Time

Paul Deane, "The Big House Revisited: Molly Keane's *Time after Time*," *NMIL* 3 (1991): 37–44.

KIELY, BENEDICT

A Ball of Malt and Madame Butterfly

Frank Kersnowski, "Ben Kiely and His *Ball of Malt*," *JSSE* 7 (Autumn 1986): 17–27.

"Bloodless Byrne of a Monday"

Ben Forkner and Benedict Kiely, "Benedict Kiely: General Remarks and a New Story: 'Bloodless Byrne of a Monday,'" *JSSE* 8 (Spring 1987): 9–34.

Nothing Happens in Carmincross

Edwin C. Epps, "Benedict Kiely and the Irish Gelignite Tradition," *VirEB* 36 (Winter 1986): 122–25.

KINGSLEY, CHARLES

Alton Locke, Tailor and Poet

Philippe Daumas, "Charles Kingsley's Style in *Alton Locke*," *LM* 63 (March–April 1969): 6975.

Frederick R. Karl, "*Alton Locke*," in *A Reader's Guide to the Nineteenth Century Novel* (New York: Farrar, Straus, 1964), 23, 146, 274, 326–27, 333–37.

Charles H. Muller, "*Alton Locke*: Kingsley's Dramatic Sermon," *UES* 14 (1976): ii–iii, 9–20.

Wanda Fraiken Neff, "Alton Locke," in *Victorian Working Women: An Historical and Literary Study of Women in British Industries and Professions 1832–1850* (New York: AMS, 1966), 133–35, 142, 145–46, 148, 177.

Alan Rauch, "The Tailor Transformed: Kingsley's *Alton Locke* and the Notion of Change," *SNNTS* 25 (Summer 1993): 196–213.

Hereward the Wake

George H. Bushnell, "*Hereward the Wake*," *N&Q* 159 (15 November 1930): 346–47.

Ernest Rhys, "Introduction," in *The Everyman Edition of "Hereward the Wake*," ed. Ernest Rhys (London: Dent, 1961), i–xvi.

Michael Young, "History as Myth: Charles Kingsley's *Hereward the Wake*," *SNNTS* 17 (Summer 1985): 174–88.

Hypatia

Valerie Grosvenor Myer, "Charles Kingsley's *Hypatia*: A Seminal Novel," *N&Q* 39 (June 1992): 179–80.

O. B. Vainshtein, "Osobennosti poetiki romana Ch. Kingsli *Ipatiia* v otsenke viktorianskoi kritiki," *VMU* 9 (January–February 1985): 69–71.

Two Years Ago

George Meredith, "Review of *Two Years Ago*," *WestR* 11 (April 1857): 609–11.

John Kimberley Roberts, "English Writers and Welsh Railways," *AWR* 17 (Fall 1968): 136–38.

The Water Babies

Dorothy Coleman, "Rabelais and *The Water Babies*," *MLR* 66 (July 1971): 511–21.

Valentine Cunningham, "Soiled Fairy: *The Water Babies* in Its Time," *EIC* 35 (April 1985): 121–48.

John C. Hawley, "*The Water Babies* as Catechetical Paradigm," *CLAQ* 14 (Spring 1989): 19–21.

Q. D. Leavis, "*The Water Babies*," *CLE* 23 (1976): 155–63.

Louis MacNeice, "*The Water Babies*," in *Varieties of Parable* (Cambridge, MA: Cambridge University Press, 1965), 13, 20–21, 83–89.

Charles H. Muller, "*The Water Babies*—Moral Lessons for Children," *UES* 24 (May 1986): 12–17.

Stephen Paget, "*The Water Babies*," in *I Have Reason to Believe* (London: Macmillan, 1921), 102–16.

Larry Uffelman and Patrick Scott, "Kingsley's Serial Novels, II: *The Water Babies*," *VPR* 19 (Winter 1986): 122–31.

Westward Ho!

John Hunter Sedgwick, "A Mid–Victorian Nordic," *NAR* 225 (January 1928): 86–93.

Yeast

John L. Kijinski, "Charles Kingsley's *Yeast*: Brotherhood and the Condition of England," *VIJ* 13 (1985): 97–109.

P. G. Scott and Larry K. Uffelman, "Kingsley's Serial Novels: *Yeast*," *VPN* 9 (June 1976): 111–19.

Shelia M. Smith, "Blue Books and Victorian Novelists," *RES* 31 (February 1971): 23–40.

Stanley T. Williams, "*Yeast*: A Victorian Heresy," *NAR* 212 (November 1920): 697–704.

"Young and Old"

Terence Hoagwood, "Kingsley's 'Young and Old,'" *Expl* 46 (Summer 1988): 18–21.

KIPLING, RUDYARD

"Below the Mill Dam"

Ann Parry, "'Take away that bauble!' Political Allegory in 'Below the Mill Dam,'" *KJ* 62 (December 1988): 10–24.

"Beyond the Pale"

Gareth Cornwell, "'Beyond the Pale': A Preface," *ESA* 27, no. 2 (1984): 123–32.

Robert H. MacDonald, "Discourse and Ideology in Kipling's 'Beyond the Pale,'" *SSF* 23 (Fall 1986): 413–18.

"The Bridge Builders"

Ann Parry, "Imperialism in 'The Bridge Builders': Metaphor or Reality?" *KJ* 60 (March 1986; June 1986): 12–22; 9–16.

R. Ramachandra, "Kipling's 'The Bridge-Builders': An Excursion into Value Structure," *LCrit* 22, no. 4 (1987): 87–91.

"The Brushwood Boy"

Zohreh T. Sullivan, "Kipling the Nightwalker," *MFS* 30 (Summer 1984): 217–35.

"The Bull That Thought"

Danielle Schaub, "Kipling's Craftsmanship in 'The Bull That Thought,'" *SSF* 22 (Summer 1985): 309–16.

"The Crab That Played with the Sea"

B. E. Smythies, "Three More or Less Malay Phrases," *KJ* 60 (March 1986): 35–36.

"Dayspring Mishandled"

E. N. Houlton, "Poor Old Castorley," *KJ* 60 (June 1986): 61–70.

"Debits and Credits"

Lisa A. F. Lewis, "Some Links between the Stories in Kipling's 'Debits and Credits,'" *ELT* 25, no. 2 (1982): 74–85.

Harry Ricketts, "Kipling and the War: A Reading of 'Debits and Credits,'" *ELT* 29, no. 1 (1986): 29–39.

"The Devil and the Deep Sea"

C. E. Moorhouse, "Mr Wardrop's Problem: Excerpts from a Talk on Kipling and Technology," *KJ* 61 (March 1987): 10–22.

"The Elephant's-Child"

Howard R. Cell, "The Socratic Pilgrimage of the Elephant Child," *ChildL* 20 (1992): 132–45.

"The Eye of Allah"

John Coates, "Memories of Mansura: The 'Tints and Textures' of Kipling's Late Art in 'The Eye of Allah,'" *MLR* 85 (July 1990): 355–69.

"Fairy Kist"

Elizabeth M. Knowles, "Seven Portugal Onions: A Note on Kipling's Reading," *KJ* 60 (December 1986): 43–48.

B. E. Smythies, "Four Pictures on the Wall," *KJ* 61 (June 1987): 50–52.

"Friendly Brook"

Philip Mason, "Two Kipling Puzzles," *KJ* 62 (December 1988): 25–34.

"His Private Honour"

Mark Paffard, "Ortheris: Private Stanley Ortheris, No. 22639, B Company," *KJ* 58 (June 1984): 18–25.

"The Killing of Hatim Tai"

D. H. Stewart, "Shooting Elephants Right," *SoR* 22 (Winter 1986): 86–92.

Kim

Radha Achar, "The Child in Kipling's Fiction: An Analysis," *LCrit* 22, no. 4 (1987): 46–53.

Jeanne F. Bedell, "The Great Game," *ArmD* 21 (Fall 1988): 380–87.

K.C. Belliappa, "The Meaning of Rudyard Kipling's *Kim*," *JCL* 26 (August 1991): 151–57.

William Blackburn, "Internationalism and Empire: *Kim* and the Art of Rudyard Kipling," in *Proceedings of the Sixth Annual Conference of the Children's*

Literature Association, University of Toronto March, 1979, ed. Priscilla A. Ord (Villanova, PA: Villanova University Press, 1980), 78–85.

Nirad C. Chaudhuri, "The Finest Story About India—in English," *Encounter* 8 (April 1957): 47–53.

Margaret Peller Feeley, "The Kim that Nobody Reads," in *Rudyard Kipling's "Kim,"* ed. Harold Bloom (New York: Chelsea House, 1987), 57–74.

Robert D. Gorchov, "The Little Friend of All the World," *OJES* 10 (1973): 1–10.

Jean-François Gournay, "Esquisse d'une lecture anthropologique de Kim," *ÉA* 35 (October–December 1982): 385–95.

Irving Howe, "The Pleasures of *Kim*," in *Rudyard Kipling's "Kim,"* ed. Harold Bloom (New York: Chelsea House, 1987), 31–41.

Cynthia A. Leenerts, "Kipling's Vision of Law in *Kim*," *LCrit* 25, no. 4 (1990): 48–61.

Philip Mason, "*Kim*: 'Life as He Would Have It,'" in *Rudyard Kipling's "Kim,"* ed. Harold Bloom (New York: Chelsea House, 1987), 25–30.

Robert F. Moss, "Kipling's Triumph: The Double Boyhood of Kimball O'Hara," in *Rudyard Kipling's "Kim,"* ed. Harold Bloom (New York: Chelsea House, 1987), 87–100.

J. Mukherjee, "The Relevance of the Irish Aspect in Rudyard Kipling's *Kim*," *LCrit* 22, no. 4 (1987): 41–45.

Judith A. Plotz, "Crossing and Double-Crossing Cultural Barriers in Kipling's *Kim*," in *Cross–Culturalism in Children's Literature: Selected Papers from the Children's Literature Association*, ed. Susan R. Gannon and Ruth Anne Thompson (New York: Pace University Press, 1988), 61–65.

Judith A. Plotz, "The Empire of Youth: Crossing and Double–Crossing Cultural Barriers in Kipling's *Kim*," *ChildL* 20 (1992): 111–31.

Alam Qamar, "Form and Pattrn of Kipling's *Kim*," *OJES* 10 (1973): 11–14.

K. Raghavendra Rao, "Collective Identity in Kipling's *Kim*: Deconstructing Imperialism," *LCrit* 22, no. 4 (1987): 22–30.

Fred Reid, "Kipling, Kim and Imperialism," *HT* 32 (August 1982): 14–20.

Constance Scheerer, "The Lost Paradise of Rudyard Kipling," *DR* 61 (Spring 1981): 27–37. Reprinted in *Rudyard Kipling's "Kim,"* ed. Harold Bloom (New York: Chelsea House, 1987), 75–85.

Vasant A. Shahane, "*Kim*: The Process of Becoming," in *Rudyard Kipling's "Kim,"* ed. Harold Bloom (New York: Chelsea House, 1987), 9–23.

David H. Stewart, "Aspects of Language in *Kim*," *KJ* 57 (June 1983): 25–39.

David H. Stewart, "Orality in Kipling's *Kim*," *JNT* 13 (Winter 1983): 47–57. Reprinted in *Rudyard Kipling's "Kim*," ed. Harold Bloom (New York: Chelsea House, 1987), 101–11.

David H. Stewart, "Structure in Kipling's *Kim*," *VN* 58 (1980): 24–26.

Angus Wilson, "Kipling's *Kim*," in *Rudyard Kipling's "Kim*," ed. Harold Bloom (New York: Chelsea House, 1987), 43–55.

The Jungle Books

Roger Lancelyn Green, "Mowgli's Jungle," *KJ* 57 (September 1983): 29–35.

John McBratney, "Imperial Subjects, Imperial Space in Kipling's *Jungle Book*," *VS* 35 (Spring 1992): 277–93.

John Murray, "The Law of *The Jungle Books*," *ChildL* 20 (1992): 1–14

Just So Stories

Celia Catlett Anderson, "'O Best Beloved': Kipling's Reading Instructions in the *Just So Stories*," in *The Child and the Story: An Exploration of Narrative Forms*, ed. Priscilla Ord (Boston: Children's Literature Association, 1983), 33–39.

Rosalind Meyer, "But Is It Art? An Appreciation of *Just So Stories*," *KJ* 58 (December 1984): 10–33.

The Light That Failed

Pierre Coustillas, "*The Light That Failed*; Or, Artistic Bohemia as Self–Revelation," *ELT* 29, no. 2 (1986): 127–39.

J. E. Monro, "'How It All Began': *The Light That Failed*: A Study in Defective Personality," *KJ* 60 (December 1986): 10–22.

Leonard Shengold, "An Attempt at Soul Murder: Rudyard Kipling's Early Life and Work," in *Lives, Events, and Other Players: Directions in Psychobiography*, ed. Joseph T. Coltrera (New York: Aronson, 1981), 203–54.

The Man Who Would Be King

Tim Bascom, "Secret Imperialism: The Reader's Response to the Narrator in *The Man Who Would Be King*," *ELT* 31, no. 2 (1988): 162–73.

Manfred Draudt, "Reality or Delusion? Narrative Technique and Meaning in Kipling's *The Man Who Would Be King*," *ES* 65 (August 1984): 316–26.

Jeffrey Meyers, "The Idea of Moral Authority in *The Man Who Would Be King*," *SEL* 8 (1968): 711–23.

David H. Stewart, "Kipling, Conrad and the Dark Heart," *Conradiana* 19 (Autumn 1987): 195–205.

"Many Inventions"

M. C. Hamard, "Ordre et desordre dans 'Many Inventions,'" *CVE* 27 (April 1988): 53–62.

"Mary Postgate"

Norman Page, "What Happens in 'Mary Postgate'?" *ELT* 29, no. 1 (1986): 41–47.

M. Tarinayya, "Kipling's 'Mary Postgate': An Analysis," *CIEFLB* 18, no. 1–2 (1982): 103–14.

"Mrs. Bathurst"

John Bayley, "'Mrs Bathurst' Again," *EIC* 38 (July 1988): 233–36.

Barbara Everett, "Kipling's Lightning-Flash," *LRB* 13 (10 January 1991): 12–15.

T. C. W. Stinton, "What Really Happened in 'Mrs. Bathurst?'" *EIC* 38 (January 1988): 55–74.

Ruth Waterhouse, "'That blindish look': Signification of Meaning in 'Mrs. Bathurst,'" *SN* 60, no. 2 (1988): 193–206.

The Naulahka

D. A. Shankar, "*The Naulahka* and Post–Kipling British Fiction on India," *LCrit* 22, no. 4 (1987): 71–79.

"The Phantom 'Rickshaw'"

William J. Scheick, "Hesitation in Kipling's 'The Phantom 'Rickshaw,'" *ELT* 29, no. 1 (1986): 48–53.

Plain Tales from the Hills

D. M. E. Roskies, "Rudyard Kipling's Wonderful Lies," *ESA* 27, no. 1 (1984): 49–60.

"Proofs of Holy Writ"

John Coates, "'Proofs of Holy Writ': Kipling's Valedictory Statement on Art," *KJ* 61 (September 1987): 12–20.

Philip Mason, "'Proofs of Holy Writ': An Introduction," *KJ* 62 (March 1988): 33–37.

"Puck of Pook's Hill"

Patricia Owen, "Kipling's View of History in Puck of Pook's Hill," *NR* 5, no. 2 (1986): 65–71.

Jack G. Voller, "Kipling's Myth of Making: Creation and Contradiction in 'Puck of Pook's Hill,'" in *The Celebration of the Fantastic: Selected Papers from the Tenth Anniversary International Conference on the Fantastic in the Arts*, ed. Donald E. Morse, Marshall B. Tymn, and Csilla Bertha (Westport, CT: Greenwood, 1992), 81–90.

"Rewards and Fairies"

John Coates, "Loyalty and Sacrifice as Aspects of 'Rewards and Fairies,'" *KJ* 62 (September 1988): 12–28.

John Coates, "Thor and Tyr: Sacrifice, Necessary Suffering and the Battle against Disorder in 'Rewards and Fairies,'" *ELT* 29, no. 1 (1986): 64–75.

"Sea Constables"

G. H. Newsom, "'Sea Constables' and the Blockade of January 1915," *KJ* 58 (March 1984): 12–29.

"The Ship That Found Herself"

Evelyne Hanquart-Turner, "Devoir et liberté: 'The Ship That Found Herself' de Kipling," *CVE* 33 (April 1991): 33–42.

"Stalky & Co."

R. J. Dingley, "Beetle's Responsibility: The Ending of 'Stalky & Co,'" *KJ* 58 (June 1984): 9–17.

G. C. K. Dunsterville, "Stalky, As Seen (at Times) by His Son," *KJ* 57 (December 1983): 34–39.

Ace G. Pilkington, "'Stalky & Co.': Kipling's School in the Absurd World," *Encyclia* 63 (1986): 126–32.

"'Stalky' (1)," *KJ* 57 (September 1983): 52–54.

"Stalky (3): Extracts from General Dunsterville's Diaries Relating to the Kipling Society," *KJ* 58 (March 1984): 36–40.

"Stalky (4): A Note by the Editor on Dunsterville's Last Year at School," *KJ* 58 (June 1984): 30.

"'Stalky' (5): More Extracts from the Dunsterville Diaries Relating to Kipling," *KJ* 58 (September 1984): 30–35.

"'Stalky' (7–8)," *KJ* 59 (September 1985; December 1985): 70–72; 51–56.

D. H. Stewart, "Stalky and the Language of Education," *ChildL* 20 (1992): 36–51.

"The Strange Ride of Morrowbie Jukes"

Evelyne Hanquart, "Une Descente en enfer: 'The Strange Ride of Morrowbie Jukes,'" *CVE* 18 (November 1983): 9–20.

"That Look"

Kent Fedorowich, "'That Look': An Unpublished Story by Rudyard Kipling," *KJ* 62 (June 1988): 34–42.

"They"

John H. Schwarz, "Hardy and Kipling's 'They,'" *ELT* 34, no. 1 (1991): 7–16.

"The Tomb of His Ancestors"

Jean-François Gournay, "Charisme et Pax Britannica dans 'The Tomb of His Ancestors,'" *CVE* 18 (November 1983): 39–48.

Philip Mason, "The Birth of a Story," *KJ* 62 (June 1988): 20–26.

KIPLING, RUDYARD, “The White Man’s Burden”

“The White Man’s Burden”

Christopher Hitchens, “Burdens and Songs: The Anglo-American Rudyard Kipling,” *GrandS* 9 (Spring 1990): 203–34.

KOESTLER, ARTHUR

Arrival and Departure

Saul Bellow, “A Revolutionist’s Testament,” *NYTBR* (21 November 1943): 1, 53.

Alex Comfort, “The Desire for Martydom: *Arrival and Departure*,” *L&L* 40 (January 1944): 55–62.

Philip Rahv, “Lost Illusions: *Arrival and Departure*,” *KR* 6 (Spring 1944): 288–92.

The Call Girls

Anatole Broyard, “Cosmos Without Characters,” *NYTBR* (3 April 1973): 41.

Herbert Lomas, “Going Off the Motorway: *The Call Girls*,” *LMag* 12 (December 1972–January 1973): 155–56.

Darkness at Noon

Robert Beum, “Epigraphs for Rubishov: Koestler’s *Darkness at Noon*,” *DR* 42 (Spring 1962): 86–91.

Francis Downing, “Koestler Revisited: The Character Gletkin in *Darkness at Noon*,” *Commonweal* 53 (9 February 1951): 444–46.

H. M. Drucker, “Koestler’s *Darkness at Noon*,” in *The Political Uses of Ideology* (New York: Barnes & Noble, 1974), 269–94.

R. G. Geering, “*Darkness at Noon* and *Nineteen Eighty-Four*, a Comparative Study,” *AusQ* 30 (September 1958): 90–96.

Alexander George, “Inconsistency in *Darkness at Noon*: Slip or Tip?” *NAR* 279 (May–June 1994): 24–25.

Freerick J. Hoffman, “*Darkness at Noon*: The Consequences of Secular Grace,” *GaR* 13 (Fall 1959): 331–45.

V. Kantor, "Nazvat' t'mu t'moiu," *LO* 2 (1989): 48–53.

Paul L. Kelly, "Kubler–Ross's Stages of Death Model Applied to *Darkness at Noon*: A Literary and Psychological Analysis of the Processes of the Prisoner," *CJ&B* 15 (June 1988): 172–78.

Reed B. Merrill, "*Darkness at Noon* and the Political Novel," *Neohelicon* 14, no. 2 (1987): 245–56.

George Orwell, "*Darkness at Noon*, by Arthur Koestler," *NewS&N* 21 (4 January 1941): 15–16.

Takashi Ozawa, "Sakka to Seiji: Arthur Koestler Mahiru no Akumuron," *Oberon* 49 (1986): 32–44.

M. S. Prabhakar, "Two Inconsistencies in *Darkness at Noon*," *N&Q* 209 (October 1964): 387–88.

David Lewis Schaefer, "The Limits of Ideology: Koestler's *Darkness at Noon*, I & II," *ModA* 29; 30 (Fall 1985; Winter 1986): 319–329; 10–21.

Mikhail Zolotonosov, "Krasnaia magiia," *LO* 2 (1989): 44–48.

Thieves in the Night

Edmund Wilson, "Arthur Koestler in Palestine: *Thieves in the Night*," *NewY* 22 (15 November 1946): 125–30.

LAVIN, MARY

"The Becker Wives"

Susan Ashbee, "Mary Lavin's 'The Becker Wives': Narrative Strategy and Reader Response," *JSSE* 8 (Spring 1987): 93–101.

Patricia K. Meszaros, "Woman as Artist: The Fiction of Mary Lavin," *Critique* 24 (Fall 1982): 39–52.

"Memory"

Janet Engleston Dunleavy, "The Making of Mary Lavin's 'A Memory,' " *Éire* 12 (Fall 1977): 90–99.

LAWRENCE, D[AVID] H[ERBERT]

Aaron's Rod

Paul G. Baker, "Profile of an Anti–Hero: Aaron Sisson Reconsidered," *DHLR* 10 (Summer 1977): 182–92.

William R. Barr, "*Aaron's Rod* as D. H. Lawrence's Picaresque Novel," *DHLR* 9 (Fall 1976): 213–25.

Sandra Barry, "Singularity of Two; the Plurality of One," *Paunch* 26 (1966): 34–39.

Jacques Debu–Bridel, "La Verge D'Aaron, par D. H. Lawrence," *NRF* 46 (1936): 606–08.

Virginia Hyde, "*Aaron's Rod*: D. H. Lawrence's Revisionist Typology," *Mosaic* 20 (Spring 1987): 111–26.

Robin Mayhead, *Understanding Literature* (Cambridge: Cambridge University Press, 1965), 30–34.

Jeanie Wagner, "A Botanical Note on *Aaron's Rod*," *DHLR* 4 (Fall 1971): 287–90.

"The Blind-Man"

Nancy Abolin, "Lawrence's 'The Blind Man': The Reality of Touch," in *A D. H. Lawrence Miscellany*, ed. Harry T. Moore (Carbondale: Southern Illinois University Press, 1959), 215–20.

Paul Delany, "Who Was 'The Blind Man'?" *ESC* 9 (March 1983): 92–99.

Regina Fadiman, "The Poet as Choreographer: Lawrence's 'The Blind Man,'" *JNT* 2 (1972): 60–67.

W. S. Marks, III, "The Psychology of Regression in D. H. Lawrence's 'The Blind Man,'" *L&P* 17 (1967): 177–92.

Sidney Warschaushy, "'The Blind Man,'" in *Insight II: Analyses of Modern British Literature*, ed. John V. Hagopian and Martin Dolch (Frankfurt: Hirschgraben, 1964), 221–28.

Ray West, "Point of View and Authority in 'The Blind Man,'" in *The Art of Writing Fiction* (New York: Crowell, 1968), 223–36.

Richard P. Wheeler, "Intimacy and Irony in 'The Blind Man,'" *DHLR* 9 (Fall 1976): 236–53.

The Boy in the Bush (with Mollie L. Skinner)

Norman Bartlett, "Mollie Skinner and *The Boy in the Bush*," *Quadrant* 28 (July–August 1984): 73–75.

Harry T. Moore, "Preface," in *The Boy in the Bush* (Carbondale: Southern Illinois University Press, 1971), vii–xxviii.

Charles Rossman, "*The Boy in the Bush* in the Lawrence Canon," in *D. H. Lawrence: The Man Who Lived*, ed. Robert B. Partlow and Harry T. Moore (Carbondale: Southern Illinois University Press, 1980), 185–94.

"The Captain's Doll"

Eugene W. Dawson, "Love Among the Mannikins: 'The Captain's Doll,'" *DHLR* 1 (Summer 1968): 137–48.

Gerald Doherty, "A 'Very Funny' Story: Figural Play in D. H. Lawrence's 'The Captain's Doll,'" *DHLR* 18 (Spring 1985–86): 5–17.

Frederick P. W. McDowell, "'The Individual in His Pure Singleness': Theme and Symbol in 'The Captain's Doll,'" in *The Challenge of D. H. Lawrence*, ed. Michael Squires and Keith Cushman (Madison: University of Wisconsin Press, 1990), 143–58.

W. R. Martin, "Hannele's 'Surrender': A Misreading of 'The Captain's Doll,'" *DHLR* 18 (Spring 1985–86): 19–23.

Elgin W. Mellown, "'The Captain's Doll': Its Origins and Literary Allusions," *DHLR* 9 (Fall 1976): 226–35.

"The Daughters of the Vicar"

Bibhu Padhi, "An Instrument of Sympathy: Irony in Lawrence's 'The Daughters of the Vicar,'" *JLSTL* 4, no. 2 (1981): 53–61.

"England, My England"

Alain Blayac, "Guerre et guerres dans 'England, My England,'" *ÉLawr* 3 (May 1988): 17–36.

David Lodge, "D. H. Lawrence," in *The Modes of Modern Writing: Metaphor, Metonymy, and The Typology of Modern Literature* (London: Arnold, 1977), 164–76.

Barbara Lucas, "Apropos of 'England, My England,'" *TC* 169 (1961): 288–93.

Volker Raddatz, "'England, My England': Ein Beitrag zum Englandbild von D. H. Lawrence sowie zum Verhaltnis von Landeskunde und Literatur–wisenschaft," in *Von Shakespeare bis Chomsky: Arbeiten zur englischen Philologie an der Freien Universitat Berlin*, ed. Thomas Fohrbeck Meier and Elfi Bettinger (Frankfurt: Peter Lang, 1987), 179–90.

Charles L. Ross, "D. H. Lawrence and World War I or History and the 'Forms of Reality': The Case of 'England, My England,'" in *Franklin Pierce Studies in Literature: 1981*, ed. James F. Maybury and Marjorie A. Zerbel (Rindge, NH: Franklin Pierce College Press, 1982), 11–21.

M. Tarinayya, "Lawrence's 'England, My England': An Analysis," *JSL* 7 (Monsoon 1980–Winter 1981): 70–83.

Weldon Thornton, "'The Flower or the Fruit': A Reading of D. H. Lawrence's 'England, My England,'" *DHLR* 16 (Fall 1983): 247–58.

Fanny and Annie

Marko Modiano, "*Fanny and Annie* and the War," *DUJ* 83 (July 1991): 215–16.

Robert Secor, "Language and Movement in *Fanny and Annie*," *SSF* 6 (1969): 395–400.

"The Fly in the Ointment"

Keith Cushman, "A Note on Lawrence's 'Fly in the Ointment,'" *ELN* 15 (1977): 47–51.

The Flying Fish

Ginette Roy, "Tel un poisson dans l'eau: Du lethal au foetal dans *The Flying Fish*," *ÉLawr* 1 (May 1986): 59–72.

"The Fox"

Edmund Bergler, "D. H. Lawrence's 'The Fox' and the Psychoanalytic Theory of Lesbianism," in *A D. H. Lawrence Miscellany*, ed. Harry T. Moore (Carbondale: Southern Illinois University Press, 1959), 49–55.

James L. Boren, "Commitment and Futility in 'The Fox,'" *UR* 31 (1965): 301–04.

Peggy Brayfield, "Lawrence's 'Male and Female Principles' and the Symbolism of 'The Fox,'" *Mosaic* 4 (Fall 1971): 41–51.

Christopher Brown, "The Eyes Have It: Vision in 'The Fox,'" *WascanaR* 15 (Fall 1980): 61–68.

Patricia Davis, "Chicken Queen's Delight: D. H. Lawrence's 'The Fox,'" *MFS* 19 (1973): 565–71.

O. Bryan Fulmer, "The Significance of the Death of the Fox in D. H. Lawrence's 'The Fox,'" *SSF* 5 (1968): 275–82.

Jan Good, "Toward a Resolution of Gender Identity Confusion: The Relationship of Henry and March in 'The Fox,'" *DHLR* 18 (Summer–Fall 1986): 217–27.

Ronald Granofsky, "A Second Caveat: D. H. Lawrence's 'The Fox,'" *ESC* 14 (March 1988): 49–63.

Ian Gregor, "'The Fox': A Caveat," *EIC* 9 (1959): 10–21.

Louis K. Greiff, "Bittersweet Dreaming in Lawrence's 'The Fox': A Freudian Perspective," *SSF* 20 (Winter 1983): 7–16.

Gerald Levin, "The Symbolism of Lawrence's 'The Fox,'" *CLAJ* 11 (1967): 135–42.

Yoshio Nakamura, "What the Death of the Fox Signifies in D. H. Lawrence's 'The Fox,'" *SELit* 59 (December 1982): 191–200.

J. P. Naugrette, "Le Renard et les rêves: Onirisme, écriture et inconscient dans 'The Fox,'" *ÉA* 37 (April–June 1984): 141–55.

Jane A. Nelson, "The Familial Isotopy in 'The Fox,'" in *The Challenge of D. H. Lawrence*, ed. Michael Squires and Keith Cushman (Madison: University of Wisconsin Press, 1990), 129–42.

Marijane Osborn, "Complexities of Gender and Genre in Lawrence's 'The Fox,'" *ELWIU* 19 (Spring 1992): 84–97.

Stanley Renner, "Sexuality and the Unconscious: Psychosexual Drama and Conflict in 'The Fox,'" *DHLR* 21 (Autumn 1990): 245–73.

Michael Ross, "Ladies and Foxes: D. H. Lawrence, David Garnett and the Female of the Species," *DHLR* 18 (Summer–Fall 1986): 229–38.

Judith Ruderman, "'The Fox' and the 'Devouring Mother,'" *DHLR* 10 (Fall 1977): 251–69.

Judith Ruderman, "The New Adam and Eve in Lawrence's 'The Fox' and Other Works," *SHR* 17 (Summer 1983): 225–36.

Judith Ruderman, "Prototypes for Lawrence's 'The Fox,'" *JML* 8 (1980): 77–98.

E. F. Shields, "Broken Vision in Lawrence's 'The Fox,'" *SSF* 9 (1972): 353–63.

A. K. Singh, "War and Lawrence: A Study of His Short Story 'The Fox,'" in *Essays on D. H. Lawrence*, ed. T. R. Sharma (Meerut, India: Shalabh, 1987), 134–38.

Claude Sinzelle, "Skinning the Fox: A Masochist's Delight," in *D. H. Lawrence in the Modern World*, ed. Peter Preston and Peter Hoare (Cambridge: Cambridge University Press, 1989), 161–79.

Suzanne Wolkenfeld, "'The Sleeping Beauty' Retold: D. H. Lawrence's 'The Fox,'" *SSF* 14 (1977): 345–52.

"A Fragment of Stained Glass"

Joseph Baim, "Past and Present in D. H. Lawrence's 'A Fragment of Stained Glass,'" *SSF* 8 (1971): 323–26.

P. G. Baker, "By the Help of Certain Notes: A Source for D. H. Lawrence's 'A Fragment of Stained Glass,'" *SSF* 17 (1980): 317–26.

"The Horse Dealer's Daughter"

Sara Betsky-Zweig, "'Floutingly in the Fine Black Mud': D. H. Lawrence's 'The Horse Dealer's Daughter,'" *DQR* 3 (1973): 159–64.

Daniel Fraustino, "Psychic Rebirth and Christian Imagery in D. H. Lawrence's 'The Horse Dealer's Daughter,'" *JEP* 9 (March 1989): 105–08.

Thomas A. Gullason, "Revelation and Evolution: A Neglected Dimension of the Short Story," *SSF* 10 (1973): 348–52.

Donald Junkins, "D. H. Lawrence's 'The Horse Dealer's Daughter,'" *SSF* 6 (1969): 210–12.

Thomas H. McCabe, "Rhythm as Form in Lawrence's 'The Horse Dealer's Daughter,'" *PMLA* 87 (1972): 64–68.

John V. McDermott, "Faith and Love: Twin Forces in 'The Rocking-Horse Winner,'" *NConL* 18 (January 1988): 6–8.

Jeffrey Meyers, "D. H. Lawrence and Tradition: 'The Horse Dealer's Daughter,'" *SSF* 26 (Summer 1989): 346–51.

Stephen R. Phillips, "The Double Pattern of D. H. Lawrence's 'The Horse Dealer's Daughter,'" *SSF* 10 (1973): 94–97.

Clyde de fL. Ryals, "D. H. Lawrence's 'The Horse Dealer's Daugher,'" *L&P* 12 (1962): 39–43.

Jack F. Stewart, "Eros and Thanatos in 'The Horse Dealer's Daughter,'" *StHUM* 12 (June 1985): 11–19.

Kangaroo

John Alexander, "D. H. Lawrence's *Kangaroo*: Fantasy, Fact, or Fiction?" *Meanjin* 24 (1965): 179–96.

Chiseki Asahi, "*Kangaroo* ni Okeru Cooley no Australia–sei," *EigoS* 133 (1987): 76–78.

Curtis Atkinson, "Was There Fact in D. H. Lawrence's *Kangaroo*?" *Meanjin* 24 (1965): 358–59.

Carla Comellini, "*Kangaroo*, ovvero l'avventura mentale," in *D. H. Lawrence cent'anni dopo: Nuove prospettive della critica Lawrenciana*, ed. Carla Comellini and Vita Fortunati (Bologna: Patron, 1991), 47–64.

Robert Darroch, "D. H. Lawrence's Australia," *Overland* 113 (December 1988): 34–38.

Andre Dommergues, "*Kangaroo*, stratégie de rupture," *ÉLawr* 3 (May 1988): 139–52.

David Ellis, "Lawrence in Australia: The Darroch Controversy," *DHLR* 21 (Summer 1989): 167–74.

Leo Gurko, "*Kangaroo*: D. H. Lawrence in Transit," *MFS* 10 (1964): 349–58.

A. D. Hope, "D. H. Lawrence's *Kangaroo*: How It Looks to an Australian," in *The Australian Experience: Critical Essays on Australian Novels*, ed. William S. Ramson (Canberra: Australian National University Press, 1976), 157–73.

John B. Humma, "Of Bits, Beasts and Bush: The Interior Wilderness in D. H. Lawrence's *Kangaroo*," *SoAR* 51 (January 1986): 83–100.

Robert Lee, "D. H. Lawrence and the Australian Ethos," *Southerly* 33 (1973): 144–51.

John Lowe, "Judas in for the Spree? The Role of Jaz in *Kangaroo*," *DHLR* 4 (Spring 1986): 30–34.

Murray S. Martin, "*Kangaroo* Revisited,'" *DHLR* 18 (Summer–Fall 1986): 201–15.

John Milfull, "Die 'Mannerphantisien' des D. H. Lawrence, *Kangaroo* und der Erste Weltkrieg," in *Ansichten vom Krieg: Vergleichende Studien zum Ersten Weltkrieg in Literatur und Gesellschaft*, ed. Bernd Huppauf (Konigstein: Forum Academy in Verlagsgruppe Athenaum, Hain, Hanstein, 1984), 177–83.

Andrew Moore, "The Historian as Detective: Pursuing the Darroch Thesis and D. H. Lawrence's Secret Army," *Overland* 113 (December 1988): 39–44.

Edward St. John, "D. H. Lawrence and Australia's Secret Army," *Quadrant* 26 (June 1982): 53–57.

Marilyn S. Samuels, "Water, Ships, and the Sea: Unifying Symbols in Lawrence's *Kangaroo*," *UR* 37 (1970): 46–57.

Daniel J. Schneider, "Psychology and Art in Lawrence's *Kangaroo*," *DHLR* 14 (Summer 1981): 156–71.

Visnja Sepcic, "The Category of Landscape in D. H. Lawrence's *Kangaroo*," *SrRAZ* 27–28 (1969): 129–52.

S. K. Vohra, "*Kangaroo*: Search for Viable Alternatives," in *Essays on D. H. Lawrence*, ed. T. R. Sharma (Meerut, India: Shalabh, 1987), 109–15.

Michael Wilding, "*Kangaroo*: 'a new show,'" in *Political Fictions* (London: Routledge & Kegan Paul, 1980), 150–91.

"Jimmy and the Desperate Woman"

Donald Gutierrez, "Getting Even with John Middleton Murry," *Interpretations* 15 (Fall 1983): 31–38.

"The Ladybird"

James C. Cowan, "D. H. Lawrence's Dualism: The Apollonian-Dionysian Polarity and 'The Ladybird,'" in *Forms of Modern British Fiction*, ed. Alan W. Friedman (Austin: University of Texas Press, 1975), 73–99.

Joost Daalder, "Background and Significance of D. H. Lawrence's 'The Ladybird,'" *DHLR* 15 (Spring–Summer 1982): 107–28.

Sandra M. Gilbert, "Potent Griselda: 'The Ladybird' and the Great Mother," in *D. H. Lawrence: A Centenary Consideration*, ed. Peter Balbert and Phillip L. Marcus (Ithaca, NY: Cornell University Press, 1985), 130–61.

John B. Humma, "Lawrence's 'The Ladybird' and the Enabling Image," *DHLR* 17 (Fall 1984): 219–32.

Laurence Steven, "From Thimble to Ladybird: D. H. Lawrence's Widening Vision," *DHLR* 18 (Summer–Fall 1986): 239–53.

Lady Chatterley's Lover

Iqbal A. Ansari, "*Lady Chatterley's Lover*: Pattern of Contrast and Conflict," *AJES* 10, no. 2 (1985): 178–87.

Peter H. Balbert, "The Loving of Lady Chatterley: D. H. Lawrence and the Phallic Imagination," in *D. H. Lawrence: The Man Who Lived*, ed. Robert B. Partlow and Harry T. Moore (Carbondale: Southern Illinois University Press, 1980), 143–58.

Wayne Burns, "*Lady Chatterley's Lover*: A Pilgrim's Progress for Our Time," *Paunch* 26 (1966): 16–33.

J. M. Coetzee, "The Taint of the Pornographic: Defending (against) *Lady Chatterley's Lover*," *Mosaic* 21 (Winter 1988): 1–11.

Émile Delavenay, "Les Trois Amants de *Lady Chatterley*," *ÉA* 29 (1976): 46–63.

John Doheny, "Lady Chatterley and Her Lover," *WCR* 8, no. 3 (1974): 51–56.

Duane Edwards, "Mr. Mellors' Lover: A Study of *Lady Chatterley*," *SHR* 19 (Spring 1985): 117–31.

Ronald Friedland, "Introduction," in *Lady Chatterley's Lover*, ed. Ronald Friedland (New York: Bantam, 1968), xiii–xxiv.

Ben Ephraim Gavriel, "The Achievement of Balance in *Lady Chatterley's Lover*," in *D. H. Lawrence's "Lady": A New Look at "Lady Chatterley's Lover*," ed. Michael Squires and Dennis Jackson (Athens: University of Georgia Press, 1985), 136–53.

Ian Gregor and Brain Nicholas, "The Novel as Prophecy: *Lady Chatterley's Lover*," in *The Moral and the Story* (London: Faber, 1962), 217–48.

Donald Gutierrez, "The Hylozoistic Vision of *Lady Chatterley's Lover*," *NAMM* 19 (Spring 1981): 25–34.

Donald Gutierrez, "'The Impossible Notation': The Sodomy Scene in *Lady Chatterley's Lover*," *Sphinx* 4, no. 2 (1982): 109–25.

Renatus Hartoga with Hans Fantel, "Intercourse with Lady Chatterley," in *Four Letter Word Games: The Psychology of Obscenity* (New York: Delacorte, 1968), 11–24.

G. B. McK Henry, "Carrying On: *Lady Chatterley's Lover*," *CR* 10 (1967): 46–62.

Evelyn J. Hinz and John J. Teunissen, "War, Love, and Industrialism: The Ares/Aphrodite/Hephaestus Complex in *Lady Chatterley's Lover*," in *D. H. Lawrence's "Lady": A New Look at "Lady Chatterley's Lover,"* ed. Michael Squires and Dennis Jackson (Athens: University of Georgia Press, 1985), 197–221.

John B. Humma, "The Interpenetrating Metaphor: Nature and Myth in *Lady Chatterley's Lover*," *PMLA* 98 (January 1983): 77–86.

Earl G. Ingersoll, "*Lady Chatterley's Lover*: 'The Bastard Offspring of This Signifying Concatenation,'" *SPsyT* 1 (Spring 1992): 59–65.

Chikai Ito, "Chatterley Fujin no Koibito Zengo: Leadership no Yukue," *EigoS* 131 (1985): 438–42.

Dennis Jackson, "*Lady Chatterley's* Color," *Interpretations* 15 (Fall 1983): 39–52.

Dennis Jackson, "The 'Old Pagan Vision': Myth and Ritual and *Lady Chatterley's Lover*," *DHLR* 11 (Fall 1978): 260–71.

Andre Malraux and Euridice Aguirre, "D. H. Lawrence y el erotismo: A proposito de *El amante de Lady Chatterley*," *Vuelta* 15 (March 1991): 30–31.

Jerome Mandel, "Medieval Romance and *Lady Chatterley's Lover*," *DHLR* 10 (Spring 1977): 20–33.

Louis L. Martz, "The Second Lady Chatterley," in *The Spirit of D. H. Lawrence: Centenary Studies*, ed. Gamini Salgado and G. K. Das (Totowa, NJ: Barnes & Noble, 1988), 106–24.

Lea Masina, "O Amante de Lady Chatterley: Um Romance Atipico e Tumultuado," *MGSL* 24 (January 1991): 11–13.

Harry T. Moore, "Afterword: *Lady Chatterley's Lover*: The Novel as Ritual," in *Lady Chatterley's Lover*, ed. Harry T. Moore (New York: New American Library, 1962), 285–99.

Harry T. Moore, "*Lady Chatterley's Lover* as Romance," in *A D. H. Lawrence Miscellany*, ed. Harry T. Moore (Carbondale: Southern Illinois University Press, 1959), 262–64.

William B. Ober, "Lady Chatterley's What?" in *Boswell's Clap, and Other Essays: Medical Analyses of Literary Men's Afflictions* (Carbondale: Southern Illinois University Press, 1979), 89–117.

Klaus Ostheeren, "Dialekt und Register in *Lady Chatterley's Lover*," in *Festschrift für Karl Schneider*, ed. Ernst Siegfried Dick and Kurt R. Jankowsky (Amsterdam: Benjamins, 1982), 517–33.

Octavio Paz, "Los amantes de Lady Chatterley," *Vuelta* 15 (March 1991): 27–29.

Joan D. Peters, "The Living and the Dead: Lawrence's Theory of the Novel and the Structure of *Lady Chatterley's Lover*," *DHLR* 20 (Spring 1988): 5–20.

Joan Ramon Resina, "The Word and the Deed in *Lady Chatterley's Lover*," *FMLS* 23 (October 1987): 351–65.

Stephen Rowley, "The Sight–Touch Metaphor in *Lady Chatterley's Lover*," *ÉLawr* 3 (May 1988): 179–88.

Scott R. Sanders, "Lady Chatterley's Loving and the Annihilation Impulse," in *D. H. Lawrence's "Lady": A New Look at "Lady Chatterley's Lover*," ed. Michael Squires and Dennis Jackson (Athens: University of Georgia Press, 1985), 1–16.

Myra Glazer Schotz, "For the Sexes: Blake's Hermaphrodite in *Lady Chatterley's Lover*," *BuR* 24, no. 1 (1978): 17–26.

Vis/nja Sepc/ic/, "The Dialogue in *Lady Chatterley's Lover*," *SrRAZ* 29–30 (1970–71): 461–80.

Daniel J. Sheerin, "John Thomas and the King of Glory: Two Analogues to D. H. Lawrence's Use of Psalm 24:7 in Chapter XIV of *Lady Chatterley's Lover*," *DHLR* 11 (Fall 1978): 297–300.

Mark Spilka, "On Lawrence's Hostility to Wilful Women: The Chatterley Solution," in *Lawrence and Women*, ed. Anne Smith (London: Vision, 1978), 189–211.

Michael Squires, "*Lady Chatterley's Lover*: 'Pure Seclusion," in *The Pastoral Novel: Studies in George Eliot, Thomas Hardy, and D. H. Lawrence* (Charlottesburg: University Press of Virginia, 1974), 196–212.

Michael Squires, "New Light on the Gamekeeper in *Lady Chatterley's Lover*," *DHLR* 11 (Fall 1978): 234–45.

Andre Topia, "La Chaîne et le circuit: Le Corps mutant dans *Lady Chatterley's Lover*," in *ÉLawr* 1 (May 1986): 29–40.

Joseph C. Voelker, "The Spirit of No-Place: Elements of the Classical Ironic Utopia in D. H. Lawrence's *Lady Chatterley's Lover*," *MFS* 25 (1979): 223–39.

"The Last Laugh"

Joseph Baim, "The Second Coming of Pan: A Note on D. H. Lawrence's 'The Last Laugh,'" *SSF* 6 (1968): 98–100.

The Lost Girl

Leo Gurko, "*The Lost Girl*: D. H. Lawrence as 'Dickens of the Midlands,'" *PMLA* 78 (1963): 601–05.

James Hafley, "*The Lost Girl*: Lawrence Really Real," *ArQ* 10 (1954): 312–22.

Phillip F. Herring, "Caliban in Nottingham: D. H. Lawrence's *The Lost Girl*," *Mosaic* 12 (Winter 1979): 9–19.

Gary A. Wiener, "Lawrence's *Little Girl Lost*," *DHLR* 19 (Fall 1987): 243–53.

Virginia Woolf, "Postscript or Prelude?" in *Contemporary Writers*, comp. Jean Guiguet (New York: Harcourt, Brace, 1966), 158–60.

John Worthen, "Introduction," in *D. H. Lawrence: "The Lost Girl,"* ed. John Worthen (London: Secker, 1920), xix–liv.

Love among the Haystacks

Mikel Vause, "The Death Instinct Reflected in D. H. Lawrence's *Love among the Haystacks*," *JEP* 9 (August 1988): 187–89.

"The Lovely Lady"

Pascal Aquien, "Le Visage et la voix dans 'The Lovely Lady,'" in *ÉLawr* 3 (May 1988): 71–80.

"The Man Who Died"

Gerald J. Butler, "'The Man Who Died' and Lawrence's Final Attitude Towards Tragedy," *RecL* 6, no. 3 (1977): 1–14.

Gerald Fiderer, "D. H. Lawrence's 'The Man Who Died': The Phallic Christ," *AI* 25 (1968): 91–96.

Evelyn J. Hinz and John J. Teunissen, "Savior and Cock: Allusion and Icon in Lawrence's 'The Man Who Died,'" *JML* 5 (1976): 279–96.

Dorothea Krook, "Messianic Humanism: D. H. Lawrence's 'The Man Who Died,'" in *Three Traditions of Moral Thought* (Cambridge: Cambridge University Press, 1959), 255–92.

Francis L. Kunkel, "Lawrence's 'The Man Who Died': The Heavenly Cock," in *Passion and the Passion: Sex and Religion in Modern Literature* (Philadelphia: Westminster, 1975), 37–57.

Gerald M. Lacy, "Commentary," in *The Escaped Cock*, ed. Gerald M. Lacy (Los Angeles: Black Sparrow, 1973), 123–70.

Elizabeth Larsen, "Lawrence's 'The Man Who Died,'" *Expl* 40 (Summer 1982): 38–40.

Larry V. LeDoux, "Christ and Isis: The Function of the Dying and Reviving God in 'The Man Who Died,'" *DHLR* 5 (Summer 1972): 132–47.

Robert H. MacDonald, "The Union of Fire and Water: An Examination of the Imagery of 'The Man Who Died,'" *DHLR* 10 (Spring 1977): 34–51.

John Middleton Murry, "'The Escaped Cock,'" *Criterion* 10 (1930): 183–88.

Rakhi, "'The Man Who Died': A Jungian Interpretation," in *Essays on D. H. Lawrence*, ed. T. R. Sharma (Meerut, India: Shalabh, 1987), 116–24.

Leslie M. Thompson, "The Christ Who Didn't Die: Analogues to D. H. Lawrence's 'The Man Who Died,'" *DHLR* 8 (Spring 1975): 19–30.

"The Man Who Loved Islands"

Corinne Alexandre Garner, "'The Man Who Loved Islands' ou l'effacement de la trace," *ÉLawr* 3 (May 1988): 91–106.

Lynn E. Harris, "The Island as a Mental Image of Withdrawal, Used in a Literary Work, D. H. Lawrence's 'The Man Who Loved Islands,'" in *Imagery 2*, ed. David G. Russell, David F. Marks, and John T. E. Richardson (Dunedin, New Zealand: Human Performance Associates, 1986), 178–81.

Frederick R. Karl, "Lawrence's 'The Man Who Loved Islands': The Crusoe Who Failed," in *A D. H. Lawrence Miscellany*, ed. Harry T. Moore (Carbondale: Southern Illinois University Press, 1979), 265–79.

Martin F. Kearney, "Spirit, Place and Psyche: Integral Integration in D. H. Lawrence's 'The Man Who Loved Islands,'" *ES* 69 (April 1988): 158–62.

Viktor Link, "D. H. Lawrence's 'The Man Who Loved Islands' in Light of Compton Mackenzie's Memoirs," *DHLR* 15 (Spring–Summer 1982): 77–86.

Takashi Toyokuni, "A Modern Man Obsessed by Time: A Note on 'The Man Who Loved Islands,'" *DHLR* 7 (Summer 1974): 78–82.

John F. Turner, "'The Capacity to Be Alone' and Its Failure in D. H. Lawrence's 'The Man Who Loved Islands,'" *DHLR* 16 (Fall 1983): 259–89.

David Willbern, "Malice in Paradise: Isolation and Projection in 'The Man Who Loved Islands,'" *DHLR* 10 (Fall 1977): 223–41.

Mr Noon

Peter Balbert, "Silver Spoon to Devil's Fork: Diana Trilling and the Sexual Ethics of *Mr Noon*," *DHLR* 20 (Summer 1988): 237–50.

Lydia Blanchard, "D. H. Lawrence and His 'Gentle Reader': The New Audience of *Mr Noon*," *DHLR* 20 (Summer 1988): 223–35.

Lydia Blanchard, "'Reading Out' a 'New Novel': Lawrence's Experiments with Story and Discourse in *Mr Noon*," in *Critical Essays on D. H. Lawrence*, ed. Dennis Jackson and Fleda Brown Jackson (Boston: G. K. Hall, 1988), 110–18.

Peter S. Christensen, "*Mr Noon*: Some Problems in a New Text," *SNNTS* 18 (Winter 1986): 415–26.

Paul Delany, "*Mr Noon* and Modern Paganism," *DHLR* 20 (Summer 1988): 251–61.

Dorrit Einersen, "Life and Fiction in D. H. Lawrence's *Mr Noon* and the Novel's Place within the Lawrence Canon," *OL* 42, no. 2 (1987): 97–117.

Dorrit Einersen, "*Mr Noon*: D. H. Lawrence's Newly Published Picaresque Romance," *Angles* 1 (Autumn 1986): 2–6.

Maria Aline Ferreira, "*Mr Noon*: The Reader in the Text," *DHLR* 20 (Summer 1988): 209–21.

Earl G. Ingersoll, "D. H. Lawrence's *Mr Noon* as a Postmodern Text," *MLR* 85 (April 1990): 304–9.

Earl G. Ingersoll, "The Progress towards Marriage in D. H. Lawrence's *Mr Noon*," *DQR* 19, no. 4 (1989): 294–306.

Earl G. Ingersoll, "The Theme of Friendship and the Genesis of D. H. Lawrence's *Mr Noon*," *DUJ* 83 (January 1991): 69–74.

Dieter Mehl, "D. H. Lawrence und sein 'neur' Roman *Mr Noon*," *Poetica* 21, no. 1–2 (1989): 164–78.

Jeffrey Meyers, "Lawrence's *Mr Noon*," *MFS* 31 (Winter 1985): 710–15.

Philip Sicker, "Surgery for the Novel: Lawrence's *Mr Noon* and the 'Gentle Reader,'" *DHLR* 20 (Summer 1988): 191–207.

Lindeth Vasey and John Worthen, "Mr Noon/*Mr Noon*," *DHLR* 20 (Summer 1988): 179–89.

Michael W. Weithmann, "D. H. Lawrence: Vom Achensee nach Welschtirol," *Schlern* 64 (February 1990): 67–86.

"Mother and Daughter"

Jeffrey Meyers, "Katherine Mansfield, Gurdjieff and Lawrence's 'Mother and Daughter,'" *TCL* 22 (1976): 444–53.

"Odour of Chrysanthemums"

Weirui Hou, "Explication of Text: The Opening Passage from D. H. Lawrence's 'Odour of Chrysanthemums,'" *Waiguoyu* 3 (May 1984): 48–53.

Robert N. Hudspeth, "Lawrence's 'Odour of Chrysanthemums': Isolation and Paradox," *SSF* 6 (1969): 630–36.

Mara Kalnins, "D. H. Lawrence's 'Odour of Chrysanthemums': The Three Endings,'" *SSF* 13 (1976): 471–79.

T. H. McCabe, "The Otherness of D. H. Lawrence's 'Odour of Chrysanthemums,'" *DHLR* 19 (Summer 1987): 149–56.

Wayne D. McGinnis, "Lawrence's 'Odour of Chrysanthemums' and Blake," *RsSt* 44 (1976): 251–52.

Walter Nash, "On a Passage from Lawrence's 'Odour of Chrysanthemums,'" in *Language and Literature: An Introductory Reader in Stylistics*, ed. Ronald Carter (London: Allen & Unwin, 1982), 101–20.

Jean Pierre Naugrette, "Le Mythe et le reel: Lecture de 'Odour of Chrysanthemums,'" in *ÉLawr* 1 (May 1986): 7–27.

Volker Schulz, "D. H. Lawrence's Early Masterpiece of Short Fiction: 'Odour of Chrysanthemums,'" *SSF* 28 (Summer 1991): 363–70.

"The Old Adam"

Keith Cushman, "Domestic Life in the Suburbs: Lawrence, the Joneses, and 'The Old Adam,'" *DHLR* 16 (Fall 1983): 221–34.

"The Overtone"

Paul Neumarkt, "Pan and Christ: An Analysis of the 'Hieros Gamos' Concept in D. H. Lawrence's Short Story 'The Overtone,'" *DCon* 9–10 (1971–72): 27–48.

The Plumed Serpent

T. E. Apter, "Let's Hear What the Male Chauvinist is Saying: *The Plumed Serpent*," in *Lawrence and Women*, ed. Anne Smith (London: Vision, 1978), 156–77.

LAWRENCE, D. H., *The Plumed Serpent*

Alice Baldwin, "The Structure of the Coatl Symbol in *The Plumed Serpent*," *Style* 5 (1971): 138–50.

Michael Ballin, "Lewis Spence and the Myth of Quetzalcoatl in D. H. Lawrence's *The Plumed Serpent*," *DHLR* 13 (Summer 1980): 63–78.

Uwe Boker, "D. H. Lawrence transpolitischer Antirassismus: *The Plumed Serpent* (1926)," *A&E* 16 (1982): 31–50.

Bruce Clarke, "The Eye and the Soul: A Moment of Clairvoyance in *The Plumed Serpent*," *SoR* 19 (Spring 1983): 298–301.

Carla Comellini, "D. H. Lawrence: Il mito infranto in *The Plumed Serpent*," *SMod* 11 (1979): 106–22.

Gerald Doherty, "The Throes of Aphrodite: The Sexual Dimension in D. H. Lawrence's *The Plumed Serpent*," *StHum* 12 (December 1985): 67–78.

Duane Edwards, "Erich Neumann and the Shadow Problem in *The Plumed Serpent*," *DHLR* 23 (Summer–Fall 1991): 129–41.

Lleana Galea, "D. H. Lawrence si cultura primitiva," *Steaua* 37 (August 1986): 47–48.

Charles I. Glicksberg, "Myth in Lawrence's Fiction," in *Modern Literary Perspectivism* (Dallas, TX: Southern Methodist University Press, 1970), 139–48.

John Humma, "The Imagery of *The Plumed Serpent*: The Going–under of Organicism," *DHLR* 15 (Fall 1982): 197–218.

Jascha Kessler, "Descent in Darkness: The Myth of *The Plumed Serpent*," in *A D. H. Lawrence Miscellany*, ed. Harry T. Moore (Carbondale: Southern Illinois University Press, 1959), 239–61.

Ozzie Mayers, "The Child as Jungian Hero in D. H. Lawrence's *The Plumed Serpent*," *JEP* 8 (August 1987): 306–17.

Jeffrey Meyers, "*The Plumed Serpent* and the Mexican Revolution," *JML* 4 (1974): 55–72.

Harry T. Moore, "*The Plumed Serpent*: Vision and Language," in *D. H. Lawrence: A Collection of Critical Essays*, ed. Mark Spilka (Englewood Cliffs, NJ: Prentice-Hall, 1963), 61–71.

Jean Paul Pichardie, "Le Mexique: Ordo ab chao," *ÉLawr* 3 (May 1988): 163–69.

Katherine Anne Porter, "Quetzalcoatl," in *The Days Before* (New York: Harcourt, Brace, 1952), 262–67.

Lawrence Clark Powell, "*The Plumed Serpent*," in *Southwest Classics: The Creative Literature of the Arid Lands, Essays on the Books and Their Writers* (Los Angeles: Ward Ritchie, 1974), 81–91.

Kameshwar Prasad, "Evil in D. H. Lawrence's *The Plumed Serpent*: The Collapse of Vision and Art," in *Modern Studies and Other Essays in Honour of Dr. R. K. Sinha*, ed. R. C. Prasad and A. K. Sharma (New Delhi: Vikas, 1987), 49–59.

Frederick Ramey, "Words in the Service of Silence: Preverbal Language in Lawrence's *The Plumed Serpent*," *MFS* 27 (Winter 1981–82): 613–21.

Fernando Garcia Ramirez, "D. H. Lawrence y la religion de la Serpiente," *Vuelta* 15 (March 1991): 35–36.

William York Tindall, "Introduction," in *The Plumed Serpent* (*Quetzalcoatl*), ed. William York Tindall (New York: Knopf, 1951), v–xv.

John B. Vickery, "*The Plumed Serpent* and the Eternal Paradox," *Criticism* 5 (1963): 119–34.

John B. Vickery, "*The Plumed Serpent* and the Reviving God," *JML* 2 (1972): 505–32.

Therese Vichy, "Le Mexique dans *The Plumed Serpent*," *Cycnos* 7 (1991): 41–50.

Frank Waters, "Quetzalcoatl Versus D. H. Lawrence's *Plumed Serpent*," *WAL* 3 (1968): 103–13.

Leonora Woodman, "D. H. Lawrence and the Hermetic Tradition," *CaudaP* 8 (Fall 1989): 1–6.

"A Prelude"

Ginette Katz Roy, "Prelude et variations," *ÉLawr* 3 (May 1988): 5–16.

"The Princess"

Robert H. MacDonald, "Images of Negative Union: The Symbolic World of D. H. Lawrence's 'The Princess,'" *SSF* 16 (1979): 289–93.

S. Ronald Weiner, "Irony and Symbolism in 'The Princess,'" in *A D. H. Lawrence Miscellany*, ed. Harry T. Moore (Carbondale: Southern Illinois University Press, 1979), 221–38.

"The Prussian Officer"

Gary Adelman, "Beyond the Pleasure Principle: An Analysis of D. H. Lawrence's 'The Prussian Officer,'" *SSF* 1 (1963): 8–15.

Walter E. Anderson, "'The Prussian Officer': Lawrence's Version of the Fall of Man Legend," *ELWIU* 12 (Fall 1985): 215–23.

M. Begliev, "Postroennie khudozhestvennogo teksta i ego funktsial'naia perspektiva v rasskaze D. G. Lourensa 'Prusskii ofitser,'" *VMU* 9 (March–April 1988): 76–80.

Rosemary Reeves Davies, "From Heat to Radiance: The Language of 'The Prussian Officer,'" *SSF* 21 (Summer 1984): 269–71.

Ann Englander, "'The Prussian Officer': The Self Divided," *SR* 71 (1963): 605–19.

Anna Grmelova, "Thematic and Structural Diversification of D. H. Lawrence's Short Story in the Wake of World War I," *LPrag* 2, no. 4 (1992): 58–69.

Jack F. Stewart, "Expressionism in 'The Prussian Officer,'" *DHLR* 18 (Summer–Fall 1986): 275–89.

The Rainbow

Ian Adam, "Lawrence's Anti–Symbol: The Ending of *The Rainbow*," *JNT* 3 (1973): 77–84.

T. H. Adamowski, "*The Rainbow* and 'Otherness,'" *DHLR* 7 (Spring 1974): 58–77.

Tamara Alinei, "Imagery and Meaning in D. H. Lawrence's *The Rainbow*," *YES* 2 (1972): 205–11.

Tamara Alinei, "The Beginning of *The Rainbow*: Novel within a Novel?" *Ling&S* 12 (1977): 161–66.

W. H. G. Armytage, "The Novel as the Hole in the Wall: D. H. Lawrence's [The] *Rainbow*," in *Yesterday's Tomorrows: A Historical Survey of Future Societies* (Toronto: University of Toronto Press, 1968), 106–8.

Peter Balbert, "'Logic of the soul': Prothalamic Pattern in *The Rainbow*," in *D. H. Lawrence: A Centenary Consideration*, ed. Peter Balbert and Phillip L. Marcus (Ithaca, NY: Cornell University Press, 1985), 45–66.

J. Barry, "Oswald Spengler and D. H. Lawrence," *ESA* 12 (1969): 151–61.

Elizabeth S. Bell, "Slang Associations of D. H. Lawrence's Image Patterns in *The Rainbow*," *ModSt* 4 (1982): 77–86.

Jacques Berthoud, "*The Rainbow* as Experimental Novel," in *D. H. Lawrence: A Critical Study of the Major Novels and Other Writings*, ed. Andor Gomme (New York: Barnes & Noble, 1978), 53–69.

Bingbin Bi, "The Era and *The Rainbow*," *FLitS* 30 (December 1985): 70–75.

A. M. Brandabur, "The Ritual Corn Harvest Scene in *The Rainbow*," *DHLR* 6 (Fall 1973): 284–302.

Ashley Brown, "Prose into Poetry: D. H. Lawrence's *The Rainbow*," in *Order in Variety: Essays and Poems in Honor of Donald E. Stanford*, ed. R. W. Crump (Newark: University of Delaware Press, 1991), 133–42.

Homer O. Brown, "'The Passionate Struggle Into Conscious Being': D. H. Lawrence's *The Rainbow*," *DHLR* 7 (Fall 1974): 275–90.

Robert Burns, "The Novel as a Metaphysical Statement: Lawrence's *The Rainbow*," *SoR* 4 (1971): 139–60.

J. A. V. Chapple, *Documentary and Imaginative Literature, 1880–1920* (New York: Barnes & Noble, 1970), 72–83, 88–90.

Peter G. Christensen, "Problems in Characterization in D. H. Lawrence's *The Rainbow*," *AUMLA* 77 (May 1992): 78–96.

Barbara Cross, "Lawrence and the Unbroken Circle," *Perspective* 11 (1959): 81–89.

Edward Davis, "*The Rainbow*," in *Readings in Modern Fiction* (Cape Town, South Africa: Simondium, 1964), 258–69.

Gerald Doherty, "The Metaphorical Imperative: From Trope to Narrative in *The Rainbow*," *SCRev* 6 (Spring 1989): 46–61.

Adelyn Dougherty, "The Concept of Person in D. H. Lawrence's *The Rainbow*," *C&L* 21, no. 4 (1972): 15–22.

Ronald P. Draper, "*The Rainbow*," *CritQ* 20, no. 3 (1978): 49–64.

Roger Ebbatson, "The Opening of *The Rainbow*,'" in *D. H. Lawrence 1885–1930: A Celebration*, ed. Andrew Cooper (Nottingham: D. H. Lawrence Society, 1985), 72–76.

Paul Eggert, "The Half-Structured Rainbow," *CR* 23 (1981): 89–97.

Edward Engelberg, "Escape from the Circles of Experience: D. H. Lawrence's *The Rainbow* as a Modern 'Bildungsroman,'" *PMLA* 78 (1963): 103–13.

Lawrence B. Gamache, "Husband Father: D. H. Lawrence's Use of Character in Structuring a Narrative," *ModSt* 4 (1982): 36–51.

Lawrence B. Gamache, "The Making of an Ugly Techocrat: Character and Structure in Lawrence's *The Rainbow*," *Mosaic* 12 (Spring 1978): 61–78.

S. L. Goldberg, "*The Rainbow*: Fiddle-Bow and Sand," *EIC* 11 (1961): 418–34.

Richard Lynn Greever, "Ursula's Struggle for Independence," *CA&E* 20 (1987): 279–81.

John Haegert, "Lawrence's World Elsewhere: Elegy and History in *The Rainbow*," *CLIO* 15 (Winter 1986): 115–35.

Adrian Harding, "Self-Parody and Ethical Satire in *The Rainbow*," *ÉLawr* 6 (May 1991): 31–38.

Lucia Henning Heldt, "Lawrence on Love: The Courtship and Marriage of Tom Brangwen and Lydia Lensky," *DHLR* 8 (Fall 1975): 358–70.

Ordelle G. Hill and Potter Woodbery, "Ursula Brangwen of *The Rainbow*: Christian Saint or Pagan Godess?" *DHLR* 4 (Fall 1971): 274–79.

Evelyn J. Hinz, "The Paradoxical Fall: Eternal Recurrence in D. H. Lawrence's *The Rainbow*," *ESC* 3 (1977): 466–81.

Evelyn J. Hinz, "*The Rainbow*: Ursula's 'Liberation,'" *ConL* 17 (1976): 24–43.

Dennis Hoerner, "Ursula, Anton, and the 'Sons of God': Armor and Core in *The Rainbow*'s Third Generation," *Paunch* 63–64 (December 1990): 173–98.

Wilhelm Hortmann, "The Nail and the Novel: Some Remarks on Style and the Unconscious in *The Rainbow*," in *Theorie und Praxis im Erzahlen des 19. und 20. Jahrhunderts: Studien zur englischen und amerikanischen Literatur zu Ehren von Willi Erzgraber*, ed. Winfried Herget, Klaus Peter Jochum, and Ingeborg Weber (Tubingen: Narr, 1986), 167–79.

Virginia Hyde, "Toward 'the Earth's New Architecture': Triads, Arches, and Angles in *The Rainbow*," *ModSt* 4 (1982): 7–35.

Earl G. Ingersoll, "Lawrence's *The Rainbow*," *Expl* 47 (Summer 1989): 46–50.

Wallace G. Kay, "Lawrence and *The Rainbow*: Apollo and Dionysus in Conflict," *SoQ* 10 (1972): 209–22.

Andrew Kennedy, "After Not So Strange Gods in *The Rainbow*," *ES* 63 (June 1982): 220–30.

Arnold Kettle, "D. H. Lawrence: *The Rainbow*," in *An Introduction to the English Novel*, vol. 2: *Henry James to the Present* (London: Hutchinson, 1951), 111–34.

David J. Kleinhard, "D. H. Lawrence and Ontological Insecurity," *PMLA* 89 (1974): 154–63.

Kyoko Kondo, "*The Rainbow* in Focus: A Study of the Form of *The Rainbow* by D. H. Lawrence," *SELit* (1985): 53–69.

Seymour Lainoff, "*The Rainbow*: The Shaping of Modern Man," *MFS* 1, no. 4 (1955): 23–27.

Ann L. McLaughlin, "The Clenched and Knotted Horses in *The Rainbow*," *DHLR* 13 (Summer 1980): 179–86.

Shanta Mahalanobis, "Pre-War Feminism in Lawrence's *The Rainbow*," *JDECU* 21, no. 1–2 (1986–1987): 30–41.

Anna Makolkina, "The Dance of Dionysos in H. Khodkevych and D. H. Lawrence," *JUkGS* 15 (Summer 1990): 31–38.

David Manicom, "An Approach to the Imagery: A Study of Selected Biblical Analogues in D. H. Lawrence's *The Rainbow*," *ESC* 11 (December 1985): 474–83.

Vida E. Markovic, "Ursula Brangwen," in *The Changing Face: Disintegration of Personality in the Twentieth–Century British Novel, 1900–1950* (Carbondale: Southern Illinois University Press, 1970), 19–37.

Jeffrey Meyers, "Fra Angelico and *The Rainbow*," in *Painting and the Novel* (Manchester, England: Manchester University Press, 1975), 53–64.

Barbara A. Miliaras, "The Collapse of Agrarian Order and the Death of Thomas Brangwen in D. H. Lawrence's *The Rainbow*," *ÉLawr* 3 (May 1988): 65–77.

Siv Monell, "On the Role of Case, Aspect and Valency in the Narrative Technique of *The Rainbow* by D. H. Lawrence," in *Papers from the Second Scandinavian Symposium on Syntactic Variation*, ed. Sven Jacobson (Stockholm: Almqvist & Wiksell, 1983), 153–68.

Siv Monell, "Three Descriptions of the Lawrence Country: On the Metaphoric Use of Case, Aspect, and Valency in the Narrative Technique of *The Rainbow*, by D. H. Lawrence," in *Proceedings from the Second Nordic Conference for English Studies*, ed. Haken Ringbom and Matti Rissanen (Abo: Abo Akademi, 1984), 559–79.

Marvin Mudrick, "The Originality of *The Rainbow*," *Spectrum* 3 (1959): 3–28.

E. L. Nicholes, "The 'Symbol of the Sparrow' in *The Rainbow* by D. H. Lawrence," *MLN* 64 (1949): 171–74.

Cornelia Nixon, "To Procreate Oneself: Ursula's Horses in *The Rainbow*," *ELH* 49 (Spring 1982): 123–42.

LAWRENCE, D. H., *The Rainbow*

Paul C. Obler, *D. H. Lawrence's World of "The Rainbow"* (Madison, NJ: Drew University Press, 1955), 1–19.

Adelyn O'Connell, RSCJ, "The Concept of Person in D. H. Lawrence's *The Rainbow*," in *Literature and Religion: Views on D. H. Lawrence*, ed. Charles A. Hutter (Holland, MI: Hope College Press, 1968), 1–7.

Stefan Oltean, "Functions of Free Indirect Discourse: The Case of a Novel," *RRL* 31 (1986): 153–64.

George Otte, "The Loss of History in the Modern Novel: The Case of *The Rainbow*," *PCP* 16 (June 1981): 67–76.

S. L. Pal, "The Meaning of *The Rainbow*," in *Essays on D. H. Lawrence*, ed. T. R. Sharma (Meerut, India: Shalabh, 1987), 147–52.

Volker Raddatz, "Lyrical Elements in D. H. Lawrence's *The Rainbow*," *RLV* 40 (1974): 235–42.

M. L. Raina, "The Wheel and the Centre: An Approach to *The Rainbow*," *LCrit* 9, no. 2 (1970): 41–55.

Paul J. Rosenzweig, "A Defense of the Second Half of *The Rainbow*: Its Structure and Characterization," *DHLR* 13 (Summer 1980): 150–60.

Lara R. Ruffolo, "Lawrence's Borrowed Bird: The Flight of Bede's Sparrow through *The Rainbow*," *AntigR* 53 (Spring 1983): 127–32.

Roger Sale, "The Narrative Technique of *The Rainbow*," *MFS* 5 (1959): 29–38.

Ronald Schleifer, "Lawrence's Rhetoric of Vision: The Ending of *The Rainbow*," *DHLR* 13 (Summer 1980): 161–78.

Daniel R. Schwarz, "Lawrence's Quest in *The Rainbow*," *Ariel* 11 (July 1980): 43–66.

Keith Selby, "D. H. Lawrence's *The Rainbow*," *Expl* 46 (Fall 1987): 41–43.

Joseph Spano, "A Study of Ursula (of *The Rainbow*) and H. M. Daleski's Commentary," *Paunch* 33 (1968): 22–31.

Logan Speirs, "Lawrence's Debt to Tolstoy in *The Rainbow*," in *Tolstoy and Chekhov* (Cambridge: Cambridge University Press, 1971), 227–37.

Michael Squires, "Recurrence as a Narrative Technique in *The Rainbow*," *MFS* 21 (1975): 230–36.

Jack F. Stewart, "Expressionism in *The Rainbow*," *Novel* 13 (1980): 296–315.

Toshiji Suzuki, "D. H. Lawrence to Bijutsu: Renaissance Bijutsuron to Niji," *EigoS* 129 (1983): 106–10.

Marlin Thomas, "Somewhere under *The Rainbow*: D. H. Lawrence and the Typology of Hermeneutics," *MidHLS* 6 (1983): 57–65.

Nancy M. Tischler, "The Rainbow and the Arch," in *Literature and Religion: Views on D. H. Lawrence*, ed. Charles A. Huttar (Holland, MI: Hope College Press, 1968), 8–29.

Patricia D. Tobin, "The Cycle Dance: D. H. Lawrence, *The Rainbow*," in *Time and the Novel: The Genealogical Imperative* (Princeton: Princeton University Press, 1978), 81–106.

B. K. Tripathy, "*The Rainbow*: Unfamiliar Quest," *AJES* 10, no. 2 (1985): 141–55.

Bjorn J. Tysdahl, "Kvinnesak og skjo/nnlitteratur: D. H. Lawrence: *The Rainbow*," *Edda* 75 (1975): 29–36.

Jan Verleun, "The Inadequate Male in D. H. Lawrence's *The Rainbow*," *Neophil* 72 (January 1988): 116–35.

Pun Tzoh Wah, "*The Rainbow* and Lawrence's Vision of a New World," *SARE* 12–13 (June–December 1986): 97–106.

William Walsh, "The Writer and the Child: Ursula in *The Rainbow*," in *The Use of the Imagination: Educational Thought and the Literary Mind* (London: Chatto & Windus, 1959), 163–74.

Richard Wasson, "Comedy and History in *The Rainbow*," *MFS* 13 (1967): 465–77.

Mark Kinkead Weekes, "The Marriage of Opposites in *The Rainbow*," in *D. H. Lawrence: Centenary Essays*, ed. Mara Kalnins (Bristol, England: Bristol Classical, 1986), 21–39.

Mark Kinkead Weekes, "The Sense of History in *The Rainbow*," in *D. H. Lawrence in the Modern World*, ed. Peter Preston and Peter Hoare (Cambridge: Cambridge University Press, 1989), 121–38.

Michael Wilding, "*The Rainbow*: 'smashing the great machine,'" in *Political Fictions* (London: Routledge & Kegan Paul, 1980), 127–49.

John Worthen, "Introduction" and "Notes," in *The Rainbow*, ed. John Worthen (Harmondsworth, England: Penguin, 1981), 11–33, 551–71.

Helen W. Wussow, "Lawrence's *The Rainbow*," *Expl* 41 (Fall 1982): 44–45.

"The Rocking-Horse Winner"

Rosemary Reeves Davies, "Lawrence, Lady Cynthia Asquith, and 'The Rocking-Horse Winner,'" *SSF* 20 (Spring–Summer 1983): 121–26.

LAWRENCE, D. H., "The Rocking-Horse Winner"

Michael Goldberg, "Lawrence's 'The Rocking-Horse Winner': A Dickensian Fable?" *MFS* 15 (1969): 525–36.

Carolyn Gordon and Allen Tate, *The House of Fiction*, ed. Carolyn Gordon and Allen Tate (New York: Scribner's, 1950), 227–30.

John B. Humma, "Pan and 'The Rocking-Horse Winner,'" *ELWIU* 5 (1978): 53–60.

Hugh J. Ingrasci, "Names as Symbolic Crowns Unifying Lawrence's 'The Rocking-Horse Winner,'" in *Festschrift in Honor of Virgil J. Vogel*, ed. Edward Callary (DeKalb: Illinois Name Society, 1985), 1–22.

Charles Koban, "Allegory and the Death of the Heart in 'The Rocking-Horse Winner,'" *SSF* 15 (1978): 391–96.

Roy Lamson, et al., "Critical Analysis of 'The Rocking-Horse Winner,'" in *The Critical Reader* (New York: Norton, 1962), 542–47.

W. S. Marks, III, "The Psychology of the Uncanny in Lawrence's 'The Rocking-Horse Winner,'" *MFS* 11 (1966): 381–92.

W. R. Martin, "Fancy or Imagination? 'The Rocking-Horse Winner,'" *CE* 24 (1962): 64–65.

Mary Rohrberger, "D. H. Lawrence: 'The Rocking-Horse Winner,'" in *Hawthorne and the Modern Short Story: A Study in Genre* (The Hague: Mouton, 1966), 74–80.

Epifanio San Juan, "Theme Versus Imitation: D. H. Lawrence's 'The Rocking-Horse Winner,'" *DHLR* 3 (Summer 1970): 136–40.

James B. Scott, "The Norton Distortion: A Dangerous Typo in 'The Rocking-Horse Winner,'" *DHLR* 21 (Summer 1990): 175–77.

W. D. Snodgrass, "A Rocking-Horse: The Symbol, the Pattern, the Way to Live," *HudR* 11 (1958): 191–200.

Frederick W. Turner, "Prancing in to a Purpose: Myths, Horses, and True Selfhood in Lawrence's 'The Rocking-Horse Winner,'" in *D. H. Lawrence: "The Rocking-Horse Winner,"* ed. Dominick P. Consolo (Columbus, OH: Bobbs Merrill, 1969), 95–106.

John F. Turner, "The Perversion of Play in D. H. Lawrence's 'The Rocking-Horse Winner,'" *DHLR* 15 (Fall 1982): 249–70.

Sidney Warschausky, "'The Rocking-Horse Winner,'" in *Insight II: Analyses of Modern British Literature*, ed. John V. Hagopian and Martin Dolch (Frankfurt: Hirschgraben, 1964), 228–33.

Daniel P. Watkins, "Labor and Religion in D. H. Lawrence's 'The Rocking-Horse Winner,'" *SSF* 24 (Summer 1987): 295–301.

Keith Wilson, "D. H. Lawrence's 'The Rocking-Horse Winner': Parable and Structure," *ESC* 13 (December 1987): 438–50.

St. Mawr

Anne Darling Barker, "The Fairy Tale and *St. Mawr*," *FMLS* 20 (January 1984): 76–83.

Keith Brown, "Welsh Red Indians: D. H. Lawrence and *St. Mawr*," *EIC* 32 (April 1982): 158–79.

Mick Gidley, "Antipodes: D. H. Lawrence's *St. Mawr*," *Ariel* 5, no. 1 (1974): 25–41.

John Haegert, "Lawrence's *St. Mawr* and the De-Creation of America," *Criticism* 34 (Winter 1992): 75–98.

Robert Liddell, "Lawrence and Dr. Leavis: The Case of *St. Mawr*," *EIC* 4 (1954): 321–27.

Frederick P. W. McDowell, "'Pioneering into the wilderness of unopened life': Lou Witt in America," in *The Spirit of D. H. Lawrence: Centenary Studies*, ed. Gamini Salgado and G. K. Das (Totowa, NJ: Barnes & Noble, 1988), 92–105.

Polanki Rama Moorthy, "*St. Mawr*: The Third Eye," *AJES* 10, no. 2 (1985): 188–204.

Horst Oppel, "D. H. Lawrence: *St. Mawr*," in *Der Moderne Englische Roman: Interpretationen*, ed. Horst Oppel (Berlin: Schmidt, 1965), 115–34.

Bibhu Padhi, "Lawrence, *St. Mawr* and Irony," *SDR* 21 (Summer 1983): 5–13.

Michael Ragussis, "The False Myth of *St. Mawr*: Lawrence and the Subterfuge of Art," *PLL* 11 (1975): 186–96.

J. F. Galvan Reula, "*St. Mawr* a traves de sus imagenes," *RCEI* 11 (November 1985): 25–34.

M. Scholtes, "*St. Mawr*: Between Degeneration and Regeneration," *DQR* 5 (1975): 253–69.

Bob L. Smith, "D. H. Lawrence's *St. Mawr*: Transposition of Myth," *ArQ* 24 (1968): 197–208.

Nicole Tartera, "*St Mawr*, de l'humour à la satire, ou les facettes de l'esprit lawrencien," *ÉLawr* 6 (May 1991): 53–68.

Jerry Wasserman, “*St. Mawr* and the Search of Community,” *Mosaic* 5 (Summer 1972): 113–23.

Alan Wilde, “The Illusion of *St. Mawr*: Technique and Vision in D. H. Lawrence’s Novel,” *PMLA* 79 (1964): 164–70.

“The Shadow in the Rose Garden”

Keith Cushman, “D. H. Lawrence at Work: ‘The Shadow in the Rose Garden,’” *DHLR* 8 (Spring 1975): 31–46.

Sons and Lovers

T. H. Adamowski, “The Father of All Things: The Oral and the Oedipal in *Sons and Lovers*,” *Mosaic* 14 (Fall 1981): 69–88.

T. H. Adamowski, “Intimacy at a Distance: Sexuality and Orality in *Sons and Lovers*,” *Mosaic* 13 (Fall 1980): 71–89.

Tamara Alinei, “D. H. Lawrence’s Natural Imagery: A Non-Vitalist Reading,” *DQR* 6 (1976): 116–38.

Tamara Alinei, “Three Times Morel: Recurrent Structure in *Sons and Lovers*,” *DQR* 5 (1975): 39–53.

Judith Arcana, “I Remember Mama: Mother–Blaming in *Sons and Lovers* Criticism,” *DHLR* 21 (Summer 1989): 137–51.

Chiseki Asahi, “Dreaming Woman: Musuko to Koibito no Hiroin–zo,” *EigoS* 135 (n.d.): 79–81.

Peter H. Balbert, “Forging and Feminism: *Sons and Lovers* and the Phallic Imagination,” *DHLR* 11 (Summer 1978): 93–113.

Helen Baron, “Jessie Chambers’ Plea for Justice to Miriam,” *Archiv* 222, no. 1 (1985): 63–84.

Richard D. Beards, “*Sons and Lovers* as ‘Bilddungsroman,’” *CollL* 1 (1974): 204–17.

Calvin Bedient, “The Vital Self,” in *Sons and Lovers*, ed. Harold Bloom (New York: Chelsea House, 1988), 71–78.

Maurice Beebe, “*Sons and Lovers*,” in *Ivory Towers and Sacred Founts: The Artist as Hero in Fiction from Goethe to Joyce* (New York: New York University Press, 1964), 103–13.

Gavriel Ben-Ephraim, "Paul's Passion," in *Sons and Lovers*, ed. Harold Bloom (New York: Chelsea House, 1988), 131–42.

Seymour Betsky, "Rhythm and Theme: D. H. Lawrence's *Sons and Lovers*," in *The Achievement of D. H. Lawrence*, ed. Frederick J. Hoffman and Harry T. Moore (Norman: University of Oklahoma Press, 1953), 131–43.

Harold Bloom, "Introduction," in *Sons and Lovers*, ed. Harold Bloom (New York: Chelsea House, 1988), 1–4.

Diane S. Bonds, "Miriam, the Narrator, and the Reader of Sons and Lovers," *DHLR* 14 (Summer 1981): 143–55.

Jerome H. Buckley, "D. H. Lawrence: The Burden of Apology," in *Season of Youth: The "Bildungsroman" from Dickens to Golding* (Cambridge, MA: Harvard University Press, 1974), 204–24.

Angus Burrell, "D. H. Lawrence: *Sons and Lovers*," in *Modern Fiction*, ed. Angus Burrell and Dorothy Brewster (New York: Columbia University Press, 1934), 137–54.

Rose Marie Burwell, "Schopenhauer, Hardy, and Lawrence: Toward a New Understanding of *Sons and Lovers*," *WHR* 28 (1974): 105–17.

Elizabeth A. Campbell, "Metonymy and Character: *Sons and Lovers* and the Metaphysic of Self," *DHLR* 20 (Spring 1988): 21–32.

Arindam Chatterji, "*Sons and Lovers*: Dynamic Sanity," *PURB* 16 (October 1985): 3–21.

Kai Chen, "Remarks on the Style of D. H. Lawrence's *Sons and Lovers*," *Waiguoyu* 1 (February 1987): 71–75.

Mario L. D'Avanzo, "On the Naming of Paul Morel and the Ending of *Sons and Lovers*," *SoR* 12 (1979): 103–07.

H. M. Daleski, "The Release: The First Period," in "*Sons and Lovers*," ed. Harold Bloom (New York: Chelsea House, 1988), 23–45.

Paul Delany, "*Sons and Lovers*: The More Marriage as a War of Position," *DHLR* 21 (Summer 1989): 153–65.

Émile Delavenay, "Lawrence's Major Work," in *D. H. Lawrence: The Man Who Lived*, ed. Robert B. Partlow and Harry T. Moore (Carbondale: Southern Illinois University Press, 1980), 139–42.

Dennis DeNitto, "*Sons and Lovers* (1913), D. H. Lawrence: Jack Cardiff, 1960: All Passion Spent," in *The English Novels and the Movies*, ed. Michael Klein and Gillian Parker (New York: Ungar, 1981), 235–47.

LAWRENCE, D. H., *Sons and Lovers*

Daniel Dervin, "Play, Creativity and Matricide: The Implications of Lawrence's 'Smashed Doll' Episode," *Mosaic* 14 (Summer 1981): 81–94.

Susan Dietz, "Miriam," *RecL* 6, no. 3 (1978): 15–22.

Richard DiMaggio, "A Note on *Sons and Lovers* and Emerson's 'Experience,'" *DHLR* 6 (Fall 1973): 214–16.

John Doheny, "The Novel Is the Book of Life: D. H. Lawrence and a Revised Version of Polymorphous Perversity," *Paunch* 26 (1966): 40–59.

Ronald P. Draper, "D. H. Lawrence on Mother Love," *EIC* 8 (1958): 285–89.

Paul Eggert, "Edward Garnett's *Sons and Lovers*," *CritQ* 28 (Winter 1986): 51–61.

John M. Eichrodt, "Doctrine and Dogma in *Sons and Lovers*," *ConnR* 4 (1970): 18–32.

Avrom Fleishman, "The Fictions of Autobiographical Fiction," *Genre* 9 (1976): 73–86.

Louis Fraiberg, "The Uattainable Self: D. H. Lawrence's *Sons and Lovers*," in *Twelve Original Essays on Great English Novels*, ed. Charles Shapiro (Detroit: Wayne State University Press, 1960), 175–201.

Michael Patrick Gillespie, "Lawrence's *Sons and Lovers*," *Expl* 40 (Summer 1982): 36–38.

Andor Gomme, "Jessie Chambers and Miriam Leivers: An Essay on *Sons and Lovers*," in *D. H. Lawrence: A Critical Study*, ed. Andor Goome (New York: Barnes & Noble, 1978), 30–52.

Charolyn Hampson, "The Morels and the Gants: Sexual Conflict as a Universal Theme," *TWN* 8, no. 1 (1984): 27–40.

John Edward Hardy, "*Sons and Lovers*: The Artist as Savior," in *Man in the Modern Novel* (Seattle: University of Washington Press, 1964), 52–66.

Geoffrey Harvey and Michael Scott, eds. *Sons and Lovers* (Atlantic Highlands, NJ: Humanities, 1987), 1–84.

Enid Hilton, "Alice Dax: D. H. Lawrence's Clara in *Sons and Lovers*," *DHLR* 22 (Fall 1990): 275–85.

Evelyn J. Hinz, "*Sons and Lovers*: The Archetypal Dimensions of Lawrence's Oedipal Tragedy," *DHLR* 5 (Spring 1972): 26–53.

Phil Joffe, "*Sons and Lovers*: The Growth of Paul Morel," *CRUX* 20 (August 1986): 49–62.

Tetsuhiko Kamimura, "D. H. Laurence no Musuko to Koibito," in *Eibungaku to no Deai*, ed. Naomi Matsuura (Kyoto: Showado, 1983), 99–111.

Alfred Kazin, "Sons, Lovers and Mothers," *PR* 29 (1962): 373–85.

Mark Kinkead–Weekes, "Eros and Metaphor in *Sons and Lovers*," in "*Sons and Lovers*," ed. Harold Bloom (New York: Chelsea House, 1988), 103–08.

David J. Kleinbard, "Laing, Lawrence, and the Maternal Cannibal," *PsyAR* 58 (1971): 5–13.

Alfred Booth Kuttner, "*Sons and Lovers*: A Freudian Appreciation," *PsyAR* 3 (1916): 295–317.

J. C. F. Littlewood, "Son and Lover," *CQ* 4 (1969–70): 323–61.

Samuel E. Longmire, "Lawrence's *Sons and Lovers*," *Expl* 42 (Spring 1984): 2–4.

Jose Mateo Martinez, "Lawrence y la naturaleza: Una empatia sinestesica," *RAEI* 1 (November 1988): 139–51.

Louis L. Martz, "Portrait of Miriam: A Study in the Design of *Sons and Lovers*," in *Imagined Worlds: Essays on Some English Novels and Novelists in Honour of John Butt*, ed. Maynard Mack and Ian Gregor (London: Methuen, 1968), 343–69. Reprinted as "Portrait of Miriam" in "*Sons and Lovers*," ed. Harold Bloom (New York: Chelsea House, 1988), 47–69.

Hirai Masako, "Chichioya fuzai no Paradox: *Sons and Lovers* o megutte," *EK* 63 (September 1986): 75–94.

Barbara Melchiori, "'Objects in the powerful light of emotion,'" *Ariel* 1 (1970): 21–30.

Giles R. Mitchell, "*Sons and Lovers* and the Oedipal Project," *DHLR* 13 (Fall 1980): 209–19.

Donald E. Mortland, "The Conclusion of *Sons and Lovers*: A Reconsideration," *SNNTS* 3 (1971): 305–15.

Edwin M. Moseley, "Christ as Artist and Lover: D. H. Lawrence's *Sons and Lovers*," in *Pseudonyms of Christ in the Modern Novel* (Pittsburgh: University of Pittsburgh Press, 1962), 69–86.

Malcolm Muggeridge, "Lawrence's *Sons and Lovers*," *NewS&N* 49 (1955): 581–82.

Ira B. Nadel, "From Fathers and Sons to *Sons and Lovers*," *DR* 59 (1979): 221–38.

LAWRENCE, D. H., *Sons and Lovers*

Thomas Nash, "'Bleeding at the Roots': The Folklore of Plants in *Sons and Lovers*," *KFR* 27 (January–June 1981): 20–32.

William H. New, "Character and Symbol: Annie's Role in *Sons and Lovers*," *DHLR* 1 (Spring 1968): 31–43.

David Newmarch, "'Death of a Young Man in London': Ernest Lawrence and William Morel in *Sons and Lovers*," *DUJ* 76 (December 1983): 73–79.

Frank O'Connor, "D. H. Lawrence: *Sons and Lovers*," in *The Mirror in the Roadway: A Study of the Modern Novel* (New York: Knopf, 1956), 270–79.

M. L. Pandit, "The Family Relationship in *Sons and Lovers*: Gertrude and Walter Morel," in *Essays on D. H. Lawrence*, ed. T. R. Sharma (Meerut, India: Shalabh, 1987), 89–94.

Shirley Panken, "Some Psychodynamics in *Sons and Lovers*: A New Look at the Oedipal Theme," *PsyAR* 61 (1974): 571–89.

Bibhu Padhi, "Man, Nature and Motions of the Spirit: Symbolic Scenes in D. H. Lawrence's *Sons and Lovers*," *WascanaR* 19 (Fall 1984): 53–67.

Roy Pascal, "The Autobiographical Novel and the Autobiography," *EIC* 9 (1959): 134–50.

Carlos A. Perez, "Husbands and Wives, Sons and Lovers: Intimate Conflict in the Fiction of D. H. Lawrence," in *The Aching Hearth: Family Violence in Life and Literature*, ed. Sara Munson Deats and Lagretta Tallent Lenker (New York: Plenum, 1991), 175–87.

Danna Phillips, "Lawrence's Understanding of Miriam through Sue," *RecL* 7, no. 1 (1979): 46–56.

Malcolm Pittock, "*Sons and Lovers*: The Price of Betrayal," *EIC* 36 (July 1986): 235–54.

Xavier Pons, "'Baptism of Fire': The Oedipal Element in D. H. Lawrence's *Sons and Lovers*," *CVE* 32 (October 1990): 101–10.

V. S. Pritchett, "*Sons and Lovers*," in *The Living Novel and Later Appreciations* (New York: Random, 1964), 182–89.

Faith Pullin, "Lawrence's Treatment of Women in *Sons and Lovers*," in *Lawrence and Women*, ed. Anne Smith (London: Vision, 1978), 49–74.

Harish Raizada, "Paul Morel: Architect of His Own Tragedy," *AJES* 10, no. 2 (1985): 122–40.

Bernard Richards, "Lawrence's *Sons and Lovers*," *Expl* 46 (Spring 1988): 32–35.

Max Vega Ritter, "*Sons and Lovers*: Roman de l'immolation," *CVE* 32 (October 1990): 111–24.

Charles Roseman, "The Gospel According to D. H. Lawrence: Religion in *Sons and Lovers*," *DHLR* 3 (Spring 1970): 31–41.

Keith Sagar, "Introduction" and "Notes," in *Sons and Lovers*, ed. Keith Sagar (Harmondsworth, England: Penguin, 1981), 11–28, 493–500.

Barry J. Scherr, "The 'Dark Fire of Desire' in D. H. Lawrence's *Sons and Lovers*," *RecL* 16 (1988): 37–67.

Daniel J. Schneider, "The Artist as Psychologist," in *Sons and Lovers*, ed. Harold Bloom (New York: Chelsea House, 1988), 143–53.

Mark Schorer, "Technique as Discovery," *HudR* 1 (1948): 67–87.

Daniel R. Schwartz, "Speaking of Paul Morel: Voice, Unity, and Meaning in *Sons and Lovers*," *SNNTS* 8 (Fall 1976): 255–77. Reprinted in "*Sons and Lovers*," ed. Harold Bloom (New York: Chelsea House, 1988), 79–101.

Visnja Sepcic/, "Realism Versus Symbolism: The Double Patterning of *Sons and Lovers*," *SrRAZ* 33–36 (1972–73): 185–208.

K. C. Shrivastava, "D. H. Lawrence's *Sons and Lovers* as a Proletarian Novel," in *Essays on D. H. Lawrence*, ed. T. R. Sharma (Meerut, India: Shalabh, 1987), 104–08.

E. P. Shrubb, "Reading *Sons and Lovers*," in *Sons and Lovers*, ed. Harold Bloom (New York: Chelsea House, 1988), 109–29.

Kuga Shunji, "Paul's Course of Life: Where Will He Go?" *SELit* 58 (December 1981): 169–81.

Grover Smith, "The Doll-Burners: D. H. Lawrence and Louise Alcott," *MLQ* 19 (1958): 28–32.

John A. Taylor, "The Greatness in *Sons and Lovers*," *MP* 71 (1973–74): 380–87.

Wayne Templeton, "The Drift towards Life: Paul Morel's Search for a Place," *DHLR* 15 (Spring–Summer 1982): 177–94.

Darlene Harbour Unrue, "The Symbolism of Names in *Sons and Lovers*," *Names* 28 (June 1980): 131–40.

Dorothy Van Ghent, "Lawrence: *Sons and Lovers*," in *The English Novel: Form and Function* (New York: Harper, 1961), 245–61, 452–62. Reprinted as "On *Sons and Lovers*," in "*Sons and Lovers*," ed. Harold Bloom (New York: Chelsea House, 1988), 5–22.

Daniel E. Van Tassel, "The Search for Manhood in D. H. Lawrence's *Sons and Lovers*," *Costerus* 3 (1972): 197–210.

Therese Vichy, "Les Formes du temps dans *Sons and Lovers*," *ÉLawr* 3 (May 1988): 23–39.

Jean Wahl, "Sur D. H. Lawrence," *NRF* 42 (1934): 115–21.

James N. Wise, "Emerson's 'Experience' and *Sons and Lovers*," *Costerus* 6 (1972): 179–221.

Howard R. Wolf, "British Fathers and Sons, 1773–1913: From Filial Submissiveness to Creativity," *PsyAR* 52 (1965): 210–14.

Virginia Woolf, "Notes on D. H. Lawrence," in *Collected Essays*, ed. Leonard Woolf (London: Hogarth, 1931), 353–55.

John Worthen, "Lawrence's Autobiographies," in *The Spirit of D. H. Lawrence: Centenary Studies*, ed. Gamini Salgado and G. K. Das (Totowa, NJ: Barnes & Noble, 1988), 1–15.

Koichi Yoshimura, "*Sons and Lovers* ni okeru shizen to jinbutsu," in *Bungaku to kotoba*, ed. Toshio Kimura, Hisao Kanaseki, and Isamu Saito (Tokyo: Nan'un do, 1986), 268–80.

"Sun"

L. D. Clark, "Lawrence's 'Maya' Drawing for 'Sun,'" *DHLR* 15 (Spring–Summer 1982): 141–46.

Francoise Dufour, "'Sun': Nouvelle, essai ou poème?" *ÉLawr* 3 (May 1988): 59–70.

"Things"

Keith Cushman, "The Serious Comedy of 'Things,'" *ÉLawr* 6 (May 1991): 83–94.

"The Thorn in the Flesh"

James C. Cowan, "Phobia and Psychological Development in D. H. Lawrence's 'The Thorn in the Flesh,'" in *The Modernists: Studies in a Literary Phenomenon: Essays in Honor of Harry T. Moore*, ed. Lawrence B. Gamache and Ian S. MacNiven (Rutherford, NJ: Fairleigh Dickinson University Press, 1987), 163–70.

"Tickets, Please"

E. Kegel-Brinkgreve, "The Dionysian Tramline," *DQR* 5 (1975): 180–94.

Seymour Lainoff, "The Wartime Setting of Lawrence's 'Tickets, Please,'" *SSF* 7 (1970): 649–51.

Paulette Michel-Michot, "D. H. Lawrence's 'Tickets, Please': The Structural Importance of the Setting," *RLV* 41 (1975): 464–70.

Kiernan Ryan, "The Revenge of the Women: Lawrence's 'Tickets, Please,'" *L&H* 7 (Autumn 1981): 210–22.

Lionel Trilling, "D. H. Lawrence: 'Tickets, Please,'" in *Prefaces to "The Experience of Literature"* (New York: Harcourt, Brace, 1979), 123–27.

Richard P. Wheeler, "'Cunning in his overthrow': Lawrence's Art in 'Tickets, Please,'" *DHLR* 10 (Fall 1977): 242–50.

Paul A. Wood, "On Teaching Lawrence: Up at the Front: A Teacher's Learning Experience with Lawrence's Sexual Politics," *DHLR* 20 (Spring 1988): 71–77.

The Trespasser

A. R. Atkins, "Recognising the 'Stranger' in D. H. Lawrence's *The Trespasser*," *CQ* 20, no. 1 (1991): 1–20.

Helen Corke, "The Writing of *The Trespasser*," *DHLR* 7 (Fall 1974): 227–39.

Leo Gurke, "*The Trespasser*: D. H. Lawrence's Neglected Novel," *CE* 24 (1962): 29–35.

Evelyn J. Hinz, "*The Trespasser*: Lawrence's Wagnerian Tragedy and Divine Comedy," *DHLR* 4 (Summer 1971): 122–41.

Herbert Howarth, "D. H. Lawrence from Island to Glacier," *UTQ* 37 (1968): 215–29.

Joseph A. Kestner, "The Literary Wagnerism of D. H. Lawrence's *The Trespasser*," *ModBL* 2 (1977): 123–38.

Elizabeth Mansfield, "Introduction," in *D. H. Lawrence: "The Trespasser,"* ed. Elizabeth Mansfield (Cambridge: Cambridge University Press, 1912), 3–37.

Robert Millett, "Great Expectations: D. H Lawrence's *The Trespasser*," in *Twenty-Seven to One*, ed. B. Broughton (Ogdensbury, NY: Ryan, 1970), 125–32.

Koya Shimizu, "D. H. Lawrence Shinyusha Ko," in *Muraoka Isamu Sensei Kiju Kinen Ronbunshu: Eibungaku Shiron* (Tokyo: Kinseido, 1983), 328–40.

Louise Wright, "Lawrence's *The Trespasser*: Its Debt to Reality," *TSLL* 20 (1978): 230–48.

Elliott Zuckerman, "Wagnerizing on the Isle of Wight," in *The First Hundred Years of Wagner's "Tristan"* (New York: Columbia University Press, 1964), 124–27.

"The Undying Man"

George J. Zytaruk, "'The Undying Man': D. H. Lawrence's Yiddish Story," *DHLR* 4 (Spring 1971): 20–27.

The Virgin and the Gipsy

Peter Balpert, "Scorched Ego, the Novel, and the Beast: Patterns of Fourth Dimensionality in *The Virgin and the Gipsy*," *PLL* 29 (Fall 1993): 395–416.

Ashby Bland Crowder and Lynn O'Malley Crowder, "Mythic Intent in D. H. Lawrence's *The Virgin and the Gipsy*," *SoAR* 49 (May 1984): 61–66.

Barnett Guttenberg, "Realism and Romance in Lawrence's *The Virgin and the Gypsy*," *SSF* 17 (1980): 99–103.

Jeffrey Meyers, "'The Voice of Water': Lawrence's *The Virgin and the Gypsy*," *EngM* 21 (1970): 199–207.

John Turner, "Purity and Danger in D. H. Lawrence's *The Virgin and the Gipsy*," in *D. H. Lawrence: Centenary Essays*, ed. Mara Kalnins (Bristol, England: Bristol Classical, 1986), 139–71.

Garry Watson, "'The Fact, and the Crucial Significance, of Desire': Lawrence's *Virgin and the Gipsy*," *Eng* 34 (Summer 1985): 131–56.

Noriyuki Yanada, "*The Virgin and the Gipsy*: Four Realms and Narrative Modes," *L&C* 20 (1991): 121–46.

The White Peacock

Christopher Brown, "As Cyril Likes It: Pastoral Reality and Illusion in *The White Peacock*," *ELWIU* 6 (1979): 187–93.

Robert E. Gajdusek, "A Reading of 'A Poem of Friendship,' a Chapter in Lawrence's *The White Peacock*," *DHLR* 3 (Spring 1970): 42–67.

Robert E. Gajdusek, "A Reading of *The White Peacock*," in *A D. H. Lawrence Miscellany*, ed. Harry T. Moore (Carbondale: Southern Illinois University Press, 1959), 188–203.

Evelyn J. Hinz, "June and *The White Peacock*: Lawrence's English Epic," *DHLR* 3 (Summer 1970): 115–35.

W. J. Keith, "D. H. Lawrence's *The White Peacock*: An Essay in Criticism," *UTQ* 37 (1977): 230–47.

H. A. Mason, "D. H. Lawrence and *The White Peacock*," *CQ* 7 (1977): 216–31.

Jeffrey Meyers, "Maurice Greiffenhagen and *The White Peacock*," in *Painting and the Novel* (Manchester, England: Manchest University Press, 1975), 46–52.

Marko Modiano, "Symbolism, Characterization, and Setting in *The White Peacock*, by D. H. Lawrence," *MSpr* 77, no. 4 (1983): 345–52.

Kristin Morrison, "Lawrence, Beardsley, and Wilde: *The White Peacock* and Sexual Ambiguity," *WHR* 30 (1976): 241–48.

Bernard Richards, "A Botanical Mistake in Lawrence's *The White Peacock*," *N&Q* 36 (June 1989): 2, 202.

Visnja Sepcic, "*The White Peacock* Reconsidered," *SrRAZ* 38 (1875): 105–14.

Michael Squires, "*The White Peacock*: 'Fit for Old Theocritus,'" in *The Pastoral Novel: Studies in George Eliot, Thomas Hardy, and D. H. Lawrence* (Charlottesville: University Press of Virginia, 1974), 174–95.

Raney Stanford, "Thomas Hardy and Lawrence's *The White Peacock*," *MFS* 5 (1959): 19–28.

Margaret Storch, "The Lacerated Male: Ambivalent Images of Women in *The White Peacock*," *DHLR* 21 (Summer 1989): 117–36.

W. M. Verhoeven, "D. H. Lawrence's Duality Concept in *The White Peacock*," *Neophil* 69 (April 1985): 294–317.

Women in Love

T. H. Adamowski, "Being Perfect: Lawrence, Sartre, and *Women in Love*," *CritI* 2 (1975): 345–68.

A. A. Ansari, "*Women in Love*: Search for Integrated Being," *AJES* 10, no. 2 (1985): 156–77.

Peter Balbert, "Ursula Brangwen and 'The Essential Criticism': The Female Corrective in *Women in Love*," *SNNTS* 17 (Fall 1985): 267–85.

David S. Barber, "Can a Radical Interpretation of *Women in Love* be Adequate?" *DHLR* 3 (Summer 1970): 168–74.

David S. Barber, "Community in *Women in Love*," *Novel* 5 (1971): 32–41.

LAWRENCE, D. H., *Women in Love*

Angelo P. Bertocci, "Symbolism in *Women in Love*," in *A D. H. Lawrence Miscellany*, ed. Harry T. Moore (Carbondale: Southern Illinois University Press, 1959), 82–102.

Lydia Blanchard, "The 'Real Quarter' of *Women in Love*: Lawrence on Brothers and Sisters," in *D. H. Lawrence: The Man Who Lived*, ed. Robert B. Partlow and Harry T. Moore (Carbondale: Southern Illinois University Press, 1980), 199–206.

Lydia Blanchard, "*Women in Love*: Mourning Becomes Narcissism," *Mosaic* 15 (Winter 1982): 105–18.

Diane S. Bonds, "Going into the Abyss: Literalization in *Women in Love*," *ELWIU* 8 (Fall 1981): 189–202.

Graham Bradshaw, "'Lapsing Out' in *Women in Love*," *Eng* 32 (Spring 1983): 17–32.

William E. Cain, "Lawrence's 'Purely Destructive' Art in *Women in Love*," *SCRev* 13 (1980): 38–47.

Douglas M. Catron, "'Jiu-Jitsu' in Lawrence's 'Gladiatorial,'" *SoCB* 43 (Winter 1983): 92–94.

Robert L. Chamberlain, "Pussum, Minette, and the Africo-Nordic Symbol in Lawrence's *Women in Love*," *PMLA* 78 (1963): 407–16.

L. D. Clark, "Lawrence/*Women in Love*: The Contravened Knot," in *Approaches to the Twentieth Century Novel*, ed. John Unterecker (New York: Crowell, 1965), 51–78.

Keith Cushman, "A Note on Lawrence's 'Fly in the Ointment,'" *ELN* 15 (1977): 47–51.

Edward Davis, "*Women in Love*," in *Readings in Modern Fiction* (Cape Town, South Africa: Simondium, 1964), 270–81.

William S. Davis, Jr., "Mountains, Metaphors, and Other Entanglements: Sexual Representation in the Prologue to *Women in Love*," *DHLR* 22 (Spring 1990): 69–76.

Maria DiBattista, "*Women in Love*: D. H. Lawrence's Judgment Book," in *D. H. Lawrence: A Centenary Consideration*, ed. Peter Balbert and Phillip L. Marcus (Ithaca, NY: Cornell University Press, 1985), 67–90.

Gerald Doherty, "The Art of Leaping: Metaphor Unbound in D. H. Lawrence's *Women in Love*," *Style* 26 (Spring 1992): 50–65.

Gerald Doherty, "The Darkest Source: D. H. Lawrence, Tantric Yoga, and *Women in Love*," *ELWIU* 11 (Fall 1984): 211–22.

Gerald Doherty, "The Salvator Mundi Touch: Messianic Typology in D. H. Lawrence's *Women in Love*," *Ariel* 13 (July 1982): 53–71.

George Donaldson, "'Men in Love?' D. H. Lawrence, Rupert Birkin and Gerald Crich," in *D. H. Lawrence: Centenary Essays*, ed. Mara Kalnins (Bristol, England: Bristol Classical, 1986), 41–67.

Richard L. Drain, "*Women in Love*," in *D. H. Lawrence: A Critical Study: A Critical Study of the Novels and Other Major Writings*, ed. Andor Gomme (New York: Barnes & Noble, 1978), 70–93.

Elizabeth Drew, "*Women in Love*," in *The Novel: A Modern Guide to Fifteen English Masterpieces* (New York: Dell, 1963), 208–23.

Donald R. Eastman, "Myth and Fate in the Characters of *Women in Love*," *DHLR* 9 (Summer 1976): 177–93.

Janet M. Eldred, "Plot and Subplot in *Women in Love*," *JNT* 20 (Fall 1990): 284–95.

Richard D. Erlich, "Catastrophism and Coition: Universal and Individual Development in *Women in Love*," *TSLL* 9 (1967): 117–28.

Stephen Farber, "*Women in Love*," *HudR* 23 (1970): 321–26.

George H. Ford, "An Introductory Note to D. H. Lawrence's 'Prologue' to *Women in Love*," *TexasQ* 1 (1963): 92–97.

George H. Ford, "Shelley or Schiller? A Note on D. H. Lawrence at Work," *TSLL* 4 (1962): 154–56.

Herve Fourtina, "La Perversion dans *Women in Love*," *ÉLawr* 4 (May 1989): 71–86.

A. L. French, "'The Whole Pulse of Social England': *Women in Love*," *CR* 21 (1979): 57–71.

Stephen Gerber, "Character, Language, and Experience in 'Water Party,'" *Paunch* 36–37 (1973): 3–29.

Stephen Gill, "Lawrence and Gerald Crich," *EIC* 27 (1977): 231–47.

David J. Gordon, "*Women in Love* and the Lawrencean Aesthetic," in *Twentieth Century Interpretations of "Women in Love,"* ed. Stephen J. Miko (Englewood Cliffs, NJ: Prentice-Hall, 1969), 50–60.

Ronald D. Gray, "English Resistance to German Literature from Coleridge to D. H. Lawrence," in *The German Tradition in Literature, 1871–1945* (Cambridge: Cambridge University Press, 1967), 341–53.

Linda S. Grimes, "Lawrence's *Women in Love*," *Expl* 46 (Winter 1988): 24–27.

LAWRENCE, D. H., *Women in Love*

William F. Hall, "The Image of the Wolf in Chapter XXX of D. H. Lawrence's *Women in Love*," *DHLR* 2 (Fall 1969): 272–74.

Howard M. Harper, "'Fantasia' and the Psychodynamics of *Women in Love*," in *The Classic British Novel*, ed. Harper and Charles Edge (Athens: University of Georgia Press, 1972), 202–19.

Lucia Henning Heldt, "Lawrence on Love: The Courtship and Marriage of Tom Brangwen and Lydia Lensky," *DHLR* 8 (Fall 1975): 358–70.

Christopher Heywood, "The Image of Africa in *Women in Love*," *DHLR* 4 (Spring 1986): 13–21.

Evelyn J. Hinz and John J. Teunissen, "*Women in Love* and the Myth of Eros and Psyche," in *D. H. Lawrence: The Man Who Lived*, ed. Robert B. Partlow and Harry T. Moore (Carbondale: Southern Illinois University Press, 1980), 207–20.

John B. Humma, "Lawrence in Another Light: *Women in Love* and Existentialism," *SNNTS* 24 (Winter 1992): 392–409.

Virginia Hyde, "Architectural Monuments: Centers of Worship in *Women in Love*," *Mosaic* 17 (Fall 1984): 53–71.

Dan Jacobson, "*Women in Love* and the Death of the Will," *GrandS* 7 (Autumn 1987): 130–39.

Sibyl Jacobson, "The Paradox of Fulfillment: A Discussion of *Women in Love*," *JNT* 3 (1973): 53–65.

Debra Journet, "Symbol and Allegory in *Women in Love*," *SoAR* 49 (May 1984): 42–60.

Joseph A. Kestner, "Sculptural Character in Lawrence's *Women in Love*," *MFS* 21 (1975): 543–53.

Robert Kiely, "Accident and Purpose: 'Bad Form' in Lawrence's Fiction," in *D. H. Lawrence: A Centenary Consideration*, ed. Peter Balbert and Phillip L. Marcus (Ithaca, NY: Cornell University Press, 1985), 91–107.

George Klawitter, "Impressionist Characterization in *Women in Love*," *UDR* 17 (Winter 1985–86): 49–55.

Murray Krieger, "The State of Monologue in D. H. Lawrence," in *The Tragic Vision: Variations on a Theme in Literary Interpretation* (Chicago: University of Chicago Press, 1966), 37–49.

F. H. Langham, "*Women in Love*," *EIC* 17 (1967): 183–206.

Robin Lee, "Darkness and 'A Heavy Gold Glamour': Lawrence's *Women in Love*," *Theoria* 42 (1974): 57–64.

Michael Levenson, "'The Passion of Opposition' in *Women in Love*: None, One, Two, Few, Many," *MLS* 17 (Spring 1987): 22–36.

Eric P. Levy, "Lawrence's Psychology of Void and Center in *Women in Love*," *DHLR* 23 (Spring 1991): 5–19.

Vida E. Markovic, "Ursula Brangwen," in *The Changing Face: Disintegration of Personality in the Twentieth-Century British Novel, 1900–1950* (Carbondale: Southern Illinois University Press, 1970), 19–37.

W. R. Martin, "'Freedom Together' in D. H. Lawrence's *Women in Love*," *ESA* 8 (1965): 111–20.

Youko Matsudaira, "Hermione Roddice in *Women in Love*," *SLRev* 18 (1984): 1–18.

Jeffrey Meyers, "Mark Gertler and *Women in Love*," in *Painting and the Novel* (Manchester, England: Manchester University Press, 1975), 65–82.

Thomas H. Miles, "Birkin's Electro-Mystical Body of Reality: D. H. Lawrence's Use of Kundalini," *DHLR* 9 (Summer 1976): 194–212.

Joyce Carol Oates, "Lawrence's Götterdämmrung: The Tragic Vision of *Women in Love*," *CritI* 4 (1978): 559–78.

Daniel O'Hara, "The Power of Nothing in *Women in Love*," *BuR* 28, no. 2 (1983): 151–64.

Jean Paul Pichardie, "*Women in Love*: Structures," *ÉLawr* 4 (May 1989): 7–19.

Colette Pirenet, "La Structure symbolique de *Women in Love*," *ÉA* 22 (1969): 137–51.

Norma Procopiow, "The Narrator's Stratagem in *Women in Love*," *CollL* 5 (1978): 114–24.

Catherine Rihoit, "D'une quete feminine de la connaissance dans *Women in Love*," *ÉLawr* 4 (May 1989): 87–104.

Shalom Rachman, "Art and Value in D. H. Lawrence's *Women in Love*," *DHLR* 5 (Spring 1972): 1–25.

Bryan D. Reddick, "Point of View and Narrative Tone in *Women in Love*: The Portrayal of Interpsychic Space," *DHLR* 7 (Summer 1974): 156–71.

Bryan D. Reddick, "Tension at the Heart of *Women in Love*," *ELT* 19 (1976): 73–86.

John Remsbury, "*Women in Love* as a Novel of Change," *DHLR* 6 (Summer 1973): 149–72.

Neil Roberts, "Lawrence's Tragic Lovers: The Story and the Tale in *Women in Love*," in *D. H. Lawrence: New Studies*, ed. Christopher Heywood (New York: St. Martin's, 1987), 34–45.

W. W. Robson, "D. H. Lawrence and *Women in Love*," in *The Modern Age*, 3d ed., ed. Boris Ford (Baltimore: Penguin, 1973), 280–300.

Charles L. Ross, "Homoerotic Feeling in *Women in Love*: Lawrence's 'Struggle for Verbal Consciousness' in the Manuscripts," in *D. H. Lawrence: The Man Who Lived*, ed. Robert B. Partlow and Harry T. Moore (Carbondale: Southern Illinois University Press, 1980), 168–82.

Charles L. Ross, "Introduction" and "Notes," in *Lawrence's "Women in Love,"* ed. Charles L. Ross (Harmondsworth, England: Penguin, 1982), 13–48; 585–93.

Ginette Katz Roy, "Les Arts plastiques et la mode dans *Women in Love*," *ÉLawr* 4 (May 1989): 53–70.

Barry J. Scherr, "Lawrence's 'Dark Flood:' A Platonic Interpretation of 'Excurse,'" *Paunch* 63–64 (December 1990): 209–46.

Claude Sinzelle, "Du poulpe à la rose dans 'Moony,'" *ÉLawr* 5 (May 1990): 77–96.

Yasu Ueyama, "Koisuru Onnatachi," in *Igirisu Bungaku: Kenkyu to Kansho 2*, ed. Yoshitsugu Uchida and Kishimoto Yoshitaka (Osaka: Sogensha, 1982), 53–67.

Thérèse Vichy, "Liberté et création dans *Women in Love*," *ÉLawr* 5 (May 1990): 7–19.

Thérèse Vichy, "Symbolisme et structures dans *Women in Love*," *ÉA* 33 (1980): 400–413.

Pierre Vitoux, "The Chapter 'Excurse' in *Women in Love*: Its Genesis and the Critical Problem," *TSLL* 17 (1976): 821–36.

Pierre Vitoux, "Le Fleuve souterrain dans *Women in Love*," *ÉA* 42 (January–March 1989): 13–26.

Sylvia Walsh, "*Women in Love*," *Soundings* 65 (Fall 1982): 352– 68.

Michael G. Yetman, "The Failure of the Un-Romantic Imagination in *Women in Love*," *Mosaic* 9 (Fall 1976): 83–98.

Yonghui Zhao, "A Fire Burning on Ice: On Lawrence and His *Women in Love*," *FLitS* 37 (September 1987): 32–36.

"The Woman Who Rode Away"

Peter Balbert, "Snake's Eye and Obsidian Knife: Art, Ideology, and 'The Women Who Rode Away,'" *DHLR* 18 (Summer–Fall 1986): 255–73.

Serena Cenni, "Fenomenologia dell'azione sospesa: D. H. Lawrence, 'The Woman Who Rode Away,'" in *Dal Novellino a Moravia: Problemi della narrativa*, ed. Ezio Raimondi and Bruno Basile (Bologna: Mulino, 1979), 167–79.

Constante Gonzalez Groba, "D. H. Lawrence y 'The Woman Who Rode Away': La imposible conexion entre dos mundos opuestos," *RCEI* 11 (November 1985): 35–46.

Sachidananda Mohanty, "'The Woman Who Rode Away': Defeat of Feminism?" *AJES* 14, no. 1 (1989): 96–107.

Bibhu Padhi, "'The Woman Who Rode Away' and Lawrence's Vision of the New World," *UDR* 17 (Winter 1985–86): 57–61.

Sigrid Renaux, "D. H. Lawrence's 'The Woman Who Rode Away': An Exploration," *EAA* 9–11 (1985–87): 68–88.

Laurence Steven, "'The Woman Who Rode Away': D. H. Lawrence's Cul de Sac," *ESC* 10 (June 1984): 209–20.

Therese Vichy, "L'Ironie dans 'The Woman Who Rode Away,'" *ÉLaw* 6 (May 1991): 69–81.

Mark Kinkead Weekes, "The Gringo Senora Who Rode Away," *DHLR* 22 (Fall 1990): 251–65.

LE CARRÉ, JOHN
(JOHN DAVID MOORE CORNWELL)

Call for the Dead

LynnDianne Beene, "A Brief History of a Sentimental Man: *Call for the Dead*," in *John le Carré* (Boston: Twayne, 1988), 28–36.

Helen S. Garson, "Enter George Smiley: Le Carré's *Call for the Dead*," *Clues* 3 (Fall–Winter 1982): 93–99.

John Kirk, "Introduction" in *The Incongruous Spy: "Call for the Dead" and "A Murder of Quality"* (New York: Walker, 1963), 1–4.

Peter Lewis, "A Far from Saintly George: *Call for the Dead*," in *John le Carré* (New York: Ungar, 1985), 14–39.

The Honourable Schoolboy

Tony Barley, "Sideshow: *The Honourable Schoolboy*," in *Taking Sides: The Fiction of John le Carré* (Philadelphia: Open University Press, 1986), 105–26.

LynnDianne Beene, "The Quest for Karla: *The Honourable Schoolboy*," in *John le Carré* (Boston: Twayne, 1988), 100–15.

James M. Buzard, "Faces, Photos, Mirrors: Image and Ideology in the Novels of John le Carré," *W&D* 7 (Spring 1989): 53–75. Reprinted in *Image and Ideology in Modern/Postmodern Discourse*, ed. David B. Downing and Susan Bazargan (Albany: State University of New York Press, 1991), 153–79.

Peter Lewis, "The Spy Who Went Into the Heat: *Honourable Schoolboy*," in *John le Carré* (New York: Ungar, 1985), 138–63.

Cheryl C. Powell, "*The Honourable Schoolboy*," in *Redemption for the Protagonist in Three Novels by John le Carré*, Ph.D. dissertation, Florida State University, 1991, 84–117.

The Little Drummer Girl

Tony Barley, "Taking Sides: *The Little Drummer Girl*," in *Taking Sides: The Fiction of John le Carré* (Philadelphia: Open University Press, 1986), 146–66.

LynnDianne Beene, "The Story within the Story within the Story: *The Little Drummer Girl*," in *John le Carré* (Boston: Twayne, 1988), 112–22.

Melvin Bragg, "*The Little Drummer Girl*: An Interview with John le Carré," in *The Quest for le Carré*, ed. Alan Bold (New York: St. Martin's, 1988), 129–43. [Interview that was first transmitted on the I.T.V. network, 27 March 1983.]

Julie Diamond, "Spies in the Promised Land: A Review Article," *R&C* 25 (1984): 35–40.

Peter Lewis, "A Country Not Ours to Give: *The Little Drummer Girl*," in *John le Carré* (New York: Ungar, 1985), 181–212.

Norman Moss, "Charlie: Fact and Fiction," *Telegraph* (15 July 1984): 16–17.

Brenda R. Silver, "Woman as Agent: The Case of Le Carré's *Little Drummer Girl*," *ConL* 28 (Spring 1987): 14–40.

The Looking-Glass War

Tony Barley, "Little Games: *The Looking-Glass War*," in *Taking Sides: The Fiction of John le Carré* (Philadelphia: Open University Press, 1986), 48–65

LynnDianne Beene, "Cold War Fiction: *The Looking-Glass War*," in *John le Carré* (Boston: Twayne, 1988), 60–65, 70–71.

Peter Lewis, "Peter Pan's Last Victim: *The Looking-Glass War*," in *John le Carré* (New York: Ungar, 1985), 78–95.

A Murder of Quality

LynnDianne Beene, "A Brief History of a Sentimental Man: *A Murder of Quality*," in *John le Carré* (Boston: Twayne, 1988), 36–45.

John Kirk, "Introduction" in *The Incongruous Spy: "Call for the Dead" and "A Murder of Quality"* (New York: Walker and Company, 1963), 4–7.

Peter Lewis, "An Exercise in Class: *A Murder of Quality*," in *John le Carré* (New York: Ungar, 1985), 40–58.

The Night Manager

Paul Berman, "*The Night Manager*," *NewR* 209 (9 August 1993): 35–37.

Nigel Fountain, "*The Night Manager*," *NewS&S* 6 (9 July 1993): 37–38.

Sean O'Brien, "*The Night Manager*," *TLS* (2 July 1993): 21.

David Remnick, "Le Carré's New World Order," *NYRB* 40 (12 August 1993): 20–23.

Julian Symons, "Our Man in Zurich," *NYTBR* 94 (27 June 1993): 1, 29.

The Naive and Sentimental Lover

LynnDianne Beene, "David and Jonathan: *The Naive and Sentimental Lover*," in *John le Carré* (Boston: Twayne, 1988), 77–87.

Betty Lou Dubois, "Regular Adverbs of Manner in Le Carré's *Naive and Sentimental Lover*: Shamus Demanded Testily, but Sandra Returned Peevishly, While Sal Waited Patiently, and Cassidy Retorted Churlishly," *SJL* 9, no. 2 (1990): 43–62.

Peter Lewis, "To Catch a Mole," in *John le Carré* (New York: Ungar, 1985), 113–15.

A Perfect Spy

LynnDianne Beene, "The Story within the Story within the Story: *A Perfect Spy*," in *John le Carré* (Boston: Twayne, 1988), 111–13, 123–28.

R. F. Brissenden, "*A Perfect Spy*: 'Like Huckleberry Finn,'" *Quadrant* 30 (December 1986): 45–49.

H. M. Daleski, "*A Perfect Spy* and a Great Tradition," *JNT* 20 (Winter 1990): 56–64.

Vivian Green, "*A Perfect Spy*: A Personal Reminiscence," in *The Quest for Le Carré*, ed. Alan Norman Bold (New York: St. Martin's, 1988), 25–40.

Gwen Griffiths, "Individual and Societal Entropy in le Carré's *A Perfect Spy*," *Critique* 31 (Winter 1990): 112–24.

Susan Laity, "'The Second Burden of a Former Child': Doubling and Repetition in *A Perfect Spy*," in *John le Carré*, ed. Harold Bloom (New York: Chelsea House, 1987): 137–64.

Thomas Loe, "The Double Plot in John Le Carré's *A Perfect Spy*," *NConL* 18 (September 1988): 5–7.

The Quest for Karla

LynnDianne Beene, "The Quest for Karla: The Quest for Smiley, Ann, and Karla," in *John le Carré* (Boston: Twayne, 1988), 92–110.

Thomas Michael Stein, "'A World Grown Old and Cold and Weary': Intertextuelle Referenzen in John Le Carres Trilogie *The Quest for Karla*," *A&E* 37 (1989): 113–30.

The Russia House

LynnDianne Beene, "The Story within the Story within the Story: *The Russia House*," in *John le Carré* (Boston: Twayne, 1988), 128–34.

Percy Kemp, "Les Nouveaux Traitres de John Le Carré," *Esprit* 157 (December 1989): 95–99.

Cheryl C. Powell, "*The Russia House*," in *Redemption for the Protagonist in Three Novels by John le Carré*, Ph.D dissertation, Florida State University, 1991, 118–45.

The Secret Pilgrim

LynnDianne Beene, "The Story within the Story within the Story: *The Secret Pilgrim*," in *John le Carré* (Boston: Twayne, 1988), 134–37.

Keith Jeffery, "*The Secret Pilgrim*," *TLS* (11 January 1991): 24.

A Small Town in Germany

Tony Barley, "A Sense of History: *A Small Town in Germany*," in *Taking Sides: The Fiction of John le Carré* (Philadelphia: Open University Press, 1986), 66–83.

LynnDianne Beene, "Cold War Fiction: The Distrusted Professional" in *John le Carré* (Boston: Twayne, 1988), 65–70.

Glenn W. Most, "The Hippocratic Smile: John le Carré and the Traditions of the Detective Novel," in *The Poetics of Murder: Detective Fiction & Literary Theory*, ed. Glenn W. Most and William W. Stowe, (New York: Harcourt, Brace, 1983), 362–64.

Smiley's People

Tony Barley, "The Sandman: *Smiley's People*," in *Taking Sides: The Fiction of John le Carré* (Philadelphia: Open University Press, 1986), 127–45.

LynnDianne Beene, "The Quest for Karla: *Smiley's People*," in *John le Carré* (Boston: Twayne, 1988), 105–11.

Peter Lewis, "Ahab Chasing His Big White Whale: *Smiley's People*," in *John le Carré* (New York: Ungar, 1985), 164–80.

The Spy Who Came in from the Cold

Tony Barley, "Cold Warriors: *The Spy Who Came in from the Cold*," in *Taking Sides: The Fiction of John le Carré* (Philadelphia: Open University Press, 1986), 27–47.

LynnDianne Beene, "Cold War Fiction: The Unreflective Professional," in *John le Carré* (Boston: Twayne, 1988), 49–59.

Robert Giddings, "The Writing on the Igloo Walls: Narrative Technique in *The Spy Who Came in from the Cold*," in *The Quest for Le Carré*, ed. Alan Norman Bold (New York: St. Martin's, 1988), 188–210.

Peter Lewis, "Blind Man's Double Bluff," in *John le Carré* (New York: Ungar, 1985), 59–77.

B. K. Martin, "Le Carré's *The Spy Who Came in from the Cold*: A Structuralist Reading," *SSEng* 14 (1988–89): 72–88.

Cheryl C. Powell, "*The Spy Who Came in from the Cold*," in *Redemption for the Protagonist in Three Novels by John le Carré*, Ph.D. dissertation, Flordia State University, 1991, 46–83.

LE CARRÉ, JOHN, *Tinker, Tailor, Soldier, Spy*

Tinker, Tailor, Soldier, Spy

Tony Barley, "Absent Friends: *Tinker, Tailor, Soldier, Spy*," in *Taking Sides: The Fiction of John le Carré* (Philadelphia: Open University Press, 1986), 84–104.

LynnDianne Beene, "The Quest for Karla: *Tinker, Tailor, Soldier, Spy*," in *John le Carré* (Boston: Twayne, 1988), 96–100.

Holly Beth King, "Child's Play in John Le Carré's *Tinker, Tailor, Soldier, Spy*," *Clues* 3 (Fall–Winter 1982): 87–92.

Victor Lasseter, "*Tinker, Tailor, Soldier, Spy*: A Story of Modern Love," *Critique* 31 (Winter 1990): 101–11.

Peter Lewis, "To Catch a Mole: *Tinker, Tailor, Solider, Spy*," in *John le Carré* (New York: Ungar, 1985), 116–37.

Glenn W. Most, "The Hippocratic Smile: John le Carré and the Traditions of the Detective Novel," in *The Poetics of Murder: Detective Fiction & Literary Theory*, ed. Glenn W. Most and William W. Stowe, (New York: Harcourt, Brace, 1983), 359–62.

LEE, TANITH

The Book of the Mad

Laura Pedrick, "*The Book of the Mad*: The Secret Books of Paradys, IV," *RCF* 13 (Fall 1993): 238–40.

The Silver Metal Lover

Sarah Lefanu, "Robots and Romance: The Science Fiction and Fantasy of Tanith Lee," in *Sweet Dreams: Sexuality, Gender and Popular Fiction*, ed. Susannah Radstone (London: Lawrence & Wishart, 1988), 121–36.

LE FANU, JOSEPH SHERIDAN

"An Account of Some Strange Disturbances in Aungier Street"

Ivan Melada, "'An Account of Some Strange Disturbances in Aungier Street,'" in *Sheridan Le Fanu* (Boston: Twayne, 1990), 120–22, 126.

"An Adventure of Hardress Fitzgerald"

Ivan Melada, "'An Adventure of Hardress Fitzgerald,'" *Sheridan Le Fanu* (Boston: Twayne, 1990), 17.

"All in the Dark"

Ivan Melada, "'All in the Dark,'" *Sheridan Le Fanu* (Boston: Twayne, 1990), 11, 68–69.

"The Authentic Narrative of a Haunted House"

Ivan Melada, "'The Authentic Narrative of a Haunted House,'" *Sheridan Le Fanu* (Boston: Twayne, 1990), 120.

"Bill Malowny's Taste for Love and Glory"

Ivan Melada, "'Bill Malowny's Taste for Love and Glory,'" *Sheridan Le Fanu* (Boston: Twayne, 1990), 13.

"The Bird of Passage"

Ivan Melada, "'The Bird of Passage,'" *Sheridan Le Fanu* (Boston: Twayne, 1990), 93.

"The Bridal of Carrivarah"

Ivan Melada, "'The Bridal of Carrivarah,'" *Sheridan Le Fanu* (Boston: Twayne, 1990), 15–17.

"Carmilla"

Nelson Browne, *Sheridan Le Fanu* (London: Arthur Barker, 1951): 83–85.

Ronald Foust, "Rite of Passage: The Vampire Tale as Cosmogonic Myth," in *Aspects of Fantasy: Selected Essays from the Second International Conference on the Fantastic in Literature and Film*, ed. William Coyle (Westport, CT: Greenwood, 1986), 73–84.

Mireille Magnier, "L'Art du conteur dans 'Carmilla,'" in *Linguistique, Civilisation, Littérature* (Paris: Didier, 1980), 268–74.

Ivan Melada, "'Carmilla,'" *Sheridan Le Fanu* (Boston: Twayne, 1990), 49, 94, 99–101.

Carol A. Senf, "Women and Power in 'Carmilla,'" *Gothic* 2 (1987): 25–33.

"A Chapter in the History of the Tyrone Family"

Ivan Melada, "'A Chapter in the History of the Tyrone Family,'" *Sheridan Le Fanu* (Boston: Twayne, 1990), 21, 83.

"Checkmate"

Ivan Melada, "'Checkmate,'" *Sheridan Le Fanu* (Boston: Twayne, 1990), 11.

"The Child That Went with the Fairies"

Ivan Melada, "'The Child That Went with the Fairies,'" *Sheridan Le Fanu* (Boston: Twayne, 1990), 110.

Chronicles of Golden Friars

Ivan Melada, "*Chronicles of Golden Friars*," *Sheridan Le Fanu* (Boston: Twayne, 1990), 11, 90–94.

"The Cock and Anchor"

Ivan Melada, "'The Cock and Anchor,'" *Sheridan Le Fanu* (Boston: Twayne, 1990), 9, 24–30, 4, 60.

"The Dead Sexton"

Ivan Melada, "'The Dead Sexton,'" *Sheridan Le Fanu* (Boston: Twayne, 1990), 111.

"Dickon the Devil"

Ivan Melada, "'Dickon the Devil,'" *Sheridan Le Fanu* (Boston: Twayne, 1990), 108–9.

"The Drunkard's Dream"

Ivan Melada, "'The Drunkard's Dream,'" *Sheridan Le Fanu* (Boston: Twayne, 1990), 20–21, 114–15.

"The Evil Guest"

Nelson Browne, *Sheridan Le Fanu* (London: Arthur Barker, 1951): 74–77.

Ivan Melada, "'The Evil Guest,'" *Sheridan Le Fanu* (Boston: Twayne, 1990), 9, 11, 44, 69–72, 83, 88.

"The Familiar"

Ivan Melada, "'The Familiar,'" *Sheridan Le Fanu* (Boston: Twayne, 1990), 9.

"The Fatal Bride"

Ivan Melada, "'The Fatal Bride,'" *Sheridan Le Fanu* (Boston: Twayne, 1990), 122.

"The Fortunes of Sir Robert Ardagh"

Ivan Melada, "'The Fortunes of Sir Robert Ardagh,'" *Sheridan Le Fanu* (Boston: Twayne, 1990), 18, 92.

"The Ghost and the Bonesetter"

Ivan Melada, "'The Ghost and the Bonesetter,'" *Sheridan Le Fanu* (Boston: Twayne, 1990), 8, 13, 14.

Ghost Stories and Tales of Mystery

Ivan Melada, "*Ghost Stories and Tales of Mystery*," *Sheridan Le Fanu* (Boston: Twayne, 1990), 9, 43.

"Ghost Stories of Chapelizod"

Ivan Melada, "'Ghost Stories of Chapelizod,'" *Sheridan Le Fanu* (Boston: Twayne, 1990), 115.

LE FANU, JOSEPH SHERIDAN, "Ghost Stories of Chapelizod"

"The Great Good Place"

Ivan Melada, "'The Great Good Place,'" *Sheridan Le Fanu* (Boston: Twayne, 1990), 96–7.

"Green Tea"

Ivan Melada, "'Green Tea,'" *Sheridan Le Fanu* (Boston: Twayne, 1990), 94–97, 101, 122, 126–28.

Guy Deverell

Ivan Melada, "*Guy Deverell*," *Sheridan Le Fanu* (Boston: Twayne, 1990), 11, 66–69, 73, 89, 126.

"The Haunted Baronet"

Ivan Melada, "'The Haunted Baronet,'" *Sheridan Le Fanu* (Boston: Twayne, 1990), 18–21, 91–92, 114–15.

"Haunted Lives"

Nelson Browne, *Sheridan Le Fanu* (London: Arthur Barker, 1951): 59–61.

The House by the Churchyard

David Gates, "'A Dish of Village Chat': Narrative Technique in Sheridan Le Fanu's *The House by the Churchyard*," *CJIS* 10 (June 1984): 63–69.

Audrey Peterson, "Joseph Sheridan Le Fanu: Horror and Suspense," in *Victorian Masters of Mystery: From Wilkie Collins to Conan Doyle* (New York: Ungar, 1984), 127–30.

"In a Glass Darkly"

Gary William Crawford, "Sheridan LeFanu and 'In a Glass Darkly,'" *Romantist* 4–5 (1980–81): 25–27.

Ivan Melada, "'In a Glass Darkly,'" *Sheridan Le Fanu* (Boston: Twayne, 1990), 9, 11, 94–101.

Harold Orel, "'Rigid Adherence to Facts': Le Fanu's 'In a Glass Darkly,'" *Éire* 20 (Winter 1985): 65–88.

Kel Roop, "Making Light in the Shadow Box: The Artistry of Le Fanu," *PLL* 21 (Fall 1985): 359–69.

"The Invisible Prince"

Ivan Melada, "'The Invisible Prince,'" *Sheridan Le Fanu* (Boston: Twayne, 1990), 12.

"Jim Sulivan's Adventures in the Great Dnow"

Ivan Melada, "'Jim Sulivan's Adventures in the Great Dnow,'" *Sheridan Le Fanu* (Boston: Twayne, 1990), 13.

"Justice Harbottle"

Ivan Melada, "'Justice Harbottle,'" *Sheridan Le Fanu* (Boston: Twayne, 1990), 94, 97–98.

"The Last Heir of Castle Connor"

Ivan Melada, "'The Last Heir of Castle Connor,'" *Sheridan Le Fanu* (Boston: Twayne, 1990), 2–3, 15, 16–17, 122.

"Laura Silver Bell"

Ivan Melada, "'Laura Silver Bell,'" *Sheridan Le Fanu* (Boston: Twayne, 1990), 112–13, 127.

A Lost Name

Ivan Melada, "*A Lost Name*," *Sheridan Le Fanu* (Boston: Twayne, 1990), 11, 16, 45, 69–72.

"Madam Crowl's Ghost"

Ivan Melada, "'Madam Crowl's Ghost,'" *Sheridan Le Fanu* (Boston: Twayne, 1990), 91.

"The Murdered Cousin"

Ivan Melada, "'The Murdered Cousin,'" *Sheridan Le Fanu* (Boston: Twayne, 1990), 9, 43, 50, 69.

"My Aunt Margaret's Adventure"

Ivan Melada, "'My Aunt Margaret's Adventure,'" *Sheridan Le Fanu* (Boston: Twayne, 1990), 122–24.

My Own Story; or Loved and Lost

Ivan Melada, "*My Own Story; or Loved and Lost,*" *Sheridan Le Fanu* (Boston: Twayne, 1990), 11.

"The Mysterious Lodger"

Jean Lozes, "'The Mysterious Lodger; Ou, Le Fanu a coeur ouvert,'" *ÉI* 12 (June 1987): 53–58.

Ivan Melada, "'The Mysterious Lodger,'" *Sheridan Le Fanu* (Boston: Twayne, 1990), 11, 117–20.

"Passage in the Secret History of an Irish Countess"

Ivan Melada, "'Passage in the Secret History of an Irish Countess,'" *Sheridan Le Fanu* (Boston: Twayne, 1990), 21–23, 43, 50, 69, 83, 91.

"The Quare Gander"

Ivan Melada, "'The Quare Gander,'" *Sheridan Le Fanu* (Boston: Twayne, 1990), 13, 14.

"Richard Marston"

Ivan Melada, "'Richard Marston,'" *Sheridan Le Fanu* (Boston: Twayne, 1990), 11, 69, 89.

"The Room in the Dragon Volant"

Ivan Melada, "'The Room in the Dragon Volant,'" *Sheridan Le Fanu* (Boston: Twayne, 1990), 98–99, 101.

The Rose and the Key

Ivan Melada, "*The Rose and the Key,*" *Sheridan Le Fanu* (Boston: Twayne, 1990), 11, 81, 83–86, 89.

"Schalken the Painter"

Gaid Girard, "Le Peintre et le sourire de Rose," in *Du Fantastique en littérature: Figures et figurations: Elements pour une poetique du fantastique sur quelques exemples anglo-saxons*, ed. Max Duperray (Aix-en-Provence: Université de Provence, 1990), 99–109.

Ivan Melada, "'Schalken the Painter,'" *Sheridan Le Fanu* (Boston: Twayne, 1990), 9, 18–20.

Kel Roop, "Making Light in the Shadow Box: The Artistry of Le Fanu," *PLL* 21 (Fall 1985): 359–69.

James Swafford, "Tradition and Guilt in Le Fanu's 'Schalken the Painter,'" *CJIS* 14 (January 1989): 48–59.

"Scraps of Hibernian Ballads"

Ivan Melada, "'Scraps of Hibernian Ballads,'" *Sheridan Le Fanu* (Boston: Twayne, 1990), 102.

"The Sexton's Adventure"

Ivan Melada, "'The Sexton's Adventure,'" *Sheridan Le Fanu* (Boston: Twayne, 1990), 105.

"Sir Dominick's Bargain"

Ivan Melada, "'Sir Dominick's Bargain,'" *Sheridan Le Fanu* (Boston: Twayne, 1990), 111–12.

"The Spectre Lovers"

Ivan Melada, "'The Spectre Lovers,'" *Sheridan Le Fanu* (Boston: Twayne, 1990), 108, 115, 116, 127.

"Squire Toby's Will"

Ivan Melada, "'Squire Toby's Will,'" *Sheridan Le Fanu* (Boston: Twayne, 1990), 117.

The Tenants of Malory

Ivan Melada, "*The Tenants of Malory*," *Sheridan Le Fanu* (Boston: Twayne, 1990), 11, 73–77, 78, 81, 83, 87, 126.

Torlogh O'Brien

Ivan Melada, "*Torlogh O'Brien*," *Sheridan Le Fanu* (Boston: Twayne, 1990), 3, 7, 9, 17, 30–34, 42.

"Ultor de Lacy"

Ivan Melada, "'Ultor de Lacy,'" *Sheridan Le Fanu* (Boston: Twayne, 1990), 108–10.

Uncle Silas

Nelson Browne, *Sheridan Le Fanu* (London: Arthur Barker, 1951): 111–15.

Marjorie Howes, "Misalliance and Anglo-Irish Tradition in Le Fanu's *Uncle Silas*," *NCF* 47 (September 1992): 164–86.

Ivan Melada, "*Uncle Silas*," *Sheridan Le Fanu* (Boston: Twayne, 1990), 11, 21–22, 41, 42–62, 63, 66, 69, 72, 83, 89, 91, 93, 125, 128.

Audrey Peterson, "Joseph Le Fanu," in *Victorian Masters of Mystery: From Wilkie Collins to Conan Doyle* (New York: Ungar, 1984), 141–54.

"The Village Bully"

Ivan Melada, "'The Village Bully,'" *Sheridan Le Fanu* (Boston: Twayne, 1990), 108.

"Vision of Tom Chuff"

Ivan Melada, "'Vision of Tom Chuff,'" *Sheridan Le Fanu* (Boston: Twayne, 1990), 114–16.

"The Watcher"

Ivan Melada, "'The Watcher,'" *Sheridan Le Fanu* (Boston: Twayne, 1990), 9, 97–8, 126.

"The White Cat of Drumgunniol"

Ivan Melada, "'The White Cat of Drumgunniol,'" *Sheridan Le Fanu* (Boston: Twayne, 1990), 111.

"Wicked Captain Walshawe of Wauling"

Ivan Melada, "'Wicked Captain Walshawe of Wauling,'" *Sheridan Le Fanu* (Boston: Twayne, 1990), 112–14, 127.

Willing to Die

Ivan Melada, "*Willing to Die*," *Sheridan Le Fanu* (Boston: Twayne, 1990), 11, 81, 86–89.

Wylder's Hand

Ivan Melada, "*Wylder's Hand*," *Sheridan Le Fanu* (Boston: Twayne, 1990), 11, 63–66, 73, 81, 89, 126.

Audrey Peterson, "Joseph Sheridan Le Fanu: Horror and Suspense," in *Victorian Masters of Mystery: From Wilkie Collins to Conan Doyle* (New York: Ungar 1984), 131–41.

John Paul Russo, "Isle of the Dead: Italy and the Uncanny in Arnold Bocklin, Sheridan Le Fanu, and James Russell Lowell," *RLAn* 1 (1989): 202–09.

The Wyvern Mystery

Ivan Melada, "*The Wyvern Mystery*," *Sheridan Le Fanu* (Boston: Twayne, 1990), 11, 21–23, 81–83.

LEHMANN, ROSAMOND

The Ballad and the Source

Sydney Janet Kaplan, "Rosamond Lehmann's 'The Ballad and the Source': A Confrontation with 'The Great Mother,'" *TCL* 27 (Summer 1981): 127–45.

The Echoing Grove

Panthea Reid Broughton, "Narrative License in 'The Echoing Grove,'" *SoCR* 1 (Spring–Summer 1984): 85–107.

LEWIS, C[LIVE] S[TAPLES]

The Chronicles of Narnia

Charles A. Huttar, "C. S. Lewis's *Narnia* and the 'Grand Design,'" in *The Longing for a Form: Essays on the Fiction of C. S. Lewis*, ed. Peter J. Schakel (Kent, OH: Kent State University Press, 1977), 119–35.

Elaine Tixier, "Imagination Baptized, or, 'Holiness' in the *Chronicles of Narnia*," in *The Longing for a Form: Essays on the Fiction of C. S. Lewis*, ed. Peter J. Schakel (Kent, OH: Kent State University Press, 1977), 136–58.

Jessica Yates, "Tolkien's Influence on *The Chronicles of Narnia*," *Mallorn* 18 (June 1982): 31–33.

Out of the Silent Planet

Evan K. Gibson, "The Solar Landscape: *Out of the Silent Planet*," in *C. S. Lewis: Spinner of Tales: A Guide to His Fiction* (Washington, DC: Christian College Consortium, 1980), 25–45.

Kath Filmer, "*Out of the Silent Planet*: Reconstructing Wells with a Few Shots at Shaw," *Inklings* 6 (1988): 43–54.

Sarah Larratt Keefer, "Houyhnhnms on Malacandra: C. S. Lewis and Jonathan Swift," *ANQ* 7, no. 14 (October 1994): 210–15.

Perelandra

Evan K. Gibson, "The Solar Landscape: *Perelandra*," in *C. S. Lewis: Spinner of Tales: A Guide to His Fiction* (Washington, DC: Christian College Consortium, 1980), 46–68.

Margaret P. Hannay, "A Preface to *Perelandra*," in *The Longing for a Form: Essays on the Fiction of C. S. Lewis*, ed. Peter J. Schakel (Kent, OH: Kent State University Press, 1977), 73–90.

The Silver Chair

John D. Cox, "Epistemological Release in *The Silver Chair*," in *The Longing for a Form: Essays on the Fiction of C. S. Lewis*, ed. Peter J. Schakel (Kent, OH: Kent State University Press, 1977), 159–68.

That Hideous Strength

Patrick J. Callahan, "The Two Gardens in C. S. Lewis's *That Hideous Strength*," in *SF: The Other Side of Realism. Essays on Modern Fantasy and Science Fiction*, ed. Thomas D. Clareson (Bowling Green, OH: Popular, 1971), 147–56.

Evan K. Gibson, "The Solar Landscape: *Perelandra*," in *C. S. Lewis: Spinner of Tales: A Guide to His Fiction* (Washington, DC: Christian College Consortium, 1980), 69–100.

Till We Have Faces

Sally A. Bartlett, "Humanistic Psychology in C. S. Lewis's *Till We Have Faces*: A Feminist Critique," *SLitI* 22 (Fall 1989): 185–94.

Joe R. Christopher, "Archetypal Patterns in *Till We Have Faces*," in *The Longing for a Form: Essays on the Fiction of C. S. Lewis*, ed. Peter J. Schakel (Kent, OH: Kent State University Press, 1977), 193–212.

Evan K. Gibson, "The Solar Landscape: *Till We Have Faces*," in *C. S. Lewis: Spinner of Tales: A Guide to His Fiction* (Washington, DC: Christian College Consortium, 1980), 221–57.

Steve J. Van der Weele, "From Mt. Olympus to Gloma: C. S. Lewis's Dislocation of Apuleis's *Cupid and Psyche* in *Till We Have Faces*," in *The Longing for a*

Form: Essays on the Fiction of C. S. Lewis, ed. Peter J. Schakel (Kent, OH: Kent State University Press, 1977), 182–92.

LEWIS, MATTHEW GREGORY

The Monk

Liliane Abensour, "Limites—non frontieres d'une oeuvre: *Le Moine* de M. G. Lewis," *Europe* 659 (March 1984): 13–18.

Fernand Baldensperger, "*Le Moine* de Lewis dans la littérature francaise," in *The English Gothic Novel: A Miscellany in Four Volumes*, ed. Thomas Meade Harwell (Salzburg: University of Salzburg, 1986), 170–90.

Max Duperroy, "*The Monk* de M. G. Lewis: Fantastique et melodrame," *ÉA* 40 (July–September 1987): 258–66.

Claude Fierobe, "Ordre et chaos dans *The Monk* de M. G. Lewis," *BSEAA* 21 (November 1985): 163–77.

Claude Fierobe, "La Topographie romanesque de M. G. Lewis dans *The Monk*," *ÉA* 39 (January– March 1986): 15–25.

Jean Gournay, "Erotisme, Sadisme et Perversion dans *The Monk*," in *L'Erotisme en Angleterre XVIIe–XVIIIe siècles*, ed. Jean Gournay (Publication de Université de Lille, 1992), 77–84.

Mark Hennelly, "'Putting My Eye to the Keyhole': Gothic Vision in *The Monk*," *JEP* 8 (August 1987): 289–305.

Gudrun Kauhl, "On the Release from Monkish Fetters: Matthew Lewis Reconsidered," *DQR* 19, no. 4 (1989): 264–80.

Wendy Jones, "Stories of Desire in *The Monk*," *ELH* 57 (Spring 1990): 129–50.

D. L. MacDonald, "The Erotic Sublime: The Marvellous in *The Monk*," *ESC* 18 (Summer 1992): 273–85.

M. Magnier, "*Le Moine* et les superstitions papistes," *MCRel* 1 (1983): 95–105.

Jean Marigny, "*The Monk* de M. G. Lewis et la pensée revolutionnaire," *Cycnos* 5 (1989): 105–12.

Nancy Caplan Mellerski, "The Exploding Matrix: The Episode of the Bleeding Nun in M. G. Lewis's *Monk*," in *Forms of the Fantastic*, ed., Jan Hokenson and Howard D. Pearce (Westport, CT: Greenwood, 1986), 41–47.

Tiziana Sabbadini, "*The Monk* di M. G. Lewis e l'attesa di svelamento," *LetP* 15 (December 1984): 69–73.

R. J. Schork, "Lewis' *The Monk*," *Expl* 44 (Spring 1986): 26–29.

Takao Tomijima, "Shudosha no Taihi Kozo," in *Shiro to Memai: Goshikku o Yomu*, ed. Shigeru Koike, Masao Shimura, and Takao Tomiyama (Tokyo: Kokusho Kankokai, 1982), 374–89.

Daniel P. Watkins, "Social Hierarchy in Matthew Lewis's *The Monk*," *SNNTS* 18 (Summer 1986): 115–24.

LEWIS, WYNDHAM

The Apes of God

Paul Edwards, "Augustan and Related Allusions in *The Apes of God*," *EN* 24 (Summer 1987): 17–21.

Hugh Kenner, "Wyndham Lewis: The Satirist as Barbarian," *English Satire and the Satiric Tradition*, ed. Claude Rawson (Oxford: Blackwell, 1984), 264–75.

The Childermass

Paul Tiessen, "Wyndham Lewis's *The Childermass* (1928): The Slaughter of the Innocents in the Age of Cinema," in *Apocalyptic Visions Past and Present: Selected Papers from Eighth & Ninth Annual Florida State University Conference on Literature & Film*, ed. JoAnn James and William J. Cloonan (Tallahassee: Florida State University Press, 1988), 25–35.

"Creativity"

Bernard Lafourcade, "'Creativity' en famille: A Study in Genetic Manipulations," in *Blast 3*, ed. Seamus Cooney, Bradford Morrow, Bernard Lafourcade, and Hugh Kenner (Santa Barbara, CA: Black Sparrow, 1984), 201–4.

Mrs. Duke's Millions

Anne Quema, "Mrs. Duke's Millions: A Mystery," *EN* 27 (Winter 1988): 12–16.

Revenge for Love

Reed Dasenbrock, "Wyndham Lewis's Fascist Imagination and the Fiction of Paranoia," *Fascism, Aesthetics, and Culture*, ed. Richard Golsan, (Hanover, NH: University Press of New England, 1992), 81–97.

Jeffrey Meyers, "Van Gogh and Lewis' *Revenge for Love*," *MFS* 29 (Summer 1983): 235–39.

John Russell, "Proletarian Tragedy: Wyndham Lewis' *Revenge for Love*," *ModA* 27 (Winter 1983): 61–66.

"Sigismund"

Alan Soons, "Sigismundo, Delbora and Wyndham Lewis's 'Sigismund,'" *Arcadia* 19, no. 2 (1984): 170–74.

Snooty Baronet

Reed Way Dasenbrock, "Lewis's Sources for the Persian Settings of *Snooty Baronet*," *EN* 22 (Spring 1986): 42–49.

Tarr

Peter Burger, "Subjektauflosung und verhartetes Ich: Moderne und Avantgarde in Wyndham Lewis' Kunstlerroman *Tarr*," in *Die Modernisierung des Ich: Studien zur Subjektkonstitution in der Vor- und Fruhmoderne*, ed. Manfred Pfister (Passau: Rothe, 1989), 286–92.

Michael Levenson, "Form's Body: Wyndham Lewis's *Tarr*," *MLQ* 45 (September 1984): 241–62.

Walter Michel, "On the Date of Writing of *Tarr*," *EN* 28 (Summer 1989): 22–23.

Walter Michel, "On the Genesis of *Tarr*," *EN* 22 (Spring 1986): 38–41.

Anne Quema, "*Tarr* and the Vortex," *EN* 26 (Summer 1988): 15–19.

Richard W. Sheppard, "Wyndham Lewis's *Tarr*: An (Anti-)Vorticist Novel?" *JEGP* 88 (October 1989): 510–30.

Alan Starr, "*Tarr* and Wyndham Lewis," *ELH* 49 (Spring 1982): 179–89.

Ina Verstl, "*Tarr*—A Joke Too Deep for Laughter? The Comic, the Body and Gender," *EN* 33 (Winter 1991): 4–9.

Michael Wutz, "The Energetics of *Tarr*: The Vortex-Machine Kreisler," *MFS* 38 (Winter 1992): 845–69.

The Wild Body

David Corbett, "Lewis's Construction of an Authorial Persona in the *Wild Body* Stories," *EN* 28 (Summer 1989): 4–15.

LODGE, DAVID

How Far Can You Go?

Beata Streichsbier, "Irony in David Lodge's *How Far Can You Go?*" in *A Yearbook in English Language and Literature*, ed. Max Gauna and Siegfried Korninger (Vienna: Braumuller, n.d), 97–110.

Nice Work

Robert S. Burton, "Standoff at the Crossroads: When Town Meets Gown in David Lodge's *Nice Work*," *Critique* 35 (Summer 1994): 237–43.

Small World

Maria Teresa Gilbert Maceda, "*Small World* . . . y baldio," *RAEI* 2 (November 1989): 83–90.

Frederick M. Holmes, "The Reader as Discoverer in David Lodge's *Small World*," *Critique* 32 (Fall 1990): 47–57.

Stuart Laing, "The Three Small Worlds of David Lodge," *CRSur* 3, no. 3 (1991): 324–30.

Siegfried Mews, "The Professor's Novel: David Lodge's *Small World*," *MLA* 104 (April 1989): 713–26.

Werner Wolf, "Literaturtheorie in der Literatur: David Lodges *Small World* als kritische Auseinandersetzung mit dem Dekonstruktivismus," *ArAA* 14, no. 1 (1989): 19–37.

LOWERY, MALCOLM

Dark as the Grave Wherein My Friend Is Laid

Elizabeth D. Rankin, "Writer as Metaphor in Malcolm Lowry's *Dark as the Grave*," *TCL* 28 (Fall 1982): 319–34.

"Elephant and Colosseum"

Elizabeth D. Rankin, "Malcolm Lowry's Comic Vision: 'Elephant and Colosseum,'" *CanL* 101 (Summer 1984): 167–71.

LOWERY, MALCOLM, "The Forest Path to the Spring"

"The Forest Path to the Spring"

Regis Durand, "'The Forest Path to the Spring' (Malcolm Lowry): Evenements d'espace," *RANAM* 16 (1983): 121–30.

"Hear Us, O Lord, from Heaven Thy Dwelling-Place"

Sherrill E. Grace, "'A Sound of Singing': Polyphony and Narrative Decentering in Malcolm Lowry's 'Hear Us O Lord,'" in *Modes of Narrative: Approaches to American, Canadian and British Fiction*, ed. Reingard M. Nischik and Barbara Korte (Wurzburg: Konigshausen & Neumann, 1990), 129–40.

Keith Harrison, "Malcolm Lowry's 'Hear Us O Lord': Visions and Revisions of the Past," *SCL* 6, NO. 2 (1981): 245–55.

Lunar Caustic

Keith Harrison, "Lowry's Allusions to Melville in *Lunar Caustic*," *CanL* 94 (Autumn 1982): 180–84.

Norman Newton, "The Loxodromic Curve: A Study of *Lunar Caustic* by Malcolm Lowry," *CanL* 126 (Autumn 1990): 65–86.

Mark Thomas, "Rereading Lowry's *Lunar Caustic*," *CanL* 112 (Spring 1987): 195–97.

October Ferry to Gabriola

Richard Hauer Costa, "The Man Who Would Be Steppenwolf," *SoCB* 42 (Winter 1982): 125–27.

Keith Harrison, "Malcolm Lowry's *October Ferry to Gabriola*: Balancing Time," *SCL* 7, no. 1 (1982): 115–21.

Antonio-Prometeo Moya, "Sobre la ultima novela de Malcolm Lowry," *Pasajes* 7 (1987): 41–51.

Through the Panama

Sherrill Grace, "'An Assembly of Apparently Incongruous Parts': Intertextuality in Lowry's *Through the Panama*," in *Proceedings of the London Conference on Malcolm Lowry 1984*, ed. Gordon Bowker and Paul Tiessen (London: Goldsmiths' College, University of London, 1985), 135–65.

Sherrill Grace, "'Listen to the Voice': Dialogism and the Canadian Novel," in *Future Indicative: Literary Theory and Canadian Literature*, ed. John Moss (Ottawa: University of Ottawa Press; 1987), 117–36.

Ultramarine

Norman Newton, "Celestial Machinery: A Study of *Ultramarine*," *MLNew* 27 (Fall 1990): 62–82.

Norman Newton, "Celestial Machinery: A Study of *Ultramarine*," *MLNew* 26 (Spring 1990): 19–45.

Norman Newton, "Celestial Machinery: A Study of *Ultramarine*," *MLNew* 23–24 (Fall 1988–Spring 1989): 93–132.

Elizabeth D. Rankin, "Beyond Autobiography: Art and Life in Malcolm Lowry's *Ultramarine*," *SCL* 6, no. 1 (1981): 53–64.

Under the Volcano

Chris J. Ackerley, "Barbarous Mexico and *Under the Volcano*," *N&Q* 31 (March 1984): 81–83.

Chris J. Ackerley, "The Consul's Book," *MLNew* 23–24 (Fall–Spring 1988–89): 78–92.

Chris J. Ackerley, "The Kashmiri Elements of *Under the Volcano*," *N&Q* 30 (August 1983): 331–33.

Chris J. Ackerley, "Lowry's Tlaxcala," *MLNew* 13 (Fall 1983): 17–30.

Chris J. Ackerley, "Malcolm Lowry's Quauhnahuac," *MLNew* 12 (Spring 1983): 14–29.

Chris J. Ackerley, "The Many and Various Threads," *MLNew* 17–18 (Fall–Spring 1985–86): 134–35.

Chris J. Ackerley, "Mexican History and *Under the Volcano*," *MLNew* 15 (Fall 1984): 24–44.

Chris J. Ackerley, "Mexican History and *Under the Volcano*: Part 2," *MLNew* 16 (Spring 1985): 32–52.

Chris J. Ackerley, "Salud y pesetas . . . y tiempo para guerrear," *MLNew* 17–18 (Fall–Spring 1985–86): 136–37.

Chris J. Ackerley, "Some Notes towards *Under the Volcano*," *CanL* 95 (Winter 1982): 185–90.

LOWERY, MALCOLM, *Under the Volcano*

Chris J. Ackerley, "Strange Comfort," *MLNew* 9 (Fall 1981): 31–33

Chris J. Ackerley, "*Under the Volcano*: A Check-List of Unknown Details," *MLNew* 17–18 (Fall–Spring 1985–86): 121–33.

Chris J. Ackerley, "*Under the Volcano*: Four Notes," *MLNew* 11 (Fall 1982): 13–16.

Chris J. Ackerley, "*Under the Volcano* and the Spanish Civil War," *MLNew* 14 (Spring 1984): 4–25.

Chris J. Ackerley, "The 'White Alps' of *Under the Volcano*," *MLNew* 17–18 (Fall–Spring 1985–86): 138–39.

Chris J. Ackerley and Lawrence J. Clipper, *A Companion to Under the Volcano* (Vancouver: University of British Columbia Press, 1984), 1–476.

Frederick Asals, "Lowry's Use of Indian Sources in *Under the Volcano*," *JML* 16 (Summer 1989): 113–40.

Frederick Asals, "Revision and Illusion in *Under the Volcano*," in *Swinging the Maelstrom: New Perspectives on Malcolm Lowry*, ed. Sherrill Grace (Montreal & Kingston: McGill-Queen's University Press, 1992), 93–111.

Shyam M. Asnani, "In Love With Damnation: A Study of Malcom Lowry's *Under the Volcano*," *PURB* 15 (October 1984): 3–12.

Ronald Binns, "Materialism and Magic," in *Malcolm Lowry: "Under the Volcano": A Casebook*, ed. Gordon Bowker (London: Macmillan, 1987), 172–86.

Ronald Binns, "The Q-Ship Incident: The Historical Source," *MLNew* 8 (Spring 1981): 5–7.

Gordon Bowker, "And the Truth of the World Became Apparent," in *Apparently Incongruous Parts: The Worlds of Malcolm Lowry*, ed. Paul Tiessen (Metuchen, NJ: Scarecrow, 1990), 3–10.

Marilyn Champan, "'Alastor': The Spirit of *Under the Volcano*," *SCL* 6, no. 2 (1981): 256–72.

Larry Clipper, "A Note on the Wibberlee Wobberlee Song," *MLNew* 10 (Spring 1982): 20–22.

Richard Hauer Costa, "The Grisly Graphics of Malcolm Lowry," *CollL* 11 (Fall 1984): 250–57. Reprinted in *Proceedings of the London Conference on Malcolm Lowry 1984*, ed. Gordon Bowker and Paul Tiessen (London: Goldsmiths' College, University of London, 1985), 98–106.

Michael Cripps, "Lost in the Wilderness: The Puritan Theme in *Under the Volcano*," *ESC* 10 (December 1984): 457–75.

Michael Cripps, "*Under the Volcano*: The Politics of the Imperial Self," *CanL* 95 (Winter 1982): 85–101.

Tara Cullis, "Science and Literature in the Twentieth Century," *CanL* 96 (Spring 1983): 87–101

Joost Daalder, "Some Renaissance Elements in Malcolm Lowry's *Under the Volcano*," *ANQ* 21 (March–April 1983): 115–16.

Hallvard Dahlie, "'A Norwegian at Heart': Lowry and the Grieg Connection," in *Swinging the Maelstrom: New Perspectives on Malcolm Lowry*, ed. Sherrill Grace (Montreal & Kingston: McGill-Queen's University Press, 1992), 31–42.

Joseph Dobrinsky, "Notes pour une psycholecture de *Under the Volcano*," in *Linguistique, civilisation, littérature*, pref. Andre Bordeaux (Paris: Didier, 1980), 276–78.

Victor Doyen, "Elements Towards a Spatial Reading," in *Malcolm Lowry: "Under the Volcano": A Casebook*, ed. Gordon Bowker (London: Macmillan, 1987), 101–13.

Dale Edmonds, "A Mosaic of Doom: A Reading of the 'Immediate Level,'" in *Malcolm Lowry: "Under the Volcano": A Casebook*, ed. Gordon Bowker (London: Macmillan, 1987), 114–29.

Wilfrid Eggleston, "Writer's Notebook: Wilfrid Eggleston on Malcolm Lowry," *MLNew* 29–30 (Fall–Spring 1991–92): 78–102.

David Falk, "The Descent into Hell of Jacques Laruelle: Chapter I of *Under the Volcano*," *CanL* 112 (Spring 1987): 72–83.

David Falk, "Self and Shadow: The Brothers Firmin in *Under the Volcano*," *TSLL* 27 (Summer 1985): 209–23.

Ileana Galea, "Romanul La poalele vulcanului in traditia literara britanica," *Steaua* 37 (March 1986): 54–55.

Thomas B. Gilmore, "The Place of Hallucinations in *Under the Volcano*," *ConL* 23 (Summer 1982): 285–305.

Sherrill Grace, "The Consul's 'Contiguity' Disorder," *MLNew* 13 (Fall 1983): 31–34.

Sherrill Grace, "The Luminous Wheel," in *Malcolm Lowry: "Under the Volcano": A Casebook*, ed. Gordon Bowker (London: Macmillan, 1987), 152–71.

LOWERY, MALCOLM, *Under the Volcano*

Dana A. Grove, "Two Notes," *MLNew* 17–18 (Fall–Spring 1985–86): 140–42.

Duncan Hadfield, "Laruelle's Left Cut: An Observation," *MLNew* 21–22 (Fall–Spring 1987–88): 133–40.

Duncan Hadfield, "Under the Tarot: A Reading of a Volcanic Sub-Level," *MLNew* 23–24 (Fall–Spring 1988–89): 40–77.

Duncan Hadfield, "*Under the Volcano* and Gogol's 'Diary of a Madman,'" *MLNew* 16 (Spring 1985): 78–81.

Duncan Hadfield, "*Under the Volcano*'s 'Central' Symbols: Trees, Towers and Their Variants," in *Proceedings of the London Conference on Malcolm Lowry 1984*, ed. Gordon Bowker and Paul Tiessen (London: Goldsmiths' College, University of London, 1985), 107–34.

Duncan Hadfield, "*Under the Volcano*'s Colour Fields," *MLNew* 19–20 (Spring–Fall 1986–87): 82–102.

Keith Harrison, "Allusions in *Under the Volcano*: Function and Pattern," *SCL* 9, no. 2 (1984): 224–32.

Keith Harrison, "Indian Traditions and *Under the Volcano*," *LHY* 23 (January 1982): 43–59.

Keith Harrison, "The Myth of Oedipus in *Under the Volcano*," *MLNew* 11 (Fall 1982): 16–19.

Keith Harrison, "'Objectivisation' in *Under the Volcano*: The Modernism of Eliot, Joyce, and Pound," *MLNew* 10 (Spring 1982): 14–17.

Keith Harrison, "The Philoctetes Myth in *Under the Volcano*," *MLNew* 10 (Spring 1982): 3–5.

Arnt Lykke Jakobsen, "Malcolm Lowry's *Under the Volcano*," in *Papers from the First Nordic Conference for English Studies*, ed. Stig Johansson and Bjorn Tysdahl (Oslo: Institute of English Studies, University of Oslo, 1981), 83–94.

D. B. Jewison, "The Uses of Intertextuality in *Under the Volcano*," in *Swinging the Maelstrom: New Perspectives on Malcolm Lowry*, ed. Sherrill Grace (Montreal & Kingston: McGill-Queen's University Press, 1992), 136–45.

Suzanne Kim, "*Autour du Volcan* (de) Malcolm Lowry," in *Linguistique, Civilisation, Littérature*, pref. Andre Bordeaux (Paris: Didier, 1980), 279–87.

Suzanne Kim, "Le Récit piège de *Under the Volcano*," *ÉA* 43 (January–March 1990): 55–73.

Russell Lowry, "Clearing Up Some Problems," *MLNew* 21–22 (Fall–Spring 1987–88): 100–04.

Russell Lowry, "Note on the Spring 1982 Note on the Wibbly Wobbly Song," *MLNew* 11 (Fall 1982): 10–12.

Patrick McCarthy, "Wrider/Espider: The Consul as Artist in *Under the Volcano*," *SCL* 17, no. 1 (1992): 30–51.

Catherine MacGregor, "Conspiring with the Addict: Yvonne's Co-Dependency in *Under the Volcano*," *Mosaic* 24 (Summer 1991): 145–62.

Jean Mambrino, "Mon ombre est la votre ou le voyage sans fin de Malcolm Lowry," *Études* 362 (January 1985; February 1985): 51–63; 211–222.

Betsy Martinez, "Saludy pesetas y amor . . . y sentido comun," *MLNew* 19–20 (Fall–Spring 1986–87): 127–28.

Betsy Martinez, "*Under the Volcano*: The Opening Sense of Closure," *MLNew* 21–22 (Fall–Spring 1987–88): 141–53.

Oscar Mata, "Lowry: A cincuenta anos de su descenso a Mexico," *Plural* 16 (September 1987): 82–90.

Tom Middlebro', "The Political Strand in Malcolm Lowry's *Under the Volcano*," *SCL* 7, no. 1 (1982): 122–26.

Micheline Miro, "Masques et mascarades: Les Representations de l'homme–dieu dans *Under the Volcano*," *ÉA* 43 (April–June 1990): 169–80.

Ken Moon, "Lowry's *Under the Volcano*," *Expl* 46 (Spring 1988): 37–39.

Kenneth Moon, "Lowry's *Under the Volcano* and Coleridge's 'Kubla Khan,'" *Expl* 44 (Winter 1986): 44–46.

Kenneth Moon, "Lowry's *Under the Volcano*," *Expl* 46 (Spring 1988): 37–39.

Miguel Morey, "Las desventuras del Buen Samaritano," *Quimera* 53 (n.d.): 32–37.

Lazlo Moussong, "*Bajo el volcan*: Un falso mito," *Plural* 16 (September 1987): 82–90.

Joan Mulholland, "The Consul as Communicator: The Voice *Under the Volcano*," in *Swinging the Maelstrom: New Perspectives on Malcolm Lowry*, ed. Sherrill Grace (Montreal & Kingston: McGill-Queen's University Press, 1992), 112–22.

Udo Nattermann, "Color in Malcolm Lowry's *Under the Volcano*," *MLNew* 19–20 (Fall–Spring 1986–87): 103–13.

Brian O'Kill, "Aspects of Language in *Under the Volcano*," in *Malcolm Lowry: "Under the Volcano": A Casebook*, ed. Gordon Bowker (London: Macmillan, 1987), 36–57.

Christine Pagnoulle and Maria Mercedes Gomis, "Mas alla de los espejos," *Quimera* 53 (n.d.): 38–43.

Juan Garcia Ponce, "Un descenso a los infiernos," *Quimera* 53 (n.d.): 44–47.

Andrew J. Pottinger, "The Consul's 'Murder,'" in *Malcolm Lowry: "Under the Volcano": A Casebook*, ed. Gordon Bowker (London: Macmillan, 1987), 130–42.

Christine Ramsay, "Apocalyptic Visions, Alcoholic Hallucinations, and Modernism: The (Gendered) Signs of Drinking and Death in *Under the Volcano*," *Dionysos* 3 (Winter 1992): 21–35.

Audrie Rankin, "Malcolm Lowry and the Old Man: A Reconciliation," *MLNew* 19–20 (Fall–Spring 1986–87): 56–81.

David Rosenwasser, "'Folded upon Itself, a Burning Castle': The End(s) of the Word in *Under the Volcano*," *EIL* 17 (Fall 1990): 22–31.

Carole Slade and Carmen Virgili, "Yvonne: Eve-One," *Quimera* 53 (n.d.): 48–52.

John Spencer, "Saving Lowry's Eden," *MLNew* 19–20 (Spring–Fall 1986–87): 131–38.

Hilda Thomas, "Praxis as Prophylaxis: A Political Reading of *Under the Volcano*," in *Swinging the Maelstrom: New Perspectives on Malcolm Lowry*, ed. Sherrill Grace (Montreal & Kingston: McGill-Queen's University Press, 1992), 82–92.

Paul Tiessen, "Something Forgotten, Something Lost: Gerald Noxon and the Creation of *Under the Volcano*," in *Proceedings of the London Conference on Malcolm Lowry 1984*, ed. Gordon Bowker and Paul Tiessen (London: Goldsmiths' College, University of London, 1985), 37–44.

Sue Vice, "Dreams—Visions—Metaphor: The Images of Manuel Alvarez Bravo and Malcolm Lowry," *MLNew* 15 (Fall 1984): 19–24.

Sue Vice, "The Mystique of Mezcal," *CanL* 112 (Spring 1987): 197–202.

Sue Vice, "The Volcano of the Postmodern Lowry," in *Swinging the Maelstrom: New Perspectives on Malcolm Lowry*, ed. Sherrill Grace (Montreal & Kingston: McGill-Queen's University Press, 1992), 123–35.

Carmen Virgili, "Hugh, la juventud del consul," *Quimera* 53 (n.d.): 54–61.

Ronald G. Walker, "'The Weight of the Past': Toward a Chronology of *Under the Volcano*," *MLNew* 9 (Fall 1981): 3–23.

Barry Wood, "'The Strands of Novel, Confession, Anatomy and Romance,'" in *Malcolm Lowry: "Under the Volcano": A Casebook*, ed. Gordon Bowker (London: Macmillan, 1987), 142–51.

Thomas York, "The Post-Mortem Point of View in Malcolm Lowry's *Under the Volcano*," *CanL* 99 (Winter 1983): 35–46.

Ornella De Zordo, "*Under the Volcano* e i due tempi del modernismo di Malcolm Lowry," *LetP* 13 (December 1982): 71–83.

MACDONALD, GEORGE

At the Back of the North Wind

Roderick McGillis, "Language and Secret Knowledge in *At the Back of the North Wind*," in *Proceedings of the Seventh Annual Conference of the Children's Literature Association* (Baylor University, March, 1980), ed. Priscilla A. Ord (New Rochelle, NY: Department of English, Iona College, 1982), 120–27.

Roderick F. McGillis, "Language and Secret Knowledge in *At the Back of the North Wind*," *DUJ* 73 (June 1981): 191–98.

"The Day Boy and the Night Girl"

Cynthia Marshall, "Allegory, Orthodoxy, Ambivalence: MacDonald's 'The Day Boy and the Night Girl,'" *ChildL* 16 (1988): 57–75.

The Golden Key

Cynthia Marshall, "Reading *The Golden Key*: Narrative Strategies of Parable," *CLAQ* 14 (Spring 1989): 22–25.

Lilith

Kath Filmer, "La Belle Dame sans merci: Cultural Criticism and the Mythopoeic Imagination in George MacDonalds's *Lilith*," *Mythlore* 15 (Summer 1989): 17–20.

Rolland Hein, "'Whence Came the Fantasia?' The Good Dream in George MacDonald's *Lilith*," *North Wind* 3 (1984): 27–40.

Roderick F. McGillis, "George MacDonald and the Lilith Legend in the XIX Century," *Mythlore* 6 (Winter 1979): 3–11.

Michael Mendelson, "George MacDonald's *Lilith* and the Conventions of Ascent," *StSL* 20 (1985): 197–218.

Karen Schaafsma, "The Demon Lover: *Lilith* and the Hero in Modern Fantasy," *Extrapolation* 28 (Spring 1987): 52–61.

Jeanne Murray Walker, "The Demoness and the Grail: Deciphering MacDonald's *Lilith*," *The Scope of the Fantastic: Culture, Biography, Themes, Children's Literature: Selected Essays from 1st International Conference on Fantastic in Literature & Film*, ed. Robert A. Collins and Howard D. Pearce III (Westport, CT: Greenwood, 1985), 179–90.

Phantastes

Sylvia Bruce, "Entering the Vision: A Novelist's View of *Phantastes*," *Seven* 9 (1988): 19–28.

Susan E. Howard, "In Search of Spiritual Maturity: George MacDonald's *Phantastes*," *Extrapolation* 30 (Fall 1989): 280–92.

Oriana Palusci, " 'The Road into Fairy-Land': Phantastes di George MacDonald," in *Nel tempo del sogno: Le forme della narrativa fantastica dall'immaginario vittoriano all'utopia contemporanea*, ed. Carlo Pagetti (Ravenna: Longo, 1988), 11–34.

John Pennington, "*Phantastes* as Metafiction: George MacDonald's Self-Reflexive Myth," *Mythlore* 14 (Spring 1988): 26–29.

Max Keith Sutton, "The Psychology of the Self in MacDonald's *Phantastes*," *Seven* 5 (1984): 9–25.

Keith Wilson, "The Quest for 'The Truth': A Reading of George MacDonald's *Phantastes*," *ÉA* 34 (April–June 1981): 141–52.

"The Princess and the Goblin"

Roderick McGillis, " 'If You Call Me Grandmother, That Will Do,' " *Mythlore* 6 (Summer 1979): 27–28.

Michael Steig, "Reading Outside Over There," *ChildL* 13 (1985): 139–53.

Lesley Willis, " 'Born Again': The Metamorphosis of Irene in George MacDonald's 'The Princess and the Goblin,' " *ScLJ* 12 (May 1985): 24–39.

MCEWAN, IAN

Black Dogs

Bette Pesetsky, "Irreconcilable Passions," *NYTBR* 97 (8 November 1992): 7, 9.

Jack Slay Jr., "An the Walls Came Tumbling Down: *The Innocent and Black Dogs*," in *Ian McEwan* (New York: Twayne, 1996), 140–45.

"The Butterflies"

Jack Slay Jr., "A Shock into Literature: *First Love, Last Rites*," in *Ian McEwan* (New York: Twayne, 1996), 25–27.

The Cement Garden

Max Duperray, "Insolite modernite: *The Cement Garden* (1979) d'Ian McEwan: Chef-d'oeuvre d'une nouvelle litterature de l'angoisse," *ÉA* 35 (October–December 1982): 420–29.

Viktors Freibergs, "Rituali pilsetas," *Gramata* 2 (February 1991): 77–79.

Ian Hamilton, "Points of Departure," *New Reviews* 5, no. 2 (1978): 9–21.

Gerard Klaus, "Le Monstrueux et la dialectique du pur et de l'impur dans *The Cement Garden* de Ian McEwan," Actes du Colloque, Aix-en-Provence, 19-20 Avril 1985, in *Le Monstrueux dans la littérature et la pensée anglaises*, ed. Nadia J. Rigaud (Aix-en-Provence: Publications Université de Provence, 1985), 239–50.

Pal Gerhard Olsen, "Litteraturens nodvendige ubehag," *Samtiden* 1 (1987): 41.

Jack Slay Jr., "The Momentum of Childhood Fantasy: *The Cement Garden*," in *Ian McEwan* (New York: Twayne, 1996), 35–50.

Wolfgang Wicht, "Ian McEwan: Der Zementgarten," *WB* 36, no. 7 (1990): 1146–156.

The Child in Time

Jack Slay Jr., "Vandalizing Time: Ian McEwan's *The Child in Time*," *Critique* 35 (Summer 1994): 205–18.

The Comfort of Strangers

J. R. Banks, "A Gondola Named Desire," *CritQ* 24 (Summer 1982): 27–31.

MCEWAN, IAN, "Conversations with a Cupboard Man"

Max Duperray, "L'Etranger dans le contexte post-moderniste: *The Comfort of Strangers* d'Ian McEwan," in *L'Etranger dans la littérature et la pensée anglaises*, ed. N. J. Rigaud (Aix-en-Provence: Université de Provence, 1989), 291–306.

Viktors Friebergs, "Rituali pilsetas," *Gramata* 2 (February 1991): 77–79.

Jack Slay Jr., "Danger in a Strange Land: *The Comfort of Strangers*," in *Ian McEwan* (New York: Twayne, 1996), 72–88.

"Conversations with a Cupboard Man"

Jack Slay Jr., "A Shock into Literature: *First Love, Last Rites*," in *Ian McEwan* (New York: Twayne, 1996), 20–21.

"Dead as They Come"

Jack Slay Jr., "Gorillas, Mannequins, and Other Lovers: *In Between the Sheets*," in *Ian McEwan* (New York: Twayne, 1996), 56–58, 63, 66.

"Disguises"

Jack Slay Jr., "A Shock into Literature: *First Love, Last Rites*," in *Ian McEwan* (New York: Twayne, 1996), 18–20.

First Love, Last Rites

Jack Slay Jr., "A Shock into Literature: *First Love, Last Rites*," in *Ian McEwan* (New York: Twayne, 1996), 9–34.

"First Love, Last Rites"

Jack Slay Jr., "A Shock into Literature: *First Love, Last Rites*," in *Ian McEwan* (New York: Twayne, 1996), 31–34.

"Homemade"

Jack Slay Jr., "A Shock into Literature: *First Love, Last Rites*," in *Ian McEwan* (New York: Twayne, 1996), 12, 13–14, 18, 20.

In Between the Sheets

Jack Slay Jr., "Gorillas, Mannequins, and Other Lovers: *In Between the Sheets*," in *Ian McEwan* (New York: Twayne, 1996), 51–71.

The Innocent

Jack Slay Jr., "And the Walls Came Tumbling Down: *The Innocent* and *Black Dogs*," in *Ian McEwan* (New York: Twayne, 1996), 134–40.

"Last Day of Summer"

Jack Slay Jr., "A Shock into Literature: *First Love, Last Rites*," in *Ian McEwan* (New York: Twayne, 1996), 15–18.

"Pornography"

Jack Slay Jr., "Gorillas, Mannequins, and Other Lovers: *In Between the Sheets*," in *Ian McEwan* (New York: Twayne, 1996), 65–68.

"Psychopolis"

Jack Slay Jr., "Gorillas, Mannequins, and Other Lovers: *In Between the Sheets*," in *Ian McEwan* (New York: Twayne, 1996), 58–62.

"Reflections of a Kept Ape"

Jack Slay Jr., "Gorillas, Mannequins, and Other Lovers: *In Between the Sheets*," in *Ian McEwan* (New York: Twayne, 1996), 53–55, 56, 57–58, 63.

"Solid Geometry"

Jack Slay Jr., "A Shock into Literature: *First Love, Last Rites*," in *Ian McEwan* (New York: Twayne, 1996), 27–30.

"To and Fro"

Jack Slay Jr., "Gorillas, Mannequins, and Other Lovers: *In Between the Sheets*," in *Ian McEwan* (New York: Twayne, 1996), 64–65.

"Two Fragments: March 199—"

Jack Slay Jr., "Gorillas, Mannequins, and Other Lovers: *In Between the Sheets*," in *Ian McEwan* (New York: Twayne, 1996), 61–63.

MCGAHERN, JOHN

Amongst Women

Antoinette Quinn, "A Prayer for My Daughters: Patriarchy in *Amongst Women*," *CJIS* 17 (July 1991): 79–90.

High Ground

Nicola Bradbury, "*High Ground*," in *Re-Reading the Short Story*, ed. Clare Hanson (New York: St. Martin's, 1989), 86–97.

Laurel Graeber, "New and Noteworthy," *NYTBR* 98 (14 February 1993): 24.

The Leavetaking

Terence Killeen, "Versions of Exile: A Reading of *The Leavetaking*," *CJIS* 17 (July 1991): 69–79.

The Pornographer

Bruce Berlind, "*The Pornographer*," *NL* 47 (Summer 1981): 140–41.

MANSFIELD, KATHERINE

"Bank Holiday"

Patrick D. Morrow, "Stories from *The Garden Part and Other Stories*," in *Katherine Mansfield's Fiction* (Bowling Green, OH: Popular, 1993), 87–89.

"Blaze"

Patrick D. Morrow, "Stories from *In a German Pension*," in *Katherine Mansfield's Fiction* (Bowling Green, OH: Popular, 1993), 44–46.

"Bliss"

Walter E. Anderson, "The Hidden Love Triangle in Mansfield's 'Bliss,'" *TCL* 28 (Winter 1982): 397–404.

Patrick D. Morrow, "Stories from *Bliss and Other Stories*," in *Katherine Mansfield's Fiction* (Bowling Green, OH: Popular, 1993), 53–55, 141–42.

Judith S. Neaman, "Allusion, Image, and Associative Pattern: The Answers in Mansfield's 'Bliss,'" *TCL* 32 (Summer 1986): 242–54.

Paola Zaccaria, "Viaggi per la beatitudine all'interno di una casa inglese anni venti," *LeS* 20 (January–March 1985): 73–87.

"The Canary"

Kiichiro Nakatami, "The Structure of Expressions in 'The Canary,'" *HSELL* 25 (1980): 78–91.

"The Child Who Was Tired"

Andree-Marie Harmat, "Un tres mansfieldien plagiat de Tchekov: 'L'Enfant qui etait fatiguée' de Katherine Mansfield," *Litt* 16 (Spring 1987): 49–68.

"A Cup of Tea"

Patrick D. Morrow, "Stories from the Posthumous Collection, *The Dove's Nest and Other Stories*," in *Katherine Mansfield's Fiction* (Bowling Green, OH: Popular, 1993), 99–100.

"The Dill Pickle"

Patrick D. Morrow, "Stories from *Bliss and Other Stories*," in *Katherine Mansfield's Fiction* (Bowling Green, OH: Popular, 1993), 65–67.

"Frau Brechenmacher Attends a Wedding"

Patrick D. Morrow, "Stories from *In a German Pension*," in *Katherine Mansfield's Fiction* (Bowling Green, OH: Popular, 1993), 31–33.

"The Garden Party"

Jayne Marek, "Class-Consciousness and Self-Consciousness in Katherine Mansfield's 'The Garden Party,'" *PostS* 7 (1990): 35–43.

Ben Satterfield, "Irony in 'The Garden Party,'" *BSUF* 23 (Winter 1982): 68–70.

Jane Wilkinson, "Feasting to Death: 'Garden Party' Variations," in *Short Fiction in the New Literatures in English: Proceedings of the Nice Conference of the European Association for Commonwealth Literature and Language Studies*, ed.

MANSFIELD, KATHERINE, "Her First Ball"

Jacqueline Bardolph (Nice: Faculti des Lettres & Sciences Humaines de Nice, 1989), 23–30.

Hubert Zapf, "Time and Space in Katherine Mansfield's 'The Garden Party,'" *OL* 40, no. 1 (1985): 44–54.

"Her First Ball"

Carol Franklin, "Mansfield and Richardson: A Short Story Dialectic," *ALS* 11 (October 1983): 227–33.

Patrick D. Morrow, "Stories from *The Garden Part and Other Stories*," in *Katherine Mansfield's Fiction* (Bowling Green, OH: Popular, 1993), 83–84.

"Late at Night"

Patrick D. Morrow, "Stories from the Posthumous Collection, *Something Childish and Other Stories*," in *Katherine Mansfield's Fiction* (Bowling Green, OH: Popular, 1993), 127–29.

"The Luftbad"

Parkin-Gounelas, Ruth, "Katherine Mansfield's piece of pink wool: feminine signification in 'The Luftbad,'" *SSF* 27 (Fall 1990): 495–507.

"The Man without a Temperament"

Gordon N. Ross, "Klaymongso in Mansfield's 'The Man without a Temperament,'" *SSF* 18 (Spring 1981): 179–80.

"Miss Brill"

Andree-Marie Harmat, "Essai d'analyse structurale d'une nouvelle lyrique anglaise: 'Miss Brill' de Katherine Mansfield," *CahiersN* 1 (1983): 49–74.

Miriam B. Mandel, "Reductive Imagery in 'Miss Brill,'" *SSF* 26 (Fall 1989): 473–77.

Patrick D. Morrow, "Stories from *The Garden Part and Other Stories*," in *Katherine Mansfield's Fiction* (Bowling Green, OH: Popular, 1993), 72, 82.

"The Stranger"

Hannelore Breuer and Horst Breuer, "Psychoanalytische Bemerkungen zu Katherine Mansfields Erzahlung 'The Stranger,'" *LWU* 20, no. 4 (1987): 505–17.

"A Suburban Fairy Tale"

Patrick D. Morrow, "Stories from the Posthumous Collection, *Something Childish and Other Stories*," in *Katherine Mansfield's Fiction* (Bowling Green, OH: Popular, 1993), 130–32.

"The Voyage"

Helmut Bonheim, "Teaching Katherine Mansfield's 'The Voyage': Metaphor Boxes," *LWU* 20, no. 1 (1987): 99–113.

Patrick D. Morrow, "Stories from *The Garden Part and Other Stories*," in *Katherine Mansfield's Fiction* (Bowling Green, OH: Popular, 1993), 80–81.

Graeme Tytler, "Mansfield's 'The Voyage,'" *Expl* 50 (Fall 1991): 42–45.

"The Wind Blows"

V. I. Kotliarova, "Muzykal'nost' kak svoistvo stiliia rasskaza K. Mensfild 'Duet veter,'" *FN* 1 (1985): 80–82.

Patrick D. Morrow, "Stories from *Bliss and Other Stories*," in *Katherine Mansfield's Fiction* (Bowling Green, OH: Popular, 1993), 55–57.

MARTINEAU, HARRIET

Deerbrook

Valerie Sanders, "'No Ordinary Case of a Village Apothecary': The Doctor as Hero in Harriet Martineau's *Deerbrook*," *N&Q* 30 (August 1983): 293–94.

"The Sickness and Health of the People of Bleaburn"

Anne Lohrli, "Harriet Martineau and the 'People of Bleaburn,'" *SSF* 20 (Spring–Summer 1983): 101–4.

MATURIN, CHARLES ROBERT

Melmoth, the Wanderer

Susanna Corradi, "Il silenzio di Melmoth: Lettura analitica del testo *Melmoth the Wanderer* di Charles Robert Maturin," *SULLA* 55 (1981–82): 123–42.

Patricia Coughlan, "The Recycling of Melmoth: 'A Very German Story,'" in *Literary Interrelations: Ireland, England and the World, II: Comparison and Impact*, ed. Wolfgang Zach and Heinz Kosok (Tubingen: Narr, 1987), 181–91.

Leigh A. Ehlers, "The 'Incommunicable Condition' of Melmoth," *RsSt* 49 (September 1981): 171-82.

Kathleen Fowler, "Hieroglyphics in Fire: *Melmoth the Wanderer*," *StRom* 25 (Winter 1986): 521-39.

Mark M. Hennelly Jr., "*Melmoth the Wanderer* and Gothic Existentialism," *SEL* 21 (Autumn 1981): 665–79.

Rosemary Lloyd, "*Melmoth the Wanderer*: The Code of Romanticism," in *Baudelaire, Mallarmé, Valery: New Essays in Honour of Lloyd Austin*, ed. Malcolm Bowie, Alison Fairlie, and Alison Finch (Cambridge: Cambridge University Press, 1982), 80–94.

Amy Elizabeth Smith, "Experimentation and 'Horrid Curiosity' in Maturin's *Melmoth the Wanderer*," *ES* 74 (December 1993): 24–35.

G. St. John Stott, "The Structure of *Melmoth the Wanderer*," *ÉI* 12 (June 1987): 41–52.

Marie-Christine Vuillemin, "*Melmoth the Wanderer*: An English Representation of Faust," *MCRel* 7 (1989): 143–49.

The Milesian Chief

Claude Fierobe, "C. R. Maturin: Nationalisme et fantastique," *ÉI* 9 (December 1984): 43–55.

MAUGHAM, W. SOMERSET

"The Ant and the Grasshopper"

H. Sopher, "Somerset Maugham's 'The Ant and the Grasshopper': The Literary Implications of its Multilayered Structure," *SSF* 31 (Winter 1994): 109–14.

Ashenden

Jeanne F. Bedell, "Somerset Maugham's *Ashenden* and the Modernization of Espionage Fiction," *SPC* 7 (1984): 40–46.

Edward Shanks, "Review," *Mercury* (May 1928): 98. Reprinted in *W. Somerset Maugham: The Critical Heritage*, ed. Anthony Curtis and John Whitehead (London: Routledge & Kegan Paul, 1987), 175–76.

Cakes and Ale

Katherine Fell, "The Unspoken Language of Edward Driffield," *Lang&Lit* 7, no. 1–3 (1982): 93–106.

Jacky Martin, "*Cakes and Ale* de W. S. Maugham ou la relation juste," *CVE* 22 (October 1985): 55–77.

R. Barton Palmer, "Artists and the Hacks: Maugham's *Cakes and Ale*," *SoAR* 46 (November 1981): 54–63.

"The Letter"

Guido Fink, "Smiling Unconcern: Tre racconti malesi di W. S. Maugham," in *Studi inglesi: Raccolta di saggi e ricerche*, ed. Agostino Lombardo (Bari: Adriatica, 1978), 261–80.

The Moon and Sixpence

M. N. Airapetova, "Osobennosti funktsionirovaniia derivatov v tekste: Na materiale proizvedenii S. Moema Luna i grosh i Teatr," *IAN* 1 (1987): 76–81.

Maxwell Anderson, "In Vishnu-Land What Avatar?" *Dial* 67 (29 November 1919): 477–78. Reprinted in *W. Somerset Maugham: The Critical Heritage*, ed. Anthony Curtis and John Whitehead (London: Routledge & Kegan Paul, 1987), 144–47.

K[atherine] M[ansfield], "Inarticulations," *Athenaeum* (9 May 1919): 302. Reprinted in *W. Somerset Maugham: The Critical Heritage*, ed. Anthony Curtis and John Whitehead (London: Routledge & Kegan Paul, 1987), 139–42.

"Mr. Know-All"

Armine Kotin Mortimer, "Second Stories: The Example of 'Mr. Know-All,'" *SSF* 25 (Summer 1988): 307–14.

Of Human Bondage

Bonnie Hoover Braendlin, "The Prostitute as Scapegoat: Mildred Rogers in Somerset Maugham's *Of Human Bondage*," in *The Image of the Prostitute in Modern Literature*, ed. Pierre L. Horn and Mary Beth Pringle (New York: Ungar, 1984), 9–18.

Joseph Dobrinsky, "The Dialectics of Art and Life in *Of Human Bondage*," *CVE* 22 (October 1985): 33–55.

Joseph Dobrinsky, "Les Non-dits de la psychologie amoureuse dans *Of Human Bondage*," *ÉA* 41 (January–March 1988): 37–47.

Theodore Dreiser, "As a Realist Sees It," *NewR* 5 (25 December 1915): 202–4. Reprinted in *W. Somerset Maugham: The Critical Heritage*, ed. Anthony Curtis and John Whitehead (London: Routledge & Kegan Paul, 1987), 130–34.

Gerald Gould, "Review," *NewS* 5 (25 September 1915): 594. Reprinted in *W. Somerset Maugham: The Critical Heritage*, ed. Anthony Curtis and John Whitehead (London: Routledge & Kegan Paul, 1987), 126–29.

Renate Noll-Wiemann, "Maughams *Of Human Bondage* und die Tradition des Entwicklungsromans," in *Motive and Themen in englischsprachiger Literatur als Indikatoren literaturgeschichtlicher Prozesse: Festschrift zum 65. Geburtstag von Theodor Wolpers*, ed. Heinz-Joachim Mullenbrock and Alfons Klein (Tubingen: Niemeyer, 1990), 321–42.

The Razor's Edge

Dalma Brunauer, "The Road Not Taken: Fragmentation as a Device for Self-Concealment in *The Razor's Edge*," *JEP* 8 (March 1987): 24–33.

"The Yellow Streak"

Philip Holden, "W. Somerset Maugham's 'Yellow Streak,'" *SSF* 29 (Fall 1992): 575–82.

MEREDITH, GEORGE

Amazing Marriage

Elizabeth M. Shore, "Godwin's Fleetwood and the Hero of Meredith's *The Amazing Marriage*," *ESC* 8 (March 1982): 38–48.

Beauchamp's Career

V. V. Babikov, "Roman Kar'era B'iuchempa v khudozhestvennoi sisteme Dzh. Meredita," *FN* 4, no. 142 (1984): 24–29.

Gary Handwerk, "On Heroes and Their Demise: Critical Liberalism in *Beauchamp's Career*," *SEL* 27 (Autumn 1987): 663–81.

Margaret Harris, "The Epistle of Dr. Shrapel to Commander Beauchamp in Meredith's *Beauchamp's Career*," *N&Q* 29 (August 1982): 317–20.

Margaret Harris, "Thomas Carlyle and Frederick Maxse in *Beauchamp's Career*," *CarN* 7 (Spring 1986): 7–11.

Michael Wilding, "George Meredith's *Beauchamp's Career*: Politics, Romance and Realism," *SSEng* 8 (1982–83): 46–69.

"Case of General Ople and Lady Camper"

Lynn E. Wolf, "A Bracing Corrective: Women and Comedy in George Meredith's 'Case of General Ople and Lady Camper,'" *ELWIU* 21 (Spring 1994): 68–81.

Diana of the Crossways

Elizabeth J. Deis, "Marriage as Crossways: George Meredith's Victorian-Modern Compromise," in *Portraits of Marriage in Literature*, ed. Anne C. Hargrove and Maurine Magliocco (Macomb, IL: Essays in Literature, 1984), 13–30.

Diane Michelle Elam, "'We pray to be defended from her cleverness': Conjugating Romance in George Meredith's *Diana of the Crossways*," *Genre* 21 (Summer 1988): 179–201.

Waldo Sumner Glock, "Theme and Metaphor in *Diana of the Crossways*," *DR* 65 (Spring 1985): 67–79.

The Egoist

Roslyn Belkin, "According to Their Age: Older Women in George Meredith's *The Egoist*," *IJWS* 7 (January–February 1984): 37–46.

Neal Bowers, "Prelude as Theory and Scenario in *The Egoist*," *BSUF* 24, no. 2 (1983): 3–8.

Alanna Kathleen Brown, "The Self and the Other: George Meredith's *The Egoist*," in *Women and Violence in Literature: An Essay Collection*, ed. Katherine Anne Ackley (New York: Garland, 1990), 105–38.

Sheila Emerson, "Imagery as Countercurrent in *The Egoist*," *Ariel* 12 (January 1981): 21–28.

Marjorie H. Goss, "Language and Sir Willoughby in Meredith's *The Egoist*," *Interpretations* 13 (Fall 1981): 18–23.

Gary J. Handwerk, "Linguistic Blindness and Ironic Vision in *The Egoist*," *NCF* 39 (September 1984): 163–85.

J. Hillis Miller, "'Herself against Herself': The Clarification of Clara Middleton," in *The Representation of Women in Fiction*, ed. Carolyn G. Heilbrun and Margaret R. Higonnet (Baltimore: Johns Hopkins University Press, 1983), 98-123.

Tokiko Sugawara, "Koteika eno Hanko," in *Igirisu Shosetsu no Joseitachi*, ed. Yaeko Sumi and Naomi Okamura (Tokyo: Keiso, 1983), 119–46.

Carolyn Williams, "Natural Selection and Narrative Form in *The Egoist*," *VS* 27 (Autumn 1983): 53–79.

Carolyn Williams, "Unbroken Patterns: Gender, Culture, and Voice in *The Egoist*," *BIS* 13 (1985): 45–70.

Evan Harrington

Natalie Cole Michta, "The Legitimate Self in George Meredith's *Evan Harrington*," *SNNTS* 21 (Spring 1989): 41–59.

"The Friend of an Engaged Couple"

Lewis Sawin, "'The Friend of an Engaged Couple': An Unpublished Short Story by George Meredith," *VIJ* 14 (1986): 135–45.

Lord Ormont and His Aminta

Yoshiko Takakuwa, "'Shiawasena Onna Aminta F.: George Meredith: *Lord Ormont and His Aminta*," *EigoS* 132 (1987): 484–85.

The Ordeal of Richard Feverel

Debra Stoner Barker, "Richard Feverel's Passage to Knighthood," *ANQ* 3 (October 1990): 168–71.

Thomas J. Campbell, "Adrian's Shrug: A Note on the 'Wise Youth,'" *VN* 61 (Spring 1982): 19–20.

Lewis Horne, "Sir Austin, His Devil, and the Well-Designed World," *SNNTS* 24 (Spring 1992): 35–47.

Nikki Lee Manos, "'The Ordeal of Richard Feverel': Bildungsroman or anti-Bildungsroman?" *VN* 70 (Fall 1986): 18–24.

Daniel Smirlock, "The Models of Richard Feverel," *JNT* 11 (Spring 1981): 91–109.

Sandra Belloni

Mihoko Higaya, "*Sandra Belloni* to Soseki," *EigoS* 132 (1987): 535–36, 598–99.

MILNE, A[LAN] A[LEXANDER]

The House at Pooh Corner

Thomas Burnett Swann, "A House for Many Summers," in *A. A. Milne* (New York: Twayne, 1971), 66, 93–97.

The Man in the Bowler Hat

Georg Buddruss, "Zum Vorbild des Einakters Naya purana von Upendranath Ask," *StII* 7 (1981): 3–10.

Once on a Time

Thomas Burnett Swann, "A House for Many Summers," in *A. A. Milne* (New York: Twayne, 1971), 66–73.

The Red House Mystery

Thomas Burnett Swann, "From Mr. Pim to Chloe Marr," in *A. A. Milne* (New York: Twayne, 1971), 98–99, 104–8, 111–12.

Toad of Toad Hall

Thomas Burnett Swann, "Drawing Rooms and Dreams" and "The Falling Star," in *A. A. Milne* (New York: Twayne, 1971), 35–36, 54–57.

When We Were Very Young

Thomas Burnett Swann, "Whisper Who Dares," in *A. A. Milne* (New York: Twayne, 1971), 74–80, 81–83.

Winnie-the-Pooh

Anthony Low, "Religious Myth in *Winnie-the-Pooh*," *Greyfriar* 22 (1981): 13–16.

Kathleen O'Brien, "Winnipeg, Winnie, and Friend," *Canoma* 16 (December 1990): 30–31.

Kazuo Ogaway, "Kuma no Pu San," *Oberon* 31 (1960): 67–70.

Caról A. Stranger, "*Winnie the Pooh* through a Feminist Lens," *L&U* 11, no. 2 (1987): 34–50.

Thomas Burnett Swann, "The Peerless Pooh" and "*Back to the Bear*," in *A. A. Milne* (New York: Twayne, 1971), 47, 55, 58, 66, 80, 89–93, 115, 123, 130–35.

Elen Tremper, "Instigorating *Winnie the Pooh*," *L&U* 1, no. 1 (1977): 33–46.

Anita Wilson, "Milne's Pooh Books: The Benevolent Forest," in *Touchstones: Reflections on the Best in Children's Literature, Volume One*, ed. Perry Nodelman (West Lafayette, WI: Children's Literature Association Press, 1985), 163–72.

Jacqueline Colombat, "Ordre et desordre dans la litterature enfantine victorienne et edouardienne ou 'Un Ordre peut en cacher un autre,'" *CVE* (27 April 1988): 73–81.

The World of Pooh

Thomas Burnett Swann, "Back to the Bear," in *A. A. Milne* (New York: Twayne, 1971), 130–31.

Wurzel-Flummery

Thomas Burnett Swann, "Drawing Rooms and Dreams," in *A. A. Milne* (New York: Twayne, 1971), 32–33, 36–37, 38–39.

Year In, Year Out

Thomas Burnett Swann, "Drawing Rooms and Dreams," in *A. A. Milne* (New York: Twayne, 1971), 29–31.

MITCHELL, JAMES LESLIE (LEWIS GRASSIC GIBBON)

A Scots Quair

Deirdre Burton, "A Feminist Reading of Lewis Grassic Gibbon's *A Scots Quair*," in *The British Working-Class Novel in the Twentieth Century*, ed. Jeremy Hawthorn (London: Arnold, 1984), 34–46.

Angus Calder, "A Mania for Self-Reliance: Grassic Gibbon's *Scots Quair*," in *The Uses of Fiction: Essays on the Modern Novel in Honour of Arnold Kettle*, ed. Douglas Jefferson and Graham Martin (Milton Keynes, England: Open University Press, 1982), 99–113.

Glenda Norquay, "Voices in Time: *A Scots Quair*," *ScLJ* 11 (May 1984): 57–68.

Ramon Lopez Ortega, "Language and Point of View in Lewis Grassic Gibbon's *A Scots Quair*," *StSL* 16 (1981): 148–59.

D. M. E. Roskies, "Language, Class and Radical Perspective in *A Scots Quair*," *ZAA* 29, no. 2 (1981): 142–53.

Jenny Wolmark, "Problems of Tone in *A Scots Quair*," *RLt* 11 (1981): 15–23

MUNRO, HECTOR HUGH (SAKI)

The Chronicles of Clovis

Joseph S. Salemi, "An Asp Lurking in an Apple-Charlotte: Animal Violence in Saki's *The Chronicles of Clovis*," *SSF* 26 (Fall 1989): 423–30.

"Mrs. Packletide's Tiger"

Gerd Stratmann, "'Mrs. Packletide's Tiger': Saki und die selbstironische Farce," *A&E* 18 (1982): 121–28.

Wratislav

Paul Larreya, "Pragmatique linguistique et analyse de discours: L'Implicite dans *Wratislav*, de Saki," *RANAM* 17 (1984): 95–107.

MURDOCH, IRIS

The Bell

David W. Beams, "The Fortunate Fall: Three Actions in *The Bell*," *TCL* 34 (Winter 1988): 416–33.

Jacques Souvage, "Symbol as Narrative Device: An Interpretation of Iris Murdoch's *The Bell*," *ES* 43 (April 1962): 81–96.

Hilda D. Spear, *Iris Murdoch* (New York: St. Martin's, 1995), 27–32, 97–98.

Toshio Tsukamoto, "Chisho ni okeru Kane no Image ni tsuite," in *Bungaku to Ningen: Nakajima Kanji Kyoju Tsuito Ronbunshu* (Tokyo: Kinseido; 1981), 178–87.

Dorothy A. Winsor, "Iris Murdoch and the Uncanny: Supernatural Events in *The Bell*," *L&P* 30, no. 3–4 (1980): 147–54.

Dorothy A. Winsor, "Solipsistic Sexuality in Murdoch's Gothic Novels," in *Iris Murdoch*, ed. Harold Bloom (New York: Chelsea House, 1986), 122–26.

Peter Wolfe, "*The Bell*: The Unheard Voice of Love," in *The Disciplined Heart: Iris Murdoch and Her Novels* (Columbia: University of Missouri Press, 1966), 113–138.

The Black Prince

Elizabeth Dipple, "*The Black Prince* and the Figure of Marsyas," in *Iris Murdoch*, ed. Harold Bloom (New York: Chelsea House, 1986), 131–58.

Peter Lamarque, "Truth and Art in Iris Murdoch's *The Black Prince*," *P&L* 2 (Fall 1978): 209–22.

Hilda D. Spear, *Iris Murdoch* (New York: St. Martin's, 1995), 75–81.

Richard Todd, "The Plausibility of *The Black Prince*," *DQR* 8, no. 2 (1978): 82–93.

Diamond Oberoi Vahali, "Inter-Textuality, Self-Reflexivity and Self-Consciousness in Murdoch's *The Black Prince*," *PURB* 21 (October 1990): 53–57.

Peter Wolfe, "'Malformed Treatise' and Prizewinner: Iris Murdoch's *The Black Prince*," in *British Novelists since 1900*, ed. Jack I. Biles (New York: AMS, 1987), 279–97.

Bruno's Dream

Frank Kermode, "*Bruno's Dream*" in *Iris Murdoch*, ed. Harold Bloom (New York: Chelsea House, 1986), 21–25.

Hilda D. Spear, *Iris Murdoch* (New York: St. Martin's, 1995), 64–67.

A Fairly Honourable Defeat

Louis L. Martz, "The London Novels" in *Iris Murdoch*, ed. Harold Bloom (New York: Chelsea House, 1986), 53–57.

Hilda D. Spear, *Iris Murdoch* (New York: St. Martin's, 1995), 64–67.

The Flight from the Enchanter

Louis L. Martz, "The London Novels," in *Iris Murdoch*, ed. Harold Bloom (New York: Chelsea House, 1986), 48–50.

Hilda D. Spear, *Iris Murdoch* (New York: St. Martin's, 1995), 24–26.

Zohreh Tawakuli Sullivan, "The Demonic: *The Flight From the Enchanter*," in *Iris Murdoch*, ed. Harold Bloom (New York: Chelsea House, 1986), 71–86.

Peter Wolfe, "*The Flight from the Enchanter*: The Fragmentation and Fusion of Society," in *The Disciplined Heart: Iris Murdoch and Her Novels* (Columbia: University of Missouri Press, 1966), 68–88.

The Good Apprentice

Harold Bloom, "Introduction," in *Iris Murdoch*, ed. Harold Bloom (New York: Chelsea House, 1986), 1–7.

William C. Carter, "Proustian Resonances in Iris Murdoch's *The Good Apprentice*," *PRAN* 25 (Summer 1986): 55–57.

Fernand Corin, "Rites of Passage in Iris Murdoch's *The Good Apprentice*," in *Multiple Worlds, Multiple Words: Essays in Honour of Irene Simon*, ed. Hena Maes-Jelinek, Pierre Michel, and Paulette Michel-Michot (Liege: Université de Liege, 1987), 15–25.

Irene Simon, "A Note on Iris Murdoch's *The Good Apprentice*," *ES* 68 (February 1987): 75–78.

Hilda D. Spear, *Iris Murdoch* (New York: St. Martin's, 1995), 108–20.

The Green Knight

Linda Simon, "The Mugger Who Came Back From the Dead," *NYTBR* (9 January 1994): 7.

Henry and Cato

Lorna Sage, "The Pursuit of Imperfection: *Henry and Cato*" in *Iris Murdoch*, ed. Harold Bloom (New York: Chelsea House, 1986), 111–19.

Hilda D. Spear, *Iris Murdoch* (New York: St. Martin's, 1995), 82–87.

The Italian Girl

Frederick J. Hoffman, "*The Italian Girl*" in *Iris Murdoch*, ed. Harold Bloom (New York: Chelsea House, 1986), 17–20.

Peter Wolfe, "*The Italian Girl*: A Weary Homecoming," in *The Disciplined Heart: Iris Murdoch and Her Novels* (Columbia: University of Missouri Press, 1966), 203–8.

The Nice and the Good

Ann M. Ashworth, "'Venus, Cupid, Folly, and Time': Bronzino's Allegory and Murdoch's Fiction," *Critique* 23, no. 1 (1981): 18–24.

Frank Baldanza, "*The Nice and the Good*," in *Iris Murdoch*, ed. Harold Bloom (New York: Chelsea House, 1986), 27–38.

Hilda D. Spear, *Iris Murdoch* (New York: St. Martin's, 1995), 67–68.

Nuns and Soldiers

Peter J. Conradi, "Useful Fictions: Iris Murdoch," *CritQ* 23 (Autumn 1981): 63–69.

Margaret Scanlon, "The Problem of the Past in Iris Murdoch's *Nuns and Soldiers*," *Renascence* 38 (Spring 1986): 170–82.

Hilda D. Spear, *Iris Murdoch* (New York: St. Martin's, 1995), 90–91.

The Philosopher's Pupil

G. E. H. Hughes, "Narrative Secrets and Reader Coercion: Iris Murdoch's *The Philosopher's Pupil*," *HSELL* 32 (1987): 1–16.

Madeline Marget, "The Water is Deep: Iris Murdoch's 'Utterly Demanding Present,'" *Commonweal* 118 (14 June 1991): 399–403.

Hilda D. Spear, *Iris Murdoch* (New York: St. Martin's, 1995), 51–54.

The Red and the Green

Colette Charpentier, "The Critical Reception of Iris Murdoch's Irish Novels (1963–1976) II: *The Red and the Green* (1)," *ÉI* 6 (December 1981): 87–98.

Louise A. DeSalvo, "'This Should Not Be': Iris Murdoch's Critique of English Policy towards Ireland in *The Red and the Green*," *CLQ* 19 (September 1983): 113–24.

Donna Gerstenberger, "*The Red and the Green*," in *Iris Murdoch*, ed. Harold Bloom (New York: Chelsea House, 1986), 59–70.

Thomas M. Leitch, "To What Is Fiction Committed?" *PSt* 6 (September 1983): 159–75.

The Sacred and Profane Love Machine

Hilda D. Spear, *Iris Murdoch* (New York: St. Martin's, 1995), 73–75.

Dorothy A. Winsor, "Iris Murdoch's Conflicting Ethical Demands: Separation versus Passivity in *The Sacred and Profane Love Machine*," *MLQ* 44 (December 1983): 394–409.

The Sandcastle

Peter Wolfe, "*The Sandcastle*: Acquiescence as Action," in *The Disciplined Heart: Iris Murdoch and Her Novels* (Columbia: University of Missouri Press, 1966), 89–112.

The Sea, the Sea

Gerd Brantenberg, "I kollisjon med virkeligheten," *Samtiden* 1 (1987): 36–37.

Angela Downing, "Recursive Premodifications as a Literary Device in Iris Murdoch's *The Sea, the Sea*," *RCEI* 10 (April 1985): 65–80.

Hilda D. Spear, *Iris Murdoch* (New York: St. Martin's, 1995), 92–100.

Lindsey Tucker, "Released from Bands: Iris Murdoch's Two Prosperos in *The Sea, the Sea*," *ConL* 27 (Fall 1986): 378–95.

A Severed Head

Ann Gossman, " Icons and Idols in Murdoch's *A Severed Head*," in *Iris Murdoch*, ed. Harold Bloom (New York: Chelsea House, 1986), 105–10.

Louis L. Martz, "The London Novels" in *Iris Murdoch*, ed. Harold Bloom (New York: Chelsea House, 1986), 50–51.

Rita Severi, "La testa tagliata dell'incantatore: Considerazioni retoriche su *A Severed Head* di Iris Murdoch," *Ling&S* 23 (September 1988): 477–88.

Hilda D. Spear, *Iris Murdoch* (New York: St. Martin's, 1995), 39–46.

Jack Turner, "Murdoch vs. Freud in *A Severed Head* and Other Novels," *L&P* 36 (Spring–Summer 1990): 110–21.

Peter Wolfe, "*The Severed Head*: The Moral of the Minuet," in *The Disciplined Heart: Iris Murdoch and Her Novels* (Columbia: University of Missouri Press, 1966), 139–60.

"Something Special"

Deborah DeZure, "The Perceiving Self as Gatekeeper: Choice in Iris Murdoch's 'Something Special,'" *SSF* 27 (Spring 1990): 211–20.

The Sovereignty of Good

Lawrence A. Blum, "Iris Murdoch and the Domain of the Moral," *PhS* 50 (November 1986): 343–67.

Hilda D. Spear, *Iris Murdoch* (New York: St. Martin's, 1995), 55–56, 64–65.

The Time of the Angels

Iu. I. Levin, "Konfiguratsionno-dispozitsionnyi podkhod k povestvovatel'nomu tekstu: Na materiale romana A. Merdok Vremia angelov," in *Semiotics and the History of Culture*, ed. Morris Halle, Krystyna Pomorska, Elena Semenka-Pankratov, and Boris Uspenskij (Columbus, OH: Slavica, 1988), 384–99.

Hilda D. Spear, *Iris Murdoch* (New York: St. Martin's, 1995), 56–63.

"*The Time of the Angels*: Self-Subversive Plot and Iris Murdoch," *PURB* 16 (October 1985): 39–46.

Dorothy A. Winsor, "Solipsistic Sexuality in Murdoch's Gothic Novels" in *Iris Murdoch*, ed. Harold Bloom (New York: Chelsea House, 1986), 128–30.

Under the Net

Marilyn Stall Fontane, "*Under the Net* of a Mid-Summer Night's Dream," *PAPA* 9 (Spring 1983): 43–54.

Susan Luck Hooks, "Development of Identity: Iris Murdoch's *Under the Net*," *NConL* 23 (September 1993): 6–8.

Steven G. Kellman, "*Under the Net*: The Self-Begetting Novel" in *Iris Murdoch*, ed. Harold Bloom (New York: Chelsea House, 1986), 95–103.

Louis L. Martz, "The London Novels" in *Iris Murdoch*, ed. Harold Bloom (New York: Chelsea House, 1986), 44–48.

Jacques Souvage, "The Unresolved Tension: An Interpretation of Iris Murdoch's *Under the Net*," *RLV* 26, no. 6 (1966): 420–30.

Hilda D. Spear, *Iris Murdoch* (New York: St. Martin's, 1995), 20–24, 33–35.

Peter Wolfe, "*Under the Net*: The Novel as Philosophical Criticism," in *The Disciplined Heart: Iris Murdoch and Her Novels* (Columbia: University of Missouri Press, 1966), 46–67.

The Unicorn

Colette Charpentier, "L'Etrange dans *The Unicorn* d'Iris Murdoch," *ÉI* 9 (December 1984): 89–94.

Joseph A. Cosenza, "Murdoch's *The Unicorn*," *Expl* 50 (Spring 1992): 175–77.

Roger Decap, "Mythe et modernite: *The Unicorn* d'Iris Murdoch," *Caliban* 27 (1990): 83–97.

Suzanne Dutruch, "*The Unicorn*: Art et artifice," *ÉA* 36 (January–March 1983): 57–66.

Hilda D. Spear, *Iris Murdoch* (New York: St. Martin's, 1995), 46–50.

Dorothy A. Winsor, "Solipsistic Sexuality in Murdoch's Gothic Novels" in *Iris Murdoch*, ed. Harold Bloom (New York: Chelsea House, 1986), 126–28.

Peter Wolfe, "*The Unicorn*: Perception as Moral Vision," in *The Disciplined Heart: Iris Murdoch and Her Novels* (Columbia: University of Missouri Press, 1966), 183–202.

The Unofficial Rose

Peter Wolfe, "*The Unofficial Rose*: Some Uses of Beauty," in *The Disciplined Heart: Iris Murdoch and Her Novels* (Columbia: University of Missouri Press, 1966), 161–82.

A Word Child

Barbara Stevens Heusel, "Iris Murdoch's *A Word Child*: Playing Games with Wittgenstein's Perspectives," *StHum* 13 (December 1986): 81–92.

Catherine E. Howard, "'Only Connect': Logical Aesthetic of Fragmentation in *A Word Child*," *TCL* 38 (Spring 1992): 54–65.

O'BRIEN, EDNA

"The Doll"

Kitti Carriker, "Edna O'Brien's 'The Doll': A Narrative of Abjection," *NMIL* 1 (1989): 6–13.

A Fanatic Heart: Selected Stories

Adam Mars-Jones, "*A Fanatic Heart: Selected Stories*," *NYRB* 32 (31 January 1985), 17–19.

House of Splendid Isolation

John L'Heureux, "The Terrorist and the Lady," *NYTBR* (26 June 1994): 7.

Helen Thompson, "*House of Splendid Isolation*," *RCF* 15 (Spring 1995): 179–80.

Lantern Slides

Jose Lanters, "*Lantern Slides*," *WLT* 65 (Spring 1991): 303–4.

"The Love Object"

Kiera O'Hara, "Love Objects: Love and Obsession in the Stories of Edna O'Brien," *SSF* 30 (Summer 1993): 317–25.

"A Nun's Mother"

Jeanette Roberts Shumaker, "Sacrificial Women in Short Stories by Mary Levin and Edna O'Brien," *SSF* 32 (Spring 1995): 185–91.

A Pagan Place

David Herman, "Textual 'You' and Double Deixis in Edna O'Brien's '*A Pagan Place*,'" *Style* 28 (Fall 1994): 378–410.

"Sister Imelda"

Jeanette Roberts Shumaker, "Sacrificial Women in Short Stories by Mary Levin and Edna O'Brien," *SSF* 32 (Spring 1995): 191–98.

O'BRIEN, FLANN (PSEUDONYM OF BRIAN O'NOLAN)

At Swim-Two-Birds

Joseph M. Conte, "Metaphor and Metonymy in Flann O'Brien's *At Swim-Two-Birds*," *RCF* 5 (Spring 1985): 128–34.

Joshua D. Esty, "Flann O'Brien's *At Swim-Two-Birds* and the Post-post Debate," *Ariel* 26 (October 1995): 23–26.

Joseph M. Hassett, "Flann O'Brien and the Idea of the City," in *The Irish Writer and the City*, ed. Maurice Harmon (Gerrards Cross, Buckinghamshire: Smyth; Totowa, NJ: Barnes & Noble, 1984), 115–24.

P. L. Henry, "The Structure of Flann O'Brien's *At Swim-Two-Birds*," *IUR* 20 (Spring 1990): 35–40.

Danielle Jacquin, "L'Etudiant d'*At Swim-Two-Birds* et la paysan de Tarry Flynn sur les chemins de la liberte," *ÉI* 15 (June 1990): 85–96.

Cathal G. O Hainle, "Fionn and Suibhne in *At Swim-Two-Birds*," *Hermathena* 142 (Summer 1987): 13–49.

Kim McMullen, "Culture as Colloquy: Flann O'Brien's Postmodern Dialogue with Irish Tradtion," *Novel* 27 (Fall 1993): 62–84.

Thomas B. O'Grady, "High Anxiety: Flann O'Brien's Portrait of the Artist," *SNNTS* 21 (Summer 1989): 200–8.

An Beal Bocht/The Poor Mouth

Declan Kiberd, "*An Beal Bocht* agus en Bearia," *Comhar* 43, no. 4 (1984): 20–27.

Danielle Jacquin, "Technique et effets de la satire dans *An Beal Bocht* (*The Poor Mouth*) de Myles na gCopaleen," *ÉI* 6 (December 1981): 61–71.

Breandan O Conaire, "Myles na Gaeilge," *Scriobh* 5 (1981): 62–79.

The Hard Life

Thomas F. Shea, "The Craft of Seeming Pedestrian: Flann O'Brien's *The Hard Life*," *CLQ* 25 (December 1989): 258–67.

The Third Policeman

M. Keith Booker, "Science, Philosophy and *The Third Policeman*: Flann O'Brien and the Epistemology of Futility," *SoAR* 56 (November 1991): 37–56.

Francis Doherty, "Flann O'Brien's Existentialist Hell," *CJIS* 15 (December 1989): 51–67.

Werner Huber, "Flann O'Brien and the Language of the Grotesque," in *Anglo-Irish and Irish Literature: Aspects of Language and Culture*, ed. Birgit Bramsback and Martin Croghan (Uppsala: Uppsala University Press, 1988), 123–30.

Charles Kemnitz, "Beyond the Zone of Middle Dimensions: A Relativistic Reading of *The Third Policeman*," *IRU* 15 (Spring 1985): 56–72.

Jerry L. McGuire, "Teasing after Death: Metatextuality in *The Third Policeman*," *Éire* 16 (Summer 1981): 107–21.

Mary A. O'Toole, "The Theory of Serialism in *The Third Policeman*," *IUR* 18 (Autumn 1988): 215–25.

O'CONNOR, FRANK (PSEUDONYM OF MICHAEL O'DONOVAN)

"The Genius"

Michael Steinman, "Frank O' Connor at Work: 'The Genius,'" *Éire* 20 (Winter 1985): 23–42.

Guests of the Nation

Marta Bardotti, "*Guests of the Nation* di Frank O'Connor: Una proposta di lettura," *StIL* 7 (1984): 273–99.

J. R. Crider, "Jupiter Pluvius in *Guests of the Nation*," *SSF* 23 (Fall 1986): 407–11.

Michael Liberman, "Unforeseen Duty in Frank O'Connor's *Guests of the Nation*," *SSF* 24 (Fall 1987): 438–41.

"The Guests of the Nation"

Patrick Rafroidi, "'Guests of the Nation': 'The Seminal Story of Modern Irish Literature?'" *JSSE* 8 (Spring 1987): 51–57.

Stanley Renner, "The Theme of Hidden Powers: Fate vs. Human Responsibility in 'Guests of the Nation,'" *SSF* 27 (Summer 1990): 371–77.

Patricia Robinson, "O'Connor's 'Guests of the Nation,'" *Expl* 45 (Fall 1986): 58.

"The Holy Door"

Albert Fowler, "Challenge to Mood in Frank O'Connor," *Approach* 23 (Spring 1957): 24–27.

"Judas"

Michael Steinman, "Frank O'Connor at Work: Creating Kitty Doherty," *ÉI* 19 (Fall 1984): 142–48.

"My Father's Son"

John Hildebidle, "Clouded Patrimonies: A Glance at 'My Father's Son,'" *TCL* 36 (Fall 1990): 303–09.

The Saint and Mary Kate

James H. Matthews, "Women, War, and Words: Frank O'Connor's First Confessions," *IRA* 1, no. 1 (1980): 73–112.

O'FAOLAIN, SEAN

"An Inside Outside Complex"

Therese Tessier, Simone Lavabre, and Maurice Pergnier, "Lecture plurielle de la nouvelle 'An Inside Outside Complex' de Sean O'Faolain," *CahiersN* 1 (1983): 127–38.

"Lovers of the Lake"

Ronald Tamplin, "Sean O'Faolain's 'Lovers of the Lake,'" *JSSE* 8 (Spring 1987): 59–69.

O'FAOLAIN, SEAN, "The Silence of the Valley"

"The Silence of the Valley"

Thomas E. Kennedy, "Sean O'Faolain's 'The Silence of the Valley,'" *Critique* 29 (Spring 1988): 188–94.

OLIPHANT, MARGARET

The Carlingford Stories: Miss Marjoribanks

Joseph H. O'Mealy, "Mrs. Oliphant, Miss Marjoribanks, and the Victorian Canon," *VN* 82 (Fall 1992): 44–49.

The Melvilles

John Stock Clarke, "Mrs. Oliphant's Unacknowledged Social Novels," *N&Q* 28 (October 1981): 408–13.

The Son of His Father

Margarete Rubik, "The Return of the Convict in Mrs. Oliphant's *The Son of His Father*," in *A Yearbook of Studies in English Language and Literature 1985/86: Festschrift für Siegfried Korninger*, ed. Otto Rauchbauer (Vienna: Braumuller, 1986), 201–15.

ORWELL, GEORGE

Animal Farm

Samir Elbarbary, "Language as Theme in *Animal Farm*," *IFR* 19, no. 1 (1992): 31–38.

Laraine Fergenson, "George Orwell's *Animal Farm*: A Twentieth-Century Beast Fable," *Bestia* 2 (May 1990): 109–18.

Averil Gardner, "*Animal Farm*," in *George Orwell* (Boston: Twayne, 1987), 96–107.

Jean Queval, "Les Voyages de George Orwell," *Critique* 40 (May 1984): 349–61.

Burmese Days

Averil Gardner, "The Road to George Orwell: *Burmese Days*," in *George Orwell* (Boston: Twayne, 1987), 25–33.

Brian Matthews, " 'Living with the Stream': George Orwell's *Burmese Days*," in *Only Connect: Literary Perspectives East and West*, ed. Guy Amirthanayagam and Syd C. Harrex (Adelaide, Honolulu: Centre for Research in the New Literatures in English; East-West Center, 1981), 93–106.

Malcolm Muggeridge, "*Burmese Days*," in *George Orwell*, ed. Harold Bloom (New York: Chelsea House, 1986), 21–24.

David Seed, "Disorientation and Committment in the Fiction of Empire: Kipling and Orwell," in *Rudyard Kipling's "Kim*," ed. Harold Bloom (New York: Chelsea House, 1987), 119–23.

The Clergyman's Daughter

Averil Gardner, "An English Novelist in the 1930's: *The Clergyman's Daughter*," in *George Orwell* (Boston: Twayne, 1987), 35–43.

Philip Rieff, "George Orwell and the Post–Liberal Imagination," in *George Orwell*, ed. Harold Bloom (New York: Chelsea House, 1986), 49–57.

Coming Up for Air

Gilbert Bonifas, "*Coming Up for Air*: Entre militantisme et defaitisme," *Annees* 1 (30 November 1983): 1–42.

Averil Gardner, "An English Novelist in the 1930's: *Coming Up for Air*," in *George Orwell* (Boston: Twayne, 1987), 54–62.

Francesco Marroni, "Retorica e struttura topologica in *Coming Up for Air*," *Trimestre* 13–14 (December 1980—March 1981): 115–25.

Jeffrey Meyers, "Orwell's Apocalypse: *Coming Up for Air*," in *George Orwell*, ed. Harold Bloom (New York: Chelsea House, 1986), 85–96.

Walter Poznar, "Orwell's George Bowling: How to Be," *WascanaR* 14 (Fall 1979): 80–90.

Robert J. Van Dellen, "George Orwell's *Coming Up For Air*: The Politics of Powerlessness," *MFS* 21 (Spring 1975): 57–68.

Keep the Aspidistra Flying

Averil Gardner, "An English Novelist in the 1930's: *Keep the Aspidistra Flying*," in *George Orwell* (Boston: Twayne, 1987), 43–53.

1984

Joseph Adelson, "The Self and Memory in *Nineteen Eighty-Four*," in *The Future of "Nineteen Eighty-Four*," ed. Ejner J. Jensen (Ann Arbor: University of Michigan Press, 1984), 111–19.

Hayward R. Alker Jr., "An Orwellian Lasswell for Today," in *The Orwellian Moment: Hindsight and Foresight in the Post–1984 World*, ed. Robert L. Savage, James Combs, and Dan Nimmo (Fayetteville: University of Arkansas Press, 1989), 131–55.

Francis A. Allen, "*Nineteen Eighty-Four* and the Eclipse of Private Worlds," *MQR* 22 (Fall 1983): 517–40. Reprinted in *The Future of "Nineteen Eighty-Four*," ed. Ejner J. Jensen (Ann Arbor: University of Michigan Press, 1984), 151–75

William Atkinson, "Big Brother George: The End of *1984*," *SCRev* 17, no. 1 (1984): 16–27.

Crispin Aubrey, "The Making of *1984*," in *"Nineteen Eighty-Four" in 1984: Autonomy, Control and Communication*, ed. Paul Chilton and Crispin Aubrey (London: Comedia, 1983), 7–14.

Richard W. Bailey, "George Orwell and the English Language," in *The Future of "Nineteen Eighty-Four*," ed. Ejner J. Jensen (Ann Arbor: University of Michigan Press, 1984), 23–46.

John H. Barnsley, "'The Last Man in Europe': A Comment on George Orwell's *1984*," *ContempR* 239 (July 1981): 30–34.

Elaine Hoffman Baruch, "'The Golden Country': Sex and Love in *1984*," in *"1984" Revisited: Totalitarianism in Our Century*, ed. Irving Howe (New York: Harper & Row, 1983), 47–56.

Beatrice Battaglia, "'The Quick and the Dead': Mito e utopia in *Nineteen Eighty-Four* di George Orwell," in *Per una definizione dell'utopia: Metodologie e discipline a confronto*, ed. Nadia Minerva (Ravenna: Longo, 1992), 121–35.

Gorman Beauchamp, "From Bingo to Big Brother: Orwell on Power and Sadism," in *The Future of "Nineteen Eighty-Four*," ed. Ejner J. Jensen (Ann Arbor: University of Michigan Press, 1984), 65–85.

Gorman Beauchamp, "*1984*: Oceania as an Ideal State," *CollL* 11 (Winter 1984): 1–12.

Hanna Behrend, "George Orwell: *1984*—The Vital Factor," *ZAA* 32, no. 3 (1984): 234–40.

Nadiia Belashova, "Slidamy orvellivs'koho bumu," *Vsesvit* 4 (April 1988): 146–47.

Bernard Bergonzi, "*Nineteen Eighty-Four* and the Literary Imagination," *DQR* 15, no. 3 1985: 211–28. Reprinted in *Between Dream and Nature: Essays on Utopia and Dystopia*, ed. Dominic Baker-Smith and C. C. Barfoot (Amsterdam: Rodopi, 1987), 211–28.

Alain Besancon and Elena Benarroch, "*1984*: Orwell y nosotros," *RO* 33–34 (1984): 65–78.

George F. Bishop, "Manipulation and Control of People's Responses to Public Opinion Polls: An Orwellian Experiment in *1984*," in *The Orwellian Moment: Hindsight and Foresight in the Post-1984 World*, ed. Robert L. Savage, James Combs, and Dan Nimmo (Fayetteville: University of Arkansas Press, 1989), 119–29.

Stephen Blakemore, "Language and Ideology in Orwell's *1984*," *ST&P* 10 (Fall 1984): 349–56.

Uwe Boker, "Zur Namengebung in Orwells *1984*," *Anglia* 104, no. 1–2 (1986): 122–31.

Gilbert Bonifas, "L'Anti-utopie face a l'histoire: Le Cas de *Nineteen Eighty-Four*," *Cycnos* 4 (1988): 107–17.

Raimond Borgmeier, "Nature in Orwell's *Nineteen Eighty-Four*," in *Essays from Oceania and Eurasia: George Orwell and "1984*," ed. Benoit J. Suykerbuyk (Antwerp: University Instelling Antwerpen, 1984), 111–19.

Karel Boullart, "Metaphor, Discursiveness, and Death, or 'Big Brother, the Eternal Drudge,'" in *Essays from Oceania and Eurasia: George Orwell and "1984*," ed. Benoit J. Suykerbuyk (Antwerp: University Instelling Antwerpen, 1984), 165–74.

J. Brooks Bouson, "The 'Hidden Agenda' of Winston Smith: Pathological Narcissism and *1984*," *HSL* 18, no. 1 (1986): 8–20.

Uwe Boker, "Der sozialistische und der totalitare Winston Smith: Ubersehene Aspekte der politischen Analyse in Orwells *1984*," *Archiv* 221, no. 2 (1984): 268–85.

Manuel Brito, "El concepto de 'doublethink' en *1984* y su relacion con el solipsismo linguistico," *RFULL* 2 (1983): 101–7.

R. Buisson, "Anti-Utopie au corruption d'un ideal dans *1984*," in *Autour de l'ideé de Nature: Histoire des ideés et civilisation* (Paris: Didier, 1977), 193–201.

Anthony Burgess, "Utopia and Science-Fiction," in *Essays from Oceania and Eurasia: George Orwell and "1984,"* ed. Benoit J. Suykerbuyk (Antwerp: University Instelling Antwerpen, 1984), 3–18.

Steve Carter, "'Freedom is Slavery': History, the Reader and *1984*," *SCRev* 17, no. 1 (1984): 3–15.

William Casement, "Another Perspective on Orwellian Pessimism," *IFR* 15 (Winter 1988): 48–50.

William Casement, "*Nineteen Eighty-Four* and Philosophical Realism," *MidWQ* 30 (Winter 1989): 215–28.

Jean Chesneaux, "De la novlangue a la nuclangue," *LQ* 411 (16–29 February 1984): 10–11.

Jean Chesneaux, "Our *1984*: The Planet-Wide Model of Compulsory Modernity: From INGSOC to PLAMOD," in *Essays from Oceania and Eurasia: George Orwell and "1984,"* ed. Benoit J. Suykerbuyk (Antwerp: University Instelling Antwerpen, 1984), 159–64.

Jean-Louis Chevalier, "Vestiges et reliques dans *1984*," *CRLI* 9 (1984): 155–64.

Paul Chilton, "Newspeak: It's The Real Thing," in *"Nineteen Eighty-Four" in 1984: Autonomy, Control and Communication*, ed. Paul Chilton and Crispin Aubrey (London: Comedia, 1983), 33–44.

Paul Chilton, "Orwell's Conception of Language," in *Essays from Oceania and Eurasia: George Orwell and "1984,"* ed. Benoit J. Suykerbuyk (Antwerp: University Instelling Antwerpen, 1984), 99–110.

Paul Chilton, "Orwell, Language and Linguistics," *Lang&C* 4, no. 2 (1984): 129–46.

Jerry B. Clavner, "Genesis XI: Orwell and Language," *CuyahogaR* 2 (Spring–Summer 1984): 23–26.

Terry Christensen, "Britain in *1984*," *SJS* 10 (Winter 1984): 6–24.

James Combs, "Towards 2084: Continuing the Orwellian Tradition," in *The Orwellian Moment: Hindsight and Foresight in the Post-1984 World*, ed. Robert L. Savage, James Combs, and Dan Nimmo (Fayetteville: University of Arkansas Press, 1989), 152–77.

Mike Cooley and Mike Johnson, "The Robots' Return?" in *"Nineteen Eighty-Four" in 1984: Autonomy, Control and Communication*, ed. Paul Chilton and Crispin Aubrey (London: Comedia, 1983), 71–78.

Thomas W. Cooper, "Fictional 1984 and Factual 1984: Ethical Questions Regarding the Control of Consciousness by Mass Media," in *The Orwellian Moment: Hindsight and Foresight in the Post-1984 World*, ed. Robert L. Savage, James Combs, and Dan Nimmo (Fayetteville: University of Arkansas Press, 1989), 83–107.

Philip Corrigan, "Hard Machines, Soft Messages," in *"Nineteen Eighty-Four" in 1984: Autonomy, Control and Communication*, ed. Paul Chilton and Crispin Aubrey (London: Comedia, 1983), 98–104.

Jean-Jacques Courtine and Laura Willett, "A Brave New Language: Orwell's Invention of Newspeak in *1984*," *SubStance* 15, no. 2 (1986): 69–74.

Bernard Crick, "*Nineteen Eighty-Four*: Satire or Prophecy?" *DQR* 13, no. 2 (1983): 90–102.

Bernard Crick, "*Nineteen Eighty-Four* and 1984: Satire or Prophecy?" in *Essays from Oceania and Eurasia: George Orwell and "1984*," ed. Benoit J. Suykerbuyk (Antwerp: University Instelling Antwerpen, 1984), 75–78. Reprinted in *The Future of Nineteen Eighty-Four*, ed. Ejner J. Jensen (Ann Arbor: University of Michigan Press, 1984), 7–21. Reprinted as "Reading Nineteen Eighty-Four as Satire," in *Reflections on America, 1984: An Orwell Symposium*, ed. Robert Mulvihill (Athens: University of Georgia Press, 1986), 15–45.

Robert Currie, "The 'Big Truth' in *Nineteen Eighty-Four*," *EIC* 34 (January 1984): 56–69.

Luk De Vos, "News-peak: He Hated B. B.," in *Essays from Oceania and Eurasia: George Orwell and "1984*," ed. Benoit J. Suykerbuyk (Antwerp: University Instelling Antwerpen, 1984), 91–98.

Thomas Dilworth, "'The Village Blacksmith' in *Nineteen Eighty-Four*," *IFR* 8 (Winter 1981): 63–65.

Kurt Dittmar, "Die Fiktionalisierung der Wirklichkeit als antiutopische Fiktion: Manipulative Realitatskontrolle in George Orwells *Nineteen Eighty-Four*," *DVLG* 58 (December 1984): 679–712.

R. Bruce Douglass, "The Fate of Orwell's Warning," *Thought* 60 (September 1985): 263–74.

Lillian Feder, "Selfhood, Language and Reality: George Orwell's *Nineteen Eighty-Four*," *GaR* 37 (Summer 1983): 392–409.

Ana Francisca Fernandez de Elio, "Neolengua y lenguaje poetico en la novela *1984* de George Orwell," *Kañina* 5 (January–June 1981): 103–9.

ORWELL, GEORGE, *1984*

Howard Fink, "Orwell versus Koestler: *Nineteen Eighty-Four* as Optimistic Satire," in *George Orwell*, ed. Courtney T. Wemyss and Alexej Ugrinsky (Westport, CT: Greenwood, 1987), 101–09.

Carl Freedman, "Antinomies of *Nineteen Eighty-Four*," *MFS* 30 (Winter 1984): 601–20.

Averil Gardner, "The Last Man in Europe: *Nineteen Eighty-Four*," in *George Orwell* (Boston: Twayne, 1987), 108–23.

Armelle Gauffenic, "*1984*: From Fiction to Reality," in *Essays from Oceania and Eurasia: George Orwell and "1984*," ed. Benoit J. Suykerbuyk (Antwerp: University Instelling Antwerpen, 1984), 121–25.

Charles Gilman, "If FORTRAN = Newspeak or BASIC = Newspeak then *1984*: Computerese as an Orwellian Language," *CuyahogaR* 2 (Spring–Summer 1984): 34–43.

Andre Glucksmann and Eva del Campo, "Camarada Big Brother," *Quimera* 35 (January 1984): 40–41.

Graham Good, " 'Ingsoc in Relation to Chess': Reversible Opposites in Orwell's *1984*," *Novel* 18 (Fall 1984): 50–63.

Erika Gottlieb, *The Orwell Conundrum: A Cry of Despair or Faith in the Spirit of Man?* (Ottawa: Carleton University Press, 1992), 1–313.

Erika Gottlieb, "Political Allegory and Psychological Realism in Orwell's *1984*," *AJES* 9, no. 1 (1984): 64–89.

Russell Gray, "*Nineteen Eighty-Four* and the Massaging of the Media," in *George Orwell*, ed. Courtney T. Wemyss and Alexej Ugrinsky (Westport, CT: Greenwood, 1987), 111–17.

Colin Greenland, "Images of *Nineteen Eighty-Four*: Fiction and Prediction," in *Storm Warnings: Science Fiction Confronts the Future*, ed. George Edgar Slusser, Colin Greenland, and Eric S. Rabkin (Carbondale: Southern Illinois University Press, 1987), 124–34.

Kathryn M. Grossman, " 'Through a glass darkly': Utopian Imagery in *Nineteen Eighty-Four*," *US* 1 (1987): 52–60.

Brigitte de Guillebon, "Le Corps dans *1984*," *CRLI* 9 (1984): 147–52.

Basia Miller Gulati, "Orwell's *Nineteen Eighty-Four*: Escape from Doublethink," *IFR* 12 (Summer 1985): 79–83.

Leah Hadomi, " 'A Look an' a Word an' the Dreams They Stirred!' " *DQR* 15, no. 2 (1985): 73–91.

Leah Hadomi, "*Nineteen Eighty-Four* as Dystopia," in *George Orwell*, ed. Courtney T. Wemyss and Alexej Ugrinsky (Westport, CT: Greenwood, 1987), 119–25.

Roy Harris, "The Misunderstanding of Newspeak," *TLS* (6 January 1984): 17. Revised and reprinted in *George Orwell*, ed. Harold Bloom (New York: Chelsea House, 1986), 113–19.

Irving Howe and Georges Giral, "*1984*: Les Enigmes du pouvoir," *QL* 411 (16–29 February 1984): 5–7.

Earl G. Ingersoll, "The Decentering of Tragic Narrative in George Orwell's *Nineteen Eighty-Four*," *StHum* 16 (December 1989): 69–83.

Marcel Janssens, "Orwell in een kadertje," *DWB* 129 (December 1984): 735–50.

Claude Jolicoeur, "George Orwell et l'imagination dans *1984* ou les metamorphoses du fantastique politique," in *Echanges: Actes du Congres de Strasbourg*, ed. G. Laprevotte (Paris: Didier, 1982), 301–07.

Claude Jolicoeur, "*1984*: La Denonciation du rêve utopique," *Moreana* 21 (June 1984): 55–70.

Claude Jolicoeur, "Orwell et l'utopie," *CRLI* 9 (1984): 111–20.

Jean-Daniel Jurgensen, "Vers *1984*: Orwell et la liberté," *NRDM* (August 1981): 285–92.

Bernd Kahrmann, "Orwells *1984*," *NG/FH* 39, no. 11–12 (1984): 150–55. Reprinted as "George Orwell, *Nineteen Eighty-Four*," in *Literarische Utopien von Morus bis zur Gegenwart*, ed. Klaus L. Berghahn and Ulrich Seeber (Konigstein/Ts.: Athenaum, 1983), 233–50.

Alfred Kazin, "'Not One of Us': George Orwell and *Nineteen Eighty-Four*," in *George Orwell & Nineteen Eighty-Four: The Man and the Book* (Washington, DC: Library of Congress, 1985), 70–78.

Nadia Khouri, "Reaction and Nihilism: The Political Genealogy of Orwell's *1984*," *SFS* 12 (July 1985): 136–47.

Daniel Kies, "The Uses of Passivity: Suppressing Agency in *Nineteen Eighty-Four*," in *Advances in Systemic Linguistics: Recent Theory and Practice*, ed. Martin Davies and Louise Ravelli (London: Pinter, 1992), 229–50.

Gunter Kunert and William Riggan, "What Orwell Did Not Foresee," *WLT* 58 (Spring 1984): 197–99.

Bernhard Kytzler, "Das literarische Genre von *1984*," *Moreana* 21 (June 1984): 49–54.

Berel Lang, "*1984*: Newspeak, Technology and the Death of Language," *Soundings* 72 (Spring 1989): 165–77.

Paul Lashmar, "Information as Power," in *"Nineteen Eighty-Four" in 1984: Autonomy, Control and Communication*, ed. Paul Chilton and Crispin Aubrey (London: Comedia, 1983), 79–88.

Maurice Levy, "Orwell: Prophete, temoin, ou psychopathe?" *CRLI* 9 (1984): 123–31.

Florence Lewis and Peter Moss, "The Tyranny of Language," in *"Nineteen Eighty-Four" in 1984: Autonomy, Control and Communication*, ed. Paul Chilton and Crispin Aubrey (London: Comedia, 1983), 45–57.

Arthur Liebman, "The Political Economic Problems of *1984*," in *George Orwell and 1984*, ed. Michael Skovmand (Aarhus, Denmark: Seklos, Department of English, University of Aarhus, 1984), 28–38.

Samuel L. Macey, "George Orwell's *1984*: The Future That Becomes the Past," *ESC* 11 (December 1985): 450–58.

James McNamara and Dennis J. O'Keeffe, "Waiting for *1984*: On Orwell & Evil," *Encounter* 59 (December 1982): 43–48.

Stefano Manferlotti, "Pozzo de Babele: Parola e morte in *1984*," *Belfagor* 39 (31 July 1984): 397–408.

Leo Mates, "Ring Out Orwell's *1984*," *ContempR* 246 (August 1985): 67–70.

Gilles Menegaldo, "L'Espace de la quête dans *1984*," *CRLI* 9 (1984): 133–45.

Arthur Mettinger, "Unendurable Unpersons Unmask Unexampled Untruths: Remarks on the Functions of Negative Prefixes in Orwell's *1984*," in *A Yearbook of Studies in English Language and Literature 1985/86*, ed. Otto Rauchbauer (Vienna: Braumuller, 1986), 109–18.

Jeffrey Meyers, "*Nineteen Eighty-Four*: A Novel of the 1930s," in *George Orwell & "Nineteen Eighty-Four": The Man and the Book* (Washington, DC: Library of Congress, 1985), 79–93. Reprinted in *George Orwell*, ed. Courtney T. Wemyss and Alexej Ugrinsky (Westport, CT: Greenwood, 1987), 135–43.

Mark Crispin Miller, "Big Brother Is You, Watching," *GaR* 38 (Winter 1984): 695–719.

Mark Crispin Miller, "The Fate of *1984*," in *1984 Revisited: Totalitarianism in Our Century*, ed. Irving Howe (New York: Harper & Row, 1983), 19–46.

Giuseppe Mininni, "Chi controlla i segni, controlla la mente," *RILA* 17 (January–April 1985): 33–49.

Juan Molla, "*1984* frente a 1984: La hora del juicio para George Orwell," *RepL* 9 (January 1984): 19–21.

Therese Moreau, "'Mon Dieu! C'est 1984! Et j'ai oublié de prendre rendez–vous chez le coiffeur!" *ÉLT* 4 (1987): 81–92.

John S. Nelson, "Orwell's Political Myths and Ours," in *The Orwellian Moment: Hindsight and Foresight in the Post-1984 World*, ed. Robert L. Savage, James Combs, and Dan Nimmo (Fayetteville: University of Arkansas Press, 1989), 11–44.

Joyce McCarl Nielsen, "Women in Dystopia/Utopia: *1984* and Beyond," *IJWS* 7 (March–April 1984): 144–54.

Robert Nisbet, "*1984* and the Conservative Imagination," in *1984 Revisited: Totalitarianism in Our Century*, ed. Irving Howe (New York: Harper & Row, 1983), 180–206.

Michael Orange, "*Nineteen Eighty-Four* and the Spirit of Schweik," in *George Orwell*, ed. Courtney T. Wemyss and Alexej Ugrinsky (Westport, CT: Greenwood, 1987), 51–57.

Nicola Pantaleo, "Un caso di scrittura pluridiscorsiva: *1984* di George Orwell," in *La performance del testo: Atti del VII Cong. Nazionale dell'Assn. It. di Anglistica, Siena, 2–4 Nov. 1984*, ed. Franco Marucci and Adriano Bruttini (Siena: Ticci, 1986), 225–33.

Daphne Patai, "Gamesmanship and Androcentrism in Orwell's *1984*," *PMLA* 97 (October 1982): 856–70.

Frederick Pohl, "Coming Up on *1984*," in *Storm Warnings: Science Fiction Confronts the Future*, ed. George Edgar Slusser, Colin Greenland, and Eric S. Rabkin (Carbondale: Southern Illinois University Press, 1987), 97–113.

Paul Poupard, "Orwell contre l'espérance," *NRDM* (May 1984): 269–83.

Patrick Reilly, "*Nineteen Eighty-Four*: The Failure of Humanism," *CritQ* 24 (Autumn 1982): 19–30.

H. Mark Roelofs, "George Orwell's Obscured Utopia," *R&L* 19 (Summer 1987): 11–33.

Christopher Roper, "Taming the Universal Machine," in *"Nineteen Eighty-Four" in 1984: Autonomy, Control and Communication*, ed. Paul Chilton and Crispin Aubrey (London: Comedia, 1983), 58–70.

Murray N. Rothbard, "George Orwell and the Cold War: A Reconsideration," in *Reflections on America, 1984: An Orwell Symposium*, ed. Robert Mulvihill (Athens: University of Georgia Press, 1986), 5–14.

James B. Rule, "*1984*—The Ingredients of Totalitarianism," in *1984 Revisited: Totalitarianism in Our Century*, ed. Irving Howe (New York: Harper & Row, 1983), 166–79.

Richard K. Sanderson, "The Two Narrators and Happy Ending of *Nineteen Eighty-Four*," *MFS* 34 (Winter 1988): 587–95.

Fernando Savater, "*1984*: Sociopatologia de la consciencia fiscal," *RO* 33–34 (1984): 177–88.

Jurgen Schmidt, "George Orwell: *Nineteen Eighty-Four* (1949)," in *Die Utopie in der angloamerikanischen Literatur: Interpretationen*, ed. Hartmut Heuermann and Bernd-Peter Lange (Dusseldorf: Bagel, 1984), 235–58.

Nathan A. Scott, "Orwell's Legacy," in *George Orwell & "Nineteen Eighty-Four": The Man and the Book,* ed. Librarian of Congress (Washington, DC: Library of Congress, 1985), 104–20.

Roger Sharrock, "*1984* and the Rupture of Desire," *EIC* 34 (October 1984): 319–38.

T. A. Shippey, "Variations on Newspeak: The Open Question of *Nineteen Eighty-Four*," in *Storm Warnings: Science Fiction Confronts the Future*, ed. George Edgar Slusser, Colin Greenland, and Eric S. Rabkin (Carbondale: Southern Illinois University Press, 1987), 172–93.

Michael Skovmand, "The Battleground of *1984*: Readings and Appropriations," in *George Orwell and 1984*, ed. Michael Skovmand (Aarhus, Denmark: Seklos, Department of English, University of Aarhus, 1984), 47–58.

Michael E. Starr, "Memories of Tomorrow: The Context of Orwell's *1984*," *CuyahogaR* 2 (Spring–Summer 1984): 5–16.

William R. Steinhoff, "Afterword: The Inner Heart," in *The Future of Nineteen Eighty-Four*, ed. Ejner J. Jensen (Ann Arbor: University of Michigan Press, 1984), 201–08.

William Steinhoff, "Utopia Reconsidered: Comments on *1984*," in *No Place Else: Explorations in Utopian and Dystopian Fiction*, ed. Eric S. Rabkin, Martin H. Greenberg, and Joseph D. Olander (Carbondale: Southern Illinois University Press, 1983), 147–61.

Ralph Stewart, "Orwell's Waste Land," *IFR* 8 (Summer 1981): 150–52.

Jenny Taylor, "Desire Is Thoughtcrime," in *"Nineteen Eighty-Four" in 1984: Autonomy, Control and Communication*, ed. Paul Chilton and Crispin Aubrey (London: Comedia, 1983), 24–32.

Malcolm R. Thorp, "The Dynamics of Terror in Orwell's *1984*," *BYUS* 24 (Winter 1984): 3–17.

Annie Verut, "*1984*: De Dieu à 'Big Brother,'" in *Aspects du sacre dans la littérature anglo-americaine* (Reims: Pubs. du Centre de Recherche sur l'Imaginaire dans les Littératures de Langue Anglaise, 1979), 93–105.

David Ward, "Translating Registers: Proletarian Language in *1984*," *QFG* 3 (1984): 297–304.

Joseph Weizenbaum, "The Computer in the Orwellian Year," in *Reflections on America, 1984: An Orwell Symposium*, ed. Robert Mulvihill (Athens: University of Georgia Press, 1986), 130–35.

Frank Winter, "Was Orwell a Secret Optimist? The Narrative Function of the 'Appendix' to *Nineteen Eighty-Four*," in *Essays from Oceania and Eurasia: George Orwell and 1984*, ed. Benoit J. Suykerbuyk (Antwerp: University Instelling Antwerpen, 1984), 79–89.

Sheldon Wolin, "Counter–Enlightenment: Orwell's *Nineteen Eighty-Four*," in *Reflections on America, 1984: An Orwell Symposium*, ed. Robert Mulvihill (Athens: University of Georgia Press, 1986), 98–113.

Michael P. Zuckert, "Orwell's Hopes, Orwell's Fears: *1984* as a Theory of Totalitarianism," in *The Orwellian Moment: Hindsight and Foresight in the Post-1984 World*, ed. Robert L. Savage, James Combs, and Dan Nimmo (Fayetteville: University of Arkansas Press, 1989), 45–67.

PAYN, JAMES

By Proxy

Audrey Peterson, "Some Minor Voices," in *Victorian Masters of Mystery: From Wilkie Collins to Conan Doyle* (New York: Ungar, 1984), 180–82.

The Clyffards of Clyffe

Audrey Peterson, "Some Minor Voices," in *Victorian Masters of Mystery: From Wilkie Collins to Conan Doyle* (New York: Ungar, 1984), 178.

A Confidential Agent

Audrey Peterson, "Some Minor Voices," in *Victorian Masters of Mystery: From Wilkie Collins to Conan Doyle* (New York: Ungar, 1984), 182–87.

Like Father, Like Son

Audrey Peterson, "Some Minor Voices," in *Victorian Masters of Mystery: From Wilkie Collins to Conan Doyle* (New York: Ungar, 1984), 178–80.

Lost Sir Massingberd: A Romance of Real Life

Audrey Peterson, "Some Minor Voices," in *Victorian Masters of Mystery: From Wilkie Collins to Conan Doyle* (New York: Ungar, 1984), 173–78.

PEACOCK, THOMAS LOVE

Crotchet Castle

Katrina E. Bachinger, "Poe's Folio Club: A Pun on Peacock's Folliott," *N&Q* 31 (March 1984): 66.

James D. Mulvihill, "Thomas Love Peacock's *Crotchet Castle*: Reconciling the Spirits of the Age," *NCF* 38 (December 1983): 253–70.

Gryll Grange

James Mulvihill, "A Source for Peacock's Satire of Spiritualism in *Gryll Grange*," *N&Q* 32 (December 1987): 491–92.

Michael Slater, "Peacock's Victorian Novel," in *Dickens and Other Victorians: Essays in Honor of Philip Collins*, ed. Joanne Shattock (New York: St. Martin's, 1988), 172–84.

Headlong Hall

Anthony Harris, "Peacock's Lord Littlebrain," *N&Q* 31 (December 1984): 474-75.

James D. Mulvihill, "Peacock and Perfectibility in *Headlong Hall*," *CLIO* 13 (Spring 1984): 227–46.

Melincourt

James Mulvihill, "A New Coleridge Source for Peacock's *Melincourt*," *N&Q* 32 (September 1985): 344–45.

James Mulvihill, "A Tookean Presence in Peacock's *Melincourt*," *ES* 67 (June 1986): 216–20.

The Misfortunes of Elphin

Roger Simpson, "A Source for Peacock's *The Misfortunes of Elphin*," *N&Q* 33 (June 1986): 165–66.

Nightmare Abbey

Mark Cunningham, 'Fatout! Who Am I?': A Model for the Honourable Mr. Listless in Thomas Love Peacock's *Nightmare Abbey*," *ELN* 39 (September 1992): 43–45.

Klaus Schwank, "From Satire to Indeterminacy: Thomas Love Peacock's *Nightmare Abbey*," in *Beyond the Suburbs of the Mind: Exploring English Romanticism: Papers Delivered at Mannheim Symposium in Honour of Hermann Fischer*, ed. Michael Gassenmeier and Norbert H. Platz (Essen: Blaue Eule, 1987), 151–62.

Julia M. Wright, "Peacock's Early Parody of Thomas Moore in *Nightmare Abbey*," *ELN* 30 (June 1993): 31–38.

POWELL, ANTHONY

A Dance to the Music of Time

Donald Williams Bruce, "Anthony Powell: The Reversals and Renewals of Time," *ConR* 256 (June 1990): 309–14.

Mark A. R. Facknitz, "Self-Effacement as Revelation: Narration and Art in Anthony Powell's *Dance to the Music of Time*," *JML* 15 (Spring 1989): 519–29.

Lynette Felber, "The Fictional Narrator as Historian: Ironic Detachment and the Project of History in Anthony Powell's *A Dance to the Music of Time*," *CLIO* 22 (Fall 1992): 21–35.

Lynette Felber, "A Text of Arrested Desire: The Anticlimax of Extended Narrative in Anthony Powell's *A Dance to the Music of Time*," *Style* 22 (Winter 1988): 576–94.

Donald Gutierrez, "The Doubleness of Anthony Powell: Point of View in *A Dance to the Music of Time*," *APC* 21 (March 1985): 5–21.

Donald Gutierrez, "Exemplary Punishment: Anthony Powell's *Dance* as Comedy," *Greyfriar* 22 (1981): 27–44.

Keith Wilson, "Pattern and Process: The Narrative Strategies of Anthony Powell's *A Dance to the Music of Time*," *ESC* 11 (June 1985): 214–22.

POWELL, ANTHONY, *Hearing Secret Harmonies*

Hearing Secret Harmonies

M. D. Lindemann, "Nicholas Jenkins's Bonfire," *ESA* 26, no. 1 (1983): 27–37.

POWYS, JOHN COWPER

Atlantis

Peter G. Christensen, "*Atlantis*: Étude de la sexualite chez Powys," *Plein-Chant* 42–43 (Fall 1988): 251–61.

The Brazen Head

Peter G. Christensen, "Wessex, 1272: History in John Cowper Powys's *The Brazen Head*," *PowR* 6, no. 1 (1987–88): 28–34.

A Glastonbury Romance

Peter G. Christensen, "The Idea of the Feminine in John Cowper Powys's *A Glastonbury Romance*," *PowN* 6 (Spring–Summer 1990): 17–32.

Dorothee von Huene Greenberg, "Stone Worship and the Search for Community in John Cowper Powys's *A Glastonbury Romance*," *PowR* 8, no. 19 (1986): 36–42.

Ben Jones, "Exile and Presences: Powys's Nihilism," *PowN* 7 (Spring–Summer 1991): 4–20.

Ben Jones, "The 'Mysterious Word Esplumeoir' and Polyphonic Structure in *A Glastonbury Romance*," in *In the Spirit of Powys: New Essays*, ed. Denis Lane (Lewisburg, PA: Bucknell University Press; London: Associated University Presses, 1990), 71–85.

Charles Lock, "Polyphonic Powys: Dostoevsky, Bakhtin, and *A Glastonbury Romance*," *UTQ* 55 (Spring 1986): 261–81.

Susan Rands, "Aspects of the Topography of *A Glastonbury Romance*," *PowR* 5, no. 4 (1987): 27–40.

The Inmates

Susan Rands, "John Cowper Powys's *The Inmates*, an Allegory," *PowR* 8, no. 2 (1991): 49–58.

Maiden Castle

W. J. Keith, "The Archaeological Background to *Maiden Castle*," *PowR* 6, no. 2 (1988): 14–19.

Charles Lock, "'To ravage and redeem': *Maiden Castle* and the Violation of Form," *PowR* 6, no. 1 (1987–88): 16–27.

Margaret Moran, "Animating Fictions in *Maiden Castle*," in *In the Spirit of Powys: New Essays*, ed. Denis Lane (Lewisburg, PA: Bucknell University Press; London: Associated University Presses, 1990), 180–92.

Susan Rands, "The Gateposts of Stalbridge Park," *PowR* 8, no. 1 (1990): 54–55.

Owen Glendower

H. W. Fawkner, "*Owen Glendower*: Love at the Margins of Being," *PowR* 6, no. 3 (1989): 48–60.

Porius

Michael Ballin, "John Cowper Powys's *Porius* and the Dialectic of History," *PowR* 8, no. 19 (1986): 20–35.

Michael Ballin, "*Porius* and the Cauldron of Rebirth," in *In the Spirit of Powys: New Essays*, ed. Denis Lane (Lewisburg, PA: Bucknell University Press; London: Associated University Presses, 1990), 214–35.

Peter Christensen, "The Marriage of Myth and History in John Cowper Powys's *Porius*," *PowR* 8, no. 1 (1990): 16–23.

Denis Lane, "Elementalism in John Cowper Powys' *Porius*," *PLL* 17 (Fall 1981): 381–404.

Mark Patterson, "The Origins of John Cowper Powys's Myrddin Wyllt," *PowR* 8, no. 1 (1990): 3–15.

Weymouth Sands

Charles Lock, "*Weymouth Sands* and the Matter of Representation: Live Dogs, Stuffed Animals and Unsealed Stones," *PowR* 6, no. 3 (1989): 25–38.

Anthony Low, "Dry Sand and Wet Sand: Margins and Thresholds in *Weymouth Sands*," in *In the Spirit of Powys: New Essays*, ed. Denis Lane (Lewisburg, PA: Bucknell University Press; London: Associated University Presses, 1990), 112–35.

Janina Nordius, "Hav och sten: Ensamheter i *Weymouth Sands*," *Studiekamraten* 74, no. 2–3 (1992): 10–12.

Colin Style, "On Hardy's Sacred Ground: John Cowper Powys's *Weymouth Sands*," *PowR* 6, no. 17 (1985): 27–38.

Wolf Solent

Peter G. Christensen, "Jason's Poems in *Wolf Solent*," in *John Cowper Powys's "Wolf Solent": Critical Studies*, ed. Belinda Humfrey (Cardiff: University of Wales Press, 1990), 143–57.

Carole Coates, "Gerda and Christie," in *John Cowper Powys's "Wolf Solent": Critical Studies*, ed. Belinda Humfrey (Cardiff: University of Wales Press, 1990), 159–71.

T. J. Diffey, "Not in the Light of Truth: Philosophy and Poetry in *Wolf Solent*," in *John Cowper Powys's "Wolf Solent": Critical Studies*, ed. Belinda Humfrey (Cardiff: University of Wales Press, 1990), 69–85.

Peter Easingwood, "The Face on the Waterloo Steps," in *John Cowper Powys's "Wolf Solent": Critical Studies*, ed. Belinda Humfrey (Cardiff: University of Wales Press, 1990), 55–67.

Tony Hallett, "Ramsgard to Blacksod Continued," *PowR* 8, no. 1 (1990): 51–53.

Tony Hallett, "Ramsguard to Blacksod: The Setting of *Wolf Solent*," *PowR* 6, no. 4 (1989): 23–30.

John Hodgson, "'A Victim of Self-Vivisection'—John Cowper Powys and *Wolf Solent*," in *John Cowper Powys's "Wolf Solent": Critical Studies*, ed. Belinda Humfrey (Cardiff: University of Wales Press, 1990), 31–53.

Ian Hughes, "Allusion, Illusion, and Reality: Fact and Fiction in *Wolf Solent*," in *John Cowper Powys's "Wolf Solent": Critical Studies*, ed. Belinda Humfrey (Cardiff: University of Wales Press; 1990), 103–15.

Ben Jones, "The Look of the Other in *Wolf Solent*," in *John Cowper Powys's "Wolf Solent": Critical Studies*, ed. Belinda Humfrey (Cardiff: University of Wales Press, 1990), 131–41.

Gerd-Klaus Kaltenbrunner, "Ein Verlaufer der Postmoderne," *NDH* 34, no.4 (1987): 790–94.

Denis Lane, "The Elemental Image in *Wolf Solent*," in *In the Spirit of Powys: New Essays*, ed. Denis Lane (Lewisburg, PA: Bucknell University Press; London: Associated University Presses, 1990), 55–70.

Charles Lock, "*Wolf Solent*: Myth and Narrative," in *John Cowper Powys's "Wolf Solent": Critical Studies*, ed. Belinda Humfrey (Cardiff: University of Wales Press, 1990), 117–30.

Ned Lukacher, "Notre Homme des Fleurs: Wolf Solent's Metaphoric Legends," *PowR* 2 (Winter–Spring 1979–80): 64–73. Reprinted in *John Cowper Powys's "Wolf Solent": Critical Studies*, ed. Belinda Humfrey (Cardiff: University of Wales Press, 1990), 87–102.

Margaret Moran, "Creative Lies," in *John Cowper Powys's "Wolf Solent": Critical Studies*, ed. Belinda Humfrey (Cardiff: University of Wales Press, 1990), 191–214.

Janina Nordius, "Behind the Pigsty: On the Duplicity of Solitude in *Wolf Solent*," *PowR* 8, no. 2 (1991): 19–28.

J. S. Rodman, "Plotting *Wolf Solent*," *PowR* 8, no. 2 (1991): 10–19.

Patrick Samway, S.J., "Meditative Thoughts on *Wolf Solent* as Ineffable History," in *In the Spirit of Powys: New Essays*, ed. Denis Lane (Lewisburg, PA: Bucknell University Press; London: Associated University Presses, 1990), 43–54.

Penny Smith, "*Wolf Solent*: Exploring the Limits of the Will," in *John Cowper Powys's "Wolf Solent": Critical Studies*, ed. Belinda Humfrey (Cardiff: University of Wales Press, 1990), 215–25.

Elizabeth Tombs, "*Wolf Solent*: Prodding the Female Substance of the Earth," in *John Cowper Powys's "Wolf Solent": Critical Studies*, ed. Belinda Humfrey (Cardiff: University of Wales Press, 1990), 173–90.

POWYS, THEODORE FRANCIS

Innocent Birds

John Williams, "T. F. Powys: Absence and Exile in *Innocent Birds*," *PowR* 8, no. 2 (1991): 3–10.

Mr. Weston's Good Wine

Deborah Wills, "Problems of Ontology and Omnipotence in *Mr. Weston's Good Wine*," *PowR* 6, no. 2 (1988): 41–45.

Unclay

Bryn Gunnell, "T. F. Powys's *Unclay*, or the Unconditional Gift," *DUJ* 85 (January 1993): 95–103.

PRITCHETT, V. S.

"The Aristocrat"

Michel Pouillard, "V. S. Pritchett's 'The Aristocrat' as a One-Act Comedy," *JSSE* 6 (Spring 1986): 93–100.

"The Diver"

Pascal Aquien, "'The Diver'; Or, The Plunge into Fantasy," *JSSE* 6 (Spring 1986): 47–57.

"A Fly in the Ointment"

Pierre Yvard, "V. S. Pritchett and the Short Narrative in 'A Fly in the Ointment,'" *JSSE* 6 (Spring 1986): 111–21.

"Many Are Disappointed"

Genevieve Doze, "Two Tentative Readings of 'Many Are Disappointed' by V. S. Pritchett," *JSSE* 6 (Spring 1986): 59–66.

READE, CHARLES

The Cloister and the Hearth

Hans-Jurgen Diller, "Charles Read: *The Cloister and the Hearth*: A Tale of the Middle Ages (1861)," *A&E* 22 (1984): 129–42.

Dianna Vitanza, "*The Cloister and the Hearth*: A Popular Response to the Oxford Movement," *R&L* 18 (Fall 1986): 71–88.

RHYS, JEAN

After Leaving Mr. Mackenzie

Nancy Hemond Brown, "On Becoming a Butterfly: Issues of Identity in Jean Rhys's *After Mr. Mackenzie*," *JRR* 2 (Fall 1987): 6–15.

Arnold E. Davidson, "The Art and Economics of Destitution in Jean Rhys' *After Leaving Mr. Mackenzie*," *SNNTS* 16 (Summer 1984): 215–27.

Good Morning, Midnight

Jack Byrne, "Jean Rhys's *Good Morning, Midnight*: The Boulevard of Broken Dreams," *RCF* 5 (Summer 1985): 151–59.

Jan Curtis, "The Room and the Black Background: A Re-Interpretation of Jean Rhys's *Good Morning, Midnight*," *WLWE* 25 (Autumn 1985): 264–70.

Arnold E. Davidson, "The Dark Is Light Enough: Affirmation from Despair in Jean Rhys's *Good Morning, Midnight*," *ConL* 24 (Fall 1983): 349–64.

Mary Lou Emery, "The Paradox of Style: Metaphor and Ritual in *Good Morning, Midnight*," *RCF* 5 (Summer 1985): 145–50.

Judith Kegan Gardiner, "*Good Morning, Midnight*; Good Night, Modernism," *boundaryII* 11 (Fall–Winter 1982): 233–51.

Bianca Tarozzi, "The Turning Point: Themes in *Good Morning, Midnight*," *JRR* 3 (Spring 1989): 2–12.

Quartet

Silvia Albertazzi, "*Quartet* di Jean Rhys: Un minuetto in trascrizione jazzistica," in *Ritratto dell'artista come donna: Saggi sull'avanguardia del Novecento*, ed. Lilla Maria Crisafulli Jones and Vita Fortunati (Urbino: QuattroVenti, 1988), 113–31.

"Till September Petronella"

Carole Angier, "Week-End in Gloucestershire: Jean Rhys, Adrian Allinson and 'Till September Petronella,'" *JRR* 4 (Spring 1990): 2–14.

Voyage in the Dark

Jan Curtis, "Jean Rhys' *Voyage in the Dark*: A Re-Assessment," *JCL* 22, no. 1 (1987): 144–58.

Chantal Delourme, "*Voyage in the Dark*: Deuil d'un mythe," *JRR* 3 (Spring 1989): 12–19.

Pearl Hochstadt, "'Connais-tu le pays?' Anna Morgan's Double Voyage," *JRR* 1 (Spring 1987): 2–7.

Deborah Kelly Kloepfer, "*Voyage in the Dark*: Jean Rhys's Masquerade for the Mother," *ConL* 26 (Winter 1985): 443–59.

Francesco Marroni, "*Voyage in the Dark*: Jean Rhys e le stanze dell'esilio," *LetP* 17 (December 1986): 78–91.

Evelyn Hawthorne Vanouse, "Jean Rhys's *Voyage in the Dark*: Histories Patterned and Resolute," *WLWE* 28 (Spring 1988): 125–33.

Lucy Wilson, "European or Caribbean: Jean Rhys and the Language of Exile," *Frontiers* 10, no. 3 (1989): 68–72.

Wide Sargasso Sea

Stephanie Branson, "Magicked by the Place: Shadow and Substance in *Wide Sargasso Sea*," *JRR* 3 (Spring 1989): 19–28.

Jan Curtis, "The Secret of *Wide Sargasso Sea*," *Critique* 31 (Spring 1990): 185–97.

Françoise Defromont, "Memoires hantées: De Jane Eyre a *Wide Sargasso Sea*," *CVE* 27 (April 1988): 149–57.

Lee Erwin, "'Like in a Looking-Glass': History and Narrative in *Wide Sargasso Sea*," *Novel* 22 (Winter 1989): 143–58.

Mona Fayad, "Unquiet Ghosts: The Struggle for Representation in Jean Rhys's *Wide Sargasso Sea*," *MFS* 34 (Autumn 1988): 437–52.

Wilson Harris, "Jean Rhys's 'Tree of Life,'" *RCF* 5 (Summer 1985): 114–17.

Kristien Hemmerechts, "*Wide Sargasso Sea* van Jean Rhys: Een intertextuele feministische lezing," *SpL* 29, no. 1–2 (1987): 69–78.

Bettina L. Knapp, "Jean Rhys: *Wide Sargossa Sea*: Mother/Daughter Identification and Alienation," *JEP* 7 (August 1986): 211–26.

Anne Koenen, "The Fantastic as Feminine Mode: *Wide Sargasso Sea*," *JRR* 4 (Spring 1990): 15–27.

Missy Dehn Kubitschek, "Charting the Empty Spaces of Jean Rhys's *Wide Sargasso Sea*," *Frontiers* 9, no. 2 (1987): 23–28.

Barbara Lalla, "Discourse of Dispossession: Ex-Centric Journeys of the Un-Living in *Wide Sargasso Sea* and the Old English 'The Wife's Lament,'" *Ariel* 24 (July 1993): 55–72.

Lori Lawson, "Mirror and Madness: A Lacanian Analysis of the Feminine Subject in *Wide Sargasso Sea*," *JRR* 4 (Summer 1991): 19–27.

Thomas Loe, "Patterns of the Zombie in Jean Rhys's *Wide Sargasso Sea*," *WLWE* 31 (Spring 1991): 34–42.

Kathy Mezei, "'And It Kept Its Secret': Narration, Memory, and Madness in Jean Rhys' *Wide Sargasso Sea*," *Critique* 28 (Summer 1987): 195–209.

Maria Olaussen, "Jean Rhys's Construction of Blackness as Escape from White Femininity in *Wide Sargasso Sea*," *Ariel* 24 (April 1993): 65–82.

Rosa Maria Garcia Rayego, "Apuntes sobre la evolucion del punto de vista en la ficcion de Jean Rhys: *Wide Sargasso Sea*," *RAEI* 3 (November 1991): 49–55.

RICHARDSON, DOROTHY MILLER

The Pilgrimage

Allen McLaurin, "'Siamese Twins': The Verbal and the Visual in Dorothy Richardson's *Pilgrimage*," *Trivium* 18 (May 1983): 73–85.

Pointed Roofs

Sarah Schuyler, "Double-Dealing Fictions," *Genders* 9 (Fall 1990): 75–92.

RUSHDIE, SALMAN

Grimus

Catherine Cundy, "'Rehearsing Voices': Salman Rushdie's *Grimus*," *JCL* 27 (August 1992): 128–38.

Ib Johansen, "The Flight from the Enchanter: Reflections on Salman Rushdie's *Grimus*," *Kunapipi* 7, no. 1 (1985): 20–32.

P. Bayapa Reddy, "*Grimus*: An Analysis," *ComR* 1, no. 2 (1990): 5–9.

Haroun and the Sea of Stories

Aron R. Aji, "All names mean something": Salman Rushdie's *Haroun* and the Legacy of Islam," *ConL* 36 (Spring 1995): 103–29.

Jean-Pierre Durix, "'The Gardner of Stories': Salman Rushdie's *Haroun and the Sea of Stories*," *JCL* 29 (August 1993): 114–22.

Suchismita Sen, "Memory, Language and Society in Salman Rushdie's *Haroun and the Sea of Stories*," *ConL* 36 (Winter 1995): 654–75.

Sushila Singh, "*Haroun and the Sea of Stories*: Rushdie's Flight to Freedom," in *The Novels of Salman Rushdie*, ed. G. R. Taneja and R. K. Dhawan (New Delhi: Indian Society for Commonwealth Studies, 1992), 209–16.

Midnight's Children

Hedi Ben Abbes, "Abracadabra ou la magie de la conclusion de *Midnight's Children*," *ÉBC* 1 (December 1992): 63–71.

Ashutosh Banerjee, "Narrative Technique in *Midnight's Children*," *ComR* 1, no. 2 (1990): 23–32.

Jacqueline Bardolph, "Bombay, ville imaginaire dans *Midnight's Children* de Salman Rushdie," *Cycnos* 1 (1984): 83–92.

Una Chaudhuri, "Imaginative Maps," *Turnstile* 2, no. 1 (1990): 36–47.

Samir Dayal, "Talking Dirty: Salman Rushdie's *Midnight's Children*," *CE* 54 (April 1992): 431–45.

Jean-Pierre Durix, "Magic Realism in *Midnight's Children*," *ComE&S* 8 (Autumn 1985): 57–63.

Kathleen Flanagan, "The Fragmented Self in Salman Rushdie's *Midnight's Children*," *ComNE* 5 (Spring 1992): 38–45.

Clement Hawes, "Leading History by the Nose: The Turn to the Eighteenth Century in *Midnight's Children*," *MFS* 39 (Spring 1993): 147–68.

E. W. Herd, "Tin Drum and Snake-Charmer's Flute: Salman Rushdie's Debt to Gunter Grass," *NewCom* 6 (Autumn 1988): 205–18.

Jean Kane, "The Migrant Intellectual and the Body of History: Salman Rushdie's *Midnight's Children*," *ConL* 37 (Spring 1996): 94–118.

Indira Karamcheti, "Salman Rushdie's *Midnight's Children* as an Alternate Genesis," *PCP* 21 (November 1986): 81–84.

Arun P. Mukherjeee, "Characterization in Salman Rushdie's *Midnight's Children*: Breaking out of the Hold of Realism and Seeking the 'Alienation Effect,'" in *The New Indian Novel in English: A Study of the 1980s*, ed. Viney Kirpal (New Delhi: Allied, 1990), 109–20.

M. K. Naik, "A Life of Fragments: The Fate of Identity in *Midnight's Children*," *ILitR* 3 (October 1985): 63–68.

Shyamala A. Narayan, "*Midnight's Children*," *LCrit* 18, no. 3 (1983): 23–32.

Sudha Pai, "Expatriate Concerns in Salman Rushdie's *Midnight's Children*," *LCrit* 23, no. 4 (1988): 36–41.

Uma Parameswaran, "'Lest He Returning Chide': Saleem Sinai's Inaction in Salman Rushdie's *Midnight's Children*," *LCrit* 18, no. 3 (1983): 57–66.

K. J. Phillips, "Salman Rushdie's *Midnight's Children*: Models for Storytelling, East and West," in *Comparative Literature East and West: Traditions and Trends*, ed. Cornelia Moore and Raymond Moody (Honolulu: University of Hawaii Press; 1989), 202–07.

David J. Piwinski, "Losing Eden in Modern Bombay: Rushdie's *Midnight Children*," *NConL* 23 (May 1993): 10–12.

David W. Price, "Salman Rushdie's 'Use and Abuse of History' in *Midnight's Children*," *Ariel* 25 (April 1994): 91–107.

M. Madhusudana Rao, "Quest for Identity: A Study of the Narrative in Rushdie's *Midnight's Children*," *LCrit* 25, no. 4 (1990): 31–42.

Ron Shepherd, "*Midnight's Children* as Fantasy," *ComR* 1, no. 2 (1990): 33–43.

Sushila Singh, "Salman Rushdie's *Midnight's Children*: Rethinking the Life and Times in Modern India," *PURB* 16 (April 1985): 55–67.

Colin Smith, "The Unbearable Lightness of Salman Rushdie," in *Critical Approaches to the New Literatures in English, I*, ed. Dieter Riemenschneider (Essen: Blaue Eule, 1989), 104–15.

"Sprak, identitet, litteratur og historie: Samtale med Salman Rushdie," *Samtiden* 93, no. 4 (1984): 34–37.

John Stephens, "*Midnight's Children*: The Parody of an Indian Novel," *SPAN* 21 (October 1985): 184–208.

Joseph Swann, "'East Is East and West Is West'? Salman Rushdie's *Midnight's Children* as an Indian Novel," *WLWE* 26 (Autumn 1986): 353–62.Reprinted in *The New Indian Novel in English: A Study of the 1980s*, ed. Viney Kirpal (New Delhi: Allied, 1990), 251–62.

Stephane Tyssens, "*Midnight's Children*: Or, The Ambiguity of Impotence," *ComE&S* 12 (Autumn 1989): 19–29.

Keith Wilson, "*Midnight's Children* and Reader Responsibility," *CritQ* 26 (Autumn 1984): 23–37.

The Satanic Verses

Fawzia Afzal-Khan, "Religion as a Colonizing Power," in *International Literature in English: Essays on the Major Writers*, ed. Robert L. Ross (New York: Garland, 1991), 351–61.

Rudolf Bader, "*The Satanic Verses*: An Intercultural Experiment by Salman Rushdie," *IFR* 19, no. 2 (1992): 65–75.

Tim Brennan, "Rushdie, Islam, and Postcolonial Criticism," *SoT* 10, no. 2–3 (1992): 271–75.

Anthony Close, "The Empirical Author: Salman Rushdie's *The Satanic Verses*," *P&L* 14 (October 1990): 248–67.

Marlena G. Corcoran, "Salman Rushdie's Satanic Narration," *IowaR* 20 (Winter 1990): 155–67.

Jurgen Donnerstag, "Of what type—satanic, angelic—was Farishta's song?: Dekonstruktion als Darstellungsprinzip in Salman Rushdies *The Satanic Verses*," *ZAA* 40, no. 3 (1992): 227–37.

David Kerr, "Migration and the Human Spirit in Salman Rushdie's *The Satanic Verses*," *ComR* 2, no. 1–2 (1990–1991): 168–80.

Feroza Jussawalla, "Post-Joycean Sub-Joycean: The Reverses of Mr. Rushdie's Tricks in *The Satanic Verses*," in *The New Indian Novel in English: A Study of the 1980s*, ed. Viney Kirpal (New Delhi: Allied, 1990), 227–38.

Ali A. Mazrui, "Moral Dilemmas of the *Satanic Verses*," *BS* 20 (March–April 1989): 19–32.

Aamir Mufti, "*The Satanic Verses* and the Cultural Politics of 'Islam': A Response to Brennan," *SoT* 10, no. 2–3 (1992): 277–82.

David Myers, "From Satiric Farce to Tragic Epiphany: Salman Rushdie's *The Satanic Verses*," *ComR* 2, no. 1–2 (1990–1991): 144–67.

Peter Nazareth, "Rushdie Wo/manichean Novel," *IowaR* 20 (Winter 1990): 168–74.

Ronny Noor, "Reclaiming 'Mahound': An Intention Misunderstood?" *NConL* 22 (May 1992): 5–6.

Pierre Pachet, "*Les Versets sataniques*: Salman Rushdie et l'heritage des religions," *Esprit* 158 (January 1990): 5–22.

Nicholas D. Rombes, Jr., "*The Satanic Verses* as a Cinematic Narrative," *LFQ* 21 (January 1993): 47–53.

Saadi A. Simawe, "Rushdie's *The Satanic Verses* and Heretical Literature in Islam," *IowaR* 20 (Winter 1990): 185–98.

Beert C. Verstraete, "Classical References and Themes in Salman Rushdie's *The Satanic Verses*," *CML* 10 (Summer 1990): 327–34.

Helen Watson-Williams, "Finding a Father: A Reading of Salman Rushdie's *The Satanic Verses*," *Westerly* 35 (March 1990): 66–71.

Shame

Rudolf Bader, "On Blood and Blushing: Bipolarity in Salman Rushie's *Shame*," *IFR* 15 (Winter 1988): 30–33.

Ashutosh Banerjee, "A Critical Study of *Shame*," *ComR* 1, no. 2 (1990): 71–76.

Indira Bhatt, "*Shame*: A Thematic Study," *ComR* 1, no. 2 (1990): 64–70.

Suresh Chandra, "The Metaphor of *Shame*: Rushdie's Fact-Fiction," *ComR* 1, no. 2 (1990): 77–84.

Jean-Pierre Durix, "The Artistic Journey in Salman Rushdie's *Shame*," *WLWE* 23 (Spring 1984): 451–63.

M. D. Fletcher, "Rushdie's *Shame* as Apologue," *JCL* 21 (August 1986): 120–32.

Inderpal Grewal, "Salman Rushdie: Marginality, Women, and *Shame*," *Genders* 3 (November 1988): 24–42.

Michael Hollington, "Salman Rushdie's *Shame*," *Meanjin* 43 (September 1984): 403–07.

Feroza Jussawalla, "Rushdie's *Shame*: Problems in Communication," in *Studies in Indian Fiction in English*, ed. G. S. Balarama Gupta (Gulgarga, India: JIWE Publications, 1987), 1–13.

O. P. Mathur, "Sense and Sensibility in *Shame*," *ComR* 1, no. 2 (1990): 85–93.

D. S. Mishra, "Narrative Techniques of Salman Rushdie's *Shame*," *PURB* 18 (April 1987): 37–44.

Stephanie Moss, "The Cream of the Crop: Female Characters in Salman Rushdie's *Shame*," *IFR* 19, no. 1 (1992): 28–30.

Susan Oommen, "Fictional Intent in Rushdie's *Shame*," *LCrit* 20, no. 2 (1985): 36–41.

Uma Parameswaran, "Salman Rushdie's *Shame*: An Overview of a Labyrinth," in *The New Indian Novel in English: A Study of the 1980s*, ed. Viney Kirpal (New Delhi: Allied, 1990), 121–30.

Sushila Singh, "*Shame*: Salman Rushdie's Judgement on Pakistan," in *Studies in Indian Fiction in English*, ed. G. S. Balarama Gupta (Gulgarga, India: JIWE Publications, 1987), 14–24.

S. K. Tikoo, "*Shame*: A Modern Comic Epic in Prose," *ComR* 1, no. 2 (1990): 44–63.

Helen Watson-Williams, "An Antique Land: Salman Rushdie's *Shame*," *Westerly* 29 (December 1984): 37–45.

SAYERS, DOROTHY L[EIGH]

Busman's Honeymoon

Mary Brian Durkin O. P., "The Later Novels—Murder and Manners," in *Dorothy L. Sayers* (Boston: Twayne, 1980), 78–81.

Dawson Gaillard, "Precarious Balance," in *Dorothy L. Sayers* (New York: Ungar, 1981), 83–87, 96–97.

Trevor H. Hall, "The Dates in *Busman's Honeymoon*," in *Dorothy L. Sayers: Nine Literary Studies* (London: Duckworth, 1980), 104–13.

Nancy-Lou Patterson, "Beneath That Ancient Roof: The House as Symbol in Dorothy L. Sayers' *Busman's Honeymoon*," *Mythlore* 10 (Winter 1984): 39–46; 48.

B. J. Rahn, "The Marriage of True Minds," in *Dorothy L. Sayers: The Centenary Celebration*, ed. Alizina Stone Dale (New York: Walker, 1993), 64–65.

William Reynolds, "Dorothy L. Sayers' *Busman's Honeymoon* and the Mind of Its Maker," *Clues* 10 (Fall–Winter 1989): 65–81.

Clouds of Witness

Mary Brian Durkin O. P., "The Early Novels—Murder and Mirth," in *Dorothy L. Sayers* (Boston: Twayne, 1980), 35–39.

Dawson Gaillard, "Detective Short Stories," in *Dorothy L. Sayers* (New York: Ungar, 1981), 29–31, 34–35, 37–39.

Sharon McCrumb, "Where the Bodies are Buried: The Real Murder Cases in the Crime Novels of Dorothy L. Sayers," in *Dorothy L. Sayers: The Centenary Celebration*, ed. Alizina Stone Dale (New York: Walker, 1993), 93–95.

The Documents in the Case
(with Robert Eustace)

Mary Brian Durkin O. P., "The Early Novels—Murder and Mirth," in *Dorothy L. Sayers* (Boston: Twayne, 1980), 46–52.

Dawson Gaillard, "Toward a Detective Novel of Manners," in *Dorothy L. Sayers* (New York: Ungar, 1981), 46–49.

Trevor H. Hall, "*The Documents in the Case*," in *Dorothy L. Sayers: Nine Literary Studies* (London: Duckworth, 1980), 62–74.

H. F. R. Keating, "Dorothy L's Mickey Finn," in *Dorothy L. Sayers: The Centenary Celebration*, ed. Alizina Stone Dale (New York: Walker, 1993), 134–38.

Catherine Kenney, "Moral Fiction," in *The Remarkable Case of Dorothy L. Sayers* (Kent, OH: Kent State University Press, 1990), 198–203.

Five Red Herrings
(U. S. Title: *Suspicious Characters*)

Mary Brian Durkin O. P., "The Later Novels—Murder and Manners," in *Dorothy L. Sayers* (Boston: Twayne, 1980), 57–61, 67.

Dawson Gaillard, "From Puzzle to Manners to Mystery," in *Dorothy L. Sayers* (New York: Ungar, 1981), 55–58, 62–65.

Gaudy Night

Miriam Brody, "The Haunting of *Gaudy Night*: Misreadings in a Work of Detective Fiction," *Style* 19 (Spring 1985): 94–116.

SueEllen Campbell, "The Detective Heroine and Death of Her Hero: Dorothy Sayers to P. D. James," in *Feminism in Women's Detective Fiction*, ed. Glenwood Irons (Toronto: University of Toronto Press, 1995), 12–28.

Stephen P. Clarke, "*Gaudy Night*'s Legacy: P. D. James's *An Unsuitable Job for a Woman*," *Sayers Review* 4, no. 1 (1977): 1–12.

Mary Brian Durkin O. P., "The Later Novels—Murder and Manners," in *Dorothy L. Sayers* (Boston: Twayne, 1980), 73–78.

Nicolas Freeling, "*Gaudy Night* in 1935," in *Julian Symons at 80: A Tribute*, ed. Patricia Craig (Helsinki: Eurographica, 1992), 121–29.

Dawson Gaillard, "Precarious Balance," in *Dorothy L. Sayers* (New York: Ungar, 1981), 71–79, 82–84, 97–98.

Margaret P. Hannay, "Head versus Heart in Dorothy L. Sayers' *Gaudy Night*," *Mythlore* 6 (Summer 1979): 33–37.

Carolyn G. Hart, "*Gaudy Night*: Quintessential Sayers," in *Dorothy L. Sayers: The Centenary Celebration*, ed. Alzinia Stone Dale (New York: Walker, 1993), 45–50.

Carolyn G. Heilbrun, "*Gaudy Night* and Its American Women Readers," Presentation published by Proceedings of the 1985 Sayers Society Seminar.

Lillian M. Heldreth, "Breaking the Rules of the Game: Shattered Patterns in Dorothy L. Sayers' *Gaudy Night*," *Clues* 3 (Spring–Summer 1982): 120–27.

Catherine Kenney, "*Gaudy Night* and the Mystery of the Human Heart," in *The Remarkable Case of Dorothy L. Sayers* (Kent, OH: Kent State University Press, 1990), 81–119.

Q. D. Leavis, "The Case of Miss Dorothy Sayers," *Scrutiny* 6 (December 1937): 621–22.

Donald G. Marshall, "*Gaudy Night*: An Investigation of Truth," *Seven* 4 (1983): 98–114.

B. J. Rahn, "The Marriage of True Minds," in *Dorothy L. Sayers: The Centenary Celebration*, ed. Alizina Stone Dale (New York: Walker, 1993), 51–52, 57–63.

William Reynolds, "Literature, Latin, and Love: Dorothy L. Sayers' *Gaudy Night*," *Clues* 6 (Spring–Summer 1985): 67–78.

Janice Rossen, "Oxford in Loco Parentis: The College as Mother in Dorothy Sayers' *Gaudy Night*," in *University Fiction*, ed. David Bevan (Amsterdam: Rodopi, 1990), 139–56.

Ian Stuart, "D. L. S.: An Unsteady Throne?" in *Dorothy L. Sayers: The Centenary Celebration*, ed. Alizina Stone Dale (New York: Walker, 1993), 26–27.

Hangman's Holiday

Mary Brian Durkin O. P., "The Stories—Short but Sinister," in *Dorothy L. Sayers* (Boston: Twayne, 1980), 88–92.

Have His Carcase

Mary Brian Durkin O. P., "The Later Novels—Murder and Manners," in *Dorothy L. Sayers* (Boston: Twayne, 1980), 61–63.

Dawson Gaillard, "From Puzzle and Manners to Mystery," in *Dorothy L. Sayers* (New York: Ungar, 1981), 58–61, 64, 65, 95–96.

In the Teeth of the Evidence

Mary Brian Durkin O. P., "The Stories—Short but Sinister," in *Dorothy L. Sayers* (Boston: Twayne, 1980), 92–95.

Lord Peter Views a Body

Mary Brian Durkin O. P., “The Stories—Short but Sinister,” in *Dorothy L. Sayers* (Boston: Twayne, 1980), 84–88.

Murder Must Advertise

Dawson Gaillard, “From Puzzle and Manners to Mystery,” in *Dorothy L. Sayers* (New York: Ungar, 1981), 61–65.

Stephen Hahn, “Theodicy in Dorothy Sayers’ *Murder Must Advertise*,” *Renascence* 41 (Spring 1989): 169–76.

Nancy-Lou Patterson, “A Comedy of Masks: Lord Peter as Harlequin in *Murder Must Advertise*,” *Mythlore* 15 (Spring 1989): 22–28.

The Nine Tailors

Sarah Beach, “Harriet in Rehearsal: Hilary Thorpe in *The Nine Tailors*,” *Mythlore* 19 (Summer 1993): 37–39.

John G. Cawelti, *Adventure, Mystery, and Romance: Formula Stories in Art and Popular Culture* (Chicago: University of Chicago Press, 1976), 106–38.

Mary Brian Durkin O. P., “The Later Novels—Murder and Manners,” in *Dorothy L. Sayers* (Boston: Twayne, 1980), 67–73.

Dawson Gaillard, “From Puzzle and Manners to Mystery,” in *Dorothy L. Sayers* (New York: Ungar, 1981), 65–69, 80–82, 90–94.

Trevor H. Hall, “The Nebuly Coat,” in *Dorothy L. Sayers: Nine Literary Studies* (London: Duckworth, 1980), 36–39.

Catherine Kenney, “The Comedy of Dorothy L. Sayers,” in *Dorothy L. Sayers: The Centenary Celebration*, ed. Alizina Stone Dale (New York: Walker, 1993), 141–43.

Catherine Kenney, “*The Nine Tailors* and the Riddle of the Universe,” in *The Remarkable Case of Dorothy L. Sayers* (Kent, OH: Kent State University Press, 1990), 53–80.

Nancy-Lou Patterson, “A Ring of Good Bells: Providence and Judgement in Dorothy L. Sayers’ *The Nine Tailors*,” *Mythlore* 16 (Autumn 1989): 50–52.

Laurence Urdang, “*Nine Tailors*,” *Verbatim* 12 (Winter 1986): 15–16.

Strong Poison

Trevor H. Hall, "Dorothy L. Sayers and Psychical Research," in *Dorothy L. Sayers: Nine Literary Studies* (London: Duckworth, 1980), 119–23.

Gayle F. Wald, "*Strong Poison*: Love and the Novelistic in Dorothy Sayers," in *The Cunning Craft: Original Essays on Detective Fiction and Contemporary Literary Theory*, ed. Ronald G. Walker and June M. Frazer (Macomb: Western Illinois University Press, 1990), 98–108.

Unnatural Death
(U. S. Title: *The Dawson Pedigree*)

Mary Brian Durkin O. P., "The Early Novels—Murder and Mirth," in *Dorothy L. Sayers* (Boston: Twayne, 1980), 39–43.

Catherine Kenney, "*Unnatural Death* and the Testimony of Superfluous Women," in *The Remarkable Case of Dorothy L. Sayers* (Kent, OH: Kent State University Press, 1990), 128–40.

Unpleasantness at the Bellona Club

Mary Brian Durkin O. P., "The Early Novels—Murder and Mirth," in *Dorothy L. Sayers* (Boston: Twayne, 1980), 19–20, 43–46.

Whose Body?

Vera Brittain, *The Women at Oxford: A Fragment of History* (New York: Macmillan, 1960), 122–24.

Christopher Dean, "The Character of Lord Peter Wimsey in *Whose Body?*" *Inklings* 12 (1994): 11–26.

Mary Brian Durkin O. P., "The Early Novels—Murder and Mirth," in *Dorothy L. Sayers* (Boston: Twayne, 1980), 27–34.

SCOTT, SIR WALTER

Waverley Novels: Anne of Geierstein

Wilson F. Engel III, "Scott's *Anne of Geierstein*," *Expl* 40 (Summer 1982): 28–30.

Waverley Novels: The Antiquary

Wilson F. Engel III, "Scott's *The Antiquary*," *Expl* 40 (Summer 1982): 26–28.

Waverley Novels: The Bride of Lammermoor

Daniel S. Butterworth, "Tinto, Pattieson and the Theories of Pictorial and Dramatic Representation in Scott's *Bride of Lammermoor*," *SoAR* 56 (January 1991): 1–15.

James Chandler, "Scott and the Scene of Explanation: Framing Contextuality in *The Bride of Lammermoor*," *SNNTS* 26 (Summer 1994): 69–98.

Caroline Franklin, "Feud and Faction in *The Bride of Lammermoor*," *ScLJ* 14 (November 1987): 18–31.

Brian Hollingworth, "The Tragedy of Lucy Ashton, *The Bride of Lammermoor*," *StSL* 19 (1984): 94–105.

James Kerr, "Scott's Dreams of the Past: *The Bride of Lammermoor* as Political Fantasy," *SNNTS* 18 (Summer 1986): 125–42.

Joseph Kestner, "Beyond Reason," *ON* 53 (February 1989): 8–12.

Harry E. Shaw, "Scott, Mackenzie, and Structure in *The Bride of Lammermoor*," *SNNTS* 13 (Winter 1981): 349–66.

Waverley Novels: Guy Mannering

Jana Davies, "Landscape Images and Epistemology in *Guy Mannering*," in *Scott and His Influence: Papers of the Aberdeen Scott Conference, 1982*, ed. J. H. Alexander and David Hewitt (Aberdeen: Association for Scottish Literary Studies, 1983), 119–28.

Jane Millgate, "The Structure of *Guy Mannering*," in *Scott and His Influence: Papers of the Aberdeen Scott Conference, 1982*, ed. J. H. Alexander and David Hewitt (Aberdeen: Association for Scottish Literary Studies, 1983), 109–18.

Waverley Novels: The Heart of Midlothian

Margaret Movshin Criscuola, "The Porteous Mob: Fact and Truth in *The Heart of Midlothian*," *ELN* 22 (September 1984): 43–50.

Thomas Dale, "The Jurists, the Dominie, and Jeanie Deans," *ScLJ* 11 (May 1984): 36–44.

Julian Meldon D'Arcy, "Davie Deans and Bothwell Bridge: A Re–Evaluation," *ScLJ* 12 (November 1985): 23–34.

Jana Davis, "Sir Walter Scott's *The Heart of Midlothian* and Scottish Common-Sense Morality," *Mosaic* 21 (Fall 1988): 55–63.

Rick A. Davies, "The Demon Lover Motif in *The Heart of Midlothian*," *StSL* 16 (1981): 91–96.

James Kerr, "Scott's Fable of Regeneration: *The Heart of Midlothian*," *ELH* 53 (Winter 1986): 801–20.

Jane Millgate, "Scott and the Law: *The Heart of Midlothian*," in *Rough Justice: Essays on Crime in Literature*, ed. M. L. Friedland (Toronto: University of Toronto Press, 1991), 95–113.

Mary Anne Schofield, "The 'Heart' of Midlothian: Jeanie Deans as Narrator," *SECC* 19 (1989): 153–64.

Harry E. Shaw, "Scott's 'Daemon' and the Voices of Historical Narration," *JEGP* 88 (January 1989): 21–33.

Jon Thompson, "Sir Walter Scott and Madge Wildfire: Strategies of Containment in *The Heart of Midlothian*," *L&H* 13 (Autumn 1987): 188–99.

Alistair D. Walker, "The Tentative Romantic: An Aspect of *The Heart of Midlothian*," *ES* 69 (April 1988): 146–57.

Daniel Whitemore, "Fagin, Effie Deans, and the Spectacle of the Courtroom," *DQu* 3 (September 1986): 132–34.

Waverley Novels: The Highland Widow

Graham Tulloch, "Imagery in *The Highland Widow*," *StSL* 21 (1986): 147–57.

Waverley Novels: Ivanhoe

Chris R. Vanden Bossche, "Culture and Economy in *Ivanhoe*," *NCF* 42 (June 1987): 46–72.

Blas Matamoro, "El lugar del heroe," *CHA* 386 (August 1982): 407–16.

Michael Ragussis, "Writing Nationalist History: England, The Conversion of the Jews, and *Ivanhoe*," *ELH* 60 (Spring 1993): 181–215.

Daniel Whitmore, "Scott's Indebtedness to the German Romantics: *Ivanhoe* Reconsidered," *WC* 15 (Spring 1984): 72–73.

Waverley Novels: Kenilworth

Wilson F. Engel, III, "Scott's *Kenilworth*," *Expl* 39 (Spring 1981): 11–12.

Waverley Novels: The Lay of the Last Minstrel

Lloyd Davis, "The Story in History: Time and Truth in Scott's *The Lay of the Last Minstrel*," *CLIO* 18 (Spring 1989): 221–39.

Waverley Novels: The Monastery

Andrzej Branny, "Walter Scott's *The Monastery* and the Myth of Romantic Middle Ages," *KN* 32, no. 4 (1985): 393–404.

Patricia Harkin, "The Fop, the Fairy, and the Genres of Scott's *Monastery*," *StSL* 19 (1984): 177–93.

Waverley Novels: Old Mortality

Deborah J. Barrett, "Balfour of Burley: The Evil Energy in Scott's *Old Mortality*," *StSL* 17 (1982): 248–53.

Jennifer B. Fleischner, "Class, Character and Landscape in *Old Mortality*," *ScLJ* 9 (December 1982): 21–36.

John B. Humma, "The Narrative Framing Apparatus of Scott's *Old Mortality*," *SNNTS* 12 (Winter 1980): 301–15.

Steven F. Klepeter, "Levels of Narration in *Old Mortality*," *WC* 13 (Winter 1982): 38–45.

Donald G. Priestman, "Old Battles Fought Anew: The Religious and Political Ramifications of Scott's *Old Mortality*," *WC* 12 (Spring 1981): 117–21.

Kenneth M. Sroka, "Scott's Aesthetic Parable: A Study of *Old Mortality*'s Two–Part Structure," *ELWIU* 10 (Fall 1983): 183–97.

Waverley Novels: The Pirate

Jana Davis, "Scott's *The Pirate*," *Expl* 45 (Spring 1987): 20–22.

Waverley Novels: Quentin Durward

R. V. Johnson, "An Assurance of Continuity: Scott's Model of Past and Present in *Quentin Durward*," *SoR* 13 (July 1980): 79–96.

Lionel Lackey, "Plausibility and the Romantic Plot Contsruction of *Quentin Durward*," *SP* 90 (Winter 1993): 101–14.

Joep Leerssen, "Image and Reality—and Belgium," in *Europa Provincia Mundi*, ed. Joep Leerssen and Karl Ulrich Syndram (Amsterdam: Rodopi, 1992), 281–91.

Waverley Novels: Redgauntlet

Bruce Beiderwell, "Scott's *Redgauntlet* as a Romance of Power," *StRom* 28 (Summer 1989): 273–90.

Margaret M. Criscuola, "Constancy and Change: The Process of History in Scott's *Redgauntlet*," *StSL* 20 (1985): 123–36.

James Kerr, "Fiction against History: Scott's *Redgauntlet* and the Power of Romance," *TSLL* 29 (Fall 1987): 237–60.

Rohan Maitzen, " 'By no means an improbable fiction': *Redgauntlet*'s novel historicism," *SNNTS* 25 (Summer 1993): 70–83.

Pierre Morere, "Historie et recit dans *Redgauntlet* de Walter Scott," *Caliban* 28 (1991): 25–35.

Mark A. Weinstein, "Law, History, and the Nightmare of Romance in *Redgauntlet*," in *Scott and His Influence: Papers of the Aberdeen Scott Conference*, 1982, ed. J. H. Alexander and David Hewitt (Aberdeen: Association for Scottish Literary Studies, 1983), 140–48.

Joanne Wilkes, "Scott's Use of Scottish Family History in *Redgauntlet*," *RES* 41 (May 1990): 200–11.

Waverley Novels: Rob Roy

Bruce Beiderwell, "Scott's *Rob Roy* and the Business of Revenge," *PQ* 67 (Spring 1988): 241–55.

Lars Hartveit, "The Hero in the Melting Pot: A Reading of Sir Walter Scott's *Rob Roy*," in *The Romantic Heritage: A Collection of Critical Essays*, ed. Karsten Engelberg (Copenhagen: University of Copenhagen, 1983), 53–80.

Lars Hartveit, "Interaction between Genre and Social Content in Sir Walter Scott, *Rob Roy*," in *Papers on Language and Literature: Presented to Alvar Ellegard and Erik Frykman*, ed. Sven Backman and Goran Kjellmer (Goteborg: ACTA University Gothoburgensis, 1985), 165–83.

David Hewitt, "*Rob Roy* and First Person Narratives," in *Scott and His Influence: Papers of the Aberdeen Scott Conf., 1982*, ed. J. H. Alexander and David Hewitt (Aberdeen: Association for Scottish Literary Studies, 1983), 372–81.

J. Derrick McClure, "Linguistic Characterisation in *Rob Roy*," *Scott and His Influence: Papers of the Aberdeen Scott Conference, 1982*, ed. J. H. Alexander and David Hewitt (Aberdeen: Association for Scottish Lit. Studies, 1983), 129–39.

Waverley Novels: St. Ronan's Well

H. Michael Buck, "A Message in Her Madness: Socio-Political Bias in Scott's Portrayal of Mad Clara Mowbray of *St. Ronan's Well*," *StSL* 24 (1989): 181–93.

Tara Ghoshal Wallace, "Walter Scott and Feminine Discourse: The Case of *St. Ronan's Well*," *JNT* 19 (Spring 1989): 233–47.

Tales of the Crusaders: The Betrothed and *The Talisman*

Michael Robertson, "Narrative Logic, Folktales and Machines," *OL* 43, no. 1 (1988): 1–19.

"The Two Drovers"

W. J. Overton, "Scott, the Short Story and History: 'The Two Drovers,'" *StSL* 21 (1986): 210–25.

Waverley Novels: Waverley

Bruce Beiderwell, "The Reasoning of Those Times: Scott's *Waverley* and the Problem of Punishment," *CLIO* 15 (Fall 1985): 15–30.

Raimund Borgmeier, "Das Gattungsmodell: Sir Walter Scott: *Waverly* (1814)," *A&E* 22 (1984): 39–55.

Ina Ferris, "Re-positioning the novel: *Waverley* and the Gender of Fiction," *StRom* 28 (Summer 1989): 291–301.

Mark M. Hennelly Jr., *Waverley* and Romanticism," *NCF* 28 (September 1873): 194–209.

Marilyn Orr, "Real and narrative time: *Waverley* and the Education of Memory," *SEL* 31 (Autumn 1991): 715–34.

Harry Shaw, "Metonymy and Realism: The Example of Scott," in *Narrative Poetics: Innovations, Limits, Challenges*, ed. James Phelan (Columbus: Center for Comparative Studies in Humanities, Ohio State University Press, 1987), 127–35.

Louise Z. Smith, "Dialectic, Rhetoric, and Anthropology in Scott's *Waverley*," *StSL* 21 (1986): 43–52.

Bruce Stovel, "*Waverley* and the Aeneid: Scott's Art of Allusion," *ESC* 11 (March 1985): 26–39.

Joseph Valente, "Upon the Braes: History and Hermeneutics in *Waverley*," *StRom* 25 (Summer 1986): 251–76.

Waverley Novels: Woodstock

Kenneth M. Sroka, "Fairy Castles and Characters in *Woodstock*," *ELWIU* 14 (Fall 1987): 189–205.

SHAW, GEORGE BERNARD

The Adventures of the Black Girl in Her Search for God

Leon H. Hugo, "The Black Girl and Some Lesser Quests: 1932–1934," *Shaw* 9 (1980): 161–84.

Cashel Byron's Profession

P. G. Wodehouse, "The Pugilist in Fiction," *Independent Shavian* 30, no. 1–2 (1992): 12–14.

The Irrational Knot

Charles A. Berst, "*The Irrational Knot*: The Art of Shaw as a Young Ibsenite," *JEGP* 85 (April 1986): 222–48.

The Unsocial Socialist

Eileen Sypher, "Fabian Anti-Novel: Shaw's *The Unsocial Socialist*," *L&H* 11 (Autumn 1985): 241–53.

SHELLEY, MARY WOLLSTONECRAFT

Frankenstein

Krishna Banerji, "Enlightenment and Romanticism in the Gothic: A Study of Mary Shelley's *Frankenstein*," in *The Romantic Tradition*, ed. Visvanath Chatterjee (Calcutta: Jadavpur University, 1984), 95–105.

Kulan Barber, "*Frankenstein*," in *Monsters Who's Who*, (New York: Crescent, 1974), 34–40.

Stephen C. Behrendt, "Language and Style in *Frankenstein*," in *Approaches to Teaching Shelley's "Frankenstein,"* ed. Stephen C. Behrendt (New York: Modern Language Association, 1990), 78–84.

Alan Bewell, "An Issue of Monstrous Desire: *Frankenstein* and Obstetrics," *YJC* 2 (Fall 1988): 105–28.

Harold Bloom, "*Frankenstein*, or the New Prometheus," *PR* 32 (Fall 1965): 611–19.

Christian Bok, "The Monstrosity of Representation: *Frankenstein* and Rousseau," *ESC* 18 (December 1992): 415–32.

Matthew C. Brennan, "The Landscape of Grief in Mary Shelley's *Frankenstein*," *StHum* 15 (June 1988): 33–44.

Nathan Cervo, "Shelley's *Frankenstein*," *Expl* 46 (Winter 1988): 14–17.

Laura P. Claridge, "Parent-Child Tensions in *Frankenstein*: The Search for Communion," *SNNTS* 17 (Spring 1985): 14–26.

John Clubbe, "Mary Shelley as Autobiographer: The Evidence of the 1831 Introduction to *Frankenstein*," *WC* 12 (Spring 1981): 102–06.

David Collings, "The Monster and the Imaginary Mother: A Lacanian Reading of *Frankenstein*," in *Mary Shelley: Frankenstein* (New York: St. Martin's, 1992), 245–58.

Daniel Cottom, "*Frankenstein* and the Monster of Representation," *Sub-Stance* 28 (1980): 60–71.

Giovanna Covi, "The Matrushka Monster of Feminist Criticism," *Textus* 2 (January–December 1989): 217–36.

Wilbur L. Cross, "Frankenstein," in *The Development of the English Novel* (New York: Macmillan, 1917), 108, 158.

James P. Davis, "*Frankenstein* and the Subversion of the Masculine Voice," *WS* 21, no. 3 (1992): 307–22.

Mary A. Favret, "A Woman Writes the Fiction of Science: The Body in *Frankenstein*," *Genders* 14 (Fall 1992): 50–65.

Paula R. Feldman, "Probing the Psychological Mystery of *Frankenstein*," in *Approaches to Teaching Shelley's "Frankenstein,"* ed. Stephen C. Behrendt (New York: MLA, 1990), 67–77.

R. E. Foust, "Monstrous Image: Theory of Fantasy Antagonists," *Genre* 13 (Winter 1980): 441–53.

M. A. Goldberg, "Moral and Myth in Mrs. Shelley's *Frankenstein*," *KSJ* 8 (Winter 1959): 27–38.

Dalton Gross and Mary J. H. Gross, "Joseph Grimaldi: An Influence on *Frankenstein*," *N&Q* 28 (October 1981): 403–04.

Lee E. Heller, "*Frankenstein* and the Cultural Uses of Gothic," in *Mary Shelley: "Frankenstein"* (New York: St. Martin's, 1992), 325–41.

Maurice Hindle, "Vital Matters: Mary Shelley's *Frankenstein* and Romantic Science," *CrSur* 2, no. 1 (1990): 29–35.

Devon Hodges, "*Frankenstein* and the Feminine Subversion of the Novel," *TSWL* 2 (Fall 1983): 155–64.

Rosemary Jackson, "Narcissism and Beyond: A Psychoanalytic Reading of *Frankenstein* and Fantasies of the Double," in *Aspects of Fantasy: Selected Essays from the Second International Conference on the Fantastic in Literature and Film*, ed. William Coyle (Westport, CT: Greenwood, 1986), 43–53.

Joseph Kestner, "Narcissism as Symptom and Structure: The Case of Mary Shelley's *Frankenstein*," in *The Nature of Identity: Essays Presented to Donald E. Haydon by the Graduate Faculty of Modern Letters, The University of Tulsa*, ed. William Weathers (Tulsa: University of Tulsa, 1981), 15–25.

Robert Kiely, "*Frankenstein*. Mary Wollstonecraft Shelly. 1818," in *The Romantic Novel in England*, (Cambridge, MA: Harvard University Press, 1972), 155–73, 241, 252, 267–268.

Laura Kranzler, "*Frankenstein* and the Technological Future," *Foundation* 44 (Winter 1988–1989): 42–49.

John B. Lamb, "Mary Shelley's *Frankenstein* and Milton's Monstrous Myth," *NCF* 47 (December 1992): 303–19.

Pierre Laszlo, "Extase sublime et declin de la nature: Note sur le *Frankenstein* de Mary Shelley," *RSH* 4, no. 188 (1982): 89–92.

Jean-Jacques Lecercle, "*Frankenstein*," in *Le Fantasme*, ed. Pierre Arnaud (Paris: Université de Paris X—Nanterre, 1987), 59–84.

George Levine, "*Frankenstein* and the Tradition of Realism," *Novel* 7 (Fall 1973): 14–30.

Frank H. McCloskey, "Mary Shelley's *Frankenstein*," in *The Humanities in the Age of Science* (Rutherford, NJ: Fairleigh Dickinson University Press, 1968), 116–38.

Peter McInerney, "*Frankenstein* and the Godlike Science of Letters," *Genre* 13 (Winter 1980): 455–75.

Lucia Magagnoli, "I prodromi della fantascienza: Il *Frankenstein* di Mary Shelley," *LetP* 20 (September 1988): 71–79.

Manfred Markus, "Erscheinungsformen des Feminismus in Mary Shelleys *Frankenstein*," *LWU* 16, no. 1 (1983): 1–17.

Anne K. Mellor, "*Frankenstein*: A Feminist Critique of Science," in *One Culture: Essays in Science and Literature*, ed. George Levine and Alan Rauch (Madison: University of Wisconsin Press, 1987), 287–312.

Anne K. Mellor, "Possessing Nature: The Female in *Frankenstein*," in *Romanticism and Feminism*, ed. Anne K. Mellor (Bloomington: Indiana University Press, 1988), 20–32.

Elsie B. Michie, "*Frankenstein* and Marx's Theories of Alienated Labor," in *Approaches to Teaching Shelley's "Frankenstein,"* ed. Stephen C. Behrendt (New York: Modern Language Association, 1990), 93–98.

Warren Montag, "'The Workshop of Filthy Creation': A Marxist Reading of *Frankenstein*," in *Mary Shelley: "Frankenstein"* (New York: St. Martin's, 1992), 300–11.

Alain Morvan, "Savoir, folie et violence dans *Frankenstein* de Mary Shelley," in *Savoir et violence en Angleterre du XVIe au XIXe siecle*, ed. Alain Morvan (Lille: Université de Lille III, 1987), 187–95.

Ross C. Murfin, "Marxist Criticism and *Frankenstein*," in *Mary Shelley: "Frankenstein"* (New York: St. Martin's, 1992), 286–99.

Beth Newman, "Narratives of Seduction and the Seductions of Narrative: The Frame Structure of *Frankenstein*," *ELH* 53 (Spring 1986): 141–63.

Margo V. Perkins, "The Nature of Otherness: Class and Difference in Mary Shelley's *Frankenstein*," *StHum* 19 (June 1992): 27–42.

Fred V. Randel, "*Frankenstein*, Feminism, and the Intertextuality of Mountains," *StRom* 23 (Winter 1984): 515–32.

Rolando Riviere, "Fascinacion de una novela desconocida: *Frankenstein*," *SupLN* (22 February 1987): 6.

Bertrand Russell, "Byron and the Modern World," *JHI* 1 (January 1940): 24–37.

Robert M. Ryan, "Mary Shelley's Christian Monster," *WC* 19 (Summer 1988): 150–55.

Richard K. Sanderson, "Glutting the Maw of Death: Suicide and Procreation in *Frankenstein*," *SoCR* 9 (Summer 1992): 49–64.

David Seed, "*Frankenstein*: Parable of Spectacle?" *Criticism* 24 (Fall 1982): 327–40.

Paul Sherwin, "*Frankenstein*: Creation as Catastrophe," *PMLA* 96 (October 1981): 883–903.

Paul Sherwin, "A Psychoaesthetic Reading of Mary Shelley's *Frankenstein*," in *CUNY English Forum* 1, ed. Saul N. Brody and Harold Schechter (New York: AMS, 1985), 199–210.

Johanna M. Smith, "'Cooped Up': Feminine Domesticity in *Frankenstein*," in *Mary Shelley: "Frankenstein"* (New York: St. Martin's, 1992), 270–85.

David Soyka, "*Frankenstein* and the Miltonic Creation of Evil," *Extrapolation* 33 (Summer 1992): 166–77.

Terry Thompson, "Shelley's *Frankenstein*," *Expl* 50 (Summer 1992): 209–11.

James B. Twitchell, "*Frankenstein* and the Anatomy of Horror," *GaR* 37 (Spring 1983): 41–78.

Samuel H. Vasbinder, "A Possible Source for the Term 'Vermicelli' in Mary Shelley's *Frankenstein*," *WC* 12 (Spring 1981): 116–17.

Anca Vlasopolos, "Frankenstein's Hidden Skeleton: The Psycho-Politics of Oppression," *SFS* 10 (July 1983): 125–36.

Barbara Frey Waxman, "Victor Frankenstein's Romantic Fate: The Tragedy of the Promethean Overreacher as Woman," *PLL* 23 (Winter 1987): 14–26.

Theodore Ziolkowski, "Science, *Frankenstein*, and Myth," *SR* 89 (Winter 1981): 34–56.

The Last Man

Gregory O'Dea, "Prophetic History and Textuality in Mary Shelley's *The Last Man*," *PLL* 28 (Summer 1992): 283–304.

Morton D. Paley, "Mary Shelley's *The Last Man*: Apocalypse without Millennium," *KSMB* 4 (Autumn 1989): 1–25.

SPARK, MURIEL

The Driver's Seat

Ian Rankin, "Surface and Structure: Reading Muriel Spark's *The Driver's Seat*," *JNT* 15 (Spring 1985): 146–55.

The Prime of Miss Jean Brodie

Anne L. Bower, "The Narrative Structure of Muriel Spark's *The Prime of Miss Jean Brodie*," *MidWQ* 31 (Summer 1990): 488–98.

Trevor Royale, "Spark and Scotland," in *Muriel Spark: An Odd Capacity for Vision*, ed. Alan Bold (London: Vision; Totowa, NJ: Barnes & Noble, 1984), 147–66.

Territorial Rights

Marc Poitou, "Les Ironies de Venise: Roman et decor dans *Territorial Rights* de Muriel Spark," *Cycnos* 1 (1984): 15–24.

"You Should Have Seen the Mess"

J. A. de Reuck, "A New Voice in Narrative," *JLSTL* 2 (July 1986): 41–56.

STAPLEDON, OLAF

Darkness and the Light

Robert Crossley, "Politics and the Artist: The Aesthetic of *Darkness and the Light*," *SFS* 9 (November 1982): 294–305.

Last and First Men

Eugene Goodheart, "Olaf Stapledon's *Last and First Men*," in *No Place Else: Explorations in Utopian and Dystopian Fiction*, ed. Eric S. Rabkin, Martin H. Greenberg, and Joseph D. Olander (Carbondale: Southern Illinois University Press, 1983), 78–93.

John Huntington, "Remembrance of Things to Come: Narrative Technique in *Last and First Men*," *SFS* 9 (November 1982): 257–64.

STAPLEDON, OLAF, *Star Maker*

Stanislaw Lem and Istvan Csicsery-Ronay, Jr., "On Stapledon's *Last and First Men*," *SFS* 13 (November 1986): 272–91.

Patrick A. McCarthy, "*Last and First Men* as Miltonic Epic," *SFS* 11 (November 1984): 244–52.

Star Maker

Stanislaw Lem, "On Stapledon's *Star Maker*," *SFS* 14 (March 1987): 1–8.

Patrick A. McCarthy, "*Star Maker*: Olaf Stapledon's Divine Tragedy," *SFS* 8 (November 1981): 266–79.

Amelia A. Rutledge, "*Star Maker*: The Agnostic Quest," *SFS* 9 (November 1982): 274–83.

STEPHENS, JAMES

The Charwoman's Daughter

Jochen Achilles, "*The Charwoman's Daughter* and the Emergency of National Psychology," *IUR* 11 (Autumn 1981): 184–97.

The Crock of Gold

Gary M. Boyer, "*The Crock of Gold*," *AntigR* 44 (Winter 1980): 91–99.

Birgit Bramsback, "James Stephens and *The Crock of Gold*," in *Homage to Ireland: Aspects of Culture, Literature and Language*, ed. Birgit Bramsback (Uppsala: University of Uppsala, 1990), 31–44.

Birgit Bramsback, "The Philosophical Quest in *The Crock of Gold*," in *Studies in Anglo-Irish Literature*, ed. Heniz Kosok (Bonn: Bouvier, 1982), 190–97.

Deirdre

Giovanna Tallone, "James Stephens' *Deirdre*: The Determining Word," *CJIS* 16 (July 1990): 75–79.

"Here Are Ladies"

Paul F. Casey, "Thrice: James Stephens's 'Here Are the Ladies,'" *Éire* 16 (Spring 1981): 128–34.

"Oisin's-Mother"

Claire Douglas, "'Oisin's Mother': Because I Would Not Give My Love to the Druid Named Dark," in *Psyche's Stories: Modern Jungian Interpretations of Fairy Tales, II*, ed. Murray Stein and Lionel Corbett (Wilmette, IL: Chiron, 1992), 33–57.

STEVENSON, ROBERT LEWIS

"The Beach of Falesa"

Katherine Bailey Linehan, "Taking up with Kanakas: Stevenson's Complex Social Criticism in 'The Beach of Falesa,'" *ELT* 33, no. 4 (1990): 407–22.

Dr. Jekyll and Mr. Hyde

Daniel V. Fraustino, "Dr. Jekyll and Mr. Hyde: Anatomy of Misperception," *ArQ* 38 (Autumn 1982): 235–40.

Daniel V. Fraustino, "'The Not So Strange Case of *Dr. Jekyll and Mr. Hyde*,'" *JEP* 5 (August 1984): 205–09.

Peter K. Garrett, "Cries and Voices: Reading *Jekyll and Hyde*," in *Dr. Jekyll and Mr. Hyde after One Hundred Years*, ed. William Veeder and Gordon Hirsh (Chicago: University of Chicago Press, 1988), 59–72.

Richard T. Gaughan, "Mr. Hyde and Mr. Seek: Utterson's Antidote," *JNT* 17 (Spring 1987): 184–97.

Stephen Heath, "Psychopathia Sexualis: Stevenson's Strange Case," *CritQ* 28 (Spring–Summer 1986): 93–108.

Jerrold E. Hogle, "The Struggle for a Dichotomy: Abjection in Jekyll and His Interpreters," in *Dr. Jekyll and Mr. Hyde after One Hundred Years*, ed. William Veeder and Gordon Hirsh (Chicago: University of Chicago Press, 1988), 161–207.

Wayne Koestenbaum, "The Shadow on the Bed: Dr. Jekyll, Mr. Hyde, and the Labouchère Amendment," *CrM* 1 (Spring 1988): 31–55.

Andre Labarrere, "Onomastique, structure et dédoublement dans *Le cas étrange du Docteur Jekyll et de Mister Hyde*," in *Hommage a Claude Digeon*, ed. Claude Faisant (Paris: Belles Lettres, 1987), 303–13.

Colin Manlove, "'Closer Than an Eye': The Interconnection of Stevenson's *Dr. Jekyll and Mr. Hyde*," *StSL* 23 (1988): 87–103.

STEVENSON, ROBERT LEWIS, "The Enchantress"

Martin Tropp, "*Dr. Jekyll and Mr. Hyde*, Schopenhauer, and the Power of the Will," *MidWQ* 32 (Winter 1991): 141–55.

"The Enchantress"

David D. Mann and Susan Garland Mann, "'The Enchantress,'" *GaR* 43 (Fall 1989): 551–68.

Kidnapped

W. W. Robson, "On *Kidnapped*," in *Stevenson and Victorian Scotland*, ed. Jenni Calder (Edinburgh: Edinburgh University Press, 1981), 88–106.

Ralph Stewart, "The Unity of *Kidnapped*," *VN* 64 (Fall 1983): 30–31.

The Master of Ballantrae

Carol Mills, "*The Master of Ballantrae*: An Experiment with Genre," in *Robert Louis Stevenson*, ed. Andrew Noble (London: Vision; Totowa, NJ: Barnes & Noble, 1983), 118–33.

Jean-Pierre Naugette, "Les Aventures du roman: En derivant de Ballantrae," *Critique* 39 (May 1983): 365–78.

Jean-Pierre Naugette, "*The Master of Ballantrae*: Fragments d'un discours aventeureux," *ÉA* 43 (January–March 1990): 29–40.

Jean-Pierre Naugette, "Robert Louis Stevenson, *The Master of Ballantrae*," *CVE* 30 (October 1989): 177–87.

"The Merry Men"

Tom Shearer, "A Strange Judgement of God's? Stevenson's 'The Merry Men,'" *StSL* 20 (1985): 71–87.

"The Misadventures of John Nicholson"

Kenneth Gelder, "R. L. Stevenson's Scottish Christmas Story: 'The Misadventures of John Nicholson,' the Free Church, and the Prodigal Son," *StSL* 23 (1988): 122–35.

"New Arabian Nights"

Barry Menikoff, "'New Arabian Nights': Stevenson's Experiment in Fiction," *NCF* 45 (December 1990): 339–62.

"Olalla"

Jean-Pierre Naugrette, "Décor, désir, espace: Une Lecture de Stevenson," *Litt* 61 (February 1986): 49–64.

"Story of the Young Man with the Cream Tart"

Rosella Mallardi, "La commedia dell'onore: Un racconto 'arabo' di R. L. Stevenson," *Ling&S* 24 (June 1989): 265–93.

Treasure Island

David H. Jackson, "*Treasure Island* as a Late–Victorian Adults' Novel," *VN* 72 (Fall 1987): 28–32.

John LeVay, "Stevenson's *Treasure Island*," *Expl* 47 (Spring 1989): 25–29.

Mary Louise Mckenzie, "The Toy Theatre, Romance, and *Treasure Island*: The Artistry of R. L. S.," *ESC* 8 (December 1982): 409–21.

David D. Mann and William H. Hardesty, "Stevenson's Method in *Treasure Island*: 'The Old Romance Retold,'" *ELWIU* 9 (Fall 1982): 180–93.

John D. Moore, "Emphasis and Suppression in Stevenson's *Treasure Island*: Fabrication of the Self in Jim Hawkins' Narrative," *CLAJ* 34 (June 1991): 436–52.

Sam Pickering, "Stevenson's "Elementary Novel of Adventure,'" *RsSt* 49 (June 1981): 99–106.

"The Vagabond"

Rudolf Stamm, "'To an Air of Schubert': R. L. Stevenson's 'The Vagabond' Re–Considered," *ES* 64 (February 1983): 36–40.

"Was It Murder?"

Roland Leibold, "Robert Louis Stevenson: 'Was It Murder?'" *A&E* 23 (1984): 37–48.

Weir of Hermiston

Kenneth G. Simpson, "Author and Narrator in *Weir of Hermiston*," in *Robert Louis Stevenson*, ed. Andrew Noble (London: Vision; Totowa, NJ: Barnes & Noble, 1983), 202–27.

Kenneth G. Simpson, "Realism and Romance: Stevenson and Scottish Values," *StSL* 20 (1985): 231–47.

STOKER, BRAM

Dracula

Stephen D. Arata, "The Occidental Tourist: *Dracula* and the Anxiety of Reverse Colonization," *VS* 33 (Summer 1990): 621–45.

Troy Boone, "'He is English and Therefore Adventurous': Politics, Decadence, and *Dracula*," *SNNTS* 25 (Spring 1993): 76–92.

Thomas B. Byers, "Good Men and Monsters: The Defenses of *Dracula*," *L&P* 31, no. 4 (1981): 24–31.

Christopher Craft, "'Kiss Me with Those Red Lips': Gender and Inversion in Bram Stoker's *Dracula*," *Representations* 8 (Fall 1984): 107–33. Reprinted in *Speaking of Gender*, ed. Elaine Showalter (New York: Routledge, 1989), 216–42.

Anne Cranny-Francis, "Sexual Politics and Political Repression in Bram Stoker's *Dracula*," in *Nineteenth-Century Suspense: From Poe to Conan Doyle*, ed. Clive Bloom, Brian Docherty, Jane Gibb, and Keith Shand (New York: St. Martin's, 1988), 64–79.

Paul Gutjahr, "Stoker's *Dracula*," *Expl* 52 (Fall 1993): 36–38.

Judith Halberstam, "Technologies of Monstrosity: Bram Stoker's *Dracula*," *VS* 36 (Spring 1993): 333–52.

Mark M. Hennelly Jr., "*Dracula*: The Gnostic Quest and Victorian Wasteland," *ELT* 20 (1977): 13–26.

Mark M. Hennelly Jr., "The Victorian Book of the Dead: *Dracula*," *JEP* 13 (August 1992): 204–11.

Marjorie Howes, "The Mediation of the Feminine: Bisexuality, Homoerotic Desire, and Self-Expression in Bram Stoker's *Dracula*," *TSLL* 30 (Spring 1988): 104–19.

Rosemary Jann, "Saved by Science? The Mixed Messages of Stoker's *Dracula*," *TSLL* 31 (Summer 1989): 273–87.

Alan P. Johnson, "Bent and Broken Necks: Signs of Design in Stoker's *Dracula*," *VN* 72 (Fall 1987): 17–24.

Alan P. Johnson, "'Dual Life': The Status of Women in Stoker's *Dracula*," *TStL* 27 (1984): 20–39.

Patrick Keats, "Stoker's *Dracula*," *Expl* 50 (Fall 1991): 26–27.

Wolfgang Lottes, "Dracula & Co.: Der Vampir in der englischen Literatur," *Archiv* 220, no. 2 (1983): 285–99.

Beth McDonald, "The Vampire as Trickster Figure in Bram Stoker's *Dracula*," *Extrapolation* 33 (Summer 1992): 128–44.

Anne McWhir, "Pollution and Redemption in *Dracula*," *MLS* 17 (Summer 1987): 31–40.

Philip Martin, "The Vampire in the Looking-Glass: Reflection and Projection in Bram Stoker's *Dracula*," in *Nineteenth-Century Suspense: From Poe to Conan Doyle*, ed. Clive Bloom, Brian Docherty, Jane Gibb, and Keith Shand (New York: St. Martin's, 1988), 80–92.

Bette B. Roberts, "Victorian Values in the Narration of *Dracula*," *StWF* 6 (Fall 1989): 10–14.

David Seed, "The Narrative Method of *Dracula*," *NCF* 40 (June 1985): 61–75.

Carol A. Senf, "*Dracula*: Stoker's Response to the New Woman," *VS* 26 (Autumn 1982): 33–49.

Kathleen Spencer, "Purity and Danger: *Dracula*, the Urban Gothic, and the Late Victorian Degeneracy Crisis," *ELH* 59 (Spring 1992): 197–225.

George Stade, "Dracula's Women," *PR* 53, no. 2 (1986): 200–215.

John Allen Stevenson, "A Vampire in the Mirror: The Sexuality of *Dracula*," *PMLA* 103 (March 1988): 139–49.

Geoffrey Wall, "'Different from Writing': *Dracula* in 1897," *L&H* 10 (Spring 1984): 15–23.

Jules Zanger, "A Sympathetic Vibration: *Dracula* and the Jews," *ELT* 34, no. 1 (1991): 33–44.

The Lady of the Shroud

Carol A. Senf, "*The Lady of the Shroud*: Stoker's Successor to Dracula," *EAS* 19 (May 1990): 82–96.

STUART, FRANCIS

Black List, Section H

Francis C. Molloy, "Autobiography and Fiction: Francis Stuart's *Black List, Section H*," *Critique* 25 (Winter 1984): 115–24.

Francis C. Molloy, "A Life Reshaped: Francis Stuart's *Black List, Section H*," *CJIS* 14 (January 1989): 37–47.

The High Consistory

Valentine Cunningham, "The Spell of the Monstrous," *TLS* (16 January 1981): 51.

Memorial

Peter Hazeldine, "Private Lives," *PNR* 15, no. 1 (1988): 28–30.

SWIFT, GRAHAM

Waterland

George P. Landow, "History, His Story, and Stories in Graham Swift's *Waterland*," *StLI* 23 (Fall 1990): 197–211.

Marc Poree, "Différences et répétition dans *Waterland* de Graham Swift," in *La Répétition*, ed. Jean-Jacques Lecercle (Paris: Centre de Recherches Anglo-America, Université de Paris, 1989), 159–89.

John Schad, "The End of the End of History: Graham Swift's *Waterland*," *MFS* 38 (Winter 1992): 910–25.

THACKERAY, WILLIAM MAKEPEACE

The Adventures of Philip on His Way Through the World, Showing Who Robbed Him, Who Helped Him, and Who Passed Him by

Ina Ferris, "Narrative Strategy in Thackeray's *The Adventures of Philip*," *ESC* 5 (1974): 448–56.

Ina Ferris, "RePlaying: Thackeray's Later Work," in *William Makepeace Thackeray* (Boston: Twayne, 1983), 107–16.

Juliet McMaster, "Funeral Baked Meats: Thackeray's Last Novel," *Studies in the Novel* 13 (Spring/Summer 1981): 133–55. Reprinted in *William Makepeace Thackeray*, ed. Harold Bloom (New York: Chelsea House, 1987), 137–52.

Catherine: A Story

Frederick C. Cabot, "The Two Voices in Thackeray's *Catherine*," *NCF* 28 (1978): 404–16.

Ina Ferris, "The Making of the Novelist," in *William Makepeace Thackeray* (Boston: Twayne, 1983), 14–17.

Denis Duvall

Ina Ferris, "RePlaying: Thackeray's Later Work," in *William Makepeace Thackeray* (Boston: Twayne, 1983), 117–19.

"An Excellent New Ballad about a Lord and a Lawyer"

David A. Haury, "Thackeray's 'An Excellent New Ballad About a Lord and a Lawyer,'" *N&Q* 28 (October 1981): 404–05.

The History of Henry Esmond, Esq. A Colonel in the Service of Her Majesty Queen Anne

Karen Chase, "The Kindness of Consanguinity: Family History in Henry Esmond," *MLS* 16 (Summer 1986): 213–26.

Micael Clarke, "Thackeray's *Henry Esmond* and Feminism: A Double Vision of Feminist Discourse and Narrative," *WW&D* 5 (Spring 1987): 85–107.

Ina Ferris, "The Uses of History: *The History of Henry Esmond*," in *William Makepeace Thackeray* (Boston: Twayne, 1983), 59–74.

Joan Garrett-Goodyear, "Stylized Emotions, Unrealized Selves: Expressive Characterization in Thackeray," *VS* 2 (Winter 1979): 173–92. Reprinted in *William Makepeace Thackeray*, ed. Harold Bloom (New York: Chelsea House, 1987), 74–76, 83–88.

Marjorie Garson, "'Knowledge and Good and Evil': Henry and Rachel in *The History of Henry Esmond*," *ESC* 9 (1983): 418–34.

Dieter Hamblock, "'The Novel Is History': Thackeray's *Henry Esmond* (1852)," *A&E* 22 (1984): 95–107.

Edgar F. Harden, "Esmond and the Search for Self," *YES* 3 (1973): 181–95.

Sylvia Manning, "Incest and the Structure of *Henry Esmond*," *NCF* 34 (1979): 194–213.

J. Hillis Miller, "*Henry Esmond*: Repetition and Irony," in *William Makepeace Thackeray*, ed. Harold Bloom (New York: Chelsea House, 1987), 179–213.

Ria Omasreiter, "The Muse of History Pulls Off Her Periwig: Thackerays Henry Esmond als Korrektur historischer Klischees," *Anglia* 106, no. 3–4 (1988): 393–410.

J. M. Rignall, "Thackeray's *Henry Esmond* and the Struggle against the Power of Time," in *The Nineteenth-Century British Novel*, ed. Jeremy Hawthorn (Baltimore: Arnold, 1986), 81–93.

Mary Rogers, "Perspective on *Henry Esmond*," *VN* 56 (Fall 1979): 26–31.

Elaine Scarry, "*Henry Esmond*: The Rookery at Castlewood," in *Literary Monographs* 7, ed. Eric Rothstein and Joseph Anthony Wittreich, Jr. (Madison: University of Wisconsin Press, 1975), 1–45.

John A. Sutherland, "*Henry Esmond* and the Virtues of Carelessness," *MP* 68 (1971): 345–54.

Henri A. Talon, "Time and Memory in Thackeray's *Henry Esmond*," *RES* 13 (n.s.) (1962): 147–56.

Terry Tierney, "Henry Esmond's Double Vision," *SNNTS* 24 (Winter 1992): 349–65.

George J. Worth, "The Unity of *Henry Esmond*," *NCF* 15 (December 1961): 345–53.

The History of Pendennis

Cates Baldridge, "The Problems of Worldliness in *Pendennis*," *NCF* 44 (March 1990): 492–513.

Robert Bledsoe, "*Pendennis* and the Power of Sentimentality: A Study of Motherly Love," *PMLA* 91 (1976): 871–83.

John Coates, "Handling Change: A Study of Thackeray's Techniques of Presenting Social and Personal Change in *Pendennis*," *DUJ* 75 (December 1982): 43–51.

Ina Ferris, "The Thackerayan Hero: *The History of Pendennis*," in *William Makepeace Thackeray* (Boston: Twayne, 1983), 43–58.

Judith Law Fisher, "Siren and Artist: Contradiction in Thackeray's Aesthetic Ideal," *NCF* 39 (March 1985): 392–419.

Peter K. Garrett, "Thackeray: Seeing Double," in *William Makepeace Thackeray*, ed. Harold Bloom (New York: Chelsea House, 1987), 90–98.

Edgar F. Harden, "Theatricality in *Pendennis*," *Ariel* 4 (1973): 74–94.

Craig Howes, "*Pendennis* and the Controversy on the 'Dignity of Literature,'" *NCF* 41 (December 1986): 269–98. Reprinted in *William Makepeace Thackeray*, ed. Harold Bloom (New York: Chelsea House, 1987), 233–53.

Thomas Jeffers, "Thackeray's *Pendennis*: Son and Gentleman," *NCF* 33 (June 1978): 175–93.

T. E. Kinsey, "Podasokus," *N&Q* 34 (December 1987): 491.

Gunther Klotz, "'A Sort of Confidential Talk between Writer and Reader'; Oder, Wast heisst und zu welchem Ende studiert man die Geschichte von *Pendennis*?" *ZAA* 34, no. 2 (1986): 109–15.

George Levine, "*Pendennis*: The Virtue of the Dilettante's Unbelief," in *William Makepeace Thackeray*, ed. Harold Bloom (New York: Chelsea House, 1987), 153–67.

Michael Lund, "Growing Up in Fiction and in Fact: Protagonist and Reader in Thackeray's *Pendennis*," *DSA* 12 (1983): 285–302.

Kenneth L. Moler, "'Leveling' Motifs in *Pendennis*: A Strategy That Does Not Always Work," *PQ* 67 (Winter 1988): 93–102.

Sylvère Monod, "'Brother Wearers of Motley,'" *E&S* 26 (1973): 66–82.

Peter L. Shillingsburg, "*Pendennis* Revisited," *ÉA* 34 (October–December 1981): 432–42.

Deborah A. Thomas, "Bondage and Freedom in Thackeray's *Pendennis*," *SNNTS* 17 (Summer 1985): 138–57.

Max Vega-Ritter, "Essai d'analyse psychocritique de *Pendennis*," *CVE* 13 (April 1981): 53–78.

Lovel the Widower

Ina Ferris, "The Breakdown of Thackeray's Narrator: *Lovel the Widower*," in *William Makepeace Thackeray*, ed. Harold Bloom (New York: Chelsea House, 1987), 55–69.

Ina Ferris, "RePlayings: Thackeray's Later Work," in *William Makepeace Thackeray* (Boston: Twayne, 1983), 117–18.

The Memoirs of Barry Lyndon, Esq. of the Kingdom of Ireland

Micael M. Clarke, "Thackeray's *Barry Lyndon*: An Irony against Misogynists," *TSLL* 29 (Fall 1987): 261–77.

Roger Decap, "*Barry Lyndon*: Thackeray et 'l'ailleurs,'" *Caliban* 28 (1991): 37–48.

Ina Ferris, "The Making of the Novelist," in *William Makepeace Thackeray* (Boston: Twayne, 1983), 17–20.

Terence McCarthy, "Chronological Inconsistencies in *Barry Lyndon*," *ELN* 21 (December 1983): 29–37.

David Parker, "Thackeray's *Barry Lyndon*," *Ariel* 6, no. 4 (1975): 68–80.

Nancy Jane Tyson, "Thackeray and Bulwer: Between the Lines in *Barry Lyndon*," *ELN* 27 (December 1989): 53–56.

The Newcomes: Memoirs of a Most Respectable Family

Ina Ferris, "The Way of the World: *The Newcomes*," in *William Makepeace Thackeray* (Boston: Twayne, 1983), 75–99, 123–24.

Peter K. Garrett, "Thackeray: Seeing Double," in *William Makepeace Thackeray*, ed. Harold Bloom (New York: Chelsea House, 1987), 116–20.

Joan Garrett-Goodyear, "Stylized Emotions, Unrealized Selves: Expressive Characterization in Thackeray," in *William Makepeace Thackeray*, ed. Harold Bloom (New York: Chelsea House, 1987), 76–80.

Michael Lund, "Reading Serially Published Novels: Old Stories in Thackeray's *The Newcomes*," *PQ* 60 (Spring 1981): 205–25.

Juliet McMaster, "Theme and Form in *The Newcomes*," *NCF* 23 (1968): 177–88.

R. D. McMaster, "London as a System of Signs in Thackeray's *The Newcomes*," *VR* 16 (Summer 1990): 1–21.

R. D. McMaster, "The Pygmalion Motif in The Newcomes," *NCF* 29 (June 1974): 22–39. Reprinted in *William Makepeace Thackeray*, ed. Harold Bloom (New York: Chelsea House, 1987), 21–35.

Margaret Diane Stetz, "Thackeray's *The Newcomes* and the Artist's World," *PreRR* 3 (May 1983): 80–95.

The Rose and the Ring, Or, The History of Prince Giglio and Prince Belbo: A Fire-Side Patonmine for Great and Small Children

Gail D. Sorensen, "Thackeray's *The Rose and the Ring*: A Novelist's Fairy Tale," *Mythlore* 15 (Spring 1989): 37–38, 43.

"A Shabby Genteel Story"

Ina Ferris, "RePlayings: Thackeray's Later Work," in *William Makepeace Thackeray* (Boston: Twayne, 1983), 107.

Vanity Fair: A Novel Without a Hero

Robert T. Bledsoe, "*Vanity Fair* and Singing," *SNNTS* 13 (Spring–Summer 1981): 51–63.

Mark H. Burch, "'The world is a looking-glass': *Vanity Fair* as Satire," *Genre* 15 (Fall 1982): 265–79.

Edward H. Cohen, "George IV and Jos Sedley in *Vanity Fair*," *ELN* 19 (December 1981): 122–30.

G. Armour Craig, "On the Style of *Vanity Fair*," in *Studies in Prose Fiction*, ed. Harold C. Martin (New York: Columbia University Press, 1959), 87–113.

H. M. Daleski, "Strategies in *Vanity Fair*," in *William Makepeace Thackeray's "Vanity Fair*," ed. Harold Bloom (New York: Chelsea House, 1987), 121–48.

Maria DiBattista, "The Triump of Clytemnestra: The Charades in *Vanity Fair*," *PMlA* 95 (October 1980): 827–37. Reprinted in *William Makepeace Thackeray's "Vanity Fair*," ed. Harold Bloom (New York: Chelsea House, 1987), 83–100. Reprinted in *William Makepeace Thackeray*, ed. Harold Bloom (New York: Chelsea House, 1987), 121–36.

D. J. Dooley, "Thackeray's Use of *Vanity Fair*," *SEL* 11 (1971): 701–13.

William R. Elkins, "Thackeray's *Vanity Fair*," *Expl* 44 (Spring 1986): 31–35.

Ina Ferris, "'The Sentiment of Reality': *Vanity Fair*," in *William Makepeace Thackeray* (Boston: Twayne, 1983), 25–42.

John P. Frazee, "George IV and Jos Sedley in *Vanity Fair*," *ELN* 19 (December 1981): 122–28.

Peter K. Garrett, "Thackeray: Seeing Double," in *William Makepeace Thackeray*, ed. Harold Bloom (New York: Chelsea House, 1987), 98–116.

John Hagan, "*Vanity Fair*: Becky Brought to Book Again," *SNNTS* 7 (1975): 479–505.

Barbara Hardy, "Art and Nature," in *William Makepeace Thackeray's "Vanity Fair*," ed. Harold Bloom (New York: Chelsea House, 1987), 19–35.

William Harmon, "Hawthorne and Thackeray: Two Notes on Eliot's Reading and Borrowing," *YER* 8, no. 1–2 (1986): 123–24.

Charles J. Heglar, "Rhoda Swartz in *Vanity Fair*: A Doll Without Admirers," *CLAJ* 37 (March 1994): 336–46.

Wolfgang Iser, "The Reader as a Component Part of the Realistic Novel: Esthetic Effects in Thackeray's *Vanity Fair*," in *William Makepeace Thackeray's "Vanity Fair*," ed. Harold Bloom (New York: Chelsea House, 1987), 37–55. Reprinted in *William Makepeace Thackeray*, ed. Harold Bloom (New York: Chelsea House, 1987), 37–53.

J. T. Klein, "The Dual Center: A Study of Narrative Structure in *Vanity Fair*," *CollL* 4, no. 2 (1977): 122–28.

Joe K. Law, "The Prima Donnas of *Vanity Fair*," *CLAJ* 31 (September 1987): 87–110.

Arno Loffler, "'What a Splendid Actress and Manager': Die satirische Funktion Becky Sharps in *Vanity Fair*," *Anglia* 105, no. 3–4 (1987): 342–65

Robert E. Lougy, "Vision and Satire: The Warped Looking Glass in *Vanity Fair*," *PMLA* 90 (March 1975): 256–69. Reprinted in *William Makepeace Thackeray's "Vanity Fair*," ed. Harold Bloom (New York: Chelsea House, 1987), 57–82.

Bruce K. Martin, "*Vanity Fair*: Narrative Ambivalence and Comic Form," *TStL* 20 (1975): 37–49.

Natalie Maynor, "Punctuation and Style in *Vanity Fair*: Thackeray versus His Compositors," *ELN* 22 (December 1984): 48–55.

Andrew Miller, "*Vanity Fair* through Plate Glass," *PMLA* 105 (October 1990): 1042–54.

Ian Milner, "Theme and Moral Vision in Thackeray's *Vanity Fair*," *PhPr* 13, no. 4 (1970): 177–85.

David Musselwhite, "Notes on a Journey to *Vanity Fair*," *L&H* 7 (Spring 1981): 62–90.

James Phelan, "*Vanity Fair*: Listening as a Rhetorician," in *Out of Bounds: Male Writers and Gender(ed) Criticism*, ed. Laura Claridge and Elizabeth Langland (Amherst: University of Massachusetts Press, 1990), 132–47.

Robert M. Polhemus, "The Comedy of Shifting Perspectives," in *William Makepeace Thackeray's "Vanity Fair,"* ed. Harold Bloom (New York: Chelsea House, 1987), 101–20.

Gordon N. Ray, "*Vanity Fair*: One Version of the Novelist's Responsiblity," *EDH* 25 (1980): 87–101.

Bruce Redwine, "The Uses of Memento Mori in *Vanity Fair*," *SELit* 17 (1977): 657–72.

Henry N. Rogers, "*Vanity Fair* as Satiric Myth," *PAPA* 8 (Fall 1982): 49–65.

Masahiko Sano, "Thackeray to Rekishi teki Shiya—Kyoei no Ichi o Chushin ni," in *Igirisu no Katari to Shiten no Shosetsu*, ed. Takeshi Uchida (Tokyo: Tokai Daigaku, 1983), 89–123.

Robin Ann Sheets, "Art and Artistry in *Vanity Fair*," *ELH* 42 (1975): 420–32.

Richard C. Stevenson, "The Problem of Judging Beck Sharp: Scene and Narrative Commentary in *Vanity Fair*," *VIJ* 6 (1977): 1–8.

John A. Sutherland, "The Expanding Narrative of *Vanity Fair*," *JNT* 3 (1973): 149–69.

Lisa Tadwin, "The Seductiveness of Female Duplicity in *Vanity Fair*," *SEL* 32 (Autumn 1992): 663–87.

Myron Taube, "Contrast as a Principle of Structure in *Vanity Fair*," *NCF* 18 (June 1963): 119–35.

Sarah Thornton, "'Blind Love an Unbounded Credit': L'Argent et le texte dans *Vanity Fair*," *CVE* 35 (April 1992): 169–76.

Max Vaga-Ritter, "Women under Judgment in *Vanity Fair*," *CVE* 3 (1976): 7–24.

Dorothy Van Ghent, "On *Vanity Fair*," in *William Makepeace Thackeray's "Vanity Fair,"* ed. Harold Bloom (New York: Chelsea House, 1987), 5–17.

Ann Y. Wilkinson, "The Tomeavsian Way of Knowing the World: Technique and Meaning in *Vanity Fair*," *ELH* 32 (1965): 370–87.

Cynthia Griffin Wolff, "Who Is the Narrator of *Vanity Fair* and Where Is He Standing?" *CollL* 1 (1974): 190–203.

The Virginians: A Tale of the Last Century

Ina Ferris, "RePlayings: Thackeray's Later Work," in *William Makepeace Thackeray* (Boston: Twayne, 1983), 102–07.

Gerald C. Sorenson, "Beginning and Ending: *The Virginians* as a Sequel," *SNNTS* 13 (Spring–Summer 1981): 109–21.

THOMAS, DYLAN

Portrait of an Artist as a Young Dog

John Ackerman, *Dylan Thomas: His Life and Work* (London: Oxford, 1964), 106–31.

D. C. Mueche, "Come Back! Come Back!: A Theme in Dylan Thomas's Prose," *Meanjin* 18 (April 1959): 74–76.

"One Warm Saturday"

Richard Kelly, "The Lost Vision in Dylan Thomas's "One Warm Saturday," *SSF* 6 (Winter 1969): 205–9.

Quite Early One Morning

Anthony West, "A Singer and a Spectre," *NewY* (22 January 1955): 106–8.

THOMAS, D[ONALD] M[ICHAEL]

Ararat

Anthony Burgess, "Let's Parler Yidglish!" *Punch* 284 (2 March 1983): 76–77.

George Kearns, "World Well Lost," *HudR* 36 (Autumn 1983): 549–62.

Peter S. Prescott, "Thomas's Enigma Variations," *Newsweek* (4 April 1983): 75.

Birthstone

Andrew Motion, "Cornish Pastiche," *TLS* (14 March 1980): 296.

Eating Pavlova

David Cohen, "*Eating Pavlova*," *NewS&S* 7 (13 May 1994): 40.

The Flute Player

Ron Kirke, "Pipe Dreams," *TLS* (30 November 1979): 77.

Nicholas Shrimpton, "Love of Flying," *NewS* 97 (22 June 1979): 922–23.

Flying in to Love

T. J. Binyon, "Dreams of Death," *TLS* (7 February 1992): 18.

Rober Houston, "*Flying in to Love*," *NYTBR* (11 October 1992): 13–14.

Lying Together

Maureen Freely, "Don's Party Tricks: *Lying Together*," *NewS&S* 3 (22 June 1990): 49.

Angeline Goreau, "The Characters Are in Charge," *NYTBR* (8 July 1990): 3, 19.

Carol Rumens, "Inviting Confusions: Review of *Lying Together*," *TLS* (13 July 1990): 746.

Pictures at an Exhibition

Frederick Busch, "The Man From Auschwitz," *NYTBR* (31 October 1993): 13, 14.

Bryan Cheyette, "A Pornographic Universe," *TLS* (29 January 1993): 20.

The White Hotel

Frances Bartkowski and Catherine Stearns, "The Lost Icon in *The White Hotel*," *JHS* 1 (October 1990): 283–95.

Catherine Bernard, "D. M. Thomas: La Danse de l'historie," in *Historicite et metafiction dans le roman contemporain des Iles Britanniques*, ed. Max Duperray (Aix-en-Provence: Université de Provence, 1994), 85–100.

Lady Falls Brown, "*The White Hotel*: D. M. Thomas's Considerable Debt to Anatoli Kuznetsov and Babi Yar," *SoCR* 2 (Summer 1985), 60–79.

David Cowart, "Being and Seeming: *The White Hotel*," *Novel* 19 (Spring 1986): 216–31.

David Cowart, "The Turning Point: Abreaction of the West: *The White Hotel*," in *History and the Contemporary Novel* (Carbondale: Southern Illinois University Press, 1989), 141–64.

Richard K. Cross, "The Soul Is Far country: D. M. Thomas and *The White Hotel*," *JLM* 18 (Winter 1992): 19–47.

Max Duperray, "Enchainements et dechainements: La Violence et la repetition dans *The White Hotel* (1981) de D. M. Thomas," in *La Violence dans la littéra-*

ture et la pensée anglaises, ed. Nadia Rigaud and Paul Denisot (Aix-en-Provence: Université de Provence, 1989), 159–174.

Chris Ellery, "Oracle and Womb: Delphic Myth in D. M. Thomas' *The White Hotel*," *NConL* 19 (May 1989): 3–4.

Irene Engclstad, "Den store gaten om livet og doden: D. M. Thomas' roman *Det hvite hotellet* og S. Freuds sykehistorier," *Vinduet* 36, no. 1 (1982): 51–56.

John Burt Foster, Jr., "Magic Realism in *The White Hotel*: Compensatory Vision and the Transformation of Classic Realism," *SHR* 20 (Summer 1986): 205–19.

Krin Gabbard, "*The White Hotel* and the Traditions of Ring Composition," *CLS* 27, no. 3 (1990): 230–48.

Diana George, "Teaching the Nightmare World of *The White Hotel*," *Proteus* 6 (Spring 1989): 57–60.

Ronald Granofsky, "Holocaust as Symbol in *Riddley Walker* and *The White Hotel*," *MLS* 16 (Summer 1986): 172–82.

Ronald Granofsky, "The Pornographic Mind and *The White Hotel*," *CollL* 20 (October 1993): 44–56.

Michael Hollington, "Hysterionics: D. M. Thomas's *The White Hotel*," *Meanjin* 41 (September 1982): 363–66.

Linda Hutcheon, "Subject in/of/to History and His Story," *Diacritics* 16 (Spring 1986): 78–91. Reprinted in *The Poetics of Postmodernism* (New York: Routledge, 1988), 158–77.

Marsha Kinder, "The Spirit of *The White Hotel*," *HumS* 4–5 (Spring–Summer 1981): 143–70.

George Levin, "No Reservation," *NYTBR* (28 May 1981): 20–23.

Penelope Lively, "Books and Writers: *The White Hotel*," *Encounter* 62 (August 1981): 55.

Robert E. Lougy, "The Wolf-Man, Freud, and D.M. Thomas: Intertextuality, Interpretation, and Narration in *The White Hotel*," *MLS* 21 (Summer 1991): 91–106.

John Macinnes, "The Case of Anna G.: *The White Hotel* and Acts of Understanding, *Soundings* 77 (Fall–Winter 1994): 253–69.

M. Pierrette Malcuzynski, "Polyphonic Theory and Contemporary Literary Practices," *StTCL* 9 (Fall 1984): 75–87.

M. Pierrette Malcuzynski, "Polyphony, Polydetermination, and Narratological Alienation since 1960," in *Proceedings of the Xth Congress of the International Comparative Liternature: Vol. 1: General Problems of Literary History*, ed. Anna Balakian, James J. Wilhelm, Douwe W. Fokkema, Claudio Guillen, and M. J. Valdes (New York: Garland, 1985), 21–26.

Keith Neilson, *White Hotel, The*," in *Survey of Modern Fantasy Litterature*, vol. 5, ed. Frank Magill,(Englewood Cliffs, NJ: Salem, 1983): 2122–125.

Robert D. Newman, "Another *White Hotel*," *NConL* 21 (September 1991): 3–4.

Robert D. Newman, "D. M. Thomas' *The White Hotel*: Mirrors, Triangles, and Sublime Repression," *MFS* 35 (Summer 1989): 193–209.

K. J. Phillips, "The Phalaris Syndrome: Alain Robbe-Grillet vs. D. M. Thomas," in *Women and Violence in Literature: An Essay Collection*, ed. Katherine Anne Ackley (New York: Garland, 1990), 186–205.

Christine Reynie, "Histoire et Histoire dans *The White Hotel* (D. M. Thomas)," in *Historicite et metafiction dans le roman contemporain des Iles Britanniques*, ed. Max Duperray (Aix-en-Provence: Université de Provence, 1994), 101–20.

Mary F. Robertson, "Hystery, Herstory, History: 'Imagining the Real' in Thomas's *The White Hotel*," *ConL* 25 (Winter 1984): 452–77.

Lars Ole Sauerberg, "When the Soul Takes Wing: D. M. Thomas's *The White Hotel*," *Critique* 31 (Fall 1989): 3–10.

Ellen Y. Siegelman, "*The White Hotel*: Visions and Revisions of the Psyche," *L&P* 33, no. 1 (1987): 69–76.

Patrick Swinden, "D. M. Thomas and *The White Hotel*, *CritQ* 24 (Winter 1982): 78.

Laura E. Tanner, "Sweet Pain and Charred Bodies: Figuring Violence in *The White Hotel*," *boundaryII* 18 (Summer 1991): 130–49.

Jim Weber, "*The White Hotel*: Freud, Medusa, and the Missing Goddess," *NConL* 21 (January 1991): 10–11.

Hana Wirth-Nesher, "The Ethics of Narration in D. M. Thomas's *The White Hotel*," *JNT* 15 (1985): 15–28.

Rowland Wymer, "Freud, Jung and the 'Myth' of Psychoanalysis in *The White Hotel*," *Mosaic* 22 (Winter 1989): 55–69.

Benzi Zhang, "The Chinese Box in D. M. Thomas's *The White Hotel*," *IFR* 20, no. 1 (1993): 54–57.

TOLKIEN, J[OHN] R[ONALD] R[EVEL]

The Adventures of Tom Bombadil

Keith Masson, "Tom Bombadil: A Critical Essay," *Mythlore* 2 (Winter 1971): 7–8.

John D. Rateliff, "J. R. R. Tolkien: 'Sir Topas' Revisited," *N&Q* 29 (August 1982): 348.

Blickling Homilies

Carl F. Hostetter, "Over Middle-Earth Sent unto Men: On the Philological Origins of Tolkien's Earendel Myth," *Mythlore* 17 (Spring 1991): 5–10.

The Book of Lost Tales

Richard Sturch, "The Theology of *The Book of Lost Tales*," *Amon Hen* 67 (May 1984): 9–10.

"Farmer Giles of Ham"

Brin Dunsire, "Of Ham, and What Became of It," *Amon Hen* 98 (July 1989): 15–17.

William H. Green, "Legendary and Historical Time in Tolkien's 'Farmer Giles of Ham,'" *NConL* 5, no. 3 (1975): 14–15.

J. A. Johnson, "'Farmer Giles of Ham': What Is It?" *Orcrist* 7 (Summer 1973): 21–24.

Steve Linley, "Farmer Giles: Beowulf for the Critics?" *Amon Hen* 98 (July 1989): 11–12.

Dylan Pugh, "A Dog's Eye View," *Amon Hen* 98 (July 1989): 17–18.

R. C. Walker, "The Little Kingdom: Some Considerations and a Map," *Mythlore* 10 (Winter 1984): 47–48.

The Father Christmas Letters

Paul Nolan Hyde, "A Philologist at the North Pole: J. R. R. Tolkien and *The Father Christmas Letters*," *Mythlore* 15 (Autumn 1988): 23–27.

Martha and Laurence Krieg, "*The Father Christmas Letters*," *Mythlore* 4 (December 1976): 24–25.

The Fellowship of the Ring

W. H. Auden, "A World Imaginary, but Real," *Encounter* 3 (November 1954): 59–62.

David Bell, "The Battle of the Pelennor Fields: An Impossible Victory?" *Mallorn* 19 (December 1982): 25–28.

H. A. Blair, "Myth or Legend," *CHR* 156 (January–March 1955): 121–22.

Anthony Boucher, "*The Fellowship of the Ring*," *MFSC* 8 (April 1955): 82.

Verlyn B. Flieger, "A Question of Time," *Mythlore* 16 (Spring 1990): 5–8.

Daniel Hughes, "The Lord of the Rings," *Spectator* (1 October 1954): 408–409.

C. S. Lewis, "The Gods Return to Earth," *T&T* 35 (14 August 1954): 1082–83.

David M. Miller, "Narrative Pattern in *The Fellowship of the Ring*," in *A Tolkien Compass*, ed. Jared Lobdell (New York: Ballantine, 1980), 95–106.

J. S. Ryan, "Paddle-Feet and Not Paddle-Paws," *MTES* 13 (November–December 1984): 8, 10.

The Hobbit

Mitzi M. Brunsdale, "Norse Mythological Elements in *The Hobbit*," *Mythlore* 9 (Winter 1983): 49–50.

Christopher L. Couch, "From Under Mountains to Beyond Stars: The Process of Riddling in Leofric's *The Exeter Book* and *The Hobbit*," *Mythlore* 14 (Autumn 1987): 9–13, 55.

John A. Ellison, "The Structure of *The Hobbit*," *Mallorn* 27 (September 1990): 29–32.

Constance B. Hieatt, "The Text of *The Hobbit*: Putting Tolkien's Notes in Order," *ESC* 7 (Summer 1981): 212–24.

James L. Hodge, "The Heroic Profile of Bilbo Baggins," *Florilegium* 8 (1986): 212–21.

James L. Hodge, "Tolkien's Mythological Calendar in *The Hobbit*," in *Aspects of Fantasy: Selected Essays from the Second International Conference on the Fantastic in Literature and Film*, ed. William Coyle (Westport, CT: Greenwood, 1986), 141–48.

Paul Nolan Hyde, "A Comprehensive Index of Proper Names and Phrases in *The Hobbit*," *Mythlore* 17 (Spring 1991): 39–42.

Lois R. Kuznets, "Tolkien and the Rhetoric of Childhood," in *Tolkien: New Critical Perspectives*, ed. Neil D. Isaacs and Rose A. Zimbardo (Lexington: University Press of Kentucky, 1981), 150–62.

Alex Lewis, "The Moving Mountains of Mirkwood," *Amon Hen* 71 (January 1985): 11–12.

Alex Lewis, "The Real Mischief," *Amon Hen* 84 (September 1987): 21–22.

Jean MacIntyre, " 'Time shall run back': Tolkien's *The Hobbit*," *CLAQ* 13 (Spring 1988): 12–17.

Dorothy Matthews, "The Psychological Journey of Bilbo Baggins," in *A Tolkien Compass*, ed. Jared Lobdell (New York: Ballantine, 1980), 29–42.

Donald O'Brien, "On the Origin of the Name *Hobbit*," *Mythlore* 16 (Winter 1989): 32–38.

Salman Rushtoes, "Colour Prejudice," *Amon Hen* 99 (September 1989): 18–20.

J. S. Ryan, "Entrance to a Smial!" *Amon Hen* 61 (May 1983): 12–13.

David Stevens, "Trolls and Dragons versus Pocket Handkerchiefs and 'Polite Nothings': Elements of the Fantastic and the Prosaic in *The Hobbit*," in *The Scope of the Fantastic: Culture, Biography, Themes, Children's Literature*, ed. Robert A. Collins and Howard D. Pearce, III (Westport, CT: Greenwood, 1985), 249–55.

Kristin Thompson, "*The Hobbit* as a Part of The Red Book of Westmarch," *Mythlore* 15 (Winter 1988): 11–16.

Steven C. Walker, "The Making of a Hobbit: Tolkien's Tantalizing Narrative Technique," *Mythlore* 7 (Autumn 1980): 6–7.

The Lord of the Rings

Joe Abbott, "Tolkien's Monsters: Concept and Function in *The Lord of the Rings* (Part 1): The Balrog of Khazad-dum," *Mythlore* 16 (Autumn 1989): 19–26, 33.

Joe Abbott, "Tolkien's Monsters: Concept and Function in *The Lord of the Rings*, I: Shelob the Great," *Mythlore* 16 (Winter 1989): 40–47.

Joe Abbott, "Tolkien's Monsters: Concept and Function in *The Lord of the Rings*, II: Shelob the Great; III: Sauron," *Mythlore* 16 (Winter 1989; Spring 1990): 40–47; 51–59.

Kevin Aldrich, "The Sense of Time in J. R. R. Tolkien's *The Lord of the Rings*," *Mythlore* 15 (Autumn 1988): 5–9.

John Algeo, "The Toponymy of Middle-Earth," *Names* 33 (March–June 1985): 80–95.

Elizabeth M. Allen, "Persian Influences in J. R. R. Tolkien's *The Lord of the Rings*," in *The Transcendent Adventure: Studies of Religion in Science Fiction/Fantasy*, ed. Robert Reilly (Westport, CT: Greenwood, 1985), 189–206.

Margaret Askew, "'Lord of the Isles': No, Sorry Mr Giddings, I Mean 'Rings,'" *Mallorn* 21 (June 1984): 15–19.

W. H. Auden, "Good and Evil in *The Lord of the Rings*," *TolJ* 3, no. 1 (1967): 5–8.

Anthony Bailey, "Power in the Third Age of the Middle Earth," *Commonweal* 64 (11 May 1956): 154.

Lionel Basney, "Myth, History, and Time in *The Lord of the Rings*," in *Tolkien: New Critical Perspectives*, ed. Neil D. Isaacs and Rose A. Zimbardo (Lexington: University Press of Kentucky, 1981), 8–18.

Rhona Beare, "Tolkien's Calendar and Ithildin," *Mythlore* 9 (Winter 1983): 23–29.

Bruce A. Beatie, "*The Lord of the Rings*: Myth, Reality, and Relevance," *WR* 4 (Winter 1967): 58–59.

William Edwin Bettridge, "Tolkien's 'New' Mythology," *Mythlore* 16 (Summer 1990): 27–31.

Dianis Bisenieks, "Power and Poetry in Middleearth," *Mythlore* 3, no. 2 (1975): 2024.

Richard Blackwelder, "Cirdan the Shipwright," *MTES* 16 (Winter 1987): 10–15.

William Blissett, "Despots of the Rings," *SoAQ* 58 (Summer 1959): 448–56.

Raimund Borgmeier, "No Message? Zur Deutung von Tolkiens *Lord of the Rings*," *Anglia* 100, no. 3–4 (1982): 397–412.

Anthony Boucher, "*The Lord of the Rings*," *MFSF* 11 (July 1956): 91–92.

Derek Brewer, "*The Lord of the Rings* as Romance," in *J. R. R. Tolkien, Scholar and Storyteller*, ed. Mary Salu and Robert T. Farrell, (Ithaca, NY: Cornell University Press, 1969), 249–64.

G. R. Brown, "Pastoralism and Industrialism in *The Lord of the Rings*," *ESA* 19, no. 2 (September 1976): 83–91.

TOLKIEN, J. R. R. , *The Lord of the Rings*

Richard P. Bullock, "The Importance of Free Will in *The Lord of the Rings*," *Mythlore* 11 (Winter–Spring 1985): 29, 56–57.

Robert A. Bunda, "Color Symbolism in *The Lord of the Rings*," *Ocrist* 8 (1977): 14–16.

Douglas A. Burger, "Tolkien's Elvish Craft and Frodo's Mithril Coat," in *The Scope of the Fantastic: Theory, Technique, Major Authors*, ed. Robert A. Collins and Howard D. Pearce (Westport, CT: Greenwood, 1985), 255–62.

Douglas A. Burger, "The Uses of the Past in *The Lord of the Rings*," *KanQ* 16 (Summer 1984): 23–28.

Michael W. Burgess, "Of Barghest, Orc and Ringwraith," *Amon Hen* 75 (September 1985):15–16.

John A. Calabrese, "Continuity with the Past: Mythic Time in Tolkien's *The Lord of the Rings*," in *The Fantastic in World Literature and the Arts*, ed. Donald E. Morse (Westport, CT: Greenwood, 1987), 31–45.

John A. Calabrese, "Dynamic Symbolism and the Mythic Resolution of Polar Extremes in *The Lord of the Rings*," in *Spectrum of the Fantastic*, ed. Donald Palumbo (Westport, CT: Greenwood, 1988), 135–40.

Patrick J. Callahan, "Animism and Magic in Tolkien's *The Lord of the Rings*," *RQ* 4 (March 1971): 240–49.

David Callaway, "Gollum: A Misunderstood Hero," *Mythlore* 10 (Winter 1984): 14–17; 22.

Christopher Clausen, "*The Lord of the Rings* and 'The Ballad of the White Horse,'" *SoAB* 39, no. 2 (May 1974): 10–16.

Paul Cockburn, "The Lore of the Rings," *Amon Hen* 99 (September 1989): 15–16.

Colin Davey, "Missing Rings—Revisited," *Amon Hen* 71 (January 1985): 18–19.

Donald Davie, "On Hobbits and Intellectuals," *Encounter* 33 (October 1969): 87–92.

Thomas S. Donahue and Paul Nolan Hyde, "A Linguist Looks at Tolkien's Elvish," *Mythlore* 10 (Winter 1984): 28–34.

Susan C. Dorman, "Conviviality in Middle-Earth," *MTES* 15 (Fall 1986): 11–14.

Angela Downing, "From Quenya to the Common Speech: Linguistic Diversification in J. R. R. Tolkien's *The Lord of the Rings*," *RCEI* 4 (April 1982): 23–31.

Roger Drury, "Providence at Elrond's Council," *Mythlore* 7 (Autumn 1980): 8–9.

John A. Ellison, "From Innocence to Experience: The 'Naivete' of J. R. R. Tolkien," *Mallorn* 23 (Summer 1986): 10–13.

John A. Ellison, "'The Legendary War and the Real One': *The Lord of the Rings* and the Climate of Its Times," *Mallorn* 26 (September 1989): 17–20.

Merle Fifield, "Fantasy in and for the Sixties: *The Lord of the Rings*," *EJ* 55 (1966): 841–44.

Verlyn Flieger, "Frodo and Aragorn: The Concept of the Hero," in *Tolkien: New Critical Perspectives*, ed. Neil D. Isaacs and Rose A. Zimbardo (Lexington: University Press of Kentucky, 1981), 40–62.

Cheryl Forbes, "Frodo Decides—Or Does He?" *CT* 20 (19 December 1975): 10–13.

Barton Friedman, "Fabricating History: Narrative Strategy in *The Lord of the Rings*," *CLIO* 2 (1973): 123–44.

Irene Garnett, "From Genesis to Revelation in Middle-Earth," *Mallorn* 22 (April 1985): 39.

Peter Damien Goselin, "Two Faces of Eve: Galadriel and Shelop as Anima Figures," *Mythlore* 6 (Summer 1979): 3–4,28.

Robert A. Hall Jr., "Silent Commands? Frodo and Gollum at the Cracks of Doom," *Mythlore* 10 (Winter 1984): 5–7.

Robert A. Hall Jr., "Who Is the Master of the 'Precious'?" *Mythlore* 11 (Winter–Spring 1985): 34–35.

Gene Hargrove, "Who Is Tom Bombadil?" *Mythlore* 13 (Autumn 1986): 20–24.

Elizabeth Harrod, "Trees in Tolkien and What Happened under Them," *Mythlore* 11 (Summer 1984): 47–52; 58.

Mark M. Hennelly Jr., "The Road and the Ring: Solid Geometry in Tolkien's Middle-Earth," *Mythlore* 9 (Autumn 1982): 3–13.

Michael R. Hickman, "The Religious Ritual and Practise of the Elves of Middle-Earth at the Time of the War of the Ring," *Mallorn* 26 (September 1989): 39–43.

Gwyneth E. Hood, "Sauron as Gorgon and Basilisk," *Seven* 8 (1987): 59–71.

John Houghton, "Rochester the Renewer: The Byronic Hero and the Messiah as Elements in King Elessar," *Mythlore* 11 (Summer 1984): 13–16, 45.

Daniel Hughes, "Pieties and Giant Forms in *The Lord of the Rings*," in *Shadows of Imagination*, ed. Mark R. Hilligas (Carbondale: Southern Illinois University Press, 1969), 81–96.

TOLKIEN, J. R. R. , *The Lord of the Rings*

Paul Nolan Hyde, "Quenti Laubaudillion: A Column on Middle-Earth Linguistics," *Mythlore* 9 (Winter 1983): 19–20.

Paul Nolan Hyde, "Translations from the Elvish: The Linguo-Cultural Foundations of Middle-Earth," *PMPA* 8 (1983): 11–16.

Betty J. Irwin, "Archaic Pronouns in *The Lord of the Rings*," *Mythlore* 14 (Autumn 1987): 46–47.

David Lyle Jeffrey, "Recovery: The Name in *The Lord of the Rings*," in *Tolkien: New Critical Perspectives*, ed. Neil D. Isaacs and Rose A. Zimbardo (Lexington: University Press of Kentucky, 1981), 106–16.

David Lyle Jeffrey, "Tolkien as Philologist," *Seven* 1 (March 1980): 47–61.

Carol Jeffs, "The Forest," *Mallorn* 22 (April 1985): 33–36.

Carol Jeffs, "*Lord of the Rings* as Tragedy," *Mallorn* 21 (June 1984): 5–10.

Nils-Lennart Johannesson, "On the Use of Syntactic Variation in *The Lord of the Rings*," in *Papers from the Second Scandinavian Symposium on Syntactic Variation, Stockholm May 15–16, 1982*, ed. Sven Jacobson (Stockholm: Almqvist & Wiksell, 1983), 135–51.

Gerald Jonas, "Triumph of the Good," *NYTBR* (31 October 1965): 78–79.

Diana Wynne Jones, "The Shape of the Narrative in *The Lord of the Rings*," in *J. R. R. Tolkien: This Far Land*, ed. Robert Giddings (London: Vision; Totowa, NJ: Barnes & Noble, 1983), 87–107.

Kathleen Jones, "The Use and Misuse of Fantasy," *Mallorn* 23 (Society 1986): 5–9.

Hugh T. Keenan, "The Appeal of *The Lord of the Rings*: A Struggle for Life," in *Tolkien and the Critics* ed. Neil D. Isaacs and Rose A. Zimbardo, (Notre Dame, IN: University of Notre Dame Press, 1968), 62–80.

Mary Quella Kelly, "The Poetry of Fantasy: Verse in *The Lord of the Rings*," in *Tolkien and the Critics* ed. Neil D. Isaacs and Rose A. Zimbardo, (Notre Dame, IN: University of Notre Dame Press, 1968), 170–200.

Wilfried Keutsch, "Kult und Allegorie: J. R. R. Tolkiens *Lord of the Rings*," *LWU* 15 (March 1982): 43–59.

Robert Kiely, "Middle Earth," *Commentary* 43 (February 1967): 93–96.

Clyde S. Kilby. "Meaning in *The Lord of the Rings*," in *Shadows of Imagination: The Fantasies of C. S. Lewis, J. R. R. Tolkien, and Charles Williams*, ed. Mark R. Hillegas, (Carbondale: Southern Illinois University Press, 1969), 70–80.

Gisbert Kranz, "Der heilende Aragorn," *Inklings* 2 (1984): 11–24.

Wojciech Kubinski, "Comprehending the Incomprehensible: On the Pragmatic Analysis of Elvish Texts in *The Lord of the Rings*," *Inklings* 7 (1989): 63–81.

Alex Lewis, "The Breaking of Frodo," *Amon Hen* 78; 81 (May 1986; September 1986): 17–18; 20–21.

Alex Lewis, "Hobbit Culture 2," *Amon Hen* 84 (March 1987): 13–14.

Edward Lense, "Sauron is Watching You: The Role of the Great Eye in *The Lord of the Rings*," *Mythlore* 4, no. 1 (September 1976): 3–6.

Alexis Levitin, "The Genre of *The Lord of the Rings*," *Orcrist* 3 (Spring–Summer 1969): 4–8, 23.

Sean Lindsay, "The Dream System in *The Lord of the Rings*," *Mythlore* 13 (Spring 1987): 7–14.

Jarded Lobdell, "J. R. R. Tolkien: Words that Sound Like Castles," *Rally* 1 (August 1966): 24–26.

Peter Lowentrout, "The Evocation of Good in Tolkien," *Mythlore* 10 (Spring 1984): 32–33.

James Lynch, "The Literary Banquet and the Eucharistic Feast: Tradition in Tolkien," *Mythlore* 5 (August 1978): 13–14.

Andrew MacColl, "Frodo Lives . . . ," *Amon Hen* 80 (July 1986): 15–16.

H. C. Mack, "A Parametric Analysis of Antithetical Conflict and Irony: Tolkien's *The Lord of the Rings*," *WORD* 31 (August 1980): 121–49.

Catherine Madsen, "Light from an Invisible Lamp: Natural Religion in *The Lord of the Rings*," *Mythlore* 14 (Spring 1988): 43–47.

Peter Marginter, "John Ronald Reuel Tolkien, der Erfinder von Mittelerde," *L&K* 183–184 (April–May 1984): 157–68.

S. Meagol, "Dealing with Denethor," *Amon Hen* 83 (January 1987): 17–18.

Janet Menzies, "Middle-Earth and the Adolescent," in *J. R. R. Tolkien: This Far Land*, ed. Robert Giddings (London: Vision; Totowa, NJ: Barnes & Noble, 1983), 35–72.

Sandra Miesel, "Some Religious Aspects of *Lord of the Rings*," *RQ* 3 (August 1968): 209–13.

Miriam Y. Miller, "The Green Sun: A Study of Color in J. R. R. Tolkien's *The Lord of the Rings*," *Mythlore* 7 (Winter 1981): 3–11.

Caroline Monks, "Christianity and Kingship in Tolkien and Lewis," *Mallorn* 19 (December 1982): 5–7, 28.

TOLKIEN, J. R. R. , *The Lord of the Rings*

Charles W. Moorman, "Heroism in *The Lord of the Rings*," *SoQ* 11 (1972): 29–39.

Paul Murphy, "The Dwarves in the Fourth Age," *Amon Hen* 67 (May 1984): 7–8.

Sam Naur, "Errors of Gandalf," *Amon Hen* 82 (November 1986): 15–17.

Donald O'Brien, "The Cross-Country Capability of Shadowfax," *MTES* 15 (Fall 1986): 3–9.

Nick Otty, "The Structuralist's Guide to Middle-Earth," in *J. R. R. Tolkien: This Far Land*, ed. Robert Giddings (London: Vision; Totowa, NJ: Barnes & Noble, 1983), 154–78.

David Paul Pace, "The Influence of Vergil's *Aeneid* on *The Lord of the Rings*," *Mythlore* 6 (Spring 1979): 37–38.

Brenda Partridge, "No Sex Please—We're Hobbits: The Construction of Female Sexuality in *The Lord of the Rings*," in *J. R. R. Tolkien: This Far Land*, ed. Robert Giddings (London: Vision; Totowa, NJ: Barnes & Noble, 1983), 179–97.

Diana Paxson, "The Tolkien Tradition," *Mythlore* 11 (Summer 1984): 23–27, 37.

Michael Percival, "The Draining of Moria," *Mallorn* 25 (September 1988): 30–32.

Agnes Perkins and Helen Hill, "The Corruption of Power," in *A Tolkien Compass*, ed. Jared Lobdell (New York: Ballantine, 1980), 57–68.

Dylan Pugh, "Atlantis and Middle-Earth," *Amon Hen* 68 (July 1984): 11–12.

Dylan Pugh, "MOR Than Meets the Eye," *Amon Hen* 85 (July 1987): 13–14.

Margaret R. Purdy, "Symbols of Immortality: A Comparison of European and Elvish Heraldry," *Mythlore* 9 (Spring 1982): 19–22.

Burton Raffel, "*The Lord of the Rings* as Literature," in *Tolkien and the Critics*, ed. Neil D. Isaacs and Rose A. Zimbardo, (Notre Dame: University of Notre Dame Press, 1968), 218–46.

John Rateliff, "Grima the Wormtongue: Tolkien and His Sources," *Mallorn* 25 (September 1988): 15–17.

Melanie Rawls, "Arwen, Shadow Bride," *Mythlore* 12 (Autumn 1985): 24–25, 37.

Melanie Rawls, "The Rings of Power," *Mythlore* 11 (Autumn 1984): 29–32.

William Reynolds, "Poetry as Metaphor in *The Lord of the Rings*," *Mythlore* 4 (June 1977): 12, 14–16.

Derek Robinson, "The Hasty Stroke Goes Oft Astray: Tolkien and Humour," in *J. R. R. Tolkien: This Far Land*, ed. Robert Giddings (London: Vision; Totowa, NJ: Barnes & Noble, 1983), 108–24.

James Robinson, "The Wizard and History: Saruman's Vision of a New Order," *Orcrist* 1 (1966–67): 17–23.

Karen Rockow, "Funeral Customs in Tolkien's Trilogy," *Unicorn* 2 (Winter 1973): 22–30.

Jerome Rosenberg, "The Humanity of Sam Gamgee," *Mythlore* 5 (May 1978): 10–11.

Mariann Russell, "'The Northern Literature' and the Ring Trilogy," *Mythlore* 5 (Autumn 1978): 41–42.

J. S. Ryan, "The Barghest as Possible Source for Tolkien's Goblins and Ring-Wraiths," *Amon Hen* 73 (May 1985): 10–11.

J. S. Ryan, "Mid-Century Perceptions of the Ancient Celtic Peoples of 'England,'" *Seven* 9 (1988): 57–65.

J. S. Ryan, "Oath-Swearing, the Stone of Erech and the Near East of the Ancient World," *Inklings* 4 (1986): 107–21.

J. S. Ryan, "The Origin of the Name 'Wetwang,'" *Amon Hen* 63 (August 1983): 10–13.

J. S. Ryan, "Saruman, 'Sharkey' and Suruman: Analogous Figures of Eastern Ingenuity and Cunning," *Mythlore* 12 (Autumn 1985): 43–44, 57.

Gloriana St. Clair, "*The Lord of the Rings* as Saga," *Mythlore* 6 (Spring 1979): 11–16.

Gary Savage, "The Culture of the Hobbit," *Amon Hen* 83 (January 1987): 15–16.

Mary Aileen Schmiel, "The Forge of Los: Tolkien and the Art of Creative Fantasy," *Mythlore* 10 (Spring 1983): 17–30.

Christina Scull, "On Reading and Re-Reading *The Lord of the Rings*," *Mallorn* 27 (September 1990): 11–14.

Karl Schoor, "The Nature of Dreams in *The Lord of the Rings*," *Mythlore* 10 (Summer 1983): 21–30.

J. A. Schulp, "The Flora of Middle Earth," *Inklings* 3 (1985): 129–39.

Walter Scheps, "The Fairy-Tale Morality of *The Lord of the Rings*," in *A Tolkien Compass*, ed. Jared Lobdell (New York: Ballantine, 1980), 43–56.

TOLKIEN, J. R. R. , *The Lord of the Rings*

Dale W. Simpson, "Names and Moral Character in J. R. R. Tolkien's *Lord of the Rings*," *PMPA* 6 (1981): 1–5.

Patricia Meyer Spacks, "Ethical Pattern in *Lord of the Rings*," *Critique* 3 (Spring–Fall 1959): 30–42.

L. Eugene Startzman, "Goldberry and Galadriel: The Quality of Joy," *Mythlore* 16 (Winter 1989): 5–13.

Jeff Stevenson, "A Delusion Unmasked," *Mallorn* 24 (September 1987): 5–7, 10.

William Stoddard, "A Critical Approach to Fantasy with Application to *The Lord of the Rings*," *Mythlore* 10 (Winter 1984): 8–13.

Leslie Stratyner, "de Us das Beagas Geaf (He Who Gave Us These Rings): Sauron and the Perversion of Anglo-Saxon Ethos," *Mythlore* 16 (Autumn 1989): 5–8.

Jefferson P. Swycaffer, "Historical Motivations for the Siege of Minas Tirith," *Mythlore* 10 (Spring 1983): 48–50.

Stephen L. Walker, "The War of the Rings Treelogy: An Elegy for Lost Innocence and Wonder," *Mythlore* 5 (May 1978): 3–5.

Nigel Walmsley, "Tolkien and the '60s," in *J. R. R. Tolkien: This Far Land*, ed. Robert Giddings (London: Vision; Totowa, NJ: Barnes & Noble, 1983), 73–86.

Andrew Wells, "Armour in the Third Age," *Amon Hen* 68 (July 1984): 16–17.

Richard C. West, "The Interlace and Professor Tolkien: Medieval Narrative Technique in *The Lord of the Rings*," *Orcrist* 1 (1966–67): 26–49.

Colin Wilson, "The Power of Darkness: J. R. R. Tolkien," in *The Strength to Dream: Literature and the Imagination* (Boston: Houghton Mifflin, 1962), 130–32.

Ralph C. Wood, "Traveling the One Road: *The Lord of the Rings* as a 'Pre-Christian' Classic," *CC* 110 (24 February 1993): 208–11.

Samuel Woods Jr., "J. R. R. Tolkien and the Hobbits," *CmRev* 1 (September 1967): 44–52.

J. R. Wytenbroek, "Apocalyptic Vision in *The Lord of the Rings*," *Mythlore* 14 (Summer 1988): 7–12.

Jessica Yates, "In Defence of Fantasy," *Mallorn* 21 (June 1984): 23–28.

Andrzej Zgorzelski, "Does Tolkien Provoke Us to Comprehend Elvish Texts?" *Inklings* 8 (1990): 47–51.

Andrzej Zgorzelski, "The Lyrical in J. R. R. Tolkien's Trilogy," *Inklings* 4 (1986): 87–106.

Rose A. Zimbardo, "The Medieval-Renaissance Vision of *The Lord of the Rings*," in *Tolkien: New Critical Perspectives*, ed. Neil D. Isaacs and Rose A. Zimbardo (Lexington: University Press of Kentucky, 1981), 63–71.

Rose A. Zimbardo, "Moral Vision in *The Lord of the Rings*," in *Tolkien and the Critics* (Notre Dame: University of Notre Dame Press, 1968), 100–08.

Manfred Zimmerman, "Miscellaneous Remarks on Gimli and on Rhythmic Prose," *Mythlore* 11 (Winter–Spring 1985): 32.

Manfred Zimmerman, "The Origin of Gandalf and Joseph Madlener," *Mythlore* 9 (Winter 1983): 22, 24.

Adam Ziolkowski and Winfried Kranz, "Tolkien oder Das rehabilitierte Marchen," *Inklings* 3 (1985): 141–47.

Mr. Bliss

Nils Ivar Agoy, "*Mr. Bliss*: The Precursor of a Precursor?" *Mallorn* 20 (September 1983): 25–27.

The Return of the King

W. H. Auden, "At the End of the Quest, Victory," *SFRB* (January 1978): 96–100.

Jane Beverley, "Aragorn and Aeneas," *Amon Hen* 99 (September 1989): 20–21.

Jenny Curtis, "The Stone of Erech," *Mallorn* 24 (September 1987): 13–15.

Kathleen Herbert, "'Other Minds and Hands': An Experiment in Reconstructing 'The Tale of Valacar and Vidumavi,'" *Mallorn* 22 (April 1985): 25–31.

Francis Huxley, "The Endless Worm," *NewS&N* 50 (5 November 1955): 587–88.

J. S. Ryan, "Before Puck: The Pukel-Men and the Puca," *Mallorn* 20 (September 1983): 5–10.

The Silmarillion

Robert M. Adams, "The Hobbit Habit," *NYRB* (24 November 1977): 22–24.

E. M. Apenko, "*Sil'marillion* Dzhona Tolkina: K voprosu ob zhanrovom eksperimente," *VLU* 1 (January 1989): 41–46.

Elizabeth Broadwell, "Esse and Narn: Name, Identity, and Narrative in the Tale of Turin Turambar," *Mythlore* 17 (Winter 1990): 34–40, 42–44.

TOLKIEN, J. R. R. , *The Silmarillion*

Richard Brookhiser, "Kicking the Hobbit," *NatLR* 9 (December 1977): 1439–440.

Michael Burgess, "Orome and the Wild Hunt: The Development of a Myth," *Mallorn* 22 (April 1985): 5–11.

Peter Conrad, "The Babbit," *NewS* 94 (23 September 1977): 408–9.

Daniel Coogan, "Failing Fantasy, Tragic Fact," *America* 137 (5 November 1977): 315–16.

Howard Davis, "The Ainulindale: Music of Creation," *Mythlore* 9 (Summer 1982): 6–8.

Susan C. Dorman, "The Morning and the Evening Star," *MTES* 16 (Winter 1987): 10–14.

Thomas M. Egan, "*The Silmarillion* and the Rise of Evil: The Birth Pains of Middle Earth," *Seven* 6 (1985): 79–85.

Verlyn Flieger, "Naming the Unnameable: The Neoplatonic 'One' in Tolkien's *Silmarillion*," in *Diakonia: Studies in Honor of Robert T. Meyer*, ed. Thomas Halton and Joseph P. Williman (Washington, DC: Catholic University of America Press, 1986), 127–32.

David Greenman, "*The Silmarillion* as Aristotelian Epic-Tragedy," *Mythlore* 14 (Spring 1988): 20–25.

Paul Kocher, "Iluvatar and the Secret Fire," *Mythlore* 12 (Autumn 1985): 36–37.

Iwan Rhys Morus, "'The Tale of Beren and Luthien,'" *Mallorn* 10 (September 1983): 19–22.

Charles Noad, "A Note on the Geography of the First Age," *Mallorn* 27 (September 1990): 40.

Melanie Rawls, "The Feminine Principle in Tolkien," *Mythlore* 10 (Spring 1984): 5–13.

J. S. Ryan, "Ancient Mosaic Tiles from Out the West: Some Romano-British 'Traditional' Motifs," *MTES* 15 (Summer 1986): 13–17.

Ian Myles Slater, "A Long and Secret Labour: The Forging of *The Silmarillion*: Songs of Light," *Fantasiae* 6 (March 1978): 6–11.

Andrzej Wicher, "The Artificial Mythology of *The Silmarillion* by J. R. R. Tolkien," *KN* 28, no. 3–4 (1981): 399–405.

Patrick Wynne, "Notes Toward a Translation of 'Luthien's Song,'" *Mythlore* 16 (Summer 1990): 37–39.

Sir Orfeo

J. S. Ryan, "The Wild Hunt, *Sir Orfeo* and J. R. R. Tolkien," *Mallorn* 24 (September 1987): 16–17.

"Smith of Wootton Major"

Hugh Crago, "Tolkien in Miniature," *CLN* 4 (May 1968): 8–10.

Margaret Sammons, "Tolkien on Fantasy in 'Smith of Wootton Major,'" *Mythlore* 12 (Autumn 1985): 3–7, 37.

Tree and Leaf

Guy Davenport, "The Persistence of Light," *NatlR* (20 April 1965): 332, 334.

Unfinished Tales

Denis Bridoux, "The Tale of Galadriel and Celeborn: An Attempt at an Integrated Reconstruction," *Amon Hen* 104 (July 1990): 19–23.

Frederick Buechner, "For Devotees of Middle-earth," *NYTBR* (16 November 1980): 15, 20.

Brian Sibley, "History for Hobbits," *Listener* (2 October 1980): 443–44.

TROLLOPE, ANTHONY

The American Senator

John G. Hynes, "*The American Senator*: Anthony Trollope's Critical 'Chronicle of a Winter at Dillsborough,'" *ES* 69 (February 1988): 48–54.

Jackson Trotter, "Foxhunting and the English Social Order in Trollope's *The American Senator*," *SNNTS* 24 (Fall 1992): 227–41.

Ayala's Angel

Nancy A. Metz, "*Ayala's Angel*: Trollope's Late Fable of Change and Choice," *DSA* 9 (1981): 217–32.

Barchester Towers

Harold Bloom, "Introduction," in *Anthony Trollope's "Barchester Towers" and "The Warden,"* ed. Harold Bloom (New York: Chelsea House, 1988), 1–6.

William Cadbury, "Character and the Mock Heroic in *Barchester Towers,*" *TSLL* 5 (1963–64): 509–19.

P. D. Edwards, "The Boundaries of Barset," in *Anthony Trollope's "Barchester Towers" and "The Warden,"* ed. Harold Bloom (New York: Chelsea House, 1988), 92–104.

Ann Frankland, "*Barchester Towers*: A Study in Dialectics," *PAPA* (1986): 197–208.

Robin Gilmour, "The Challenge of *Barchester Towers,*" in *Anthony Trollope's "Barchester Towers" and "The Warden,"* ed. Harold Bloom (New York: Chelsea House, 1988), 141–56.

Christopher Herbert, "*Barchester Towers* and the Charms of Imperfection," in *Anthony Trollope's "Barchester Towers" and "The Warden,"* ed. Harold Bloom (New York: Chelsea House, 1988), 157–63.

Edward H. Kelly, "Trollope's *Barchester Towers,*" *Expl* 44 (Winter 1986): 27–29.

James R. Kincaid, "*The Warden* and *Barchester Towers*: The Pastoral Defined," in *Anthony Trollope's "Barchester Towers" and "The Warden,"* ed. Harold Bloom (New York: Chelsea House, 1988), 69–81.

U. C. Knoepflmacher, "*Barchester Towers*: The Comedy of Change," in *Anthony Trollope's "Barchester Towers" and "The Warden,"* ed. Harold Bloom (New York: Chelsea House, 1988), 43–63.

Robert James Merrett, "Port and Claret: The Politics of Wine in Trollope's *Barsetshire* Novels," *Mosaic* 24 (Summer–Fall 1991): 107–25.

D. A. Miller, "The Novel as Usual: Trollope's 'Barchester Towers,'" in *Sex, Politics, and Science in the Nineteenth-Century Novel*, ed. Ruth Bernard Yeazell (Baltimore: Johns Hopkins University Press, 1986), 1–38.

Jane Nardin, "Conservative Comedy and the Women of *Barchester Towers,*" *SNNTS* 18 (Winter 1986): 381–94.

Robert M. Polhemus, "Trollope's *Barchester Towers*: Comic Reformation," in *Anthony Trollope's "Barchester Towers" and "The Warden,"* ed. Harold Bloom (New York: Chelsea House, 1988), 105–29.

Gay Sibley, "The Spectrum of 'Taste' in *Barchester Towers,*" *SNNTS* 17 (Spring 1985): 38–52.

Andrew Wright, "*Barchester Towers*: Victory's Defeat," in *Anthony Trollope's "Barchester Towers" and "The Warden,"* ed. Harold Bloom (New York: Chelsea House, 1988), 131–39.

The Bertrams

Lawrence Jay Dessner, "The Autobiographical Matrix of Trollope's *The Bertrams*," *NCF* 45 (June 1990): 26–58.

The Duke's Children

James R. Kincaid, "Anthony Trollope and the Unmannerly Novel," in *Reading and Writing Women's Lives: A Study of the Novel of Manners*, ed. Bege K. Bowers and Barbara Brothers (Ann Arbor, MI: University Microfilms International Research Press, 1990), 87–104.

"The Eustace Diamonds"

Henry James Wye Milley, "'The Eustace Diamonds' and *The Moonstone*," *SP* 36 (October 1939): 651–63.

Alan Roth, "He Thought He Was Right (But Wasn't): Property Law in Anthony Trollope's 'The Eustace Diamonds,'" *SLR* 44 (April 1992): 879–97.

Patricia A. Vernon, "Reading and Misreading in 'The Eustace Diamonds,'" *VIJ* 12 (1984): 1–8.

An Eye for an Eye

John G. Hynes, "*An Eye for an Eye*: Anthony Trollope's Irish Masterpiece," *JIL* 16 (May 1987): 54–58.

He Knew He Was Right

Wendy Jones, "Feminism, Fiction and Contract Theory: Trollope's *He Knew He Was Right*," *Criticism* 36 (Summer 1994): 401–14.

Jane Nardin, "Tragedy, Farce, and Comedy in Trollope's *He Knew He Was Right*," *Genre* 15 (Fall 1982): 303–13.

"The Journey to Panama"

Denise Kohn, "'The Journey to Panama': One of Trollope's Best 'Tarts'—Or, Why You Should Read 'The Journey to Panama' to Develop Your Taste for Trollope," *SSF* 30 (Winter 1993): 15–22.

Lady Anna

Deborah Morse, "Trollope's *Lady Anna*: 'Corrupt Relations' or 'Erotic Faith'?" *The Anna Book: Searching for Anna in Literary History* (Westport, CT: Greenwood, 1992), 49–58.

The Landleaguers

John Hynes, "A Note on Trollope's *Landleaguers*," *ÉI* 11 (December 1986): 65–70.

The Last Chronicle of Barset

Robert Pattison, "Trollope among the Textuaries," in *Reconstructing Literature*, ed. Laurence Lerner (Totowa, NJ: Barnes & Noble, 1983), 142–59.

The Macdermots of Ballycloran

Conor Johnston, "*The Macdermots of Ballycloran*: Trollope as Convervative-Liberal," *Éire* 16 (Summer 1981): 71–92.

Sarah Gilead, "Trollope's Ground of Meaning: *The Macdermots of Ballycloran*," *VN* 69 (Spring 1986): 23–26.

Mr. Scarborough's Family

Geoffrey Harvey, "A Parable of Justice: Drama and Rhetoric in *Mr. Scarborough's Family*," *NCF* 37 (December 1982): 419–29.

R. D. McMaster, "Trollope and the Terrible Meshes of the Law: *Mr. Scarborough's Family*," *NCF* 36 (September 1981): 135–56.

Orley Farm

Laura Hapke, "The Lady as Criminal: Contradiction and Resolution in Trollope's *Orley Farm*," *VN* 66 (Fall 1984): 18–21.

Glynn-Ellen Fisichelli, "The Language of Law and Love: Anthony Trollope's *Orley Farm*, *ELH* 61 (Fall 1994): 635–53.

Palliser

Patricia A. Vernon, "The Poor Fictionist's Conscience: Point of View in the *Palliser* Novels," *VN* 71 (Spring 1987): 16–20.

The Prime Minister

Adam Roberts, "Trollope in *The Prime Minister*," *N&Q* 39 (June 1992): 183–84.

Rachel Ray

Jane Nardin, "Comic Tradition in Trollope's *Rachel Ray*," *PLL* 22 (Winter 1986): 39–50.

Sir Harry Hotspur of Humblethwaite

David Pearson, "'The Letter Killeth': Epistolary Purposes and Techniques in *Sir Harry Hotspur of Humblethwaite*," *NCF* 37 (December 1982): 396–418.

The Small House of Allington

Sarah Gilead, "Trollope's *The Small House of Allington*," *Expl* 42 (Winter 1984): 12–14.

The Three Clerks

Henry N. Rogers, III, "Trollope's Fourth Clerk: 'Crinoline and Macassar' in *The Three Clerks*," *PAPA* 13 (Fall 1987): 81–100.

The Warden

J. C. Eade, "'That's The Way the Money Goes': Accounting in *The Warden*," *N&Q* 39 (June 1992): 182–83.

P. D. Edwards, "The Boundaries of Barset," in *Anthony Trollope's "Barchester Towers" and "The Warden,"* ed. Harold Bloom (New York: Chelsea House, 1988), 83–92.

Sherman Hawkins, "Mr. Harding's Church Music," in *Anthony Trollope's "Barchester Towers" and "The Warden,"* ed. Harold Bloom (New York: Chelsea House, 1988), 7–26.

Hugh L. Hennedy, "*The Warden*: Novel of Vocation," in *Anthony Trollope's "Barchester Towers" and "The Warden,"* ed. Harold Bloom (New York: Chelsea House, 1988), 27–41.

James R. Kincaid, "*The Warden* and *Barchester Towers*: The Pastoral Defined," in *Anthony Trollope's "Barchester Towers" and "The Warden,"* ed. Harold Bloom (New York: Chelsea House, 1988), 65–69.

Thomas A. Langford, "Trollope's Satire in *The Warden*," *SNNTS* 19 (Winter 1987): 435–47.

Barry M. Maid, "Trollope, Idealists, Reality, and Play," *VIJ* 12 (1984): 9–21.

Jerome Meckier, "The Cant of Reform: Trollope Rewrites Dickens in *The Warden*," *SNNTS* 15 (Fall 1983): 202–23.

Ross C. Murfin, "The Gap in Trollope's Fiction: *The Warden* as Example," *SNNTS* 14 (Spring 1982): 17–30.

Geoff Ridden, "Trollope, Salisbury, and Winchester," *HRev* 3 (Spring 1989): 330–35.

Ramón Saldivar, "Trollope's *The Warden* and the Fiction of Realism," *JNT* 11 (Fall 1981): 166–83.

The Way We Live Now

A. Abbott Ikeler, "That Peculiar Book: Critics, Common Readers and *The Way We Live Now*," *CLAJ* 30 (December 1986): 219–40.

Iva G. Jones, "Patterns of Estrangement in Trollope's *The Way We Live Now*," in *Amid Visions and Revisions: Poetry and Criticism on Literature and the Arts*, ed. Burney J. Hollis (Baltimore, MD: Morgan State University Press, 1985), 47–58.

H. P. Lisova, "Satyra na viktorians'ku diisnist': Pro roman A. Trollopa Ik my zhyvemo teper," *IF* 68 (1982): 124–29.

R. D. McMaster, "Women in *The Way We Live Now*," *ESC* 7 (Spring 1981): 68–80.

Stephen Wall, "Trollope, Satire, and *The Way We Live Now*," *EIC* 37 (January 1987): 43–61.

WAUGH, EVELYN

Basil Seal Rides Again

Ian Littlewood, *The Writings of Evelyn Waugh* (Oxford: Blackwell, 1983), 122–23.

Stuart Wright, "A Note on Evelyn Waugh's *Basil Seal Rides Again*," *EWNS* 17 (Autumn 1983): 6–7.

Black Mischief

Stanley R. Kaplan, "Circularity and Futility in *Black Mischief*," *EWNS* 15 (Winter 1981): 1–4.

Ian Littlewood, *The Writings of Evelyn Waugh* (Oxford: Blackwell, 1983), 38–41, 44–45, 48–51, 54–55, 72–73, 84–85.

Brideshead Revisited

David Bittner, "The Thread with a Built-In Twitch; Or, The Case for Lady Marchmain," *EWNS* 21 (Autumn 1987): 1–3.

Deborah Core, "The City and the Garden in *Brideshead Revisited*," *KPAB* (1984): 7–13.

Robert Murray Davis, "Chronology in *Brideshead Revisited*," *EWNS* 23 (Autumn 1989): 4–6.

Delia V. Galvan, "Las heroinas de Elena Garro," *La Palabra y el Hombre* 65 (January–March 1988): 145–53.

William T. Going, "Pre-Raphaelitism in *Brideshead Revisited*," *JPRS* 7 (May 1987): 90–93.

Donald Greene, "Charles Ryder's Conversion?" *EWNS* 22 (Winter 1988): 5–7.

Donald Greene, "The Fountain in *Brideshead Revisited*," *EWNS* 23 (Autumn 1989): 4.

Donald Greene, "More on Charles Ryder's Conversion," *EWNS* 23 (Winter 1989: 1–3.

Donald Greene, "Peerage Nomenclature in *Brideshead Revisited*," *EWNS* 16 (Autumn 1982): 5–6.

WAUGH, EVELYN, *Brideshead Revisited*

Ann Hitt, "The Fountain at *Brideshead Castle*," *EWNS* 23 (Winter 1989): 6–7.

Ann Hitt, "Possible Additional Sources of the Fountain in *Brideshead Revisited*," *EWNS* 24 (Winter 1990): 3–4.

Richard G. Hodgson, "Remembrance of Things Past: Proustian Elements in Evelyn Waugh's *Brideshead Revisited*," *EWNS* 18 (Winter 1984): 1–5.

Valerie Kennedy, "Evelyn Waugh's *Brideshead Revisited*: Paradise Lost or Paradise Regained?" *Ariel* 21 (January 1990): 23–39.

Simon Leys, "*Brideshead* Reconsidered, I," *Quadrant* 26 (September 1982): 61–62.

Rhonda Linholm and Elaine E. Whitaker, "Jerusalem Revisited," *EWNS* 24 (Winter 1990): 1–2.

Ian Littlewood, *The Writings of Evelyn Waugh* (Oxford: Blackwell, 1983), 86–87, 104–5, 114–16, 190–92, 208–9.

John W. Mahon, "Charles Ryder's Catholicism," *EWNS* 23 (Spring 1989): 5–7.

Laura Mooneyham, "The Triple Conversions of *Brideshead Revisited*," *Renascence* 45 (Summer 1993): 225–35.

John W. Osborne, "Charles Ryder's Conversion Revisited," *EWNS* 24 (Autumn 1990): 3–4.

John W. Osborne, "Hints of Charles Ryder's Conversion in *Brideshead Revisited*," *EWNS* 22 (Winter 1988): 4–5.

John W. Osborne, "A Problem of Chronology in *Brideshead Revisited*," *EWNS* 22 (Spring 1988): 3–4.

John W. Osborne, "A Reply to Donald Greene about Charles Ryder's Conversion," *EWNS* 23 (Spring 1989): 3–5.

John W. Osborne, "Sebastian Flyte as a Homosexual," *EWNS* 23 (Winter 1989): 7–8.

John W. Osborne, "The Source of a Quotation in *Brideshead*," *EWNS* 21 (Winter 1987): 3.

Kurt Schlueter, "Anno Domini 1943," *EWNS* 20 (Autumn 1986): 4–6.

Kurt Schlueter, "Dimensions of Time and Levels of Representation in *Brideshead Revisited*," in *Elizabethan and Modern Studies: Presented to Professor Willem Schrickx on the Occasion of His Retirement*," ed. J. P. Vander Motten (Ghent: Seminarie voor English & American Literature, Rijksuniversiteit Gent, 1985), 211–17.

Ulf Schonberg, "Architecture and Environment in Evelyn Waugh's *Brideshead Revisited*," *OL* 45, no. 1 (1990): 84–95.

Edmund Wilson, "Splendors and Miseries of Evelyn Waugh," in *Classics and Commercials* (New York: Farrar, Straus, 1950), 298–301. Reprinted in *Critical Essays on Evelyn Waugh*, ed. James F. Carens (Boston: G. K. Hall, 1987), 117–19.

Ruth Wilson, "*Brideshead* Reconsidered, II," *Quadrant* 26 (September 1982): 63–65.

Decline and Fall

Ian Littlewood, *The Writings of Evelyn Waugh* (Oxford: Blackwell, 1983), 46–47, 106–7, 145–46, 185–87.

Shelley Walia, "Sense of an Ending: Evelyn Waugh's *Decline and Fall*," *PURB* 19 (April 1988): 23–40.

A Handful of Dust

Edwin J. Blesch, "(W)Awe-Inspiring: Waugh's *A Handful of Dust* on Screen," *EWNS* 22 (Autumn 1988): 3–6.

Jean-Louis Chevalier, "La Subjectivite du narrateur impersonnel dans *A Handful of Dust*," *Cycnos* 3 (Winter 1986–1987): 51–74.

Roger Decap, "*A Handful of Dust*: Des souris et des hommes," *Caliban* 24 (1987): 109–23.

D. J. Dooley, "*A Handful of Dust* on Film: The Missing Implications," *EWNS* 23 (Autumn 1989): 1–3.

Donald Greene, "Another Waugh Identification: Mrs. Beaver," *EWNS* 21 (Spring 1987): 1–2.

Eric Jager, "A Handful of Dusty Books: Orality and Literacy in Waugh," *EWNS* 24 (Autumn 1990): 4–5.

Pamela R. Johnson, "Tony Last's Search for Order and Justice in *A Handful of Dust*," *EWNS* 18 (Spring 1984): 6–7.

Robert J. Kloss, "Waugh's *A Handful of Dust* as Autobiography," *JEP* 10 (August 1989): 372–82.

Leszek Kolek, "'Uncinematic Devices' in Evelyn Waugh's *A Handful of Dust*," *LWU* 15 (December 1982): 353–65.

Ian Littlewood, *The Writings of Evelyn Waugh* (Oxford: Blackwell, 1983), 23–24, 87–88, 94–98, 120–21, 146–48.

Ann Pasternak Slater, "Waugh's *A Handful of Dust*: Right Things in Wrong Places," *EIC* 32 (January 1982): 48–68.

Yvon Tosser, "Repetition et difference dans *A Handful of Dust*," *ÉA* 40 (January–March 1987): 39–50.

Richard Wasson, "*A Handful of Dust*: Critique of Victorianism," *MFS* 7 (Winter 1961): 327–37. Reprinted in *Critical Essays on Evelyn Waugh*, ed. James F. Carens (Boston: G. K. Hall, 1987), 133–43.

John Howard Wilson, "A Note on the Ending of *A Handful of Dust*," *EWNS* 24 (Winter 1990): 2.

Helena

Patrick Adcock, "*Helena*: Waugh's Englishwoman on the Frontier of Faith," *PAPA* 14 (Spring 1988): 61–67.

Ian Littlewood, *The Writings of Evelyn Waugh* (Oxford: Blackwell, 1983), 155–57, 165–66.

R. J. MacSween, "*Helena*: Waugh's Failure," *AntigR* 73 (Spring 1988): 27–31.

Aubrey Menen, "The Baroque and Mr. Waugh," *Month* 5 (April 1951): 226–37. Reprinted in *Critical Essays on Evelyn Waugh*, ed. James F. Carens (Boston: G. K. Hall, 1987), 120–27.

Love Among the Ruins

Ian Littlewood, *The Writings of Evelyn Waugh* (Oxford: Blackwell, 1983), 55–56.

Peter Miles, "Improving Culture: The Politics of Illustration in Evelyn Waugh's *Love Among the Ruins*," *Trivium* 18 (May 1983): 7–38.

The Loved One

Paul A. Doyle, "That Poem in *The Loved One*," *EWNS* 15 (Winter 1981): 6–7.

Donald Greene, "Evelyn Waugh's Hollywood," *EWNS* 16 (Winter 1982): 1–4.

John Louis Lepage, "Waugh's *The Loved One*," *Expl* 42 (Spring 1984): 51–52.

Ian Littlewood, *The Writings of Evelyn Waugh* (Oxford: Blackwell, 1983), 56–59.

Francis A. Williams, "Waugh's *The Loved One*: Responses to the Dream Machine Philosophy," *EWNS* 21 (Spring 1987): 2–5.

Men at Arms

Mark L. Gnerro, "Echoes of the Anima Christi in a Pivotal Paragraph of Evelyn Waugh's *Men at Arms*," *EWNS* 20 (Winter 1986): 3–6.

Ian Littlewood, *The Writings of Evelyn Waugh* (Oxford: Blackwell, 1983), 99–101, 218–19.

James J. Lynch, "An Allusion to Dante in *Men at Arms*," *EWNS* 18 (Winter 1984): 7.

Officers and Gentlemen

James F. Carens, "All Gentlemen Are Now Very Old," in *The Satiric Art of Evelyn Waugh* (Seattle and London: University of Washington Press, 1966), 157–73. Reprinted in *Critical Essays on Evelyn Waugh*, ed. James F. Carens (Boston: G. K. Hall, 1987), 143–54.

The Ordeal of Gilbert Pinfold

Pamela White Hadas, "Madness and Medicine: The Graphomaniac's Cure," *L&M* 9 (1990): 181–93.

Daniel L. Hurst and Mary Jane Hurst, "Bromide Psychosis: A Literary Case," *CINP* 7 (October 1983): 259–64.

Mary Jane Hurst and Daniel L. Hurst, "Bromide Poisoning in *The Ordeal of Gilbert Pinfold*," *EWNS* 16 (Autumn 1982): 1–5.

Robert J. Kloss, "Evelyn Waugh: His Ordeal," *AI* 42 (Spring 1985): 99–110.

Ian Littlewood, *The Writings of Evelyn Waugh* (Oxford: Blackwell, 1983), 219–30.

J. B. Priestly, "What Was Wrong with Pinfold?" *NS&S* 31 (August 1957): 244. Reprinted in *Critical Essays on Evelyn Waugh*, ed. James F. Carens (Boston: G. K. Hall, 1987), 127–30.

"Period Piece"

Robert Murray Davis, "Waugh Reshapes 'Period Piece,'" *SSF* 21 (Winter 1984): 65–68.

Put Out More Flags

Claire Hopley, "The Significance of Exhilaration and Silence in *Put Out More Flags*," *MFS* 30 (Spring 1984): 83–97.

Ian Littlewood, *The Writings of Evelyn Waugh* (Oxford: Blackwell, 1983), 27–29.

"Ryder by Gaslight"

Jerome Meckier, "Evelyn Waugh's 'Ryder by Gaslight': A Postmortem," *TCL* 31 (Winter 1985): 399–409.

Scoop

Leonard R. N. Ashley, "'Up to a Point': Onomastic Devices and Satire in Evelyn Waugh's *Scoop*," *LOS* 15 (1988): 75–92.

Frederick L. Beaty, "Echoes of A Doll's House in Waugh's *Scoop*," *EWNS* 21 (Winter 1987): 1–2.

Ian Littlewood, *The Writings of Evelyn Waugh* (Oxford: Blackwell, 1983), 51–52, 113–14, 118–19, 148–49.

Sword of Honour

Robert Blow, "*Sword of Honour*: A Novel with a Hero," *DUJ* 80 (June 1988): 305–11.

Robert Murray Davis, "The Magnum Opus: *Sword of Honour*," in *Evelyn Waugh, Writer* (Norman, OK: Pilgrim Books, 1981), 326–32. Reprinted in *Critical Essays on Evelyn Waugh*, ed. James F. Carens (Boston: G. K. Hall, 1987), 157–63.

Thomas Gribble, "The Nature of a Trimmer," *EWNS* 15 (Autumn 1981): 1–3.

Hubertus Schulte Herbruggen, "Der unsterbliche Ritter: Evelyn Waughs *Sword of Honour*," in *Das Ritterbild in Mittelalter und Renaissance*, ed. Hubertus Schulte Herbruggen (Dusseldorf: Droste 1985), 131–48.

Vile Bodies

Kurt Bangert, "The Use of Short Story Techniques in *Vile Bodies*," *EWNS* 21 (Autumn 1987): 3–6.

Emily Dalgarno, "The Title of *Vile Bodies*," *EWNS* 21 (Autumn 1987): 7–8.

Ian Littlewood, *The Writings of Evelyn Waugh* (Oxford: Blackwell, 1983), 11–23, 187–89.

Andreas Mahler, "Zwischenkriegsbewusstsein und die Inszenierung satirischen Erzahlens am Beispiel von Evelyn Waughs *Vile Bodies*," *DVLG* 64 (June 1990): 311–37.

Randall Toye, "Waugh's *Vile Bodies*," *Expl* 43 (Fall 1984): 55–56.

WELLS, H[ERBERT] G[EORGE]

Ann Veronica

Josette Ducamp, "La Signification historique de *Ann Veronica*," *CVE* 30 (October 1989): 79–92.

The Autocracy of Mr. Parham

William J. Scheick, "Lost Places in Dreams and Texts: H. G. Wells's *The Autocracy of Mr. Parham*," *KRev* 4 (Winter 1983): 56–64.

"The Country of the Blind"

Giulia Pissarello, "Un apologo darwiniano: 'The Country of the Blind' di H. G. Wells," *RLMC* 43 (October–December 1990): 399–409.

A. Langley Searles, "Concerning 'The Country of the Blind,'" *Wellsian* 14 (Summer 1991): 29–33.

The First Men in the Moon

Mark R. Hillegas, "A Road Not Taken," *Extrapolation* 30 (Winter 1989): 364–71.

David Lake, "Mr Bedford's Brush with God: Fantastic Tradition and Mysticism in *The First Men in the Moon*," *Wellsian* 13 (Summer 1990): 2–17.

Carlo Pagetti, "H. G. Wells: *The First Men in the Moon*," in *Studi inglesi: Raccolta di saggi e ricerche*, ed. Agostino Lombardo (Bari: Adriatica, 1978), 189–210.

"In the Abyss"

William J. Scheick, "The In-Struction of Wells's 'In the Abyss,'" *SSF* 24 (Spring 1987): 155–59.

The Invisible Man

Philip Holt, "H. G. Wells and the Ring of Gyges," *SFS* 19 (July 1992): 236–47.

Anne B. Simpson, "The 'Tangible Antagonist': H. G. Wells and the Discourse of Otherness," *Extrapolation* 31 (Summer 1990): 134–57.

Margaret Diane Stetz, "Visible and Invisible Ills: H. G. Wells's 'Scientific Romances' as Social Criticism," *VIJ* 19 (1991): 1–24.

Jeanne Murray Walker, "Exchange Short-Circuited: The Isolated Scientist in H. G. Wells's 'The Invisible Man,'" *JNT* 15 (Spring 1985): 156–68.

The Island of Dr. Moreau

Roger Bozzetto, et al. "Moreau's Tragi-Farcical Island," *SFC* 20 (March 1993): 34–44.

Maria Teresa Chialant, "A proposito dell'isola del Dottor Moreau," in *Nel tempo del sogno: Le forme della narrativa fantastica dall'immaginario vittoriano all'u-topia contemporanea*, ed. Carlo Pagetti (Ravenna: Longo, 1988), 75–93.

R. D. Haynes, "The Unholy Alliance of Science in *The Island of Doctor Moreau*," *Wellsian* 11 (Summer 1988): 13–24.

Frances M. Malpezzi, "Sons of Circe: Milton's Comus and H. G. Well's Dr. Moreau," *L&FAR* 4 (July 1984): 1–6.

Michele Paris, "La Femme et le monstrueux: Réflexion à partir de *L'Ile du Docteur Moreau* (1896)," in *Le Monstrueux dans la littérature et la pensée anglaises*, ed. Nadia J. Rigaud (Aix-en-Provence: Publications Université de Provence, 1985), 171–84.

Robert M. Philmus, "The Satiric Ambivalence of *The Island of Doctor Moreau*," *SCF* 8 (March 1981): 2–11.

Robert M. Philmus, "The Strange Case of Moreau Gets Stranger," *SFS* 19 (July 1992): 248–50.

John R. Reed, "The Vanity of Law in *The Island of Doctor Moreau*," in *H. G. Wells Under Revision*, ed. Patrick Parrinder and Christopher Rolfe (Selinsgrove, PA: Susquehanna University Press; London: Associated University Presses, 1990), 134–44.

A Modern Utopia

June Deery, "H. G. Wells's *A Modern Utopia* as a Work in Progress," *Extrapolation* 34 (Fall 1993): 216–29.

Bruno Schultze, "Herbert George Wells: *A Modern Utopia* (1905)," in *Die Utopie in der angloamerikanischen Literatur: Interpretationen*, ed. Hartmut Heuermann and Bernd Peter Lange (Dusseldorf: Bagel, 1984), 161–75.

The Passionate Friends

William J. Scheick, "Revisionary Artistry in Wells's *The Passionate Friends*," in *British Novelists Since 1900*, ed. Jack I. Biles (New York: AMS, 1987), 29–39.

The Sea Lady

William J. Scheick, "The De-Forming In-Struction of Wells's *The Wonderful Visit* and *The Sea Lady*," *ELT* 30, no. 4 (1987): 397–409.

Leon Stover, "H. G. Wells and *The Sea Lady*—a Platonic Affair in the 'Great Outside'?" *Wellsian* 12 (Summer 1989): 2–16.

Star Begotten

William J. Scheick, "Towards the Ultra-Science-Fiction Novel: H. G. Wells's *Star Begotten*," *SFS* 8 (March 1981): 19–25.

"A Story of the Days to Come"

Robert M. Philmus, " 'A Story of the Days to Come' and News from Nowhere: H. G. Wells as a Writer of Anti-Utopian Fiction," *ELT* 30, no. 4 (1987): 450–55.

The Time Machine

Merritt Abrash, "The Hubris of Science: Wells's Time Traveller," in *Patterns of the Fantastic II*, ed. Donald M. Hassler (Mercer Island, WA: Starmont, 1985), 5–11.

Robert J. Begiebing, "The Mythic Hero in H. G. Wells's *The Time Machine*," *ELWIU* 11 (Fall 1984): 201–10.

Lars Gustafsson, "The Present as the Museum of the Future," in *Utopian Vision, Technological Innovation and Poetic Imagination*, ed. Klaus L. Berghahn, Reinhold Grimm, and Helmut Kreuzer (Heidelberg: Winter, 1990), 105–10.

Veronica Hollinger, "Deconstructing *The Time Machine*," *SFS* 14 (July 1987): 201–221.

Kathryn Hume, "Eat or Be Eaten: H. G. Wells's *Time Machine*," *PQ* 69 (Spring 1990): 233–51.

David Ketterer, "Oedipus as Time Traveller," *SFS* 9 (November 1982): 340–41.

Robert M. Philmus, "Futurological Congress as Metageneric Text," *SFS* 13 (November 1986): 313–28.

Frank Scafella, "The White Sphinx and *The Time Machine*," *SFS* 8 (November 1981): 255–65.

Kenneth Tucker, "The Time Machine: H. G. Wells's Early Fable of Human Identity," *JEP* 9 (August 1988): 352–63.

Tono-Bungay

John Allett, "The Durkheimian Theme of Suicide in *Tono-Bungay*," *Wellsian* 13 (Summer 1990): 35–43.

John Allett, "*Tono-Bungay*: The Metaphor of Disease in H. G. Wells's Novel," *QQ* 93 (Summer 1986): 365–74.

John Allett, "*Tono-Bungay*: A Study in Suicide," *UTQ* 60 (Summer 1991): 469–475.

Maria Teresa Chialant, "Dickensian Motifs in Wells's Novels: The Disease Metaphor in *Tono-Bungay*," in *H. G. Wells Under Revision*, ed. Patrick Parrinder and Christopher Rolfe (Selinsgrove, PA: Susquehanna University Press; London: Associated University Presses, 1990), 97–107.

J. R. Hammond, "The Narrative Voice in *Tono-Bungay*," *Wellsian* 12 (Summer 1989): 16–21.

J. R. Hammond, "The Timescale of *Tono-Bungay*: A Problem in Literary Detection," *Wellsian* 14 (Summer 1991): 34–36.

Jeffrey Sommers, "Wells's *Tono-Bungay*: The Novel within the Novel," *SNNTS* 17 (Spring 1985): 69–79.

The War of the Worlds

Brian W. Aldiss, "Introduction to *The War of the Worlds*, Part 1," *NYRSF* 50 (October 1992): 8–10.

Michael J. Bugeja, "Culture and Anarchy in *The War of the Worlds*," *NDQ* 54 (Spring 1986): 79–83.

Hans Esselborn, "Science Fiction als Lehr—und Forschungsgegenstand interkultureller Deutschstudien," *JDF* 18 (1992): 87–107.

Tom Gibbons, "H. G. Wells's Fire Sermon: *The War of the Worlds* and the Book of Revelation," *SFic* 6 (March 1984): 5–14.

Kathryn Hume, "The Hidden Dynamics of *The War of the Worlds*," *PQ* 62 (Summer 1983): 279–92.

Philip Klass, "Wells, Welles and the Martians," *NYTBR* 30 (October 1988): 1, 8–49.

Peter Lowentrout, "*The War of the Worlds* Revisited: Science Fiction and the Angst of Secularization," *Extrapolation* 33 (Winter 1992): 351–59.

Werner von Koppenfelds, "Of Ants and Aliens: Wells's *The War of the Worlds* as Menippean Satire," in *Telling Stories: Studies in Honour of Ulrich Broich on the Occasion of his 60th Birthday*, ed. Elmar Lehmann and Bernd Lenz (Amsterdam: Gruner, 1992), 147–62.

Bruno Schultze, "Herbert George Wells, *The War of the Worlds* (1898)," in *Der Science Fiction Roman in der Angloamerikanischen Literatur: Interpretationen*, ed. Hartmut Heuermann (Dusseldorf: Bagel, 1986), 47–64.

Iain Wakeford, "Wells, Woking and *The War of the Worlds*," *Wellsian* 14 (Summer 1991): 18–29.

The Wheels of Chance

Michel Ballard, "Dualité et duplicité dans *The Wheels of Chance*," *ÉA* 34 (April–June 1981): 153–64.

WHITE, T[ERENCE] H[ANBURY]

Candle in the Wind

John K. Crane, "The Once and Future King," in *T. H. White* (New York: Twayne, 1974), 112–22.

Darkness at Pemberley

John K. Crane, "A Gray White," in *T. H. White* (New York: Twayne, 1974), 37–42.

Dead Mr. Nixon

John K. Crane, "A Gray White," in *T. H. White* (New York: Twayne, 1974), 31–37.

The Elephant and the Kangaroo

John K. Crane, "The Neoclassicist," in *T. H. White* (New York: Twayne, 1974), 134–41.

First Lesson

John K. Crane, "A Gray White," in *T. H. White* (New York: Twayne, 1974), 46–51.

Ill-Made Knight

John K. Crane, "The Once and Future King," in *T. H. White* (New York: Twayne, 1974), 99–112.

The Master

John K. Crane, "The Last Ten Years," in *T. H. White* (New York: Twayne, 1974), 168–72.

Mistress Masham's Repose

John K. Crane, "The Neoclassicist," in *T. H. White* (New York: Twayne, 1974), 123–34.

Cynthia A. Eby, "White's *Mistress Masham's Repose*," *Expl* 40 (Summer 1982): 52–54.

The Once and Future King

John K. Crane, "The Once and Future King," in *T. H. White* (New York: Twayne, 1974), 75–122.

Barbara Floyd, "A Critique of T. H. White's *The Once and Future King*," *RQ* 1 (1965): 175–80.

François Gallix, "T. H. White et le legende du roi Arthur: De la fantaisie animale au moralisme politique," *ÉA* 34 (April–June 1981): 192–203.

Siriol Hugh-Jones, "A Visible Export: T. H. White, Merlyn's Last Pupil," *TLS* (7 August 1969): ix.

Nancy Merrell, "Merlin's Magic," *VirEB* 36 (Winter 1986): 106–7.

Queen of Air and Darkness

John K. Crane, "The Once and Future King," in *T. H. White* (New York: Twayne, 1974), 85–99.

The Sword in the Stone

John K. Crane, "The Once and Future King," in *T. H. White* (New York: Twayne, 1974), 75–85.

Judith N. Mitchell, "The Boy Who Would Be King," *JPC* 17 (Spring 1984): 134–37.

They Winter Abroad

John K. Crane, "A Gray White," in *T. H. White* (New York: Twayne, 1974), 42–46.

WILDE, OSCAR

"The Birthday of the Infanta"

Horst Schroeder, "Some Historical and Literary References in Oscar Wilde's 'The Birthday of the Infanta,'" *LWU* 21, no. 4 (1988): 289–92.

"The Canterville Ghost"

Lydia Reineck Willburn, "Oscar Wilde's 'The Canterville Ghost': The Power of an Audience," *PLL* 23 (Winter 1987): 41–55.

"The Harlot's House"

Bobby Fong, "Wilde's 'The Harlot's House,'" *Expl* 48 (Spring 1990): 198–201.

"Lord Arthur Savile's Crime"

Alfons Klein, "Motive und Themen in Oscar Wildes 'Lord Arthur Savile's Crime,'" in *Motive une Themen in Erzahlungen des spaten 19. Jahrhunderts*, ed. Theodor Wolpers (Gottingen: Vandenhoeck & Ruprecht, 1982), 66–87.

"The Nightingale and the Rose"

Guy Willoughby, "The Marvellous Rose: Christ and the Meaning of Art in 'The Nightingale and the Rose,'" *ESA* 31, no. 2 (1988): 107–17.

The Picture of Dorian Gray

Karl Beckson, "Wilde's Autobiographical Signature in *The Picture of Dorian Gray*," *VN* 69 (Spring 1986): 30–32.

Rachel Bowlby, "Promoting *Dorian Gray*, *OLR* 9, no. 1–2 (1987): 147–62.

Joseph Bristo, "Wilde, Dorian Gray, and Gross Indecency," in *Sexual Sameness: Textual Differences in Lesbian and Gay Writing*, ed. Joseph Bristow (London: Routledge, 1992), 44–63.

William E. Buckler, "*The Picture of Dorian Gray*: An Essay in Aesthetic Exploration," *VIJ* 18 (1990): 135–74.

Nathan Cervo, "Wilde's Closet Self: A Solo at One Remove," *VN* 67 (Spring 1985): 17–19.

Alan Corkhill, "Tiecks William Lovell und Wildes *The Picture of Dorian Gray*: Eine kontinuierliche Tradition," *Archiv* 224, no. 2 (1987): 346–52.

Terence Dawson, "The Dandy in *The Picture of Dorian Gray*: Towards an Archetypal Theory of Wit," *NewComp* 3 (Summer 1987): 133–42.

Richard Dellamora, "Representation and Homophobia in *The Picture of Dorian Gray*," *VN* 73 (Spring 1988): 28–31. Reprinted in *Homosexual Themes in Literary Studies*, ed. Wayne R. Dynes and Stephen Donaldson (New York: Garland, 1992), 82–85.

Donald R. Dickson, "'In a mirror that mirrors the soul': Masks and Mirrors in *Dorian Gray*," *ELT* 26, no. 1 (1983): 5–15.

Sylvette Gendre Dusuzeau, "Dorian Gray ou l'Anti-Narcisse," in *Eighth International Conference on Literature and Psychoanalysis*, ed. Frederico Pereira (Lisbon: Institue Superior de Psicologia Aplicada, 1992), 101–06.

Madame Eusebi, "The Devil in *Dorian Gray*," *CRel* 5 (1987): 85–89.

John Gall, "The Pregnant Death of *Dorian Gray*," *VN* 82 (Fall 1992): 55–58.

Michael Patrick Gillespie, "Picturing Dorian Gray: Resistant Readings in Wilde's Novel," *ELT* 35, no. 1 (1992): 7–25.

Apryl L. D. Heath, "An Unnoted Allusion to Matthew Arnold in *The Picture of Dorian Gray*," *N&Q* 35 (September 1988): 332.

Kathryn Humphreys, "The Artistic Exchange: Dorian Gray at the Sacred Fount," *TSLL* 32 (Winter 1990): 522–35.

Alfons Klein, "Asthetisches Rollenspiel: Zum Motiv der 'gelebten Literatur' in Oscar Wildes *The Picture of Dorian Gray*," in *Gelebte Literatur in der Literatur: Studien zu Erscheinungsformen und Geschichte eines literarischen Motivs*, ed. Theodor Wolpers (Gottingen: Vandenhoeck & Ruprecht, 1986), 272–97.

Dominic Manganiello, "Ethics and Aesthetics in *The Picture of Dorian Gray*," *CJIS* 9 (December 1983): 25–33.

Frederic Monneyron, "Une Lecture nietzscheenne de *Dorian Gray*," *CVE* 16 (October 1982): 139–45.

Jeff Nunokawa, "Homosexual Desire and the Effacement of the Self in *The Picture of Dorian Gray*," *AI* 49 (Fall 1992): 311–21.

Kerry Powell, "Tom, Dick, and Dorian Gray: Magic-Picture Mania in Late Victorian Fiction," *PQ* 62 (Spring 1983): 147–70.

Kerry Powell, "Who Was Basil Hallward?" *ELN* 24 (September 1986): 84-91.

Eric S. Rabkin, "Fantastic Verbal Portraits of Fantastic Visual Portraits," *Mosaic* 21 (Fall 1988): 87-97.

Ellie Ragland-Sullivan, "The Phenomenon of Aging in Oscar Wilde's *Picture of Dorian Gray*: A Lacanian View," in *Memory and Desire: Aging—Literature—Psychoanalysis*, ed. Kathleen Woodward and Murray M. Schwartz (Bloomington: Indiana University Press, 1986), 114–33.

Douglas Robillard, Jr., "Self-Reflexive Art and Wilde's *The Picture of Dorian Gray*," *EAS* 18 (May 1989): 29–38.

Horst Schroeder, "A Quotation in *Dorian Gray*," *N&Q* 38 (September 1991): 327–28.

Charles Swann, "*The Picture of Dorian Gray*, the Bible, and the Unpardonable Sin," *N&Q* 38 (September 1991): 326–27.

WILDE, OSCAR, "The Portrait of Mr. W. H."

Martine Vieron, "Le Mythe du double dans 'Le Portrait de Dorian Gray' d'Oscar Wilde," in *Mythe—Rite—Symbole*, ed. Georges Cesbron (Angers: Université d'Angers, 1985), 77–90.

Stanley Weintraub, "Disraeli and Wilde's *Dorian Gray*," *CVE* 36 (October 1992): 19–27.

"The Portrait of Mr. W. H."

Bruce Bashford, "Hermeneutics in Oscar Wilde's 'The Portrait of Mr. W. H.,'" *PLL* 24 (Fall 1988): 412–22.

William E. Buckler, "The Agnostic's Apology: A New Reading of Oscar Wilde's 'The Portrait of Mr. W. H.,'" *VN* 76 (Fall 1989): 17–22.

William A. Cohen, "Willie and Wilde: Reading 'The Portrait of Mr. W. H.,'" *SoAQ* 88 (Winter 1989): 219–45.

WILLIAMSON, HENRY

A Chronicle of Ancient Sunlight

J. W. Blench, "Henry Williamson and the Romantic Appeal of Fascism, II," *DUJ* 81 (June 1989): 289–305.

The Flax of Dream

J. W. Blench, "Henry Williamson's *The Flax of Dream*: A Reappraisal," *DUJ* 76 (December 1983): 81–97.

Salar the Salmon

J. W. Blench, "Henry Williamson's *Salar the Salmon*: An Appraisal," *DUJ* 83 (July 1991): 223–34.

Tarka the Otter

J. W. Blench, "How Good Is Henry Williamson's *Tarka the Otter* as Literature?" *DUJ* 80 (December 1987): 99–110.

WILSON, ANGUS

Anglo-Saxon Attitudes

Angus Wilson, "The Genesis of *Anglo-Saxon Attitudes*," *BatI* 34 (April 1981): 3–8.

As If by Magic

Jai Dev, "The Function of The Idiot Motifs in *As If by Magic*," *TCL* 29 (Summer 1983): 223–30.

Frederick P. W. McDowell, "An Exchange of Letters and Some Reflections on *As If by Magic*," *TCL* 29 (Summer 1983): 231–35.

No Laughing Matter

Andela Zander, "Tradition und Innovation in Angus Wilsons *No Laughing Matter*," *ZAA* 37, no. 1 (1989): 43–46.

"Raspberry Jam"

Mary Dell Fletcher, "Wilson's 'Raspberry Jam,'" *Expl* 40 (Spring 1982): 49–51.

Setting the World on Fire

Ted Billy, "*Setting the World on Fire*: Phaeton's Fall and Wilson's Redemption," in *Critical Essays on Angus Wilson*, ed. Jay L. Halio (Boston: G. K. Hall, 1985), 192–202.

James M. Haule, "*Setting the World on Fire*: Angus Wilson and the Problem of Evil," *TCL* 28 (Winter 1982): 453–66.

Frederick P. W. McDowell, "Chaos and the Forms of Order in *Setting the World on Fire*," *TCL* 29 (Summer 1983): 236–48.

Michael O'Shea, "Sources and Analogues in Angus Wilson's *Setting the World on Fire*," in *Critical Essays on Angus Wilson*, ed. Jay L. Halio (Boston: G. K. Hall, 1985), 203–17.

Sumans Sen-Bagchee, "Some Joycean Echoes in Wilson's *Setting the World on Fire*," *NConL* 17 (May 1987): 9–11.

WILSON, COLIN

Adrift in Soho

John A. Weigel, *Colin Wilson* (New York: Twayne, 1975), 29, 71–74.

The Black Room

John A. Weigel, *Colin Wilson* (New York: Twayne, 1975), 30, 104–7.

Slaves of the Death Spiders

Brian Stableford, "*Slaves of the Death Spiders*: Colin Wilson and Existentialist Science Fiction," *Foundation* 38 (Winter 1986–1987): 63–67.

The Space Vampires

Jean Marigny, "Science-fiction et fantastique in *The Space Vampires* de Colin Wilson," *ÉA* 41 (July–September 1988): 319–27.

WODEHOUSE, P. G.

The Head of Kay's

Richard J. Voorhees, "The School Novels," in *P. G. Wodehouse* (New York: Twayne, 1966), 54–55.

Love Among the Chickens

Richard J. Voorhees, "Experiments and Transitions," in *P. G. Wodehouse* (New York: Twayne, 1966), 66–72.

Mike and Psmith

Richard J. Voorhees, "Experiments and Transitions," in *P. G. Wodehouse* (New York: Twayne, 1966), 72–74.

Pigs Have Wings

John Sykes, "The German for P. G. Wodehouse," *IL* 24 (Winter 1985): 55–58.

Psmith in the City

Richard J. Voorhees, "Experiments and Transitions," in *P. G. Wodehouse* (New York: Twayne, 1966), 74–77.

Psmith Journalist

Richard J. Voorhees, "Experiments and Transitions," in *P. G. Wodehouse* (New York: Twayne, 1966), 77–82.

"Valley Fields"

Robert A. Hall, "Valley Fields," *PLS* 4 (November 1983): 1–8.

Richard Usborne, "Valley Fields," in *P. G. Wodehouse: A Centenary Celebration, 1881–1981*, ed. James H Heineman and Donald R. Bensen (New York: Pierpont Morgan Library; London: Oxford University Press, 1981), 67–69.

"Ukridge's Accident Syndicate"

Christopher Holcomb, "Nodal Humor in Comic Narrative: A Semantic Analysis of Two Stories by Twain and Wodehouse," *Humor* 5, no. 3 (1992): 233–50.

WOOLF, VIRIGINIA

Between the Acts

Barbara A. Babcock, "Mud, Mirrors, and Making Up: Liminality and Reflexivity in *Between the Acts*," in *Victor Turner and the Construction of Cultural Criticism*, ed. Kathleen M. Ashley (Bloomington: Indiana University Press; 1990), 86–116.

Eileen Barrett, "Matriarchal Myth on a Patriarchal Stage: Virginia Woolf's *Between the Acts*," *TCL* 33 (Spring 1987): 18–37.

Shulamith Barzilai, "The Principle of the Chinese Dagger: Synecdoche in *Between the Acts*," *BRH* 87, no. 1 (1986–87): 128–46.

Harriet Blodgett, "The Nature of *Between the Acts*," *MLS* 13 (Summer 1983): 27–37.

Mari Boyd, "The Art Theme in *Between the Acts*," *SELit* 59 (1983): 49–64.

Jacqueline Buckman, "Virginia Woolf's *Between the Acts* and Some Problems of Periodisation," *DUJ* 84 (July 1992): 279–89.

Stuart N. Clarke, "The Horse with a Green Tail," *VWM* 34 (Spring 1990): 3–4.

Patricia Cramer, "Virginia Woolf's Matriarchal Family of Origins in *Between the Acts*," *TCL* 39 (Summer 1993): 166–84.

Maria DiBattista, "*Between the Acts*: The Play of Wills," in *Virginia Woolf*, ed. Harold Bloom (New York: Chelsea House, 1986), 137–52.

Harold Fromm, "*Between the Acts*: The Demiurge Made Flesh," *SHR* 15 (Summer 1981): 209–17.

Mark Hussey, " '"I" Rejected, "We" Substituted': Self and Society in *Between the Acts*," in *Reading and Writing Women's Lives: A Study of the Novel of Manners*, ed. Bege K. Bowers and Barbara Brothers (Ann Arbor, MI: University Microfilms International Research Press, 1990), 141–52.

Judith L. Johnston, "The Remediable Flaw: Revisioning Cultural History in *Between the Acts*," in *Virginia Woolf and Bloomsbury: A Centenary Celebration*, ed. Jane Marcus (Bloomington: Indiana University Press, 1987), 253–77.

Patricia Klindienst Joplin, "The Authority of Illusion: Feminism and Fascism in Virginia Woolf's *Between the Acts*," *SoCR* 6 (Summer 1989): 88–104.

Melba Cuddy Keane, "The Politics of Comic Modes in Virginia Woolf's *Between the Acts*," *PMLA* 105 (March 1990): 273–85.

Ann Lane, "A Strength Won from Weakness: *Between the Acts*," *CR* 26 (1984): 101–13.

Anne Leblans, "*Between the Acts* als poging tot kommunikatie," *Restant* 10 (Fall 1982): 347–85.

Richard S. Lyons, "The Intellectual Structure of Woolf's *Between the Acts*," *MLQ* 38 (1977): 149–66.

Herbert Marder, "Alienation Effects: Dramatic Satire in *Between the Acts*," *PLL* 24 (Fall 1988): 423–35.

Pamela Mills, "Narrative Techniques in *Between the Acts*," *IlD* 24, no. 2 (1990): 27–37.

Penny Painter, "Two New Notes on Woolf's Novels: The Summer of 1897: The Origin of Some Character and Place Names in Virginia Woolf's *Between the Acts*," *VWM* 35 (Fall 1990): 6–7.

Shaista Rahman, "Names as History in Virginia Woolf's *Between the Acts*," *LOS* 11 (1984): 115–33.

Sangeeta Ray, "The Discourse of Silence: Narrative Interruption and Female Speech in Woolf's *Between the Acts*," *W&D* 8 (Spring 1990): 37–50.

Karen Schneider, "Of Two Minds: Woolf, the War and *Between the Acts*," *JML* 16 (Summer 1989): 93–106.

Jack F. Stewart, "Cubist Elements in *Between the Acts*," *Mosaic* 18 (Spring 1985): 65–89.

Ingeborg Weber, "Die Sprache des Schweigens in Virginia Woolfs Roman *Between the Acts*," in *Theorie und Praxis im Erzahlen des 19. und 20. Jahrhunderts: Studien zur englischen und amerikanischen Literatur zu Ehren von Willi Erzgraber*, ed. Winfried Herget, Klaus Peter Jochum, and Ingeborg Weber (Tubingen: Narr, 1986), 141–52.

Ned Williams, "The Plurisignificance of the Names of Female Characters in Virginia Woolf's *Between the Acts*," *LOS* 11 (1984): 135–46.

G. Patton Wright, "Virginia Woolf's Uncommon Reader: Allusions in *Between the Acts*," in *Virginia Woolf Miscellanies: Proceedings of the First Annual Conference on Virginia Woolf*, ed. Mark Hussey and Vara Neverow Turk (New York: Pace University Press, 1992), 230–33.

"A Haunted House"

Elizabeth Steele, "'A Haunted House': Virginia Woolf's Noh Story," *SSF* 26 (Spring 1989): 151–61.

"In the Orchard"

Sandra Cavicchioli, "I sensi, lo spazio, gli umori: Micro-analisi di 'In the Orchard' di Virginia Woolf," *Versus* 57 (September–December 1990): 11–27.

Jacob's Room

Jane Archer, "The Characterization of Gender-Malaise: Gazing Up at the Windows of *Jacob's Room*," in *Gender Studies: New Directions in Feminist Criticism*, ed. Judith Spector (Bowling Green, OH: Popular Press, 1986), 30–42.

Edward L. Bishop, "The Subject in *Jacob's Room*," *MFS* 38 (Spring 1992): 147–75.

Jean-Louis Chevalier, "La Lettre comme poétique dans *Jacob's Room*," in *Poétique(s): Domaine anglais*, ed. Alain Bony (Lyon: Publication Université de Lyon, 1983), 33–48.

Kathleen Dobie, "This Is the Room That Class Built: The Structures of Sex and Class in *Jacob's Room*," in *Virginia Woolf and Bloomsbury: A Centenary Celebration*, ed. Jane Marcus (Bloomington: Indiana University Press, 1987), 195–207.

William R. Handley, "War and the Politics of Narration in *Jacob's Room*," in *Virginia Woolf and War: Fiction, Reality, and Myth*, ed. Mark Hussey (Syracuse, NY: Syracuse University Press, 1991), 110–33.

Tamotsu Ito, "The British Museum Is Falling Down: A Study of *Jacob's Room*," *HSELL* 28 (1983): 36–46.

Francesca Kazan, "Description and the Pictorial in *Jacob's Room*," *ELH* 55 (Fall 1988): 701–19.

Judy Little, "*Jacob's Room* as Comedy: Woolf's Parodic Bildungsroman," in *New Feminist Essays on Virginia Woolf*, ed. Jane Marcus (Lincoln: University of Nebraska Press, 1981), 105–24.

Carol Ohmann, "Culture and Anarchy in *Jacob's Room*," *ConL* 18 (1977): 160–72.

Susan Bennett Smith, "What the Duke of Wellington Is Doing in *Jacob's Room*," *VWM* 36 (Spring 1991): 2.

Masami Usui, "The German Raid on Scarborough in *Jacob's Room*," *VWM* 35 (Fall 1990): 7.

Alex Zwerdling, "*Jacob's Room*: Woolf's Satiric Elegy," *ELH* 48 (Winter 1981): 894–913.

"Kew Gardens"

Edward L. Bishop, "Pursuing 'It' through 'Kew Gardens,'" *SSF* 19 (Summer 1982): 269–75.

Karl J. Haussler, "Das beispielhafte Experiment: Virginia Woolfs 'Kew Gardens,'" *LWU* 15 (September 1982): 241–67.

Jeanette McVicker, "Vast Nests of Chinese Boxes, or Getting from Q to R: Critiquing Empire in 'Kew Gardens' and *To the Lighthouse*," in *Virginia Woolf Miscellanies: Proceedings of the First Annual Conference on Virginia Woolf*, ed. Mark Hussey and Vara Neverow-Turk (New York: Pace University Press, 1992), 40–42.

John Oakland, "Virginia Woolf's 'Kew Gardens,'" *ES* 68 (June 1987): 264–73.

Pierre Yvard, "Forme et significations dans 'Kew Gardens' de Virginia Woolf," *CahiersN* 1 (1983): 159–63.

"The Mark on the Wall"

Janet Lumpkin, "Woolf's 'Mark on the Wall' as a Voice in Transition," *CCTEP* 54 (September 1989): 28–33.

Wayne Narey, "Virginia Woolf's 'The Mark on the Wall': An Einsteinian View of Art," *SSF* 29 (Winter 1992): 35–42.

Melymbrosia

Elizabeth Heine, "New Light on *Melymbrosia*," in *Virginia Woolf Miscellanies: Proceedings of the First Annual Conference on Virginia Woolf*, ed. Mark Hussey and Vara Neverow-Turk (New York: Pace University Press, 1992), 227–30

Mrs. Dalloway

Elizabeth Abel, "Narrative Structure(s) and Female Development: The Case of *Mrs. Dalloway*," in *The Voyage In: Fictions of Female Development*, ed. Elizabeth Abel, Marianne Hirsch, and Elizabeth Langland (Hanover, NH: University Press of New England for Dartmouth College, 1983), 161–85. Reprinted in *Virginia Woolf*, ed. Harold Bloom (New York: Chelsea House, 1986), 243–64.

Nancy Armstrong, "A Language of One's Own: Communication-Modeling Systems in *Mrs. Dalloway*," *L&S* 16 (Summer 1983): 343–60.

Miroslav Beker, "London as a Principle of Structure in *Mrs. Dalloway*," *MFS* 18 (1972): 375–85.

Morris Benja, "Virginia Woolf: Matches Struck in the Dark," in *Epiphany in the Modern Novel* (Seattle: University of Washington Press, 1971), 133–39. Reprinted in *Major Literary Characters: Clarissa Dalloway*, ed., Harold Bloom (New York: Chelsea House, 1990), 36–40.

Joan Bennett, "Characters and Human Beings," in *Virginia Woolf: Her Art as a Novelist* (New York: Harcourt, Brace, 1945), 24, 29–30, 33, 47–49. Reprinted in *Clarissa Dalloway*, ed., Harold Bloom (New York: Chelsea House, 1990), 25–27.

Edward Bishop, "Writing, Speech, and Silence in *Mrs. Dalloway*," *ESC* 12 (December 1986): 397–423.

Reuben Brower, "Something Central Which Permeated: *Mrs. Dalloway*," in *The Fields of Light: An Experiment in Critical Reading* (New York: Oxford University Press, 1951), 123–37. Reprinted in *Virginia Woolf*, ed. Harold Bloom (New York: Chelsea House, 1986), 7–18. Reprinted in *Major Literary Characters: Clarissa Dalloway*, ed. Harold Bloom (New York: Chelsea House, 1990), 67–77.

WOOLF, VIRIGINIA, *Mrs. Dalloway*

Keith Brower, "*Mrs. Dalloway* on Mount Caburn: A Garden Extended," *CbR* (29 January 1982): 100–05.

Megan C. Burroughs, "Septimus Smith: A Man of Many Words," *UWR* 22, no. 1 (1989): 70–78.

Kai Chen, "A Probe into the Language Features of *Mrs. Dalloway*," *Waiguoyu* 6 (December 1990): 47–52.

Peter Conradi, "The Metaphysical Hostess: The Cult of Personal Relations in the Modern English Novel," *ELH* 48 (Summer 1981):432–36, 445–46. Reprinted in *Major Literary Characters: Clarissa Dalloway*, ed. Harold Bloom (New York: Chelsea House, 1990), 50–54.

David Daiches, "Virginia Woolf," in *The Novel and the Modern World* (Chicago: University of Chicago Press, 1939; rev. ed. 1960), 202–12. Reprinted in *Major Literary Characters: Clarissa Dalloway*, ed. Harold Bloom (New York: Chelsea House, 1990), 30–36.

Elizabeth A. Drew, "A Note on Technique," *The Modern Novel: Some Aspects of Contemporary Fiction* (New York: Harcourt Brace, 1926), 254–62. Reprinted in *Major Literary Characters: Clarissa Dalloway*, ed. Harold Bloom (New York: Chelsea House, 1990), 12–16.

Teresa L. Ebert, "Metaphor, Metonymy, and Ideology: Language and Perception in *Mrs. Dalloway*," *L&S* 18 (Spring 1985): 152–64.

Lee R. Edwards, "War and Roses: The Politics of *Mrs. Dalloway*," in *The Authority of Experience: Essays in Feminist Criticism*, ed. Arlyn Diamond and Lee R. Edwards (Amherst: University of Massachusetts Press, 1977), 161–77. Reprinted in *Major Literary Characters: Clarissa Dalloway*, ed. Harold Bloom (New York: Chelsea House, 1990), 99–112.

E. M. Forster, "Virginia Woolf," in *Two Cheers for Democracy* (New York: Harcourt, Brace, 1951), 247, 250. Reprinted in *Major Literary Characters: Clarissa Dalloway*, ed. Harold Bloom (New York: Chelsea House, 1990), 24–25.

June M. Frazer, "*Mrs. Dalloway*: Virginia Woolf's Greek Novel," *RsSt* 47 (1979): 221–28.

Joanne S. Frye, "*Mrs. Dalloway* as Lyrical Paradox," *BSUF* 23 (Winter 1982): 42–56.

Blanche H. Gelfant, "Love and Conversion in *Mrs. Dalloway*," *Criticism* 8 (Summer 1966): 299–45. Reprinted in *Major Literary Characters: Clarissa Dalloway*, ed. Harold Bloom (New York: Chelsea House, 1990), 86–98.

Deborah Guth, "Rituals of Self-Deception: Clarissa Dalloway's Final Moment of Vision," *TCL* 36 (Spring 1990): 35–42.

Deborah Guth, "'What a Lark! What a Plunge!': Fiction as Self-Evasion in *Mrs. Dalloway*," *MLR* 84 (January 1989): 18–25.

Howard Harper, "*Mrs. Dalloway*," *Between Language and Silence: The Novels of Virginia Woolf* (Baton Rouge: Louisiana State University Press, 1982), 107–17, 122–31. Reprinted in *Major Literary Characters: Clarissa Dalloway*, ed. Harold Bloom (New York: Chelsea House, 1990), 158–70.

Geoffrey H. Hartman, "Virginia's Web," *ChR* 14 (Spring 1961): 20–32. Reprinted in *Beyond Formalism: Literary Essays 1958–1970* (New Haven: Yale University Press, 1970), 71–81. Reprinted in *Major Literary Characters: Clarissa Dalloway*, ed. Harold Bloom (New York: Chelsea House, 1990), 78–85.

Jeremy Hawthorne, "Together and Apart," in *Virginia Woolf's "Mrs. Dalloway": A Study in Alienation* (London: Sussex University Press/Chatto & Windus, 1975), 9–17. Reprinted in *Clarissa Dalloway*, ed. Harold Bloom (New York: Chelsea House, 1990), 41–45.

Suzette A. Henke, "*Mrs. Dalloway*: The Communion of Saints," in *New Feminist Essays on Virginia Woolf*, ed. Jane Marcus (Lincoln: University of Nebraska Press, 1981), 125–47.

Suzette A. Henke, "Virginia Woolf's Septimus Smith: An Analysis of 'Paraphrenic' and the Schizophrenic Use of Language," *L&P* 31, no. 4 (1981): 13–23.

John G. Hessler, "Moral Accountability in *Mrs. Dalloway*," *Renascence* 30 (1978): 126–36. Reprinted in *Major Literary Characters: Clarissa Dalloway*, ed. Harold Bloom (New York: Chelsea House, 1990), 126–36.

Dorothy M. Hoare, "Virginia Woolf, in *Some Studies in the Modern Novel* (London: Chatto & Windus, 1938), 50–53. Reprinted in *Major Literary Characters: Clarissa Dalloway*, ed. Harold Bloom (New York: Chelsea House, 1990), 21–23.

Molly Hoff, "The Midday Topos in *Mrs. Dalloway*," *TCL* 36 (Winter 1990): 449–63.

Molly Hoff, "People Like Ott," *VWM* 37 (Fall 1991): 2–3.

Molly Hoff, "Woolf's *Mrs. Dalloway*," *Expl* 50 (Spring 1992): 161–63.

Edward A. Hungerford, "'My Tunnelling Process': The Method of *Mrs. Dalloway*," *MFS* 3 (Summer 1957): 164–67. Reprinted in *Major Literary Characters: Clarissa Dalloway*, ed. Harold Bloom (New York: Chelsea House, 1990), 27–30.

Mark Hussey, "Identity and Self," in *The Singing of the Real World: The Philosophy of Virginia Woolf's Fiction* (Columbus: Ohio State University Press, 1986), 21–29. Reprinted in *Major Literary Characters: Clarissa Dalloway*, ed. Harold Bloom (New York: Chelsea House, 1990), 55–61.

WOOLF, VIRIGINIA, *Mrs. Dalloway*

Samuel Hynes, "The Whole Contention between Mr. Bennett and Mrs. Woolf," *Novel* 1 (1967): 34–44.

William D. Jenkins, "From Bloomsbury to Baker Street: Who's Afraid of Mrs. Turner?" *BSJ* 33 (September 1983): 137–39.

Emily Jensen, "Clarissa Dalloway's Respectable Suicide," in *Virginia Woolf: A Feminist Slant*, ed. Jane Marcus (Lincoln: University of Nebraska Press, 1983), 162–79.

Vijay Kapoor, "A Jungian Interpretation of *Mrs. Dalloway*," *AJES* 7, no. 2 (1982): 207–24.

Robert Kiely, "A Long Event of Perpetual Change," *Beyond Egotism: The Fiction of James Joyce, Virginia Woolf, and D. H. Lawrence* (Cambridge, MA: Harvard University Press, 1980), 119–30. Reprinted in *Major Literary Characters: Clarissa Dalloway*, ed. Harold Bloom (New York: Chelsea House, 1990), 137–46.

Deborah Kuhlmann, "Woolf's *Mrs. Dalloway*," *Expl* 43 (Winter 1985): 30–32.

So-Hee Lee, "Madness, Marginalization and Power in *Mrs. Dalloway*," *JELL* 36 (Winter 1990): 691–712.

Karen L. Levenback, "Clarissa Dalloway, Doris Kilman and the Great War," *VWM* 37 (Fall 1991): 3–4.

Wyndham Lewis, "Virginia Woolf: 'Mind' and 'Matter' on the Plane of Literary Controversy," in *Men without Art* (Santa Rosa, CA: Black Sparrow Press, 1987), 133–40. Reprinted in *Major Literary Characters: Clarissa Dalloway*, ed. Harold Bloom (New York: Chelsea House, 1990), 16–21.

Jeanette McVicker, "Identity and Difference in Woolf's *Mrs. Dalloway*," in *Translation Perspectives IV: Selected Papers, 1986–87*, ed. Marilyn Gaddis Rose (Binghamton: State University of New York Press, 1988), 171–84.

Herbert Marder, "Split Perspective: Types of Incongruity in *Mrs. Dalloway*," *PLL* 22 (Winter 1986): 51–69. Reprinted in *Major Literary Characters: Clarissa Dalloway*, ed. Harold Bloom (New York: Chelsea House, 1990), 61–63.

Edward Mendelson, "The Death of *Mrs. Dalloway*: Two Readings," in *Textual Analysis: Some Readers Reading*, ed. Mary Ann Caws (New York: Modern Language Association, 1986), 272–80.

Yasuko Mikami, "A Poet's Passion in *Mrs. Dalloway*," *VWR* 8 (1991): 48–63.

J. Hillis Miller, "*Mrs. Dalloway*: Repetition as the Raising of the Dead," in *Fiction and Repetition: Seven English Novels* (Cambridge, MA: Harvard University Press, 1982), 176–202. Reprinted in *Virginia Woolf*, ed. Harold Bloom (New York: Chelsea House, 1986), 169–90.

Makiko Minow-Pinkney, "The Problem of the Subject in *Mrs. Dalloway*," in *Virginia Woolf and the Problem of the Subject* (New Brunswick, NJ: Rutgers University Press, 1987), 60–64, 67–72, 80–83. Reprinted in *Major Literary Characters: Clarissa Dalloway*, ed. Harold Bloom (New York: Chelsea House, 1990), 171–82.

N. Elizabeth Monroe, "The Inception of Mrs. Woolf's Art," *CE*, 2 (December 1940): 218–20. Reprinted in *Major Literary Characters: Clarissa Dalloway*, ed. Harold Bloom (New York: Chelsea House, 1990), 23–24.

Kenneth Moon, "Where is Clarissa? Doris Kilman in *Mrs. Dalloway*," *CLAJ* 23 (March 1980): 273–86. Reprinted in *Major Literary Characters: Clarissa Dalloway*, ed. Harold Bloom (New York: Chelsea House, 1990), 147–57.

Tetsuya Ogoshi, " 'Kyori' no Gyakusetsu: *Mrs. Dalloway* o Megutte," *EigoS* 130 (1985): 522–26.

Stefan Oltean, "Textual Functions of Free Indirect Discourse in the Novel *Mrs. Dalloway* by Virginia Woolf," *RRLing* 26 (November–December 1981): 533–47.

Shijing Qu, "Characterization, Theme and Structure of *Mrs. Dalloway*," *FLitS* 31 (March 1986): 105–09.

Susanna Lippoczy Rich, "Woolf's *Mrs. Dalloway*," *Expl* 47 (Winter 1989): 45–47.

Harvena Richter, "The Canonical Hours in *Mrs. Dalloway*," *MFS* 28 (Summer 1982): 236–40.

Margaret Moan Rowe, "Balancing Two Worlds: Setting and Characterization in *Mrs. Dalloway*," *VWQ* 3 (1978): 268–75.

Lucio P. Ruotolo, "Clarissa Dalloway," in *Six Existential Heroes: The Politics of Faith* (Cambridge, MA: Harvard University Press, 1973), 13–35.

Lucio P. Ruotolo, "*Mrs. Dalloway*: The Journey Out of Subjectivity," *WS* 4 (1977): 173–78.

Ikuko Sato, "Dalloway Fujin: 'Shi' no Sekai tono Tataki," in *Bungaku to Ningen: Nakajima Kanji Kyoju Tsuito Ronbunshu* (Tokyo: Kinseido, 1981), 165–77.

Judith P. Saunders, "Mortal Stain: Literary Allusion and Female Sexuality in *Mrs. Dalloway* in Bond Street,' " *SSF* 15 (Spring 1978): 139–44. Reprinted in *Major Literary Characters: Clarissa Dalloway*, ed. Harold Bloom (New York: Chelsea House, 1990), 45–50.

Mark Spilka, "On Mrs. Dalloway's Absent Grief: A Psycho-Literary Speculation," *ConL* 20 (1979): 316–38.

Susan M. Squier, "Carnival and Funeral," in *Virginia Woolf and London: The Sexual Politics of the City* (Chapel Hill: University of North Carolina Press, 1985), 91–104, 108–10, 121. Reprinted in *Major Literary Characters: Clarissa Dalloway*, ed. Harold Bloom (New York: Chelsea House, 1990), 171–82.

Sharon Stockton, "Turbulence in the Text: Narrative Complexity in *Mrs. Dalloway*," *NOR* 18 (Spring 1991): 46–55.

Minoru Tada, "Dalloway Fujin Oboegaki," in *Suga Yasuo, Ogoshi Kazugo: Ryokyoju Taikan Kinen Ronbunshu* (Kyoto: Apollonsha, 1980), 515–27.

Kazuhisa Takahashi, "Shinya no Vision: Dalloway Fujin No Eta Mono," in *Suga Yasuo, Ogoshi Kazugo: Ryokyoju Taikan Kinen Ronbunshu* (Kyoto: Apollonsha, 1980), 541–55.

Jeremy Tambling, "Repression in Mrs Dalloway's London," *EIC* 39 (April 1989): 137–55.

Nancy Taylor, "Erasure of Definition: Androgyny in *Mrs. Dalloway*," *WS* 18 (January 1991): 367–77.

Victor Udwin, "Reading the Red Ball—a Phenomenology of Narrative Process," in *Narrative Poetics: Innovations, Limits, Challenges*, ed. James Phelan (Columbus: Center for Comparative Studies in Humanities, Ohio State University Press 1987), 115–26.

Masami Usui, "The Female Victims of the War in *Mrs. Dalloway*," in *Virginia Woolf and War: Fiction, Reality, and Myth*, ed. Mark Hussey (Syracuse, NY: Syracuse University Press, 1991), 151–63.

Therese Vichy, "Schemes imaginaires dans *Mrs. Dalloway*," in *Poétique(s): Domaine anglais*, ed. Alain Bony (Lyon: Publication Université de Lyon, 1983), 115–26.

Michel Wade, "Mrs. Dalloway's Affirmation of Value," *HUSL* 7 (1979): 245–70.

Ronald G. Walker, "Leaden Circles Dissolving in Air: Narrative Rhythm and Meaning in *Mrs. Dalloway*," *EELWIU* 13 (Spring 1986): 57–87.

Ban Wang, "'I' on the Run: Crisis of Identity in *Mrs. Dalloway*," *MFS* 38 (Spring 1992): 177–91.

Virginia Woolf, "Mr. Bennett and Mrs. Brown," in *The Captain's Death Bed and Other Essays* (New York: Harcourt, Brace, 1950), 94–102, 109–11, 115–17. Reprinted in *Major Literary Characters: Clarissa Dalloway*, ed. Harold Bloom (New York: Chelsea House, 1990), 5–11.

Virginia Woolf, "Diary (June 18, 1925), in *The Diary of Virginia Woolf*, vol. 3, ed. Anne Alivier Bell and Andrew McNeillie (New York: Harcourt Brace, 1980),

32. Reprinted in *Major Literary Characters: Clarissa Dalloway*, ed. Harold Bloom (New York: Chelsea House, 1990), 11.

Jean Wyatt, "Avoiding Self-Definition: In Defense of Women's Right to Merge," *WS* 13, no. 1–2 (1986): 115–26.

Jean Wyatt, "*Mrs. Dalloway*: Literary Allusion as Structural Metaphor," *PMLA* 88 (1973): 440–51

Alex Zwerdling, "*Mrs. Dalloway* and the Social System," *PMLA* 92 (1977): 69–82.

Night and Day

T. E. Apter, "An Uncertain Balance: *Night and Day*," in *Virginia Woolf*, ed. Harold Bloom (New York: Chelsea House, 1986), 119–28.

Elizabeth Cooley, "Discovering the 'Enchanted Region': A Revisionary Reading of *Night and Day*," *CEA* 54 (Spring 1992): 4–17.

David Galef, "Mrs Woolf and Mr Browne," *N&Q* 36 (June 1989): 202–03.

Shirley Nelson Garner, "'Women Together' in Virginia Woolf's *Night and Day*," in *The (M)other Tongue: Essays in Feminist Psychoanalytic Interpretation*, ed. Shirley Nelson Garner, Claire Kahane, and Madelon Sprengnether (Ithaca, NY: Cornell University Press, 1985), 318–33.

Susan J. Leonardi, "Bare Places and Ancient Blemishes: Virginia Woolf's Search for New Language in *Night and Day*," *Novel* 19 (Winter 1986): 150–63.

Randy Malamud, "Splitting the Husks: Woolf's Modernist Language in *Night and Day*," *SoCR* 6 (Spring 1989): 32–45.

Sonya Rudikoff, "A Possible Source for Night and Day's Cassandra Otway," *VWM* 28 (Spring 1987): 4–5.

Susan Merrill Squier, "Tradition and Revision: The Classic City Novel and Virginia Woolf's *Night and Day*," in *Women Writers and the City: Essays in Feminist Literary Criticism*, ed. Susan Merrill Squier (Knoxville: University of Tennessee Press, 1984), 114–33.

Helen Wussow, "Conflict of Language in Virginia Woolf's *Night and Day*," *JML* 16 (Summer 1989): 61–73.

Orlando

Barbara Currier Bell, "*Orlando*: Mockery with a Grin or with a Vengeance?" *ModST* 4 (1982): 207–17.

Vita Fortunati, "Parodia e ironia in 'Orlando' di Virginia Woolf," in *Ritratto dell'artista come donna: Saggi sull' avanguardia del Novecento*, ed. Lilla Maria Crisafulli Jones and Vita Fortunati (Urbino: Quattro Venti, 1988), 71–90.

Sherron E. Knopp, "'If I saw you would you kiss me?' Sapphism and the Subversiveness of Virginia Woolf's *Orlando*," *PMLA* 103 (January 1988): 24–34. Reprinted in *Homosexual Themes in Literary Studies*, ed. Wayne R. Dynes and Stephen Donaldson (New York: Garland, 1992), 192–202.

Karen R. Lawrence, "Orlando's Voyage Out," *MFS* 38 (Spring 1992): 253–77.

Judy Little, "(En)gendering Laughter: Woolf's *Orlando* as Contraband in the Age of Joyce," *WS* 15, no. 1–3 (1988): 179–91.

Judy Little, "The Politics of Holiday: *Orlando*," in *Virginia Woolf*, ed. Harold Bloom (New York: Chelsea House, 1986), 223–29.

Kari Elise Lokke, "*Orlando* and Incandescence: Virginia Woolf's Comic Sublime," *MFS* 38 (Spring 1992): 235–52.

Elizabeth Meese, "When Virginia Looked at Vita, What Did She See; Or, Lesbian: Feminist: Woman—What's the Differ(e/a)nce?" *FS* 18 (Spring 1992): 99–117.

Françoise Pellan, "Virginia Woolf's Posthumous Poem," *MFS* 29 (Winter 1983): 695–700.

David Roessel, "The Significance of Constantinople in *Orlando*," *PLL* 28 (Fall 1992): 398–416.

Klaus Schwank, "'Granite and Rainbow': Virginia Woolfs *Orlando* (1928) zwischen Historiographie und Fiktion," *A&E* 24 (1984): 7–21.

Susan M. Squier, "Tradition and Revision in Woolf's *Orlando*: Defoe and 'The Jessamy Brides,'" *WS* 12, no. 2 (1986): 167–78.

Paul West, "Enigmas of Imagination: *Orlando* Through the Looking Glass," in *Virginia Woolf*, ed. Harold Bloom (New York: Chelsea House, 1986), 83–100.

J. J. Wilson, "Why Is 'Orlando' Difficult?" in *New Feminist Essays on Virginia Woolf*, ed. Jane Marcus (Lincoln: University of Nebraska Press, 1981), 170–84.

"A Society"

Susan Dick, "'What Fools We Were!' Virginia Woolf's 'A Society,'" *TCL* 33 (Spring 1987): 51–66.

Edward A. Hungerford, "Is 'A Society' a Short Story?" *VWM* 21 (Fall 1983): 3–4.

"Solid Objects"

Robert A. Watson, "'Solid Objects' as Allegory," *VWM* 16 (Spring 1981): 3–4.

Three Guineas

Susan Groag Bell, "'I Am an Outsider': The Politics of Virginia Woolf," *VWM* 20 (Spring 1983): 2–3.

Glynis Carr, "Waging Peace: Virginia Woolf's *Three Guineas*," *Proteus* 3 (Fall 1986): 13–21.

Lynne T. Hanley, "Virginia Woolf and the Romance of Oxbridge," *MR* 25 (Summer 1984): 421–36.

Victoria Middleton, "*Three Guineas*: Subversion and Survival in the Professions," *TCL* 28 (Winter 1982): 405–17.

Brenda R. Silver, "The Authority of Anger: *Three Guineas* as Case Study," *Signs* 16 (Winter 1991): 340–70.

Catherine F. Smith, "*Three Guineas*: Virginia Woolf's Prophecy," in *Virginia Woolf and Bloomsbury: A Centenary Celebration*, ed. Jane Marcus (Bloomington: Indiana University Press, 1987), 225–41.

To the Lighthouse

Elizabeth Abel, "'Cam the Wicked': Woolf's Portrait of the Artist as Her Father's Daughter," *Virginia Woolf and Bloomsbury: A Centenary Celebration*, ed. Jane Marcus (Bloomington: Indiana University Press, 1987), 170–94.

Kate Adams, "Root and Branch: Mrs. Ramsay and Lily Briscoe in *To the Lighthouse*," *SJS* 9 (Spring 1983): 93–109.

William Rodney Allen, "Woolf's *To the Lighthouse*," *Expl* 47 (Spring 1989): 37–38.

A. A. Ansari, "Structure of Correspondences in *To the Lighthouse*," *AJES* 7, no. 2 (1982): 248–52.

Eric Auerbach, "The Brown Stocking," in *Virginia Woolf*, ed. Harold Bloom (New York: Chelsea House, 1986), 22–40.

Tina Barr, "Divine Politics: Virginia Woolf's Journey toward Eleusis in *To the Lighthouse*," *boundaryII* 20 (Spring 1993): 125–45.

Bruce Bassoff, "Tables in Trees: Realism in *To the Lighthouse*," *SNNTS* 16 (Winter 1984): 424–34.

Gillian Beer, "Hume, Stephen, and Elegy in *To the Lighthouse*," *EIC* 34 (January 1984): 33–55. Reprinted in *Virginia Woolf's "To the Lighthouse,"* ed. Harold Bloom (New York: Chelsea House, 1988), 75–93.

Ilona Bell, "'Haunted by Great Ghosts': Virginia Woolf and *To the Lighthouse*," *Biography* 9 (Spring 1986): 150–75.

John W. Bicknell, "Mr Ramsay Was Young Once," in *Virginia Woolf and Bloomsbury: A Centenary Celebration*, ed. Jane Marcus (Bloomington: Indiana University Press, 1987), 52–67.

Sheldon Brivic, "Love as Destruction in Woolf's *To the Lighthouse*," *Mosaic* 27 (September 1994): 65–85.

William J. Burling, "Virginia Woolf's *Lighthouse*: An Allusion to Shelley's Queen Mab?" *ELN* 22 (December 1984): 62–65.

John Burt, "Irreconcilable Habits of Thought in 'A Room of One's Own' and *To the Lighthouse*," *ELH* 49 (Winter 1982): 894–907. Reprinted in *Virginia Woolf*, ed. Harold Bloom (New York: Chelsea House, 1986), 197–206. Reprinted in *Virginia Woolf's "To the Lighthouse,"* ed. Harold Bloom (New York: Chelsea House, 1988), 59–74.

Miriam Marty Clark, "Consciousness, Stream and Quanta, in *To the Lighthouse*," *SNNTS* 21 (Winter 1989): 413–23.

Martin Corner, "Mysticism and Atheism in *To the Lighthouse*," *SNNTS* 13 (Winter 1981): 408–23. Reprinted in *Virginia Woolf's "To the Lighthouse,"* ed. Harold Bloom (New York: Chelsea House, 1988), 43–58.

Helen Storm Corsa, "Death, Mourning, and Transfiguation in *To the Lighthouse*," *L&P* 21 (3 November 1971): 120–22.

Beth Rigel Daugherty, "'There She Sat': The Power of the Feminist Imagination in *To the Lighthouse*," *TCL* 37 (Fall 1991): 289–308.

Susan Dick, "The Restless Searcher: A Discussion of the Evolution of 'Time Passes' in *To the Lighthouse*," *ESC* 5 (1979): 311–29.

Sandra M. Donaldson, "Where does Q leave Mr. Ramsay?" *TSWL* 11 (Fall 1992): 329–36.

Laura Doyle, "'These Emotions of the Body'": Intercorporeal Narrative in *To the Lighthouse*," *TCL* 40 (Spring 1994): 42–71.

Mary Lou Emery, "'Robbed of Meaning': The Work at the Center of *To the Lighthouse*," *MFS* 38 (Spring 1992): 217–34.

Deborah Esch, "'Think of a kitchen table': Hume, Woolf, and the Translation of Example," in *Literature as Philosophy/Philosophy as Literature*, ed. Donald G.

Marshall (Iowa City: University of Iowa Press, 1987), 262–76. Reprinted as "'Think of a Kitchen Table': Hume, Virginia Woolf and the Translation of Example," in *Perspectives on Perception: Philosophy, Art, and Literature*, ed. Mary Ann Caws (New York: Peter Lang, 1989), 79–94.

John Ferguson, "A Sea Change: Thomas De Quincey and Mr. Carmichael in *To the Lighthouse*," *JML* 14 (Summer 1987): 45–63.

Kate Flint, "Virginia Woolf and the General Strike," *EIC* 36 (October 1986): 319–34.

Martin Gliserman, "Virginia Woolf's *To the Lighthouse*: Syntax and the Female Center," *AI* 40 (Spring 1983): 51–101.

Elissa Greenwald, "Casting off from 'The Castaway': *To the Lighthouse* as Prose Elegy," *Genre* 19 (Spring 1986): 37–57.

Deborah Guth, "Virginia Woolf: Myth and *To the Lighthouse*," *CollL* 11 (Fall 1984): 233–49.

William R. Handley, "The Housemaid and the Kitchen Table: Incorporating the Frame in *To the Lighthouse*," *TCL* 40 (Spring 1994): 15–31.

Harry R. Harrington, "The Central Line Down the Middle of *To the Lighthouse*," *ConL* 21 (1980): 363–83.

Mark M. Hennely, "Romantic Symbol and Psyche in *To the Lighthouse*," *JEP* 4 (August 1983): 145–62.

Anne Golomb Hoffman, "Demeter and Poseidon: Fusion and Distance in *To the Lighthouse*," *SNNTS* 16 (Summer 1984): 182–96.

Earl G. Ingersoll, "Woolf's *To the Lighthouse*," *Expl* 50 (Winter 1992): 93–96.

Mary Jacobus, "'The Third Stroke': Reading Woolf with Freud," in *Grafts: Feminist Cultural Criticism*, ed. Susan Sheridan (London: Verso, 1988), 93–110.

Bettina L. Knapp, "Virginia Woolf's 'Boeuf en Daube,' *Literary Gastronomy*, ed. David Bevan (Amsterdam: Rodopi, 1988), 29–36.

Peter Knox-Shaw, "*To the Lighthouse*: The Novel as Elegy," *ESA* 29, no. 1 (1986): 31–52.

John Kunat, "The Function of Augustus Carmichael in Virginia Woolf's *To the Lighthouse*," *Xanadu* 13 (1990): 48–59.

Hermione Lee, "To the Lighthouse: Completed Forms," in *Virginia Woolf's "To the Lighthouse*," ed. Harold Bloom (New York: Chelsea House, 1988), 9–26.

Joan Lidoff, "Virginia Woolf's Feminine Sentence: The Mother-Daughter World of *To the Lighthouse*," *L&P* 32, no. 3 (1986): 43–59.

Jane Lilienfeld, "'Like a Lion Seeking Whom He Could Devour': Domestic Violence in *To the Lighthouse*," in *Virginia Woolf Miscellanies: Proceedings of the First Annual Conference on Virginia Woolf*, ed. Mark Hussey and Vara Neverow Turk (New York: Pace University Press, 1992), 154–64.

Jane Lilienfeld, "Where the Spear Plants Grew: The Ramsay's Marriage in *To the Lighthouse*," in *New Feminist Essays on Virginia Woolf*, ed. Jane Marcus (Lincoln: University of Nebraska Press, 1981), 148–69.

Lisa Low, "Two Figures Standing in Dense Violet Light: John Milton, Virginia Woolf, and the Epic Vision of Marriage," in *Virginia Woolf Miscellanies: Proceedings of the First Annual Conference on Virginia Woolf*, ed. Mark Hussey and Vara Neverow Turk (New York: Pace University Press, 1992), 144–45.

Frank McCombie, "Flounders in *To the Lighthouse*," *N&Q* 38 (September 1991): 343–45.

Bill Martin, "*To the Lighthouse* and the Feminist Path to Postmodernity," *P&L* 13 (October 1989): 307–15.

Keith M. May, "The Symbol of Painting in Virginia Woolf's *To the Lighthouse*," *REL* 8 (April 1967): 91–98.

Perry Meisel, "Deferred Action in *To the Lighthouse*," in *The Myth of the Modern: A Study in British Literature and Criticism after 1850* (New Haven: Yale University Press, 1987), 102–4. *Virginia Woolf's "To the Lighthouse*," ed. Harold Bloom (New York: Chelsea House, 1988), 139–48. Reprinted in *Major Literary Characters: Clarissa Dalloway*, ed. Harold Bloom (New York: Chelsea House, 1990), 63–65.

Margaret E. Melia, "Portrait of an Artist as a Mature Woman: A Study of Virginia Woolf's Androgynous Aesthetics in *To the Lighthouse*," *ESRS* 37 (Summer 1988): 5–17.

John Mepham, "Figures of Desire: Narration and Fiction in *To the Lighthouse*," in *The Modern English Novel*, ed. G. Josipovici (London: Open Books, 1976), 149–85.

J. Hillis Miller, "Mr. Carmichael and Lily Briscoe: The Rhythm of Creativity in *To the Lighthouse*," in *Modernism Reconsidered*, ed. Robert Kiely and John Hildebidle (Cambridge, MA: Harvard University Press, 1983), 167–89.

Christian Moser, "Der Blick der Kunstlerin: Zur Revision asthetischer Wahrnehmungsformen in Virginia Woolfs *To the Lighthouse*," *Poetica* 22, no. 3–4: 384–412.

Pierre Nordon, "*To the Lighthouse* et l'expérience existentielle," in *Genese de la conscience moderne: Études sur le développement de la conscience de soi dans les littératures du monde occidental*, ed. Robert Ellrodt (Paris: Publication Université de France, 1983), 403–07.

Solange Ribeiro de Oliveira, "A Arte como Conhecimento: *To the Lighthouse* de Virginia Woolf," *IID* 24, no. 2 (1990): 39–63.

Kyoko Ono, "*To the Lighthouse* as a Criticism on Modern Civilization: Why Does Mr. Carmichael Stand There?" *SELit* 59 (September 1982): 57–69.

Graham Parkes, "Imagining Reality in *To the Lighthouse*," *P&L* 6, no. 1–2 (1982): 33–44.

M. L. Raina, "Novel as Aesthetic: An Aspect of *To the Lighthouse*," *AJES* 7, no. 2 (1982): 225–47.

Beverly Schlack Randles, "Virginia Woolf's Poetic Imagination: Patterns of Light and Darkness in *To the Lighthouse*," in *The Elemental Dialectic of Light and Darkness: The Passions of the Soul in the Onto-Poiesis of Life*, ed. Anna Theresa Tymieniecka (Dordrecht: Kluwer, 1992), 193–205.

Um Mi sook, "Multiple Inner Points of View in *To the Lighthouse*," *JELL* 37 (Autumn 1991): 667–87.

Mark Spilka, "On Lily Briscoe's Borrowed Grief: A Psycho-Literary Speculation," *Criticism* 21 (1979): 1–33.

Gayatri C. Spivak, "Unmaking and Making in *To the Lighthouse*," in *Women and Language in Literature and Society*, ed. Sally McConnell-Ginet, Ruth Borker, and Nelly Furman, (New York: Praeger, 1980), 310–27.

Erwin R. Steinberg, "G. E. Moore's Table and Chair in *To the Lighthouse*," *JML* 15 (Summer 1988): 161–68.

Jack F. Stewart, "Color in *To the Lighthouse*," *TCL* 31 (Winter 1985): 438–58.

Jack F. Stewart, "Light in *To the Lighthouse*," *TCL* 23 (Fall 1977): 377–89.

Vara Neverow Turk, "'Mrs. Rayley Is Out, Sir': Re-Reading That Hole in Minta's Stocking," *VWM* 39 (Fall 1992): 9.

John Wareham, "Woolf's *To the Lighthouse*," *Expl* 52 (Spring 1994): 167–69.

Anita Weston, "Of Meat and Metaphor: The Life of Signifier in *To the Lighthouse*," in *La performance del testo*, ed. Franco Marucci and Adriano Bruttini (Siena: Ticci, 1986), 383–92.

Rob Wolfs, "Passage(s) in *To the Lighthouse*," *Restant* 15, no. 2 (1987): 229–44.

Jean Wyatt, "The Celebrations of Eros: Greek Concepts of Love and Beauty in *To the Lighthouse*," *P&L* 2 (Fall 1978): 160–75.

The Voyage Out

E. L. Bishop, "Toward the Far Side of Language: Virginia Woolf's *The Voyage Out*," *TCL* 27 (Winter 1981): 343–61. Reprinted in *Virginia Woolf*, ed. Harold Bloom (New York: Chelsea House, 1986), 153–68.

Virginia Blain, "Narrative Voice and the Female Perspective in *The Voyage Out*" in *Virginia Woolf*, ed. Harold Bloom (New York: Chelsea House, 1986), 231–41.

Christine Froula, "Out of the Chrysalis: Female Initiation and Female Authority in Virginia Woolf's *The Voyage Out*," *TSWL* 5 (Spring 1986): 63–90.

Madeline Moore, "Some Female Versions of Pastoral: *The Voyage Out* and Matriarchal Mythologies," in *New Feminist Essays on Virginia Woolf*, ed. Jane Marcus (Lincoln: University of Nebraska Press, 1981), 82–104.

Ai Tanji, "Surely Order Did Prevail: *The Voyage Out* as a Bildungsroman," *Lang&C* 1 (1982): 143–57.

Anca Vlasopolos, "Shelley's Triumph of Death in Virginia Woolf's *Voyage Out*," *MLQ* 47 (June 1986): 130–53.

Helen Wussow, "War and Conflict in *The Voyage Out*," in *Virginia Woolf and War: Fiction, Reality, and Myth*, ed. Mark Hussey (Syracuse, NY: Syracuse University Press, 1991), 101–09.

The Waves

Shulamith Barzilai, "The Knot of Consciouness in *The Waves*," *HUSL* 7 (1979): 214–44.

Darlene Beaman, "'Like as the Waves Make toward the Pebbled Shore': Shakespeare's Influence in *The Waves*," *CCTEP* 48 (September 1983): 79–88.

M. Keith Booker, "Tradition, Authority, and Subjectivity: Narrative Constitution of the Self in *The Waves*," *LIT* 3, no. 1 (1991): 33–55.

Joseph Allen Boone, "The Meaning of Elvedon in *The Waves*: A Key to Bernard's Experience and Woolf's Vision," *MFS* 27 (Winter 1981–82): 629–37.

Susan Dick, "I Remembered, I Forgotten: Bernard's Final Soliloquy in *The Waves*," *MLS* 13 (Summer 1983): 38–52.

J. W. Graham, "Manuscript Revision and the Heroic Theme of *The Waves*," *TCL* 3, no. 20 (1983): 312–32.

Robin Hackett, "Shakespeare's Sonnet 7 in Woolf's *The Waves*," *VWM* 36 (Spring 1991): 6.

Suzette A. Henke, "Virginia Woolf's *The Waves*: A Phenomenological Reading," *Neophil* 73 (July 1989): 461–72.

John F. Hulcoop, "Percival and the Porpoise: Woolf's Heroic Theme in *The Waves*," *TCL* 34 (Winter 1988): 468–88.

Peter Kaye, "Arnold Bennett and *The Waves*: Presence within Absence," *VWM* 27 (Fall 1986): 2–3.

Hermione Lee, "*The Waves*," in *Virginia Woolf*, ed. Harold Bloom (New York: Chelsea House, 1986), 101–17.

Judith Lee, "'This Hideous Shaping and Moulding': War and *The Waves*," in *Virginia Woolf and War: Fiction, Reality, and Myth*, ed. Mark Hussey (Syracuse, NY: Syracuse University Press, 1991), 180–202.

Gerald Levin, "The Musical Style of *The Waves*," *JNT* 13 (Fall 1983): 164–71. Reprinted in *Virginia Woolf*, ed. Harold Bloom (New York: Chelsea House, 1986), 215–22.

Susan E. Lorsch, "Structure and Rhythm in *The Waves*: The Ebb and Flow of Meaning," *ELWIU* 6 (1979): 195–206

Frank D. McConnell, "'Death Among the Apple Trees': *The Waves*" and the World of Things," in *Virginia Woolf*, ed. Harold Bloom (New York: Chelsea House, 1986), 53–65.

Patrick McGee, "The Politics of Modernist Form; or, Who Rules *The Waves*," *MFS* 38 (Fall 1992): 631–50.

Stephen J. Miko, "Reflections on *The Waves*: Virginia Woolf at the Limits of Her Art," *Criticism* 39 (Winter 1988): 63–90.

Kenneth Moon, "The Two Kisses: Human Sexuality in Virginia Woolf's *The Waves*," *AUMLA* 70 (November 1988): 321–35.

James Phelan, "Character and Judgment in Narrative and in Lyric: Toward an Understanding of the Audience's Engagement in *The Waves*," *Style* 24 (Fall 1990): 408–21.

Louise Poresky, "Eternal Renewal: Life and Death in Virginia Woolf's *The Waves*," in *Virginia Woolf Miscellanies: Proceedings of the First Annual Conference on Virginia Woolf*, ed. Mark Hussey and Vara Neverow Turk (New York: Pace University Press, 1992), 64–70.

Raymonde Praly, "A Neoplatonic Variation from the Bird's Songs of Innocence to Their Songs of Experience in *The Waves*," *CVE* 25 (April 1987): 49–61.

Beverly Schlack Randles, "The Waves of Life in Virginia Woolf's *The Waves*," in *Poetics of the Elements in the Human Condition: The Sea: From Elemental

Stirrings to Symbolic Inspiration, Language, and Life-Significance in Literary Interpretation and Theory, ed. Anna-Teresa Tymieniecka (Dordrecht: Reidel, 1985), 45–56.

Mary W. Schneider, "The Arnoldian Voice in Woolf's *The Waves*," *Arnoldian* 10 (Spring 1983): 7–20.

Motoko Seo, "Koga to Shi: *The Waves* no Sekai," in *Yamakawa Kozo Kyoju Taikan Kinen Ronbunshu* (Toyonaka: N.p., 1981), 420–33.

Garrett Stewart, "Catching the Stylistic Drift: Sound Effects in *The Waves*," *ELH* 54 (Summer 1987): 421–61.

Jack F. Stewart, "Spatial Form and Color in *The Waves*," *TCL* 28 (Spring 1982): 86–107.

Eileen B. Sypher, "*The Waves*: A Utopia of Androgyny?" in *Virginia Woolf: Centennial Essays*, ed. Elaine K. Ginsberg and Laura Moss Gottlieb (Troy, NY: Whitston, 1983), 187–213.

Judith Wilt, "God's Spies: The Knower in *The Waves*," *JEGP 92 (April 1993): 179–99.*

The Years

Patricia Cramer, "'Loving in the War Years': The War of Images in *The Years*," in *Virginia Woolf and War: Fiction, Reality, and Myth*, ed. Mark Hussey (Syracuse, NY: Syracuse University Press, 1991), 203–24.

Sharon Friedman, "Virginia Woolf's *The Years*: The Feminine Tradition Recreated by Three Women Characters," *MidHLS* 4 (1981): 107–18.

Laura Moss Gottlieb, "*The Years*: A Feminist Novel," in *Virginia Woolf: Centennial Essays*, ed. Elaine K. Ginsberg and Laura Moss Gottlieb (Troy, NY: Whitston, 1983), 215–29.

N. Janardanan, "The Problem of Unity in Virginia Woolf's *The Years*," *JEngS* 3 (1980): 28–37.

Michael Lucey, "Voice to Voice: Self-affirmation in *The Years*," *Novel* 24 (Spring 1991): 257–81.

James Naremore, "Nature and History in *The Years*," in *Virginia Woolf*, ed. Harold Bloom (New York: Chelsea House, 1986), 67–82.

Kathy J. Phillips, "Woolf's Criticism of the British Empire in *The Years*," in *Virginia Woolf Miscellanies: Proceedings of the First Annual Conference on Virginia Woolf*, ed. Mark Hussey and Vara Neverow-Turk (New York: Pace University Press, 1992), 30–31.

Marie-Paule Vigne, "Les Lieux de la parole dans *The Years*," *ÉA* 38 (January–March 1985): 49–59.

ZANGWILL, ISRAEL

The Big Bow Mystery

Meri-Jane Rochelson, "*The Big Bow Mystery*: Jewish Identity and the English Detective Novel," *VR* 17 (Winter 1991): 11–20.

Children of the Ghetto

Meri-Jane Rochelson, "Language, Gender, and Ethnic Anxiety in Zangwill's *Children of the Ghetto*," *ELT* 31, no. 4 (1988): 399–412.

Main Sources Consulted

Books listed as main sources are those containing either numerous or particularly important explications of individual works or elements of a work. Periodicals listed as main sources are those that frequently publish explications. For periodical abbreviations, see the list following the preface.

The ABAC Journal 12 (September–December 1992).

ABEL, ELIZABETH, **MARIANNE HIRSCH**, and **ELIZABETH LANGLAND**, eds. *The Voyage In: Fictions of Female Development*. Hanover, NH: University Press of New England for Dartmouth College Press, 1983.

Accent 4 (Winter 1944)–16 (Spring–Summer 1956).

ACKERMAN, JOHN. *Dylan Thomas: His Life and Work*. London: Oxford University Press, 1964.

ACKLEY, KATHERINE ANNE, ed. *Women and Violence in Literature: An Essay Collection*. New York: Garland, 1990.

———, ed. *Misogyny in Literature: An Essay Collection*. New York: Garland, 1992.

Acme: Annali della Facoltà di Lettere e Filosofia dell'Università degli Studi di Milano 38 (September–December 1985).

ACTES DU CONGRÈS DE POITIERS, ed. *Société des Anglicistes de l'Enseignement Supérieur*. Paris: Didier, 1984.

ADAM International Review 18 (1950).

ADAM, IAN, and **HELEN TIFFIN**, eds. *Past the Last Post: Theorizing Post-Colonialism and Post-Modernism*. Calgary: University of Calgary Press, 1990.

AGGELER, GEOFFREY. *Anthony Burgess: The Artist as Novelist*. University: University of Alabama Press, 1979.

———, ed. *Critical Essays on Anthony Burgess*. Boston: G. K. Hall, 1986.

Albion 8 (Summer 1976).

Alei-Siah 17–18 (1983).

The Aligarh Journal of English Studies 6, no. 1 (1981)–14, no. 1 (1989).

ALLOTT, MIRIAM, ed. *Emily Brontë: "Wuthering Heights": A Casebook*. London: Macmillan, 1970. Rev. ed. 1992.

ALEXANDER, J. H., **DAVID HEWITT**, and **THOMAS CRAWFORD**, eds. *Scott and His Influence: Papers of the Aberdeen Scott Conference, 1982*. Aberdeen: Association for Scottish Literary Studies, 1983.

The Aligarh Critical Miscellany 2 (1989).

AMALRIC, JEAN-CLAUDE, ed. *Studies in the Later Dickens*. Montpellier: Université Paul Valéry, 1973.

America 105 (9 September 1961)–136 (17 June 1978).

The American Bar Association Journal 8 (1922).

The American Benedictine Review 40 (September 1989).

American Humor 8 (Fall 1981).

American Imago: A Psychoanalytic Journal for Culture, Science, and the Arts 9 (Spring 1952)–47 (Fall–Winter 1990).

The American Journal of Psychoanalysis 52 (December 1992).

American Opinion 9 (April 1966).

The American Philosophical Quarterly 26 (October 1989).

The American Scholar 42 (Winter 1972–73).

Amon Hen 67 (May 1984)–104 (July 1990).

Analele Stiintiface ale Universitatii "Al.I. Cuza" din Iasi, Serie noua, e. Lingvistica 33 (1987).

Analele Universitatii, Burcuresti, Limbi Germanice 21 (1972).

Analog: Science Fiction-Science Fact 108 (February 1988)–113 (September 1993).

ANDREW, R. V. *Wilkie Collins: A Critical Survey of his Prose Fiction with a Bibliography*. New York: Garland, 1979.

Angel's Flight 4 (Fall–Spring 1978–1979).

Angles on English Speaking World 1 (Autumn 1986).

Anglia: Zietschrift für Englische Philologie 75 (1957)–108, no. 1–2 (1990).

Anglistik & Englishunterricht 16 (1982)–37 (1989).

The Anglo-Welsh Review 15 (Summer 1965)–86 (Fall 1987).

Annali della Scuola Normale Superiore di Pisa: Classe di lettere e Filosophia 13, no. 4 (1983).

Annali di Ca' Foscari: Rivista della Facoltà di Lingue e Letterature Straniere dell'Università di Venezia 22, no. 1–2 (1983).

The Annals of Internal Medicine 80 (June 1974).

Annees 1 (30 November 1983).

The Anthony Powell Communication 21 (March 1985).

The Antigonish Review 6 (Spring 1975)–53 (Spring 1983).

The Antioch Review 40 (Fall 1982)–46 (Fall 1988).

Antithesis 6, no. 2 (1993).

ANQ: A Quarterly Journal of Short Articles, Notes, and Reviews 5 (September/December 1966)–7 (October 1994).

AOYAMA, SEIKO and **HIROSHI NAKAOKA**, eds. *Bronte Kenkyu: Sakuhin to Haikei*. Tokyo: Kaibunsha, 1983.

Applied Linguistics 10 (September 1989).

Approach 23 (Spring 1957).

Arbeiten aus Auglistik und Amerikanistik 7, no. 1 (1982)–14, no. 1 (1989).

Arbor 303 (1971)–387 (1978).

Arcadia: Zeitschrift für Vergleichende Literaturewissenschaft 19, no. 2 (1984)–20, no. 3 (1985).

Archiv für das Studium der Neueren Sprachen und Literaturen 148 (1925)–224, no. 2 (1987).

Ariel: A Review of International English Literature 4 (1973)–26, no. 2 (1995).

The Arizona English Bulletin 15 (Fall 1972)–16 (April 1974).

The Arizona Quarterly: A Journal of American Literature, Culture, and Theory 10 (Fall 1954)–38 (Winter 1982).

The Armchair Detective: A Quarterly Journal Devoted to the Appreciation of Mystery, Detective, and Suspense Fiction 4 (April 1971)–14 (Winter 1981).

ARMYTAGE, W. H. G. *Yesterday's Tomorrows: A Historical Survey of Future Societies*. Tornonto: University of Toronto Press, 1968.

The Arnoldian: A Review of Mid-Victorian Culture 4 (April 1971)–11 (Spring 1984).

Artes 6 (1983).

ASH, BRIAN. *Faces of the Future: The Lessons of Science Fiction*. New York: Taplinger, 1975.

ASHLEY, LEONARD R. N., and **STUART ASTOR**, eds. *British Short Stories: Classics and Criticism*. Englewood Cliffs, NJ: Prentice-Hall, 1968.

Athenaeum: Studi Periodici di Letteratura e Storia dell'Antichità (23 November 1850)–(9 May 1919).

Atlantic Monthly 184 (December 1949)–240 (December 1977).

Atlantis: A Women's Studies Journal/Revue d'Études sur la Femme (formerly *Atlantis: A Women's Studies Journal/Journal d'Études sur la Femme*) 8 (Spring 1983)–12 (November 1991).

ATTRIDGE, DEREK, ed. *Cambridge Companion to James Joyce*. Cambridge: Cambridge University Press, 1990.

———, and **DANIEL FERRER**, eds. *Post-Structuralist Joyce: Essays from the French*. Cambridge: Cambridge University Press, 1988.

AUSTIN, ALLAN E. *Elizabeth Bowen*. New York: Twayne, 1971.

The Australian Journal of French Studies 18 (January–April 1981)–19 (January–April 1982).

The Australian Literary Studies 6 (October 1976).

Australian Quarterly 30 (September 1958).

AUMLA: Australian Universities Language and Literature Association: A Jounal of Literary Criticism and Linguistics 73 (May 1990)–78 (November 1992).

BACKMAN, SVEN, and **GORDON KJELLMER**, eds. *Papers on Language and Literature: Presented to Alvar Ellegard and Erik Frykman*. Goteborg: ACTA Universite Gothoburgensis, 1985.

BAKER, JAMES R., ed. *Critical Essays on William Golding*. Boston: G. K. Hall, 1988.

The Baker Street Journal: An Irregular Quarterly of the Sherlockiana 32 (March 1982)–41 (March 1991).

BAKKER, J., **A. VERLEUN**, and **J. VRIESENAERDE**, eds. *Essays on American Literature and a Sheaf of Poems*. Amsterdam: Rodopi, 1987.

BALAKIAN, ANNA, et al., eds. *Proceedings of the Xth Congress on the International Comparative Literature*. Vol. 1: *General Problems of Literary History*. New York: Garland, 1985.

BALBERT, PETER, and **PHILIP L. MARCUS**, eds. *D. H. Lawrence: A Centenary Consideration*. Ithaca, NY: Cornell University Press, 1985.

Ball State University Forum 9 (Spring 1968)–23 (Winter 1982).

BALOTA, NICOLAE. *Umanitati: Eseuri*. Bucharest: Eminescu, 1973.

The Barat Review 5 (1970).

BARGAINNIER, EARL F. *The Gentle Art of Murder: The Detective Fiction of Agatha Christie*. Bowling Green, OH: Popular, 1980.

BARKER, FRANCIS, and **THE ESSEX CONFERENCE ON THE SOCIOLOGY OF LITERATURE**, eds. *1848: The Sociology of Literature: Proceedings of the Essex Conference on the Sociology of Literature, July 1977*. Colchester: University of Essex Press, 1978.

BERKER, FRANCIS, ed. *Literature, Society and the Sociology of Literature: Proceedings of a Conference Held at the University of Essex, July 1976*. Colchester: University of Essex Press, 1977.

BARNES, MELVYN. *Dick Francis*. New York: Ungar, 1986.

BARRECA, REGINA, ed. *Sex and Death in Victorian Literature*. Bloomington: Indiana University Press, 1990.

The Basilian Teacher 8 (1963).

BAUER, ROGER, et al., eds. *II: Space and Boundaries in Literature/Espace et frontieres dans la littérature*. Munich: Iudicium, 1990.

BECK, WARREN. *Joyce's "Dubliners": Substance, Vision, and Art*. Durham, NC: Duke University Press, 1969.

BEEBE, MAURICE. *Ivory Towers and Sacred Founts: The Artist as Hero in Fiction from Goethe to Joyce*. New York: New York University Press, 1964.

BEENE, LYNNDIANE. *John le Carré*. Boston: Twayne, 1988.

BEER, JOHN, ed. *Passage to India: Essays in Interpretation*. Totowa, NJ: Barnes & Noble, 1986.

BEHRENDT, STEPHEN C., ed. *Approaches to Teaching Shelley's "Frankenstein."* New York: Modern Language Association Press, 1990.

BEJA, MORRIS, and **SHARI BENSTOCK**, eds. *Coping with Joyce: Essays from the Copenhagen Symposium*. Columbus: Ohio State University Press, 1989.

Belfagor: Rassengna di Varia Umanita 38 (31 July 1983).

BEGNAL, MICHAEL H., ed. *On Miracle Ground: Essays on the Fiction of Lawrence Durrell*. Lewisburg, PA: Bucknell University Press, 1990.

BEN-MERRE, DIANA A., and **MAUREEN MURPHY**, eds. *James Joyce and His Contemporaries*. Westport, CT: Greenwood, 1989.

BENNETT, ANDREW, and **NICHOLAS ROYLE**. *Elizabeth Bowen and the Dissolution of the Novel: Still Lives*. New York: St. Martin's, 1995.

BENSON, JAMES D., and **WILLIAM S. GREAVES**, eds. *Systemic Perspectives on Discourse, II: Selected Applied Papers from the 9th International Systemic Workshop*. Norwood, NJ: Ablex, 1985.

BENTLEY, E. C. *Those Days*. London: Constable, 1940.

BENSTOCK, BERNARD, ed. *James Joyce: The Augmented Ninth: Proceedings of the Ninth International James Joyce Symposium, Frankfurt, 1984*. Syracuse, NY: Syracuse University Press, 1988.

———, ed. *The Seventh of Joyce*. Bloomington: Indiana University Press, 1982; Brighton: Harvester, 1982.

BARLEY, TONY. *Taking Sides: The Fiction of John le Carré*. Philadelphia: Open University Press, 1986.

BERGMANN, HELENA. *Between Obedience and Freedom: Woman's Role in the Mid-Nineteenth Century Industrial Novel*. Götheborg: Acta Universitatis Gothoburgensis, 1979.

BERMAN, JEFFREY. *Narcissism and the Novel*. New York: New York University Press, 1990.

BERTHOLF, ROBERT J., and **ANNETTE S. LEVITT**, eds. *William Blake and the Moderns*. Albany: State University of New York Press, 1982.

BESSIERE, JEAN, ed. *Recit et histoire*. Paris: Publication Université de France, 1984.

Bestia 2 (May 1990).

BEVAN, DAVID, ed. *Literature and War*. Amsterdam: Rodopi, 1990.

BILES, JACK I., ed. *British Novelists Since 1990*. New York: AMS, 1987.

BILLY, TED, ed. *Critical Essays on Joseph Conrad*. Boston: G. K. Hall, 1987.

Biography: An Interdisciplinary Quarterly 9 (Spring 1986).

BIRCH, DAVID, and **MICHAEL O'TOOLE**, eds. *Functions of Style*. London: Pinter, 1988.

BISHOP, A. G., ed. *Selected Essays*. London: Michael Joseph, 1976.

BLACK, MICHAEL. *The Literature of Fidelity*. New York: Barnes & Noble, 1975.

Blackfriars 21 (May 1940)–42 (November 1961).

Black Orpheus: Journal of African and Afro-American Literature 4 (October 1958).

The Black Scholar 20 (March–April 1989).

BLAKE, KATHLEEN, ed. *Approaches to Teaching Eliot's "Middlemarch."* New York: Modern Language Association Press, 1990.

BLINKENA, A., **B. LAUMANE**, and **B. SKUJINA**, eds. *Valodas aktualitates 1988, I: III Valodas nedela; II: Vietvardi un personvardi*. Riga: Zinatne, 1989.

BLONDEL, J. *Du verbe au geste: Melanges en l'honneur de Pierre Danchin*. Nancy: Pus de Nancy, 1986.

BLOOM, CLIVE, ed. *Spy Thrillers: From Buchan to le Carré*. New York: St. Martin's, 1990.

———, et al., eds. *Nineteenth-Century Suspense: From Poe to Conan Doyle*. New York: St. Martin's, 1988.

BLOOM, HAROLD, ed. *Major Literary Characters: Clarissa Dalloway*. New York: Chelsea House, 1990.

———, ed. *Modern Critical Interpretations of Anthony Trollope's "Barchester Towers" and "The Warden."* New York: Chelsea House, 1988.

———, ed. *Modern Critical Interpretations of the Brontës*. New York: Chelsea House, 1987.

———, ed. *Modern Critical Interpretations of Charles Dickens*. New York: Chelsea House, 1987.

———, ed. *Modern Critical Interpretations of Charles Dickens's "Bleak House."* New York: Chelsea House, 1987.

———, ed. *Modern Critical Interpretations of Charles Dickens's "David Copperfield."* New York: Chelsea House, 1987.

———, ed. *Modern Critical Interpretations of Charles Dickens's "David Copperfield."* New York: Chelsea House, 1992.

———, ed. *Modern Critical Interpretations of Charles Dickens's "Hard Times."* New York: Chelsea House, 1987.

———, ed. *Modern Critical Interpretations of Charles Dickens's "A Tale of Two Cities."* New York: Chelsea House, 1987.

———, ed. *Modern Critical Interpretations of Charlotte Brontë's "Jane Eyre."* New York: Chelsea House, 1987.

———, ed. *Modern Critical Interpretations of Clarissa Dalloway*. New York: Chelsea House, 1990.

———, ed. *Modern Critical Interpretations of D. H. Lawrence's "Sons and Lovers."* New York: Chelsea House, 1988.

———, ed. *Modern Critical Interpretations of Elizabeth Bowen*. New York: Chelsea House, 1987.

———, ed. *Modern Critical Interpretations of E. M. Forster's "A Passage to India."* New York: Chelsea House, 1987.

———, ed. *Modern Critical Interpretations of Emily Brontë's "Wuthering Heights."* New York: Chelsea House, 1987.

———, ed. *Modern Critical Interpretations of George Eliot's "Middlemarch."* New York: Chelsea House, 1987.

———, ed. *Modern Critical Interpretations of George Eliot's "Mill on the Floss."* New York: Chelsea House, 1988.

———, ed. *Modern Critical Interpretations of George Orwell*. New York: Chelsea House, 1988.

———, ed. *Modern Critical Interpretations of Heathcliff*. New York: Chelsea House, 1993.

———, ed. *Modern Critical Interpretations of Iris Murdoch*. New York: Chelsea House, 1986.

———, ed. *Modern Critical Interpretations of James Joyce's "Dubliners."* New York: Chelsea House, 1988.

———, ed. *Modern Critical Interpretations of James Joyce's "A Portrait of the Artist as a Young Man."* New York: Chelsea House, 1988.

———, ed. *Modern Critical Interpretations of John le Carré*. New York: Chelsea House, 1987.

———, ed. *Modern Critical Interpretations of Joseph Conrad*. New York: Chelsea House, 1986.

———, ed. *Modern Critical Interpretations of Joseph Conrad's "Heart of Darkness."* New York: Chelsea House, 1987.

———, ed. *Modern Critical Interpretations of Joseph Conrad's "Nostromo."* New York: Chelsea House, 1987.

———, ed. *Modern Critical Interpretations of Rudyard Kipling's "Kim."* New York: Chelsea House, 1987.

———, ed. *Modern Critical Interpretations of Thomas Hardy's "Tess of the d'Urbervilles."* New York: Chelsea House, 1987.

———, ed. *Modern Critical Interpretations of Virginia Woolf*. New York: Chelsea House, 1986.

———, ed. *Modern Critical Interpretations of Virginia Woolf's "To the Lighthouse."* New York: Chelsea House, 1988.

———, ed. *Modern Critical Interpretations of William Makepeace Thackery*. New York: Chelsea House, 1987.

———, ed. *Modern Critical Interpretations of William Makepeace Thackery's "Vanity Fair."* New York: Chelsea House, 1987.

BLOOMFIELD, MORTON W., ed. *The Interpretation of Narrative: Theory and Practice*. Cambridge, MA: Harvard University Press, 1970.

BLOTNER, JOSEPH L. *The Political Novel*. Garden City, NY: Doubleday, 1955.

BLY, PETER, ed. *Galdos y la Historia*. Ottawa: Dovehouse, 1988.

BOHEEMEN, CHRISTINE VAN, ed. *Joyce, Modernity, and Its Mediation*. Amsterdam: Rodopi, 1989.

BOLD, ALLAN, ed. *The Quest for le Carré*. New York: St. Martin's, 1988.

BOLTON, FRANCOISE. *Le Genre du roman—les genres de romans*. Paris: Publication Université de France, 1980.

BOMB 28 (Summer 1989).

BONNELL, HENRY HOUSTON. *Charlotte Brontë, George Eliot, Jane Austin: Studies in Their Works*. London: Longmans, Green, 1902.

Bonniers Litterara Magasin 56 (February 1987)–58 (November 1989).

The Booklover's Magazine 1 (May 1903).

Books Abroad 35 (1961).

Books at Iowa 34 (April 1981).

Booster 2 (1937).

BORDEAUX, ANDRÉ, pref. *Linguistique, Civilisation, Littérature*. Paris: Didier, 1980.

BOSINELLI, ROSA, et al., eds. *The Languages of Joyce: Selected Papers from the 11th International James Joyce Symposium*. Philadelphia: Benjamins, 1992.

———, **PAOLA PUGLIATTI**, and **ROMANA ZACCHI**, eds. *Myriadminded Man: Jottings on Joyce*. Bologna: Cooperativa Librari Universiti Educational Bologna, 1986.

The [Boston] *Evening Transcript* (11 September 1937).

Boston University Studies in English 1 (Autumn 1955).

LE BOUILLE, LUCIEN, ed. *Fins de romans: Aspects de la conclusion dans la littérature anglaise*. Caen: Publication Université de Caen, 1993.

boundaryII: A Journal of Postmodern Literature and Culture 7 (Spring 1979)–18 (Summer 1991).

BOWEN, ELIZABETH. *Seven Winters Memories of a Dublin Childhood & Afterthoughts: Pieces on Writing*. New York: Knopf, 1951.

BOWEN, ZACK, and **JAMES F. CARENS**, eds. *A Companion to Joyce Studies*. Westport, CT: Greenwood, 1984.

BOWERS, BEGE K., and **BARBARA BROTHERS**, eds. *Reading and Writing Women's Lives: A Study of the Novel of Manners*. Ann Arbor, MI: University Microfilms International Research Press, 1990.

BOWKER, GORDON, ed. *Malcolm Lowry: "Under the Volcano": A Casebook*. London: Macmillan, 1987.

BOYLE, NICOLAS, MARTIN SWALES, and **RICHARD BRINKMANN**, eds. *Realism in European Literature*. Cambridge: Cambridge University Press, 1986.

BRADBURY, MALCOLM, ed. *E. M. Forster: "A Passage to India": A Casebook*. London: Macmillan, 1970.

———, ed. *Forster: A Collection of Critical Essays*. Englewood Cliffs, NJ: Prentice Hall, 1966.

BRADY, MARK. *Four Fits of Anger: Essays on the Angry Young Men*. Udine: Campanotto, 1986.

BRAMSBACK, BIRGIT, and **MARTIN CROGHAN**, eds. *The Anglo-Irish and Irish Literature: Aspects of Language and Culture*. Uppsala: Uppsala University Press, 1988.

BRIDGES, MARGARET, ed. *On Strangeness*. Tubingen: Gunter Narr, 1990.

Brigham Young University Studies 24 (Winter 1984).

The British Journal of Aesthetics 23 (Winter 1983)–33 (January 1993).

Britain Today 148 (August 1948).

BRITTAIN, VERA. *The Women at Oxford: A Fragment of History*. New York: Macmillan, 1960.

Brontë Society Transactions 16 (Winter 1971–72)–19 (1989).

Broom 5 (August 1923).

BROPHY, BRIGID, **MICHAEL LEVEY**, and **CHARLES OSBOURNE**. *Fifty Works of English Literature We Could Do Without*. London: Rapp & Carroll, 1967.

BROUGHTON, B., ed. *Twenty Seven to One*. Ogdensbury, NY: Ryan, 1970.

BROWER, REUBEN ARTHUR. *The Fields of Light: An Experiment in Critical Reading*. New York: Oxford University Press, 1951.

BROWN, ARTHER W. *Sexual Analysis of Dickens' Props*. New York: Emerson, 1971.

BROWN, E[DWARD] K[ILLORAN]. *Rhythm in the Novel*. Toronto: University of Toronto Press, 1950.

BROWNE, NELSON. *Sheridan le Fanu*. London: Arthur Barker, Ltd., 1951.

BROWNE, PAT, ed. *Heroines of Popular Culture*. Bowling Green, OH: Popular, 1987.

The Browning Institute Studies: An Annual of Victorian Literary and Cultural History 13 (1985).

Browning Newsletter 6 (1987).

Bruxelles Revue des Langues Vivantes 24 (1958).

BUCKLEY, JEROME H., ed. *The Worlds of Victorian Fiction: Harvard English Studies 6*. Cambridge, MA: Harvard University Press, 1975.

———. *Seasons of Youth: The 'Bildungsroman' from Dickens to Golding*. Cambridge, MA: Harvard University Press, 1974.

The Bucknell Review: A Scholarly Journal of Letters, Arts and Sciences 24, no. 1 (1978)–34, no. 2 (1990).

BUDD, ELAINE. *13 Mistresses of Murder*. New York: Frederick Ungar, 1986.

Bulletin de l'ACLA/Bulletin of the ACLA 11 (Spring 1989).

Bulletin de la Société d'Études Anglo-Américaines des XVII et XVII Siecles 21 (November 1985).

Bulletin de la Société de Stylistique Anglaise 7 (1985).

Bulletin: Municiple University of Wichita 16 (April 1941).

Bulletin of Research in the Humanities 87, no. 1 (1986–87).

Bulletin of the [Calcutta] Department of English 6 (1970–71).

Bulletin of the John Rylands University Library 52 (Spring 1970).

Bulletin of the New York C. S. Lewis Society 18 (May 1987)–21 (November 1989).

Bulletin of the New York Public Library 76 (1972).

Bulletin of the West Virginia Association of College English Teachers 2, no. 2 (1975).

BURKE, KENNETH. *Language as Symbolic Action*. Los Angeles: University of California Press, 1968.

BURRELL, ANGUS, and **DOROTHY BREWSTER**, eds. *Modern Fiction*. New York: Columbia University Press, 1934.

BUSSE, WILHELM G., ed. *Anglistentag 1991*. Tubingen: Niemeyer, 1992.

BUTLER, LANCE ST. JOHN, and **ROBERT DAVIS**, eds. *Rethinking Beckett: A Collection of Critical Essays*. London: Macmillan, 1990.

BUTT, JOHN, and **KATHLEEN TILLOTSON**. *Dickens at Work*. London: Methuen, 1957.

Les Cahiers de la Nouvelle: Journal of the Short Story in English 1 (1983)–8 (Spring 1987).

Les Cahiers du Centre d'Études Irlandaises 7 (1982)–9 (1984).

Les Cahiers du Centre d'Études et de Recherches sur les Littéraires de l'Imaginaire 9 (1984).

Les Cahiers Victoriens et Edouardiens: Revue du Centre d'Études et de Recherches Victoriennes et Edouardiennes de l'Université Paul Valéry (August 1982)–35 (April 1992).

The Calcutta Review n.s. 2 (January–March 1971).

Calcutta University Bulletin n.s. 5, no. 2 (1969–70)–6, no. 2 (1970–71).

Caliban 8 (1971)–27 (1990).

CALINESCU, MATEI, and **DOUWE FOKKEMA**, eds. *Exploring Postmodernism*. Amsterdam: Benjamins, 1987.

CALLARY, EDWARD, ed. *Festschrift in Honor of Virgil J. Vogel*. DeKalb: Illinois Name Society, 1985.

The Cambridge Journal 5 (April 1952).

The Cambridge Quarterly 4 (Winter 1969)–20, no. 1 (1991).

The Cambridge Review (29 January 1982).

The Canadian Holmes 8 (Spring 1985).

The Canadian Journal of History/Annales Canadiennes d'Histoire 18 (April 1983).

The Canadian Journal of Irish Studies 10 (June 1984)–17 (July 1991).

Canadian Literature 126 (Autumn 1990)–137 (Summer 1993).

The Canadian Review of Comparative Literature/Revue Canadienne de Littérature Comparée 1 (Winter 1974).

Canoma 16 (December 1990).

CARABINE, KEITH, **OWEN KNOWLES**, and **WIESLAW KRAJKA**, eds. *Conrad's Literary Career*. Lublin: Maria Curie-Skldowska University Press, 1992.

CARENS, JAMES F., ed. *Critical Essays on Evelyn Waugh*. Boston: G. K. Hall, 1987.

———. *The Satiric Art of Evelyn Waugh*. Seattle: University of Washington Press, 1966.

CAREY, JOHN, ed. *William Golding: The Man and His Books*. London: Farrar, Straus, 1986; New York: Faber, 1987.

CAREY, PHYLLIS, and **ED JEWINSKI**, eds. *RE: Joyce 'n Beckett*. New York: Fordham University Press, 1992.

CARGAS, HARRY J., ed. *Graham Greene*. St. Louis, MO: Herder, 1969.

CARLSON, PATRICIA ANN, ed. *Literature and Lore of the Sea*. Amsterdam: Rodopi, 1986.

The Carlyle Newsletter 7 (Spring 1986).

The Carnegie Magazine 39 (1965).

The Carolina Quarterly 9 (Summer 1957).

CARRABINO, VICTOR, ed. *The Power of Myth in Literature and Film*. Tallahassee: University Press of Florida, 1980.

CARRÉ, JACQUES. *Hommage a Georges Fourrier*. Paris: Université de Besancon, 1973.

CARTER, RONALD, ed. *Language and Literature: An Introductory Reader in Stylistics*. London: Allen & Unwin, 1982.

Casopis pro Moderníi Filologii 37 (1955).

LA CASSAGNERE, CHRISTIAN, pref. *Romantisme Anglais et Eros*. Clermont-Ferrand: Université de Clermont-Ferrand II, 1982.

———, ed. *Visages de l'angoisse*. Clermont-Ferrand: Publications de la faculte des lettres de Clermont, 1989.

CASTANGT, JEAN-CLAUDE, and **RENE GALLET**, eds. *Études sur "The French Lieutenant's Woman" de John Fowles*. Caen: Centre National de Documentation Pédagogique, 1977.

The Catholic World 194 (October 1961).

Cauda Pavonis: Studies in Hermeticism 8 (Fall 1989).

CAWELTI, JOHN G. *Adventure, Mystery and Romance: Formula Stories as Art and Popular Culture*. Chicago: University of Chicago Press, 1976.

CAWS, MARY ANN, ed. *Perspectives on Perception: Philosophy, Art, and Literature*. New York: Peter Lang, 1989.

———, ed. *Some Readers Reading*. New York: Modern Language Association, 1986.

CAZAMIAN, LOUIS. *Le Roman Social en Angleterre (1830–1950): Dickens—Disraeli—Mrs. Gaskell—Kingsley*. Paris: Société Nouvelle de Librairie et d'Edition, 1904.

The CEA Critic: An Official Journal of the College English Association 48 (Fall 1985)–54 (Spring 1992).

CECIL, LORD DAVID. *Early Victorian Novelists*. Indianapolis: Bobbs-Merrill, 1935. Reprinted by Chicago: University of Chicago Press, 1958.

The Centennial Review 15 (1971)–27 (Winter 1983).

The Central Institute of English and Foreign Languages Bulletin 18, no. 1–2 (1982).

Century (4 July 1970).

CHAPPLE, J. A. V. *Documentary and Imaginative Literature, 1880–1920*. New York: Barnes & Noble, 1970.

CHARNEY, MAURICE, and **JOSEPH REPPEN**, eds. *Psychoanalytic Approaches to Literature and Film*. Rutherford, NJ: Fairleigh Dickinson University Press, 1987.

CHARQUES, RICHARD D. *Contemporary Literature and Social Revolution*. London: Secker, 1933.

Chatelaine 60 (April 1987).

CHATTERJEE, VISVANATH, ed. *The Romantic Tradition*. Calcutta: Jadavpur University, 1984.

CHENG, VINCENT J., and **TIMOTHY MARTIN**, eds. *Joyce in Context*. Cambridge: Cambridge University Press, 1992.

CHESTERTON, G. K. *Appreciations and Criticisms of the Work of Charles Dickens*. London: Dent, 1911.

———. *Autobiography*. London: Hutchinson, 1969; New York: Sheed & Ward, 1936.

———. *The Spice of Life and Other Essays*. Beaconsfield: Bucks, Darween Finlayson, 1967.

The Chesterton Review: The Journal of the Chesterton Society 4 (1977–78)–19 (Spring 1993).

Chicago Review 14 (Spring 1961).

The Children's Libraries Newsletter 4 (May 1968).

The Children's Literature Association Quarterly 9 (Winter 1984–85)–17 (Fall 1992).

Children's Literature: Annual of the Modern Language Association Division on Children's Literature 9 (1981)–22 (1994).

Children's Literature in Education 23 (1976).

CHILTON, PAUL, and **CRISPIN AUBREY**, eds. *Nineteen Eighty-Four in 1984: Autonomy, Control and Communication*. London: Comedia, 1983.

The Christian Century 110 (24 February 1993).

Christianity and Literature 21 (Winter 1972)–33 (Spring 1984).

Christianity Today 20 (19 December 1975)–22 (2 June 1978).

The Christian Science Monitor (23 October 1952).

The Chung-wai Literary Monthly: Publicacion Cuatrimestral del Centro di Estudios Teologicos de San Esteban 13 (January 1985).

The Church Quarterly Review 156 (January–March 1955).

The Cimarron Review 1 (September 1967).

Citbara: Essays in the Judaeo-Christian Tradition 13 (May 1974)–15 (November 1975).

CLAEYS, GREGORY and **LISELOTTE GLAGE**, eds. *Radikalismus in Literatur und Gesellschaft de 19. Jahrhunderts*. Frankfurt: Peter Lang, 1987.

CLARESON, THOMAS D., ed. *Many Futures, Many Worlds*. Kent, OH: Kent State University Press, 1978.

———. *A Spectrum of Worlds*. Garden City, NY: Doubleday, 1972.

CLARIDGE, LAURA, and **ELIZABETH LANGLAND**, eds. *Out of Bounds: Male Writers and Gender(ed) Criticism*. Amherst: University of Massachusetts Press, 1990.

Classical and Modern Literature: A Quarterly 1 (Winter 1981)–10 (Summer 1990).

CLAYTON, JAY. *Romantic Vision and the Novel*. Cambridge: Cambridge University Press, 1987.

The Clearing House 47 (1973).

The Clergy Review 59 (October 1974)–61 (September 1976).

Clinical Neuropharmacology 7 (October 1983).

CLIO: A Jounal of Literature, History, and the Philosophy of History 2 (June 1973)–19 (Winter 1990).

Clues: A Journal of Detection 1 (Fall–Winter 1980)–13 (Fall–Winter 1992).

COCKSHUT, A. O. J. *The Imagination of Charles Dickens*. London: Collins, 1961.

The Colby Library Quarterly 18 (March 1982)–28 (March 1992).

COLBY, ROBERT A. *Fiction With a Purpose: Major and Minor Nineteenth-Century Novels*. Bloomington: Indiana University Press, 1967.

College English 21 (November 1959)–54 (April 1992).

The College Language Association Journal 6 (March 1963)–37 (March 1994).

College Literature 1 (1974)–18 (October 1991).

College of Arts and Essays (Hanuk University of Foreign Studies, Seoul) 20 (1987).

COLLINGS, DAVID, ed. *Mary Shelley: "Frankenstein."* New York: St. Martin's, 1992.

COLLINGS, MICHAEL R., ed. *Reflections on the Fantastic*. Westport, CT: Greenwood, 1986.

COLLINS, PHILIP. *A Critical Commentary on Dickens's "Bleak House."* London: Macmillan, 1971.

Colóquio/Letras 77 (January 1984).

COLUM, PADRACI, ed. *Dubliners*. New York: Modern Library, 1926.

COMELLINI, CARLA, and **VITA FORTUNATI**, eds. *D. H. Lawrence cent'anni dopo: Nuove prospettive della critica Lawrenciana*. Bologna: Patron, 1991.

Comhar 43, no. 4 (1984).

Commentary 64 (December 1977).

Commonweal 53 (9 February 1953)–120 (26 March 1993).

Commonwealth Essays and Studies 8 (Autumn 1985)–12 (August 1989).

Commonwealth Novel in English 5 (Spring 1992).

The Commonwealth Review 1, no. 2 (1990)–2, no. 1–2 (1990–91).

Communique (Petersburg) 5, no. 1 (1980).

Comparative Criticism: A Yearbook 2 (1980).

Comparative Literature 42 (Winter 1990).

Comparative Literature Studies 27, no. 3 (1990).

Conference of College Teachers of English Studies 48 (September 1983)–54 (September 1989).

CONGER, SYNDY MCMILLEN, ed. *Sensibility in Transformation: Creative Resistance to Sentiment from the Augustans to the Romantics*. Rutherford, NJ: Fairleigh Dickinson University Press, 1990.

The Connecticut Review 4 (1970)–14 (Fall 1992).

The Conradian 8 (Winter 1983)–15 (June 1990).

Conradiana: A Journal of Joseph Conrad Studies 4 (1972)–21 (Summer 1989).

CONSOLO, DOMINICK P., ed. *D. H. Lawrence: "The Rocking-Horse Winner."* Columbus, OH: Bobbs Merril, 1969.

Dos Continentes 9–10 (1971–72).

Contemporary Literature 10 (Winter 1969)–37 (Spring 1996).

Contemporary Review 220 (April 1972)–260 (February 1992).

COONEY, SEAMUS, et al., eds. *Blast 3*. Santa Barbara, CA: Black Sparrow, 1984.

COOPER, ANDREW, ed. *D. H. Lawrence 1885–1930: A Celebration*. Nottingham: D. H. Lawrence Society, 1985.

COPE, JACKSON I. *Joyce's Cities: Archeologies of the Soul*. Baltimore: Johns Hopkins University Press, 1981.

CRONEN, JOHN. *The Anglo-Irish Novel Vol 1: The Nineteenth Century*. Belfast: Appletree Press, 1980.

Costerus 3 (1972).

COUSTILLAS, PIERRE, JEAN-PIERRE PETIT, and **JEAN RAIMOND**, eds. *Le roman anglais aux XIXe siècle*. Paris: Presses Universités de France, 1978.

COWART, DAVID. *History and the Contemporary Novel*. Carbondale: Southern Illinois University Press, 1989.

COYLE, WILLIAM, ed. *Aspects of Fantasy: Selected Essays from the Second International Conference on the Fantastic in Literature and Film*. Westport, CT: Greenwood, 1986.

CRAIG, DAVID. *The Real Foundation: Literature and Social Change*. London: Chatto & Windus; New York: Oxford University Press, 1974.

CRANE, JOHN K. *T. H. White*. New York: Twayne, 1974.

CRAWFORD, JOHN W. *Discourse: Essay* [sic] *on English and American Literature*. Amsterdam: Rodopi, 1978.

Cresset 43 (March 1980).

CREWS, FREDERICK. *E. M. Forster and the Perils of Humanism*. Princeton: Princeton University Press, 1962.

———, ed. *Psychoanalysis and Literary Process*. Cambridge, MA: Winthrop, 1970.

Criminal Justice and Behavior 15 (June 1988).

The Critic 1 (Autumn 1947)–30 (January–February 1972).

Critical Inquiry 1 (Winter 1959)–29 (Autumn 1987).

Critical Matrix: Princeton Journal of Women, Gender, and Culture (formerly *Critical Matrix: Princeton Working Papers in Women's Studies*) 1 (Spring 1988).

Critical Quarterly 1 (Winter 1959)–36 (Summer 1994).

The Critical Review 6 (1973)–27 (1985).

Critical Survey 2, no. 1 (1990).

Criterion 10 (1930)–18 (1939).

Criticism: A Quarterly Review for Literature and the Arts 1 (1959)–36 (Summer 1994).

Critique: Revue Générale des Publications Françaises et Etrangéres 3 (Spring–Fall 1959)–35 (Summer 1994).

Critique: Studies in Contemporary Fiction 28 (Summer 1987)–32 (Fall 1990).

Critique: Studies in Modern Fiction 4 (Spring/Summer 1961)–35 (Summer 1994).

Crosscurrents 1 (Winter 1951).

Crotocos 13 (Fall 1971).

CRUMP, R. W., ed. *Order in Variety: Essays and Poems in Honor of Donald E. Stanford*. Newark: University of Delaware Press, 1991.

CRUSE, AMY. *Famous English Books and Their Stories*. New York: Thomas Y. Crowell, 1926.

CRUX: A Journal on the Teaching of English 5 (August 1975)–22 (August 1988).

Cuadernos de Poética 1 (January–April 1984).

Cuadernos Hispanoamericanos: Revista Mensual de Cultura Hispanica 386 (August 1982)–464 (February 1989).

CURTIS, ANTHONY, and **JOHN WHITEHEAD**, eds. *W. Somerset Maugham: The Critical Heritage*. London: Routledge & Kegan Paul, 1987.

The Cuyahoga Review 2 (Spring–Summer 1984).

Cycnos 1 (1984)–7 (1991).

DABNEY, ROSS H. *Love and Property in the Novels of Dickens*. London: Chatto & Windus; Berkeley: University of California Press, 1967.

DABYDEEN, DAVID, ed. *The Black Presence in English Literature*. Manchester: Manchester University Press, 1985.

DAICHES, DAVID. *George Eliot: Middlemarch*. London: Arnold, 1962.

———. *The Novel and the Modern World*. Chicago: University of Chicago Press, 1960.

The Daily Telegraph (17 December 1977).

Daedalus: Journal of the American Academy of Arts and Sciences 101 (Winter 1972).

DALDRY, GRAHAM. *Charles Dickens and the Form of the Novel: Fiction and Narrative in Dickens's Work*. Totawa, NJ: Barnes & Noble, 1987.

DALE, ALIZINA STONE, ed. *Dorothy L. Sayers: The Centenary Celebration*. New York: Walker, 1993.

DALESKI, H[ILLEL] M[ATTHEW]. *Dickens and the Art of Analogy*. New York: Schocken, 1970.

———. *The Divided Heroine: A Recurrent Pattern in Six English Novels*. New York: Holmes & Meier, 1984.

Dalhousie Review 40 (Fall 1960)–73 (Spring 1993).

DAVIS, EDWARD. *Readings in Modern Fiction*. Cape Town, South Africa: Simondium, 1964.

DAVIS, EARLE. *The Flint and the Flame: The Artistry of Charles Dickens*. Columbia: University of Missouri Press, 1963.

DAVIS, ROBERT MURRAY. *Evelyn Waugh, Writer*. Norman, OK: Pilgrim Books, 1981.

DAY, GARY, and **CLIVE BLOOM**, eds. *Perspectives on Pornography: Sexuality in Film and Literature*. New York: St. Martin's, 1988.

DEELY, JOHN, ed. *Semiotics 1984*. Lanham, MD: University Press of America, 1985.

DEMERS, PATRICIA, ed. *The Creating Word: Papers from an International Conference on the Learning and Teaching of English in the 1980s*. Edmonton: University of Alberta Press, 1986.

Descant 23, no. 3 (1979).

Deus Loci: The Lawrence Durrell Journal 5 (September 1981)–11 (Spring 1992).

Deutsche Shakespeare-Gesellschaft West: Jahrbuch (1988).

Deutsche Vierteljahrsschrift für Literaturwissenschaft und Geistesgeschichte 42 (1968)–64 (June 1990).

D. H. Lawrence: The Journal of the D. H. Lawrence Society 4, no. 1 (1986).

The D. H. Lawrence Review 1 (Summer 1968)–23 (Spring 1991).

Diacritics: A Review of Contemporary Criticism 16 (Spring 1986)–19 (Summer 1989).

Dial Magazine 67 (29 November 1919)–72 (June 1922).

Dialoog 14, no. 1–2 (1973–74).

DICK, ERNST SIEGFRIED, and **KURT R. JANKOWSKY**, eds. *Festschrift für Karl Schneider*. Amsterdam: Benjamins, 1982.

The Dickensian 1 (1905)–88 (Summer 1992).

Dickens Quarterly 1 (March 1984)–9 (June 1992).

Dickens Studies Annual: Essays on Victorian Fiction 1 (1970)–21 (1992).

Dickens Studies 1, no. 2 (1965)–5 (May 1969).

The Dickens Studies Newsletter 1 (March 1970)–14 (September 1983).

Dietsche Warande en Belfort: Tijdschrift voor Letterkunde en Geestesleven 6 (1955)–129 (December 1984).

Dieu Vivant 16 (1950).

Diliman Review 14 (July 1966).

Dionysos: The Literature and Addiction TriQuarterly (formerly *Dionysos: The Literature and Intoxication TriQuarterly*) 3 (Fall 1992).

Discourse: Journal for Theoretical Studies in Media and Culture 12 (1969)–14 (Winter 1991–92).

DLSU Dialogue 23, no. 2 (1988).

DLSU Graduate Journal 13, no. 1 (1988)–no. 2 (1988).

DOBIE, ANN B., ed. *Explorations: The Nineteenth Century*. Lafayette, LA: Levy Humanities Series, 1988.

DONALDSON, NORMAN, ed. *Lady Audley's Secret*. New York: Dover, 1974.

DONOVAN, FRANK R. *Dickens and Youth.* New York: Dodd, Mead, 1968.

DOWNING, DAVID B., and **SUSAN BAZARGAN**, eds. *Image and Ideology in Modern/Postmodern Discourse.* Albany: State University of New York Press, 1991.

DRABBLE, MARGARET. *The Genius of Thomas Hardy.* London: Weidenfeld, 1976.

DREW, ELIZABETH. *The Novel: A Modern Guide to Fifteen English Masterpieces.* New York: Dell, 1963.

DRUCE, ROBERT, ed. *Centre of Excellence: Essay Presented to Seymour Betsky.* Amsterdam: Rodopi, 1987.

The Dublin Review 449 (Spring 1949)–226 (First Quarter, 1952).

DUNLEAVY, JANET E., **MELVIN J. FRIEDMAN**, and **MICHAEL PATRICK GILLESPIE**, eds. *Joycean Occasions: Essays from the Milwaukee James Joyce Conference.* Newark: University of Delaware Press, 1991.

DUNNE, TOM, ed. *The Writer as Witness: Literature as Historical Evidence.* Cork: Cork University Press, 1987.

DUPERRAY, MAX, ed. *Historicite et metafiction dans le roman contemporain des Iles Britanniques.* Aix-en-Provence: Université de Provence, 1994.

———, ed. *Du Fantastique en littérature: Figures et figurations: Elements pour une poetique du fantastique sur quelques exemples anglo-saxons.* Aix-en-Provence: Université de Provence, 1990.

Durham University Journal 34 (1973)–83 (July 1991).

DURKIN, MARY BRIAN, O. P. *Dorothy L. Sayers.* Boston: Twayne, 1980.

Dutch Dickensian 6 (December 1976)–7 (December 1978).

The Dutch Quarterly Review of Anglo American Letters 3 (1973)–19, no. 4 (1989).

DYNES, WAYNE R., and **STEPHEN DONALDSON**, eds. *Homosexual Themes in Literary Studies.* New York: Garland, 1992.

DYSON, A. E. *The Inimitable Dickens: A Reading of the Novels.* London: Macmillan, 1970.

———, ed. *Dickens: Modern Judgements.* London: Macmillan, 1968; Nashville: Aurora, 1970.

EAGLETON, TERRY. *Myths of Power.* New York: Barnes & Noble, 1975.

ECO, UMBERTO, and **THOMAS SEBEOK**, eds. *The Sign of Three: Dupin, Holmes, Peirce*. Bloomington: Indiana University Press, 1983.

Edda: Nordisk Tidsskrift for Littératurforskning/Scandinavian Journal of Literary Research 75 (1975)–81 (1981).

The Edinburgh Times 71 (January 1960).

Egoist 1 (15 July 1914).

Eibungaku Kenkyu 63 (September 1986).

Eighteen-Century Fiction 1 (October 1988(–4 (October 1991).

Eighteenth-Century Life 10 (January 1986).

The Eighteenth Century: Theory and Interpretation 29 (Fall 1988).

Eigo Seinen 126 (1981)–134 (1988).

Éire-Ireland: A Journal of Irish Studies 5 (Spring 1970)–21 (Fall 1986).

ELEKTOROWICZ, LESZEK. *Motywy zachodnie* Cracow: Wydawnictow, 1973.

ELLISON, EUGENIA ADAMS. *The Innocent Child in Dickens and Other Writers*. Edinburg, TX: Eakin, 1982.

ELLRODT, ROBERT, and **BERNARD BRUIGERE**, eds. *Age d'or et apocalypse*. Paris: Publications de la Sorbonne, 1986.

ELMALIH, N. *Récit et Roman: Formes du Roman Anglais du XVIe au Xxe Siècle*. Paris: Didier, 1972.

Emporia State Research Studies 37 (Summer 1988).

Enclitic 7 (Spring 1983).

Encounter 2 (June 1954)–71 (November 1988).

Encyclia: The Journal of the Utah Academy of Sciences, Arts, and Letters 63 (1986).

Enemy News: Journal of the Wynham Lewis Society 22 (Spring 1986)–30 (Winter 1991).

ENGELBERG, KARSTEN, ed. *The Romantic Heritage: A Collection of Critical Essays*. Copenhagen: University of Copenhagen, 1983.

ENGELL, JAMES, ed. *Johnson and His Age*. Cambridge, MA: Harvard University Press, 1984.

ENGLER, BALZ, ed. *Writing and Culture*. Zurich: Swiss Papers in English Language and Literature, 1992.

ELH (formerly *English Literary History*) 23 (Fall 1956)–61 (Summer 1994).

English Journal 54 (1965)–74 (March 1985).

English: The Journal of the English Association 20 (Spring 1991)–42 (Summer 1993).

English Language Notes 4 (March 1966)–31 (June 1994).

English Literature in Transition (1880–1920) 27, no. 2 (1984)–35, no. 2 (1992).

English Miscellany 21 (1970).

English Record 14 (April 1964).

English Studies for College 1 (September 1976).

English Studies: A Journal of English Language and Literature 47 (December 1966)–75 (January 1994).

English Studies in Africa: A Journal of the Humanities 5 (September 1962)–29 (January 1986).

English Studies in Canada 3 (Summer 1977)–16 (March 1990).

ENRIGHT, DENNIS JOSEPH. *Man Is an Onion*. London: Chatto & Windus, 1972.

ENZENBERGER, CHRISTIAN. *Leteratur und Interesse: Eine Politische Åsthetic mit zwei Beispielen aus der Englischen Literatur*. Munich and Vienna: Hanser, 1977.

L'Epoque Conradienne 18 (1992).

Epos: Revista de Filologia 4 (1988)–6 (1990).

ERLICH, RICHARD D., and **THOMAS P. DUNN**, eds. *Clockwork Worlds: Mechanized Environments in SF*. Westport, CT: Greenwood, 1983.

ERMARTH, ELIZABETH DEEDS. *George Eliot*. Boston: Twayne, 1985.

Espirit 158 (January 1990).

Essays by Divers Hands 25 (1980).

Essays in Arts and Sciences 9 (May 1980)–19 (May 1990).

Essays and Studies 23 (1970)–26 (1973).

Essays in Criticism: A Quarterly Journal of Literary Criticism 2 (April 1952)–39 (April 1989).

Essays in Literature 2 (Spring 1975)–21 (Spring 1994).

Essays on Canadian Writing 48 (Winter 1992).

Estudos Anglo-Americanos 9–11 (1985–87)–12–13 1988–89).

ETC: A Review of General Semantics 18, no. 1 (1961).

Études 260 (March 1949)–362 (February 1985).

Études Anglaises et Américaines 2 (1964).

Études Anglaises: Grande Bretagne, Etats-Unis 23 (April–June 1970)–43 (January–March 1990).

Études Britanniques Contemporaines: Revue de la Société s'Etudes Anglaises Contemporaines 1 (December 1992).

Études de Lettres 4 (1987).

Études Irlandaises: Revue Française d'Histoire, Civilisation et Littérature de l'Irelande 9 (December 1984)–15 (June 1990).

Études Lawrenciennes 1 (May 1986)–6 (May 1991).

Études Philosophiques 1 (January–March 1990).

EUBANK, INGA STINA, ed. *Their Proper Sphere: A Study of the Brontë Sisters as Early Victorian Female Novelists*. Cambridge, MA: Harvard University Press, 1966.

Europe: Revue Littéraire Mensuelle 488 (December 1969)–70 (June–July 1992).

EVANS, BERTRAND, JOSEPHINE MILES, and **WILLIAM STEINHOFF**, eds. *The Image of the Work: Essays in Criticism*. Berkeley: University of California Press, 1955.

EVANS, MAURICE. *G. K. Chesterton*. Cambridge: Cambridge University Press, 1939.

EVANS, ROBERT O., ed. *Graham Greene: Some Critical Considerations*. Lexington: University of Kentucky Press, 1963.

Evelyn Waugh Newsletter and Studies. (superseded by *The Evelyn Waugh Newsletter*) 17 (Autumn 1983)–24 (Winter 1990).

Explicator 19 (January 1961)–52 (Winter 1994).

Extrapolation: A Journal of Science Fiction and Fantasy 11 (December 1969)–35 (Spring 1994).

Fabula: Zeitschrift für Erzählforschung/Journal of Folktale Studies/Revue d'Études sur le Conte Populaire 6 (1985).

Faith and Reason 12, no. 3–4 (1986).

The Family Digest 30 (December 1974).

Fantasiae 6 (March 1978).

The Feminist Review 42 (Autumn 1992).

Feminist Studies 10 (Spring 1984)–18 (Spring 1992).

FIDO, MARTIN. *Charles Dickens: Profiles in Literature*. London: Routledge & Kegan Paul, 1968.

FIELDING, K. J. *Charles Dickens: A Critical Introduction*. London: Longmans, Green, 1965.

FIEROBE, CLAUDE. *Visages de l'harmonie dans la littérature anglo-américaine*. Reims: Centre de Recherche sur l'Imaginaire dans les Littératures de Langue Anglaise, Université de Reims, 1982.

Le Figaro 5 (December 1931).

Filologicheskie Nauki 107 (1978)–5, no. 161 (1987).

FINKLESTEIN, BONNIE BLUMENTHAL. *Forster's Women: Eternal Differences*. New York: Columbia University Press, 1973.

FISCHER-SEIDEL, THERESE, ed. *Frauen und Frauendarstellung in der englischen und amerikanischen Literatur*. Tubingen: Gunter Narr, 1991.

FLEENOR, JULIAN E., ed. *The Female Gothic*. Montreal: Eden, 1983.

FLEISHMAN, AVROM. *Fiction and the Ways of Knowing: Essays on British Novels*. Austin: University of Texas Press, 1978.

Florilegium: Carleton University Annual Papers on Late Antiquity and the Middle Ages 8 (1986).

Folklore 94, no. 2 (1983).

Folklore Forum 20, no. 1–2 (1987).

Folio: Essays on Foreign Languages and Literatures 11 (August 1978).

FORD, BORIS, ed. *The Modern Age,* 3rd ed. Baltimore: Penguin, 1973.

FORD, GEORGE H., and **LAURIAT LANE**, eds. *The Dickens Critics*. Ithaca, NY: Cornell University Press, 1961.

———, and **SYLVÉRE MONOD**, eds. *Bleak House*. New York: Norton, 1977.

Foreign Literary Studies (China) 30 (December 1985)–39 (March 1988).

FORSTER, JOHN. *The Life of Charles Dickens*. London: Chapman and Hall, 1872.

Fortnightly 160 (August 1946).

Forum 4 (Summer 1965).

Forum for Modern Language Studies 20 (January 1984)–

Foundation: The Review of Science Fiction 6 (May 1974)–49 (Summer 1990).

FRIEDMAN, ALAN WARREN, ed. *Critical Essays on Lawrence Durrell.* Boston: G. K. Hall, 1987.

———, ed. *Forms of Modern British Fiction.* Austin: University of Texas Press, 1975.

FRIEDMAN, ELLEN G., and **MIRIAN FUCHS**, eds. *Breaking the Sequence: Women's Experimental Fiction.* Princeton: Princeton University Press, 1989.

FRIEDMAN, NORMAN. *Form and Meaning in Fiction.* Athens: University of Georgia Press, 1975.

Frontiers: A Journal of Women Studies 9 (Spring 1987)–14 (Spring 1994).

Fu Jen Studies: Literature & Linguistics 15 (1982)–20 (1987).

FUKUSHIMA, OSAMU, et al., eds. *Eigakuronso: Ishii Shonosuke Sensei Kokikines Ronbunshu.* Tokyo: Kinseido, 1982.

FUSSELL, PAUL. *The Great War and Modern Memory.* New York: Oxford University Press, 1975.

GALLIARD, DAWSON. *Dorothy L. Sayers.* New York: Ungar, 1981.

GAISER, GOTTLIEB, ed. *International Perspectives on James Joyce.* Troy, NY: Whitston, 1986.

GAMACHE, LAWRENCE B., and **IAN S. MACNIVEN**, eds. *The Modernists: Studies in a Literary Phenomenon: Essays in Honor of Harry T. Moore.* Rutherford, NJ: Fairleigh Dickinson University Press, 1987.

GANNON, SUSAN R., and **RUTH ANN THOMPSON**, eds. *Cross-Culturalism in Children's Literature: Selected Papers from the Children's Literature Association.* New York: Pace University Press, 1988.

GARDNER, AVERIL. *George Orwell.* Boston: Twayne, 1987.

GARDNER, PHILIP, ed. *E. M. Forster: The Critical Heritage.* London and Boston: Routledge & Kegan Paul, 1973.

GARIS, ROBERT D. *The Dickens Theatre.* Oxford: Clarendon, 1965.

GASKELL, PHILIP. *From Writer to Reader Studies in Editorial Method.* Oxford: Clarendon, 1978.

Gaskell Society Journal 1 (Summer 1987)–6 (1992).

GASSENMEIR, MICHAEL, and **NORBERT H. PLATZ**, eds. *Beyond the Suburbs of the Mind.* Essen: Blaue Eule, 1987.

GATRELL, SIMON, ed. *The Ends of the Earth*. London: Ashfield, 1992.

GELBER, MARK, ed. *Identity and Ethos: Festschrift for Sol Liptzin on Occasion of His 85th Birthday*. New York: Peter Lang, 1986.

GENTILI, VANNA. *Atre e letteratura: Scritti in ricordo di Gabriele Baldini*. Rome: Edizioni di Storia e Letteratura, 1972.

Genders 1 (March 1988)–10 (Spring 1991).

Genre 9 (Summer 1976)–21 (Summer 1988).

The George Eliot Review: Journal of the George Eliot Fellowship 11 (1980)–20 (1989).

George Eliot-George Henry Lewes Studies (formerly *The George Eliot-George Henry Lewes Newsletter*) 3 (September 1983)–20–21 (September 1992).

The Georgia Review 13 (Fall 1959)–39 (Spring 1985).

GERALD, MICHAEL C. *The Poisonous Pen of Agatha Christie*. Austin: University of Texas Press, 1993.

Germanisch-Romanische Monatsschrift 34, no. 3 (1984)–40, no. 3 (1990).

German Life and Letters 45 (Spring 1992).

The Gettysburg Review 3 (Autumn 1990)–4 (Spring 1991).

GIBSON, EVAN K. *C. S. Lewis: Spinner of Tales: A Guide to His Fiction*. Washington, DC: Christian College Consortium, 1980.

GILBERT, SANDRA M., and **SUSAN GUBAR**. *The Madwoman in the Attic: The Woman Writer and the Nineteenth-Century Literary Imagination*. New Haven: Yale University Press, 1979.

GIDDINGS, ROBERT, ed. *The Changing World of Charles Dickens*. London: Vision; Totawa, NJ: Barnes & Noble, 1983.

———, ed. *J. R. R. Tolkien: This Far Land*. London: Vision; Totawa, NJ: Barnes & Noble, 1983.

GIFFORD, DON. *Notes for Joyce: "Dubliners" and "A Portrait of the Artist as a Young Man."* New York: Dutton, 1967.

GILLON, ADAM. *Joseph Conrad*. Boston: Twayne, 1987.

The Gissing Journal (formerly *The Gissing Newsletter*) 17 (July 1981)–25 (October 1989).

G. K.'s Weekly 24 (8 October 1936).

GLICKSBERG, CHARLES I. *Modern Literary Perspectivism*. Dallas: Southern Methodist University Press, 1970.

Glyph Textual Studies 3 (Spring 1978)–8 (1981).

GOETSCH, PAUL, et al., eds. *Der Englische Roman im 19 Jahrhundrert: Interpretationen*. Berlin: Schmidt, 1973.

GOLD, JOSEPH. *Charles Dickens: Radical Moralist*. Minneapolis: University of Minneapolis Press, 1975.

GOLDBERG, MICHAEL. *Carlyle and Dickens*. Athens: University of Georgia Press, 1972.

GOLDKNOPF, DAVID. *The Life of the Novel*. Chicago: University of Chicago Press, 1972.

Golsuorsi 4, no. 130 (1982).

GOMME, ANDOR, ed. *D. H. Lawrence: A Critical Study of the Major Novels and Other Writings*. New York: Barnes & Noble, 1978.

GONTARSKI, S. E., ed. *The Beckett Studies Reader*. Gainesville: University Press of Florida, 1987.

GOODIN, GEORGE, ed. *The English Novel in the Nineteenth Century: Essays on the Literary Mediation of Human Values*. Urbana: University of Illinois Press, 1972.

GONZÁLEZ, PADILLA, ed. *Charles Dickens 1812–1870: Homenaje en al primer centenario de su muerte*. Mexico City: University Nacional Autònoma de México, 1971.

GORDON, CAROLYN, and **ALLEN TATE**, eds. *The House of Fiction: A Collection of Short Stories with Commentary*. New York: Scribner's, 1950.

GORDON, ROBERT. *The Expanded Moment: A Short Story Anthology*. Boston: Heath, 1963.

GOSE, ELLIOT B., JR. *Imagination Indulged: The Irrational in the Nineteenth-Century Novel*. Montreal: McGill-Queen's University Press, 1972.

Gothic 2 (1987).

GOURNAY, JEAN, ed. *L'Erotisme en Angleterre XVIIe–XVIIIe siècles*. Paris: Publication de Université de Lille, 1992.

GOWDA, H. H. ANNIAH, ed. *A Garland for E, M. Forster*. Mysore, India: The Literary Half-Yearly, 1969.

GRACE, SHERRILL, ed. *Swinging the Maelstrom: New Perspectives on Malcolm Lowry*. Montreal and Kingston: McGill-Queen's University Press, 1992.

Granata 2 (February 1991).

Grand Street 7 (Autumn 1987)–9 (Autumn 1989).

GRANDSDEN, K. W. *E. M. Forster*. Edinburgh: Oliver & Boyd, 1962.

GRASSIN, JEAN-MARIE, ed. *Mythes, Images, Representations*. Paris: Didier, 1981; Limoges: Trames Université de Limoges, 1981.

GRAY, RONALD D. *The German Tradition in Literature, 1981–1945*. Cambridge: Cambridge University Press, 1967.

GREGOR, IAN, ed. *Reading the Victorian Novel: Detail into Form*. London: Vision, 1980.

———, and **BRIAN NICOLAS**, eds. *The Moral and the Story*. London: Faber, 1962.

GREY, J. DAVID, ed. *Jane Austen's Beginnings: The Juvenalia and Lady Susan*. Ann Arbor, MI: University Microfilms International Research Press, 1989.

Greyfriar: Siena Studies in Literature 17 (1976)–22 (1981).

GROSS, JOHN, and **GABRIEL PEARSON**, eds. *Dickens and the Twentieth Century*. London: Routledge & Kegan Paul, 1962.

GUETTI, JAMES. *Word-Music: The Aesthetic Aspect of Narrative Fiction*. New Brunswick, NJ: Rutgers University Press, 1980.

GUIGUET, JEAN, comp. *Contemporary Writers*. New York: Harcourt, Brace, 1966.

Guilde du Livre 16 (July 1951).

GUILIANO, EDWARD, ed. *Lewis Carroll: A Celebration: Essays on the Occasion of the 150th Anniversary of the Birth of Charles Lutwidge Dodgson*. New York: Potter, 1982.

GUPTA, G. S. BALARAMA, ed. *Studies in Indian Fiction in English*. Culgarga, India: JIWE, 1987.

Gypsy Scholar 2 (Fall 1974).

D'HAEN, THEO, and **HANS BERTENS**, eds. *History and Post-War Writing*. Amsterdam: Rodopi, 1990.

HAGOPIAN, JOHN V., and **MARTIN DOLCH**, eds. *Insight II: Analyses of Modern British Literature*. Frankfurt: Hirschgraben, 1964.

HAIGHT, GORDON SHERMAN, and **ROSEMARY T. VANARSDEL**, eds. *George Eliot: A Centenary Tribute*. London: Macmillan, 1982.

HALE, NANCY. *The Realities of Fiction: A Book About Writing*. Boston: Little, Brown, 1962.

HALIO, JAY L., ed. *Critical Essays on Angus Wilson*. Boston: G. K. Hall, 1985.

HALL, TREVOR H. *Dorothy L. Sayers: Nine Literary Studies*. London: Duckworth, 1980.

HALLE, MORRIS, et al., eds. *Semiotics and the History of Culture*. Columbus, OH: Slavica, 1988.

HALL, JOHN. *The Tragic Comedians: Seven Modern British Novelists*. Bloomington: Indiana University Press, 1963.

HALPERIN, JOHN, ed. *The Theory of the Novel: New Essays*. New York: Oxford University Press, 1974.

HALSTON, THOMAS, and **JOSEPH P. WILLIMAN**, eds. *Diakonia: Studies in Honor of Robert T. Meyer*. Washington, DC: Catholic University of America Press, 1986.

HAMILTON, ALASTAIR, tr. and ed. *Literature and Evil*. London: Calder & Boyars, 1973.

Hamlet Studies: An Internation Journal of Research on "The Tragedie of Hamlet, Prince of Denmarke" 9 (Summer–Winter 1987).

HANNAH, BARBARA. *Striving Towards Wholeness*. New York: Putnam's, 1971.

HAMARD, MARIE-CLAIRE, ed. *Home, Sweet Home or Bleak House? Art et littérature à l'époque Victorienne*. Paris: Belles Lettres, 1985.

HARDY, BARBARA. *The Appropriate Form: An Essay on the Novel*. London: Athlone, 1964.

———, ed. *Middlemarch: Critical Approaches*. New York: Oxford University Press, 1967.

———. *The Moral Art of Dickens*. New York: Oxford University Press, 1970.

———. *Tellers and Listeners: The Narrative Imagination*. London: Athlone, 1975.

HARDY, JOHN EDWARD. *Man in the Modern Novel*. Seattle: University of Washington Press, 1964.

HARGROVE, ANNE C., and **MAURINE MAGLIOCCO**, eds. *Portraits of Marriage in Literature*. Macomb, IL: Essays in Literature, 1984.

HARPER, HOWARD M., and **CHARLES EDGE**, eds. *The Classic British Novel*. Athens: University of Georgia Press, 1972.

Harpers Magazine 239 (November 1969).

HARPHAM, GEOFFREY FALT. *On the Grotesque: Strategies of Contradiction in Art and Literature*. Princeton: Princeton University Press, 1982.

HARRISON, ANTHONY, and **BEVERLY TAYLOR**, eds. *Gender and Discourse in Victorian Literature and Art*. Dekalb, Northern Illinois University Press, 1992.

HART, CLIVE, ed. *James Joyce's Dubliners*. London: Faber, 1969.

HARTOGA, RENATUS with **HANS FANTEL**. *Four Letter Word Games: The Psychology of Obscenity*. New York: Delacorte, 1968.

The Harvard Magazine 81 (January–February 1978).

HARTVEIT, LARS. *The Art of Persuasion: A Study of Six Novels*. Bergen: Universitetsforlaget, 1977.

HARVEY, GEOFFREY, and **MICHAEL SCOTT**, eds. *Sons and Lovers*. Atlantic Highlands, NJ: Humanities, 1987.

HASLER, JORG, ed. *Anglistentag 1981: Vortrage*. Frankfurt am Main: Lang, 1983.

The Hatcher Review 3 (Spring 1989).

HAWTHORN, JEREMY, ed. *The Nineteenth-Century British Novel*. Baltimore: Arnold, 1986.

HAYCRAFT, HOWARD. *The Art of the Mystery Story*. New York: Simon & Schuster, 1946.

———, ed. *E. C. Bentley's "Trent's Last Case."* San Diego: University Extension, University of California Press, 1977.

HAYS, PETER. *The Limping Hero: Grotesques in Literature*. New York: New York University Press, 1971.

Hebrew University Studies in Literature and the Arts 1 (Spring 1973)–13 (Spring 1985).

HEILBRUN, CAROLYN G. *Toward a Recognition of Androgyny*. New York: Knopf, 1973.

———, and **MARGARET R. HIGONNET**, eds. *The Representation of Women in Fiction*. Baltimore: Johns Hopkins University Press, 1983.

HELMER, HERMANN, ed. *Verfremdung in der Literatur*. Darmstadt: Wissenschaftliche Buchgesellschaft, 1984.

The Hemingway Review 3 (Spring 1984).

HENKE, SUZETTE, and **ELAINE UNKELESS**, eds. *Women in Joyce*. Urbana: University of Illinois Press, 1982.

HERGET, WINIFRED, **KLAUS PETER JOCHUM**, and **INGEBORD WEBER**, eds. *Theorie und Praxis im Erzahlen des 19. und 20. Jahrhunderts: Studien zur englischen und amerikanischen Literatur zu Ehren von Willi Erzgraber*. Turbingen: Gunter Narr, 1986.

Hermathena: A Trinity College Dublin Review 120 (Summer 1976)–142 (Summer 1987).

HERZ, JUDITH SCHERER, and **ROBERT K. MARTIN**, eds. *E. M. Forster: Centenary Revaluations*. Toronto: University of Toronto Press, 1982.

HEUERMANN, HARTMUT, and **BERND-PETER LANGE**, eds. *Die Utopie in der angloamerikanischen Literatur: Interpretationen*. Dusseldorf: Bagel, 1984.

HEUERMANN, HARTMUT, ed. *Der Science Fiction Roman in der Angloamerikanischen Literatur: Interpretationen*. Dusseldorf: Bagel, 1986.

HEWITT, DOUGLAS. *The Approach to Fiction: Good and Bad Readings of Novels*. London: Longman, 1972.

HEYWOOD, CHRISTOPHER, ed. *D. H. Lawrence: New Studies*. New York: St. Martin's, 1987.

Hibbert Journal 31 (October 1932).

Hibernia (12 December 1975).

HICKEY, LEO, ed. *The Pragmatics of Style*. London: Routledge, 1989.

HILLEGAS, MARK E. *The Future as Nightmare: H. G. Wells and the Anti-Utopians*. New York: Oxford University Press, 1967.

———. *Shadows of Imagination: The Fantasies of C. S. Lewis, J. R. R. Tolkien, and Charles Williams*. Carbondale: Southern Illinois University Press, 1969.

Hiroshima Studies in English Language and Literature 25 (1980)–32 (1987).

Hiroshima University Studies 29, no. 2 (1970)–33 (1974).

Hispanic Review 49 (Autumn 1981).

Hispanófila 28 (September 1984).

The History of Medicine 1 (Summer 1969).

History Today 32 (August 1982).

HOBSBAUM, PHILLIP. *A Reader's Guide to Charles Dickens* London: Thames & Hudson, 1972.

HOCHMAN, BARUCH. *The Test of Character: From the Victorian Novel to the Modern*. Rutherford, NJ: Fairleigh Dickinson University Press, 1983.

Hochland 59 (1966).

HOFFMAN, FREDERICK J. *The Mortal No: Death and the Modern Imagination*. Princeton: Princeton University Press, 1964.

———, and **HARRY T. MOORE**, eds. *The Achievement of D. H. Lawrence.* Norman: University of Oklahoma Press, 1953.

HOKENSON, JAN, and **HOWARD D. PEARCE**, eds. *Forms of the Fantastic: Selected Essays from the Third International Conference on the Fantastic in Literature and Film*. Westport, CT: Greenwood, 1986.

HOMANS, MARGARET. *Bearing the Word: Language and Female Experience in Nineteenth-Century Women's Writing*. Chicago: University of Chicago Press, 1986.

HOTTOIS, GILBERT, ed. *Philosophie et littérature*. Brussells: Université de Bruxelles, 1985.

Hong Kong Baptist College Academic Journal 4 (July 1977).

HORNBACK, BERT G. *Noah's Arkitecture: A Study of Dickens's Mythology*. Athens: Ohio University Press, 1972.

Die Horen: Zeitschrift für Literature, Kunst und Kritik 31, no. 2 (1986)–34, no. 2 (1989).

The Horn Book Magazine 58 (December 1982).

HOWE, FLORENCE, ed. *Tradition and the Talents of Women*. Urbana: University of Illinois Press, 1991.

HOWE, IRVING, ed. *Classics of Modern Fiction, 2nd Ed.*. New York: Harcourt, Brace, 1972.

———, ed. *"1984" Revisited: Totalitarianism in Our Century*. New York: Harper & Row, 1983.

HOWE, QUINCY, JR., ed. *Humanitas: Essays in Honor of Ralph Ross*. Claremont, CA: Scripps, 1977.

HOWES, ALAN B. *Arthur C. Clarke*. New York: Taplinger, 1977.

The Hudson Review 1 (1948)–39 (Summer 1986).

The Humanist 85 (July 1970).

The Humanities Association Review/La Revue de l'Association des Humanites 31 (Winter–Spring 1980).

Humanities in Society 4 (Spring–Summer 1981).

HUMFREY, BELINDA, ed. *John Cowper Powys's "Wolf Solent": Critical Studies*. Cardiff: University of Wales Press.

Humor: International Journal of Humor Research 5, no. 3 (1992).

Hungarian Studies in English 21 (December 1990).

The Huntington Library Quarterly: A Journal for the History and Interpretation of English and American Civilization 19 (1955–56).

HUPPAUF, BERND-RUDINGER, ed. *Ansichten vom Krieg: Verleichende Studien zum Ersten Weltkrieg in Literatur und Gesellschaft*. Konigstein: Forum Acad. In Verlagsgruppe Athenaum, Hain, Hanstein, 1984.

HUSSEY, MARK, ed. *Virginia Woolf and War: Fiction, Reality, and Myth*. Syracuse, NY: Syracuse University Press, 1991.

HUSSEY, MARK, and **VARA NEVEROW TURK**, eds. *Virginia Woolf Miscellanies: Proceedings of the First Annual Conferance on Virginia Woolf*. New York: Pace University Press, 1992.

HUTTER, CHARLES A., ed. *Literature and Religion: Views on D. H. Lawrence*. Holland, MI: Hope College Press, 1968.

HYNES, SAMUEL, ed. *Graham Greene: A Collection of Critical Essays*. Englewood Cliffs, NJ: Prentice-Hall, 1973.

Ibadan Studies in English 1 (1969).

Igirisu Shosetsu Panfuletto 3 (1972).

Ilha do Desterro: A Journal of Language and Literature 24, no. 2 (1990).

The Illinois Quarterly 33 (September 1970)–36 (September 1973).

Il Lettore di Provincia 13 (December 1982)–18 (December 1987).

The Illustrated [London] News 275 (April 1987).

The Incorporated Linguist 24 (Winter 1985).

The Independent Shavian 30, no. 1–2 (1992).

The Indian Journal of English Studies 1 (December 1960)–18 (1978–79).

The Indian Literary Review: A Tri-Quarterly of Indian Literature 3 (October 1985).

The Indian P.E.N. 51 (October–December 1990).

Inklings: Jahrbuch für Literatur und Asthetik 2 (1984)–6 (1988).

Inozemna Filolohiia 61 (1981)–68 (1982).

Insula: Revista de Letras y Ciencias Humanas 37 (September 1982).

The International Journal of Women's Studies 5 (May–June 1982)–7 (January–February 1984).

The International Fiction Review 8 (Winter 1981)–9 (Fall 1992).

Interpretation: A Journal of Political Philosophy 7 (January 1978)–16 (Winter 1988–89).

Interpretations: A Journal of Ideas, Analysis, and Criticism 13 (Fall 1981)–15 (Fall 1983).

The Iowa Review 20 (Winter 1990).

The Irish Press (9 October 1971).

The Irish University Review: A Journal of Irish Studies 11 (Autumn 1981)–22 (Spring 1992).

ISAACS, NEIL D., and **ROSE A. ZIMBARDO**, eds. *Tolkien: New Critical Perspectives*. Lexington: University Press of Kentucky, 1981.

Italica 34 (1957).

Izvestiia Akademii Nauk, Seriia Literatury I Iazyka (formerly *Izvestiia Akademii Nauk S. S. S. R., Seriia Literatury I Iazyka*) 44 (September–October 1985).

Izvestiia Akademii Nauk Turkmenskoi SSR, Seriia Obshchestvennykh Nauk 1 (1987).

Jabberwocky: The Journal of the Lewis Carroll Society 1 (1969)–10 (Winter 1980–81).

JACKSON, DENNIS, and **FLEDA BROWN JACKSON**, eds. *Critical Essays on D. H. Lawrence*. Boston: G. K. Hall, 1988.

JACKSON, PHILIP W., and **SOPHIE HAROUTUNIAN-GORDON**, eds. *From Socrates to Software: The Teacher as Text and the Text as Teacher*. Chicago: National Society for Study of Education, 1989.

JACOBSON, SVEN, ed. *Papers from the Second Scandinavian Symposium on Syntactic Variation*. Stockholm: Almqvist & Wiskell, 1983.

JACOBUS, MARY, ed. *Women Writing and Writing About Women*. London: Croom Helm, 1984.

Jahrbuch Deutsch als Fremdsprache 18 (1992).

Jahrbuch der Deutschen Schillergesellschaft 34 (1990).

JAMES, A. R. W., ed. *Victor Hugo et la Grande-Bretagne*. Liverpool: Cairns, 1986.

James Joyce Broadsheet 17 (June 1985).

James Joyce Literary Supplement 4 (Spring 1990).

James Joyce Quarterly 1 (1964)–31 (Winter 1994).

James Joyce Review 3, no. 1–2 (1959).

Jammu and Kashmir University Review 1 (November 1958).

JARMUTH, SYLVIA L. *Dickens' Use of Women in His Novels*. New York: Excelsior, 1967.

JASPER, DAVID, ed. *Images of Belief in Literature*. New York: St. Martin's, 1984.

Jean Rhys Review 1 (Spring 1987)–2 (Fall 1987).

JEFFERSON, DOUGLAS, and **GRAHAM MARTIN**, eds. *The Uses of Fiction: Essays on the Modern Novel in Honour of Arnold Kettle*. Bristol, England: Open University Press, 1982.

JENSEN, EINER J., ed. *The Future on Nineteen Eighty-Four*. Ann Arbor: University of Michigan Press, 1984.

Jezik in Slovstvo 34 (March 1988–89).

JOHNSON, MARY LYNN, and **SERAPHIA LEYDA**, eds. *Reconciliations: Studies in Honor of Richard Harter Fogle*. Salzburg: Institute für Anglistik & Amerikanistik, Universite Salzburg, 1983.

JONES, WILLIAM POWELL. *James Joyce and the Common Reader*. Norman: University of Oklahoma Press, 1955.

JONES, WILLIAM POWELL, LILLA MARIA CRISAFULLI, and **VITA FORTUNATI**, eds. *Ritratto dell'artista come donna: Saggi sull'avanguardia del Novecento*. Urbina: Quattro Venti, 1988.

JORDANOVA, L. J., ed. *Languages of Nature: Critical Essays on Science and Literature*. New Brunswick, NJ: Rutgers University Press, 1986.

JOSIPOVICI, GABRIEL, ed. *The Modern English Novel: The Reader, the Writer and the Work.* London: Open Books, 1976.

Journal of American Folklore 96 (October–December 1983).

Journal of Asian Studies 27 (February 1968).

The Journal of Beckett Studies 11–12 (1989)–15 (Autumn 1992).

The Journal of British Studies 22 (Fall 1982).

The Journal of King Saud University 11, no. 2 (1984).

The Journal of Commonwealth Literature 21 (August 1986)–29 (August 1993).

The Journal of English and Germanic Philology 72 (January 1973)–92 (April 1993).

The Journal of English Language and Literature 29 (Spring 1988)–39 (Summer 1993).

The Journal of English Teaching Techniques 10 (Summer 1980).

The Journal of European Studies 12 (March 1982)–17 (September 1987).

The Journal of Evolutionary Psychology 1 (June 1979)–13 (August 1992).

The Journal of Irish Literature 20 (September 1991).

The Journal of Literary Studies/Tydskrif Vir Literaturwetenskap 2 (July 1986).

The Journal of Modern Literature 1 (March 1971)–17 (Spring 1991).

The Journal of Narrative Technique 1 (September 1971)–23 (Spring 1993).

The Journal of Popular Culture 6 (Fall 1972)–19 (Fall 1985).

The Journal of Pre–Raphaelite Studies 7 (May 1987).

The Journal of Reading 35 (April 1992).

The Journal of the Department of English (Calcutta University) 17, no. 1 (1981–82)–21, no. 1–2 (1986–87).

The Journal of the History of Ideas 1 (January 1940).

The Journal of the History of Sexuality 1 (October 1990).

The Journal of the Midwest Modern Language Association 23 (Spring 1990).

The Journal of the School of Languages 7 (Monsoon 1980–Winter 1981).

The Journal of the Short Story in English 7 (Autumn 1986)–8 (Spring 1987).

The Journal of Ukranian Studies 15 (Summer 1990).

The Journal of Women's Studies in Literature 1 (Autumn 1979).

Joyce Studies Annual 1 (1990)– 4 (Summer 1993).

Junction (1972).

KADAR, MARLENE, ed. *Essays on Life Writing: From Genre to Critical Practice*. Toronto: University of Toronto Press, 1992.

KAKOURIOTIS, A., and **R. PARKER-GOUNELAS**, eds. *Working Papers in Linguistics and Literature*. Thessaloniki: Aristotle University Press, 1989.

Kaleidoscope (Summer–Fall 1986).

KALNINS, MARA, ed. *D. H. Lawrence: Centenary Essays*. Bristol, England: Bristol Classical, 1986.

Kañina: Revista de Artes y Letras de la Universidad de Costa Rica 4 (January–June 1980)–5 (January–June 1981).

The Kansas Quarterly 7 (Fall 1975)–16 (Summer 1984).

KARL, FREDERICK R. *A Reader's Guide to the Nineteenth Century Novel*. New York: Farrar, Straus, 1964.

The Keats-Shelley Journal: Keats, Shelley, Byron, Hunt, and Their Circles 8 (Winter 1959).

The Keats-Shelley Review 36 (1985)–4 (Autumn 1989).

Kenkyu Shuroku 21 (March 1973).

KENNEY, CATHERINE. *The Remarkable Case of Dorothy L. Sayers*. Kent, OH: Kent State University Press, 1990.

The Kentucky Folklore Record 27 (January–June 1981).

The Kentucky Philological Association Bulletin (1982)–(1984).

The Kentucky Review 4 (Winter 1983).

The Kenyon Review 13 (Spring 1951)–10 (Fall 1988).

KERMODE, FRANK, ed. *Puzzles and Epiphanies: Essays and Reviews, 1958–1961*. London: Routledge & Kegan Paul, 1962.

KERSNOWSII, FRANK, ed. *Into the Labyrinth: Essays on the Art of Lawrence Durrell*. Ann Arbor, MI: University Microfilms International Research Press, 1989.

KETTLE, ARNOLD. *An Introduction to the English Novel, II: Henry James to the Present.* London: Hutchinson, 1953.

———, *The Nineteenth-Century Novel: Critical Essays and Documents.* London: Hutchinson, 1972.

KIMURA, SHIGEKO, *Yamakawa Kozo Kyoju Taikan Kinen Ronbunshu.* Toyonaka: N.P., 1981.

KIMURA, TOSHIO, HISAO KANAEKI, and **ISAMU SAITO**, eds. *Bungaku to kotoba.* Tokyo: Nan'un do, 1986.

KINCAID, JAMES R. *Dickens and the Rhetoric of Laughter.* Oxford: Claredon, 1971.

———, and **ALBERT J. KUHN**, eds. *Victorian Literature and Society: Essays Presented to Richard D. Altick.* Columbus: Ohio State University Press, 1984.

KINASHI, YURI. *Jane Austen: Shosetsu no Kenkyu.* Tokyo: Aratake, 1981.

The Kipling Journal 57 (June 1983)–62 (December 1988).

KIRK, JOHN, ed. *The Incongruous Spy:* Call for the Dead *and* A Murder of Quality. New York: Walker, 1963.

KIRPAL, VINEY, ed. *The New Indian Novel in English: A Study of the 1980s.* New Delhi: Allied, 1990.

KLIEN, MICHAEL, and **GILLIAN PARKER**, eds. *The English Novels and Movies.* New York: Ungar, 1981.

KNOEPFLMACHER, U. C. *Laughter & Despair: Readings in Ten Novels of the Victorian Era.* Berkeley: University of California Press, 1971.

KONDO, INEKO, ed. *E. M. Forster.* Tokyo: Kentyusha, 1967.

KORSHIN, PAUL J., and **ROBERT R. ALLEN**, eds. *Greene Centennial Studies: Essays Presented to Donald Greene in the Centennial Year of the University of Southern California.* Charlottesville: University Press of Virginia, 1984.

KOSOK, HENIZ, ed. *Studies in Anglo-Irish Literature.* Bonn: Bouvier, 1982.

KRAMER, DALE, ed. *Critical Approaches to the Fiction of Thomas Hardy.* London: Macmillan, 1979.

———, ed. *Critical Essays on Thomas Hardy: The Novels.* Boston: G. K. Hall, 1990.

KRIEGER, MURRAY. *The Tragic Vision: Variations on a Theme in Literary Interpretation.* Chicago: University of Chicago Press, 1966.

KROOK, DOROTHEA, *Three Traditions of Moral Thought*. Cambridge: Cambridge University Press, 1959.

KUNKEL, FRANCIS L. *Passion and the Passion: Sex and Religion in Modern Literature*. Philadelphia: Westminster, 1975.

Kultur og Klasse: Kritik og Kulturanalyse 17, no. 3 (1990).

Kultura: Szkice, Opowiadania, Sprawozdania 6 (June 1983).

Kultuur Leven (28 October 1961).

Kunapipi 7, no. 1 (1985)–14, no. 1 (1992).

Kwartalnik Neofilologiczny 28, no. 3–4 (1981)–32, no. 4 (1985).

Labrys 5 (1979).

LACY, GERALD M. *The Escaped Cock*. Los Angeles: Black Sparrow, 1973.

The Lamar Journal of the Humanities 8 (Fall 1982)–9 (Spring 1983).

LAMBERT, GAVIN. *The Dangerous Edge*. New York: Grossman, 1976.

LAMSON, ROY, and **WALLACE W. DOUGLAS**, eds. *The Critical Reader: Essays in Criticism*. New York: Norton, 1962.

LANDOW, GEORGE P., ed. *Approaches to Victorian Autobiography*. Athens: Ohio University Press, 1979.

Le Langage et l'Homme: Recherches Pluridisciplinaires sur le Langage 26 (March 1991).

Language & Communictation: An Interdisciplinary Journal 4, no. 2 (1984).

Language and Culture 1 (1982)–22 (1992).

Language and Literature: Journal of the Poetics and Linguistics Association 7, no. 1–3 (1982).

Language and Style: An International Journal 16 (Summer 1983)–20 (Fall 1987).

The Language Quarterly 30 (Winter–Spring 1992).

La Licorne 8 (1984).

LASSNER, PHYLLIS. *Elizabeth Bowen*. New York: Macmillan, 1970.

———. *Elzabeth Bowen: A Study of Her Short Fiction*. New York: Twayne, 1991.

The Law Quarterly Review 60 (1944).

LEAVIS, F. R. *Anna Karenina and Other Essays*. London: Chatto & Windus, 1967.

———, and **Q. D. LEAVIS**, eds. *Lectures in America*. New York: Pantheon, 1969.

LEBOWITZ, NAOMI. *Humanism and the Absurd in the Modern Novel*. Evanston, IL: Northwestern University Press, 1971.

LECERCLE, JEAN-JACQUES, ed. *L'Errance*. Paris: Université de Paris X, 1991.

LEE, HERMOINE, ed. *The Mulberry Tree: Writings of Elizabeth Bowen*. New York: Harcourt, Brace, 1958.

Les Langues Modernes 59 (1965)–70 (1976).

LEHMAN, B. H., et al., eds. *The Image of the Work*. Berkeley: University of California Press, 1955.

LENSING, LEO A., and **PETER HANS-WERNER**, eds. *Wilhelm Rabbe: Studien zu seinem Leben und Werk*. Braunschweig: pp–Verl, 1981.

LERNER, LAURENCE, ed. *The Victorians*. New York: Holmes & Meier, 1978.

LERNER, LIA SCHWARTZ, and **ISAIAS LERNER**, eds. *Homenaje a Ana Maria Barrenechea*. Madrid: Castilia, 1984.

LEVINE, GEORGE, and **WILLIAM MADDEN**, eds. *The Art of Victorian Prose*. London: Oxford University Press, 1968.

———, and **ALAN RAUCH**, eds. *One Culture: Essays in Science and Literature*. Madison: University of Wisconsin Press, 1987.

LEVIN, HARRY. *James Joyce: A Critical Introduction*. Norfolk, CT: New Directions, 1960.

LEWIS, PETER, *John le Carré*. New York: Ungar, 1985.

The Liberal and Fine Arts Review 1 (July 1981)–4 (July 1984).

The Library Review 22 (Autumn 1970).

Life and Letters 40 (January 1944).

Life and Letters and The London Mercury 62 (1949).

Lingua é Stile: Trimestrale di Linguistica e Critica Letteraria (formerly *Lingua é Stile: Trimestrale di Linguistics e Critica Letteraria*) 12 (1977)–24 (June 1989).

Linguistics and Literature 1, no. 1 (1975).

The Lion and the Unicorn: A Critical Journal of Children's Literature 1, no. 1 (1977–11, no. 2 (1987).

Literature in North Queensland 11, no. 3 (1983).

The Listener 45 (22 February 1951)–117 (7 May 1987).

Literary and Linguistic Computing: Journal of the Association for Literary and Linguistic Computing 5, no. 4 (1990).

The Literary Criterion 4 (December 1960)–23, no. 4 (1988).

The Literary Endeavour: A Quarterly Journal Devoted to English Studies 3 (July–December 1960)–9, no. 1–4 (1987–88).

The Literary Half-Yearly 27 (January 1986).

Literary Onomastics Studies 12 (1985)–15 (1988).

The Literary Review: An International Journal of Contemporary Writing 24 (Winter 1981)–25 (Fall 1981).

Literary World (9 May 1879)–(16 May 1979).

Literature and Belief 12 (1992).

Literature and History 2 (October 1975)–13 (Autumn 1987).

Literature and Medicine 9 (1990).

Literature and Psychology 12 (1962)–40 (Spring–Summer 1994).

Literature East and West 16 (January 1972)–21 (January–December 1977).

Literature/Film Quarterly 9, no. 3 (1981)–21 (January 1993).

Literature of the Oppressed 1 (Fall 1987).

Literatur in Wissenschaft und Unterricht 7 (October 1974)–21 (December 1988).

Literaturnoe Obozrenie: Organ Soiuza Pisatelei S.S.S.R. 8 (August 1985)–2 (1989).

Literatur und Kritik 183–184 (April–May 1984).

Literatur und Leben 3, no. 1 (1970).

LIT: Literature Interpretation Theory 3, no. 1 (1991).

Littéraria Pragensia: Studies in Literature and Culture 2, no. 4 (1992).

Literaturwissenschaftliches Jahrbuch im Auftrage der Görres-Gesellschaft 30 (1989).

Littératures 16 (Spring 1987).

LITTLEWOOD, IAN. *The Writings of Evelyn Waugh*. Oxford: Basil Blackwell, 1983.

Living Age 339 (September 1930).

LOBDELL, JARED, ed. *A Tolkien Compass*. New York: Ballentine, 1980.

The Lock Haven Bulletin 1, no. 3 (1961).

LODGE, DAVID. *The Language of Fiction*. London: Routledge & Kegan Paul, 1966.

———. *The Modes of Modern Writing: Metaphor, Metonymy, and the Typology of Modern Literature*. London: Arnold, 1977.

———. *Working With Structuralism*. Boston: Routledge & Kegan Paul, 1981.

LOMBARD, FRANÇOIS. *Rhetorique et communication*. Paris: Didier, 1979.

LOMBARDO, AGOSTINO, ed. *Studi inglesi: Raccolta di saggi e ricerche*. Bari: Adriatica, 1978.

The London Magazine 7 (1960)–17 (December 1977).

The London Review of Books 13 (10 January 1991).

LUCAS, JOHN. *Melancholy Man: A Study of Dicken's Novels* (London: Methuen, 1970).

The Lugano Review 1 (Summer 1966).

Maatstaf 2 (1989).

MACCABE, COLIN, ed. *James Joyce: New Perspectives*. Brighton, England: Harvester, 1982; Bloomington: Indiana University Press, 1982.

MCCLEARY, G. F., ed. *On Detective Fiction and Other Things*. London: Hollis and Carter, 1960.

MCCOWN, ROBERTA A., ed. *The Life and Times of Leigh Hunt*. Iowa City: Friends of the University of Iowa Libraries, 1985.

MCCULLOUGH, BRUCE. *Representative English Novelists: Defoe to Conrad*. New York: Harper, 1946.

MCGANN, JEROME J., ed. *Historical Studies and Literary Criticism*. Madison: University of Wisconsin Press, 1985.

MCCARTHY, PATRICK, ed. *Critical Essays on James Joyce's "Finnegan's Wake."* New York: G. K. Hall, 1992.

MCILWRAITH, JEAN N., ed. *Wuthering Heights*. New York: Doubleday, 1907.

MACK, MAYNARD, and **IAN GREGOR**, eds. *Imagined Worlds: Essays on Some English Novels and Novelists in Honour of John Butt*. London: Methuen, 1968.

MCDOWELL, FREDERICK P. E. *E. M. Forster*. New York: Twayne, 1969.

MAES-JELINEK, HENA, PIERRE MICHEL, and **PAULETTE MICHEL-MICHOT**, eds. *Multiple Worlds, Multiple Words*. Liege: Université de Liege, 1987.

Magazine (19 April 1969).

The Magazine of Fantasy and Science Fiction 8 (April 1955).

MAGILL, FRANK N., ed. *Survey of Contemporary Literature*. New York: Salem, 1971.

———, ed. *Survey of Modern Fantasy Literature* (Englewood Cliffs, NJ: Salem, 1979).

———, ed. *Magill's Literary Annual, 1977*, vol. 2. Englewood Cliffs, NJ: Salem, 1977.

MALACHI, ZVI, ed. *Proceedings of the International Conference on Literary and Linguistic Computing*. Tel Aviv: Tel Aviv University Faculty of Humanities, n.d.

The Malahat Review 10 (April 1969)–44 (October 1977).

The Malcolm Lowry Review 8 (Spring 1981)–17–18 (Fall–Spring 1985–86).

Mallorn: The Journal of the Tolkien Society 18 (June 1982)–27 (September 1990).

MALLORY, WILLIAM E., and **PAUL SIMPSON-HOUSELEY**, eds. *Geography and Literature: A Meeting of the Discipline*. Syracuse, NY: Syracuse University Press, 1987.

MANNING, SYLVIA B. *Dickens As Satirist*. New Haven: Yale University Press, 1971.

MANSFIELD, ELIZABETH, ed. *D. H. Lawrence: The Trespasser*. Cambridge: Cambridge University Press, 1912.

MANUEL, M. and **K. AYYAPPA PARKER**, eds. *English and India: Essays Presented to Professor Samuel Mathai on His Seventieth Birthday*. Madras, India: Wasani for Macmillan, 1978.

MARCUS, JANE, ed. *New Feminist Essays on Virginia Woolf*. Lincoln: University of Nebraska Press, 1981.

———, ed. *Virginia Woolf and Bloomsbury: A Centenary Celebration*. Bloomington: Indiana University Press, 1987.

———, ed. *Virginia Woolf: A Feminist Slant.* Lincoln: University of Nebraska Press, 1983.

MARCUS, STEVEN. *Dickens: From Pickwick to Dombey.* New York: Basic Books, 1965.

———. *Representatives: Essays on Literature and Society.* New York: Random House, 1975.

MARKOVIC, VIDA E. *The Changing Face: Disintegration of Personlity in the Twentieth-Century British Novel, 1900–1950.* Carbondale: Southern Illinois University Press, 1970.

The Mark Twain Journal 21 (Fall 1983).

MARSHALL, DONALD G., ed. *Literature as Philosophy/Philosophy as Literature.* Iowa City: University of Iowa Press, 1987.

MARTIN, AUGUSTINE. *Charles Dickens: Hard Times.* Dublin: Gill & Macmillan, 1974.

The Massachusetts Review: A Quarterly of Literature, the Arts and Public Affairs 25 (Summer 1984).

Massachusetts Studies in English 3 (Fall 1972)–10 (Fall 1985).

MASUL, MICHIO, and **MASAMI TANABE**, eds. *Literature and Language of Dickens: Essays and Studies in Commemoration of the Centenary of the Death of Dickens.* Tokyo: Sanseido, 1972.

MARUCCI, FRANCO, and **ADRIANO BRUTTINI**, ed. *La performance del testo.* Siena: Ticci, 1986.

Mathematics Teacher (May 1962).

MATEJKA, LADISLAW, and **KRYSTYNA POMORSKA**. *Readings in Russian Poetics: Formalist and Structualist Views.* Cambridge, MA: MIT Press, 1971.

MATSUURA, NAOMI, ed. *Eibungaku to no Deai.* Kyoto: Showado, 1983.

MAUGHAM, W. SOMERSET. *The Art of Fiction: An Introduction to Ten Novels and Their Authors.* London: Heinemann, 1954.

MAYBURY, JAMES F., and **MARJORIE A. ZERBEL**, eds. *Franklin Pierce Studies in Literature: 1981.* Rindge, NH: Franklin Pierce College Press, 1982.

MAYHEAD, ROBIN. *Understanding Literature.* Cambridge: Cambridge University Press, 1965.

Meanjin 24 (1965)–44 (June 1985).

DE MEESTER, MARIE E. *Oriental Influence in English Literature of the Nineteenth Century*. Amsterdam: Swets & Zeitlunger, 1967.

MEIER, THOMAS FOHRBECK, and **ELFI BETTINGER**, eds. *Von Shakespeare bis Chomsky: Arbeiten zur englischen Philologie an der Freien Universitat Berlin*. Frankfurt: Peter Lang, 1987.

MELADA, IVAN. *The Capital of Industry in English Fiction, 1821–1871*. Albuquerque: University of New Mexico Press, 1970.

———. *Sheridan La Fanu*. Boston: Twayne, 1987.

MENDILOW, A. A., ed. *Further Studies in English Language and Literature*. Jerusalem: The Hebrew University, 1973.

[London] *Mercury* (May 1928).

Merkur: Deutsche Zeitschrift fur Europaisches Denken 38 (April 1984)–41 (November 1987).

MERRY, BRUCE. *The Anatomy of the Spy Thriller*. London: Macmillan, 1977.

MEYERS, JEFFREY. *Painting and the Novel*. Manchester, England: Manchester University Press, 1975.

———. *Fiction and the Colonial Experience*. Totowa, NJ: Rowman & Littlefield; Ipswitch: Boydell, 1975.

———, ed. *Graham Greene: A Revaluation*. New York: St. Martin's, 1990.

MFS: Modern Fiction Studies 1 (November 1955)–39 (Spring 1993).

The Michigan Quarterly Review 16 (1977)–22 (Fall 1983).

The Mid–American Review 12, no. 2 (1992).

The Mid–Hudson Language Studies 4 (1981)–12, no. 1 (1989).

The Midwest Quarterly: A Journal of Contemporary Thought 19 (Winter 1978)–35 (Spring 1994).

MIKO, STEPHEN, ed. *Twentieth Century Interpretations of "Women in Love."* Englewood Cliffs, NJ: Prentice-Hall, 1969.

MILLER, J. HILLIS. *Charles Dickens: The World of His Novels*. Cambridge, MA: Harvard University Press, 1958.

———. *The Disappearance of God: Five Nineteenth-Century Writers*. Cambridge, MA: Harvard University Press, 1963.

———. *Fiction and Repetition: Seven English Novels*. Cambridge, MA: Harvard University Press, 1982.

Minas Gerais, Suplemento Literario 24 (January 1991).

Minas Tirith Evening Star: Journal of the American Tolkien Society 13 (November–December 1984)–16 (Winter 1987).

MINERVA, NADIA, and **VITA FORTUNATI**, eds. *Per una definizione dell'utopia: Metodologie e discipline a confronto*. Ravenna: Longo, 1992.

MINTZ, SAMUEL I., ALICE CHANDLER, and **CHRISTOPHER MULVEY**, eds. *From Smollet to James: Studies in the Novel and Other Essays Presented to Edgar Johnson*. Charlottesville: University Press of Virginia, 1981.

Mirror 2 (December 1847).

Miscellanea 1 (1971).

Mississippi Quarterly: The Journal of Southern Culture 40 (Spring 1987).

The Missouri Review 3 (Fall 1979).

Mitteilungen des Verbandes deutscher Anglisten 4 (March 1993).

MJLF 12 (Spring 1986).

MLN (formerly *Modern Language Notes*) 38 (1923)–108 (December 1993).

MLQ: Modern Language Quarterly: A Journal of Literary History (formerly *Modern Language Quarterly*) 11 (July 1950)–89 (April 1994).

The Modern Age: A Quarterly Review 27 (Winter 1983)–33 (Summer 1991).

Moderna Språk 67, no. 4 (1973)–86, no. 2 (1992).

The Modern Austrian Literature 26, no. 1 (1993).

Modern British Literature 2 (1977).

Der Moderne Englische Roman 51 (1966).

Modernist Studies: Literature and Culture 1920–1940 4 (1982).

The Modern Language Review 39 (March 1944)–89 (April 1994).

Modern Language Studies 1 (1971)–16 (Summer 1986).

Modern Philology: A Journal Devoted to Research in Medieval and Modern Literature 57 (1960)–86 (August 1988).

MONAGHAN, DAVID, ed. *Jane Austen in a Social Context*. Totowa, NJ: Barnes & Noble, 1981.

MONOD, SYLVÉRE. *Dickens the Novelist*. Norman: University of Oklahoma Press, 1968.

———. Preface. *De William Shakespeare à William Golding: Mélanges dediés à la mémoire de Jean-Pierre Vernier*. Rouen: Université de Rouen, 1984.

Month 5 (April 1951).

MOORE, GENE M., ed. *Conrad's Cities: Essays for Hans van Marle*. Amsterdam: Rodopi, 1992.

MOORE, HARRY T., ed. *The Boy in the Bush*. Carbondale: Southern Illinois University Press, 1971.

———, ed. *A D. H. Lawrence Miscellany*. Carbondale: Southern Illinois University Press, 1959.

———. *Lady Chamberlain's Lover*. New York: New American Library, 1962.

MORAN, CHARLES, and **ELIZABETH F. PENFIELD**, eds. *Conversations: Contemporary Critical Thinking and the Teaching of Literature*, Urbana, IL: National Council of Teachers of English, 1990.

MORDELL, ALBERT, ed. *Literary Reviews and Essays on American, English, and French Literature*. New York: Twayne, 1957.

Moreana: Bulletin Thomas More 21 (June 1984).

MORIMATSU, KENSUKE. *Eikoku Shosetsu Kenkyu Dai 13 satsu*. Tokyo: Shinozaki, 1981.

MORREAL, JOHN, ed. *The Ninth LACUS Forum 1982*. Columbia, SC: Hornbeam, 1983.

MORRIS, ROBERT K., ed. *Old Lines, New Forces: Essays on the Contemporary British Novels, 1960–1970*. Rutherford, NJ: Fairleigh Dickinson University Press, 1976.

MORROW, PATRICK D. *Katherine Mansfield's Fiction*. Bowling Green, OH: Popular, 1993.

MORSE, DONALD E., MARSHALL B. TYMN, and **CSILLA BERTHA**, eds. *The Celebration of the Fantastic: Selected Papers from the Tenth Anniversary International Conference on the Fantastic in the Arts*. Westport, CT: Greenwood Press, 1992.

Mosaic: A Journal for the Interdisciplinary Study of Literature 10 (Fall 1977)–27 (September 1994).

MOSELEY, EDWIN M. *Pseudonyms of Christ in the Modern Novel: Motifs and Methods*. Pittsburgh: University of Pittsburgh Press, 1962.

MOST, GLENN W., and **WILLIAM W. STOWE**, eds. *The Poetics of Murder: Detective Fiction and Literary Theory*. New York: Harcourt, Brace, 1983.

MORTIMER, ANTHONY, ed. *Contemporary Approaches to Narrative*. Tubingen: Gunter Narr, 1984.

MORTON, A. L. *The Matter of Britain: Essays on a Living Culture*. London: Laurence & Wishart, 1966.

Mount Olive Review 3 (Spring 1989).

MOYNIHAN, WILLIAM T., ed. *Joyce's 'The Dead.'* Boston: Allyn & Bacon, 1965.

MULLENBROCK, HEINZ-JOACHIM, and **ALFONS KLEIN**, eds. *Motive and Themen in englischsprachiger Literatur als Indikatoren literaturgeschichtlicher Prozesse: Festschrift zum 65. Geburtstag von Theodor Wolpers*. Tubingen: Niemeyer, 1990.

———, and **RENATE NOLL-WIEMANN**, eds. *Anglistentag 1988 Gottingen: Vortrage*. Tubingen: Niemeyer, 1989.

MURFIN, ROSS C., ed. *Conrad Revisited: Essays for the Eighties*. University: University of Alabama Press, 1985.

———, ed. *Joseph Conrad: "Heart of Darkness,"* New York: St. Martin's, 1989.

Mystery & Detection Annual 1972.

Mystery FANcier 4 (March 1980)–8 (May–June 1984).

Mythes, Croyances et Religions dans le Monde Anglo–Saxon 1 (1983)–7 (1989).

Mythlore: A Journal of the J. R. R. Tolkien, C. S. Lewis, Charles Williams, and the Genres of Myth and Fantasy Studies 2 (Winter 1971)–19 (Summer 1993).

Nabokovian 20 (Spring 1988).

Names: Journal of the American Name Society 28 (June 1980) 29 (June 1981)–40 (June 1992).

NAGEL, JAMES. *Suggestions for Teaching 'Vision and Value: A Thematic Introduction to the Short Story*. Belmont, CA: Dickenson, 1970.

The Nassau Review: The Journal of Nassau Community College Devoted to Arts, Letters, and Sciences 4, no. 3 (1982)–5, no. 2 (1986).

NATHAN, RHODA B., ed. *Nineteenth-Century Women Writers of the English-Speaking World*. Westport, CT: Greenwood, 1986.

The Nation 100 (11 February 1915)–223 (18 December 1976).

The Nation and Athenaeum 37 (1925).

The National Review 29 (23 December 1977)–47 (May 1995).

The Natal University Law Review 1, no. 4 (1975).

NATOLI, JOSEPH, ed. *Psychological Perspectives on Literature: Freudian Dissidents and Non-Freudians: A Casebook.* Hamden, CT: Archon, 1984.

Neohelicon: Acta Comparationis Litterarum Universarum 10, no. 2 (1983)–14, no. 2 (1987).

Neophilologus 72 (January 1988)–73 (April 1989).

NERSESOVA, M. A. *Kholodnii dom Dikkensa.* Moscow: Khudozh, Lit., 1971.

NESTOR, PAULINE, ed. *Charlotte Brontë's "Jane Eyre."* New York: St. Martin's, 1992.

Die Neue Deutsche Hefte 34, no. 4 (1987).

Die Neue Gesellschoft/Frankfurt Hefte 39, no. 11–12 (1984).

Die Neueren Sprachen 6 (April 1957)–86 (April 1987).

Die Neue Schweizer Rundschau n.s. 19 (July 1951)

Neusprachliche Mitteilungen aus Wissenschaft und Praxis 36, no. 3 (1983)–37 (February 1984).

New Blackfriars 53 (October 1972).

New Comparison: A Journal of Comparative and General Literary Studies 3 (Summer 1987)–9 (Spring 1990).

The New Criterion 6 (March 1988)–11 (March 1992).

The New England Quarterly: A Historical Review of New England Life and Letters 21 (September 1948).

The New Hampshire College Journal 6 (Spring 1989).

New Letters: A Magazine of Fine Writing 47 (Summer 1981).

The New Literary History: A Journal of Theory and Interpretation 3 (Autumn 1971)–24 (Summer 1993).

New Orleans Review 8 (Winter 1981)–18 (Spring 1991).

New Quest 77 (July–August 1972).

The New Republic 5 (25 December 1915)–214 (29 April 1996).

New Review 5, no. 2 (1978).

The Newsletter of Victorian Studies Association of Western Canada 11 (Spring 1985)–13 (Fall 1987).

The New Statesman 5 (25 September 1915)–100 (11 July 1980).

The New Statesman and Leader (13 September 1841).

The New Statesman and Nation 17 (18 March 1939)–50 (5 November 1955).

The New Statesman and Society 4 (6 September 1991)–7 (24 June 1994).

Newsweek 78 (October 1971).

The New Yorker 22 (15 November 1946)–53 (26 December 1977).

The New York Literary Forum 7 (1980).

The New York Review of Books 14 (9 November 1967)–43 (15 February 1996).

The New York Review of Science Fiction 50 (October 1992).

The New York State Journal of Medicine 71 (15 December 1971).

The New York Times Book Review (10 December 1922)–(14 January 1996).

The New Welsh Review 1 (Autumn 1988)–3 (Spring 1991).

The New Worlds 48 (September/October 1964)–50 (July 1966).

NICHOLS, DUANE, ed. *Kansas English.* Lawrence: University of Kansas Press, 1970.

De Nieuwe Taalids: Tijdschrift voor Neerlandici 75 (May 1982).

Nineteenth-Century Literature (formerly *Nineteenth-Century Fiction*) 4 (1949–50)–49 (June 1994).

Nineteenth-Century Studies 2 (1988).

NISBET, ADA, and **BLAKE NEVIUS**, eds. *Dickens Centennial Essays.* Berkeley and Los Angeles: University of California Press, 1971.

NISCHIK, REINGARD M., and **BARBARA KORTE**, eds. *Modes of Narrative: Approaches to American, Canadian and British Fiction.* Wurzburg: Konigshausen & Neumann, 1990.

NOBILE, ANDREW, ed. *Robert Lewis Stevenson.* London: Vision; Totowa, NJ: Barnes & Noble, 1983.

NODELMAN, PERRY, ed. *Touchstones: Reflections on the Best in Children's Literature, Volume One.* West Lafayette, WI: Children's Literature Association Press, 1985.

NOLL-WIEMANN, RENATE. *Der Kunstler im englischen Roman des 19. Jahrhunderts*. Heidelberg: Winter 1977.

The North American Mentor Magazine 19 (Spring 1981)–24 (Fall 1986).

The North American Review 212 (November 1920)–225 (January 1928).

North Dakota Quarterly 34 (Spring 1969)–57 (Summer 1989).

The Northern New England Review 10 (1983).

Northhamptonshire Past and Present 6 (1980).

The North Wind: Journal of the George MacDonald Society 3 (1984).

Notes and Queries 159 (15 Novemeber 1930)–n.s. 40 (December 1993).

Notes on Contemporary Literature 2 (November 1972) 23 (May 1993).

Notes on Modern Irish Literature 1 (1989)–4 (1992).

The Notre Dame English Journal 8 (Summer 1981).

Nouvelle Revue Française 42 (1934)–n.s. 36 (November 1970).

Novel: A Forum on Fiction 1 (Fall 1967)–26 (Fall 1992).

NOVY, MARIANNE, ed. *Women's Re-Visions of Shakespeare: On the Responses of Dickinson, Woolf, Rich, H. D. George Eliot, and Other*. Urbana: University of Illinois Press, 1990.

NOWAKOWSKI, JAN, ed. *Littrae et Lingua: In Honorem Premislavi Mroczkowski*. Wroclaw: Polish Akademi Nauk, 1984.

Nueva Revista de Filologia Hispanica 35, no. 2 (1987)–36, no. 2 (1988).

Nueva Revista del Pacifico 19–20 (1981).

OBER, WILLIAM B. *Boswell's Clap, and Other Essays: Medical Analyses of Literary Men's Afflictions*. Carbondale: Southern Illinois University Press, 1979.

Oberon: Magazine for the Study of English and American Literature 31 (1960)–49 (1986).

OBLER, PAUL C. *D. H. Lawrence's World of "The Rainbow,"* Madison, NJ: Drew University Press, 1955.

The Observer (19 July 1964)–(29 October 1980).

O'CONNOR, FRANK. *The Mirror in the Roadway: A Study of the Modern Novel*. New York: Knopf, 1956.

ODDIE, WILLIAM. *Dickens and Carlyle: The Question of Influence*. London: Centenary, 1972.

O'FAOLAIN, SEAN. *Elizabeth Bowen; or Romance Does Not Pay in the Vanishing Hero: Studies in Novelties of the Twenties*. London: Eyre and Spottiswoode, 1956.

———. *The Short Story: A Study in Pleasure*. New York: Devin-Adair, 1951.

Okike: An African Journal of New Writing 13 (1979).

OLANDER, JOSEPH D., and **MARTIN HARRY GREENBERG**, eds. *Arthur C. Clarke*. New York: Taplinger, 1977.

Ons Erfdeel: Algemeen-Nederlands Tweemaandelijks Cultureel Tijdschrift 23 (November–December 1980).

Onomastica Canadiana 70 (December 1988).

The Opera News 53 (February 1989).

The Opera Quarterly 7 (Spring 1990).

OPPEL, HORST, ed. *Der Moderne Englische Roman: Interpretationen*. Berlin: Erich Schmidt Verlag, 1965.

Orbis Litterarum: International Review of Literary Studies 38, no. 2 (1983)–45, no. 1 (1990).

Orcrist 1 (1966–67)–7 (Summer 1973).

ORD, PRISCILLA, ed. *The Child and the Story: An Exploration of Narrative Forms*. Boston: Children's Literature Association, 1983.

The Orient West 9 (May–June 1964).

ORTEGA, RAMÓN LÓPEZ. *Movimiento obrero y novela inglesa*. Salamanca: Universidad de Salamanca, 1976.

OUSBY, IAN. *Bloodhounds of Heaven: The Detective in English Fiction from Godwin to Doyle*. Cambridge, MA: Harvard University Press, 1976.

The Osmania Journal of English Studies 9 (1972)–10 (1973).

The Overland 113 (December 1988).

OWENS, COLIN, ed. *Family Chronicles: Maria Edgeworth's "Castle Rackrent."* Dublin: Wolfhound; Totowa, NJ: Barnes & Noble, 1987.

The Oxford Literary Review 9, no. 1–2 (1987).

Pacific Coast Philology 16 (June 1981)–21 (November 1986).

PAGE, NORMAN. *Dickens: "Hard Times," "Great Expectations," and "Our Mutual Friend": A Casebook*. London: Macmillan, 1979.

———. *Speech in the English Novel*. London: Longman, 1973.

La Palabra y el Hombre: Revista de la Universidad Veracruzana. 65 (January–March 1988).

PALUMBO, DONALD, ed. *Spectrum of the Fantastic: Selected Essays from Sixth International Conference on Fantastic in Arts.* Westport, CT: Greenwood, 1988.

Panjab University Research Bulletin (Arts) 6 (June 1975)–8 (April–October 1977).

Papers on Language and Literature: A Journal for Scholars and Critics of Language and Literature 6 (Spring 1970)–30 (Fall 1994).

PARADIS, JAMES, and **THOMAS POSTLEWAIT**, ed. *Victorian Science and Victorian Values: Literary Perspectives.* New York: New York Academy of Sciences, 1981.

Paragraph: A Journal of Modern Critical Theory 9 (March 1987).

PARIS, BERNARD J., ed. *Third Force Psychology and the Study of Literature.* Rutherford, NJ: Fairleigh Dickinson University Press, 1986.

The Paris Critique 2 (Spring–Summer 1958).

The Paris Review 35 (Summer 1993).

PARKINSON, KATHLEEN, and **MARTIN PRIESTMAN**, eds. *Peasants and Countrymen in Literature.* London: Roehampton Institute, 1982.

Par Rapport: A Journal of the Humanities 3–4 (1980–81).

Partisan Review 16 (March 1949)–59 (Winter 1992).

PARTLOW, ROBERT B., JR., ed. *Dickens the Craftsman: Strategies of Presentation.* Carbondale: Southern Illinois University Press, 1970.

———, and **HARRY T. MOORE**, eds. *D. H. Lawrence: The Man Who Lived.* Carbondale: Southern Illinois University Press, 1980.

Pasajes 7 (1987).

PASCAL, ROY. *The Dual Voice: Free Indirect Speech and its Functioning in the Nineteenth-Century European Novel.* Manchester: Manchester University Press, 1977.

PATE, JANET. *The Black Book of Villians.* London: David & Charles, 1975.

———. *The Book of Skeuths.* London: New English Library, 1977.

Paunch 26 (1966).

PE 12 (Spring 1986).

Peake Studies 1 (Summer 1990).

PENNINGER, FREIDA ELAINE, ed. *A Festschrift for Professor Marguerite Roberts*. Richmond VA: University of Richmond Press.

PEARCE, T. S. *George Eliot*. London: Evans, 1973.

Permskii Universitet 188 (1968).

Perspective 9 (Summer 1957)–11 (1959).

Perspectives on Contemporary Literature 11 (1985).

Persuasions: Journal of the Jane Austen Society of North America 1 (December 1979)–13 (16 December 1991).

PETERSON, AUDREY. *Victorian Masters of Mystery: From Wilkie Collins to Conan Doyle*. New York: Ungar, 1984.

PETERSON, RICHARD F., ALAN M. COHN, and **EDMUND L. EPSTEIN**, eds. *Work in Progress: Joyce Centenary Essays*. Carbondale: Southern Illinois University Press, 1983.

DE PIETRIS, CARLA, ed. *Joyce Studies in Italy, II*. Rome: Bulzoni, 1988.

PFISTER, MANFRED, ed. *Alternative Welten*. Munich: Fink; 1982.

PHELAN, JAMES, ed. *Narrative Poetics: Innovations, Limits, Challenges*. Columbus: Center for Comparative Studies in Humanities, Ohio State University, 1987.

———, ed. *Reading Narrative: Form, Ethics, Ideology*. Colombus: Ohio States University Press, 1989.

PHELPS, GILBERT. *A Reader's Guide to Fifty British Novels 1600–1900*. London: Heinemann, 1979.

Philologia Pragensia 9 (1966)–13, no. 4 (1970).

Philological Quarterly 32 (October 1953)–68 (Fall 1989).

Philosophical Studies: An International Journal for Philosophy in the Analytic Tradition 50 (November 1986)–51 (January 1987).

Philosophy: The Journal of the British Institute of Philosophical Studies 65 (April 1990)–67 (April 1992).

Philosophy and Literature 2 (Fall 1978)–16 (April 1992).

Philosophy and Phenomenological Research 27 (March 1967).

PICKERING, SAMUEL F. *The Moral Tradition in English Fiction, 1785–1850*. Hanover, NH: Dartmouth College Press, 1976.

PILLING, JOHN, and **MARY BRYDEN**, eds. *The Ideal Core of the Onion: Reading Beckett Archives*. Bristol: Beckett International Foundation, 1992.

Platte Valley Review 11 (Spring 1983).

Plein–Chant 42–43 (Fall 1988).

The Plum Lines Supplement 3 (November 1982).

Plural: Revista Cultural de Excelsior 16 (September 1987).

PN Review 15, no. 1–15, no. 4 (1989).

Poetica: Zeitschrift für Sprach- und Literaturwissenschaft 12, no. 1 (1980)–23, no. 1–2 (1991).

Poetics Today 2 (Winter 1981)–8 (Summer 1987).

Poétique: Revue de Theorie et d'Analyse Litteraires 11 (November 1980)–23 (November 1992).

POLHEMUS, ROBERT M. *Erotic Faith: Being in Love from Jane Austen to D. H. Lawrence*. Chicago: University of Chicago Press, 1990.

Polish Review 29, no. 3 (1984).

PORTER, KATHERINE ANNE. *The Days Before*. New York: Harcourt, 1952.

Postscript: Publication of the Philological Association of the Carolinas 4 (1987)–7 (1990).

POTTER, ROSANNE G., ed. *Literary Computing and Literary Criticism: Theoretical and Practical Essays on Theme and Rhetoric*. Philadelphia: University of Pennsylvania Press, 1989.

POTYHET, LUCIEN. *Littérature linguistique civilisation pédagogie*. Paris: Didier, 1976.

POWELL, CHERYL C. *Redemption for the Protagonist in Three Novels by John le Carré*. Tallahassee: Florida State University, 1991.

POWELL, LAWRENCE CLARK. *Southwest Classics: The Creative Literature of the Arid Lands, Essays on the Books and Their Writers*. Los Angeles: Ward Ritchie, 1974.

Powys Notes 6 (Spring–Summer 1990)–7 (Spring–Summer 1991).

The Powys Review 6, no. 1 (1987–88)–8, no. 2 (1991).

Prague Studies in English 12 (1967).

The Prairie Schooner 55 (Spring–Summer 1981).

The Pre-Raphaelite Review 3 (November 1982)–3 (May 1983).

Pretexts: Studies in Writing and Culture 2 (Winter 1990).

The Princeton University Library Chronicle 35 (Autumn–Winter 1973)–44 (Spring 1983).

Problemi: Periodico Quadrimestrale di Cultura (Yugoslavia) 25, no. 6 (1987).

The Proceedings of the Conference of College Teachers of English of Texas 41 (September 1976).

Prose Studies: History, Theory, Criticism 6 (September 1983)–9 (May 1986).

Proteus: A Journal of Ideas 3 (Fall 1986)–6 (Spring 1989).

Proverbium: Yearbook of International Proverb Scholarship 6 (1989).

Proust Research Association Newsletter 25 (Summer 1986).

The Psychoanalytic Review 3 (1916)–62 (1975–76).

The Psychocultural Review 1 (Winter 1977).

The Psychohistory Review 12 (Fall 1983).

Psychological Reports 72 (February 1993).

Publications of the Arkansas Philological Association 1 (Fall 1974)–15 (April 1989).

Publications of the Mississippi Philological Association (1984)–(1986).

PMLA: Publications of the Modern Language Association 54 (March 1939)–109 (March 1994).

PRASAD, R. C., and **A. K. SHARMA**, eds. *Modern Studies and Other Essays in Honour of Dr. R. K. Sinha*. New Delhi: Vikas, 1987.

PRESTON, PETER, and **PETER HOARE**, eds. *D. H. Lawrence in the Modern World*. Cambridge: Cambridge University Press, 1989.

PRICKETT, STEPHEN. *Victorian Fantasy*. Hassocks, Sussex: Harvester, 1979.

PRIESTLY, J. B. *The English Comic Characters*. Staten Island, NY: Phaeton, 1972.

PRITCHETT, V. S. *The Living Novel and Later Appreciations*. New York: Random House, 1964.

———, ed. *Wuthering Heights*. Boston: Houghton Mifflin, 1956.

Prose Studies: History, Theory, Criticism 6 (September 1983).

Punch 26 (October 1966)–(2 March 1983).

PYKETT, LYN, *Emily Brontë*. Basingstoke, England: Macmillan Educational, 1989.

Quaderni di Filologia Germanica della Facolta di Lettere e Filosofia dell'Universita di Bologna 3 (1984).

Quaderni di Lingue e Letterature 2 (1977)–6 (1981).

Quadrant 26 (June 1982)–28 (July–August 1984).

The Queen's Quarterly 77 (Summer 1970)–93 (Summer 1986).

Quimera: Revista de Literatura 53 (n.d.)–65 (n.d.).

La Quinzaine Littéraire 316 (January 1980)–463 (16–31 May 1986).

RABAN, JONATHAN. *The Technique of Modern Fiction: Essays in Practical Criticism*. London: Arnold, 1968; Notre Dame: University of Notre Dame Press, 1969.

RABKIN, ERIC S. *Narrative Suspense: 'When Slim turned Sideways . . . .'* Ann Arbor: University of Michigan Press, 1973.

———, **MARTIN H. GREENBERG**, and **JOSEPH D. OLANDER**, eds. *No Place Else: Explorations in Utopian and Disutopian Fiction*. Carbondale: Southern Illinois University Press, 1983.

Race & Class 25 (1984).

The Rag: Abiko Literary Quarterly 11 (Winter 1992–1993).

RAIMONDI, EZIO, and **BRUNO BASILE**, eds. *Dal Novellino a Moravia: Problemi della narrativa*. Bologna: Mulino, 1979.

VON RAINER LENGELER, HRSG, ed. *Englische Literatur der Gegenwart*. Dusseldorf: August Bogek, 1977.

Rajasthau University Studies in English 6 (1972).

Rally 1 (August 1966).

RAMSON, WILLIAM S., ed. *The Australian Experience: Critical Essays on Australian Novels*. Canberra: Australian National University Press, 1976.

RANCE, NICHOLAS. *The Historical Novel and Popular Politics in Nineteenth-Century England*. London: Vision; New York: Barnes & Noble, 1975.

Raritan: A Quarterly Review 9 (Fall 1989)–11 (Spring 1991).

RATHBURN, ROBERT C., and **MARTIN STEINMANN, JR.**, eds. *From Jane Austen to Joseph Conrad.* Minneapolis: University of Minnesota Press, 1958.

RAWSON, CLAUDE, ed. *English Satire and the Satiric Tradition.* Oxford: Basil Blackwell, 1984.

Razgledi: Spisanie za Literatura Umetnost I Kultura 10 (December 1983).

REAL: The Yearbook of Research in English and American Literature 9 (1992).

Recherches Anglaises et Americaines 15 (1982)–17 (1984).

Recovering Literature: A Journal of Contextualist Criticism 1 (Fall 1972)–16 (1988).

Red Letters: A Journal of Cultural Politics 11 (1981).

REDMAN, BEN RAY, ed. *Trent's Case Book.* New York: Knopf, 1964.

REDMOND, JAMES, ed. *Melodrama.* Cambridge: Cambridge University Press, 1992.

REED, WALTER L., *Meditations on the Hero: A Study of the Romantic Hero in Nineteenth-Century Fiction.* New Haven: Yale University Press, 1974.

Regionalism and the Female Imagination 4 (Fall 1978).

Religion and Literature 16 (Autumn 1984)–22 (Spring 1990).

Renaissance and Modern Studies 10 (1966).

Renascence: Essays on Value in Literature 1 (Spring 1949)–38 (Spring 1986).

Representation 1 (February 1983).

Representations 6 (Spring 1984)–31 (Summer 1990).

República de las Letras 9 (January 1984).

Research in African Literatures 12 (Spring 1981).

Research Studies 44 (1976)–50 (June 1982).

Restant: Tijdschrift voor Recente Semiotische Teorievorming en de Analyse van Teksten/Review for Semiotic Theory 10 (Fall 1982)–15, no. 2 (1987).

La Revue Hebdomadaire 44 (4 May 1935).

The Review of Contemporary Fiction 5 (Spring 1985)–5 (Spring 1995).

The Review of English Studies: A Quarterly Journal of English Literature and the English Language 1 (1950)–45 (February 1994).

The Review of Politics 27 (July 1965).

Revista Alicantina de Estudios Ingleses 1 (November 1987)–5 (November 1992).

Revista Canaria de Estudios Ingleses 10 (April 1985)–15 (November 1987).

Revista Chilena de Literatura 29 (April 1987).

Revista da Faculdade de Letras 3, no. 3 (1959).

Revista de Filologia de la Universidad de La Lingua 2 (1983)–3 (1984).

Revista de Occidente 33–34 (1984).

Revue de la Pensée Française 10 (April 1951).

Revue de la Universidad de Costa Rica 41 (1975).

Revue de Littérature Comparée 59 (January–March 1985)–64 (July–September 1990).

Revue des langues vivantes (*Tidschrift voor Levende Talen*) 26, no. 6 (1966)–41 (1975).

La Revue des Lettres Modernes: Histoire des Idées et des Littératures 953–958 (1990).

La Revue de Paris 72 (1965).

Revue des Sciences Humaines 4, no. 188 (1982).

Revue Roumaine de Linguistique (incorporates *Cahiers de Linguistique Théorique et Appliquée*). 26 (November–December 1981)–31 (1986).

REYNOLDS, MARY T., ed. *James Joyce: A Collection of Critical Essays.* Englewood Cliffs, NJ: Prentice-Hall, 1993.

REXROTH, KENNETH. *The Elastic Retort: Essays in Lterature and Ideas.* New York: Seabury, 1973.

RHYS, ERNEST, ed. *Modern English Essays, 1870–1920 vol. I.* London: Dent, 1922.

Rice University Studies 61 (Winter 1975).

RICHARDSON, MAURICE, and **U. C. KNOEPFLMACHER**, eds. *Novels of Mystery from the Victorian Age.* London: Pilot, 1945.

RIGAUD, NADIA, J., ed. *La Estranger dans la littérature et la pensée.* Aix-en-Provence: Université de Provence, 1989.

———, ed. *L'Implicite dans la littérature et la pensée anglaises.* Aix-en-Provence: Université de Provence, 1984.

———, ed. *La Marginalite dans la littérature et la pensée anglaises*. Aix-en-Provence: Université de Provence, 1983.

———, ed. *Le Monstrueux dans la littérature et la pensée anglaises*. Aix-en-Provence: Université de Provence, 1985.

———, and **DENISOT, PAUL**, eds. *La Violence dans la littérature et la pensée anglaises*. Aix-en-Provence: Université de Provence, 1989.

RIGNEY, BARBARA HILL. *Lilith's Daughters: Women and Religion in Contemporary Fiction*. Madison: University of Wisconsin Press, 1982.

RILEY, DICK, ed. *Critical Encounters: Writiers and Themes in Science Fiction*. New York: Ungar, 1978.

RINGBOM, HAKEN, and **MATTI RISSANEN**, eds. *Proceedings from the Second Nordic Conference for English Studies*. Abo: Abo Akademi, 1984.

Riverside Quarterly 1 (Auguest 1965)–8 (July 1990).

Rivista di Letterature Moderne e Comparate 24 (1973)–43 (October–December 1990).

RLA: Romance Languages Annual 1 (1989).

The Rocky Mountain Review of Language and Literature 29 (Spring 1975).

ROHRBERGER, MARY. *Hawthorne and the Modern Short Story: A Study in Genre*. Hague: Mouton, 1966.

Romance Notes 19 (Winter 1978)–24 (Winter 1983).

The Romantist 4–5 (1980–81).

ROSE, ELLEN CRONAN, ed. *Critical Essays on Margaret Drabble*. Boston: G. K. Hall, 1985.

ROSE, PHYLLIS. *The Writing of Women: Essays in Renaissance*. Middletown, CT: Wesleyan University Press, 1985.

ROSS, CHARLES L. ed. *Lawrence's "Women in Love."* Harmondsworth, England: Penguin, 1982.

ROSS, ROBERT L., ed. *International Literature in English: Essays on the Major Writers*. New York: Garland, 1991.

The Round Table (1913).

The Round Table of South Central College English Association 27 (Fall 1987).

RUSSELL, DAVID G., DAVID F. MARKS, and **JOHN T. E. RICHARDSON**, eds. *Imagery* 2. Dunedin, New Zealand: Human Performance Associates, 1986.

Russkaia Literatura: Istoriko-Literaturnyî Zhurnal 3 (1981).

RUTHERFORD, ANDREW, ed. *Twentieth Century Interpretations of "A Passage to India,"* Englewood Cliffs, NJ: Prentice Hall, 1970.

DE RYALS, CLYDE L., ed. *Nineteenth-Century Literary Perspectives: Essays in Honor of Lionel Stevenson*. Durham, NC: Duke University Press, 1974.

RYCROFT, CHARLES, ed. *Imagination and Reality: Psycho-Analytic Essays, 1951–1961*. London: Hogarth Press and the Institute of Psycho-Analysis, 1968.

RYF, ROBERT S. *A New Approach to Joyce: The Portrait of the Artist as a Guidebook*. Berkely: University of California Press, 1962.

SACIUK, OLENA H., ed. *The Shape of the Fantastic: Selected Essays from the Seventh International Conference on the Fantastic in the Arts*. Westbrook, CT: Greenwood, 1990.

SACKVILLE-WEST, EDWARD, *Inclinations*. London: Secker & Warburg, 1949.

SAGAR, KEITH, ed. "*Sons and Lovers*." Harmondsworth, England: Penguin, 1981.

St Inglesi 2 (1975).

Saint Louis University Research Journal of the Graduate School of Arts and Sciences 15 (June 1984).

SAKURAI, MARIKO. *Phoenix o Motomete: Eibei Shosetsu no Yukue*. Tokyo: Nan'undo, 1982.

SALE, WILLIAM M., JR., ed. *Wuthering Heights*. New York: Norton, 1972.

SALGADO, GAMINI, and **G. K. DAS**, ed. *The Spirit of D. H. Lawrence: Centenary Studies*. Totowa, NJ: Barnes & Noble, 1988.

SAN JUAN, EPIFANIO, JR. *James Joyce and the Craft of Fiction: An Interpretation of "Dubliners*." Rutherford, NJ: Fairleigh Dickinson University Press, 1972.

Samtiden: Tidsskrift for Politikk, Litteratur og Samfunnssporsmal 1 (1987).

The San Francisco Review of Books (January 1978).

San José Studies 8 (1982)–9 (Spring 1983).

SANTANA, PEDRO. *Actas de las Ijornadas de Lenguay Literatura Inglesa y Norteamericana*. Legrono: Publications Del Colegio Universidad de Logrono, 1990.

The Saturday Review of Literature, Arts (6 September 1902)–5 (7 January 1978).

SAVAGE, ROBERT L., JAMES COMBA, and **DAN NIMMO**, eds. *The Orwellian Moment: Hindsight and Foresight in the Post-1984 World*. Fayetteville: University of Arkansas Press, 1989.

Sayers Review 4, no. (1977).

Schlern (Bolzano) 64 (February 1990).

The Science Fiction: A Review of Speculative Literature 1 (June 1977)–19 (July 1992).

Science Fiction Studies 1 (Spring 1973)–18 (November 1991).

SCHILLING, BERNARD N. *The Comic Spirit: Boccaccio to Thomas Mann*. Detroit, MI: Wayne State University Press, 1965.

SCHMIDT, DOREY, and **JAN SEALE**, eds. *Margaret Drabble: Golden Realms*. Edinburg, TX: School of Humanities, Pan American University Press, 1982.

SCHOFIELD, MARY ANNE, and **CECILIA MACHESKI**, eds. *Fetter'd or Free? British Women Novelists, 1670–1815*. Athens: Ohio University Press, 1986.

SCHOENBAUM, SAMUEL. *Shakespeare's Lives*. Oxford: Claredon, 1970.

SCHORER, MARK, ed. *Modern British Fiction: Essays in Criticism*. New York: Oxford University Press, 1961.

SCHUHMANN, KUNO, et al., eds. *Miscellanea Anglo-Americana: Festschrift fü Helmut Vierbrock*. Munich: Pressler, 1974.

SCHWARZBACH, F. S. *Dickens and the City*. London: Athlone, 1979.

SCOTT, PAUL. *Essays by Divers Hands*. London: Oxford University Press, 1970.

Scottish Literary Journal: A Review of Studies in Scottish Language and Literature 8 (May 1981)–19 (May 1992).

SCOTT, PETER JAMES MALCOLM. *Reality and Comic Confidence in Charles Dickens*. London: Macmillan, 1979.

Scriobh 5 (1981).

Scrutiny 6 (1937)–14 (1946–47).

SEEBER, HANS ULRICH, and **PAUL GERHARD KLUSSMANN**, eds. *Idylle und Modernisierung in der europaischen Literatur des 19. Jahrhunderts*. Bonn: Bouvier, 1986.

SEEHASE, GEORG. *Charles Dickens, zu einer Besonderheit seines Realismus*. Halle: Niemeyer, 1961.

SEKINE, MASARU, ed. *Irish Writers and Society at Large*. Gerrards Cross, Buckinghamshire: Smythe; Totowa, NJ: Barnes & Noble, 1985.

Seven: An Anglo–American Literary Review 1 (March 1980)–9 (March 1988).

Sewanee Review 71 (1963)–89 (Winter 1989).

SHAHANE, VASANT A., ed. *Perspectives on E. M. Forster's "A Passage to India."* New York: Barnes & Noble, 1968.

———, ed. *Approaches to E. M. Forster: A Centenary Volume*. New Delhi: Arnold-Heinemann; Atlantic Highlands, NJ: Humanities, 1981.

———, ed. *Focus on Forster's "A Passage to India."* Madras: Orient Longman, 1975.

SHALVI, ALICE, and **A. A. MENDILOW**, eds. *Studies in English Language and Literature*. Jerusalem: Hebrew University Press, 1966.

SHAPIRO, CHARLES, ed. *Contemporary British Novelists*. Carbondale: Southern Illinois University Press, 1965.

SHARMA, T. R., ed. *Influence of Bhagavadgita on Literature Written in English*. Meerut: Shalabh, 1988.

SHATTOCK, JOANNE, ed. *Dickens and Other Victorians: Essays in Honor of Philip Collins*. New York: St. Martin's, 1988.

SHAW, W. DAVID. *Victorians and Mystery: Crises of Representation*. Ithaca, NY: Cornell University Press, 1990.

Shenandoah: The Washington & Lee University Review (formerly *Shenandoah*) 18 (1967).

The Sherlock Holmes Review 2, no. 1 (n.d.).

SHIMIZU, KOYA. *Muraoka Isamu Sensei Kiju Kinen Ronbunshu: Eibungaku Shiron*. Tokyo: Kinseido, 1983.

SHIRES, LINDA M., ed. *Rewriting the Victorians: Theory, History, and the Politics of Gender*. New York: Routledge, 1922.

Shiron 24 (1985)–25 (1986).

Shoin Literature Review 18 (1984).

SHOWALTER, ELAINE, ed. *Speaking of Gender*. New York: Routledge, 1989.

SIEBENHELLER, NORMA. *P. D. James*. New York: Ungar, 1981.

Signs: Journal of Women in Culture and Society 16 (Winter 1991).

Sky & Telescope 80 (July 1990).

SLADE, JOSEPH W., and **JUDITH YAROSS LEE**, eds. *Beyond the Two Cultures: Essays on Science, Technology, and Literature*. Ames: Iowa State University Press, 1990.

SLATER, MICHAEL, ed. *Dickens 1970*. London: Chapman & Hall, 1970.

Slavic and Eastern European Journal 29 (Winter 1985).

SLAY, JACK, JR. *Ian McEwan*. New York: Twayne, 1996.

SLUSSER, GEORGE EDGAR, COLIN GREELAND, and **ERIC S. RABKIN**, eds. *Storm Warnings: Science Fiction Confronts the Future*. Carbondale: Southern Illinois University Press, 1987.

———, and **ERIC S. RABIN**, eds. *Mindscapes: The Geographies of Imagined Worlds*. Carbondale: Southern Illinois University Press, 1989.

SMITH, ANNE, ed. *Lawrence and Women*. London: Vision, 1978.

———, ed. *The Novels of Thomas Hardy*. London: Vision, 1979.

SMITH, GRAHAME. *Charles Dickens: "Bleak House."* London: Arnold, 1974.

SMITH, JOHN HAZEL, ed. *Brandeis Essays in Litterature*. Waltman, MA: Department of English & American Literature, Brandeis University, 1983.

SMITH, JOSEPH H., and **WILLIAM KERRIGAN**, eds. *Interpreting Lacan*. New Haven: Yale University Press, 1983.

SMITH, MARBELL S. C. *Studies in Dickens*. Chautauqua, NY: Chautauqua Press, 1910; New York: Haskell House, 1972.

Smithsonian Magazine 22 (June 1991).

Social Theory and Practice 10 (Fall 1984).

Social Text 10, no. 2–3 (1992).

SOCIÉTÉ DES ANGLICISTES DE L'ENSEIGNEMENT SUPÉRIEUR, ed. *Actes du Congres de Poitiers*. Paris: Didier, 1984.

SOCIÉTÉ DES ANGLICISTES DE L'ENSEIGNEMENT SUPÉRIEUR, ed. *Echanges: Actes du Congres de Strasbourg*. Paris: Didier, 1982.

Society of Social History Medical Bulletin 8 (September 1972).

Sociocriticism 4, no. 1 (1988).

Sophia English Studies 7 (1982).

Soundings: An Interdisciplinary Journal 64 (Winter 1981)–77 (Fall–Winter 1994).

The South Atlantic Bulletin 42 (May 1977).

The South Atlantic Quarterly 58 (Winter 1959)–55 (January 1990).

The South Atlantic Review 46 (November 1981)–55 (January 1990).

D'SOUZA, FRANK, and **JAGDISH SHIVPURI**, eds. *Siddha III*. Bombay: Siddarth College of Arts and Sciences Press, 1968.

The South Carolina Review 13 (1980).

The South Central Bulletin 30 (October 1970)–43 (Winter 1983).

The South Central Review: The Journal of the South Central Modern Language Association 1 (Spring–Summer 1984)–6 (Spring 1989).

The South Dakota Review 21 (Summer 1983).

The Southeast Asian Review of English 12–13 (June–December 1986).

Southerly: A Review of Australian Literature 9 (1948)–33 (1973).

The Southern Folklore Quarterly 43, no. 3–4 (1979).

The Southern Humanities Review 17 (Summer 1983) 22 (Spring 1988).

The Southern Quarterly: A Journal of the Arts in the South 11 (1972).

The Southern Review: Literary and Interdisciplinary Essays 1 (Winter 1964)–22 (Winter 1986).

Southwest Journal of Linguistics 9, no. 2 (1990).

Sovremenost: Spisanie za Literatura, Wmetnost I Opstestveni Prasanja 21 (1971).

SPAN: Journal of the South Pacific Association for Commonwealth Literature and Language Studies 21 (October 1985)–33 (May 1992).

SPACKS, PATRICIA MEYER. *The Female Imagination*. New York: Knopf, 1975.

SPEARS, HILDA D. *Iris Murdoch*. New York: St. Martin's, 1995.

The Spectator (26 March 1887)–275 (30 September 1995).

SPECTOR, JUDITH, ed. *Gender Studies: New Directions in Feminist Criticism*. Bowling Green, OH: Popular, 1986.

Spectrum 3 (1959)–27, no. 1–2 (1985).

SPIERS, LOGAN. *Tolstoy and Chekov*. Cambridge: Cambridge University Press, 1971.

SPENGEMANN, WILLIAM C., *The Forms of Autobiography: Episodes in the History of a Literary Genre*. New Haven: Yale University Press, 1980.

The Sphinx 9 (1979)–4 (1984).

Spicilegio Moderno: Letteratura, Lingua, Idee 11 (1979).

Spiegel der Letteren: Tijdschrift voor Nederlandse Literatuurgeschiedenis en voor Literatuurwetenschap 29, no. 1–2 (1987).

SPILKA, MARK, and **CAROLINE MCCRACKEN-FLESHER**, eds. *Why the Novel Matters: Postmodern Perplex*. Bloomington: Indiana University Press, 1990.

SPODSBERG, JORGEN. *Familiens Dodskamp: En Analyse of Charles Dickens Roman "Bleak House."* Grena: GMT, 1976.

Sprachkunst: Beiträge zur Literaturwissenschaft 16, no. 1 (1985).

Springfield Sunday Republican (1 January 1922).

SQUIRES, MICHAEL. *The Pastoral Novel: Studies in George Eliot, Thomas Hardy, and D. H. Lawrence*. Charlottesville: University Press of Virginia, 1974.

———, and **DENNIS JACKSON**, eds. *D. H. Lawrence's 'Lady': A New Look at "Lady Chatterly's Lover."* Athens: University of Georgia Press, 1985.

———, and **KEITH CUSHMAN**, eds. *The Challenge of D. H. Lawrence*. Madison: University of Wisconsin Press, 1990.

STALLYBRASS, OLIVER, ed. *Aspects of E. M. Forster*. New York: Harcourt, Brace, 1969.

———, ed. *Goldsworthy Lowes Dickinson and Related Writings*. London: Arnold, 1973.

La Stampa: Tuttolibri 16 (6 August 1988).

Standpoint 97 (1971).

Standpunte 24 (August 1971).

The Stanford Law Review 44 (April 1992).

STANG, SONDRA J., *The Presence of Ford Maddox Ford: A Memorial Volume of Essays, Poems, and Memoirs*. Philadelphia: University of Pennsylvania Press, 1981.

Steaua 37 (August 1986).

STEIG, MICHAEL. *Dickens and Phiz*. Bloomington: Indiana University Press, 1978.

STEINER, WENDY, ed. *The Sign in Music and Literature*. Austin: University of Texas Press, 1981.

The Stendhal Club: Revue Internationale d'Études Stendhaliennes. Nouvelle Série 15 (April 1985).

STEWART, DOUGLAS ALEXANDER. *The Flesh and the Spirit: An Outlook on Literature*. Sydney: Angus & Roberton, 1948.

STEWART, GARRETT. *Dickens and the Trails of Imagination*. Cambridge, MA: Harvard University Press, 1974.

Stimmen der Zeit 143 (February 1949)–146 (April 1950).

STOEHR, TAYLOR. *Dickens: The Dreamer's Stance*. Ithaca, NY: Cornell University Press, 1965.

STOKES, JOHN, ed. *Fin de Siècle/Fin du Globe: Fears and Fantasies of the Late Nineteenth-Century*. New York: St. Martin's, 1992.

STONE, HARRY. *Dickens and the Invisible World: Fairy Tales, Fantasy, and Novel*. Bloomington: Indiana University Press, 1979.

Streven 6 (November 1961).

Studia Anglica Posnaniensia: An International Review of English Studies 8 (1975).

Studia Mystic 8 (Fall 1985).

Studia Neophilologica: A Journal of Germanic and Romance Languages and Literature 55, no. 1 (1983)–64, no. 1 (1992).

Studia Romanica et Anglica Zagrabiensia 27–28 (1969)–38 (1975).

Studi dell'Istituto Linguistico 7 (1984).

Studi Urbinati, Serie B3: Linguistica, Letteratur, Arte 5 (1981–82).

Studien zur Indologie und Iranistik 7 (1981).

Studies in Canadian Literature Études en Litterature Canadienne 6, no. 2 (1981)–17, no. 1 (1992).

Studies in Eighteenth–Century Culture 19 (1989).

Studies in English Language and Literature 31 (January 1981)–29 (March 1989).

Studies in English Language and Literature Chuo-ku 43 (February 1993).

Studies in English Literature 50 (1973).

Studies in English Literature 1500–1900 5 (1965)–32 (Autumn 1992).

Studies in Hogg and His World 1 (1990)–3 (1992).

Studies in the Humanities 6 (March 1978)–15 (June 1988).

Studies in the Literary Imagination 3 (October 1970)–24 (Spring 1991).

Studies in the Novel 1 (Summer 1969)–25 (Fall 1993).

Studies in Philology 36 (October 1939)–90 (Winter 1993).

Studies in Popular Culture 7 (1984).

Studies in Psychoanalytic Theory 1 (Spring 1992).

Studies in Romanticism 23 (Winter 1983)–32 (Spring 1993).

Studies in Scottish Literature 16 (1981)–24 (1989).

Studies in Short Fiction 1 (1963)–32 (Spring 1995).

Studies in Twentieth-Century Literature 9 (Fall 1984)–38 (Spring 1992).

Studies in Weird Fiction 6 (Fall 1989)–7 (Spring 1990).

Studiu de literatura Universala 15 (1970).

STUMP, DONALD E., et al., eds. *Hamartia: The Concept of Error in the Western Tradition: Essays in Honor of John M. Crossett*. New York: Mellen, 1983.

Style 5 (1971)–28 (Fall 1994).

SubStance: A Review of Theory and Literary Criticism 15, no. 2 (1986).

SUMI, YAEKO, and **NAOMI OKAMURA**, ed. *Igirisu Shosetsu no Joseitachi*. Tokyo: Keiso, 1983.

Suplemento Literario La Nacion, Buenos Aires 22 (February 1987)–27 (October 1991).

The Survey Graphic 24 (November 1935).

SUYKERBUYK, BENOITO J., ed. *Essays from Oceania and Eurasia: George Orwell and "1984."* Antwerp: University Instelling Antwerpen, 1984.

Sydney Studies in English 2 (1976–77)–15 (1989–90).

SUZUKI, YUKIO, ed. *Joyce kara Joyce e*. Tokyo: Tokyodo Shuppan, 1982.

SWANN, THOMAS BURNETT. *A. A. Milne*. New York: Twayne, 1971.

SYMONS, JULIAN. *Critical Occations*. London: Hamish Hamilton, 1966.

Symposium: A Quarterly Journal in Modern Foreign Literatures 18 (1964)–46 (Winter 1992).

Synthésis: Bulletin du Comité National de Littérature Comparée et de l'Institut d'Historie et Théorie Littéraire "G. Câlinescu" de l'Academie de Roumanie 14 (1987).

Tamkang Review: A Quarterly of Comparative Studies between Chinese and Foreign Literatures 3 (October 1972).

Tampere English Studies (1 March 1991)–(24 December 1993).

TANEJA, G. R., and **R. K. DHAWAN**, eds. *The Novels of Salman Rushdie*. New Delhi: Indian Society for Commonwealth Studies, 1992.

Telegraph [Sunday] *Magazine* (15 July 1984).

Temps Modernes 5 (February 1950).

TENNENHOUSE, LEONARD, ed. *The Practice of Psychologianalytic Criticism*. Detroit: Wayne State University Press, 1976.

Tennessee Philological Bulletin: Proceedings of the Annual Meeting of the Tennessee Philological Association 11 (July 1974).

Tennessee Studies in Literature 5 (1960)–27 (1984).

TENNYSON, G. B., and **U. C. KNOEPFLACHER**, eds. *Nature and the Victorian Imagination*. Berkeley: University of California Press, 1977.

The Texas Quarterly 1 (1963)–16 (Autumn 1973).

The Texas Review 2 (Fall 1981).

Texas Studies in Language and Literature 3 (Autumn 1961) 281/91–35 (Fall 1993).

Textual Practice 3 (Winter 1989).

Textus: Annual of the Hebrew University Bible Project 2 (January–December 1989).

Thalia: Studies in Literary Humor 3 (Spring–Summer 1980)–10 (Spring–Summer 1988).

The [Sunday] *Telegraph* (10 October 1971).

Theology Today 46 (October 1989)–51 (July 1994).

Theoria: A Journal of Studies in the Arts, Humanities and Social Sciences 23 (1964)–72 (October 1988).

*The Thomas Hardy Annual*1 (1982)–5 (1987).

The Thomas Hardy Journal 2 (January 1986)–8 (May 1992).

The Thomas Hardy Yearbook 10 (1980)–14 (1987).

THOMAS, RONALD R. *Dreams of Authority: Freud and the Fictions of the Unconscious*. Ithaca, NY: Cornell University Press, 1990.

The Thomas Wolfe Review 8, no. 1 (1984).

THOMSEN, CHRISTIAN W., and **JENS MALTE FISCHER**, eds. *Phantastik in Literatur und Kunst*. Darmstadt: Wissenschaftliche Buchgesellschaft, 1980.

THOMSON, HENRY DOUGLAS. *Masters of Mystery: A Study of the Detective Story*. New York: Dover, 1978.

Thoth 12 (Fall 1971).

Thought 33 (Summer 1958)–60 (September 1985).

THURLEY, GEOFFREY. *The Dicken's Myth: Its Genesis and Structure*. New York: St. Martin's, 1976.

TILLOTSON, GEOFFREY. *Criticism and the Nineteenth Century*. New York: Barnes & Noble, 1951.

TILTON, JOHN WIGHTMAN. *Comic Satire in the Contemporary Novel*. Lewisburg, PA: Bucknell University Press, 1977.

The [London] *Times* (5 July 1956–7 October 1971).

TINDALL, WILLIAM YORK, ed. *The Plumed Serpent (Quetzalcoatl)*. New York: Knopf, 1951.

Time and Tide 35 (14 Auguest 1954).

The Times [London] *Educational Supplement* (27 August 1993)–4026 (24 December 1993).

Tirade 29 (September–December 1985).

TLS: [London] *Times Literary Supplement* (12 August 1915)–(22 March 1996).

Today (October 1948).

TOBIN, PATRICIA D. *Time and the Novel: The Genealogical Imperative*. Princeton: Princeton University Press, 1978.

TOOLAN, MICHAEL, ed. *Language, Text, and Context: Essays in Stylistics*. London: Routledge, 1992.

Tradition: A Journal of Orthodox Jewish Thought 22 (Fall 1986).

Transactions of the Yorkshire Dialect Society 17, no. 87 (1988).

TRILLING, LIONEL. *The Opposing Self: Nine Essays in Criticism*, New York: Harcourt, Brace, 1978.

———. *Prefaces to the Experience of Literature*. New York: Harcourt, Brace, 1979.

Trimestre 16 (July–December 1983).

Trivium 1 (1966)–18 (May 1983).

The Trollopian 3 (1948).

Tsuda Review 12 (November 1967).

The Tulsa Studies in Women's Literature 2 (Fall 1983)–11 (Fall 1992).

Turn of the Century Women 1 (Winter 1984).

The Twentieth Century 169 (1961).

Twentieth Century Literature: A Scholarly and Critical Journal 3 (April 1957)–39 (Spring 1993).

TYMIENIECKS, ANNA-TERESA, ed. *Poetics of the Elements in the Human Condition: The Sea: From Elemental Stirrings to Symbolic Inspiration, Language, and Life-Significance in Literary Interpretation and Theory*. Dordrecht: Reidel, 1985.

UCHIDA, YOSHITSUGU, and **KISHIMOTO YOSHITAKA**, eds. *Igirisu Bungaku: Kenkyu to Kansho*. Osaka: Sogensha, 1982.

Unicorn 2 (Winter 1973).

Unisa English Studies: Journal of the Department of English 7 (November 1970)–29 (April 1991).

University of Cape Town Studies in English 6 (October 1976).

University of Dayton Review 9 (Summer 1972)–17 (Winter 1985–86).

University of Hartford Studies in Literature: A Journal of Interdisciplinary Criticism 1 (March 1979)–19, no. 2–3 (1987).

University of Kansas Review 23 (1957)–27 (March 1961).

The University of Mississippi Studies in English 1 (1980)–10 (1992).

University of Portland Review 21 (September 1969).

UNTERECKER, JOHN, ed. *Approaches to the Twentieth Cantury Novel*. New York: Crowell, 1965.

University of Toronto Quarterly: A Canadian Journal of the Humanities 6 (January 1937)–63 (Winter 1993).

University of Windsor Review 22, no. 1 (1989).

University Review 31 (1965)–37 (1970).

Uomini e Libri: Periodico Bimestrale di Critica ed Informazione Letteraria 16 (September–October 1980) 17 (January–February 1981).

Use of English 16 (Summer 1965)–20 (Summer 1977).

Utopian Studies: Journal of the Society for Utopian Studies 1 (1987).

VALDES, MARIO J., and **OWEN MILLER**, eds. *Identity of the Literary Text*. Toronto: University of Toronto Press, 1985.

VAN GHENT, DOROTHY. *The English Novel: Form and Function*. New York: Holt, Rinehart, 1953.

Vector 31 (March 1965).

VEEDER, WILLIAM, and **GORDON HIRSCH**, eds. *Dr. Jekyll and Mr. Hyde after One Hundred Years*. Chicago: University of Chicago Press, 1988.

Venture 2 (March 1961).

Verbatim: The Language Quarterly 12 (Winter 1986).

Versus: Quaderni di Studi Semiotici 57 (September–December 1990).

Vestnik Sanki-Peterburgskogo Universiteta. Seriia 2, Istoriia, Iazykoznanie, Literaturovedenie (formerly *Vestnik Leningradskogo Universiteta Universiteta, Seriia 2 Istoriia, Iazykoznanie, Literaturovedenie*) 24 (December 1969)–n.s., no 1 (January 1989).

Vestnik Moskovskogo Universiteta. Seriia 9, Filoogiia 9 (January–February 1985)–9 (March–April 1988).

VIJ: Victorians Institute Journal 1 (July 1972)–18 (1990).

The Victorian Newsletter 30 (Fall 1966)–82 (Fall 1992).

The Victorian Periodicals Review 18 (Winter 1985)–23 (Spring 1990).

The Victorian Review: The Journal of the Victorian Studies Association of Western Canada 16 (Summer 1990)–17 (Winter 1991).

Victorian Studies: A Journal of the Humanities, Arts and Sciences 1 (December 1957)–37 (Autumn 1993).

The Village Voice (8 June 1972).

The Village Voice Literary Supplement 91 (December 1990).

Vinduet 36, no. 1 (1982)–45, no. 3 (1991).

The Virginia English Bulletin 36 (Winter 1986).

The Virginia Quarterly Review: A National Journal of Literature and Discussio 49 (Winter 1973)–58 (Winter 1982).

The Virginia Woolf Miscellany 18 (Spring 1982)–39 (Fall 1992).

The Virginia Woolf Quarterly 1 (Fall 1972)–3 (1978).

The Virginia Woolf Review 8 (1991).

VISWANATHAM, K. *India in English Fiction*. Waltair, India: Andhra University Press, 1971.

DE VITIS, A. A. *Anthony Burgess*. New York: Twayne, 1972.

Vladmir Nabakov Research Newslett 6 (Spring 1981).

VOGLER, THOMAS A., ed. *Twentieth-Century Interpretations of "Wuthering Heights*." Englewood Cliffs, NJ: Prentice-Hall, 1968.

VOORHEES, RICHARD J. *P. G. Wodehouse*. New York: Twayne, 1966.

DE VOS, LUK, ed. *Just the Other Day: Essays on the Suture of the Future*. Antwerp: EXA, 1985.

Vsesvit: Zhurnal Inozemnoï Literatury. Literaturno-Mystets 'kyita Hromads 'ko-Politychnyi Misiachnyk. Orhan Spilky Pys'mennykiv Ukraïny, Ukrains 'koiRady Myru 4 (April 1978)–7 (July 1986).

Vuelta 15 (March 1991).

Waiguoyu 3 (May 1984)–6 (December 1990).

Waiyu Jiaoxue Yu Yanjiu 2 (June 1982).

Wake Newsletter: Studies in James Joyce's "Finnegans Wake." 16 (December 1979).

WALKER, RONALD G., and **JUNE M. FRAZER**, eds. *The Cunning Craft: Original Essays on Detective Fiction and Contemporary Literary Theory*. Macomb: Westen Illinois University Press, 1990.

WALLACE, A. DAYLE, and **ROSS WOODBURN**, eds. *Studies in Honor of John Wilcox*. Detroit: Wayne University Press, 1958.

WALLACE, GAVIN, ed. *The Scottish Novel Since the Seventies: New Visions, Old Dreams*. Edinburgh: Edinburgh University Press, 1993.

WALSH, WILLIAM. *The Use of the Imagination: Educational Thought and the Literary Mind*. London: Chatto & Windus, 1959.

WARREN, ROBERT PENN. *Selected Essays*. New York: Vintage, 1966.

Wascana Review of Contemporary Poetry and Short Fiction (formerly *Wascana Review*) 15 (Fall 1980)–19 (Fall 1984).

WATERSON, ELIZABETH, ed. *John Galt: Reappraisals*. Guelph: University of Guelph Press, 1985.

WATT, IAN, ed. *The Victorian Novel: Modern Essays in Critics*. London: Oxford University Press, 1971.

WATTS-DUNTON, THEODORE, ed. *"The Professor" by Charlotte Brontë: To Which Are Added the Poems of Charlotte, Emily and Anne Brontë*. London: Oxford University Press, 1906.

Weimarer Beitrage: Zeitschrift für Literaturwisseenschaft, Asthetik und Kakturtheorie (formerly *Weimarer Beiträge: Zeitschrift für Literaturwisseenschaft, Ästhetik und Kakturtheorie*) 36, no. 7 (1990).

WEINSTEIN, PHILIP M. *The Semantics of Desire: Changing Models of Identity from Joyce to Dickens*. Princeton: Princeton University Press, 1984.

The Wellsian: The Journal of the H. G. Wells Society 11 (Summer 1988)–14 (Summer 1991).

WELSH, ALEXANDER. *From Copyright to Copperfield: The Identity of Dickens*. Cambridge, MA: Harvard University Press, 1987.

WEST, ANTHONY. *D. H. Lawrence*. London: Arthur Barker, 1950.

WEST, RAY. *The Art of Writing Fiction*. New York: Crowell, 1968.

WESTAROM, KARL HEINZ, ed. *Joyce Centenary Offshoots: James Joyce, 1882–1892*. Aarhus, Denmark: Seklos, Department of English, University of Aarhus, 1983.

West Coast Review 8, no. 3 (1974)–23 (Fall 1988).

Western Speech 20 (Fall 1956).

Westerly: A Quarterly Review 35 (March 1990).

Western American Literature 3 (1968).

Western Folklore 28 (October 1979).

Western Humanities Review 15 (Summer 1961)–27 (Autumn 1973).

Western Review 21 (Autumn 1956)–4 (Winter 1967).

Westminster Review 11 (April 1857).

The West Virginia University Philological Papers 28 (1982)–36 (1990).

WHEELER, MICHAEL. *The Art of Allusion in Victorian Fiction*. London: Macmillan; New York: Barnes & Noble, 1979.

WILDE, ALAN. *Art and Order: A Study of E. M. Forster*. New York: New York University Press, 1964.

WILDING, MICHAEL. *Political Fictions*. London: Routledge & Kegan Paul, 1980.

Wilkie Collins Society Journal 3 (1983)–7 (1987).

WILLIAMS, ORLO. *Some Great English Novels: Studies in the Art of Fiction*. London: Macmillan, 1926.

WILSON, ANGUS. *The World of Charles Dickens*. London: Martin Secker & Warburg, 1970.

WILSON, EDMUND. *Axel's Castle: A Study in the Imaginative Literature of 1879–1930*. New York: Scribner's, 1948.

———. *Classics and Commercials*. New York: Farar, Straus, 1950.

The Wilson Library Bulletin 39 (May 1965).

Wind and the Rain 6 (Summer 1949).

Wirkendes Wort: Deutsche Sprache in Forschung und Lehre 36 (November–December 1986).

Wisconsin Studies in Contemporary Literature 7 (1966).

Wiseman Review 237 (Summer 1963).

Wissenschaftliche Zeitschrift der Wilhelm Pieck Universität Rostock Gesellschaftswissenschaftlich 33, no. 7 (1984).

WOLFE, PETER. *The Disciplined Heart: Iris Murdoch and her Novels*. Columbia: University of Missouri Press, 1966.

WOLFE, PETER, ed. *Essays on Graham Greene*. Greenwood, FL: Penkevill, 1987.

WOLPERS, THEODOR, ed. *Gelebte Literatur in der Literatur: Studien zu Erscheiningsformen und Geschichte eines literarischen Motivs*. Gottingen: Vandenhoeck & Ruprecht, 1986.

Women & Literature 2 (1982)–3 (1983).

Women's Review of Books 11 (July 1994).

Women's Studies: An Interdisciplinary Journal 13, no. 1–2 (1986)–21, no. 3 (1992).

WOOLF, LEONARD, ed. *Collected Essays of Virginia Woolf.* London: Hagarth, 1931.

WOOLF, VIRGINIA. *The Moment and Other Essays*. London: Hogarth, 1947.

WORD: Journal of the International Linguistic Association 31 (August 1980).

Word and Image: A Journal of Verbal Visual Enquiry 2 (July–September 1986)–8 (April–June 1992).

The Wordsworth Circle 12 (Spring 1982)–19 (Summer 1988).

Work in Progress 3 (1980).

Works and Days: Essays in the Socio-Historical Dimensions of Literature and the Arts 5 (Fall 1987)–5 (Spring 1987).

World Literature Today: A Literary Quarterly of the University of Oklahoma 58 (Spring 1984)–65 (Spring 1991).

World Literature Written in English 23 (Spring 1984)–31 (Spring 1991).

World Review n.s. 13 (March 1950).

WORTH, GEORGE J. *Dickensian Melodrama: A Reading of the Novels.* Lawrence: University of Kansas Press, 1978.

WORTHEN, JOHN, ed. *D. H. Lawrence: "The Lost Girl,"* London: Secker, 1920.

———, ed. *D. H. Lawrence: "The Rainbow."* Harmondsworth, England: Penguin, 1981.

Writer 85 (December 1972).

Xanadu: A Literary Journal 13 (1990).

YAEGER, PATRICIA. *Honey-Mad Women: Emancipatory Strategies in Women's Writing*. New York: Columbia University Press, 1988.

———, and **BETH KOWALESKI-WALLACE**, eds. *Refiguring the Father: New Feminist Readings of Patriarchy*. Carbondale: University of Illinois Press, 1989.

Yale French Studies 43 (1969).

The Yale Journal of Criticism: Interpetation in the Humanities 2 (Fall 1988)–3 (Fall 1989).

The Yale Review 37 (1947–48)–80 (April 1992).

YASUO, OGOSHI SUGA, ed. *Kazugo: Ryokyoju Taikan Kinen Ronbunshu.* Kyoto: Appolonsha, 1980.

Yearbook of English Studies 2 (1972)–11 (1981).

Yeats Eliot Review: A Journal of Criticism and Scholarship 8, no. 1–2 (1986).

YEAZELL, RUTH BERNARD, ed. *Sex, Politics, and Science in the Nieteenth-Century Novel.* Baltimore: Johns Hopkins University Press, 1986.

YOKE, CARL B., and **DONALD M. HASSLER**, eds. *Death and the Serpent: Immortality in Science Fiction and Fantasy.* Westport, CT: Greenwood, 1985.

YOUNG, ROBERT, ed. *Untying the Text: A Post-Structuralist Reader.* New York: Routledge, 1981.

Zagadnienia Rodzajów Literackich: Woprosy Literaturnych Zanrov/Les Problèmes des Genres Littéraires 32, no. 2 (1989).

Zeitschrift für Anglistik und Amerikanistik: A Quarterly of Language, Literature, and Culture 21 (1973)–40, no. 3 (1992).

Zeitschrift für Slavische Philologie 51, no. 1 (1991).

Zeitschrift für Slawistik 35, no. 1 (1990).

ZUCKERMAN, ELLIOT. *The First Hundred Years of Wagner's Tristan.* New York: Columbia University Press, 1964.